Bioarchaeology of East Asia

Movement, Contact, Health

✳

Edited by Kate Pechenkina and Marc Oxenham

Foreword by Clark Spencer Larsen

University Press of Florida

Gainesville/Tallahassee/Tampa/Boca Raton

Pensacola/Orlando/Miami/Jacksonville/Ft. Myers/Sarasota

The publication of this book is made possible in part by a grant from
Queens College of the City University of New York.

First cloth printing, 2013
First paperback printing, 2025

30 29 28 27 26 25   6 5 4 3 2 1

A record of cataloging-in-publication data is available from the Library of Congress.
ISBN 978-0-8130-4427-9 (cloth)
ISBN 978-0-8130-8111-3 (pbk.)

The University Press of Florida is the scholarly publishing agency for the State University System
of Florida, comprising Florida A&M University, Florida Atlantic University, Florida Gulf Coast
University, Florida International University, Florida State University, New College of Florida, University of Central Florida, University of Florida, University of North Florida, University of South
Florida, and University of West Florida.

University Press of Florida
2046 NE Waldo Rod
Suite 2100
Gainesville, FL 32609
http://upress.ufl.edu

GPSR EU Authorized Representative: Mare Nostrum Group B.V., Mauritskade 21D, 1091 GC
Amsterdam, The Netherlands, gpsr@mare-nostrum.co.uk

Bioarchaeology of East Asia

Bioarchaeological Interpretations of the Human Past:
Local, Regional, and Global Perspectives

UNIVERSITY PRESS OF FLORIDA

Florida A&M University, Tallahassee
Florida Atlantic University, Boca Raton
Florida Gulf Coast University, Ft. Myers
Florida International University, Miami
Florida State University, Tallahassee
New College of Florida, Sarasota
University of Central Florida, Orlando
University of Florida, Gainesville
University of North Florida, Jacksonville
University of South Florida, Tampa
University of West Florida, Pensacola

Contents

Part II. Community Health

Figures

Tables

Foreword

Bioarchaeological Perspectives
on Migration and Health in Ancient East Asia

Bioarchaeological research provides a unique and valuable platform from which to address key attributes of lifeways and living conditions, especially in those areas of the world where large samples of human remains from archaeological settings are available. East Asia is just such a data-rich region. In particular, and as is so well illustrated by the contributions presented in this book, there is a remarkable human skeletal record derived from numerous contexts, ranging from simple-scale societies in early Japan to expansive empires in late-period China. Virtually everywhere in East Asia, societies at one point or another underwent economic change from foraging to farming or pastoralism. This gives us the opportunity to characterize the impacts of these fundamental adaptive transitions. Among the sources to draw on for some areas of East Asia are the historical records and medical texts that describe a range of characteristics, including, for example, illness, population movement, and demographic context. In addition, for at least some regions, there is an archaeological record that provides important insights into diet, material culture, social complexity, and settlement, areas that are crucial for understanding the human biological record as it is represented by skeletal remains.

Like all other regions of the world, the early work on human remains in East Asia was motivated by widespread interest in population history, especially classification and racial reconstruction based on measurement of skulls. Indeed, some of the great early twentieth-century biological anthropologists—such as Sir Arthur Keith—investigated remains from a variety of settings to explain the origins of cultures. The leading early twentieth-century East Asian biological anthropologist, Wu Dingliang (吴定良), published extensively in one of the leading journals of his day, *Biometrika*.

During the past decade or so, bioarchaeology in East Asia has begun to develop, moving beyond the near-singular focus on population history and descriptions of skeletons, and turning to the study of health and well-being, biocultural adaptation, and behavioral and dietary inference (e.g., Pietrusewsky and Douglas 2002; Pechenkina et al. 2002; Oxenham and Tayles 2006). Although still in its embryonic stage, bioarchaeological research in this region is revealing key facets of the human condition as they apply to the study of this vast region of the world during the past 10,000 years of human evolution.

The present volume represents an exciting contribution to the ongoing discussions by anthropologists, other social and behavioral scientists, and historians about past populations in Asia, addressing such central questions as: What were the consequences for health in the transition from foraging to rice farming? How was the transition different in this setting from other regions where agriculture developed, such as North America and Europe? Where do modern Japanese (and other Asian groups) derive from? What is the earliest record of infectious diseases (such tuberculosis and treponematosis)? What is the record of conflict and aggression in East Asia? How did rising social complexity impact human health? The chapters presented in this important volume provide us with a major stepping-off point for promoting new studies in a region of the world that will yield answers to long-standing questions. Importantly, the book brings together a group of scholars from diverse backgrounds and perspectives who study human behavior in the past from various points of view and help us to address important questions from multiple contexts.

Clark Spencer Larsen
Series Editor

Literature Cited

Oxenham M, Tayles N (eds.). 2006. *Bioarchaeology of Southeast Asia.* Cambridge: Cambridge University Press.

Pechenkina EA, Benfer RA Jr., Zhijun W. 2002. Diet and health change with the intensification of millet agriculture at the end of the Chinese Neolithic. *American Journal of Physical Anthropology* 117: 15–36.

Pietrusewsky M, Douglas MT. 2002. *Ban Chiang: A prehistoric village site in northeast Thailand, I: The human skeletal remains.* Philadelphia: University of Pennsylvania Press.

Preface

The overarching theme of this volume is human interaction and its consequences for the human condition across the vast expanse of East Asia during
the Holocene, examined through the lens of human remains. The volume is
also an exploration of human interaction at an entirely different level, bringing together chapters written by scholars from several distinct academic
schools of thought. The contributors stem from a range of culturally mediated scholarly traditions in biological anthropology that were isolated to varying degrees by the tumultuous politics of the twentieth century. Conceptual
frameworks, underlying assumptions, goals, and even styles of presentation
vary considerably among the chapters, reflecting our goal of creating a fo-
rum within which a highly diverse and international group of scholars could
engage in their particular approaches to examining human skeletal remains
drawn from archaeological contexts.

For a bioarchaeologist, East Asia presents a number of unique opportunities and challenges. First of all, human lives during the East Asian past were
defined by complex population movements and contact among a variety of
human groups. Starting with the arrival of fully modern *Homo sapiens* in East
Asia and their interactions with older species of humans, these movements
shaped morphogenetic variation, the ecology and subsistence networks of
early communities, pathogen distribution, patterns of violence, and technological development. Thus, from the beginning of the previous century on,
the analysis of skeletal remains from archaeological contexts in East Asia
targeted reconstruction of the processes involved in the initial peopling of
this part of the world, human expansion onto the Japanese Archipelago and
Taiwan, along with later interactions along the northern Chinese frontier,
among geographically remote continental groups via the trade routes, as well
as between insular and continental communities. Considering the intensity
of these migrations and other population exchanges, the large number of
prior skeletal studies reconstructing population interaction and the biological roots of ancient peoples based on metric and nonmetric cranial and dental
traits is not surprising (e.g., Yan 1962; Zhang et al. 1977; Han and Pan 1979,

1982; Han 1986; Turner 1987; Chen 1989; Brace et al. 1989; Zhang and Han 1998; Shang 2004, to name just a few).

Second, an array of subsistence strategies, not all of which were pursued in other parts of the world, resulted in somewhat unusual interactions between human communities and their local environments. In East Asia, at least four different prehistoric subsistence complexes can be identified: maritime sedentary populations with limited horticulture and arboriculture focused on nuts, as in the Jomon (縄文) tradition of Japan (Crawford 1983; Chisholm et al. 1992; Matsui 1996; Matsui and Kanehara 2006); wetland rice agriculture, with continued exploitation of marine resources in coastal areas, as in prehistoric Taiwan and during Yayoi (弥生) in Japan (Crawford and Lee 2003); a millet/pig agricultural complex with developed horticulture and limited farming of dry/wetland rice, along with continued hunting and inland fishing, as during Yangshao (仰韶), in the Yellow River basin of northern China (Yan 1992, 2005; Yuan and Flad 2002); and mobile pastoralism, with very limited farming of millet and symbiotic ties to sedentary farmers, such as on the Mongolian steppe (Xie 1972; Di Cosmo 1994). Chemical analyses of bone samples, as well as exploration of bone lesions and parameters of oral health, can contribute to our understanding of how these subsistence strategies became established and also test their effects on physical well-being and on the life histories of ancient East Asians.

The two-part organization of this volume provides a framework for presenting the results of bioarchaeological inquiry into both of the major topical issues summarized above. Chapters in the first part, "Biological Indicators of Population Histories in East Asia," address the effects of population movement in a broad sense. The contributions gathered together in this part of the volume not only reconstruct biological distances among populations and discuss morphological variation in cranial and dental samples but also explore the consequences of population movement in terms of patterns of the spread of pathogens across East Asia. Studies in the second part of the volume, "Community Health," are aimed at examining the effects of changing subsistence practices on morbidity, mortality, traumatic injuries, and oral health in relation to contact with neighboring communities.

The skeletal collections discussed in this volume are derived from a landscape spanning more than 8,000,000 km^2 and a time period extending from the Early Neolithic (c. 12,000 years ago) to the Iron Age (400 BC–AD 500). Collections from medieval cemeteries and data on modern populations are also used in some chapters for comparative purposes. Several studies in the volume are synthetic in scope, drawing on a large number of archaeological skeletal collections from across East Asia. Collectively, the chapters demonstrate how research hypotheses of great value to archaeologists can be tested through examination and analysis of human skeletal remains. If only for that reason, we hope this volume will spark increased interest in the study of human skeletal remains among archaeologists working in East Asia. We also hope that this volume will stimulate further international exchange of ideas and promote collaboration among the very diverse group of biological anthropologists with research interests in prehistoric and early historic East Asia.

Acknowledgments

The editors are indebted to Daniel Temple and Arthur Rostoker for substantial editorial help with many of the chapters in this volume. Liu Chinhsin translated chapter 11. Liu Yifang, Wei Miao, Yuko Shiratori, and Ji Yingbiao kindly helped us obtain reprints of several relevant Chinese publications and also helped with translations. Helpful comments were provided by Rowan Flad, Sara Stinson, Warren DeBoer, Sian Halcrow, and an anonymous reviewer. KP is grateful to her children, Tim and Yulia, for their unreserved enthusiasm about this project, as well as to their friends Nikita, Roma, Denis, Grisha, Zariya, Gino, Michal, and Roni for helping us all to get through it.

Preparation of this volume was supported by Research Enhancement Grant #90915-00 07 from the Social Science Division of Queens College and PSC-CUNY Research Grant #63645-00 41.

Literature Cited

Brace CL, Brace ML, Leonard WR. 1989. Reflections on the face of Japan: A multivariate craniofacial and odontometric perspective. *American Journal of Physical Anthropology* 78: 93–113.

Chen D. 1989. The taxonomy of Neolithic man and its phylogenetic relationship to later Paleolithic man and modern man in China. *Human Evolution* 4: 73–86.

Chisholm BS, Koike H, Nakai N. 1992. Carbon isotopic determination of paleodiet in Japan: Marine versus terrestrial sources. In: Aikens CM, Rhee SN, editors. *Pacific Northeast Asia in prehistory: Hunter-fisher-gatherers, farmers and sociopolitical elites*. Pullman: Washington State University Press. Pp. 69–73.

Crawford GW. 1983. *Paleoethnobotany of the Kameda Peninsula Jomon*. Ann Arbor: Museum of Anthropology, University of Michigan.

Crawford GW, Lee G. 2003. Agricultural origins in the Korean peninsula. *Antiquity* 77: 87–95.

Di Cosmo N. 1994. Ancient Inner Asian nomads: Their economic basis and its significance in Chinese history. *Journal of Asian Studies* 53: 1092–1126.

Han K. 1986. Study of human skeletons excavated from trench tombs in Kongquehe, Xinjiang. *Acta Archaeologica Sinica* (考古学报) 3: 361–84.

Han K, Pan Q. 1979. A study of the human skeletal remains unearthed from the tombs of Miaodigou II culture at Shanxian, Henan Province. *Acta Archaeologica Sinica* (考古学报) 2: 255–70.

Han K, Pan Q. 1982. Late Neolithic human skeletons from Hedang site, Foshan, Guangdong. *Acta Anthropologica Sinica* (人类学学报) 1: 42–51.

Matsui A. 1996. Archaeological investigation of anadromous salmon fishing in Japan. *World Archaeology* 27: 444–60.

Matsui A, Kanehara M. 2006. The question of prehistoric plant husbandry during the Jomon period in Japan. *World Archaeology* 38: 259–73.

Shang H. 2004. Distribution of the physical features of the Neolithic populations in China. In: *Proceedings of the Ninth Annual Symposium of the Chinese Society of Vertebrate Paleontology* (第九届中国古脊椎动物学学术年会论文集). Beijing: China Ocean Press. Pp. 153–63.

Turner CG II. 1987. Late Pleistocene and Holocene population history of East Asia based on dental variation. *American Journal of Physical Anthropology* 73: 305–21.

Xie J. 1972. The bases of Xiongnu subsistence. *Zhongyang Yanjiuyuan Minzuxue Yanjiusuo Jikan* 32: 163–90.

Yan W. 1992. Origins of agriculture and animal husbandry in China. In: Aikens CM, Rhee SN, editors. *Pacific Northeast Asia in prehistory: Hunter-fisher-gatherers, farmers and sociopolitical elites.* Pullman: Washington State University Press. Pp. 113–23.

Yan W. 2005. The beginning of farming. In: Allan S, editor. *The formation of Chinese civilization: An archaeological perspective.* New Haven, CT: Yale University and New World Press. Pp. 27–42.

Yan Y. 1962. The Neolithic human skeletons unearthed at Huaxian, Shaanxi. *Acta Archaeologica Sinica* (考古学报) 2: 85–104.

Yuan J, Flad RK. 2002. Pig domestication in ancient China. *Antiquity* 76: 724–32.

Zhang J, Han K. 1998. The observation and identification of the people of Neolithic Age at Yuchisi, Anhui Province. *Acta Anthropologica Sinica* (人类学学报) 17: 22–31.

Zhang Y, Wang L, Dong X. 1977. The human skulls from Zengpiyan Neolithic site at Guilin, Guangxi. *Vertebrata Palasiatica* (古脊椎动物学报) 15: 4–13.

1

Research on Human Skeletal Biology in East Asia

A Historical Overview

KATE PECHENKINA AND MARC OXENHAM

Bioarchaeology, perhaps best defined as a discipline focused on regionally based analysis of human remains within their archaeological contexts, with the objective of reconstructing human lives in past communities (see Buikstra 1977: 69; Larsen 1997; Buikstra 2006; Larsen 2006), became self-aware only fairly recently. The term was introduced by J.G.D. Clark in the title of his 1972 book *Star Carr: A Case Study in Bioarchaeology,* referring to the way in which concentrating on the recovery and interpretation of preserved organic materials produced an "archaeology of how men occupied territories and maintained life" (Clark 1973: 466). However, its meaning changed in the North American literature through the work of Jane Buikstra and her colleagues, who started using it specifically to describe research carried out on archaeologically recovered human tissue. In the dedication to a recent edited volume, Jane Buikstra and Lane Beck (2006) write that the contemporary meaning of *bioarchaeology* was first codified in 1977 during a symposium organized by Robert Blakely. It also appeared in print in the same year, in reference to "a new form of regionally based, interdisciplinary research in mortuary site archaeology and human osteology" (Buikstra 1977: 69).

The principal strength of this kind of regionally based approach to skeletal analysis, as pursued in this volume, is the integration of different modes of inquiry into the human past, including bioanthropological, archaeological, historiographic, and paleoecological research, in order to achieve holistic understanding of the human condition in a particular geographic area. Broadly based overview studies that draw on multiple geographical areas to reveal global or secular trends in relation to widespread phenomena such as the adoption of agriculture often overlook or dismiss variation between skeletal collections from the same timeframe or environmental zone. A regionally based bioarchaeological approach allows the derivation and testing of re-search hypotheses based on local archaeological and historical records that are relevant to a specific region, and it is well suited to addressing the factors leading to biological variation within a single area and/or departures from globally expected trends.

Of the large number of studies that had been carried out on East Asian human remains prior to the last decade, only a relative few (e.g., Gao and Lee 1993; Zheng 1993; Zhu and Lu 1997; Nakai et al. 1999; Chen 2001) were bioarchaeological in the sense earlier recommended by Buikstra (1977). The results of many more such studies have appeared during the last decade (e.g., for China, Pechenkina et al. 2005; Gao et al. 2007; Eng et al. 2010; Guo et al. 2011; or for Japan, Suzuki et al. 2005; Nagaoka et al. 2006; Temple 2011). Nevertheless, in terms of scholarship on East Asia, the idea that studying ancient human skeletons from a biological perspective can produce useful information about the lives of ancient peoples goes back to at least the second half of the nineteenth century.

Early Textual Evidence

In East Asia, a plethora of early medical texts and detailed historical records on population movement, morbidity, and mortality, as well as census information, provide a rich context for interpreting bioarchaeological data acquired through examination of human remains from past communities. Probably the earliest surviving medical texts are contained within *Huangdi Neijing* (黄帝内经) (*The Inner Canon of the Yellow Emperor*), a collection of medical treatises, the oldest of which likely predate the Qin dynasty (221–206 BC) (Sivin 1993: 201). Of great interest are parts of the opus dedicated to the correspondence between environment and the functioning of the human body, noting correlation between morbidity and climatic changes, and implicating environment as lending variability in susceptibility to different illness (Kong 2010: 11–15, 238–40). One of the chronologically later texts, possibly dated to the first century BC or AD, mentions autopsy as an approach to determining the size and shape of the internal organs (Unschuld 1985: 78), suggesting an early development of anatomical exploration in China. Another assemblage of early medical texts, excavated in 1973 from Mawangdui (马王堆) Tomb 3 (168 BC), in Changsha, Hunan (Unschuld 1985: 73–74), provides a detailed account of ancient diagnostic techniques and recipes for curative substances to be used in combination with healing rituals.

While these early medical texts furnish substantial information on the range of diseases affecting Chinese people during early historic times, the likelihood of their recovery, and possible treatments, some slightly later medical texts document early epidemics and can be employed to reconstruct the arrival of new pathogens in China. For instance, Ge Hong (葛洪), a fourth-century physician, describes an epidemic with a 40 percent to 50 percent death toll following a battle against the Yue people in AD 42–43 (Hanson 2006: 133). Ge Hong's description of skin rashes suggests that this outbreak might represent the introduction of smallpox to China.

Development of specific branches of medicine is documented by texts of the previous millennium. *Youyou Xinshu* (幼幼新書) (*The New Book on Juveniles*), compiled in the 1140s by Liu Fang (劉昉), not only gave extensive attention to traditional remedies for the treatment of illnesses common among children but also described variation in pediatric congenital deformities. The *Xiyuan Jilu* (洗冤集录) (*Collected Writings on the Washing Away of Wrongs*), assembled by Song Ci (宋慈) (c. 1247) during the last phase of the Southern Song dynasty, may have been the earliest treatment of the forensic examination of human remains. In listing different types of traumatic injury and approaches to reconstructing causes of death from biological evidence, the *Xiyuan Jilu* conclusively demonstrates that a tradition of systematically using human remains as a source of knowledge on life and death dates back in China to at least as early as the thirteenth century.

Skeletal Research during the Nineteenth Century

Evidence of the specific characteristics of skeletal collections recovered from archaeological sites in China and Japan became part of a more universal anthropological conversation during the second half of the nineteenth century, mainly in connection with European and Euro-American research on the origins of Native Americans and widely scattered Oceanic populations. This discourse was dominated by a prevailing assumption that variation in human cranial shape is determined primarily by differing biological ancestry or "racial difference." Eventually that supposition was questioned (Müller 1891; Ripley 1896) and it continues to be subjected to more recent criticism (van Gerven et al. 1973; Gould 1978; Goodman and Armelagos 1996).

As one example of this approach to determining the origins of "native" peoples, Arnold Schetelig (1869) published a treatise on the indigenes of Formosa (Taiwan). Comparing evidence derived from examination of a cranial series with the results of linguistic analysis and references to folklore, he discerned substantial inconsistencies, ultimately settling on the idea that three different ethnic groups were represented among the natives of the island. In his conception, one group had clear ties to "the Malayan and Polynesian races" (Schetelig 1869: 229); the second differed from the Malayo-Polynesian group with respect to cranial morphology but was linked to it by dialect; and the third group was unrelated to either, consisting of small immigrant tribes from nearby islands.

In a similar vein, Daniel Brinton (1888) and Herman ten Kate (1888) addressed cranial variation alongside linguistic and folkloristic lines of evidence in the course of a rather contentious dispute over the alleged Asian origins of Native Americans. The effect on cranial shape of the Japanese custom of using hard wooden blocks as pillows was discussed during the Congress of German Naturalists and Physicians in 1868 (Schaafhausen 1869). Skulls from Japan therefore became an element in a subsequent debate over environmental influence on cranial form, which developed, in part, in response to the aforementioned criticism of racial reconstructions from craniometry leveled by Max Müller (1891; as well as in earlier oral addresses).

Paleontology of East Asia in the Early Twentieth Century: Its Impact on Skeletal Biology

Although research on human skeletal biology in East Asia developed largely in parallel with the discipline in other parts of the world, several discoveries at the brink of the twentieth century gave unique features to its trajectory. Recovery in Java of "a great man-like mammal . . . an intermediate form between man and the apes[,] . . . named accordingly *Pithecanthropus erectus*" by Marie Eugène François Thomas Dubois (1896: 241), attracted attention to East Asia as a likely region in which to look for evidence of human origins (Matthew 1915; Berry 1916; Berkey and Morris 1927: 419). Inspired by this revelation, as well as by the infamous promotion of *Eoanthropus dawsoni* (Piltdown), Henry Fairfield Osborn (1923a, 1927, 1928; Osborn and Reeds 1922), then president of the American Museum of Natural History, proposed the high plateau regions of Tibet and Mongolia as the probable cradle of the "Dawn Man."

Following the Xinhai revolution in 1911–12, which resulted in the abdication of last emperor of China, Puyí (溥仪), the National Geological Survey of China was founded by the provisional government in Nanking. This institution initiated major exploratory work, along with specimen collection and curation, as well as the training of support staff and indigenous scholars for geological research (Andersson 1921). During this time, fieldwork was introduced as a new approach to exploration of the past, and large-scale collaborative projects were initiated (Chang 1981). Reflecting on the rapid invasion of western archaeologists into China, Nels Christian Nelson, the curator of prehistoric archaeology at the American Museum of Natural History, wrote in 1927, "China has at last been invaded by the prehistorians and a flood of light has suddenly been thrown on this the last archaeologically dark domain of the Asiatic continent" (1927: 177).

In subsequent years, major expeditions were carried out by joint teams from the American Museum of Natural History and the National Geological Survey of China (Osborn 1923a,b,c, 1924), aimed in part at discovering evidence of fossil humans (Andrews 1926). The scale of these projects can be appreciated from Osborn's (1923b: 90) description: "by the means of a train of seventy-five camels and two freight and five light automobiles, a three-thousand mile reconnaissance was made . . . between April 18 and September 20, 1922." Under the leadership of Roy Chapman Andrews, this expedition recovered a large number of fossils—including dinosaur bones, fossilized fish and insects, and early mammals (Osborn 1923b,c)—helping to bring the potential importance of the fossiliferous deposits of China and Mongolia into focus.

Already on the staff of the National Geological Survey of China as a mining adviser, Johan Gunnar Andersson, known in China as An Tesheng (安特生), directed several prominent paleontological and archaeological projects (Andersson 1923, 1929a,b, 1930). In 1918, Andersson learned about rich fossil deposits at Zhoukoudian (周口店), where he carried out a small-scale exploration (Andersson 1919). In 1921, he assigned excavation of this cave to a young paleontologist, Otto Zdansky, who had just arrived in China after studying in Uppsala (Andersson 1929a: 20). During the first excavation season, the cave yielded two hominid molars, which Zdansky (1927) conservatively identified as *Homo*(?).

The importance of Zdansky's discovery was recognized by Canadian anatomist Davidson Black (达生), at that time a professor at Peking Union Medical College, who published an article on the significance and possible dating of the Zhoukoudian molars in *Nature* (Black 1926). Following Zdansky's return to Uppsala after three years in China, excavations at Zhoukoudian during the late 1920s were supervised by Birger Bohlin, Yang Zhongjian (杨钟健), and Pei Wenzhong (裴文中).[1] Black analyzed the new hominid fossils recovered from Zhoukoudian and in 1928 proposed placing them into a new genus, *Sinanthropus* (Black 1928a: 136).

Around the time of the *Sinanthropus* discovery, Pierre Teilhard de Chardin also recovered a human-like incisor, along with other fossilized animal bones, in the loess deposits of Huang He, on the border of Inner Mongolia (Wu Rukang 1959a). During the next few years, six additional *Sinanthropus* fossils were recovered at Zhoukoudian, including mandibular fragments and the

teeth of both adult and juvenile hominids (Black 1928a, 1933). Although relying on comparison of the *Sinanthropus* mandible with that of *Eoanthropus*,
Black (1929) correctly inferred a large cranial capacity for the Chinese hominid. His interpretation was soon confirmed by the find of a well-preserved
hominid calvarium northwest of Zhoukoudian by Pei Wenzhong (1929).

Franz Weidenreich, who took over the ongoing research on human fossils
in China following Black's sudden death in 1934, was quite skeptical of the
authenticity of the *Eoanthropus* fossil. In his 1943 monograph, *The Skull of
Sinanthropus pekinensis: A Comparative Study on a Primitive Hominid Skull*,
an entire chapter was dedicated to debunking the British find. Commenting
on the incongruity among the different cranial and dental elements attributed
to Piltdown, Weidenreich concluded by saying, "The sooner the chimera
'*Eoanthropus*' is erased from the list of human fossils, the better for science"
(1943: 220) and "It is an artificial combination of fragments of a modern-
human braincase with orangutan-like mandible and teeth" (1943: 273).

Among Weidenreich's principal contributions to the paleoanthropological
debate was proposing that early hominid populations from Africa, Europe,
and Asia all had a role in the rise of modern humans, with each having greater
input into the origins of its respective local population (Weidenreich 1943,
1947a,b). This model presaged an unresolved argument between supporters
of multiregional continuity and single origin/replacement models of modern
human origins (Aigner and Laughlin 1973; Wu and Wu 1978; Wolpoff et al.
1984; Zhang 1998; Liu and Yang 1999). As a field, human skeletal biology
in East Asia was crafted by scholars for whom morphological continuity between fossil and modern humans was a topic of central interest. This is the
backdrop to an ongoing interest in variation in cranial and dental morphology, the effects of population movements and other interactions on cranial
shapes, and more recently, ancient DNA, the heritability of morphological
traits, and genetic relationships among contemporary populations.

The continuity model of modern human origins figured most prominently
in research carried out by Wu Rukang (吴汝康) and Wu Xinzhi (吴新智)
of the Institute of Vertebrate Paleontology and Paleoanthropology (IVPP)
in Beijing (Wu Rukang 1956; Wu Rukang and Wu X 1978, 1984; Wu X and
Zhang 1985; Wu Rukang 1999). In recent years, Wu Xinzhi (1998, 2006a,b)
has developed a "continuity with hybridization" model. Wu found a narrower range of variation in a number of morphological traits for both
anatomically modern and archaic *Homo sapiens* crania from East Asia as
compared with African skulls. He suggested that genetic drift resulted in
a reduction in morphological variation in East Asia before the emergence
of modern humans and proposed interbreeding between archaic and ana-

tomically modern humans as the most parsimonious explanation for persistence of this situation over time.

Studies of Human Remains from Archaeological Contexts in China

In December 1920, Johan Gunnar Andersson was presented with a collection of lithic artifacts from Yangshao village, in Henan Province. Recognizing these tools as products of a Neolithic technology (Andersson 1929a: 19), he carried out a reconnaissance of the Yangshao site a number of months later, during which he recovered a sample of thin-walled ceramic wares painted in black and red, along with occasional white. Similarities between these wares and painted pottery typical of Late Neolithic sites in the eastern Mediterranean, Mesopotamia, and Russian Turkestan reinforced his prior conclusion that the site was Neolithic (Andersson 1923).

Yangshao was subsequently excavated under the direction of Yuan Fuli (袁复礼) of the Geological Survey of China, with recovery of human burials supervised by Black and Zdansky (Andersson 1929a: 20). Based on his analysis of those remains, Davidson Black (1928b) proposed that large-scale population replacement had occurred in northern China sometime following the Neolithic, pointing to significant morphological differences between the Yangshao crania and those from previously known early Chinese sites where metal was present. The twin objectives of reconstructing population histories and identifying waves of migration persist to this day as the dominant themes underlying much of the research being carried out in China on ancient and even more recent human remains.

Another early twentieth-century study of skeletal materials from an archaeological site in East Asia was Sir Arthur Keith's (1929) analysis of crania and a mummified head recovered by Sir Aurel Stein in the Tarim Basin during his expedition of 1913–15. Regarding contact between human populations of differing geographic origin in this frontier zone, Keith wrote, "No doubt there had been traffic in women in ancient Kashgaria and coming and going of hordes of various peoples" (1929: 158). In addition to a routinely detailed appraisal of the variation in cranial shapes, Keith ventured somewhat beyond traditional craniometry, noting dental pathology and traumas. On page 152, Keith gave a detailed description of a cranial base fracture, discussing its possible causes in relation to burial context and inferred life history of the individual represented by the skull.

A number of important Chinese anthropologists and paleontologists were educated abroad during the 1920s and early 1930s, including Yang Zhongjian[2] (杨钟健), trained at Munich University by Ferdinand Broili[3] and Max Schlosser (Smith 1931; Lucas 2001: 26). Yang published a comprehensive

volume on the *Sinanthropus* fossils in 1933 but later emerged as a specialist in the study of fossil reptiles. Following World War II, Yang was instru-
mental in reviving Chinese paleontology (Lucas 2001: 26), directing the
Institute of Vertebrate Paleontology and Paleoanthropology in Beijing for
many years.

In the same way that Yang Zhongjian became the central figure in Chinese
vertebrate paleontology, Wu Dingliang (吴定良)[4] (1893–1969) should be
considered the keystone personage of modern Chinese physical anthropology (Zhu Hong, pers. comm. 2007). During the late 1920s, Wu studied at
Columbia University, in the Department of Psychology. Subsequently, in
London, he trained in statistical analysis under Karl Pearson, who virtually
invented biometrics and statistical analysis as we know them today. Wu devised mathematically grounded schemes for classifying indigenous Chinese
groups based on the analysis of human skeletal remains, as well as on analysis
of the physical characteristics of living members of ethnic minority groups.

Early in his career, Wu published extensively in *Biometrika*, including a
series of papers as sole author (Woo TL 1928, 1929, 1930, 1931, 1937), as
well as others coauthored with Karl Pearson (Woo TL and Pearson 1927;
Pearson and Woo TL 1935), Geoffrey Morant (Woo TL and Morant 1932,
1934), and Ethel Elderton (Elderton and Woo TL 1932). Cranial measurements that he took in Switzerland on large skeletal series from different parts
of the world became the empirical foundation for many of these papers, the
most influential of which was almost certainly "Preliminary Classification of
Asiatic Races Based on Cranial Measurements" (Woo TL and Morant 1934),
first published in Chinese (Wu D and Mo Rende[5] 1932).

Wu and Morant had examined biological distances among 26 craniometric data sets from India, China, Japan, and the East Asian part of Russia,
among which they recognized three distinct morphological clusters, or "racial groups": Indian, Northern Oriental, and Southern Oriental. This publication established one of the main theses in Chinese studies of human skeletal
remains, what could now be called ethnic epigenetics, or the study of biological ancestry based on the examination of morphological traits (as defined by
Kozintsev 1992).

Wu Dingliang went back to China in 1935, assuming a position as a full-
time researcher and a division director at the Institute of History and Anthropology Academia Sinica (Wu Rongyou 2005). While he continued to study
morphological variation in human crania (Wu D 1940, 1956, 1960; Woo TL
1941), he expanded his interests to include the study of morphological variation among living indigenous populations, along with applied anthropology.
In the 1940s and '50s, he published extensively on the physical characteristics

and health of the ethnic minorities of China (Woo TL 1942; Wu D 1957a,b). Wu was appointed chair of the newly founded anthropology department at Fudan University in 1952. At Fudan, he trained many students, including Wu Rukang (吴汝康) and Han Kangxin (韩康信). Persecuted during the cultural revolution, Wu Dingliang died in April 1969, following a raid on his home in which his notes and manuscripts, tools, and collection of books were taken to be destroyed (Wu Rongyou 2005).

Development of Biological Anthropology in Japan

Physical anthropology in Japan has been dominated for well over a hundred years by research and debates into the origins and nature of the Japanese people. In an important analysis of postwar developments in Japanese physical anthropology, Arnaud Nanta (2008) outlines the dichotomization of a nationalist discourse over Japanese identity, ultimately rooted in the origins and genetic purity, or otherwise, of the Japanese people. This debate, one that would govern the focus of Japanese physical anthropology, particularly in the post–WWII period, was dominated by several charismatic players. Hasebe Kotondo (長谷部 言人, 1882–1969), and his intellectual successor Suzuki Hisashi (鈴木 尚, d. 2004), supported an ideologically popular model of Japanese "racial" homogeneity and evolutionary continuity from the ancient Jomon through to recent times. In opposition to this school of thought stood Kanaseki Takeo (金関 丈夫, 1897–1983), working in what was then an academically peripheral region, Kyoto, supporting a "mixed-race" model. This position was later taken up (more successfully, albeit in a very different intellectual climate) by Hanihara Kazuro (埴原 和郎, d. 2004) in the form of the dual-structure model. But how did this particular discourse come about? What were its origins, and what shaped the nature of debate over Japanese origins? To answer these questions we need to shift our discussion away from developments in post–WWII Japan and review the nature of nineteenth-century physical anthropology in Japan.

While noting that the earliest reference to a prehistoric site in Japan dates to the early eighth century, Askew (2004) argues that the first systematic theorizing on Japanese origins began in the early Edo (江戸) period (1603–1868). In direct response to questions regarding the origins of stone tools discovered at the time, a number of theories were presented in the Edo period. The two most prominent were that they were created by gods or giants, or else made by one of several ancient peoples, including the Koro-pok-garu (コロポックル), mythical ancestors of modern Japanese, or ancestors of the Ainu (アイヌ) (Askew 2004: 65). According to Askew, this early theorizing came to influence Western debate over Japanese origins in the nineteenth century, which in turn fueled Japanese discussion of the issue. One of the most prominent Western authors in this regard during the nineteenth century was Edward Morse (1879a,b), who, among other things, developed a racial history of Japan wherein peoples making cord-marked pottery (translated into English as "Jomon" (縄文)) were replaced by non-pottery-making Ainu and, subsequently, the modern Japanese. Working at the same time in Japan as Morse, John Milne argued that Morse's pottery-making peoples were in fact the Ainu, who had been displaced by modern Japanese populations (Milne 1881). The displaced Ainu in turn superseded the Koro-pok-garu, whom Milne believed had inhabited Hokkaido. A final influential protagonist was Heinrich von Siebold, who argued that the Japanese were a product of intermixture between numerous races and that the Japanese had systematically supplanted indigenous Ainu populations over time (Askew 2004: 71). Another version of the melting pot thesis was forwarded by Erwin Balz, who saw the modern Japanese as having some degree of Ainu blood but for the most part as originating on the Korean peninsula (Askew 2004: 72). While there was limited agreement among these early Western theorists, they did share a common belief that the ancestors of the modern Japanese were not indigenous to the archipelago (Allen 2008).

Around the same time, and as part of the institutionalization of the discipline, Japanese scholars were also debating the issue of the origins of the Japanese people. Askew (2004: 63; see also Nobayashi 2003) notes that Tsuboi Shogoro (坪井 正五郎, d. 1913), a founding father of Japanese anthropology, argued for a pre-Ainu Koro-pok-garu people, while the founding father of Japanese physical anthropology, Koganei Yoshikiyo (小金井 良精, d. 1944), saw the Ainu as the original Stone Age inhabitants of Japan. Torii Ryuzo (鳥居 龍蔵, d. 1953) supported the latter view but elaborated on this theme and proposed a hybrid people (a mixture of various Northeast and Southeast Asian groups) as a second Stone Age people, the Japanese proper (Askew 2004: 63; Allen 2008: 108). The post–WWII era saw a radical polarization of views regarding Japanese origins (see below).

Biological Anthropology in East Asia after World War II

China

The political turmoil of the mid-twentieth century severely limited any exchange of ideas between biological anthropologists the United States, Western Europe, and Japan on the one hand and China, Mongolia, parts of Eastern Europe, and the Soviet Union on the other, albeit the barriers were by no means impenetrable. Anthropologists were no exception. Wu Rukang,[6] studying in the Department of Anatomy at the Washington University School of Medicine between 1946 and 1949, was probably the last Chinese anthropologist awarded a Ph.D. in the United States before the Cold War came to an end. Influenced by assertions of the mosaic evolution of *Homo*, in his dissertation research Wu focused on variation in the development and morphology of palatal torii among modern human populations (Woo J 1948, 1949), a high frequency of development of mandibular and maxillar torii being one of the morphological traits that purportedly links modern Asian populations to *Sinanthropus* (Weidenreich 1936, 1943).

The severing of diplomatic relations between the United States and the newly emergent People's Republic of China under Communist leadership greatly complicated Wu's return to China upon completion of his doctorate, in 1949, forcing him to travel first to Taiwan and then cross secretly onto the Chinese mainland. Once in China, Wu joined the IVPP and continued his research in paleoanthropology. He was particularly interested in primate fossils from Miocene/Pliocene deposits, including those of *Ramapithecus*, *Dryopithecus*, and *Gigantopithecus*, expecting to find the roots of the human lineage and the origins of apes in East Asia (Wu Rukang 1957, 1958; Pei and Wu 1956). Wu also published on the place of *Sivapithecus* with respect to pongid origins (Wu Rukang et al. 1983), as well as the morphology of Pleistocene hominids from China and their relationships to anatomically modern *Homo sapiens* in China (Wu Rukang 1956, 1959a,b, 1989; Woo J 1958; Pei and Wu 1957; Wu Rukang and Dong 1982).

The 1950s witnessed development of collaborative projects between Chinese and Soviet anthropologists (e.g., Perelomov 1964; Wu Rukang 1959a; Wu Rukang and Cheboksarov 1959). Based on his study of a large number of human cranial collections from East Asia, Nikolai Cheboksarov (Николай Чебоксаров) (1947, 1978) of Moscow State University conceived of four distinct Asian morphotypes, some of which he suggested could be recognized as far back as the Late Paleolithic. It should be kept in mind that the meaning of *race* in Soviet anthropology departed considerably from the popular concept, with its colonial-era legacy of discriminatory overtones (for a detailed discussion, see Hirsch 2002). In the pertinent Soviet studies, the term "race" refers to a statistically distinct dynamic complex of genotypic and phenotypic traits (Bunak 1961) showing no behavioral correspondence (Roginskiy 1961) and never to be arranged into hierarchical schemes or interpreted as being more or less evolved (e.g., Debets et al. 1952; Bunak 1961; Alekseev 1967), ostensibly rendering "racial purity" a nonissue (Hirsch 2002). The era of collaboration between Russian and Chinese anthropologists was fairly brief. Chinese-Soviet political relations went steeply downhill after Nikita Khrushchev ascended to power and reformed the ideology of the Soviet Communist party, changes that did not find favor with Mao Zedong.

Interest in studying human skeletal remains from archaeological sites increased during the 1960s among Chinese anthropologists, as exemplified in the work of Yan Yan (颜訚). Yan was a medical doctor who turned to anthropology as the result of briefly collaborating with Wu Dingliang during the late 1930s (Woo TL and Yan 1940). In a seminal 1961 paper (Yan 1961), he reviewed the potential of skeletal analysis for archaeological interpretation, as a means of helping to establish the relationship between social institutions and human life. Yan specifically emphasized the utility of reconstructing demographic profiles of ancient populations through skeletal analysis and further proposed that consideration of funerary contexts could aid in the refinement of age and sex assessment of skeletal remains.

The development of indigenous ethnic groups in relation to intense population movements and contacts between human populations from different geographic areas fascinated Chinese physical anthropologists through the second half of the twentieth century. Founded on rigorous statistical analysis of craniometric data, this research lead to a plethora of publications aimed at reconstructing the biological ancestry of people associated with specific archaeological traditions of the past and tracking their movements across the landscape (Yan et al. 1960; Yan 1962, 1972; Pan 1975, 1982, 1985, 1986, 1987, 1989; Han and Pan 1979, 1982, 1983; Chen and Wu 1985; Han 1986, 2005; Shang 2004). The work of Wu Dinliang's student Han Kangxin, Yan Yan, and Yan Yan's student Pan Qifeng (潘其风) (figure 1.1) helped establish ethnic epigenetics as an integral part of the archaeological investigation of human skeletal remains in China. In further developing this scholarly tradition, the same approach was employed to assess marriage patterns and kinship in early Chinese communities. Thus, based on factor analysis of craniometric data on skulls from a Neolithic Yangshao skeletal collection, Gao Qiang and Lee Yunkuen (1993) proposed that the community of origin was patrilocal, contrary to an established assumption of matriarchy and matrilocality during the Neolithic.

Intensification of collaboration between archaeologists and skeletal biologists during the 1980s and 1990s stimulated a reevaluation of old techniques and the development of new ones for assessing the basic demographic parameters of skeletal populations representing different ethnic groups of East Asia. Sex differences in pelvic shape for people of Han ancestry were evaluated in studies by Wu and colleagues (1982) and Sun and Qu (1986). Going beyond adaptation of traditional techniques of age assessment based on morphological and degenerative changes in the pubic symphysis (Zhang 1982, 1986; Liu et al. 1989) and cranial sutures (Mo et al. 1989), changes in dental structure

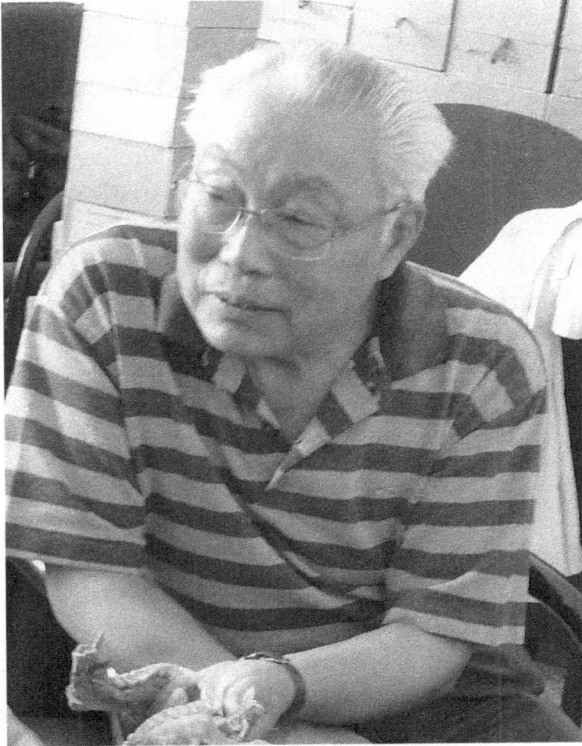

Figure 1.1. Pan Qifeng (潘其风), on June 18, 2008, at Jilin University.

(Feng 1985), as well as bone histology (Zhu 1983a), and radiographs of the *os pubis* (Zhang et al. 1996) were also looked at in relation to age.

Zhu Fangwu (朱芳武) (1983a) produced a study aimed at adapting Ellis R. Kerley's (1965, 1969) method of age estimation from bone histology for use on Chinese populations. Building on Kerley's technique, Zhu measured four microscopic parameters—the numbers of osteons, of osteon fragments, of non-Haversian canals, and the relative thickness of the lamellae—to construct an extremely accurate equation for age estimation. Linear regression equations were also developed to generate quantitative age estimates based on epiphyseal fusion and the long bone length of juveniles (Xi 1985), as well as tooth wear in adults (Wei et al. 1983; Wei and Feng 1984). Wei's method relied on the pulp-dentine index, computed as (height + width of pulp chamber)/(height + width of dentine). Discriminant functions were proposed for sex assessment based on the mandible (Yang et al. 1988), scapula (Ren 1987), tibia (Zheng and Pang 1988), arm bones (Liu et al. 1989), and patella (Zhou et al. 1997). Regression equations for stature estimates were developed based on virtually every bone (Mo 1983; Peng and Zhu 1983; Zhu 1983b; Xi 1985; Hua et al. 1994). As assessment of basic demographic characteristics of a skeletal population became a routine component of archaeological research, discussions of gender roles in the past, kinship, and the rise of social complexity often began to refer to the skeletal evidence (Underhill 2000; Liu 2004: 134–45).

Han Kangxin (1985) took the position that information afforded by examination of a human skeleton can go far beyond the simple appraisal of sex and age, making a particular issue of the utility of oral health assessment for enabling dietary reconstruction. Zhan Longdan (1986), in studying a small Neolithic to Bronze Age cranial series, took note of the individuals' fairly poor oral health. Among the other earlier Chinese comparative studies of oral health are those by Wei Boyuan and colleagues (1988), who presented an analysis of the distribution of carious lesions, periodontal disease, occlusion, eruption and mal-eruption of the third molars, as well as patterns of dental wear, for a collection of skulls from the Western Han dynasty, as compared with the oral health of modern Chinese. Zhu Fangwu and Lu Weisan (1997) compared the frequencies of carious teeth in a Neolithic collection from the Zengpiyan Cave (甑皮岩) to those for crania from both Paleolithic and modern populations. They attribute an observed increase in rates of caries during the Neolithic to a dietary shift, emphasizing the probable role of cereals.

During the 1990s, studies of oral health in early Chinese communities recruited archaeological data to produce a more nuanced interpretation of observed patterns of wear and oral pathology. Li Ruiyu and colleagues (1991) tested the association of oral pathology indicators with the location of burials, as well as sex and age at death, for a set of human remains from the Late Neolithic site of Xiawanggang (下王岗), in Henan. The only significant correspondence they found was that between periodontal disease and age. More recently, Liu and colleagues (2005) reported on their analysis of dental wear patterns for Bronze and Iron Age skeletal populations from Xinjiang and Inner Mongolia in relation to archaeological evidence on subsistence and mobility patterns in those areas, noting evidence for generally heavy masticatory demands on the chewing apparatus.

Research on artificial body modification, including artificial cranial deformation (Han and Pan 1980), ablation of the lateral incisors (Han and Pan 1982; Han and Nakahashi 1996), and trephination (Han and Chen 1999), documented the origins of these customs in China during the Neolithic and their spread through contact with other populations. Tracing the distribution across space and time of intentional tooth removal/ablation in relation to cultural contact, population movements, and the sex and age at death of the affected individuals affords us a better understanding of this peculiar custom.

Based on a cranial series from the 4,000-year-old Late Neolithic Hedang (河宕) site in Guangdong, Han Kangxin and Pan Qifeng (1982) reported male/female differences in both burial orientation and the frequency of ablation of the upper lateral incisors.

Evidence of a similar custom of extracting the upper incisors, as well as the upper premolars, was found in another Late Neolithic context at Youyu Hill (鱿鱼岗), also in Guangdong (Huang and Lui 1988). Examining the distribution of tooth removal or ablation in relation to sex and age across a wide range of Chinese and Japanese skeletal collections, Han and Nakahashi (1996) found that while the practice was widespread in eastern China and in a number of Japanese populations, customs differed with regard to the sex of the individuals so treated and also as to how early in life the affected teeth were extracted or ablated.

Paleopathological research that aimed to assess the distribution of traumatic injuries and systemic infectious disease in early China was initiated by Zhang Zhenbiao[7] (张振标) of the IVPP. During the 1990s, he performed a comprehensive analysis of changes in ancient health through the Chinese Neolithic and Dynastic periods. He reported on the frequency and distribution of cranial and postcranial traumas in a number of collections from the Neolithic, the Bronze Age, the Han dynasty, and the Northern Wei dynasty, finding a considerable increase in their frequency from the Neolithic onward (Zhang 1993). In another publication, Zhang (1994) discussed the evidence for possible cases of syphilis and leprosy found on skeletons from the Han and Song dynasties, proposing that these infectious diseases began in East Asia sometime during the Neolithic. He also performed a thorough examination of ankylosing spondylitis cases in an array of skeletal collections from ancient China, spanning the time from the Neolithic to the Northern Wei dynasty, describing patterns of ankylosis and its distribution along the vertebral column and comparing frequencies of occurrence between the sexes (Zhang Zhenbiao 1995).

Japan

Diversity of debate over Japanese origins was reduced to two polarized and diametrically opposed views in the post–WWII era, with one of these standpoints virtually dominating the Japanese physical anthropological discourse right up to the 1980s. Nanta (2008: 13) outlines the central role of Hasebe Kotondo in the discourse over ethnic purity and racial continuity, whereby the "people of the Jomon prehistoric era were seen as the direct linear ancestors of modern Japanese[;] there had been no mixing of the race during the proto-historic Yayoi period." Hasebe is also seen as one of the first physical anthropologists to introduce statistical rigor into the study of human variation (see Nobayashi 2003). Suzuki Hisashi, a former student of both Hasebe Kotondo and Koganei Yoshikiyo, developed the continuity arguments through his microevolutionary model, introduced in the 1950s–60s.

In essence, this model argued for the genetic continuity of the Japanese people from prehistory through to the present, looking to environmental and cultural influences as mediators of any observed morphological change over time and space (Nanta 2008: 35). Of course, such a standpoint is a variant of the regional continuity model, first espoused by Franz Weidenreich in China (see Tayles and Oxenham 2006: 7–8 for a more detailed discussion of this) and later promoted by his local successors, Wu Rukang and Wu Xinzhi (see discussion in this chapter).

In direct opposition to Suzuki's pure-race hegemony, Kaneseki Takeo (金關丈夫, d. 1983) argued, from his position on the periphery of the main intellectual developments in Japan centered on Tokyo, for a continental origin of the Yayoi (Nanta 2008: 37). This mixed-race model was also pursued in another peripheral area by Hanihara Kazuro, among others, in Hokkaido. Ultimately, the mixed-race (which later became referred to as the dual structure model—see Hanihara 1991) theorists were effectively silenced during the 1950s to the 1970s, with headway by the dual structure theorists only being made in the 1980s (Nanta 2008: 42). Useful summaries of biological (cranial, dental, and genetic) evidence for the dual structure hypothesis in English can be found in Hudson 1999 and Kumar 2009.

This brief review of the history of Japanese physical anthropology has focused on the question of Japanese origins for the simple reason that this topic was the focus of considerable attention for well over a century by Japanese physical anthropologists. Nonetheless, an enormous range of other topics were dealt with by biological anthropologists both during the immediate post–WWII period and in more recent decades. Reviews of this literature include general bioanthropological studies up to the beginning of the 1960s (Sofue 1961) and the 1990s (Hanihara 1992) and studies of growth and development in Japan (Kimura 1984), while references to the increasing literature on more bioarchaeological and/or paleohealth research are listed in publications such as Suzuki 1991, Temple and Larsen 2007, and Oxenham and Matsumura 2008.

Conclusion

Although an increasing number of publications have appeared over the past fifteen years that aim to reconstruct the well-being of humans in the ancient communities of East Asia (e.g., Han and Nakahashi 1996; Sakashita et al. 1997a,b; Han and Chen 1999; Hukuda et al. 2000; Chen 2001; Li Fajun 2004, 2008; Pechenkina et al. 2002, 2005; Hu et al. 2006; Zhang and Zhu 2006; Zhang et al. 2009; Temple 2007; Temple and Larsen 2007; Oxenham and Matsumura 2008; Eng et al. 2010), the bioarchaeology of this geographic domain remains nascent. The number of skeletal samples that have been analyzed for indicators of diet and health is miniscule and there are large space and time gaps for which no analysis of human bone has been done. This hampers our ability to reconstruct the chronology of health changes and distinguish between differences in the distribution of skeletal indicators caused by variation in local environments and general trends occurring over extended periods of time. The chapters in this volume explicitly underscore the potential value of such collaboration. The following chapter reviews human ecology and paleoeconomies in continental and insular East Asia and underscores the range of related questions that can be investigated through bioarchaeological inquiry.

Notes

1. Pei Wenzhong (裴文中), also known as Pei Wen-chung, was trained in the field by Yang Zhongjian, Davidson Black, and later by Teilhard de Chardin (Chang 1984).
2. Yang Zhongjian also published as Chung Chien Young, or C. C. Young.
3. Ferdinand Broili was also the academic supervisor of von Koenigswald.
4. Wu published under the name Woo Ting Liang (Woo TL) in European journals.
5. Mo Rende (莫仁德) is a Pinyin transliteration of Geoffrey Morant's last name.
6. Wu Rukang (吴汝康) published as Woo Ju-kang (Woo JK) in English and as У Рукан and у жу-кан in the Russian literature.
7. Zhang Zhenbiao (张振标) was trained by Wu Rukang and Wu Xinzhi in classical craniometry and somatometry. Through the 1980s Zhang's research was focused on reconstructing the biological ancestry of the natives of Heinan Island and Guanxi, based on the somatometry of contemporary populations (Zhang Zhenbiao and Zhang Jianjun 1982, 1983; Wu Rukang et al. 1993). However, during the 1990s he turned to analysis of changes in health marker distribution over time (Zhang Zhenbiao 1993, 1994, 1995).

Literature Cited

Aigner JS, Laughlin WS. 1973. The dating of Lantian man and his significance for analyzing trends in human evolution. *American Journal of Physical Anthropology* 39: 97–109.
Alekseev VP. 1967. Human races in modern science. *Voprosy istorii* (Вопросы Истории) 7: 71–86.
Allen CT. 2008. Early migrations, conquests, and common ancestry: Theorizing Japanese origins in relation with Korea. *Sungkyun Journal of East Asian Studies* 8: 105–30.

Andersson JG. 1919. Preliminary description of a bone-deposit at Chow-Kou-Tien in Fang-Shan-Hsien, Chili Province. *Geografiska Annaler* 1: 265–68.

Andersson JG. 1921. The National Geological Survey of China. *Geografiska Annaler* 3: 305–10.

Andersson JG. 1923. *An early Chinese culture.* Beijing: Ministry of Agriculture and Commerce, the Geological Survey of China.

Andersson JG. 1929a. The origin and aims of the Museum of Far Eastern Antiquities. *Bulletin of the Museum of Far Eastern Antiquities* 1: 11–27.

Andersson JG. 1929b. On symbolism in the prehistoric painted ceramics of China. *Bulletin of the Museum of Far Eastern Antiquities* 1: 65–69.

Andersson JG. 1930. The tenth anniversary of the Swedish China Research Committee and the Karlbeck Exhibition. *Bulletin of the Museum of Far Eastern Antiquities* 2: 233–36.

Andrews RC. 1926. *On the trail of Ancient Man: A narrative of the field work of the Central Asiatic Expeditions.* New York: G. P. Putnam and Sons.

Askew D. 2004. Debating the "Japanese" race in Meiji Japan: Towards a history of early Japanese anthropology. In: Yamashita S, Bosco J, Eades JS, editors. *The making of anthropology in East and Southeast Asia.* New York: Berghahn Books. Pp. 57–89.

Berkey CP, Morris FK. 1927. *Geology of Mongolia.* New York: American Museum of Natural History.

Berry EW. 1916. The environment of the Ape Man. *Scientific Monthly* 3: 161–69.

Black D. 1926. The Chou Kou Tien discovery. *Science* 64: 586–87.

Black D. 1928a. Discovery of further hominid remains of Lower Quaternry age from the Chou Kou Tien deposit. *Science* 67: 135–36.

Black D. 1928b. *A study of Kansu and Honan Aeneolithic skulls and specimens from later Kansu prehistoric sites in comparison with North China and other recent crania. Part 1: On measurements and identification.* Palaeontologia Sinica, Series D, vol. 6.

Black D. 1929. *Sinanthropus pekinensis:* The recovery of further fossil remains of this early hominid from the Chou Kou Tien deposit. *Science* 69: 674–76.

Black D. 1933. On the endocranial cast of the adolescent *Sinanthropus* skull. *Proceedings of the Royal Society of London* 112: 263–76.

Brinton DG. 1888. On the alleged Mongolian affinities of the American race. *Science* 12: 121–23.

Buikstra J. 1977. Biocultural dimensions of archeological study: A regional perspective. In: Blakely RL, editor. *Biocultural adaptation in prehistoric America.* Southern Anthropological Society Proceedings no. 11. Athens: University of Georgia Press. Pp. 67–84.

Buikstra J. 2006. A historical introduction. In: Buikstra J, Beck L, editors. *Bioarchaeology: The contextual analysis of human remains.* Burlington, MA: Academic Press. Pp. 7–26.

Buikstra J, Beck L, editors. 2006. *Bioarchaeology: The contextual analysis of human remains.* Burlington, MA: Academic Press.

Bunak VV. 1961. Race as a historical category. In: Bunak VV, Roginskiy YY, Debets GF, Levin MG, Cheboksarov NN, editors. *Contemporary raciology and racism.* International Journal of Linguistics, vol. 27, no. 3, pt. 2. Bloomington: Indiana University Research Center in Anthropology, Folklore, and Linguistics. Pp. 1–43.

Chang KC. 1981. Archaeology and Chinese historiography. *World Archaeology* 13: 156–69.

Cheboksarov NN. 1947. *The main trends in racial differentiation in East Asia.* Moscow: Institute of Ethnography.

Cheboksarov NN. 1978. Differentiation of the peoples of East Asia. In: Krukov MV, Sofronov MV, Cheboksarov NN, editors. *Ancient Chinese: Problems of ethnogenesis.* Moscow: Nauka. Pp. 46–52.

Chen D, Wu X. 1985. Early Neolithic human skeletons from Shigu, Changge, Henan Province. *Acta Anthropologica Sinica* (人类学学报) 4: 205–14, 314–23.

Chen X. 2001. Ancient scalping custom in China and related issues. *Chinese Archaeology* 1: 11–14.

Clark JGD. 1972. *Star Carr: A case study in bioarchaeology.* New York: Addison-Wesley.

Clark J. 1973. Bioarchaeology: Some extracts on the theme. *Current Anthropology* 14: 464–70.

Dang R, Yang Y, Zheng J, Li Y. 1985. Sex difference in the skulls of Xi'an area. *Acta Anthropologica Sinica* (人类学学报) 4: 378–83.

Debets GF, Levin MG, Trofimova TA. 1952. Anthropological material as a source on questions of ethnogenesis. *Soviet Ethnography* (Советская этнография) 1: 4–35.

Dubois E. 1896. On *Pithecanthropus erectus:* A transitional form between man and the apes. *Journal of the Anthropological Institute of Great Britain and Ireland* 25: 240–55.

Elderton EM, Woo TL [Wu, Dingliang]. 1932. On the normality or want of normality in the frequency distributions of cranial measurements. *Biometrika* 24: 45–54.

Eng JT, Zhang Q, Zhu H. 2010. Skeletal effects of castration on two eunuchs of Ming China. *Anthropological Science* 118: 107–16.

Feng J. 1985. Age determination from structure of teeth. *Acta Anthropologica Sinica* (人类学学报) 4: 379–84.

Gao Q, Lee Y. 1993. A biological perspective on Yangshao kinship. *Journal of Anthropological Archaeology* 12: 266–98.

Gao S, Yang Y, Xu Y, Zhang Q, Zhu H, Zhou H. 2007. Tracing the genetic history of the Chinese people: Mitochondrial DNA analysis of Aeneolithic population from the Lajia site. *American Journal of Physical Anthropology* 133: 1128–36.

Goodman AH, Armelagos GJ. 1996. Race, racism and the new physical anthropology. In: Reynolds L, Lieberman L, editors. *Race and other misadventures: Essays in honor of Ashley Montagu in his ninetieth year.* New York: General Hall. Pp. 174–86.

Gould SJ. 1978. Morton's ranking of races by cranial capacity. *Science* 200: 503–9.

Guo Y, Hu Y, Gao Q, Wang C, Richards MP. 2011. Stable carbon and nitrogen isotope evidence in human diets based on evidence from the Jiangzhai site, China. *Acta Anthropologica Sinica* (人类学学报) 20: 149–57.

Han K. 1985. Skeleton anthropology appraisal to archaeology research function. *Archaeology and Cultural Relics* (考古与文物) 3: 50–55.

Han K. 1986. Study of human skeletons excavated from trench tombs in Kongquehe, Xinjiang. *Acta Archaeologica Sinica* (考古学报) 3: 361–84.

Han K. 2005. A racial study of the human skeleton from Xia, Shang and Zhou dynasty in China. In: Institute of Archaeology, Chinese Academy of Social Science. *Archaeological study on new century in China* (中国社会科学院考古研究所编.新世纪的中国考古学). Beijing: Science Press. Pp. 925–66.

Han K, Chen X. 1999. Archaeological evidence of ancient Chinese open cranial surgery. *Kaogu* 7: 639–44.

Han K, Nakahashi T. 1996. A comparative study of ritual tooth ablation in ancient China and Japan. *Anthropological Science* 104: 43–64.

Han K, Pan Q. 1979. A study of the human skeletal remains unearthed from the tombs of Miaodigou II culture at Shanxian, Henan Province. *Acta Archaeologica Sinica* (考古学报) 2: 255–70.

Han K, Pan Q. 1980. Signs of artificial head modifications in Neolithic cranial series. *Kaogu* 2: 187–91.

Han K, Pan Q. 1982. Late Neolithic human skeletons from Hedang site, Foshan, Guangdong. *Acta Anthropologica Sinica* (人类学学报) 1: 42–51.

Han K, Pan Q. 1983. Early Neolithic human skulls from Hemudu, Yuyao, Zhejiang. *Acta Anthropologica Sinica* (人类学学报) 2: 124–31.

Han K, Pan Q. 1984. The study of Chinese ancient races. *Kaogu Xuebao* (考古学报) 2: 245–63.

Hanihara K. 1991. Dual structure model for the population history of the Japanese. *Japan Review* 2: 1–33.

Hanihara K. 1992. Current trends in physical anthropology in Japan. *Japan Review* 3: 131–39.

Hanson ME. 2006. The significance of Manchu medical sources in the Qing. In: Stephen W, Naeher C, Dede K, editors. *Proceedings of the First North American Conference on Manchu Studies (Portland, OR, May 9–10, 2003).* Tunguso Sibirica 15, vol. 1: Studies in Manchu Literature and History. Weisbaden: Harrassowitz. Pp. 131–75.

Hirsch F. 2002. Race without the practice of racial politics. *Slavic Review* 61: 30–43.

Hu Y, Ambrose SH, Wang C. 2006. Stable isotopic analysis of human bones from Jiahu site, Henan, China: Implications for the transition to agriculture. *Journal of Archaeological Science* 33: 1319–30.

Hua F, Zhang J, Tian X, Sun J. 1994. Estimation of stature based on Chinese male os coxae. *Acta Anthropologica Sinica* 13: 138–54.

Huang X, Lui J. 1988. Late Neolithic human skeletons from Youyu hill, Nanhai County, Guangdong Province. *Acta Anthropologica Sinica* (人类学学报) 7: 102–5.

Huang X, Wei G, Liu Y, Zhang J, Zhang S. 1985. An investigation of the physical characters of the boatmen at the Lotus hill, Guangzhou. *Acta Anthropologica Sinica* 4: 173–81.

Hudson MJ. 1999. *Ruins of identity: Ethnogenesis in the Japanese Islands.* University of Hawai'i Press: Honolulu.

Hukuda S, Inoue K, Toshio U, Saruhashi Y, Iwasaki A, Huang J, Mayeda A, Nakai M, Li F, Yang Z. 2000. Spinal degenerative lesions and spinal ligamentous ossifications in ancient Chinese populations of the Yellow River civilization. *International Journal of Osteoarchaeology* 10: 108–24.

Jia M, Wang N, Liu B, Zhang F, Yam Z, Zhu J, Pu S, Yang Z. 1989. The length of the second metacarpal and the body height. *Acta Anthropologica Sinica* (人类学学报) 8: 240–44.

Kate HT. 1888. On the alleged Mongolian affinities of the American race: A reply to Dr. Daniel G. Brinton. *Science* 12: 227–28.

Keith A. 1929. Human skeletal remains in the Tarim Basin. *Journal of the Royal Anthropological Institute of Great Britain and Ireland* 59: 149–80.

Kerley ER. 1965. The microscopic determination of age in human bone. *American Journal of Physical Anthropology* 23: 149–64.

Kerley ER. 1969. Age determination of bone fragments. *Journal of Forensic Science* 14: 59–67.

Kimura K. 1984. Studies on growth and development in Japan. *Yearbook of Physical Anthropology* 27: 179–214.

Kong YC. 2010. *Huangdi Neijing: A synopsis with commentaries.* Hong Kong: Chinese University Press.

Kozintsev AG. 1992. Ethnic epigenetics: a new approach. *Homo* 43: 213–44.

Kumar A. 2009. *Globalizing the prehistory of Japan: Language, genes and civilization.* New York: Routledge.

Larsen CS. 1997. *Bioarchaeology: Interpreting behavior from the human skeleton.* Cambridge: Cambridge University Press.

Larsen CS. 2006. The changing face of bioarchaeology: an interdisciplinary science. In: Buikstra J, Beck L, editors. 2006. *Bioarchaeology: The contextual analysis of human remains.* Burlington, MA: Academic Press. Pp. 359–74.

Li F. 2004. A research of the Neolithic human skeletons from Jiangjialiang, Yangyuan in Hebei Province, China (河北阳原姜家梁新石器时代人骨研究). Ph.D. dissertation, Department of Anthropology, Jilin University.

Li F. 2008. *A research of the Neolithic human skeletons from Jiangjialiang, Yangyuan in Hebei Province, China* (河北阳原姜家梁新石器时代人骨研究). Beijing: Science Press.

Li R, Huang J, Han L. 1991. Dental disease of the Neolithic population from Xiawanggang. *Acta Anthropologica Sinica* (人类学学报) 10: 200–205.

Liu L. 2004. *The Chinese Neolithic: Trajectories to early states.* Cambridge: Cambridge University Press.

Liu W, Yang M. 1999. The changes of tooth size of Chinese and the systematic status of *Homo erectus* in East Asia. *Acta Anthropologica Sinica* (人类学学报) 18: 176–92.

Liu W, Yang M, Tai F. 1989. Sex discriminant analysis of long bones of lower limb. *Acta Anthropologica Sinica* (人类学学报) 8: 147–54.

Liu W, Zhang Q, Wu X, Zhu H. 2005. Tooth wear and dental pathology of the Bronze–Iron Age people in Xinjiang, Northwest China: Implications for their diet and lifestyle. *Homo* 61: 102–16.

Lucas SG. 2001. *Chinese fossil vertebrates.* New York: Columbia University Press.

Matthew WD. 1915. Climate and evolution. *Annals of the New York Academy of Sciences* 24: 209–14.

Milne J. 1881. The Stone Age in Japan: With notes on recent geological changes which have taken place. *Journal of the Anthropological Institute of Great Britain and Ireland* 10: 389–423.

Mo S. 1983. Estimation of stature by long bones of Chinese male adults in South China. *Acta Anthropologica Sinica* (人类学学报) 2: 80–85.

Mo S, Peng S. 1983. Attrition of upper and lower molars with relation to age in Southern Chinese skulls. *Acta Anthropologica Sinica* (人类学学报) 2: 374–79.

Mo S, Zhang W, Lei S, Wang X, Qiu K. 1989. The relation between the age and changes in Chinese skull suture. *Acta Anthropologica Sinica* 8: 131–38.

Morse ES. 1879a. *Shell mounds of Omori.* Memoirs of the Science Department, University of Tokio, vol. 1, pt. 1.

Morse ES. 1879b. Traces of an early race in Japan. *Popular Science Monthly* 14: 257–66.

Müller M. 1891. Anthropology past and present. *Science* 18: 169–72.

Nagaoka T, Hirata K, Yokota E, Matsu'ura S. 2006. Paleodemography of a medieval population in Japan: Analysis of human skeletal remains from the Yuigahama-minami site. *American Journal of Physical Anthropology* 131: 1–14.

Nakai M, Inoue K, Hukuda S. 1999. Healed bone fractures in a Jomon skeletal population from the Yoshigo shell mound, Aichi Prefecture, Japan. *International Journal of Osteoarchaeology* 9: 77–82.

Nanta A. 2008. Physical anthropology and the reconstruction of Japanese identity in postcolonial Japan. *Social Science Japan Journal* 11: 29–47.

Nelson NC. 1927. Archaeological research in North China. *American Anthropologist* 29: 177–201.

Nobayashi A. 2003. Physical anthropology in wartime Japan. In: Shimizu A, van Bremen J, editors. *Wartime Japanese anthropology in Asia and the Pacific.* Osaka: National Museum of Ethnology. Pp. 143–50.

Osborn HF. 1923a. Why Mongolia may be the home of primitive man. Oral address in Beijing, China, cited in Osborn 1928 (p. 11).

Osborn HF. 1923b. The explorations of the American Museum of Natural History in China and Mongolia. *Proceedings of the American Philosophical Society* 62: 90–94.

Osborn HF. 1923c. Ancient fauna of Mongolia discovered by the Third Asiatic Expedition of American Museum of Natural History. *Science* 57: 729–32.

Osborn HF. 1924. Discoveries during the season of 1923 by the third Asiatic expedition in Mongolia. *Paleontology* 10: 23–24.

Osborn HF. 1927. Recent discoveries relating to the origin and antiquity of man. *Science* 20: 481–88.

Osborn HF. 1928. Present status of the problem of human ancestry. *Proceedings of the American Philosophical Society* 67: 151–56.

Osborn HF, Reeds CA. 1922. Old and new standards of Pleistocene division in relation to the prehistory of man in Europe. *Geological Society of America Bulletin* 33: 411–90.

Oxenham MF, Matsumura H. 2008. Oral and physiological paleohealth in cold adapted peoples: Northeast Asia, Hokkaido. *American Journal of Physical Anthropology* 135: 64–74.

Oxenham MF, Matsumura H, Nishimoto T. 2006. Diffuse idiopathic skeletal hyperostosis in Late Jomon Hokkaido, Japan. *International Journal of Osteoarchaeology* 16: 34–46.

Pan Q. 1975. Study on human bone in Chifeng and Ningcheng at Xiajiadian Upper Culture. *Acta Archaeologica Sinica* (考古学报) 2: 157–72.

Pan Q. 1982. Study on human bone of grassland nomad in north China, East Han. *Acta Archaeologica Sinica* (考古学报) 2: 117–36.

Pan Q. 1985. *Study on skulls in Yin ruin* (安阳殷墟头骨研究). Beijing: Culture Relics Press.

Pan Q. 1986. Hun race from skull remains. In: *Archaeology research in China: Paper collection in memory of Mr. Xia Nai*, vol. 2 (中国考古学研究－夏鼐先生考古五十年纪念文集二). Beijing: Science Press. Pp. 292–300.

Pan Q. 1987. *A study on the races of Chinese ancient populations: Analects on archaeological culture* (考古学文化论集). Beijing: Culture Relics Press.

Pan Q. 1989. *The distribution and change tendency of Chinese cranial types in Bronze Age: Analects to celebrate the 55th anniversary of Mr. Su Bingqi* (庆祝苏秉琦五十五年论文集). Beijing: Culture Relics Press.

Pearson K, Woo TL [Wu, Dingliang]. 1935. Further investigation of the morphometric characters of the individual bones of the human skull. *Biometrika* 27: 424–65.

Pechenkina EA, Ambrose SH, Ma X, Benfer RA Jr. 2005. Reconstructing northern Chinese Neolithic subsistence practices by isotopic analysis. *Journal of Archaeological Science* 32: 1176–89.

Pechenkina EA, Benfer RA Jr., Zhijun W. 2002. Diet and health changes at the end of the Chinese Neolithic: The Yangshao/Longshan transition in Shaanxi province. *American Journal of Physical Anthropology* 117: 15–36.

Pei W. 1929. An account of the discovery of an adult *Sinanthropus* skull in the Chou Kou Tien deposit. *Bulletin of the Geological Society of China* 8: 203–5.

Pei W, Wu R. 1956. New materials of *Gigantopithecus* teeth from South China. *Acta Paleontologica Sinica* (古生物學報) 4: 477–90.

Pei W, Wu R. 1957. Tzeyang Paleolithic man. *Institute of Vertebrate Paleontology Academia Sinica Memoir* (中国科学院古脊椎动物与古人类研究所甲种专刊) 1: 13–49. Beijing: Science Press.

Peng S. 1983. Attribution of upper and lower molars with relation to ageing Southern Chinese skulls. *Acta Anthropologica Sinica* (人类学学报) 2: 368–74.

Peng S, Zhu F. 1983. Estimation of stature from skull, clavicle, scapula and os coxa of male adult of southern Chinese. *Acta Anthropologica Sinica* (人类学学报) 2: 253–59.

Perelomov LS. 1964. Community and family in ancient China from 300 BC to AD 300. In: *Papers presented at VIII International Congress of Anthropological and Ethnographic Sciences* (Материалы VIII Международного Конгресса Антропологических и Этнографических наук). Moscow: Nauka. P. 8.

Ren G. 1987. Sexual diagnosis of scapula by discriminant functional analysis. *Acta Anthropologica Sinica* (人类学学报) 6: 144–46.

Ripley WZ. 1896. The form of the head as influenced by growth. *Science* 3: 888–89.

Roginskiy YY. 1961. Racial differentiation and the psyche. In: Bunak VV, Roginskiy YY, Debets GF, Levin MG, Cheboksarov NN, editors. *Contemporary raciology and racism*. International Journal of Linguistics, vol. 27, no. 3, pt. 2. Bloomington: Indiana University Research Center in Anthropology, Folklore, and Linguistics. Pp. 44–69.

Sakashita R, Inoue M, Inoue N, Pan Q, Zhu H. 1997b. Dental disease in the Chinese Yin-Shang period with respect to relationships between citizens and slaves. *American Journal of Physical Anthropology* 103: 401–8.

Sakashita R, Inoue N, Pan Q, Zhu H. 1997a. Diet and discrepancy between tooth and jaw size in the Yin-Shang period of China. *American Journal of Physical Anthropology* 103: 497–505.

Schaafhausen H. 1869. Report of the transactions of the Section for Anthropology and Ethnology at the Congress of German Naturalists and Physicians. *Anthropological Review* 7: 366–75.

Schetelig A. 1869. On the natives of Formosa. *Transactions of the Ethnological Society of London* 7: 215–29.

Shang H. 2004. Distribution of the physical features of the Neolithic populations in China. In: Dong W, editor. *Proceedings of the Ninth Annual Symposium of the Chinese Society of Vertebrate Paleontology* (第九届中国古脊椎动物学学术年会论文集). Beijing: China Ocean Press. Pp. 153–63.

Sheng K. 1984. Measurements and analyses of Chinese elite boatmen humeri by X-ray. *Acta Anthropologica Sinica* (人类学学报) 3: 132–40.

Sivin N. 1993. Huang ti nei ching (黃帝內經). In: Loewe M, editor. *Early Chinese texts: A bibliographical guide*. Berkeley: University of California Press. Pp. 196–215.

Smith GE. 1931. *Sinanthropus*—Peking Man, its discovery and significance. *Scientific Monthly* 33: 193–211.

Sofue T. 1961. Anthropology in Japan: Historical review and modern trends. *Biennial Review of Anthropology* 2: 173–214.

Sun S, Qu Y. 1986. The measurements and sexual diagnosis of the great sciatic notch in Chinese. *Acta Anthropologica Sinica* 5: 368–71.

Suzuki T. 1991. Paleopathological study on infectious disease in Japan. In: Ortner DJ, Aufderheide AC, editors. *Human paleopathology: Current syntheses and future options*. Washington, DC: Smithsonian Institution Press. Pp. 128–39.

Suzuki T, Matsushita T, Han K. 2005. On the possible case of treponematosis from the Bronze Age in China. *Anthropological Science* 113: 253–58.

Tayles N, Oxenham M. 2006. Southeast Asian bioarchaeology: Past and present. In: Oxenham M, Tayles N, editors. *Bioarchaeology of Southeast Asia*. Cambridge: Cambridge University Press. Pp. 1–30.

Temple DH. 2007. Dietary variation and stress among prehistoric Jomon foragers from Japan. *American Journal of Physical Anthropology* 133: 1035–46.

Temple DH. 2011. Evolution of postcranial morphology during agricultural transition in prehistoric Japan. In: Pinhasi R, Stock JT, editors. *Human bioarchaeology of the transition to agriculture*. Chichester, UK: Wiley-Blackwell. Pp. 235–64.

Temple DH, Larsen CS. 2007. Dental caries prevalence as evidence for agriculture and subsistence variation during the Yayoi period in prehistoric Japan: Biocultural interpretations of an economy in transition. *American Journal of Physical Anthropology* 134: 501–12.

Underhill AP. 2000. An analysis of mortuary ritual at the Dawenkou site, Shandong, China. *Journal of East Asian Archaeology* 2: 93–127.

Unschuld PU. 1985. *Medicine in China: A history of ideas*. Berkeley: University of California Press.

Van Gerven DP, Carlson DS, Armelagos GJ. 1973. Racial history and bio-cultural adaptation of Nubian archaeological populations. *Journal of African History* 14: 555–64.

Wei B, Feng J. 1984. A trinomial regression formula of estimation age with both the degree of tooth attrition and the tooth index. *Acta Anthropologica Sinica* (人类学学报) 3: 270–76.

Wei B, Feng J, Fang Z. 1983. The relationship between the construction of maxillary first molar and age. *Acta Anthropologica Sinica* (人类学学报) 2: 72–79.

Wei B, Peng S, Zhang W. 1988. The oral conditions of human skulls of the Western Han dynasty. *Acta Anthropologica Sinica* (人类学学报)7: 249–54.

Weidenreich F. 1936. *The mandibles of* Sinanthropus pekinensis: *A comparative study*. Palaeontologia Sinica, Series D, vol. 7. Beijing: Geological Survey of China.

Weidenreich F. 1943. *The skull of* Sinanthropus pekinensis: *A comparative study on a primitive hominid skull*. Lancaster, PA: Lancaster Press.

Weidenreich F. 1947a. Facts and speculations concerning the origin of *Homo sapiens*. *American Anthropologist* 49: 187–203.

Weidenreich F. 1947b. The trend of human evolution. *Evolution* 1: 221–36.

Wolpoff M, Wu X, Thorne A. 1984. Modern *Homo sapiens* origins: A general theory of hominid evolution involving the fossil evidence from East Asia. In: Smith F, Spencer F, editors. *The origins of modern humans: A world survey of the fossil evidence*. New York: Alan R. Liss. Pp. 411–83.

Woo J [Wu Rukang]. 1948. "Anterior" and "posterior" medio-palatine bones. MA thesis, Department of Anatomy, Washington University, St. Louis, MO.

Woo J [Wu Rukang]. 1949. Ossification, growth and variation of the human maxilla and palate bone. Ph.D. dissertation, Department of Anatomy, Washington University, St. Louis, MO.

Woo J [Wu Rukang]. 1958. Tzeyang Paleolithic man—earliest representative of modern man in China. *American Journal of Physical Anthropology* 16: 459–71.

Woo TL [Wu Dingliang]. 1928. Dextrality and sinistrality of hand and eye: Second memoir. *Biometrika* 20A: 79–148.

Woo TL [Wu Dingliang]. 1929. Tables for ascertaining the significance or non-significance of association measured by the correlation ratio. *Biometrika* 21: 1–66.

Woo TL [Wu Dingliang]. 1930. A study of seventy-one Ninth Dynasty Egyptian skulls from Sedment. *Biometrika* 22: 65–93.

Woo TL [Wu Dingliang]. 1931. On the asymmetry of the human skull. *Biometrika* 22: 324–52.

Woo TL [Wu Dingliang]. 1937. A biometric study of the human malar bone. *Biometrika* 29: 113–23.

Woo TL [Wu Dingliang]. 1941. On the glabella prominence of the human cranium. *Anthropological Journal of the Institute of History and Philology* 1: 205–21.

Woo TL [Wu Dingliang]. 1942. The physical characteristics of the Pa Miao people of Kweichow and other peoples of South China. *Journal of the Royal Asiatic Institute* 72: 45–53.

Woo TL [Wu Dingliang], Morant GM. 1932. A preliminary classification of Asiatic races based on cranial measurements. *Biometrika* 24: 108–34.

Woo TL [Wu Dingliang], Morant GM. 1934. A biometric study of the "flatness" of the facial skeleton in man. *Biometrika* 26: 196–250.

Woo TL [Wu Dingliang], Pearson K. 1927. Dextrality and sinistrality of hand and eye. *Biometrika* 19: 165–99.

Woo TL [Wu Dingliang], Yan Y. 1940. Index of measure [for] the position of front and back of mentale. *Academia Sinica, Monograph of the National Research Institute of History and Language, Anthropology Collected Papers* (国立中央研究院历史语言研究所人类学集刊) 2: 99–106.

Wu D. 1940. Review of relations among frontal bone measurements and glabella prominence in Chinese crania. *Bulletin of the Institute of History and Philology, Academia Sinica* (国立中央研究院历史语言研究所集刊) 2: 91–98.

Wu D. 1956. Evolutionary changes in chin position. *Fudan Journal* (Natural Science) (复旦学报) (自然科学) 1: 159–68.

Wu D. 1957a. Children's physical conditions in recent twenty years of Nanjing. *Fudan Journal* (Science Edition) (复旦学报) (自然科学) 2: 439–49.

Wu D. 1957b. Children's physical conditions in recent twenty years of Danyang County. *Fudan Journal* (Science Edition) (复旦学报) (自然科学) 2: 244–53.

Wu D. 1960. Comparative study of the ape-man supraorbital torii. *Vertebrate Paleontology and Paleoanthropology* (古脊椎动物与古人类) 2: 22–24.

Wu D, Mo R. 1932. *A preliminary classification of Asiatic races based on cranial measurements* (亚洲人种初步分类). Nanking: Academia Sinica.

Wu Rongyou. 2005. *The founders of Chinese anthropology—Wu Dingliang.* Center for Sociological Research and Anthropology of China (online publication).

Wu Rukang. 1956. Human fossils found in China and their significance in human evolution. *Scientia Sinica* (科学) 5: 389–97.

Wu Rukang. 1957. *Dryopithecus* teeth from Keiyuan, Yunnan Province. *Vertebrata Palasiatica* (古脊椎动物学报) 1: 25–31.

Wu Rukang. 1958. New materials of *Dryopithecus* from Keiyuan, Yunnan. *Vertebrata Palasiatica* (古脊椎动物学报) 2: 38–43.

Wu Rukang. 1959a. Anthropology in China. *Soviet Anthropology* (Советская Антропология) 1: 107–11.

Wu Rukang. 1959b. Groundbreaking discovery of ancient human fossils in Shaoguan City, Guangdong Province. *Vertebrate Paleontology and Paleoanthropology* (古脊椎动物与古人类) 1: 159–63.

Wu Rukang. 1989. *Paleoanthropology* (古人类学). Beijing: Cultural Relics.

Wu Rukang. 1999. On Weidenreich's work of *Sinanthropus pekinensis* and his theories of human origins. *Acta Anthropologica Sinica* (人类学学报) 18: 161–64.

Wu Rukang, Cheboksarov NN. 1959. On the continuity of the development of physical type, economic activity and culture of humans of ancient time in the territory of China. *Soviet Ethnography* (Советская Этнография) 4: 3–25.

Wu Rukang, Dong X. 1982. Preliminary study of *Homo erectus* remains from Hexian, Anhui. *Acta Anthropologica Sinica* (人类学学报) 1: 2–13.

Wu Rukang, Wu X. 1978. *The history of human development* (人类发展史). Beijing: Science Publishing House.

Wu Rukang, Wu X. 1984. Hominid fossils from China and their relation to those of neighboring regions. In: Whyte RO, editor. *The evolution of the East Asian environment.* Vol. 2. Hong Kong: University of Hong Kong. Pp. 787–95.

Wu Rukang, Xu Q, Lu Q. 1983. Morphological features of *Ramapithecus* and *Sivapithecus* and their phylogenetic relationships: Morphology and comparison of the crania. *Acta Anthropologica Sinica* (人类学学报) 2: 1–10.

Wu X. 1998. Origin of modern humans of China viewed from cranio-dental characteristics of late *Homo sapiens* in China. *Acta Anthropologica Sinica* (人类学学报) 17: 276–82.

Wu X. 2006a. New arguments on continuity of human evolution in China. *Acta Anthropologica Sinica* (人类学学报) 25: 17–25.

Wu X. 2006b. Evidence of multiregional human evolution hypothesis from China. *Quaternary Sciences* (第四纪研究) 26: 702–9.

Wu X, Shao X, Wang H. 1982. Sex differences and sex determination of the innominate bone of modern Han nationality. *Acta Anthropologica Sinica* (人类学学报) 1: 118–31.

Wu X, Zhang Zhenbiao. 1985. *Homo sapiens* remains from Late Palaeolithic and Neolithic in China. In: Wu Rukang, Olsen JW, editors. *Palaeoanthropology and Palaeolithic archeology in the People's Republic of China.* Orlando, FL: Academic Press. Pp. 107–33.

Wu X, Zhang Zhenbiao, Din X. 1984. Age determination of Chinese clavicles. *Acta Anthropologica Sinica* (人类学学报) 3: 30–31.

Xi H. 1985. Regression formulae for estimating age and stature from epiphyseal fusion and linear measurements. *Acta Anthropologica Sinica* (人类学学报) 4: 264–67.

Xie X. 1984. Effects on the inner and outer diameters of tibia by different sports on X-ray film. *Acta Anthropologica Sinica* (人类学学报) 3: 118–25.

Yan Y. 1961. The relationship between archaeology and anthropology—the estimation of sex and ages of human bones. *Kaogu* (考古) 7: 364–70.

Yan Y. 1962. The Neolithic human skeletons unearthed at Huaxian, Shaanxi. *Acta Archaeologica Sinica* (考古学报) 2: 85–104.

Yan Y. 1972. Report of the Dawenkou Neolithic human bones. *Acta Archaeologica Sinica* (考古学报) 1: 91–122.

Yan Y, Wu X, Liu C, Gu Y. 1960. A study of human skeletons from Banpo, Xi'an, Shaanxi. *Kaogu* (考古) 9: 36–47.

Yang M, Liu W, Tai F. 1988. Sex determination of mandible by discriminant analysis. *Acta Anthropologica Sinica* (人类学学报) 7: 329–34.

Zdansky O. 1927. Preliminary notice on two teeth of a hominid from a cave in Chihli (China). *Bulletin of the Geological Society of China* 5: 281–84.

Zhan L. 1986. A preliminary survey on dental alveolar diseases of Neolithic human beings in China. *Acta Anthropologica Sinica* (人类学学报) 5: 352–57.

Zhang J, Han B. 1994. The sexing clavicles of Chinese Han. *Acta Anthropologica Sinica* (人类学学报) 13: 314–20.

Zhang J, Ji Y. 1988. Tooth attrition and age estimation of Chinese males. *Acta Anthropologica Sinica* (人类学学报) 7: 230–34.

Zhang J, Tian X. 2001. The sexing of Chinese Han clavicles with Fisher's linear discriminant functions. *Acta Anthropologica Sinica* (人类学学报) 20: 209–16.

Zhang Q, Cao J, Zhu Hong. 2009. Research on dental caries of ancient populations during Bronze Age and Early Iron Age in southern central Inner Mongolia. *Acta Anthropologica Sinica* (人类学学报) 28: 372–78.

Zhang Q, Zhu H. 2006. Cribra orbitalia on the Bronze Age skulls from Yanghai Cemetery in Shanshan, Xinjiang. *Acta Anthropologica Sinica* (人类学学报) 25: 102–5.

Zhang Y. 1998. Variation of upper-facial flatness, referring to the human crania from Upper Cave in Zhoukoudian. *Acta Anthropologica Sinica* (人类学学报) 17: 247–54.

Zhang Zhenbiao. 1993. The observation on the fracture of human remains from several archaeological sites in China. *Acta Anthropologica Sinica* (人类学学报) 12: 319–26.

Zhang Zhenbiao. 1994. The skeletal evidence of human leprosy and syphilis in ancient China. *Acta Anthropologica Sinica* (人类学学报) 13: 294–99.

Zhang Zhenbiao. 1995. The skeletal evidence of the ankylosing spondylitis in ancient China. *Acta Anthropologica Sinica* (人类学学报) 14: 110–17.

Zhang Zhenbiao, Lu D, Liu Y, Re J, Bian J, Wang Y, Zhu G. 1996. Estimating pubic age by photograph of soft X-ray. *Acta Anthropologica Sinica* (人类学学报) 15: 145–50.

Zhang Zhongyao. 1982. A preliminary study of estimation of age by morphological changes in the symphysis pubis. *Acta Anthropologica Sinica* (人类学学报) 1: 132–36.

Zhang Zhongyao. 1986. A further study on the relationship between morphologic features of pubic symphyses and age estimation. *Acta Anthropologica Sinica* (人类学学报) 5: 30–37, 101–3.

Zheng T, Pang T. 1988. Determination of sex from the tibia by the stepwise discriminatory analysis. *Acta Anthropologica Sinica* (人类学学报) 7: 154–59.

Zheng X. 1993. Chemical element analysis of Bronze Age human femurs in China. *Acta Anthropologica Sinica* (人类学学报) 12: 241–50.

Zhou D. 1984. The oral conditions of Emperor Wan Li of the Ming dynasty and his two queens. *Acta Anthropologica Sinica* (人类学学报) 3: 20–24.

Zhou S, Zhang B, Rong Y, Yu X. 1997. Sex determination of patella of Chinese Han nationality. *Acta Anthropologica Sinica* (人类学学报) 16: 31–37.

Zhu F. 1983a. Preliminary study on determination of bone age by microscopic method. *Acta Anthropologica Sinica* (人类学学报) 2: 142–51.

Zhu F. 1983b. Study on the estimation of stature from phalanges of middle finger. *Acta Anthropologica Sinica* (人类学学报) 2: 375–79.

Zhu F, Lu W. 1997. The dental caries of the Neolithic population from Zengpiyan cave of Guilin, China. *Acta Anthropologica Sinica* (人类学学报) 16: 271–73.

2

Human Ecology in Continental and Insular East Asia

KATE PECHENKINA AND MARC OXENHAM

People, plants, animals, the land, and everything else on earth
are interlaced in singular and sometimes dysfunctional ways.

Daniel W. Gade 1999: 1

Continental East Asia is loosely demarcated by the Tibetan plateau in the west, the Tian Shan and Altai mountain ranges in the northwest, the Yablonevy and Stanovoy ridges in the northeast, several distinct mountain ranges including Hengduan Shan and Fan Si Pan Sa Phin in the south, and the expanse of the Pacific Ocean on the east and southeast (figure 2.1). For *Homo sapiens*, with their capacity to move from place to place, these geographic boundaries are relatively permeable. Nevertheless, during prehistory and early history they circumscribed a conglomerate of human communities that formed an inter-action network, an ancient *oikoumene*, within which genes and ideas were traded more freely than with outsiders.

Kwang-Chih Chang proposed the concept of a Chinese interaction sphere[1] to represent the indigenous cultures of the Huang He (Yellow River) and Chang Jiang (Yangtze River) valleys that were interlinked since at least the time of the Neolithic (Chang 1986: 241). However, developments within early human communities across East Asia, including innovations in lithic technology (Sagawa 1998), the transition to farming (Crawford and Shen 1998; Crawford and Lee 2003; Bettinger et al. 2007; Barton et al. 2009; Crawford 2009; Jones and Liu 2009; Ahn 2010; Zhao 2010; Cohen 2011; Fuller and Qin 2011; Zhao 2011), and technological advances in pottery making and metallurgy (Linduff 1995, 1998; Wagner 1999) often involved interaction over a much wider territory, encompassing both continental and insular populations; not all were centered on the Chinese core.

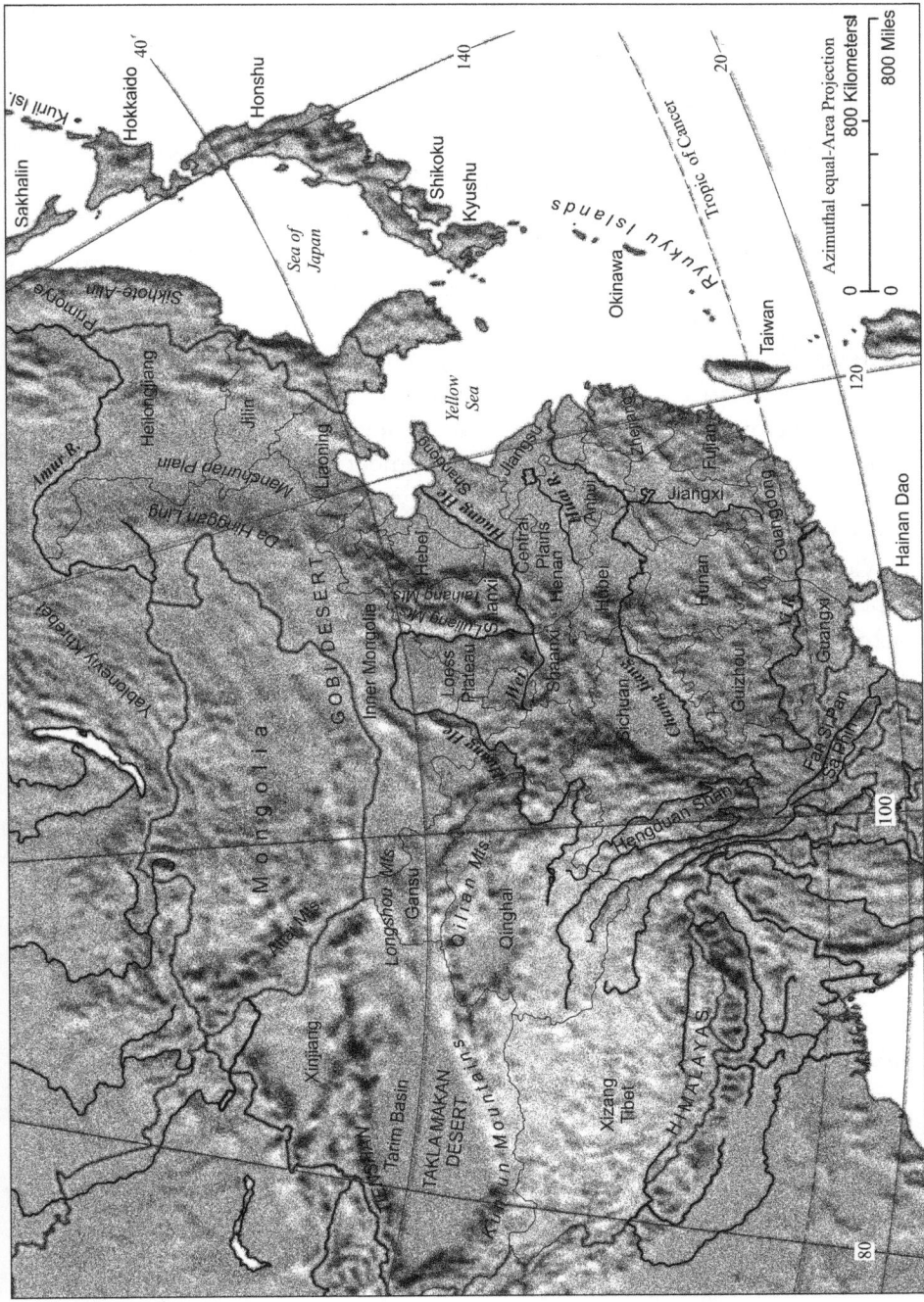

Figure 2.1. Continental East Asia.

To say that an area of over 12,000,000 km^2 encompasses diverse ecological settings would be to state the obvious. The East Asian landscape, often dominated by hills or low mountains, gives ample opportunity for microclimate formation. Ecosystems range from dense subtropical forests in the south to deciduous and coniferous forests in the north, as well as alpine grasslands at higher altitudes. However, when the large extent of continental East Asia is considered, environmental settings are fairly monotonous when compared with the extreme zonality found in the South American Andes, New Guinea, or Madagascar. From southeast to northwest, climate gradually changes from monsoon-dominated subtropics to temperate continental with well-expressed seasonality. This is not to say that climate in the area is stable or predictable, as severe droughts and heavy rainfall causing floods show great interannual variability across the region (Yang and Lau 2004). Limited zonality, overshadowed by considerable climatic change from season to season and year to year, likely favored population movement and did not considerably obstruct the exchange of farming technology and other innovations among distant communities.

Cold boreal climate dominates Manchuria, as well as northern Hokkaido. Japan, with four main islands and numerous smaller ones, extends from the subtropical latitudes in the south (Okinawa, 24° north) to the subarctic north (45° north). Nonetheless, with very limited lowland areas, much of the land falls within the temperate zone. The archipelago is mountainous, extensively forested even today, and experiences very high levels of rainfall. Vegetation ranges from warm, broad-leaved evergreen forests in Kyushu, Shikoku, and the south of Honshu, to deciduous and mixed forests in Honshu and coniferous forests in Hokkaido, with alpine and subalpine vegetation at higher elevations (Aikens and Higuchi 1982: 1–2).

Initial Peopling of the Region

When and in what manner our conspecifics first reached East Asia is a subject of vigorous debate among the supporters of various multiregional continuity, assimilation, and out-of-Africa or replacement models of human origins (e.g., Pope 1992; Aiello 1993; Wu X 1998, 2004; Wu R 1999; Wolpoff et al. 2000; Liu et al. 2010). That discussion is outside the scope of this volume. No scientist would contest that modern humans were well established in continental East Asia by the Late Pleistocene. A mandibular fragment with symphyseal morphology characteristic of anatomically modern humans, found in 2007 at Zhiren Cave (智人洞) in southern Guangxi Province, seems to document that anatomically modern humans entered East Asia very early, possibly at the very beginning of the Late Pleistocene (Liu et al. 2010). Other anatomically modern fossils found in China include a calvarium from the south slope of Xujiafen Hill in Huanglong (黄龙) (Wang and Li 1983) and a tooth from the Changwu (长武) site in the Yaotouguo Valley (Huang and Zheng 1982), both in Shaanxi Province; the perfectly preserved Liujiang (柳江) skull and a hip bone from the Tongtianyan Cave in Guangxi (Wu R 1982; Wu X 1997); and five teeth from Fox Cave (Lidong—狸洞) at Qingliu (清流) in Fujian (Dong and Fan 1996).

Because many of these specimens were recovered during the first half of the twentieth century, there is considerable ambiguity in their dating. Direct AMS dating of collagen extracted from a Xarus Valley human femur, formerly presumed to be a Pleistocene fossil, yielded dates as recent as 300–190 BP (Keates et al. 2007). Uranium series dating of breccias presumed to have been associated with the Liujiang find are suggested to indicate that the skull dates to no less than 67,000 BP and more likely to 111,000–139,000 BP (Shen et al. 2002; Wang et al. 2004). According to alternative stratigraphic assumptions, the same skull may be approximately 153,000 years old (Shen et al. 2002). However, doubts about the precise relationship between the dated breccias and the fossil allow considerable uncertainty about the Liujiang skull's actual age (Brown 1999). *Homo sapiens* crania from the Upper Cave at Zhoukoudian probably date to the terminal Pleistocene or early Holocene. Radiocarbon dates obtained directly from animal bone recovered inside the cave include 10,770+360 BP for bone found in the vicinity of the burials and 18,865+420 BP for a deer bone found in the Lower Recess (Institute of Archaeology–CASS 1991: 17; An 1991).

Through colder phases of the Middle and Late Pleistocene, land bridges formed between continental East Asia and the islands of the Japanese archipelago, both in the north, joining Hokkaido and Sakhalin with outer Manchuria, and in the south, across the Korean strait from the Korean peninsula to the consolidated mass of Honshu, Kyushu, and Shikoku (Aikens and Higuchi 1982: 27–28). Taiwan and hundreds of smaller islands south and east of China were also periodically consolidated with the continental land mass. In eastern Taiwan, the Paleolithic Changbin (長濱) culture in the south and Zuozhen (左鎮) culture in the west mark human presence in that area by 30,000 years ago (Song 1969). The advancement of China's coastline up to 600 km during the Younger Dryas (12,700–11,500 BP), the last glacial maximum of the terminal Pleistocene (Peng et al. 1984), also made that a likely time for human migration from the continent onto what are now islands off East Asia.

A series of Late Pleistocene human fossil material has been recovered in

Japan and its vicinity over the years (see Matsu'ura 1999 for a summary), the earliest of which thus far came from the Minatogawa (港川) Fissure of Okinawa Island and was dated by radiocarbon to between 18,250+650 and 16,600+300 BP (Matsu'ura 1982). These specimens show morphological resemblances to both the Liujiang skull from southern China and later Jomon (縄文) fishers and foragers occupying the Japanese archipelago between 12,000 and 2300 years ago (Suzuki and Hanihara 1982; Baba and Narasaki 1991). However, the pertinent literature emphasizes that the Minatogawa skeletal material does not represent direct ancestors of Jomon people in Japan but instead shared a common continental ancestry with them. Cranial and dental features, in turn, suggest that Jomon people resembled the Ainu (アイヌ) of Hokkaido (北海道) and, to a lesser degree, the Ryukyu (琉球) of Okinawa (沖縄) (Hanihara 1984; Brace et al. 1989; Hanihara 1991, 1993; Kozintsev 1992; Pietrusewsky 2000; Fukumine et al. 2006), as also seen in their mtDNA (Horai et al. 1991). Consequently, indigenous Ainu and Ryukyu are assumed to have retained some of the genetic distinctiveness of the Late Pleistocene migrants from the continent.

The Japanese archaeological record dates back to 25,000–30,000 BP, when edge-ground axes and associated wet-stones appeared in many parts of the archipelago, with the exception of Hokkaido (Imamura 1996a: 24). These are only a little later than the most reliably dated and provenienced edge-ground axes in the world, recently reported from northern Australia at 35,000+410 cal BP (Geneste et al. 2010). The Japanese Late Paleolithic is traditionally divided into pre- and post-Aira-Tanzawa (始良丹沢) phases (a volcanic ash layer, well dated to 21,000–22,000 BP), with relative lithic artifact homogeneity during pre-AT and more marked regional forms appearing post-AT (Imamura 1996a: 23). Given that Japan lacks an Early or Middle Paleolithic,[2] evidence for the movement of obsidian from the Asian mainland to Japan in the Late Paleolithic, as well as mainland blade lithic precursors to this same technology in the late stages of the Late Paleolithic (Imamura 1996a: 34), is consistent with the likelihood that the Late Paleolithic witnessed the first colonization of the archipelago by anatomically modern humans.

Exactly which continental populations were the first to settle in Japan and via which route is still unresolved, with somewhat different scenarios supported by differing classes of evidence. Strong ties between modern Ainu, Jomon foragers of the early Holocene, and the natives of Polynesia and Micronesia are evidenced by cranial and dental characteristics (Turner and Hanihara 1977; Turner 1979; Brace et al. 1989), which implies that the earliest inhabitants of the Japanese archipelago were Austronesian and Southeast Asian (Hanihara 1991). Classical genetic markers found in modern Ainu and

Ryukyu link Pleistocene migrations into Japan to Northeast Asia (Omoto and Saitou 1997).

A somewhat different scenario for the peopling of Japan is suggested by the distribution of Y-chromosome haplogroups (Hammer et al. 2006). Mutation sequences of Haplogroup D, the most common in Ainu and Ryukyu people, are ultimately traced to Central Asia and offer evidence of geographic expansion into the Japanese archipelago at approximately 20,000 BP. In contrast, Y-chromosome Haplogroup O, the most common in Japan overall, is associated with population expansion in Northeast Asia dated to 4000 BP, culminating in substantial migrations to the Japanese archipelago around 2500 BP (Hammer et al. 2006). These genetic results are supported by cranial and odontometric studies indicating that Jomon foragers were similar to North Asian people (Pietrusewsky 1999; Seguchi et al. 2007), while Yayoi (弥生) agriculturalists, along with the modern population of Japan, are more similar to migrant groups from Korea or northern China (Brace and Nagai 1982; Turner 1990; Nakahashi 1995; Pietrusewsky 1999; Nakahashi et al. 2002).

Following the Upper Paleolithic, population movement and interaction within continental East Asia, as well as between the continent and the islands, became extremely complex. Because these phenomena shaped the morphogenetic, cultural, and linguistic variation of both ancient peoples and their descendants, affected the trajectories of indigenous agriculture, animal husbandry, and technological development, and altered the epidemiological landscape, their accurate reconstruction serves as one of the overarching themes of bioarchaeological research in this area. As such, population movement and interaction are treated in detail throughout this volume. The most prominent routes of biological and cultural exchange followed on periodic invasions of China from the steppe, incessant movement along the Silk Road (Han 1994; Guo et al. 2001; Suzuki et al. 2005; Tan and Han 2007), and the aforementioned expansion into Japan, which began at about 300 BC (Imamura 1996b).

Paleoeconomy

Only a modest number of studies focused on human skeletal remains have considered the possible impacts of the introduction of new types of cooking vessels or other changes in ceramic technology and metallurgy on indicators of diet and health, as well as on cranial and dental morphology (Brace 1962; Scott 1979; Hinton 1982; Kaifu 1999; Eshed et al. 2006; Mahoney 2006). Nevertheless, the development of pottery and—much later—the use of metals for vessel production probably had profound effects on the distribution of skeletal markers. More effective heating and boiling of food in ceramic containers alters its texture and dietary value, while helping to extirpate some pathogens and break down toxins, thus affecting patterns of dental wear, as well as the distribution of dietary deficiencies and parasitic loads. With improvements in pottery technology, more heat-resistant vessels would have allowed prolonged cooking, simmering, or sautéing at higher temperatures (Braun 1983; O'Brien et al. 1994). The sharing of utensils both within and between families may help to propagate certain pathogens and intestinal parasites across a community. Finally, the use of certain metal alloys in the manufacture of cooking vessels can introduce traces of lead and other heavy metals into food.

East Asia was peculiar in its early development of pottery, predating plant and animal domestication by a substantial margin. Pottery appeared during the terminal Pleistocene in the Russian Far East and southern China and only slightly later in northern China and Japan (Kuzmin and Orlova 2000; Kuzmin 2002, 2006; Keally et al. 2004; Wang 2005; Boaretto et al. 2009). In the Amur area and Primorye, containers made of fired clay were recovered from six archaeological sites with radiocarbon dates spanning a time period from 14,510+240 to 9,360+30 BP (Zhushchikhovskaya 2005: 24). In China, at least two centers of early pottery making have been identified. The southern area is represented by early pottery from archaeological sites left by foragers and fishers in Jiangxi, Hunan, Guangxi, and Zhejiang, with radiocarbon dates possibly as early as 17,238+237 BP from Guangxi. The northern area encompasses sites in the Beijing area and in Hebei Province dated to the earliest Holocene (Wang 2005). Nanzhouangtou (南庄头), in Hebei Province, is one of the earliest pottery-bearing sites in the north, with associated radiocarbon dates ranging from 10,815+140 to 9,690+95 BP (Yuan 2007). Even earlier dates (18,300 to 15,430 cal BP) were obtained based on charcoal and collagen from animal bones associated with pottery from Yuchanyan (玉蟾岩) Cave (Boaretto et al. 2009).

During the time of the Middle Neolithic Yangshao (仰韶) (c. 5000 to 3000 BC) and Dawenkou (大汶口) (4100 to 2600 BC) cultures, the technical quality of pottery and perhaps its resistance to heat increased in northeastern China with the development of new pastes and pottery kilns that allowed higher firing temperatures. There was further technological improvement in Late Neolithic Longshan (龙山) (3000 to 2000 BC), with the introduction of the pottery wheel (An 1988a; Liu 2003). Wheel-thrown, thin-walled pottery of the Late Neolithic was probably more heat resistant than earlier wares, affording the use of different food processing techniques or more prolonged cooking (Braun 1983; O'Brien et al. 1994).

Residue analyses of Late Neolithic pots from Shandong indicate that some of them were used for the production or serving of fermented beverages (McGovern et al. 2004, 2005). Further refinement of vessel forms and decoration, as well as the unequal distribution of fine and coarse wares in archaeological sites from the Late Neolithic and subsequent Dynastic period on, marked a shift toward using pottery as an elite good and in rituals (Liu 2003), thus redefining the extent to which these wares were shared among community members and the routes via which pathogens could spread.

Copper and bronze apparently first entered the Yellow River valley from the steppe area via a northwestern route during the Late Neolithic (c. 3000 BC) (Linduff 1998). Among the earliest uses of these metals in northern China was production of drinking vessels imitating those made of clay, as well as to make other utilitarian objects (Liu 2003). Use of these utensils provided ample opportunities for the introduction of toxic residues into human food.

Subsistence

Continental East Asia

Plant and Animal Domestication

Initial experimentation with cereal cultivation in China has generally been thought to have begun about 10,000–9,000 years ago (Wu Z 1998; Xu 1998; Xiang 2000; Yi 2000). However, recent AMS radiocarbon dates determined directly from grains of broomcorn millet (*Panicum miliaceum*) recovered at the Early Neolithic Cishan (磁山) site in Hebei suggest that millet-based food production was already well established in northern China by ~10,400–10,100 cal BP, on the brink of the Holocene (Crawford 2009; Lu 2006). With increasing warmth and humidity during the early Holocene, reliance on domesticated monogastric animals and on cereal agriculture combined with vegetable horticulture and some foraging activities became more widespread (Ho 1977; Liu and Chen 2003; Yan 2005; Jiang and Liu 2006; Flad et al. 2007; Yang et al. 2009). During this favorable climatic episode, cereals were apparently cultivated not only for human consumption but also as support for large numbers of domesticated animals, including pigs and dogs (Pechenkina et al. 2005; Barton et al. 2009).

Staple cereals grown in ancient China included five species of grasses with somewhat complementary qualities. Rice (*Oryza sativa*) is a warmth- and water-loving cereal that is resistant to overwatering. When grown in paddies under favorable environmental conditions, it is probably the most productive Old World cereal, with crop yields as high as 1,290–1,385 kg per ha (Allan

1970). However, when cultivated on dry land, rice yields only about half of its potential. Although the overall protein content of rice is low, it is not as lysine deficient as the majority of other cereals. The two species of millet grown in East Asia, foxtail millet (*Setaria italica*) and broomcorn millet (*Panicum miliaceum*), are among the least fastidious of cereals, resistant to heat, cold, drought, and poor soil quality. Both can produce reasonable crop yields over a short growth season with very little care (Zohary and Hopf 2001: 83, 86; Lu 1999, 2002). Millet grains are tiny and fairly rich in protein (9.5–13 percent of dry weight) but are very lysine deficient, even more so than maize. Wheat (*Triticum aestivum*) is a cereal with a very high output, moderately resistant to cold, but it requires watering, especially during the dry springtime of the north. Wheat is also rich in protein (8–14 percent) (Zohary and Hopf 2001: 19; Zhao 2002). Finally, barley (*Hordeum vulgare*) also has a fairly high protein content and is very cold resistant but gives only modest yields (Zhao 2002; FAO 1972).

During the early Holocene, a warmer climate and increased annual rainfall allowed the spread of wild rice, *Oryza rufipogon*, into the Yangtze Valley (Yan 1989, 1997; Zhao 1998; Zhao and Piperno 2000) and central Henan (Zhang and Wang 1998), much farther north than it grows today. Consequently, a broad front of domestication for this cereal seems possible. Phytoliths of domesticated rice were recovered from the 9,000–10,000-year-old zone of Diaotonghuan (吊桶环) Cave, located in the middle reaches of the Yangtze (Zhao 1998). Rice phytoliths dated to around 10,000 years ago were also recovered from the Shangshan (上山) site, Zhejiang Province, in the lower reaches of the Yangtze (Jiang and Liu 2006). A sequence of rice phytoliths evidencing progressive domestication between 7000 and 5800 BC has been reported from Jiahu (贾湖), in the Huai River area (Chen et al. 1995a,b,c). However, Fuller and colleagues (2007) note that Jiahu rice is small and morphologically similar to its wild progenitor.

Grains of rice morphologically intermediate between the domestic and wild species were recovered from the Yuchanyan (玉蟾岩) site in Hunan Province, with radiocarbon dates ranging between 14,080+270 and 12,320+120 BP. The earliest direct AMS dates on grains of carbonized rice were determined from specimens recovered at the Pengtoushan (彭头山) site on the Lake Dongting plain (7,775+90 and 7,259+150 BP), confirming that rice agriculture was being practiced in that area by over 7,000 radiocarbon years ago (Crawford and Shen 1998). Rice agriculture apparently reached Taiwan via seafaring from southern China around 6,000 years ago, as evidenced by the Dapenkeng (大盆坑) Neolithic tradition on the island (6000–4500 BP) (Chang 1969).

Despite the evidence for early domestication of rice, its role in the subsistence of ancient Chinese is far from clear. Analysis of phytolith sequences from Qingpu (青浦), south of the Yangtze (Itzstein-Davey et al. 2007), suggests that cultivation of domesticated rice in this region did not commence until approximately 300 BC, while collecting wild rice retained its importance for another 250 years. Stable isotope analysis of human bones from Jiahu (Hu et al. 2006) indicates strong reliance on C3 plants, which might include rice, with highly variable amounts of meat and freshwater aquatic resources also being exploited. Poor oral health at this site suggests a heavy emphasis on cereal agriculture (Smith 2005). However, the dental sample available for Jiahu is tiny, and it is not always clear with which strata the analyzed skeletons were associated.

Historically, rice agriculture in southern China relied on paddy construction using the swamp buffalo (genus *Bubalus*) as a draft animal, increasing rice yields and helping to extirpate less water-resistant weeds. Use of paddies for rice agriculture probably became established sometime before 4000 BC, as suggested by preserved features at Hemudu (河姆渡) in Zhejiang (Zhao and Wu 1987; Zhao 1998). Small, shallow depressions found in the vicinity of the Jiahu and Pengtoushan sites, oval or round in shape and dated to between 7000 and 6000 BC, have been commonly interpreted as paddies, although they might have been fishponds or water reservoirs (Liu 2000).

When domesticated buffalo became an integral part of the wetland rice agriculture complex is more uncertain. Chen and Li (1989) proposed that *Bubalus* was domesticated circa 5000 BC, based on common finds of its skeletal elements in early archaeological contexts. Because *Bubalus* remains were recovered at Hemudu, Zhao (1998) argued that buffalo were employed for paddy construction as early as 4000 BC. However, reexamination of bovid remains from a number of archaeological sites and tests of ancient DNA by Liu and colleagues (2006) have resulted in the conclusion that buffalo remains from Neolithic archaeological contexts are of those of wild animals and that domesticated *Bubalus bubalus* was introduced from South Asia as late as 1000 BC.

In the Yellow and Wei River valleys of northern China, millets were the dominant crop plants during the Neolithic. During the third millennium BC, wheat and barley were introduced to northern territories of China from the steppe through the Hexi (河西) corridor (Flad et al. 2010) and then spread into the Central Plains by 1600–1300 BC (Lee et al. 2007). Both foxtail and broomcorn millet were probably domesticated locally, as their earliest appearances in the paleobotanical record of the Old World were in northern China. *Setaria viridis*, the wild progenitor of foxtail millet (*Setaria italica*), still grows there (Lu 2002), whereas the wild ancestor of *Panicum miliaceum* has not been conclusively identified and might no longer exist (Zohary and Hopf 2001: 83). Through the Neolithic, foxtail millet was the preponderant crop on the Central Plains, and broomcorn millet was grown in smaller quantities (Ho 1977; Yan 1992, 2005; Lee et al. 2007).

Carbonized millet and abundant agricultural tools have been recovered from Early Neolithic sites of the Peiligang (裴李崗), Cishan (磁山), and Dadiwan (大地灣) cultures (An 1984; Ren 1994; Lu 2006). In archaeological sites of the Middle Neolithic Yangshao culture, grains of carbonized millet, agricultural tools, large storage pits, and grinding stones are ubiquitous, indicative of a well-developed dryland agricultural regime (Chang 1968). During the Erlitou (二里头) culture, all four cereals were cultivated, possibly to help ensure greater crop stability and caloric output as an adaptation to the onset of more adverse and unpredictable environmental conditions between 1900 and 1500 BC (Lee and Bestel 2007; Liu 2009: 226).

Rice does not grow very well in the north, because of insufficient rainfall and lower temperatures. Nevertheless, rice cultivation apparently spread into the Yellow River valley around 5,000 years ago, where it was probably grown in small quantities near the waterways (Yan 1982; An 1988b; Jiang and Zhang 1998; Lee et al. 2007). Analysis of pottery residues from the Liangchengzhen site in Shandong indicates that rice was the main component of fermented beverages mixed with honey, fruit, plant resin, and possibly other ingredients; millet, while common in the archaeobotanical record of the site, evidently was not used in this way (McGovern et al. 2005). Thus, the rice grown in small quantities in northern China might have been defined by its importance as a component of specific recipes.

The husbandry of monogastric animals (pigs, dogs, and chickens) in China probably developed in parallel with agriculture. On the one hand, cereal agriculture was necessary to generate fodder for these animals. On the other hand, consumption of human food leftovers by pigs and dogs allowed conversion of calories that otherwise would have been wasted into dietary fat and protein. The earliest known domesticated dog, as diagnosed by size reduction, comes from the early pottery-bearing site of Nanzhouangtou (8000–6000 BC), in Hebei (Yuan 2007). Wild boar, native to the forests of ancient East Asia, was probably domesticated independently in several areas of northern and southern China (Zhou 1981; Wang 1985; Yuan and Flad 2002; Yuan 2007).

The Xinglongwa (興隆洼) site in Inner Mongolia (6200–5000 BC), which has produced evidence of early millet agriculture, the Cishan site (6000–5000 BC), and the early rice-bearing site of Kuahuqiao (跨湖桥) (6200–5000

BC) in Zhejiang Province of southeastern China all have evidence of incipient pig domestication (Yuan 2007). The frequency of pig remains in archaeological assemblages increased through the Middle Neolithic, so that by 3500 BC pig bones were predominant in some faunal assemblages from northern China (Yuan and Flad 2002; Ma 2005). When and where chickens were domesticated remains controversial, mainly due to poor preservation of small bones and the difficulty of species diagnosis (Yuan 2001). Nevertheless, finds of chicken bones have been reported from Chinese Middle Neolithic sites, including Beishouling in Baoji Province, Banpo in Xi'an, Jiangzhai in Lintong, and Nanzheng in Longgangsi, as well as Miaodigou in Shanxian and Baiying in Tangyin (Ren 1994).

The modes of millet use during the Neolithic and Early Dynastic periods in China are still being investigated. Judging from abundant grinding stones and some serendipitously preserved millet noodles from Lajia (喇家) (c. 2000 BC), in Qinghai Province, northwestern China (Lu et al. 2005), millet grain was being converted into flour and dough for human consumption in some places by about 4,000 years ago. As previously mentioned, millet also seems to have played an important role as fodder for domesticated animals, such as pigs, dogs, and fowl (Pechenkina et al. 2005; Barton et al. 2009). Studies of oral pathology (Pechenkina et al. 2002; Smith 2005) carried out on the remains of Middle Neolithic farmers from the Wei River valley—presumably engaged in millet agriculture circa 5000 to 4000 BC—found low to moderate frequencies of carious lesions, with a subsequent sharp increase in oral pathologies thereafter. This suggests either that until about 4000 BC millet was only consumed in modest quantities or that millet processing and cooking techniques changed at around that time in such a way as to increase its cariogenicity.

Agriculture and Animal Husbandry in Northeast Asia

North of the Kunlun and Longshou Mountains and beyond the Yellow River valley, a continental climate with low precipitation and harsh winters made plant cultivation both challenging and unreliable. Instead, mobile economies reliant on herding sheep/goats, cattle, and horses became established between 3000 and 2000 BC in northern and northwestern Mongolia (Allard and Erdenebaatar 2005). The Andronovo (Андроново) culture of horseback riders and herders in western Siberia (2300–1000 BC) had a pronounced influence on populations of the Tarim basin, as suggested by the presence there of typical Andronovo implements (Mei and Shell 1999), as well as by cranial morphologies that are usually linked to Andronovo nomads (Han 1986). Hills and mountain ridges separate the area of Xinjiang from northeastern

China. Interaction between peoples in Takla Makan with communities of the Wei and Yellow River valleys likely proceeded via the Hexi corridor, which lies between the Longshou and Qiliam Mountains in Gansu (Flad et al. 2007). Recovery of sheep and horse bones from Qijia (齊家) sites (4200 to 3800 years ago) in the Hexi corridor suggests that some exotic domesticated herbivores were passed on via that route into northeastern China at approximately 2000 BC (Flad et al. 2007).

Cereal agriculture seems to have played a secondary role in the subsistence of pastoralists in Xinjiang and Mongolia. Nevertheless, small-scale cultivation of drought-resistant crops, such as oats, millets, and spring wheat, was apparently practiced in the Tarim basin by sedentary communities incorporated within the range of the nomadic peoples of Xiongnu (匈奴), who controlled the steppe area during the third century BC (Xie 1972; Di Cosmo 1994). Symbiotic or perhaps parasitic relations between the mobile herders of the steppe and neighboring sedentary farmers resulted in exchange of the products of these two subsistence strategies. Barfield (2001: 10) proposed that "shadow empires" were established during the Bronze Age by mobile herders who routinely extracted resources from farming communities in northern China.

Dispersal of Agricultural Crops in, out of, and within East Asia

Millet agriculture reached Korea by 3400 BC, in Middle Chulmun (즐문 or Bit-sal-mu-ni), while rice agriculture arrived within the next thousand years, probably by 2500–2200 BC, during Late Chulmun (Crawford and Lee 2003). In Russian Primorye, north of the Amur River, *Setaria* millet was cultivated as early as 2800–2100 BC (Kuzmin et al. 1998). Millets spread into the Japanese archipelago around 900 BC, where traces of *Setaria* and *Panicum*, along with individual grains of rice, are reported from northeastern Honshu (reported AMS radiocarbon dates are 2540+240 BP and 2810+270 BP) (D'Andrea et al. 1995). This early rice could have arrived in Japan by three different routes: (1) via the Ryukyu Islands from Taiwan, where rice agriculture is documented during the time of the Dapenkeng (大盆坑) culture of the third millennium BC (Chang 1969); (2) from northeastern China into northern Kyushu, either directly or indirectly from southern Korea; or (3) from the Shandong peninsula via the western Korean coast into Kyushu (Kotani 1979). The presence of substantial quantities of dietary carbohydrates in the food of Late Jomonese, suggesting reliance on horticulture and cereal agriculture as early as 1000 BC, is supported by high frequencies of carious lesions documented for human remains from this period (Turner 1979). At the same time, reliance on wild resources continued to be important for the early cereal-growing economies of Korea and Japan, while farming played a fairly minor role (Kuzmin 2002; Crawford and Lee 2003).

While cereal agriculture took a fairly long time to reach Korea, the domesticated soybean, *Glycine max*, entered the paleobotanical record of both Korea and northern China almost simultaneously. Evidence of wild legumes, which are common in northern China even today, is frequently recovered via flotation in soil samples from Late Neolithic sites, but in small quantities and showing no seed size increase that would imply domestication (Lee et al. 2007). Nevertheless, the ubiquity of legumes suggests that they were important in human subsistence networks even before domestication. Morphological changes in the seeds of wild soybean (*Glycine* sp.) suggestive of domestication are documented no earlier than during the Shang dynasty, in paleobotanical collections from the Zaojiaoshu (皂角树) site in Henan, dated to 1900–1500 BC (Luoyang Archaeological Team, 2002; cited in Lee at al. 2007). The earliest known domesticated soybeans in Korea date from about 1000–900 BC (Crawford and Lee 2003).

Within the same time frame as the initial spread of domesticated millets and rice into Korea, Primorye, and insular East Asia, domesticated wheat and barley seem to have trickled into northeastern China. These new plant foods gradually began to surpass millets in their caloric contribution to the human diet (Zhao and He 2006). Liu Li (1996) suggested that intensive interethnic exchanges in the area of the Central Plains were stimulated by climatic fluctuations and changes in the course of the Yellow River that occurred between 3000 and 2000 BC. These changes made the fertile lands of the Yellow and Wei River valleys particularly attractive for the peoples in surrounding areas, resulting in population relocation, and possibly introduction of new crops and small domesticated herbivores (sheep and goats) from the north or northwest during the time of the Late Neolithic (2600–1900 BC). Several individual grains of wheat were reported from the Liangchengzhen site of the Late Neolithic Longshan culture in Shandong (Crawford et al. 2005), while analyses of food residues on pottery from the same site suggest the presence of barley (McGovern et al. 2005). Thirteen charred seeds resembling barley were recovered from another Longshan site, Taosi (陶寺), dated to between 2300 BC and 1900 BC (Zhao and He 2006). However, *Setaria* millet apparently remained the principal staple through the Neolithic, accounting for 70.1 percent of all seeds recovered by soil flotation at Taosi.

Based on analysis of Shang dynasty (商朝) characters engraved on turtle shells, Zhao Zhijun (2002) proposed that millet, rice, wheat, and barley were all grown in the Yellow River valley by approximately 1600 BC. He noted that wheat and barley are complementary staples, because wheat has a high output and is easy to process, while barley gives smaller yields but is very cold resistant. Heavier rainfall and warmer climate during the Shang period may have favored easy adoption of these new cereals. However, it remains unclear what other factors may have contributed to the eventual replacement of indigenous millets, grown in the Yellow and Wei River valleys for thousands of years, by these foreign crops. Considering the importance of millet, not only as a human staple but also as fodder for domestic animals, and the longer growth period of wheat, a substantial restructuring of the subsistence network would have been necessary with a shift to wheat agriculture.

Japan

Developments in the Japanese archipelago were very different from those on the mainland, although the generalized theme of complexity and heterogeneity over time and space was very much apparent there as well. Following the relatively well documented (and real) Late Paleolithic came the Jomon. Perhaps the most important review in recent years of the Jomon, whether in English or Japanese, is Junko Habu's (2004) *Ancient Jomon of Japan*, from which much of the following summary is derived, unless otherwise stated. Habu notes that the enormous wealth of data on the Jomon is a direct consequence of the extraordinary number of large-scale rescue excavations undertaken by cultural resource management (CRM) organizations since the 1970s. While it comes at the expense of research-driven archaeology, which has fluctuated between approximately 100 and 400 excavations per annum as compared to an increase from 1,040 rescue excavations in 1973 to 10,164 in 1995, the amount of available data is unique in global terms.

The emergence of the Jomon is seen by Japanese archaeologists as a function of both the appearance of pottery and change in lithic technologies. Relatively recent efforts at the absolute dating of archaeological sites in Japan indicate that undecorated pottery was used at Odai Yamamoto (大平山元) I, Aomori (青森) Prefecture, northern Honshu (本州), by approximately 16,500 cal BP. This is earlier than the better-known linear-relief and nail-impressed pottery from various layers in Fukui (福井) Cave, with dates in a range of approximately 12,500–15,800 cal BP (Habu 2004: 29). Habu notes that similarly early dates for pottery in the Russian Far East (especially the Amur River region), as well as similarities in lithics, tend to suggest this area as the point of origin, at least for Jomon material culture.

In general, Habu sees the transition from the Late Paleolithic to Incipient Jomon as being associated with a forager subsistence strategy, with a shift to smaller-sized terrestrial game at the beginning of the Jomon. Moreover, there appears to be limited evidence for any significant role of marine/freshwater fish exploitation during this transition, while there are data supporting plant exploitation (particularly grinding technology) in southern Kyushu (九州) and Tanegashima (種子島) Island (Habu 2004: 247). For the most part Habu suggests that the subsistence strategy of much of the Incipient Jomon can be characterized as residentially mobile foraging.

In terms of chronological phases, for the most part dated and distinguished by way of pottery typologies, the Jomon spans more than 10,000 years: Incipient followed by Initial (variously dated up to 6000 or 7000 uncal BP), Early followed by Middle (dated up to 3500 to 4000 uncal BP), then Late followed by Final (dated to the emergence of the Yayoi at approximately 2500 uncal BP) (Habu 2004: 38–41). Despite the Jomon being both temporally and geographically extensive, Habu (2004: 62) notes that there still exists a somewhat simplistic understanding of Jomon subsistence in that a basic calendar of activities was followed: summer marine fishing/hunting; autumn plant/nut collecting; winter terrestrial mammal hunting; spring shellfish collecting. Habu prefers to use Lewis Binford's (1980, 1982) collector-forager model to address Jomon subsistence strategies. Based on reconstructions of Jomon climate, environment, and resource availability, Habu (2004: 63) argues for Jomon communities to have been more collectors than foragers and highly specialized in their organized collecting forays—targeting a limited number of items: "acorns, chestnuts, fish and marine mammals."

However, this is a subsistence economy that developed after the Incipient and Initial Jomon periods, during the Early Jomon. During the Initial Jomon, we see the first intensive exploitation of marine resources, particularly in the Tokyo Bay area. However, this was more the exception than the rule, with much of the rest of the archipelago involved in a residentially mobile forager system (Habu 2004: 249). Exceptions include Hokkaido, where sites with extensive storage facilities suggest a move to the collector end of the forager-collector continuum, and southern Kyushu, where larger settlements and a sophisticated ceremonial material culture were present (e.g., Uenohara (上野原) site #4 in Kagoshima (鹿児島) Prefecture) (Habu 2004: 250). Extensive stable isotopic work by Chisholm and Koike (1999) supports the view of a significant marine dietary input in coastally located Jomon cultures relative to inland communities (see also Akazawa 1999).

The shift to a more collector-oriented subsistence economy is clearly seen in the Early Jomon, with extensive evidence for food storage, earliest at the Higashi-Kurotsuchida (東黒土田) site, Kagoshima Prefecture, southern Kyushu, dated to approximately 13,000 cal BP (Habu 2004: 64). Both wet and dry storage pits have been excavated, with the former generally found to contain various nuts (buckeyes, walnuts, and acorns) on the rare occasion when plant materials are preserved. Wet storage pits may have served to leach out the toxins found naturally in buckeyes and acorns, although this is by no means a certainty. Because dry storage pits are not ideal for the preservation of plant materials, it is unclear what foodstuffs they were used to store. The clear importance of nut collection and storage at Jomon sites has led to speculation that a range of trees (chestnut, oak, beech, buckeye) may have been cultivated/tended (or even domesticated) to some degree. Habu (2004: 251) generalizes the Early Jomon as serial foraging with a focus on bulk exploitation of limited, albeit critical, resources. This trend is associated with a decline in residentially mobile foragers and an increase in site size, as well as site differentiation, and a concomitant increase in ceremonial material culture.

Minagawa and Akazawa (1992) describe the Jomon strategy as that of highly flexible hunter-gatherer-fishers, whereas Crawford (2008) emphasizes the importance of food and resource production for the Jomon people, proposing that they should be labeled neither as foragers nor as farmers. The high density of Jomon sites in southern Hokkaido and northern Honshu, particularly on the coasts facing the Tsugaru Strait, can in part be linked to reliance on anadromous salmon and trout fishing (Yamanouchi 1969: 94–95; Matsui 1996). The zooarchaeological assemblage from the Early Jomon Matsugasaki (松ヶ崎) site in Kyoto (京都) included bones of deer, wild boar, Japanese macaque, and flying squirrel, as well as sea perch, sea bream, and many other species of fish (Matsui and Miyaji 1998).

At more inland sites, highly negative stable isotope carbon signatures imply greater exploitation of terrestrial resources and only limited fishing (Yoneda et al. 1996, 2004). Developed arboriculture and horticulture, similar in some respects to that of prehistoric foragers in the North American Northwest, was already evident by the Initial Jomon (Matsui 1996). Large quantities of nuts were collected and processed through the duration of the Jomon (Takahashi and Hosoya 2002; Hosoya 2011). Depending on the site location, various amounts of sweet Japanese chestnut (*Castanea crenata*), Manchurian walnut (*Juglans mandshurica*), water chestnut (*Trapa bispinosa*), and bitter horse chestnut (*Aesculus turbinata*), as well as acorns were consumed. Cultivated plants included bottle gourd (*Lagenaria siceraria*), burdock (*Arctium lappa* or *Lappa major*), perilla (*Perilla ocymoides*), and goosefoot (*Chenopodium* var. *album*). By the Middle Jomon, barnyard millet (*Echinochloa utilis*), beans (*Vigna* spp.), buckwheat (*Fagopyrum esculentum*), yam (*Dioscorea* sp.) and some other cultivars were added to the repertoire (Crawford et al. 1976; Kotani 1979; Matsui 1996; Matsui and Kanehara 2006).

During the Middle Jomon, large settlement sites were common in the east, which have been interpreted, not as indicating large population sizes, but as

Human Ecology in Continental and Insular East Asia   45

exhibiting rather frequent reuse and return to the same sites: a characteristic of seasonally sedentary collectors rather than fully sedentary ones (Habu 2004: 252). At the same time, large sites were not common in western Japan, and this may be interpreted as a more residentially mobile foraging system in comparison to the east. During the Middle Jomon, a generalized intensification and specialization in plant food collecting and a decrease in hunting (as evidenced by a significant decrease in arrowheads) also took place. Further evidence that there was more to subsistence strategies in the Jomon than hunting and gathering (and the possible arboriculture noted above) comes from the numerous domesticated plant species utilized, albeit not as staples. The following cultigens were targeted: "egoma and/or shiso mint, bottle gourd (*Lagenaria* sp.), various beans or green gram (*Vigna radiata*), barnyard millet, buckwheat (*Fagopyrum* sp.), barley (*Hordeum vulgare*), burdock (*Arctium lappa*) and rice (*Oryza sativa*)" (Habu 2004: 59; see also Imamura 1996a: 107–8; Hudson 1999: 106).

Of particular interest is the utilization of root tubers by Jomon communities, particularly given the ostensible association of such tubers with elevated levels of oral disease (see discussion in final chapter). Virtually the only direct evidence for the use of yam comes from a single Early Jomon site, Matsugasaki in Kyoto Prefecture (Habu 2004: 70). Hudson (1999: 155–16) notes that despite common assertions of the presence of taro (*Colocasia* sp.), evidence for its cultivation is scant. Imamura (1996a: 106–9) has argued that chipped-stone axes were used for digging out tubers (likely the indigenous yam, *Dioscorea japonica*) in the Middle Jomon of the Chubu (中部) Highlands and western Kanto (関東). The lack of chipped-stone axes in sites with storage pits, and vice versa, in this region indicates that axes were probably used for other purposes, as tubers cannot be stored for any length of time. Imamura argues that in lieu of any strong evidence for the cultivation of a staple such as buckwheat at this time, the only viable option was yam digging.

Also associated with the Middle Jomon is a general increase in social complexity, as measured by the elevated frequency of ceremonial material culture and long-distance exchange networks. Nonetheless, the end of the Middle Jomon witnessed a significant decline, which has been blamed on everything from climate cooling to the emergence of major epidemics; neither of these putative causes is supported by archaeological evidence. Habu (2004: 255) suggests that this decline, in the east at least, may have been a function of overspecialization, which subsequently rendered Jomon communities more sensitive to minor environmental fluctuations. In western Japan, the situation was quite different, in that oscillations in growth and decline were more the norm, rather than any major unidirectional collapse of extant economic systems. Temple (2007) has argued that elevated levels of physiological stress among western/inland communities relative to the Eastern Jomon gives emphasis to the pitfalls associated with reliance on seasonally available resources, while an increase in caries rates from the Middle to Late Jomon suggests that major dietary changes took place.

In the Late Jomon, eastern Japan saw a decline in the number of large sites, a decrease in site density, and a reduction in subsistence and settlement complexity, albeit in the face of a rise in social complexity (Habu 2004: 255). One exception was the Tokyo Bay area, where more than half of the known shell middens in Japan (of which there are over 1,000) can be found in the Kanto district (Tokyo and surrounding areas) (Habu 2004: 71; Imamura 1996a: 78). Midden size and the time required to accumulate them suggest that shellfish would have provided limited calorific and/or protein value. Middens therefore seem to be the remains of quite seasonal exploitation, and shellfish were unlikely to have formed a staple, even in the areas where middens abound. Evidence for fishing (e.g., bone hooks and pumice floats for line fishing, stone and ceramic net sinkers for netting, bone spears and harpoons, and even the rare weir) is abundant in Jomon sites, particularly in middens.

Regarding terrestrial hunting, Imamura (1996a: 79–88) has argued that the presence of numerous shallow pits throughout the Japanese islands (some with evidence of wooden stakes on their floors) is evidence for a long, and geographically dispersed, history of pit trapping (boar being the most likely victim). Less specific forms of terrestrial hunting were carried out using the ubiquitous arrowhead (Imamura 1996a: 88), which does not appear to have been used in the Late Paleolithic. Other forms of hunting tools include spearheads and tanged points, at least during the Initial Jomon, although they had a longer history in Hokkaido and Tohoku (東北). Imamura notes a significant decline in the number of hunting tools with a major increase in population during the Middle Jomon. Coastally (specifically in Kanto District), an increase in large middens took place during this period, while large inland sites attest to a more terrestrially oriented subsistence economy. Heading into the Late Jomon, again in the Kanto District, there was an increase in the number and density of coastal sites, at the expense of inland sites, which Imamura (1996a: 90) argues was due to overexploitation of inland plant resources. In the Final Jomon of the Kanto District, marine overexploitation led to a resurgence in terrestrial subsistence activities.

The end of the Final Jomon saw the transition to the Yayoi period. While archaeological data on the transition is reasonably robust, very little in the way of human skeletal material exists for the end of the Jomon and Early Yayoi (Nakahashi 1999). The agricultural transition in Korea occurred during the Jeulmum period (3500 to 2000 BC) with the adoption of foxtail millet and rice (Choy and Richards 2009). However, not until the Mumun period (1500 to 300 BC) was there any significant—and in this case far-reaching—influence on Japan, at least in the west. Traditionally, the transitional phase lasted from about 500 to 300 BC, when the Early Yayoi began (300 to 100 BC), but only in western Japan, followed by Middle Yayoi (100 BC–AD 100), and then Late Yayoi (AD 100 to 300). The reasons for the transition are still unclear, but some evidence for a population decline in western Japan may suggest changes in subsistence strategies, which may in turn have favored the adoption of intensive agricultural practices. Until there is clarification of what was happening on the Korean peninsula at the same time, a satisfactory answer may not be forthcoming. Interestingly, evidence collected at Nukdo, one of the largest southern Korean sites of the Mumun period (1500 to 300 BC), indicates that during the Mumun/Yayoi interface, agriculture, terrestrial game, and some marine resources were important in the Mumun diet, while contemporaneous communities in Kyushu had a greater focus on marine-sourced dietary components (Cho and Richards 2009). Given evidence for the early presence of agriculture in Kyushu, the initial transition from the Jomon to the Yayoi in southern Japan may have been more about changing subsistence emphases, rather than wholesale (and wholescale) new and abrupt change.

What is clear, however, is that a major development in terms of human behavior and biology occurred with the transition to the Yayoi. While dryland rice cultivation likely occurred during the Jomon to some degree (Sato 1999), the Yayoi period was characterized by the emergence of wet-rice cultivation, as well as trade in and local manufacture of metal goods, trade and exchange at all levels and ways with mainland polities, and clear social stratification, which was a precursor to the formation of polities that later led to state formation (Imamura 1996a: 127). Whatever the reason for the significant hiatus between the emergence of wet-rice agriculture in China and its emergence in Japan, when it did arrive approximately 500 BC (possibly as early as 1000 BC), it only took around 300 years to travel as far as northern Honshu. The earliest wet-rice fields with clear evidence of water control are found at the Itatsuke (板付) site in northern Kyushu. Evidence for early use of swampy sites (which produce lower yields) also comes from northern Kyushu (e.g., Nabatake 菜畑), which Imamura (1996a: 137) has argued may indicate the use of less optimal but also less labor-intensive sites during the initial stages of the adoption of rice agriculture in Japan.

While the north and eastward spread of wet-rice agriculture was rapid, it did not cross the Tsugaru (津軽) Strait onto Hokkaido, where an essentially marine-oriented foraging system persisted until historic times. Oxenham and colleagues (Oxenham and Matsumura 2008; Oxenham et al., this volume) discuss the human biological costs and responses to subsistence and climate on Hokkaido, which are quite different from the conditions facing their contemporaries in Honshu. Further, the northern boundary crept back to the middle of the Tohoku region, ostensibly because of the resistance of specialized subsistence systems (especially fishing) in northeastern Honshu (Imamura 1996a: 139), although the reason is still essentially unclear. Rice storage in the earlier period of the Yayoi included earthen pits, although these seem to have been replaced by elevated storage structures, which were much more efficient, after the Middle Yayoi (Imamura 1996a: 144). Wet-rice agriculture was not the only form of intensive agriculture seen during the Yayoi.

Evidence for dry farming of foxtail millet, adzuki (小豆) beans, and barley is seen at the Nabatake site, and dry-field farming is assumed to have been common in the more suitable soils of northeastern Japan as well (Imamura 1996a: 144). Moreover, the Yayoi agriculturalists added to the Jomon's repertoire of cultigens and are believed to have grown some 37 different plant forms. Yayoi communities continued to exploit marine resources, with stable isotopic signatures suggesting levels of marine input similar to those of inland Jomon communities (Chisholm and Koike 1999). Finally, there is some evidence for pig domestication during the Yayoi, although horse and cattle seem to have been absent until the Kofun (古墳) period. In terms of physiological stress, Temple (2010) notes that Yayoi communities experienced reduced levels of linear enamel hypoplasia in comparison to earlier Western Jomon populations in the same region. This has been interpreted as reduced stress in the Yayoi in the context of predictable resources brought about by intensive wet-rice agriculture (Temple 2010).

Conclusions

In summary, our understanding of human ecology in ancient East Asia is full of questions and controversies that can be resolved through bioarchaeological inquiry. What effects did complex population movements evidenced by archaeological and genetic studies in this area have on human morphological variation, on the spread of pathogens, and on patterns of violence? Did reliance on multiple cereals and domesticated animals in this area afford more balanced diets than in other parts of the world or help to defray starvation episodes? Was the introduction of new cereals and soybeans beneficial for community health in general, or was it driven by population movement and other interactions, disrupting established subsistence practices and leading to greater stress? Were changes in subsistence practices accompanied by gene flow or population replacement? Were interactions between populations peaceful or violent? Did interactions among communities that brought in new crops and new animals also contribute to the spread of new pathogens in the area? Targeted examination of human remains is pivotal for understanding the processes involved in shaping the paleoeconomies and prehistoric societies of East Asia, as illustrated in the chapters that follow.

Notes

1. Resonant with the "Hopewell interaction sphere" introduced by J. R. Caldwell in 1964.

2. From the mid- to late 1970s until November 2000, a Japanese Early Paleolithic dating back some half a million years was believed by virtually all Japanese archaeologists—and a great many non-Japanese—to be represented at a little under two hundred sites in eastern Japan. While the academic implications of this hoax will no doubt haunt Japanese archaeology for years to come, the reasons behind its long and uncritical acceptance are dealt with exceptionally well by Hudson (2005).

Literature Cited

Ahn S. 2010. The emergence of rice agriculture in Korea: archaeobotanical perspectives. *Archaeological and Anthropological Sciences* 2: 89–98.

Aiello LC. 1993. The fossil evidence for modern human origins in Africa: A revised view. *American Anthropologist* 95: 73–96.

Aikens CM, Higuchi T. 1982. *Prehistory of Japan*. New York: Academic Press.

Akazawa T. 1999. Regional variation in Jomon hunting-fishing-gathering societies. In: Omoto K, editor. *Interdisciplinary perspectives on the origins of the Japanese*. Proceedings of the 11th International Symposium of the International Research Center for Japanese Studies, Kyoto, 1996. Pp. 223–31.

Allan W. 1970. Ecology, techniques and settlement patterns. In: Ucko PH, Tringham R, Dimbleby GW, editors. *Man, settlement and urbanism*. London: Duckworth. Pp. 211–26.

Allard F, Erdenebaatar D. 2005. Khirigsuurs, ritual and mobility in the Bronze Age of Mongolia. *Antiquity* 79: 547–63.

An Z. 1984. Early Neolithic culture in North China. *Kaogu* (考古) 10: 936–44.

An Z. 1988a. Archaeological research on Neolithic China. *Current Anthropology* 29: 753–59.

An Z. 1988b. Chinese prehistoric agriculture. *Kaogu* (考古) 4: 375–84.

An Z. 1991. Radiocarbon dating and the prehistoric archaeology of China. *World Archaeology* 23: 193–200.

Baba H, Narasaki S. 1991. Minatogawa Man, the oldest type of modern *Homo sapiens* in East Asia. *Quaternary Research* 30: 221–30.

Barfield TJ. 2001. The shadow empires: Imperial state formation along the Chinese-nomad frontier. In: Alcock SE, D'Altroy TN, Morrison KD, Sinopoli CM, editors. *Empires: Perspectives from archaeology and history*. Cambridge: Cambridge University Press. Pp. 10–41.

Barton LS, Newsome D, Chen F-H, Wang H, Guilderson TP, Bettinger RL. 2009. Agricultural origins and the isotopic identity of domestication in northern China. *Proceedings of the National Academy of Sciences* 106: 5523–28.

Bettinger RL, Barton L, Richerson PJ, Boyd R, Wang H, Choi W. 2007. The transition to agriculture in Northwestern China. In: Madsen DB, Chen F, Gao X, editors. *Late Quaternary climate change and human adaptation in arid China*. Amsterdam: Elsevier. Pp. 83–103.

Binford LR. 1980. Willow smoke and dog's tails. *American Antiquity* 45: 4–20.

Binford LR. 1982. The archaeology of place. *Journal of Anthropological Archaeology* 1: 5–31.

Boaretto E, Wuc X, Yuand J, Bar-Yosefe O, Chub V, Panc Y, Liuf K, Coheng D, Jiaoh T, Lic S, Gud H, Goldbergi P, Weinerj S. 2009. Radiocarbon dating of charcoal and bone collagen associated with early pottery at Yuchanyan Cave, Hunan Province, China. *Proceedings of the National Academy of Sciences* 106: 9595–9600.

Brace CL 1962. Cultural factors in the evolution of the human dentition. In: Montagu MFA, editor. *Culture and the evolution of man*. New York: Oxford University Press. Pp. 343–54.

Brace CL, Brace ML, Leonard WR. 1989. Reflections on the face of Japan: A multivariate craniofacial and odontometric perspective. *American Journal of Physical Anthropology* 78: 93–113.

Brace CL, Nagai M. 1982. Japanese tooth size: Past and present. *American Journal of Physical Anthropology* 59: 399–411.

Braun DP. 1983. Pots as tools. In: Moore JA, Keene A, editors. *Archaeological hammers and theories*. New York: Academic Press. Pp. 107–34.

Brown P. 1999. The first modern East Asians? Another look at Upper Cave 101, Liujiang and Minatogawa 1. In: Omoto K, editor. *Interdisciplinary perspectives on the origins of the Japanese*. Proceedings of the 11th International Symposium of the International Research Center for Japanese Studies, Kyoto, 1996. Pp. 105–30.

Chang KC. 1968. *The archaeology of ancient China*. New Haven, CT: Yale University Press.

Chang KC. 1969. *Fengpitou, Tapenkeng and the prehistory of Taiwan*. New Haven, CT: Yale University Press.

Chang KC. 1986. *The archaeology of ancient China*. 4th ed. New Haven, CT: Yale University Press.

Chen B, Wang X, Zhang J. 1995a. Finds and morphological analysis of carbonized rice in the Jiahu Neolithic site in Wuyang County, Henan Province. *Chinese Journal of Rice Science* (中国水稻科学) 9: 129–34.

Chen B, Wang X, Zhang J. 1995b. The discovery and significance of *Oryza* phytoliths in the Neolithic site at Jiahu, Wuyang County, Henan Province. *Chinese Science Bulletin* (科学通报) 40: 339–42.

Chen B, Zhang J, Lu H. 1995c. Discovery of Rice Phytoliths in the Neolithic site at Jiahu of Henan Province and Its Significance. Chinese Science Bulletin (科学通报) 40: 339–42.

Chen YS, Li XH. 1989. New evidence of the origin and domestication of the Chinese swamp buffalo (*Bubalus bubalis*). *Buffalo Journal* 1: 51–55.

Chisholm BS, Koike H. 1999. Reconstructing prehistoric Japanese diet using stable isotopic analysis. In: Omoto K, editor. *Interdisciplinary perspectives on the origins of the Japanese*. Proceedings of the 11th International Symposium of the International Research Center for Japanese Studies, Kyoto, 1996. Pp. 199–222.

Choy K, Richards MP. 2009. Stable isotope evidence of human diet at the Nukdo shell midden site, South Korea. *Journal of Archaeological Science* 36: 1312–18.

Cohen DJ. 2011. The beginnings of agriculture in China: a multiregional view. *Current Anthropology* 52: S273–S293.

Crawford GW. 2006. East Asian plant domestication. In: Stark ML, editor. *Archaeology of Asia.* Malden, MA: Blackwell. Pp. 77–95.

Crawford GW. 2008. The Jomon in early agriculture discourse: Issues arising from Matsui, Kanehara, and Pearson. *World Archaeology* 40: 445–65.

Crawford GW. 2009. Agricultural origins in North China pushed back to the Pleistocene-Holocene boundary. *Proceedings of the National Academy of Sciences* 106: 7271–72.

Crawford GW, Hurley W, Yoshizaki M. 1976. Implications of plant remains from the Early Jomon Hamanasuno site, Hokkaido. *Asian Perspectives* 19: 145–55.

Crawford GW, Lee G-A. 2003. Agricultural origins in the Korean peninsula. *Antiquity* 77: 87–95.

Crawford GW, Shen C. 1998. The origins of rice agriculture: Recent progress in East Asia. *Antiquity* 72: 858–67.

Crawford GW, Underhill A, Zhao Z, Lee G, Feinman G, Nicholas L, Luan F, Yu H, Fang H, Cai F. 2005. Late Neolithic plant remains from northern China: Preliminary results from Liangchengzhen, Shandong. *Current Anthropology* 46: 309–17.

D'Andrea AC, Crawford GW, Yoshizaki M, Kudo T. 1995. Late Jomon cultigens in northeastern Japan. *Antiquity* 69: 146–52.

Di Cosmo N. 1994. Ancient Inner Asian nomads: Their economic basis and its significance in Chinese history. *The Journal of Asian Studies* 53: 1092–1126.

Dong X, Fan X. 1996. Note on fossil human teeth from Fox cave at Qingliu. *Acta Anthropologica Sinica* (人类学学报) 15: 315–19.

Eshed V, Gopher A, Hershkovitz I. 2006. Tooth wear and dental pathology at the advent of agriculture: New evidence from the Levant. *American Journal of Physical Anthropology* 130: 145–59.

FAO. 1972. *Food composition table for use in East Asia.* Rome: Food Policy and Nutrition Division, Food and Agriculture Organization of the United Nations.

Flad RK, Yuan J, Li S. 2007. Zooarcheological evidence for animal domestication in northwest China. In: Madsen DB, Chen FH, Gao X, editors. *Late Quaternary climate change and human adaptation in arid China.* Developments in Quaternary Science vol. 9. Amsterdam: Elsevier. Pp. 163–99.

Flad R, Li S, Wu X, Zhao Z. 2010. Early wheat in China: Results from new studies at Donghuishan in the Hexi Corridor. *The Holocene* 20: 955–65.

Fukumine T, Hanihara T, Nishime A, Ishida H. 2006. Nonmetric cranial variation of early modern human skeletal remains from Kumejima, Okinawa, and the peopling of the Ryukyu Islands. *Anthropological Science* 114: 141–51.

Fuller DQ, Harvey E, Qin L. 2007. Presumed domestication? Evidence for wild rice cultivation and domestication in the fifth millennium BC of the Lower Yangtze region. *Antiquity* 81: 316–31.

Fuller DQ, Qin L. 2011. Declining oaks, increasing artistry, and cultivating rice: The environmental and social context of the emergence of farming in the Lower Yangtze Region. *Environmental Archaeology* 15: 139–59.

Gade DW. 1999. *Nature and culture in the Andes.* Madison: University of Wisconsin Press.

Geneste J-M, David B, Pilsson H, Clarkson C, Delannoy J-J, Petchey F, Whear R. 2010. Earliest evidence for ground-edge axes: 35,400+410 cal BP from Jawoyn Country, Arnhem Land. *Australian Archaeology* 71: 66–69.

Guo Z, Zheng S, Sugimoto C, Wang Y, Zheng H, Takasaka T, Kitamura T, Guo J, Yogo Y. 2001. JC virus genotypes in northwestern China: Implications for its population history. *Anthropological Science* 109: 203–12.

Habu J. 2004. *Ancient Jomon of Japan.* Cambridge: Cambridge University Press.

Hammer MF, Karafet TM, Park H, Omoto K, Harihara S, Stoneking M, Horai S. 2006. Dual origins of the Japanese: Common ground for hunter-gatherer and farmer Y chromosomes. *Journal of Human Genetics* 51: 47–58.

Han K. 1986. Study of human skeletons excavated from trench tombs in Kongquehe, Xinjiang. *Acta Archaeologica Sinica* (考古学报) 3: 361–84.

Han K. 1994. The study of ancient human skeletons from Xinjiang, China. *Sino-Platonic Papers* 51: 1–13.

Hanihara K. 1984. Origins and affinities of Japanese viewed from cranial measurements. *Acta Anthropogenetica* 8: 149–58.

Hanihara K. 1991. Dual structure model for the population history of the Japanese. *Japanese Review* 2: 1–33.

Hanihara K. 1993. The population history of the Japanese. *Nippon Ronen Igakkai Zasshi* 30: 923–31.

Hinton RJ. 1982. Differences in interproximal and occlusal tooth wear among prehistoric Tennessee Indians: Implications for masticatory function. *American Journal of Physical Anthropology* 57: 103–15.

Ho P. 1977. The indigenous origins of Chinese agriculture. In: Reed CA, editor. *Origins of agriculture.* The Hague: Mouton. Pp. 413–47.

Horai S, Kondo R, Murayama K, Hayashi S, Koike H, Nakai N. 1991. Phylogenetic affiliation of ancient and contemporary humans inferred from mitochondrial DNA. *Philosophical Transactions of the Royal Society of London B: Biological Sciences* 333: 409–17.

Hosoya L. 2011. Staple or famine food? Ethnographic and archaeological approaches to nut processing in East Asian prehistory. *Archaeological and Anthropological Sciences* 3: 7–17.

Hu Y, Ambrose SH, Wang C. 2006. Stable isotopic analysis of human bones from the Jiahu site, Henan, China: Implications for the transition to agriculture. *Journal of Archaeological Science* 33: 1319–30.

Huang W, Zheng S. 1982. An Upper Pleistocene human tooth and mammalian fossils from Zhangwu, Shaanxi. *Acta Anthropologica Sinica* (人类学学报) 1: 14.

Hudson MJ. 1999. *Ruins of identity: Ethnogenesis in the Japanese Islands.* Honolulu: University of Hawai'i Press.

Hudson MJ. 2005. For the people, by the people: Postwar Japanese archaeology and the Early Paleolithic hoax. *Anthropological Science* 113: 131–39.

Imamura K. 1996a. *Prehistoric Japan: New perspectives on insular East Asia.* London: UCL Press.

Imamura K. 1996b. Jomon and Yayoi: The transition to agriculture in Japanese prehistory. In: Harris DR, editor. *The origins of agriculture and pastoralism in Eurasia.* Washington, DC: Smithsonian Institution Press. Pp. 442–64.

Institute of Archaeology–CASS. 1991. *Radiocarbon dates in Chinese archaeology.* Beijing: Cultural Relics.

Itzstein-Davey F, Taylor D, Dodson J, Atahan P, Zheng H. 2007. Wild and domesticated forms of rice (*Oryza sp.*) in early agriculture at Qingpu, lower Yangtze, China: Evidence from phytoliths. *Journal of Archaeological Science* 34: 2101–08.

Jiang J, Zhang Q. 1998. Phytolith evidence for rice cultivation during prehistoric periods at Baligang site of Baizhuang, Dengzhou City, Henan Province. *Geology and Geography* 34: 66–71.

Jiang L, Liu L. 2006. New evidence for the origins of sedentism and rice domestication in the Lower Yangzi River, China. *Antiquity* 80: 355–61.

Jones MK, Liu X. 2009. Origins of agriculture in East Asia. *Science* 324: 730–31.

Kaifu Y. 1999. Changes in the pattern of tooth wear from prehistoric to recent periods in Japan. *American Journal of Physical Anthropology* 109: 485–99.

Keally CT, Taniguchi Y, Kuzmin YV, Shewkomud IY. 2004. Chronology of the beginning of pottery manufacture in East Asia. *Radiocarbon* 46: 345–51.

Keates SG, Hodgins GWL, Kuzmin YV, Orlova LA. 2007. First direct dating of a presumed Pleistocene hominid from China: AMS radiocarbon age of a femur from the Ordos Plateau. *Journal of Human Evolution* 53: 1–5.

Kotani Y. 1979. Evidence of plant cultivation in Jomon Japan: Some implications. In: Koyama S, Thomas DH, editors. *Affluent foragers: Pacific coasts east and west*. Senri Ethnological Studies 9. Osaka: National Museum of Ethnology. Pp. 202–12.

Kozintsev AG. 1992. Prehistoric and recent populations of Japan: Multivariate analysis of cranioscopic data. *Arctic Anthropology* 29: 104–11.

Kuzmin YV. 2002. Radiocarbon chronology of Paleolithic and Neolithic cultural complexes from the Russian Far East. *Journal of East Asian Archaeology* 3: 227–54.

Kuzmin YV. 2006. Chronology of the earliest pottery in East Asia: Progress and pitfalls. *Antiquity* 80: 362–71.

Kuzmin YV, Jull AJT, Jones GA. 1998. Early agriculture in Primorye, Russian Far East: New radiocarbon and pollen data from late Neolithic sites. *Journal of Archaeological Science* 25: 813–16.

Kuzmin YV, Orlova LA. 2000. The Neolithization of Siberia and the Russian Far East: Radiocarbon evidence. *Antiquity* 74: 356–64.

Lee G, Bestel S. 2007. Contextual analysis of plant remains at the Erlitou-period Huizui site, Henan, China. *Bulletin of the Indo-Pacific Prehistorical Association* 27: 49–60.

Lee G, Crawford G, Chen X. 2007. Plants and people from the Early Neolithic to Shang periods in North China. *Proceedings of the National Academy of Sciences* 104: 1087–92.

Li Q. 2009. Earliest domestication of common millet (*Panicum miliaceum*) in East Asia extended to 10,000 years ago. *Proceedings of the National Academy of Sciences* 106: 7367–72.

Linduff K. 1995. Zhukaigou, steppe culture and the rise of Chinese civilization. *Antiquity* 69: 133–45.

Linduff K. 1998. The emergence and demise of bronze-producing cultures outside the Central Plain of China. In: Mair VH, editor. *The Bronze Age and Early Iron Age peoples of eastern Central Asia*. Vol. 2. Journal of Indo-European Studies Monograph no. 26. Washington, DC. Pp. 619–46.

Liu L. 1996. Settlement patterns, chiefdom variability, and the development of early states in North China. *Journal of Anthropological Archaeology* 15: 237–88.

Liu L. 2003. The products of minds as well as of hands: Production of prestige goods in the Neolithic and early state periods of China. *Asian Perspectives* 42: 1–40.

Liu L. 2009. State emergence in early China. *Annual Review of Anthropology* 38: 217–23.

Liu L, Chen X. 2003. *State formation in early China*. London: Duckworth.

Liu L, Yang D, Chen X. 2006. On the origin of the *Bubalus bubalis* in China. *Acta Archaeologica Sinica* (考古学报) 2: 141–78.

Liu W, Jin C, Zhang Y, Cai Y, Xing S, Wu X, Cheng H, Edwards RL, Pan W, Qin D, An Z, Trinkaus E, Wu X. 2010. Human remains from Zhirendong, South China, and modern human emergence in East Asia. *Proceedings of the National Academy of Sciences* 107: 19201–206.

Liu Z. 2000. Were "rice paddies" near Pengtoushan and Jiahu sites? *Agricultural Archaeology* (农业考古) 3: 70–72.

Lu H, Yang X, Ye M, Liu K-B, Xia Z, Ren X, Cai L, Wu N, Liu T-S. 2005. Culinary archaeology: Millet noodles in Late Neolithic China. *Nature* 437: 967–68.

Lu T. 1999. *The transition from foraging to farming and the origin of agriculture in China.* BAR International Series 774. Oxford: British Archaeological Reports.

Lu T. 2002. A green foxtail (*Setaria viridis*) cultivation experiment in the Middle Yellow River valley and some related issues. *Asian Perspectives* 41: 1–14.

Lu TLD. 2006. The occurrence of cereal cultivation in China. *Asian Perspectives* 45 (2): 130–58.

Luoyang Archaeological Team of Culture and Relics. 2002. *Luoyang Zaojiaoshu: Excavation report on Erlitou settlement site of Zaojiaoshu, Luoyang between 1992 and 1993.* Beijing: Science Press.

Ma X. 2005. *Emergent social complexity in the Yangshao Culture: Analyses of settlement patterns and faunal remains from Lingbao, western Henan, China (c. 4900–3000 BC).* BAR International Series 1453. Oxford: British Archaeological Reports.

Mahoney P. 2006. Dental microwear from Natufian hunter-gatherers and early Neolithic farmers: Comparisons within and between samples. *American Journal of Physical Anthropology* 130: 308–19.

Matsui A. 1996. Archaeological investigation of anadromous salmon fishing in Japan. *World Archaeology* 27: 444–60.

Matsui A, Kanehara M. 2006. The question of prehistoric plant husbandry during the Jomon period in Japan. *World Archaeology* 38: 259–73.

Matsui A, Miyaji A. 1998. *Faunal and floral remains recovered from Matsugasaki site.* Matsugasaki Site Excavation No. 5, Preliminary Reports of No. 82-1. Kyoto: Kyoto Prefectural Archaeological Center (京都府埋蔵文化財調査研究センター). Pp. 20–21.

Matsu'ura S. 1982. Relative dating of the Minatogawa man by fluorine analysis. In: Suzuki H, Hanihara K, editors. *The Minatogawa Man: The Upper Pleistocene man from the Island of Okinawa.* Bulletin no. 19. Tokyo: University Museum, University of Tokyo. Pp. 205–8.

Matsu'ura S. 1984. Fluorine dating of Upper Minatogawa man. *Journal of the Anthropological Society of Nippon* 92: 111–12.

Matsu'ura S. 1999. A chronological review of Pleistocene human remains from the Japanese archipelago. In: Omoto K, editor. *Interdisciplinary perspectives on the origins of the Japanese.* Proceedings of the 11th International Symposium of the International Research Center for Japanese Studies, Kyoto, 1996. p 181–97.

McGovern PE, Zhang J, Tang J, Zhang Z, Hall GR, Moreau RA, Nuñez A, Butrym ED, Richards MP, Wang C, Cheng G, Zhao Z, Wang C. 2004. Fermented beverages of Pre and Protohistoric China. *Proceedings of the National Academy of Sciences of the United States of America* 101: 17593–98.

McGovern PE, Underhill AP, Fang H, Luan F, R. Hall G, Yu H, Wang C, Cai F, Zhao Z, Feinman GM. 2005. Chemical identification and cultural implications of a mixed fermented beverage from late prehistoric China. *Asian Perspectives* 44: 249–76.

Mei J, Shell CA. 1999. The existence of Andronovo cultural influence in Xinjiang during the 2nd millennium BC. *Antiquity* 73: 570–78.

Milne J. 1881. The Stone Age in Japan: With notes on recent geological changes which have taken place. *Journal of the Anthropological Institute of Great Britain and Ireland* 10: 389–423.

Minagawa T, Akazawa T. 1992. Dietary patterns among Jomon hunter-gatherers: Stable nitrogen and isotope analyses of human bones. In: Aikens CM, Rhee SN, editors. *Pacific Northeast Asia in prehistory: Hunter-fisher-gatherers, farmers, and sociopolitical elites.* Pullman: Washington State University Press. Pp. 69–73.

Morse ES. 1879a. *Shell mounds of Omori.* Memoirs of the Science Department, University of Tokio, vol. 1, pt. 1.

Morse ES. 1879b. Traces of an early race in Japan. *Popular Science Monthly* 14: 257–66.

Nakahashi T. 1995. Temporal craniometric changes from the Jomon to the Modern period in western Japan. *American Journal of Physical Anthropology* 90: 409–25.

Nakahashi T. 1999. Transition from the Jomon to the Yayoi period in the northern Kyushu and Yamaguchi region as viewed from ritual tooth ablation and skeletal morphology. In: Omoto K, editor. *Interdisciplinary perspectives on the origins of the Japanese.* Proceedings of the 11th International Symposium of the International Research Center for Japanese Studies, Kyoto, 1996. Pp. 127–42.

Nakahashi T, Minchang L, Yamaguchi B. 2002. Anthropological study on the cranial measurements of the human remains from Jiangnan region, China. In: Nakahashi T, Minchang L, editors. *Ancient people in the Jiangnan region, China: Anthropological study on the origin of the Yayoi People in northern Kyushu.* Kyushu: Kyushu University Press. Pp. 17–33.

O'Brien MJ, Holland TD, Hoard RJ, Fox GL. 1994. Evolutionary implications of design and performance characteristics of prehistoric pottery. *Journal of Archaeological Method and Theory* 1: 259–304.

Omoto K, Saitou N. 1997. Genetic origins of the Japanese: Partial support for the dual structure hypothesis. *American Journal of Physical Anthropology* 102: 437–46.

Oxenham MF, Matsumura H. 2008. Oral and physiological paleohealth in cold adapted peoples: Northeast Asia, Hokkaido. *American Journal of Physical Anthropology* 135: 64–74.

Pearson R. 2005. The social context of early pottery in the Lingnan region of South China. *Antiquity* 79: 819–29.

Pechenkina EA, Ambrose SH, Ma X, and Benfer RA Jr. 2005. Reconstructing northern Chinese Neolithic subsistence practices by isotopic analysis. *Journal of Archaeological Science* 32: 1176–89.

Pechenkina EA, Benfer RA Jr., Wang Z. 2002. Diet and health changes at the end of the Chinese Neolithic: The Yangshao/Longshan transition in Shaanxi province. *American Journal of Physical Anthropology* 117: 15–36.

Peng F, Sui L, Liang J, Shen H. 1984. Data on lowest sea level of the East China Sea in Late Pleistocene. *Scientia Sinica* (科学) 27: 865–76.

Pietrusewsky M. 1999. Multivariate craniometric investigations of Japanese, Asians, and Pacific Islanders. In: Omoto K, editor. *Interdisciplinary perspectives on the origins of the Japanese.* Proceedings of the 11th International Symposium of the International Research Center for Japanese Studies, Kyoto, 1996. Pp. 65–104.

Pietrusewsky M. 2000. Metric analysis of skeletal remains: methods and applications. In: Katzenberg MA, Saunders SR, editors. *Biological anthropology of the human skeleton.* New York: Wiley-Liss. Pp. 375–415.

Pope GG. 1992. Craniofacial evidence for the origin of modern humans in China. *American Journal of Physical Anthropology Supplement* 35: 243–98.

Ren S. 1994. Several major achievements in early Neolithic China ca. 5000 BC. *Kaogu* (考古) 1: 37–49.

Sagawa M. 1998. Recent progress in studies on the Early and Middle Paleolithic period of the Japanese archipelago and their possible relations with northern and eastern Asia. *Acta Anthropologica Sinica* (人类学学报) 17: 1–21.

Sato Y. 1999. Origin and dissemination of cultivated rice in Asia. In: Omoto K, editor. *Interdisciplinary perspectives on the origins of the Japanese.* Proceedings of the 11th International Symposium of the International Research Center for Japanese Studies, Kyoto, 1996. Pp. 143–53.

Scott EC. 1979. Increase of tooth size in prehistoric coastal Peru, 10,000 B.P.–1,000 B.P. *American Journal of Physical Anthropology* 50: 251–58.

Seguchi N, Umeda H, Nelson AR, Brace CL. 2007. Population movement into the Japanese archipelago during antiquity: A craniofacial and odontometric perspective. *American Journal of Physical Anthropology Supplement* 44: 213.

Shen G, Wang W, Wang Q, Zhao J, Collerson K, Zhou C, Tobias PV. 2002. U-Series dating of Liujiang hominid site in Guangxi, Southern China. *Journal of Human Evolution* 43: 817–29.

Shi X. 1998. From Xiachuan civilization to the origin of Chinese agricultural civilization. *Nongye Kaogu* (农业考古) 1: 354.

Smith BL. 2005. Diet, health, and lifestyle in Neolithic North China. Ph.D. dissertation, Harvard University.

Song W. 1969. Changbing culture—The first discovery of Paleolithic culture in Taiwan. *Newsletter of Chinese Ethnology* (中國民族學通訊) 9: 1–27.

Suzuki H, Hanihara K. 1982. *The Minatogawa man: The Upper Pleistocene man from the Island of Okinawa.* Tokyo: University of Tokyo Press.

Suzuki T, Matsushita T, Han K. 2005. On the possible case of treponematosis from the Bronze Age in China. *Anthropological Science* 113: 253–58.

Takahashi R, Hosoya L. 2002. Nut exploitation in Jomon Society. In: Mason SLR, Hather JG, editors. *Hunter-gatherer archaeobotany: Perspective from the northern temperate zone.* London: UCL Press. Pp. 146–55.

Tan J, Han K. 2007. Physical characters and ethnic affiliations of several ancient nationalities in North China. Communication on Contemporary Anthropology (现代人类学通讯) 1: 58–66.

Temple DH. 2007. Dietary variation and stress among prehistoric Jomon foragers from Japan. *American Journal of Physical Anthropology* 133: 1035–46.

Temple DH. 2010. Pattern of systemic stress during the agricultural transition in prehistoric Japan. *American Journal of Physical Anthropology* 142: 112–24.

Turner CG II. 1979. Dental anthropological indications of agriculture among the Jomon people of central Japan. *American Journal of Physical Anthropology* 51: 619–36.

Turner CG II. 1990. Major features of Sundadonty and Sinodonty, including suggestions about East Asian microevolution, population history, and Late Pleistocene relationships with Australian Aboriginals. *American Journal of Physical Anthropology* 82: 295–317.

Turner CG II, Hanihara K. 1977. Additional features of Ainu dentition. V. Peopling of the Pacific. *American Journal of Physical Anthropology* 46: 13–24.

Wagner DB. 1999. The earliest use of iron in China. In: Young SMM, Pollard AM, Budd P, Ixer RA, editors. *Metals in antiquity.* BAR International Series 792. Oxford: British Archaeological Reports. Pp. 1–9.

Wang J. 1985. Earlier agriculture in Henan Province and surroundings according to Peiligang site tools. *Agricultural Archaeology* (农业考古) 2: 81–85.

Wang L, Li Y. 1983. On a fossil human calva unearthed from Huanglong County, Shaanxi Province. *Acta Anthropologica Sinica* (人类学学报) 2: 314–19.

Wang T. 2005. A study on early pottery in China. Ph.D. dissertation, Beijing University.

Wang W, Shen G, Zhou C, Wang Q, Zhao J. 2004. Stratigraphy and chronology of deposits in "Liujiang hominid cave," Guangxi, China. *Quaternary Sciences* (第四纪研究) 24: 272–77.

Wolpoff MH, Hawks J, Caspari R. 2000. Multiregional, not multiple origins. *American Journal of Physical Anthropology* 112: 129–36.

Wu R. 1982. Paleoanthropology in China, 1949–79. *Current Anthropology* 23: 473–77.

Wu R. 1999. On Weidenreich's work of *Sinanthropus pekinensis* and his theories of human origins. *Acta Anthropologica Sinica* (人类学学报) 18: 161–64.

Wu X. 1997. Sexing Liujiang fossil innominate bone. *Acta Anthropologica Sinica* (人类学学报) 16: 107–11.

Wu X. 1998. Origin of modern humans of China viewed from cranio-dental characteristics of late *Homo sapiens* in China. *Acta Anthropologica Sinica* (人类学学报) 17: 276–82.

Wu X. 2004. On the origin of modern humans in China. *Quaternary International* 117: 131–40.

Wu Z. 1998. Brief discussion on the origin and development of primitive paddy rice agriculture in China. *Agricultural Archaeology* (农业考古) 1: 87–93.

Xiang A. 2000. Pengtoushan rice agriculture did not spread from Jiahu: New thought on the origin of Chinese rice. *Agricultural Archaeology* (农业考古) 3: 73–77.

Xie J. 1972. The bases of Xiongnu subsistence. *Zhongyang Yanjiuyuan Minzuxue Yanjiusuo Jikan* 32: 163–90.

Xu Y. 1998. Origin and distribution of rice. *Agricultural Archaeology* (农业考古) 1: 246–54.

Yamanouchi S. 1969. On the current status of Jomon studies. In: *History of Japan and the world* (日本と世界の歴史), Vol. 1. Tokyo: Gakushu Kenkyusha. Pp. 81–97.

Yan W. 1982. Origin of rice agriculture in China. *Nongye Kaogu* (农业考古).

Yan W. 1989. Second discussion on the origin of rice horticulture in China. *Nongye Kaogu* (农业考古) 2: 72–80.

Yan W. 1992. Origins of agriculture and animal husbandry in China. In: Aikens CM, Rhee SN, editors. *Pacific Northeast Asia in prehistory: Hunter-fisher-gatherers, farmers, and sociopolitical elites.* Pullman: Washington State University Press. Pp. 113–23.

Yan W. 1997. New achievements on the origins of growing rice in China. *Kaogu* (考古) 7: 71–76.

Yan W. 2005. The beginning of farming. In: Allan S, editor. *The formation of Chinese civilization: An archaeological perspective.* New Haven, CT: Yale University and New World Press. Pp. 27–42.

Yang F, Lau K. 2004. Trend and variability of China precipitation in spring and summer: Linkage to sea-surface temperatures. *International Journal of Climatology* 24: 1625–44.

Yang X, Yu J, Lu H, Cui T, Guo J, Ge Q. 2009. Starch grain analysis reveals function of grinding stone tools at Shangzhai site, Beijing. *Science in China Series D: Earth Sciences* 52: 1164–71.

Yi X. 2000. Origin of Chinese rice cultivation according to new archaeological finds. *Agricultural Archaeology* (农业考古) 1: 61–67.

Yoneda M, Suzuki R, Shibata Y, Morita M, Sukegawa T, Shigehara N, Akazawa T. 2004. Isotopic evidence of inland fishing by a Jomon population excavated from the Boji site, Nagano, Japan. *Journal of Archaeological Science* 31: 97–107.

Yoneda M, Yoshida K, Yoshinaga J, Morita M, Akazawa T. 1996. Reconstruction of paleodiet in Nagano Prefecture based on the carbon and nitrogen isotope analysis and the trace elemental analysis. *Quaternary Research* 35: 293–303.

Yuan J. 2001. Some problems about the origin of Chinese poultry. *Nongye Kaogu* (农业考古) 3: 26–28.

Yuan J. 2007. Origin of Chinese domestic animals: New research developments. Paper presented at the International Conference of Zooarchaeology and the 20th Anniversary of Huaxia Archaeology, Zhengzhou, Henan, China.

Yuan J, Flad RK. 2002. Pig domestication in ancient China. *Antiquity* 76: 724–32.

Zhang J, Wang X. 1998. Notes on the recent discovery of ancient cultivated rice at Jiahu, Henan

Province: A new theory concerning the origin of *Oryza japonica* in China. *Antiquity* 72: 897–901.

Zhao S, Wu W. 1987. Early Neolithic Hemudu culture along the Hangzhou estuary and the origin of domestic paddy rice in China. *Asian Perspectives* 27: 29–34.

Zhao Z. 1998. The Middle Yangtze region in China is one place where rice was domesticated: Phytolith evidence from the Diaotonghuan Cave, Northern Jiangxi. *Antiquity* 72: 885–97.

Zhao Z. 2002. What was the staple crop in Shang agriculture? *Research Center for Ancient Civilization, Chinese Academy of Social Sciences* (中国古代文明研究中心) 3: 52.

Zhao Z. 2010. New data and new issues for the study of origin of rice agriculture in China. *Archaeological and Anthropological Sciences* 2: 99–105.

Zhao Z. 2011. New archaeobotanic data for the study of the origins of agriculture in China. *Current Anthropology* 52: S295–S306.

Zhao Z, He N. 2006. Results and analysis of 2002 soil sample flotation from Taosi. *Kaogu* (考古) 5: 77–90.

Zhao Z, Piperno DR. 2000. Late Pleistocene/Holocene environments in the middle Yangtze River valley, China, and rice (*Oryza sativa* L.) domestication: The phytolith evidence. *Geoarchaeology* 15: 203–22.

Zhou B. 1981. Animal skeleton at Cishan site in WuAn, Hebei Province. *Kaogu* (考古) 3: 343–46.

Zhushchikhovskaya IS. 2005. Prehistoric pottery making of the Russian Far East. British Archaeological Reports International Series 1434. Oxford: Archaeopress.

Zohary D, Hopf M. 2001. *Domestication of plants in the Old World: The origin and spread of cultivated plants in West Asia, Europe, and the Nile Valley.* Oxford: Oxford University Press.

Part I

Biological Indicators
of Population Histories
in East Asia

3

The Population History of China and Mongolia from the Bronze Age to the Medieval Period (2500 BC–AD 1500)

CHRISTINE LEE

China and Mongolia together have experienced a unique and complex population history that has seldom been explored in detail within the context of microevolutionary studies. These two countries encompass a total area of more than 10,000,000 km² and contain one-fifth of the world's total population. China witnessed very early large-scale human settlement, while Mongolia has been populated by nomadic peoples for at least 9,000 years (Derevyanko and Dorj 1992; Chang 1994; Fung 1994; Barnes 1999; Weber et al. 2002). Presently, more than 50 different ethnic groups are found within their combined borders, including the familiar Chinese, Mongolians, Koreans, and Tibetans, and the less-well-known Kazak, Uighur, and Manchurians.

To determine the population history of this area, dental nonmetric traits were scored for the remains of more than 900 individuals derived from 56 different archaeological sites. The population samples include the well-studied ethnic Han Chinese and Mongolians but also archaeological populations little known outside of Asia, such as the Xiongnu, Xianbei, Qidan, Qiang, Huimo, and Wanggu, as well as the non-Asian mummies of western China. The majority of the groups included in this study have had little representation in previously published large-scale population studies. In addition, the geographic scope and time depth of this study allow a more thorough and detailed examination of population interaction and movement in China and Mongolia than has previously been reported.

The Regional Divisions

To facilitate discussion of the large number of samples considered in this study, they have been divided into groups pertaining to four geographic regions: the Central Plains, the Northern Zone, Manchuria, and the Western Regions (figure 3.1). While these labels broadly refer to specific geographic areas, the groupings are really intended to represent division of the samples on the basis of cultural or ethnic affiliation, and therefore the actual physical boundaries are somewhat fluid.

The majority of the Central Plains samples come from sites located along the Yellow River in northern China and comprise groups of individuals considered culturally Chinese or ancestral to modern Chinese. The Northern Zone includes samples from archaeological sites left by the nomadic populations of central and eastern Mongolia. Manchuria refers to populations that resided in Manchuria, Inner Mongolia, and eastern Mongolia, which were ethnically, but not always culturally, distinct from the populations of the Central Plains and the Northern Zone. Finally, the Western Regions incorporates samplings of the European-descended populations of western Mongolia and Xinjiang Province, as well as Asian-descended populations from west of the Central Plains. The Asian samples were included with the non-Asian sam-

Figure 3.1. Regional divisions of the study area.

ples, as there appears to have been a long period of interaction and admixture among these groups within the region.

Previous Population History Studies of China and Mongolia

The following section summarizes the results of previous studies of population history in China and Mongolia. The most common methodologies used in this area are the study of cranial metric traits and DNA analysis. Recently, cranial and dental nonmetric traits have gained some popularity as subjects for investigation. Most prior studies of population history in China and Mongolia have been relatively limited in geographic or temporal scope.

Cranial Metric Studies

Until recently, the majority of the physical anthropological studies carried out in China and Mongolia used cranial metric traits to determine population relatedness. Tumen (2004), using cranial metric traits, found Bronze Age Mongolians not to be closely related to the Bronze Age Chinese. She did find cranial metric continuity within Mongolia from the Bronze Age through to the Iron Age. She concluded that the peoples of Mongolia had a long unbroken history of cranial metric distinctiveness from the Chinese.

Matsumura and colleagues (1998) examined crania from the Chandman site, located in Uvs, western Mongolia. This site was heterogeneous, with mainly non-Asian skulls and a few Asian crania. Based on cranial metric results, the population of Chandman was more closely related to modern-day Russians than to modern-day Mongolians.

Alekseev and Gochman (1983) studied two non-Asian Iron Age populations from western Mongolia and one Asian Iron Age population from eastern Mongolia, with some evidence of admixture. They found skulls from Mongolia overall to be fairly homogeneous, with population continuity from the Iron Age to the Medieval period.

Han (2001) surveyed archaeological samples from eastern Xinjiang and found the Yingpan population to be 40 percent Asian and that of the Lopnur site to be 18 percent Asian. He found three non-Asian skull types in eastern Xinjiang Province. He suggests that there were at least three separate migrations into Xinjiang Province from the west. The Asian skulls from these sites were found to be most similar to modern-day Tibetans.

Zhu (1991) compared a Qidan population from the Shanzuizi site to various Asian populations and found them most similar to contemporary Xianbei and modern Mongolians. The results of this research support historical evidence that Mongolians are descended from the Xianbei and Qidan people.

DNA-Based Studies

DNA studies have recently gained popularity in East Asia. Keyser and colleagues (2003) conducted mtDNA and Y-chromosome analyses on 62 skeletons found at the Xiongnu (300 BC–AD 154) Egiin Gol site, in Bulgan, northern Mongolia. The majority of the individuals sampled were of Asian descent, as would be expected of a Xiongnu cemetery, but a few later-period burials exhibited Turkic, and therefore non-Asian, genetic markers. This supports the idea that through time Mongolia experienced waves of migration by Turkic speakers from the west.

Fu and colleagues (2007) studied the mtDNA of 16 individuals from the Chengbozi (Chengpuzi) site in Inner Mongolia. The Chengbozi site was occupied by people of the Wanggu culture. The Wanggu individuals at Chengbozi were found to be closely related to Turkic speakers, such as the Uzbek, Uighur, and Kazak, and also to Mongolians from Mongolia. The Wanggu were not as closely related to Mongolians living in the same geographic area of Inner Mongolia. The authors concluded the Wanggu exhibited a complex population history and were an Asian population with substantial non-Asian admixture from Turkic speakers.

The Western Regions of China have been inhabited by non-Asian populations from the Bronze Age to the present. Cui (2003) looked at gene flow along the Silk Road in eastern Xinjiang Province, China. MtDNA was collected from 31 individuals from Turfan (the Subeishi, Yanghai, and Tai sites) and Lopnur (the Conqie site). The Turfan populations were found to be intermediate between Asian and non-Asian populations. This suggests some Asian genetic admixture into the populations of Turfan. The Lopnur sample was closest genetically to European populations, without evidence of Asian admixture. The archaeological populations of Xinjiang appear to have been resident on the frontier between Asian and non-Asian population expansion.

Nonmetric Traits

Nonmetric trait studies have not been used widely in China and Mongolia, but these approaches are slowly gaining broader appeal. The majority of nonmetric trait studies are skewed toward the Neolithic and Modern periods, leaving several thousand years of population history unaccounted for, including the formation of the Chinese and Mongolian empires.

Japanese researchers have used cranial nonmetric traits in several worldwide surveys, which have included populations from Mongolia and adjacent regions. Modern-day northern Chinese and Mongolians were consistently found to be closely related. Mongolian crania were also very similar to those from Lake Baikal and the Kazaks (Turkic speakers) from Central Asia, implying some non-Asian admixture. This was not unexpected, as these populations are geographically close and have had a long history of interaction (Ishida 1997; Hanihara 2000; Hanihara and Ishida 2001a–e; Hanihara et al. 2003).

One of the earliest dental nonmetric trait studies in East Asia was conducted by Turner (1987, 1990). Twenty-eight dental nonmetric traits were used to determine worldwide trait frequencies and the relationships implied. Asian samples were found to cluster into two large groups. The northern group, or Sinodont dental complex, included the populations of Mongolia, North China, South China, Hong Kong, and Japan. The southern trait complex, or Sundadont, incorporated populations from Southeast Asia, as well as the Jomon and Ainu of Japan. Turner found a north-to-south clinal variation of traits within China. This may be evidence that the major axis of human migration through time in that part of the world was north/south instead of east/west.

Matsumura and colleagues (1998) examined dental nonmetric traits from the Bronze Age Chandman site (700–400 BC), in Uvs, Mongolia. Non-Asian and Asian individuals were both buried at the Chandman site. The dental trait frequencies at Chandman were intermediate between modern-day Mediterranean Europeans and Mongolians. The trait frequencies were closest to those of modern-day Turkic speakers. This suggests that the population at Chandman was non-Asian with some Asian admixture.

Materials and Methods

Institutes

The skeletal collections used in this study were chosen based on their state of skeletal and dental preservation, the availability of large archaeological sample sizes, and the breadth of time and geography represented. The largest concentration of such Asian skeletal material is housed at the Chinese Center for Frontier Archaeology at Jilin University in Changchun, China. The collection houses over 3000 skeletons, dating from the Neolithic to the Qing dynasty. The vast majority derive from previous and continuing archaeological excavations in the northern frontier provinces of China. Most of the archaeological cultures referred to in this study are represented in this collection. These cultures include the Xiajiadian, Chinese, Xiongnu, Xianbei, Qidan, Huimo, Wanggu, Qiang, and those of the non-Asian oasis states of Xinjiang Province.

The Institute of Vertebrate Paleontology and Paleoanthropology (IVPP), located at the Chinese Academy of Sciences in Beijing, houses roughly 700 skeletons. The majority of those collections date from the eighteenth through twentieth centuries, and the whole was assembled mainly as a teaching collection for medical students. Most individuals are represented only by skulls, the postcranial material having been discarded. The IVPP also houses a few excavated Iron Age archaeological samples from the Central Plains region.

The largest skeletal collection in Mongolia is located in the Department of Anthropology and Archaeology, National University of Mongolia, in Ulaan Baatar. This collection numbers over 400 individuals, dating from the Neolithic period to the present. All of the archaeological cultures of Mongolia that have yielded skeletal remains are represented in this collection. The majority of the skeletons represent the Xiongnu and Mongol archaeological cultures, but there are also the remains of some Scythian, Afanasievo, Turkic, and modern Mongolian individuals.

For the purposes of this study, a few individuals were included from the collections of the Institute of History and the Institute of Archaeology, both part of the Mongolian Academy of Sciences in Ulaan Baatar. The individuals from the Institute of History represent burials from a royal Xiongnu tomb complex at the Golmod 2 site. The individuals curated at the Institute of Archaeology were recovered from the craftsman quarters of the Mongol period capital of Karakhorum. These remains were included in this study in order to increase the size of the Xiongnu and Mongol period samples.

Archaeological Samples

The following section summarizes the samples from each geographical region of the Bronze Age to the Medieval period. Each summary provides a brief description of the archaeological samples, along with available historical and excavation information.

Bronze Age Central Plains remains from two archaeological cultures are represented in the Central Plains region: the Shang and their successors, the Zhou (table 3.1). It is from the Shang dynasty that the earliest form of Chinese writing survives (Pulleyblank 1983; Boltz 1999). The Zhou dynasty succeeded the Shang dynasty, but whether there was any change in ethnicity is uncertain (So and Bunker 1995; Barnes 1999; Rawson 1999; Yang 1999). There is also confusion as to whether the peoples of both or either of those cultures were ancestral to modern-day Chinese.

Shang (1500–1000 BC)

The Shang archaeological culture is represented in this study by remains from the Xicha site, Inner Mongolia. The age of this site's occupation ranges across the periods of both the Shang and Zhou dynasties. The individuals from this site are considered to have been ethnically Shang. They probably spoke a form of the Chinese language.

Table 3.1. Bronze Age samples

Culture	Location	#	Time period	Dates	Institution
Central Plains					
Shang	Inner Mongolia	11	Shang–Zhou	1500–1000 BC	Jilin
Zhou	Shaanxi	15	Pre-Zhou	1200–1000 BC	Jilin
Northern Zone					
Slab Grave	Arkhangai, Dornod, Khentii, Khovsgol, Omnogobi, Ovorkhangai, Tov, Uvs	16	Bronze	1200–300 BC	NUM
Manchuria					
Upper Xiajiadian	Inner Mongolia	14	Warring States	1000–300 BC	Jilin
Pre-Xiongnu	Inner Mongolia	26	Eastern Zhou	770–221 BC	Jilin
Western Regions					
Xindian	Qinghai	22	Bronze	1200–500 BC	Jilin
Khirigsuur	Bayankhongor, Bayan Olgii, Khovd, Uvs	19	Bronze	2500–1200 BC	NUM
Chandman	Uvs	97	Bronze	700–400 BC	NUM

Sources: Jilin University (Jilin); National University of Mongolia (NUM).

Zhou (1200–1000 BC)

The Zhou archaeological culture is represented in this study by remains from the Wayaopu site, in Shaanxi, China. The age of the occupation of this site slightly predates the time of the Zhou dynasty. The individuals from this site are considered to have been ethnically Zhou. They probably spoke a form of the Chinese language.

Bronze Age Northern Zone Slab Grave (1200–300 BC)

The Slab Grave archaeological culture is represented by 11 sites in northern, central, and eastern Mongolia. Burials consisted of a limited number of individuals, possibly because of nomadic cultural practices or archaeological sampling procedures. This type of burial is found over a wide geographic area in Mongolia, northeastern China, and southern Siberia. The burial objects are related to the nomadic cultures of the Eurasian steppes. A few burials have been radiocarbon dated to 1200–300 BC (Erdenebaatar 2002; Batsaikhan 2003).

Bronze Age Manchuria Upper Xiajiadian (1000–300 BC)

The Upper Xiajiadian people practiced agriculture and raised domesticated pigs but moved more often and relied more heavily on herd animals than the preceding Lower Xiajiadian people did. Horse riding was introduced into Manchuria around 700 BC. At the same time, the quality of pottery declined, but bronze and iron metalwork became more elaborate; metal objects were related stylistically to Siberian forms. The Upper Xiajiadian people may have had more cultural ties to peoples of the northern steppes than to the Chinese (Di Cosmo 2002). The Upper Xiajiadian archaeological culture is represented by the Dashanquian site, Inner Mongolia, China.

Pre-Xiongnu (770–221 BC)

Pre-Xiongnu archaeological sites in Inner Mongolia have yielded artifactual and other evidence of non-Chinese lifeways and are believed to have been settled by Xiongnu people from central Mongolia. Recently, many archaeologists have argued that these sites were left by local populations that adopted cultural aspects of the Xiongnu, without there having been any significant migration of people (Psarras 1995; Di Cosmo 1999).

The two sites considered here are Yinniugou and Guoxian Yaozi, both from Inner Mongolia. The Yinniugou and Guoxian Yaozi sites appear to have been of the same archaeological culture. Burials were made in wood coffins with a niche at the skull. Offerings such as cattle, sheep, horse, and deer bones, as well as ceramic objects, were placed within the burials. The burial style and offerings suggest a relationship with neighboring nomadic cultures (Di Cosmo 1999; Yang 2004).

Bronze Age Western Regions Xindian (1200–500 BC)

The Xindian culture developed from preceding local cultures in Gansu and Qinghai Provinces. Burials were flexed and included pottery, sheep bones, stone mortars and pestles, shovels, arrows, hoes, pig bones, bronze knives, and bronze buttons as grave goods. They appear to be predominantly those of nomadic pastoralists who practiced limited farming. The burial artifacts appear to have been stylistically related to those of the Western Zhou. The people are hypothesized to have been ethnically Qiang, who were possibly ancestral to modern-day Tibetans (Yu 1986; An 1992; Debaine-Francfort 1995; Di Cosmo 1999). The Xindian sample is represented by remains from two sites, Xiao Handi and Mapai, in Qinghai, China.

Khirigsuur (3000–400 BC)

Non-Asians entering western Mongolia and Xinjiang Province during the Bronze Age from the west possibly were members of an extension of the Afanasevo culture. These people were nomadic pastoralists tending cattle, horses, sheep, and goats. Burials were predominantly contained in round stone mounds, called *khirigsuurs* in Mongolian, and often associated with deerstones. Deerstones are freestanding stelae carved with stylized faces, suns, deer, and other motifs. Animal offerings were buried in smaller stone satellite mounds, separate from the individual interred in the central burial. Khirigsuur burials were related to kurgan burials in Kazakhstan, Kyrgyzstan, and Tuva. Similarities in ceramics, lithics, and burial practices suggest that these people may have been ancestral to the Scythians (Jettmar 1981; Mallory 1989; Askarov et al. 1992; Erdenebaatar 2002; Honeychurch and Amartuvshin 2006).

The sample consists of non-Asian burials associated with large stone mounds in western Mongolia. The dating, cultural, and ethnic affiliation of these sites are uncertain. The slight variation in burial styles found in western Mongolia may represent something other than an ethnic difference in burial populations.

Chandman (700–400 BC)

The term *Scythian,* or *Saka,* is a relatively broad label applied to various sites in western Mongolia and Xinjiang Province, based on the presence of non-Asian burials unassociated with large stone mounds. This terminology may not be a valid cultural or ethnic designation. Scythian burials appeared in this area around 700 BC (Di Cosmo 1999).

Individuals at the Chandman site in Uvs, Mongolia, were buried in stone coffins within a timber-lined pit. They were possibly related ethnically to members of the societies associated with khirigsuur burials and those of the Uyuk culture in Kazakhstan (Askarov et al. 1992).

Iron Age Central Plains Longxian (475–221 BC)

The Longxian site is located in Shaanxi Province, China (table 3.2). This site dates to the Warring States period, and the burials recovered there represent individuals from the state of Zhao. The state of Zhao was eventually conquered by the state of Qin and incorporated into the first Chinese empire (Ramsey 1987; Yu 1990). The sample remains are assumed to be those of persons who were ethnically and linguistically Chinese. About one-half of the sample consists of fragmentary maxillae and mandibles.

Iron Age Northern Zone Xiongnu (300 BC–AD 200)

The Xiongnu period burials in this sample were collected from all over Mongolia. The burials from the royal tombs are probably culturally and ethnically Xiongnu. The remains recovered from common burials were culturally Xiongnu but probably ethnically representative of a more diverse group of peoples within the greater Xiongnu Empire. The Xiongnu did not have a formal written language, but pottery and game pieces have been excavated

Table 3.2. Iron Age samples

Name	Location	#	Time period	Dates	Institution
Central Plains					
Longxian	Shaanxi	87	Warring States	475–221 BC	IVPP
Northern Zone					
Xiongnu	Arkhangai, Bayankhongor, Bulgan, Dornod, Khentii, Khovd, Khovsgol, Ovorkhangai, Selenge, Sukhbaatar, Tov, Uvs, Zavkhan	95	Hunnu	300 BC–AD 200	MIH, NUM
Manchuria					
Shuiquan	I. Mongolia	36	Warring States	475–221 BC	Jilin
Xianbei	I. Mongolia, Liaoning, Shanxi	96	Eastern Han	25 BC–AD 534	Jilin, IVPP
Western Regions					
Nileke	Xinjiang	45	Early Iron	500–221 BC	Jilin
Yanghai	Xinjiang	52	Warring States–Han	475 BC–AD 220	Jilin
Yingpan	Xinjiang	54	Han–Jin	206 BC–AD 420	Jilin

Sources: Institute of Vertebrate Paleontology and Paleoanthropology (IVPP); Jilin University (Jilin); National University of Mongolia (NUM); Mongolian Institute of History (MIH).

that bear symbols possibly related to later Turkic runes (Miller et al. 2006). Few Xiongnu period cemeteries have been systematically excavated, so most of the sites have fewer than 10 individuals represented in the sample. While each site represents only a few individuals, Xiongnu cemeteries commonly contained over 200 burials. Most individuals were buried in wooden coffins, which varied in the elaboration of their ornate painted or applied metal decoration, depending on the occupant's social status. Burial goods included gold earrings, stone and glass beads, iron arrow points, Chinese mirrors, Chinese lacquer, Chinese coins, bronze cauldrons, and large quantities of animal bone (Miller et al. 2006; Purcell and Spurr 2006).

Iron Age Manchuria Huimo (475–221 BC)

The sample considered here is from the Shuiquan site, in Inner Mongolia, which dates to the Warring States period. The individuals buried at Shuiquan were affiliated with the Huimo archaeological culture. The Huimo may have been ethnically similar to the nomadic peoples that Chinese sources refer to as the Donghu (Di Cosmo 2002).

Xianbei (25 BC–AD 534)

The Xianbei sample consists of remains from three sites in northeastern China. The earliest is the Sandaowan site (25 BC–AD 220), Inner Mongolia.

This site dates to the Eastern Han dynasty, when the Xianbei were part of the Xiongnu Empire. From 1983 through 1984, 39 tombs were excavated at Sandaowan. Burial artifacts included ceramics, sheep bones, Chinese mirrors, bronze plaques, and bone ornaments (Wei and Zhu 2003).

The second part of the Xianbei sample is from the Lamadong site (AD 337–410) in Liaoning, China. This site dates to a period of disunion after the fall of the Xiongnu Empire and the Han dynasty, which is referred to as the three Yan states period (Former Yan, Later Yan, and Southern Yan). The buried individuals possibly represent the Murong division of the Xianbei (Twitchett and Tietze 1994; Watt 2004). In 1998, 369 tombs were excavated at the Lamadong site (Liaoning Institute of Archaeology 1999).

The final Xianbei site represented in this study is Beiwei (AD 386–534) in Shanxi, China. Beiwei was the capital of the Xianbei Northern Wei state. The burial sample possibly represents the Tuoba division of the Xianbei (Huang 2000). The Tuoba Xianbei were known to have adopted Chinese customs and intermarried with Chinese (Su 1980).

Iron Age Western Regions Nileke (550–221 BC)

Nileke dates to the early Iron Age. This site is located in northwestern Xinjiang, in the Tian Shan Mountains, near the border with Kazakhstan. These burials may represent the Saka/Scythian culture. The Nileke site is thought to have been a copper-producing center (Di Cosmo 1999). Nileke was excavated in 2001 (Liu and Li 2002).

Yanghai (475 BC–AD 220)

This site, in Xinjiang, China, dates from the Warring States period to the Han dynasty. It is located in the Turpan basin, at the foot of the Tian Shan Mountains. The language spoken in this area may have been related to Tocharian or Iranian (Mallory and Mair 2000). In 2003, 510 burials were excavated at Yanghai. Burial artifacts included ceramics, wooden bowls, bronze knives, adzes, gold earrings, turquoise necklaces, wool, leather, and silk (Lu et al. 2004). Many of the remains were naturally mummified.

Yingpan (206 BC–AD 420)

The Yingpan site, located in the Tarim basin in Xinjiang, China, was associated with the Loulan/Lopnur (Kroran) oasis state. Yingpan dates to the Han and Jin dynasties. The burials have been identified as of the Cheshi ethnicity. These individuals may have spoken an Indo-Afghan language (Mallory and Mair 2000). Many of the remains were naturally mummified and exhibit cranial modeling. Some individuals also had blond hair. In 1995, 150 burials were excavated at Yingpan. Individuals were buried in tree trunks hollowed out in the shape of boats. Burial objects included silk, wool, ceramics, bronze vessels, pearls, sheep bones, turquoise jewelry, and lacquer bowls. The silk cloth, bronze ware, and ceramics were originally from China. Wool blankets decorated with Greek motifs, glass vessels, and copper objects were originally from Central and West Asia (Li and Zhou 1998).

Medieval Period Central Plains Zhenzishan (AD 1279–1368)

The Zhenzishan site is located in Inner Mongolia (table 3.3). This site dates to the Yuan dynasty, when the Mongols ruled over China. Zhenzishan is considered Chinese, both ethnically and linguistically. In 1998–99, a total of 33 tombs were excavated at Zhenzishan. The tombs consisted of brick chambers containing individuals buried in wood coffins. Burial objects included Chinese ceramics, Chinese coins, and gold jewelry (Institute of Archaeology 2001).

Medieval Period Northern Zone Mongol (AD 1100–1500)

The Mongol sample comes from 15 archaeological sites distributed all over Mongolia. Mongol burials appear to have been sporadic, possibly because of their nomadic lifeways or perhaps as an artifact of archaeological sampling. These sites are considered to have been archaeologically and ethnically Mongolian. The Mongolian language was spoken in this region.

Table 3.3. Medieval period samples

Name	Location	#	Time period	Dates	Institution
Central Plains					
Chinese	Inner Mongolia	35	Yuan	AD 1279–1368	Jilin
Northern Zone					
Mongol	Arkhangai, Bulgan, Dornod, Khentii, Khovd, Ovorkhangai, Sukhbaatar, Selenge, Tov	54	Mongol	AD 1100–1500	NUM, MIA
Manchuria					
Qidan	Dornod, Inner Mongolia	22	Liao	AD 916–1125	Jilin, NUM
Wanggu	Inner Mongolia	16	Yuan	AD 1279–1368	Jilin

Sources: Jlin University (Jilin); National University of Mongolia (NUM); Mongolian Institute of Archaeology (MIA).

Medieval Period Manchuria Qidan (AD 916–1125)

Qidan tombs were traditionally Chinese in architecture with an underground chamber. Burial objects included horse equipment, falconry equipment, jade, rock crystal, and amber from the Baltic, as well as bows and arrows. Luxury goods acquired by long-distance trade included glass from Persia, rock crystal from India, ceramics, and silk from Song China, as well as ceramics and jewelry from Korea (Kessler 1993; Twitchett and Tietze 1994; Huang 2000; Kuhn 2006; Shen 2006; Ta and Zhang 2006).

Remains from three sites were included in the Qidan sample. These date to the Liao dynasty, when the Qidan ruled parts of northern China and Mongolia. The first Qidan sample comes from the Shanzuizi site, Inner Mongolia. The second sample is from the Alukeqinqi site, Inner Mongolia. The third Qidan sample comes from the Kholonbuir site, Dornod, Mongolia. The Qidan were probably Mongolian or Tungus language speakers (Franke 1990; Twitchett and Tietze 1994).

Wanggu (AD 1279–1368)

The Chengpuzi site is located in Inner Mongolia, China. This sample dates to the Yuan dynasty, when the Mongols ruled over China. The Wanggu are documented as having moved to Inner Mongolia from the Western Regions in AD 1124 (Gai 1991).

Dental Nonmetric Traits

Nonmetric trait studies have made significant diachronic and synchronic contributions to our knowledge of human history and to modern anthropology. Nonmetric traits are minor morphological variations in the bones and teeth, assumed to be passed genetically from parent to offspring. These variations are found in modern and fossil humans, as well as in other animals. They are considered minor, in that they do not affect the basic functions of the bones and teeth. These skeletal variants are not easily observed in living beings and are considered not to be under the control of strong sexual selection. The term *nonmetric* refers to traits measured on a either a nominal scale (absent, present) or an ordinal scale (ranked data), rather on a numerical scale (interval scale), thereby distinguishing them from metric traits (Ossenberg 1969; Scott and Turner 1997).

Modern skeletal and older archaeological populations can be compared to one another using nonmetric traits. Cranial and dental nonmetric traits are useful when dealing with many older archaeological and medical collections, as the majority of these contain only skulls lacking their associated postcranial elements. The results of studies using nonmetric traits are supported by previous research utilizing methods from a variety of disciplines, including metric, linguistic, fossil, historical, archaeological, serological, ethnographic, and DNA studies (Turner 1987, 1990; Irish 1993; Coppa et al. 1998).

Dental nonmetric trait studies have been standardized by the use of plaster dental plaques to score permanent and deciduous teeth (Hanihara 1967; Turner et al. 1991). The Arizona State University (ASU) dental anthropology system has been used successfully by researchers around the world. Absence of a trait is usually scored as 0, with degrees of trait expression beginning with the number 1. The larger the number, the more pronounced the trait expression. This system allows some flexibility to add numbers if needed, and it is adaptable to a variety of statistical analyses and computer databases. Researchers have used traits from this system to test global, continent-wide (Irish 1993), country-specific (Hawkey 1998), and taxonomic (Bailey 2002) relationships.

Sources of dental nonmetric variation include an abnormal number of teeth (congenital absence of the third molar, supernumerary teeth), unusual shape or size (extra cusps and roots, peg incisors 2, cusp 7), abnormal enamel formation (odontomes, enamel extensions), and disruptions in tooth eruption (winging, diastema).

Scoring Procedures

Twenty-eight dental nonmetric traits were scored for this study (table 3.4). Traits were chosen based on their previously documented occurrence in East Asian and European populations. The traits were scored using a numerical scale that corresponds to the degree of differences in trait expression. Each trait is scored beginning at 0 for the absence of a trait, with up to six possible variations for certain traits. The results for each trait are then dichotomized, in which a number above a certain break point is considered presence of a trait, and below this break point is considered absence of a trait.

The ASU dental plaque system was chosen because it provides a standardized scoring procedure for dental nonmetric traits. This system allows any data collected to be compared with those collected by other researchers, therefore minimizing interobserver error (Turner et al. 1991). This is the most widely used system of dental nonmetric trait scoring used in Asia and much of the rest of the world.

After data collection, traits found to be difficult to score consistently, as well as extremely rare traits, were excluded. Rare traits may occur because of

Table 3.4. Dental traits scored

Dental trait	Key teeth scored	Trait scale	Trait presence
Maxillary traits			
1. Winging	Incisor 1	1–4	1–2
2. Shoveling	Incisor 1	0–6	3–6
3. Double shoveling	Incisor 1	0–6	2–6
4. Interruption grooves	Incisor 2	0	Midline, mesial, distal
5. Tuberculum dentale	Incisor 2	0	1–6
6. Hypocone	Molar 2	0–5	0–1
7. Cusp 5	Molar 1	0–5	1–5
8. Carabelli's cusp	Molar 1	0–7	2–7
9. Parastyle	Molar 3	0–5	1–5
10. Enamel extensions	Molar 1	0–3	1–3
11. Root number	Molar 2	1–4	3
12. Root number	Premolar 1	1–2	2
13. Peg/congenital absence	Molar 3	0	1–2
14. Odontome	Premolars	0	1
15. Uto-Aztecan premolar	Premolar 1	0	1
Mandibular traits			
16. Cusp number	Premolar 1	0–9	2–9
17. Cusp number	Premolar 2	0–9	2–9
18. Y-groove pattern	Molar 2	Y, X, +	Y
19. Molar cusp number	Molar 1	4–6	6
20. Molar cusp number	Molar 2	4–6	4
21. Deflecting wrinkle	Molar 1	0–3	3
22. Protostylid	Molar 1	0–7	2–7
23. Cusp 6	Molar 1	0–5	1–5
24. Cusp 7	Molar 1	0–5	1–5
25. Root number	Molar 1	1–3	3
26. Root number	Molar 2	1–2	1
27. Root number	Premolar 1	1–2	2
28. Root number	Premolar 2	1–2	2

random mutation and therefore do not measure interpopulation variability. Whenever possible, each archaeological site equals one sample. This is based on the assumption that a burial population to some extent is also a breeding population; therefore, each individual contributes to the unique makeup of each site's profile. However, certain regions have produced small sample sizes because of culturally determined burial customs or national biases in archaeological sampling. Sites with a small sample size may be pooled as long as they share a common history or archaeological culture. The data are compared synchronically to look for patterns of population movement between geographic regions. Then the same data are examined diachronically to look for patterns through time.

Statistical Analysis

Presently the most widespread statistic used in nonmetric studies is the mean measure of divergence (MMD) developed by C.A.B. Smith (Berry and Berry 1967; Sjøvold 1977). The MMD statistic is usually modified by the Freeman-Tukey transformation suggested by Green and Suchey (1976) to mitigate for small sample sizes and trait correlations:

$$MMD = \sum_{i=1}^{r} \frac{(\Theta_{1i} - \Theta_{2i})^2 - (\frac{1}{n_{1i}} + \frac{1}{n_{2i}})}{r}$$

Small sample size is always a concern when studying archaeologically derived skeletal populations. Each nonmetric trait is first specified as to the number of individuals with presence of a trait and the total number of individuals observed for that trait, for example, 50/100. The mean measure of divergence program then compares all of the nonmetric traits between two samples. The mean measure of divergence calculates the average of the differences between two populations for N number of traits. An MMD score is considered statistically significant at the $p = .025$ level when equal to or greater than twice its standard deviation. If the MMD score is significant between two samples, the interpretation is that the two populations are not similar and do not share a common ancestry. A minimum of three samples is necessary in order to meaningfully compare population distances (Sjøvold 1973).

Any negative MMD values are read as a .0000 score. In addition, MMD scores from 0 through .0999 can be interpreted as both populations being fairly similar and probably sharing a common ancestry. A score of .1–.1999 means both samples are moderately dissimilar, and a score over .2000 means they are two distinct populations (Hawkey 1998).

Intraregional Dental Results

Mean measure of divergence scores were averaged for the samples within each of the four regional divisions (table 3.5). This gives an idea of how homogeneous or heterogeneous the population samples are within each region.

Table 3.5. Dental mean measure of divergence, intraregional averages

Intraregional samples	MMD average
Central Plains–Central Plains	.023619
Northern Zone–Northern Zone	.002629
Manchuria–Manchuria	.009170
Western Regions–Western Regions	.027564

The Northern Zone and Manchurian samples are very homogeneous within their respective regions. The Central Plains and Western Regions samples are more heterogeneous within their regions. This implies more movement and admixture within the Northern Zone and Manchurian regions. The mobile nature of these two sets of populations may have contributed to the movement and distribution of genes also. The Central Plains and Western Regions experienced more isolation, possibly due to a combination of culture, geography, and politics. The individual populations within these regions appear to have remained somewhat distinct from one another.

Dental Interregional Trait Frequencies

The dental mean measure of divergence scores were then averaged between the four regions (table 3.6). This gives an idea of the relationships, movement, and admixture between the four regions.

The Northern Zone and Manchurian populations appear to have interacted and admixed to some extent with those of the Central Plains. There was slightly less movement between the Manchurian and Northern Zone regions. The Western Regions population samples are the most divergent from the other regional samples. This is probably due to a combination of geographic remoteness, linguistic differences, and their non-Asian appearance. The hub of population movement in northern East Asia appears to have been through the Central Plains region. However, all of the MMD results are fairly minimal, which implies that there was a long history of population interaction and/or common descent among all of the four regions.

Bronze Age Cluster Analysis

The next step in analysis was to create an overview of the population history of the area through time. Mean measure of divergence scores were run through SPSS using Ward's (1963) method for cluster analysis. The popula-

Table 3.6. Dental mean measure of divergence, interregional averages

Interregional samples	MMD average
Central Plains–Northern Zone	.023564
Central Plains–Manchuria	.022867
Central Plains–Western Regions	.076821
Manchuria–Western Regions	.075612
Northern Zone–Manchuria	.045198
Northern Zone–Western Regions	.077462

```
C A S E        0      5      10     15     20     25
Label      Num ┝ ─ ─ ─ ┝ ─ ─ ─ ┝ ─ ─ ─ ┝ ─ ─ ─ ┝ ─ ─ ─ ┝

Shang-Zhou    1
Xindian       5
Xiajiadian    3
Slab grave    2
Chandman      6
Pre-Xiongnu   4
```

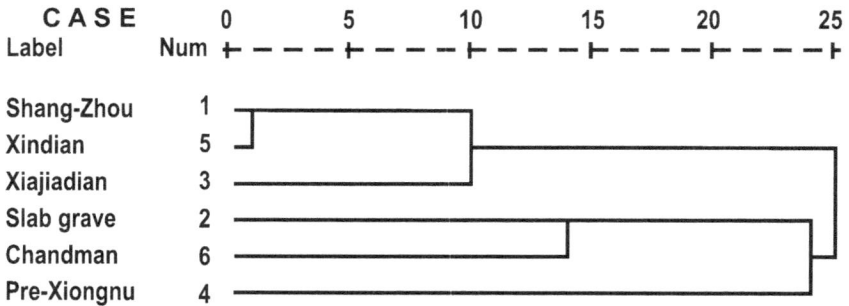

Figure 3.2. Bronze Age cluster analysis.

tions from the Bronze Age were fairly heterogeneous (figure 3.2). There are at least four spheres of interaction represented. The Central Plains (Shang-Zhou) population sample clustered closely with the Western Regions (Xindian) and with one sample from Manchuria (Xiajiadian). The unusually wide geographic scope of this cluster may point to the large-scale movement of people across all of these regions during the Bronze Age. The introduction of the horse and associated technologies may have aided this migration (Di Cosmo 2002). Another Manchurian population, the Pre-Xiongnu, constitutes its own cluster. This population may have moved into the Manchurian region from the north. The two samples from Mongolia form another cluster, even though one is Asian (Slab Grave) and another is non-Asian (Chandman). This may have been the result of a large amount of admixture between these two populations. The Bronze Age population samples show a complex pattern of interaction and heterogeneity not based on straightforward ethnicity, cultural ties, or geographic proximity.

Several factors contributed to population complexity during this time period. The introduction of the horse and chariot facilitated the movement of people over longer distances. Widespread improvement of agricultural and cooking practices increased the population density. The drying and cooling of the environment rendered the northern regions unsuitable for farming, with mass migrations southward. The rise of a ruling class, long-distance trading networks, state-mandated warfare, and sacrificial burials all point to a rapidly changing and unpredictable time (Murphy 1994; So and Bunker 1995; Yang 1999).

Iron Age Cluster Analysis

For the Iron Age samples, three clusters appear to follow the political lines of the time (figure 3.3). One cluster represents the Xiongnu Empire, encompassing the Northern Zone (Xiongnu) and the Manchurian (Xianbei, Huimo)

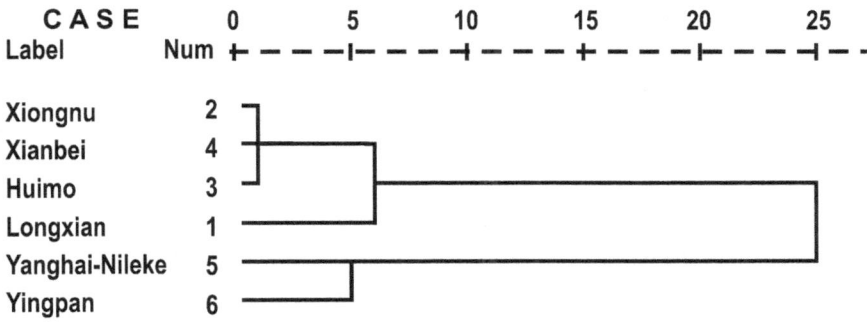

Figure 3.3. Iron Age cluster analysis.

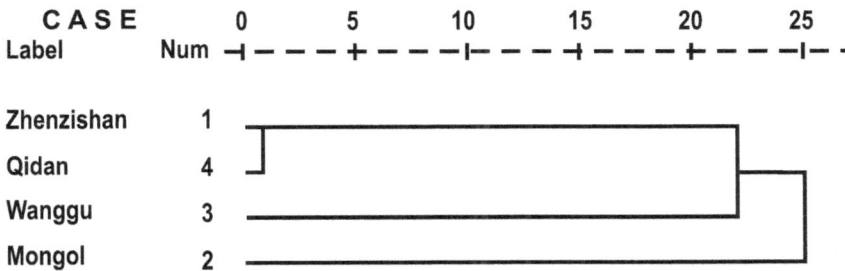

Figure 3.4. Medieval period cluster analysis.

samples. The second cluster represents the Chinese empire with the Longxian sample. The last cluster represents the semi-independent oasis states of present-day Xinjiang Province (Yanghai-Nileke, Yingpan), along the Silk Road. Populations within each cluster appear to have become more homogeneous than during the Bronze Age. This may be evidence of the various states having controlled population movement within each area.

During the Iron Age, the Great Wall was truly a physical and psychological barrier. With the formation of the Xiongnu Empire to the north and the Chinese empire to the south, movement of people was restricted. Both empires practiced colonization and the assimilation of new populations along their frontiers. This was the first widespread attempt to create a national identity for the Xiongnu and the Chinese (Yu 1990; Ebrey 1996).

Medieval Period Cluster Analysis

The Medieval period population samples appear to have been more heterogeneous than those of the preceding Iron Age. Three separate clusters are present: the Mongols in the Northern Zone and two more clusters in Manchuria (figure 3.4). The Central Plains population (Zhenzishan) was closely related to one Manchurian sample (Qidan). Population movement appears to have become more fluid again between the Northern Zone, the Central Plains, and Manchuria. No Western Regions samples were available for this time period.

Conclusions

1. Within China and Mongolia, Asian- and European-descended populations had a long history of interaction dating to the Bronze Age.
2. During the Bronze Age, many different populations were present within the study area. Their pattern of interaction was not solely based on biological relatedness, cultural ties, or geographic proximity.
3. During the Iron Age, political factors appear to have been the main driving force for controlling population movement and admixture. Three population spheres emerged, coincident with the Chinese empire, the Xiongnu Empire, and the oasis states along the Silk Road.
4. During the Medieval period there was an increase in population heterogeneity, especially within Manchuria. This may imply that populations were once again fragmented along ethnic, tribal, cultural, or linguistic lines, instead of according to political alliances.
5. Populations within the Northern Zone and Manchuria experienced a higher degree of migration and admixture than did the populations of the Central Plains and the Western Regions. The introduction of the horse and subsequent technologies to the Northern Zone and Manchuria may have been a causal factor in the homogenization of the populations within these two regions.

Acknowledgments

I would like to thank the following institutions and individuals for access to their collections: Xing Gao, Xiujie Wu, and Wu Liu at IVPP; Hong Zhu, Qi Fang, and Linhu Zhang at Jilin University; Yajun Zhang and Minghui Wang at the Chinese Institute of Archaeology; Tumen Dashtseveg and Erdene Myagmar at the Mongolian National University; Erdenebaatar Diimaajav at the Mongolian Institute of History; and Bayar Dovdoi and Ernst Pohl at the Mongolian Institute of Archaeology. I would also like to thank Christy G. Turner II and John W. Olsen for their guidance. Funding for this research was provided by the Arizona State University School of Human Evolution and Social Change and the Wenner-Gren Foundation.

Literature Cited

Alekseev VP, Gochman II. 1983. *Rassengeschichte der Menscheit*. Munich: R. Oldenbourg.

Allsen T. 1994. The rise of the Mongolian empire and Mongolian rule in North China. In: Franke H, Twitchett D, editors. *The Cambridge history of China*. Vol. 6: *Alien regimes and border states*. Cambridge: Cambridge University Press. Pp. 321–413.

An Z. 1992. Bronze Age in eastern parts of Central Asia. In: Dani AH, Masson VM, editors. *History of civilizations of Central Asia*. Vol. 1: *The dawn of civilization: Earliest times to 700 BC*. Paris: UNESCO Publishing. Pp. 319–36.

Askarov A, Volkov V, Ser-Odjav N. 1992. Pastoral and nomadic tribes at the beginning of the first millennium BC. In: Dani AH, Masson VM, editors. *History of civilizations of Central Asia*. Vol. 1: *The dawn of civilization: Earliest times to 700 BC*. Paris: UNESCO Publishing. Pp. 459–72.

Bailey SE. 2002. Neandertal dental morphology: Implications for modern human origins. Ph.D. dissertation, Arizona State University.

Barnes GL. 1999. *The rise of civilization in East Asia: The archaeology of China, Korea, and Japan*. London: Thames and Hudson.

Batsaikhan Z. 2003. *Hunnu*. Ulaanbaater: National University of Mongolia.

Berry AC, Berry RJ. 1967. Epigenetic variation in the human cranium. *Journal of Anatomy* 101: 361–79.

Boltz WG. 1999. Language and writing. In: Loewe M, Shaughnessy EL, editors. *The Cambridge history of ancient China: From the origins of civilization to 221 BC*. Cambridge: Cambridge University Press. Pp. 74–123.

Chang KC. 1994. Ritual and power. In: Murowchick RE, editor. *Cradles of civilization: China*. Norman: University of Oklahoma Press. Pp. 61–69.

Coppa A, Cuccina A, Mancinelli D, Vargiu R, Calcagno JM. 1998. Dental morphology of central-southern Iron Age Italy: The evidence of metric versus nonmetric traits. *American Journal of Physical Anthropology* 107: 371–86.

Cui Y. 2003. *Ancient DNA analysis of human population in Xinjiang: Turfan and Lopnur*. Changchun: Jilin University Press.

Debaine-Francfort C. 1995. *Du neolithique à l'age du bronze en Chine du nord-ouest: La culture de Qijia et ses connexions*. Paris: Editions Recherche sur les Civilisations.

Derevyanko AP, Dorj D. 1992. Neolithic tribes in northern parts of Central Asia. In: Dani AH, Masson VM, editors. *History of civilizations of Central Asia*. Vol. 1: *The dawn of civilization: Earliest times to 700 BC*. Paris: UNESCO Publishing. Pp. 169–90.

Di Cosmo N. 1999. The northern frontier in pre-Imperial China. In: Loewe M, Shaughnessy EL, editors. *The Cambridge history of ancient China: From the origins of civilization to 221 BC*. Cambridge: Cambridge University Press. Pp. 885–966.

Di Cosmo N. 2002. *Ancient China and its enemies: The rise of nomadic power in East Asian history*. Cambridge: Cambridge University Press.

Ebrey PB. 1996. *The Cambridge illustrated history of China*. Cambridge: Cambridge University Press.

Erdenebaatar D. 2002. *Mongolian slab grave and khirigsuur cultures*. Ulaanbaatar: National University of Mongolia.

Franke H. 1990. The forest peoples of Manchuria: Kitans and Jurchens. In: Sinor D, editor. *The Cambridge history of early Inner Asia*. Cambridge: Cambridge University Press. Pp. 400–423.

Fu Y, Zhao H, Cui Y, Zhang Q, Xu X, Zhou H, Zhu Z. 2007. Molecular genetic analysis of Wanggu remains, Inner Mongolia, China. *American Journal of Physical Anthropology* 132: 285–91.

Fung C. 1994. The beginnings of settled life. In: Murowchick RE, editor. *Cradles of civilization: China.* Norman: University of Oklahoma. Pp. 51–59.

Gai SL. 1991. *Yinshan Wanggu.* Hohhot: Inner Mongolia People's Press.

Green RF, Suchey JM. 1976. The use of inverse sine transformations in the analysis of non-metric cranial data. *American Journal of Physical Anthropology* 45: 61–68.

Han K. 2001. Physical anthropological studies on the racial affinities of the inhabitants of ancient Xinjiang. In: Wang B, editor. *The ancient corpses of Xinjiang: The peoples of ancient Xinjiang and their culture.* Urumqi: Xinjiang Peoples Press. Pp. 224–41.

Hanihara K. 1967. Racial characteristics in the dentition. *Journal of Dental Research* 46: 923–26.

Hanihara T. 2000. Frontal and facial flatness of major human populations. *American Journal of Physical Anthropology* 111: 105–34.

Hanihara T, Ishida H. 2001a. Os incae: Variation in frequency in major human population groups. *Journal of Anatomy* 198: 137–52.

Hanihara T, Ishida H. 2001b. Frequency variations of discrete cranial traits in major human populations. I: Supernumerary ossicle variations. *Journal of Anatomy* 198: 689–706.

Hanihara T, Ishida H. 2001c. Frequency variations of discrete cranial traits in major human populations. II: Hypostotic variations. *Journal of Anatomy* 198: 707–25.

Hanihara T, Ishida H. 2001d. Frequency variations of discrete cranial traits in major human populations. III: Hyperostotic variations. *Journal of Anatomy* 199: 251–72.

Hanihara T, Ishida H. 2001e. Frequency variations of discrete cranial traits in major human populations. IV: Vessel and nerve relations variations. *Journal of Anatomy* 199: 273–87.

Hanihara T, Ishida H, Dodo Y. 2003. Characterization of biological diversity through analysis of discrete cranial traits. *American Journal of Physical Anthropology* 121: 241–51.

Hawkey DE. 1998. Out of Asia: Dental evidence for affinities and microevolution of early populations from India and Sri Lanka. Ph.D. dissertation, Arizona State University.

Honeychurch W, Amartuvshin C. 2006. States on horseback: The rise of inner Asian confederations and empires. In: Stark MT, editor. *Archaeology of Asia.* Malden, MA: Blackwell. Pp. 255–78.

Huang X. 2000. Prosperity of the steppe empire from the Mongol Khan empire to the unification by the Yuan dynasty. In: Chen X, Wang Q, editors. *Treasures on grassland: Archaeological finds from the Inner Mongolian Autonomous Region.* Shanghai: Shanghai Museum. Pp. 59–60.

Institute of Archaeology, Chinese Academy of Social Sciences, and Archaeology Department, Jilin University. 2001. Excavation of the tombs at Zhenzishan to the southeast of the upper capital of the Yuan dynasty. *Wenwu* 9: 37–51.

Irish JD. 1993. Biological affinities of late Pleistocene through modern African aboriginal populations: The dental evidence. Ph.D. dissertation, Arizona State University.

Ishida H. 1997. Craniometric variation of the northeast Asian populations. *Homo* 48: 106–24.

Jettmar K. 1981. Cultures and ethnic groups west of China in the second and first millennia BC. *Asian Perspectives* 24: 145–61.

Kessler AT. 1993. *Empires beyond the great wall: The heritage of Genghis Khan.* Los Angeles: Natural History Museum of Los Angeles.

Keyser-Tracqui C, Crubezy E, Ludes B. 2003. Nuclear and mitochondrial DNA analysis of a 2,000-year-old necropolis in the Egyin Gol valley of Mongolia. *American Journal of Human Genetics* 73: 247–60.

Kuhn D. 2006. An introduction to Chinese archaeology of the Liao. In: Shen H, editor. *Gilded splendor: Treasures of China's Liao empire, 907–1125*. New York: Asia Society. Pp. 25–39.

Li W, Zhou J. 1998. Archaeological finds at the burial site of Yingpan and some related questions. In: Ma C, Yue F, editors. *Archaeological treasures of the Silk Road in Xinjiang Uygur autonomous region*. P. 75.

Liaoning Institute of Archaeology. 1999. Lamadong cemetery. In: *Chinese Archaeology Almanac: New archaeological discoveries*. Beijing: Chinese Institute of Archaeology. Pp. 154–55.

Liu X, Li S. 2002. Yili River basin, Xinjiang Province: new archaeological discoveries. *The Western Regions Studies* 1: 109–10.

Lu E, Zhang Y, Zu L, Xu D. 2004. New results from the Yanghai site archaeological tombs, Shanshan County, Xinjiang Province. *Kaogu* 5: 3–7.

Mallory JP. 1989. *In search of the Indo-Europeans: Language, archaeology, and myth*. New York: Thames and Hudson.

Mallory JP, Mair VH. 2000. *The Tarim mummies*. London: Thames and Hudson.

Matsumura H, Tumen D, Takai M. 1998. Dental and facial morphology of the human skeletons unearthed at the Chandman site in western Mongolia. *Bulletin of the National Science Museum (Tokyo) Series D* (Anthropology) 24: 9–18.

Miller BK, Allard F, Erdenebaatar D, Lee C. 2006. A Xiongnu tomb complex: Excavations at Gol Mod 2 cemetery, Mongolia (2002–5). *Mongolian Journal of Anthropology, Archaeology, and Ethnology* 2: 1–21.

Mote FW. 1994. Chinese society under Mongol rule 1214–1368. In: Franke H, Twitchett D, editors. *The Cambridge history of China*. Vol. 6: *Alien regimes and border states*. Cambridge: Cambridge University Press. Pp. 616–64.

Murphy R. 1994. The land. In: Murowchick RE, editor. *Cradles of civilization: China*. Norman: University of Oklahoma. Pp. 12–23.

Ossenberg NS. 1969. Discontinuous morphological variation in the human cranium. Ph.D. dissertation, University of Toronto.

Psarras S. 1995. Xiongnu culture: Identification and dating. *Central Asiatic Journal* 39: 102–36.

Pulleyblank EG. 1983. The Chinese and their neighbors in prehistoric and early historic times. In: Keightley DN, editor. *The origins of Chinese civilization*. Berkeley: University of California Press. Pp. 411–66.

Purcell DE, Spurr KC. 2006. Archaeological investigations of Xiongnu sites in the Tamir River valley. *Silk Road Newsletter* 4: 20–32.

Ramsey SR. 1987. *The languages of China*. Princeton: Princeton University Press.

Rawson J. 1999. Western Zhou archaeology. In: Loewe M, Shaughnessy EL, editors. *The Cambridge history of ancient China: From the origins of civilization to 221 BC*. Cambridge: Cambridge University Press. Pp. 352–449.

Scott GR, Turner CG II. 1997. *The anthropology of modern human teeth: Dental morphology and its variation in recent human populations*. Cambridge: Cambridge University Press.

Shen H. 2006. The nomadic heritage. In: Shen H, editor. *Gilded splendor: Treasures of China's Liao empire, 907–1125*. New York: Asia Society. Pp. 96–187.

Sjøvold T. 1973. The occurrence of minor non-metrical variants in the skeleton and their quantitative treatment of population comparisons. *Homo* 24: 204–33.

Sjøvold T. 1977. Non-metrical divergence between skeletal populations. *Ossa* 4: xii–133.

So JF, Bunker EC. 1995. *Traders and raiders on China's northern frontier*. Washington, DC: Smithsonian Institution.

Su B. 1980. Xianbei remains in Manchuria and Inner Mongolia. *Chinese Studies in Archaeology* 2: 3–43.

Ta L, Zhang Y. 2006. A Liao dynasty tomb on Tuerji Hill. In: Shen H, editor. *Gilded splendor: Treasures of China's Liao empire, 907–1125*. New York: Asia Society. Pp. 61–66.

Tumen D. 2004. Linguistic, cultural, and morphological characteristics of Mongolian populations. *Senri Ethnological Studies* 66: 309–24.

Turner CG II. 1987. Late Pleistocene and Holocene population history of East Asia based on dental variation. *American Journal of Physical Anthropology* 73: 605–321.

Turner CG II. 1990. The major features of Sundadonty and Sinodonty, including suggestions about East Asia microevolution, population history, and late Pleistocene relationships with Australian Aboriginals. *American Journal of Physical Anthropology* 82: 295–317.

Turner CG II, Nichol CR, Scott GR. 1991. Scoring procedures for key morphological traits of the permanent dentition: The Arizona State University dental anthropology system. In: Kelley MA, Larsen CS, editors. *Advances in dental anthropology*. New York: Wiley-Liss. Pp. 13–31.

Twitchett D, Tietze K. 1994. Liao. In: Franke H, Twitchett D, editors. *The Cambridge history of China*. Vol. 6: *Alien regimes and border states*. Cambridge: Cambridge University Press. Pp. 43–153.

Ward JH. 1963. Hierarchical grouping to optimize an objective function. *Journal of the American Statistical Association* 58: 236–44.

Watt J. 2004. Art and history in China from the 3rd–8th centuries. In: Watt J, editor. *China: Dawn of a golden age, 200–750 AD*. New York: Metropolitan Museum of Art. Pp. 3–43.

Weber AW, Link DW, Katzenberg MA. 2002. Hunter-gatherer culture change and continuity in the middle Holocene of the Cis-Baikal, Siberia. *Journal of Anthropological Archaeology* 21: 230–99.

Wei J, Zhu B. 2003. *Research on the newly discovered Xianbei tombs of the Inner Mongolia region*. Beijing: Science Press.

Yang J. 2004. *The formation of northern Chinese frontier belt during the Spring and Autumn and Warring States periods*. Beijing: Beijing Cultural Relics Publishing House.

Yang X. 1999. *The golden age of Chinese archaeology: Celebrated discoveries from the People's Republic of China*. Washington, DC: National Gallery of Art.

Yu Y. 1986. Han foreign relations. In: Twitchett D, Loewe M, editors. *The Cambridge history of China*. Vol. 1: *The Ch'in and Han Empires, 221 BC–AD 220*. Cambridge: Cambridge University Press. Pp. 377–462.

Yu Y. 1990. The Hsiung-nu. In: Sinor D, editor. *The Cambridge history of early Inner Asia*. Cambridge: Cambridge University Press. Pp. 118–50.

Zhu H. 1991. Human skulls of Qidan nationality from Liao dynasty tombs in Shanzuizi site, Ningcheng County, Inner Mongolia. *Acta Anthropologica Sinica* 10: 278–87.

4

Mongolian Origins and Cranio-Morphometric Variability

Neolithic to Mongolian Period

TUMEN DASHTSEVEG

This chapter explores the issue of cranio-morphological variability in samples from the Neolithic, Bronze and Iron Ages, and Xiongnu to Mongolian periods, as well as examining the question of the origins and genetic relationships of these ancient populations. In Mongolia, the Neolithic is known from abundant surface finds in the proximity of present or former watercourses and lakes, characterized by microblades and other small tools associated with pottery. It is generally divided into three chronological stages. The earliest ostensible evidence for Neolithic occupation in eastern Mongolia is found at the sixth millennium BC Tamsagbulag site in Dornod aimag (Gunchinsuren 2000). Traditionally, the first stage of the Mongolian Neolithic belongs to the fourth millennium BC, the second to the third millennium BC, and the third stage belongs to the end of the second millennium BC. Mongolian Neolithic populations are thought to have been seminomadic and nomadic hunters (Okladnikov 1963, 1964; Dorj 1971).

Archaeological studies reveal that during the Bronze and Early Iron Age (third millennium through third century BC) there were significant cultural differences between the western and eastern parts of Mongolia (Volkov 1967, 1981; Novgorodova 1987; Erdenebaatar 2002). In western Mongolia, a culture associated with stone kurgans, deerstone monuments, and rock art was widely distributed. The western Mongolian Bronze and Early Iron Age culture belongs to the Altai-Sayan variant of the southern Siberian Bronze and Iron Age culture. During this period there was intensive cultural admixture between the western and eastern regions of Mongolia. However, remains dated to the Bronze and Early Iron Age in eastern and central Mongolia are characteristic of the so-called Slab Grave culture: rectangular enclosures built using stone slabs set on edge, sometimes grouped in cemeteries.

The Slab Grave culture was widely distributed, not only all over eastern and central Mongolia but also in surrounding areas, from the Lake Baikal region in the north to the Ordos in the south, as well as from the Khangai Mountains in the west to Manchuria in the east. In spite of its wide distribution, remains of the Slab Grave culture are homogeneous in terms of surface and subsurface construction techniques and the range of associated material culture (Navaan 1975; Tsybekhtarov 1998; Erdenebaatar 2002). Mongolian archaeologists suggest that the people associated with the Slab Grave culture were the direct ancestors of the Xiongnu (Sukhbaatar 1980).

In recent years, hitherto unknown monuments belonging to the Early Bronze Age were discovered in the Altai Mountain region of western Mongolia as a result of work by members of the joint Mongolian-Russian Central Asian Archaeology 2002–7 project. Construction of these monuments is attributed to peoples successively affiliated with the Afanasevo (Афанасьево) culture (2800–2500 BC) of southern Siberia and the Chemurchek culture (2500–1800 BC) of northwestern China, followed by the local Munkh Khairkhan culture (1800–1500 BC), Baitag culture (1500–1200 BC), and Tevsh culture (1300–1100 BC) (Erdenebaatar and Kovalev 2006, 2007).

Xiongnu (c. 3rd century BC–2nd century AD) played an important role in the ethnic as well as the political history and culture of Eurasia (Bernshtam 1951; Gumilev 1960). In terms of Mongolian archaeology, the Xiongnu period is one of the most thoroughly investigated, although the ethnic identity of the Xiongnu is still a problematic issue. There are three main hypotheses regarding the identity of the Xiongnu: (1) Xiongnu = the Turkic tribal confederation; (2) Xiongnu = a confederacy of Mongolian tribes; and (3) Xiongnu represented a confederacy of Mongolian, Turkic, and Tungus-Manchurian tribes. In fact, the history of debate over the ethnic origins of the Xiongnu has not been resolved (a useful overview of the debate [Western, Chinese, and Mongolian] and opposing theories can be found in Di Cosmo 2002: 163–66).

Archaeological investigation has shown that Xiongnu monuments or graves varied considerably in terms of size, surface and subsurface grave construction, and associated grave goods. These differences have been interpreted as reflecting a pronounced gradient in social status (high status versus commoners) (Tseveendorj 1987; Batsaikhan 2002; Turbat 2004). Davydova (1995, 1996) suggests that Xiongnu grave construction can be divided into seven types: (1) burial without intraburial construction; (2) flat graves without coffins; (3) frame coffins made of thin logs; (4) stone cists; (5) coffins; (6) whole log coffins; and (7) double chamber burials.

Most archaeologists and historians propose that the Xiongnu were the direct ancestors of early, medieval, and contemporary Mongolians (Dorjsuren 1961; Navaan 1975; Sukhbaatar 1980; Tseveendorj 1987; Batsaikhan 2002; Turbat 2004). According to Chinese historical sources, during the first millennium AD, or the Early Mongolian period, there were several tribal unions in Mongolia, such as Xianbei (2nd–3rd centuries AD), Joujan (4th–5th centuries AD), Turkic (6th–8th centuries AD), Uighur (8th–9th centuries AD), and Qidan (10th–12th centuries AD). However, archaeological monuments, especially grave monuments, from the historic period are not well studied, with the exception of those dating to the Turkic and Uighur periods. The principal archaeological monuments of the Turkic and Uighur periods include stone men (anthropomorphic stone carvings/statues), runic inscriptions, sacrificial monuments, settlement ruins, and graves. Approximately 400 stone men from the Turkic and Uighur periods have been discovered to date in Mongolia, mostly in the western and central regions (Bayar 1999).

The Mongolian period (12th–15th century AD) is the best studied from a historical perspective, based on the availability of numerous texts written in Persian, Chinese, Arabic, and other languages. One of the main historical sources is *The Secret History of Mongols*, which was written in the thirteenth century AD. Archaeological investigation in Mongolia as well as in surrounding territories has identified numerous sites stemming from the historic period, including settlements, stone men, inscriptions, rock art, and graves. About 300 historic period graves have been excavated in Mongolia and Buryatia. Typically, such burials were clustered in groups of 2–3 or 5–10, connected at the surface, and often had sheep tibia as grave inclusions.

Archaeological human remains from a number of different Mongolian historic periods have been studied by Tumen (1976, 1979, 1985, 1987, 1992, 1996, 2002, 2003, 2006), Alekseev and colleagues (1987), and Mamonova (1979). Results from studies of such Mongolian samples indicate that these ancient populations were characterized by great heterogeneity in cranio-morphology. People with Caucasoid (in the general sense of being essentially of European descent) features inhabited western Mongolia, while populations with developed Mongoloid (in the general sense of being essentially of East Asian descent) traits occupied central and eastern Mongolia (see Lahr 1996 for current understanding and use of the terms *Mongoloid* and *Caucasoid*). However, the western Mongolian population of the Bronze Age exhibited more pronounced Mongoloid features than those seen from earlier times. It can be hypothesized that the Early Bronze Age was characterized by population movements from eastern Mongolia into western Mongolia, where intensive admixture between local Caucasoid and Mongoloid populations took place.

In the context of the brief overview of the archaeology and physical anthropology of Mongolia provided here, the chief aims of this study are to (1) compare and contrast the cranio-morphology of a range of ancient Mongolian populations in order to assess the degree of intra-Mongolian heterogeneity or homogeneity; and (2) compare and contrast the cranio-morphology of Mongolian populations with Northeast Asian samples in order to explore questions relating to the origins of and genetic relationships among these ancient populations. A quantitative morphological assessment of human remains from a range of archaeological sites in Mongolia is important, not only for addressing the problem of the origins of the Mongols but also in exploring the issues of prehistoric migrations and the biological, cultural, and historical relationships among ancient Eurasian populations.

Materials and Methods

For the purposes of this study, wherever possible, a suite of 15 cranial measurements were taken on each skull—5 on the neurocranium and 10 on the facial skeleton (as defined by Martin [see the notes for tables 4.1 and 4.2 for definitions])—a protocol followed previously by a number of other investigators (Alekseev and Debets 1964; Howells 1973; Bass 1987; Knusmann 1988; Khrisanfova and Perevozchikov 1999). Variable preservation of the available remains dictated the use of several different approaches to sex and age-at-death estimation. Sex was determined using standard techniques based on sexually dimorphic variation in the cranium and ossa coxae, as well as long bone dimensions, where appropriate (Alekseev 1966; Bass 1987). Age at death was determined in accord with occlusal tooth wear, cranial suture synostosis scores, degree of epiphyseal fusion, and pubic symphyseal morphology (Alekseev 1966; Bass 1987).

Table 4.3 summarizes the geographic location, sample size, temporal period, and institution curating each of the Mongolian subsamples. These comprise a total of 573 crania, with the largest subsamples stemming from more recent time periods. Sample distribution maps for the Mongolian and Northeast Asian comparative samples are detailed below. The Neolithic Mongolian and comparative Northeast Asian samples used for comparison in this study total 21 subsamples (figure 4.1). The 12 Bronze and Early Iron Age samples from Mongolia are provided in figure 4.2, while the 27 comparative Bronze and Early Iron Age samples adjoining Mongolia can be seen in figure 4.3. Some 15 subsamples representing the Xiongnu period in Mongolia are given in figure 4.4, and 11 comparative and contemporaneous subsamples are included in figure 4.5. This data set encompasses craniometric data from Central Asia, southern Siberia, the Russian Far East, China, Korea, and Japan

(Rykushina 1976; Kruykov et al. 1978; Alekseev and Gokhman 1983; Wu and Olsen 1985) and covers a range of time extending from the Neolithic (8000–6000 BC) through the Xiongnu period (2nd century AD). Finally, the 15 subsamples representing the Mongolian period of Mongolia are provided in figure 4.6, with 30 comparative and contemporaneous subsamples given in figure 4.7.

In analyzing the resultant data set, Penrose shape distances were calculated for each paired combination of samples defined by each prehistoric or historic period. The shape distance actually measures the precision of the mean difference between two populations and is thus considered to be a reliable indicator of morphological difference based on morphology, rather than difference based on absolute size (Penrose 1954; Brothwell 1965). The resultant diagonal matrix of Penrose distance values was then put into the cluster analysis function of SPSS (version 15).

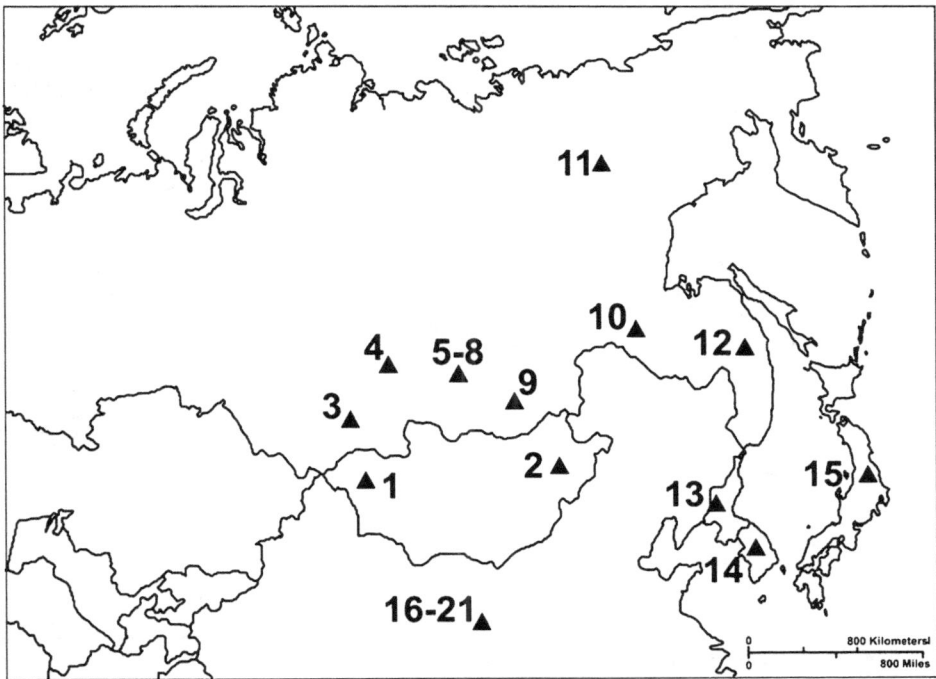

Figure 4.1. Geographic location of comparative Neolithic populations from Asia: (1) Shatar-Chuluun, Erdenetsogt soum, Bayankhongor aimag, western Mongolia; (2) Norivlon, Bulgan soum, Dornod aimag, and Tamsagbulag, Sumber soum, Dornod aimag; (3) Altai Mountains; (4) Minusin basin, southern Siberia; (5) Kitoj period, Cis-Baikalia; (6) Isakov period, Cis-Baikalia; (7) Serov period, Cis-Baikalia; (8) southern Cis-Baikalia; (9) Transbaikalia; (10) Amur River basin (Shilka River); (11) Yakutiya; (12) Primor'e; (13) North Korea; (14) South Korea; (15) Jomon, Japan; (16) Dawenkou, eastern China; (17) Huaxian culture, central China; (18) Baoji culture, central China; (19) Xixiahou culture, eastern China; (20) Banpo culture, central China; (21) Banshan culture, northwestern China.

Figure 4.2. Geographic location of studied human remains from the Bronze and Early Iron Age of Mongolia: (1) Nomgon, Ömnögovi; (2) Khujirt soum, Uberkhangai aimag; (3) Matad soum, Dornod aimag; (4) Khyargas soum, Uvs aimag; (5) Must soum, Khovd aimag; (6) Altanbulag soum, Töv aimag; (7) Ugiinuur soum, Arkhangai aimag; (8) Chandmani, Uvs aimag; (9) Khurgakh gobi, Ulaankhus soum, Bayan-Ölgii aimag; (10) Kheviin am, Bulgan soum, Bayan-Ölgii aimag; (11) Khukh Tolgoi, Munkh Khairkhan soum, Khovd aimag; (12) Telengudiin am, Munkh Khairkhan soum, Khovd aimag.

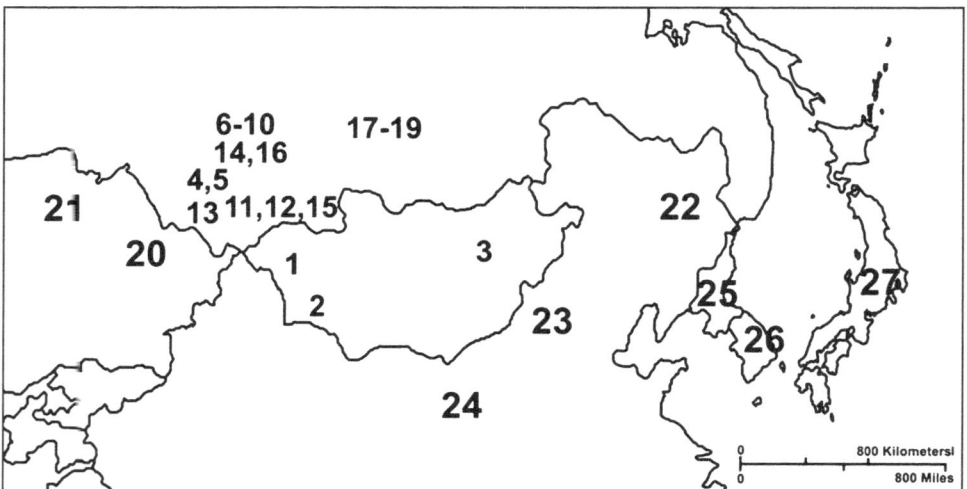

Figure 4.3. Geographic location of compared populations from the Bronze and Early Iron Age of Asia: (1) Chandman culture, western Mongolia; (2) graves without inventory, western Mongolia; (3) Slab Grave culture, eastern Mongolia; (4) Scythian culture, Altai Mountains; (5) Scythian culture, Altai Mountain spurs; (6) Afanasevo culture, southern Siberia; (7) Tagar culture, Minusinsk basin; (8) Tashtyk-Tagar culture, Minusinsk basin; (9) Tashtyk culture, southern Siberia; (10) Karasuk culture, southern Siberia; (11) graves without inventory, western Tuva; (12) Scythian culture, central Tuva; (13) Afanasevo culture, Altai Mountains; (14) Andronovo culture, Minusinsk basin; (15) Karasuk culture, central Tuva; (16) Okunev culture, Minusinsk basin; (17) Glazkov culture, Cis-Baikalia; (18) Glazkov culture, Lena River; (19) Slab Grave culture, Cis-Baikalia; (20) Usunin culture, eastern Kazakhstan; (21) Usunain culture, northern Kazakhstan; (22) Manchuria; (23) Inner Mongolia; (24) An'yang culture, central China; (25) North Korea; (26) South Korea; (27) Yayoi culture, Japan.

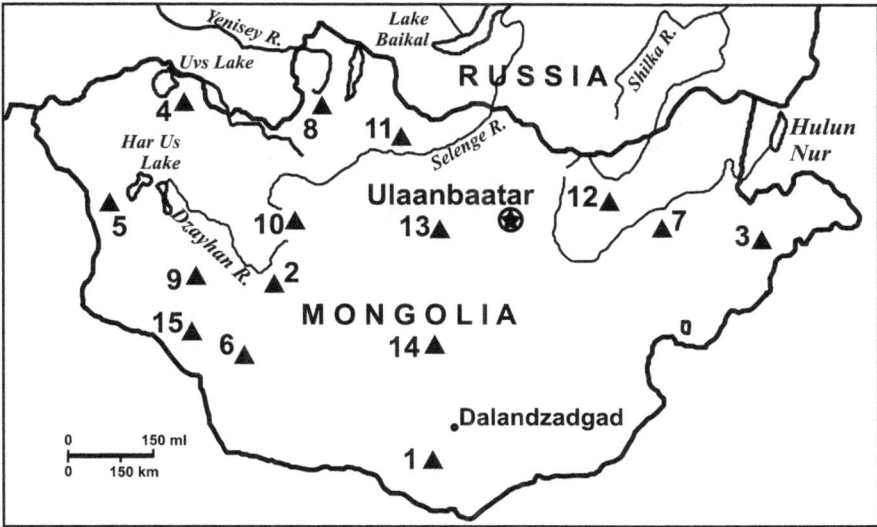

Figure 4.4. Geographic location of studied human remains from Xiongnu period of Mongolia: (1) Nomgon, Umengobi; (2) Naimaa Tolgoi, Erdenetsogt soum, Arkhangai aimag; (3) Erdenetsagaan soum, Sükhbaatar aimag; (4) Chandmani, Uvs aimag; (5) Mankhan soum, Khovd aimag; (6) Galuut, Bayankhongor; (7) Duulga Uul, Jargaltkhaan soum, Khentii aimag; (8) Galt soum, Khövsgöl aimag; (9) Delger soum, Govi-Altai aimag; (10) Battsengel soum, Arkhangai aimag; (11) Darkhan soum, Selenge aimag; (12) Khulenbuuir, Dornod aimag; (13) Altanbulag soum, Töv aimag; (14) Adaatsag soum, Dundgovi aimag; (15) Altai soum, Govi-Altai aimag.

Figure 4.5. Geographic location of compared populations from Xiongnu period of Asia: (1) western Mongolian Xiongnu; (2) central Mongolian Xiongnu; (3) eastern Mongolian Xiongnu; (4) Xiongnu from Russian Altai; (5) Xiongnu from Russian Altai spurs; (6) Xiongnu from central Tuva; (7) Xiongnu from eastern Tuva; (8) Xiongnu, Kyrgyzstan; (9) Xiongnu from Transbaikalia; (10) southern Chukotka; (11) eastern Chukotka.

Figure 4.6. Geographic location of studied human remains from the Mongolian period of Mongolia: (1) Kharahkorum, Övörkhangai aimag; (2) Tevsh Uul, Bogd soum, Övörkhangai aimag; (3) Burkhant Gatsaa, Altanbulag soum, Töv aimag; (4) Tooroin-Am, Altanbulag soum, Töv aimag; (5) Khanui Brigad, Under-Ulaan soum, Arkhangai aimag; (6) Barzangiin enger, Zuil soum, Övörkhangai aimag; (7) Buura-lin enger, Khngor soum, Selenge aimag; (8) Duulga Uul, Jargaltkhaan soum, Khentii aimag; (9) Aurgyn Rashaan, Delgerkhaan soum, Khentii aimag; (10) Delgerkhaan Uul, Tuvshinshiree soum, Sükhbaatar aimag; (11) Tarvagtain am, Mankhan soum, Khovd aimag; (12) Takhiltin khotgor, Mankhan soum, Khovd aimag; (13) Tavan Tolgoi, Ongon soum, Sükhbaatar aimag; (14) Tsuvraa Uul, Khulenbuir soum, Dornod aimag; (15) Baga Gazrin chuluu, Delgertsogt soum, Dundgovi aimag.

Results and Discussion

Summaries of the respective craniometric datasets, including sample size (n), mean values (mean), and standard deviations (SD) are provided for the male (table 4.1) and female Mongolian subsamples (table 4.2).

Neolithic Northeast Asian Relationships

When the interrelationships among the comparative Neolithic Northeast Asian samples are examined by way of the Penrose shape distance analysis and subsequent cluster analysis, five major groupings or clusters are apparent (figure 4.8). These clusters include samples from (1) eastern China and Primor'e; (2) the Amur River basin and Yakutiya; (3) the Altai Mountains, southern Siberia, Japan (Jomon period), and western Mongolia (a region characterized by a Caucasoid morphology); (4) China and Korea; and (5) eastern Mongolia, the Lake Baikal region (Cis-Baikalia and Transbaikalia), and northern China.

The results of this cluster analysis confirm that eastern Mongolian Neo-

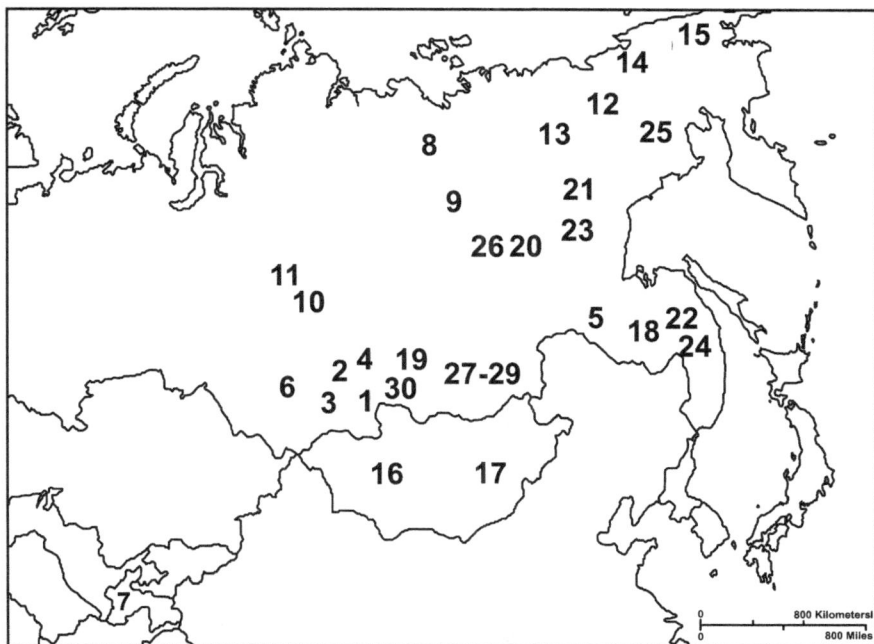

Figure 4.7. Geographic location of compared medieval and contemporary populations from Asia: (1) Tofalars; (2) Shors; (3) Kachas; (4) Sagais; (5) Nivkhs; (6) Koibals; (7) Kirgizs, or Kyrgyzs; (8) Khants; (9) Mansi; (10) Tatars-Chulim; (11) Selkups; (12) Chukchi; (13) Reindeer Chukchi; (14) Coast Chukchi; (15) Eskimos; (16) and (17) medieval and contemporary Mongolians; (18) Orochi; (19) Telengets; (20) Nents, or Nenets; (21) Yakuts; (22) Negidals; (23) Reindeer Evenks; (24) Nanais; (25) Ulchi; (26) Kets; (27) Transbaikalian Buryats; (28) West Buryats; (29) Tunkh Buryats; (30) Tuva.

lithic populations shared close phenotypic—and by implication biological—affinities with the Neolithic people of the Lake Baikal region. Previous investigators have described the Neolithic people of the Baikal region both as proto-Mongoloid (Roginskii 1978) and as the Baikalian form of the Continental Mongoloids (Debets 1948; Alekseev et al. 1987). Archaeological evidence also supports the view that there was a Neolithic culture common to eastern Mongolia and the Lake Baikal region (Dorj 1971).

Bronze and Early Iron Age Relationships

Examination of the Northeast Asian Bronze and Early Iron Age subsamples reveals that eastern Mongolian Bronze Age people were morphologically more similar to the Mongoloid population from the Baikal Lake region (figure 4.9). The Bronze Age subsamples can be separated into five major clusters, with the first cluster further divided into three subclusters (1a, 1b, 1c).

Table 4.1. Craniofacial data on archaeological populations from Mongolia (male)

Measurement #	Neolithic				Bronze and Early Iron Age						Xiongnu (3rd century BC–2nd century AD)			Mongolian period (12th–14th centuries AD)			Modern Mongolians		
	East Mongolia		West Mongolia		Eastern Mongolia (Slab Grave culture)			Western Mongolia (Chandman culture)											
	N	Mean	N	Mean	N	Mean	SD	N	Mean	SD	N	Mean	SD	N	Mean	SD	N	Mean	SD
1	3	192.00	2	196.50	8	182.31	5.79	53	182.7	9.15	47	183.63	6.16	23	182.91	8.52	200	182.15	6.56
8	3	149.00	2	141.50	9	149.67	9.41	40	138.03	3.03	47	145.94	5.04	24	147.04	8.16	201	148.01	6.34
8/1	3	77.50	2	72.40	8	81.95	5.19	37	77.34	4.7	47	77.98	12.16	21	80.07	4.28	199	81.32	3.76
17	3	147.10	2	140.10	6	129.83	3.49	45	131.46	6.1	41	131.17	5.92	22	129.05	7.29	199	130.14	4.96
17/1	3	76.61	2	71.30	6	61.21	27.2	41	72.69	2.56	40	71.42	3.23	21	70.42	5.44	198	71.45	3.15
17/8	3	98.72	2	99.01	8	88.74	6.81	33	93.26	5.88	44	81.85	6.65	22	87.81	7.97	198	88.15	4.91
5	2	120.00	2	104.00	6	99.33	3.61	43	101.36	4.26	34	99.75	5.07	22	100.95	4.8	197	100.06	4.59
9	2	96.50	2	96.00	9	92.78	3.23	52	95.59	5.35	49	93.65	4.77	27	95.96	5.63	202	94.90	4.55
10	3	128.00	2	121.50	8	124.75	5.28	41	120.45	18.5	39	121.9	5.52	23	123.52	7.48	200	121.94	9.00
32	2	81.00	2	85.00	6	82.50	6.60	42	81.8	3.92	33	78.11	5.98	20	79.45	5.5	163	82.00	6.60
40	2	119.00	2	100.00	5	99.80	3.83	40	99.24	5.38	33	97.54	4.49	21	98.5	4.86	155	97.57	5.13
45	3	150.50	2	144.50	8	139.75	6.32	49	136.18	5.83	41	140.05	5.36	23	143.87	12.1	186	140.32	10.22

48	3	82.50	2	64.70	8	74.88	5.00	55	71.36	5.15	46	74.65	5.44	24	73.89	4.74	165	74.90	4.59
48/45	3	54.82	2	44.78	8	53.59	2.99	47	52.4	2.91	40	53.95	4.33	22	51.37	4.51	156	54.65	17.58
55	3	61.00	2	46.50	8	53.89	3.30	57	50.74	3.58	47	53.19	3.18	26	55.4	4.19	199	56.46	3.30
54	3	28.00	2	27.00	4	27.06	1.29	54	25.13	2.18	45	26.62	1.61	25	26.38	1.82	195	28.22	4.08
54/55	3	44.30	2	58.10	9	50.38	4.12	54	49.69	6.01	45	50.23	3.6	25	47.91	4.63	194	50.14	7.51
51	3	41.00	2	41.50	8	42.22	2.77	55	42.34	2.06	48	42.61	2.19	26	44.06	2.59	200	42.89	2.55
52	3	35.00	2	30.50	9	35.22	2.11	55	33.24	2.87	42	34.84	1.93	26	36.38	2.35	200	36.66	2.34
52/51	3	85.30	2	73.50	9	83.63	5.79	53	78.89	6.77	42	81.75	5.8	26	82.8	6.58	200	85.27	8.72
<77	3	156.60	2	138.10	8	150.99	3.87	50	145.06	14.85	37	145.54	4.76	20	148.08	6.96	186	143.11	6.24
<zm	3	149.70	2	131.50	6	140.50	2.07	47	130.95	6.04	36	136.81	6.34	20	135.08	6.73	177	143.50	6.47
SS/SC	3	36.50	2	52.60	9	37.26	10.87	52	12.53	12.53	29	48.41	15.21	9	38.66	7.92	76	42.02	15.22
DC/DS	3	41.50	2	40.90	9	42.55	3.86	44	9.26	9.26	26	51.79	17.96	10	46.56	17.94	44	47.82	11.42
72	2	87.00	2	83.50	4	87.00	1.41	41	86.73	3.56	35	84.27	11.90	20	87.00	3.67	139	88.91	4.09
74	2	79.00	2	81.00	4	74.25	12.34	39	80.64	6.99	33	77.45	13.23	20	75.95	5.50	117	78.03	6.52
75/1	2	19.00	2	36.00	4	22.75	5.32	42	28.76	5.46	36	23.59	8.87	20	24.05	5.38	90	21.83	4.79

Note: 1 = cranial length, 8 = maximal cranial breadth, 8/1 = cranial index, 17 = basian-bregma height, 17/1 = cranial length-height index, 17/8 = cranial breadth-height index, 5 = basi-cranial length, 9 = min. frontal breadth, 10 = max. frontal breadth, 32 = frontal angle, 40 = basi-facial length, 45 = bizygomatic breadth, 48 = upper facial height, 48/45 = upper facial index, 55 = nasal height, 54 = nasal breadth, 51 = orbital breadth, 52 = orbital height, 52/51 = orbital index, <77 = nasomalar angle, <zm = zygomaxillary angle, SS/SC = Simotic index, DC/DS = Dakrial index, 72 = nasal profile angle, 74 = alveolar angle, 75/1 = nasal profile angle.

Table 4.2. Craniofacial data on archaeological populations from Mongolia (female)

Measurement #	Bronze and Early Iron Age						Xiongnu (3rd century BC–2nd century AD)			Mongolian period (12th–14th centuries AD)			Modern Mongolians		
	Eastern Mongolia (Slab Grave culture)			Western Mongolia (Chandman culture)											
	N	Mean	SD	N	Mean	SD	N	Mean	SD	N	Mean	SD	N	Mean	SD
1	5	173.2	3.27	32	175.53	10.57	24	174.46	6.35	32	171.06	7.71	95	171.75	6.34
8	4	145.25	3.5	25	136.3	7.68	23	140.78	4.74	27	142.96	7	95	142.24	5.94
8/1	4	83.77	3.61	24	76.70	3.45	21	79.60	4.42	29	78.24	22.35	95	82.93	4.39
17	4	125.25	8.66	26	126.74	7.95	22	127.61	5.5	28	122.2	10.5	92	124.63	10.97
17/1	4	72.1	5.15	26	76.70	2.96	22	69.83	16.05	29	69.22	15.45	92	72.61	6.64
17/8	3	89.83	2.34	21	92.79	6.38	23	82.63	26.5	27	82.2	18.3	92	87.66	8.05
5	4	91.25	8.18	25	97.32	5.96	17	96.88	4.81	30	96.31	10.18	91	94.05	4.34
9	5	93.6	2.3	28	93.14	6.08	24	92.77	3.86	32	94.69	10.23	95	89.89	9.32
10	5	123.4	8.26	24	118.02	6.19	21	117.24	5.79	25	122.6	9.86	95	117.83	5.28
32	5	85	3.24	19	83.29	4.44	11	80.55	7.97	10	84.67	7.66	77	86.10	4.67
40	3	93.33	5.03	24	93.01	6.6	12	92.25	4.99	24	91.44	7.07	83	92.04	5.30
45	4	137.25	2.63	23	128.39	7.92	19	129.79	7.08	24	129.81	9.06	84	129.74	11.32
48	5	70.9	2.25	30	67.07	4.61	19	70.74	4.96	26	69.5	4.06	88	68.69	4.25
48/45	4	52.01	1.42	21	52.44	2.62	19	51.34	12.7	21	52.82	2.72	77	54.31	13.63

55	5	52.26	2.06	32	47.8	3.7	18	49.72	2.97	24	52	2.94	93	26.25	1.87
54	5	26.36	0.91	33	24.16	2.42	17	26.44	3.11	22	26.54	1.86	93	52.59	2.80
54/55	5	50.47	1.58	32	50.89	5.57	17	53.23	5.94	22	51.3	3.75	92	49.92	4.29
51	5	43	3.06	29	40.24	1.81	19	40.55	2.09	24	39.1	3.76	92	40.19	2.56
52	5	35.42	1.5	29	33.26	2.21	17	33.41	2.03	24	34.63	2.31	93	35.74	1.90
52/51	5	82.83	8.28	28	82.36	6.12	16	82.33	5.33	19	89.47	9.36	92	89.37	8.90
<77	5	147.70	5.73	24	142.28	7.01	16	146.88	6	18	144.92	4.75	88	142.01	6.49
<zm	4	139.15	1.53	27	134.12	7.43	12	139.4	5.3	18	133.94	5.58	82	144.79	7.16
SS/SC	5	41.42	8.31	27	44.05	15.17	11	44.37	17.49	18	36.64	9.74	28	34.16	13.19
DC/DS	4	46.24	6.61	15	49.2	9.79	11	48.42	13.03	15	44.56	15.2	15	54.34	44.35
72	3	89	4.58	21	84.62	4.7	12	71	29.09	11	87.17	5.01	71	88.82	3.72
74	2	74.5	0.71	19	81.79	12.27	8	86.13	25.97	18	73.25	14.03	65	76.74	7.47
75/1	3	20.33	2.52	17	27.71	16.09	7	22.43	6.83	16	17.73	5.71	43	18.74	3.67

Note: 1 = cranial length, 8 = maximal cranial breadth, 8/1 = cranial index, 17 = basian-bregma height, 17/1 = cranial length-height index, 17/8 = cranial breadth-height index, 5 = basi-cranial length, 40/5, 9 = min. frontal breadth, 10 = max. frontal breadth, 32 = frontal angle, 40 = basi-facial length, 45 = bizygomatic breadth, 48 = upper facial height, 48/45 = upper facial index, 55 = nasal height, 54 = nasal breadth, 54/55 = nasal index, 51 = orbital breadth, 52 = orbital height, 52/51 = orbital index, <77 = nasomalar angle, <zm = zygomaxillary angle, SS/SC = Simotic index, DC/DS = Dakrial index, 72 = nasal profile angle, 74 = alveolar angle, 75/1 = nasal profile angle.

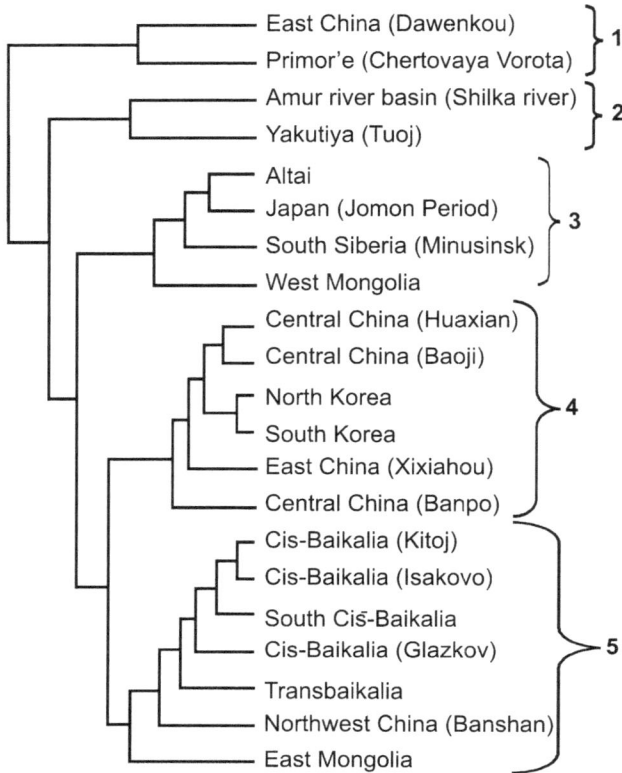

Figure 4.8. Dendrogram showing relationships among the Neolithic populations of Asia (Penrose shape distance analysis for 15 cranial variables).

While the Manchurian subsample groups with the fifth cluster, it is for all intents and purposes an outlier. Regarding cluster 1—which encompasses most of the populations from the Altai region, southern Siberia, western Mongolia (Chandman culture), and Japan (Yayoi period)—the subgrouping comprises (1a) Korea, the Lena River basin, and Cis-Baikalia; (1b) the Chandman culture of western Mongolia, as well as the Tagar and Tashtyk cultures from southern Siberia; and (1c) the Scythian culture of the Altai Mountains and central Tuva, Karasuk from southern Siberia, Usunian from eastern Kazakhstan, and a sample without associated grave inclusions to enable the ascription of cultural affinities. Interestingly, the Yayoi period sample (Japan) is also associated with this cluster, albeit quite distantly. In contrast, the southern Siberian Afanasevo subsample is situated in subcluster 1b.

The second major cluster includes samples from the Altai region (Afanasevo culture), northern Kazakhstan (Usunian culture) and southern Siberia (Minusinsk and Andronovo cultures), while the third major cluster includes

Table 4.3. Characteristics of the archaeological populations of Mongolia utilized in the study

Chronology	Sample size	Culture area	Curating institution	References
Neolithic (10,000–2000 BC)	4	Western Mongolia, eastern Mongolia	Dept. of Anthropology and Archaeology, NUM	Tumen 1980, 1981; Mamonova 1979
Bronze Age (3000–700 BC)	11	Slab Grave culture, eastern and central Mongolia	Dept. of Anthropology and Archaeology, NUM	Tumen 1985, 2007
	19	Chemurchek, Afanasevo, and Munkh Khairkhan culture, western Mongolia		
Early Iron Age (7th–3rd centuries BC)	55	Chandman culture	Dept. of Anthropology and Archaeology, NUM	Tumen 1978, 1992, 2007
Xiongnu (3rd century BC–2nd century AD)	73	Xiongnu culture	Dept. of Anthropology and Archaeology, NUM	Tumen 1987, 2002, 2007
Mongolian period (13th–15th centuries AD)	68	Mongolian culture	Dept. of Anthropology and Archaeology, NUM	Tumen 1979, 1985, 2007
Modern Mongolian period	49		Dept. of Anthropology and Archaeology, NUM	Tumen 1985, 2006, 2007
	81		Anthropological Museum, Saint Petersburg, Russia	Tumen 1985, 2006, 2007
	213		National Museum of Natural History, Smithsonian Institution, Washington, DC	Tumen (unpublished observations)

samples from Inner Mongolia, as well as central and northwestern China. A fourth cluster is formed by samples representing the Bronze Age Slab Grave culture from eastern Mongolia and the Karasuk culture from central Tuva. The final, fifth, cluster includes samples from Trans-Baikalia (Slab Grave culture), Minusinsk (Okunev culture), and western Mongolia (another sample without associated grave inclusions to enable the ascription of cultural affinities).

The separation of the Northeast Asian Bronze Age populations into several clusters and subclusters can be explained by extensive and intensive cross-regional migration and admixture between Caucasoid and Mongoloid populations during this period. According to Ismagulov (1970) and Alekseev and

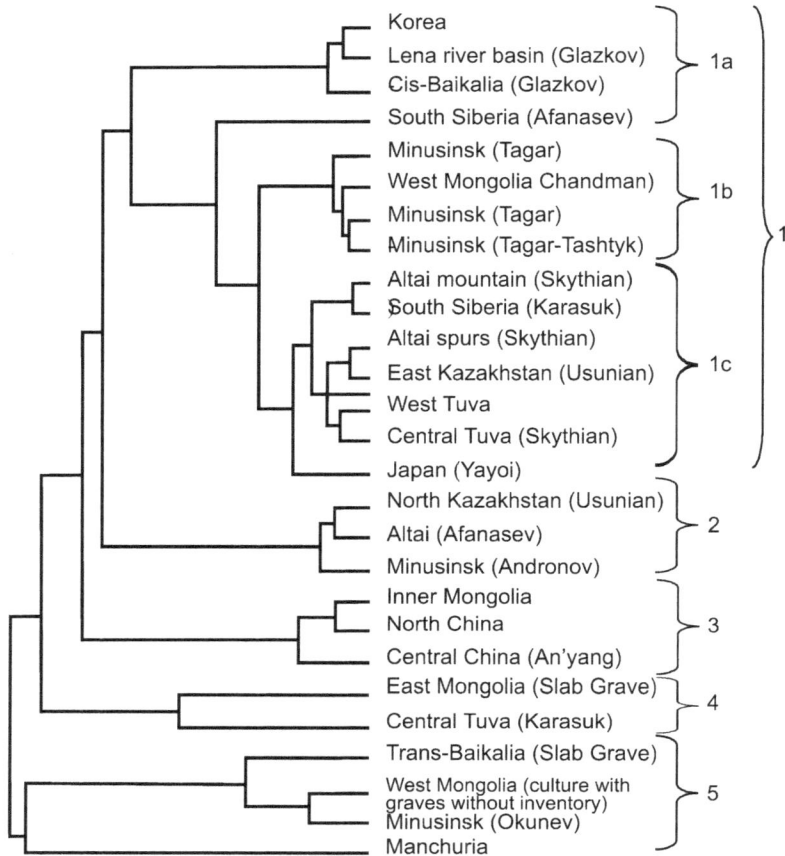

Figure 4.9. Dendrogram showing relationships among Bronze and Early Iron Age populations from Asia (Penrose shape distance analysis for 15 cranial variables).

Gokhman (1983), Mongoloid and Caucasoid genetic exchange in Central Asia (Kazakhstan and Kyrgyzstan) and southern Siberia increased gradually, beginning at the end of the Neolithic and Early Bronze Age. Moreover, Trans-baikalian and Cis-Baikalian Bronze and Early Iron Age populations affiliated with the Slab Grave culture are suggested to have in fact been Mongoloids, characterized by brachycrany, along with moderate high, broad, and flattened faces, as well as flat nasal roots (Alekseev and Gokhman 1983).

As mentioned above, the eastern Mongolian Bronze and Early Iron Age (Slab Grave culture) and Karasuk subsamples from southern Siberia are included in the same cluster, which provides supporting evidence for their biological and historical affinities, as hypothesized several decades ago by Alekseev (1961), Alekseev and Gokhman (1983), and Rykushina (1976). According to some researchers, there was indeed some eastern Mongoloid genetic exchange with the Karasuk population. Given a raft of common decorative elements and other material associations, Novgorodova (1987, 1989) and Volkov (1967, 1981) have both argued that the origins of the Karasuk culture can be seen in the Bronze Age cultures of Mongolia and Inner Mongolia. It has been suggested that extensive cross-regional migration took place in southern Siberia, Mongolia, and North China during the Bronze Age.

Xiongnu Relationships

Xiongnu skulls from Mongolia have moderate dimensions in terms of maximum cranial length and maximum cranial breadth, as well as generally low skull vaults. The Xiongnu of Mongolia were characteristically meso- or brachycranic, with narrow foreheads and medium broad, high, and flattened faces, low horizontal facial profiles, and flat nasal roots. However, some skulls from eastern Mongolia exhibit alveolar prognathism, and several skulls from eastern and central Mongolia have features intermediate between Mongoloids and Caucasoids, or even more Caucasoid-like features. The Xiongnu of Mongolia would appear to have been somewhat heterogeneous, both genetically and ethnically.

Cluster analysis of the Xiongnu subsamples indicates two major clusters (figure 4.10), with the first cluster including subsamples from southern Siberia and the second cluster including Xiongnu subsamples from western, central, and eastern Mongolia, as well as the Lake Baikal region. In the second cluster, the Xiongnu from eastern Mongolia are closer to the Baikalian Xiongnu than to the central or western Mongolian Xiongnu. The clustering pattern of Xiongnu populations from Inner Asia clearly demonstrates that the Xiongnu were very heterogeneous. Moreover, there appear to have been two distinct forms: the Xiongnu from Mongolia and the Baikal region, who may have belonged to a Central Asiatic variant of the Northern Mongoloid group; and the Xiongnu from Altai and Tuva, who may have belonged to one of the mixed variants of southern Siberian forms.

Alekseev and Gokhman (1983) have suggested that Xiongnu migration from Mongolia westward through Altai and Tuva played an important role in past ethnogenetic processes, resulting in an important anthropological signature in the region. Alekseev and Gokhman (1983) have noted that the Mongoloid component is elevated among local Caucasoid inhabitants of the region, probably as a result of the in-migration of Mongolians in the Late Bronze Age and Xiongnu period. This population movement would have been contemporaneous with the formation of the Xiongnu tribal union in Mongolia and on the Baikalian steppe, as well as with the extension of Xion-

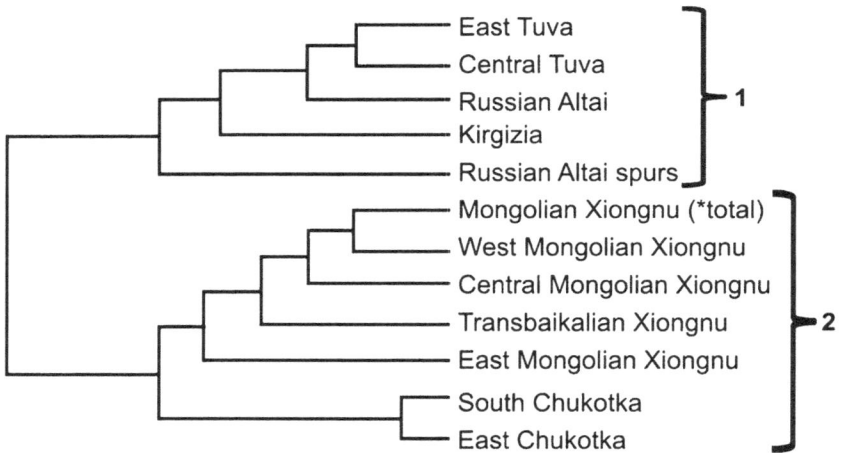

Figure 4.10. Dendrogram showing relationships among populations from the Xiongnu period of Asia (Penrose shape distance analysis for 15 cranial variables).

gnu influence both south and west (Alekseev and Gokhman 1983). A number of other authors have suggested that Xiongnu skulls from the Lake Baikal region and the Russian Far East exhibit some limited Caucasoid features, as well as possible genetic input from the Far East (Debets 1948; Mamonova 1979). These observations are consistent with both archaeological data and written Chinese sources (Alekseev and Gokhman 1983).

Mongolian Period Relationships

Mongolian period skulls are morphologically North Asian, with the exception of material from the Muslim cemetery in Kharakorum, the Medieval period capital of the Mongolian empire. Crania (9 males, 8 females) from this cemetery, excavated by Ser-Odjav, were studied by Tumen (1979), who concluded that they were morphologically very similar to medieval crania from a Nestorian cemetery in Semirechiya, Central Asia.

A comparative analysis of medieval and modern Mongolians, along with North Asians, reveals two major clusters (figure 4.11), which can be further divided into a number of subclusters. Cluster 2 includes medieval and modern Mongolians, Buryats, Yakuts, and members of some groups from the Amur River basin, which suggests some level of relatedness among these diverse populations. Nevertheless, medieval and modern Mongols form quite a distinct subcluster.

When only ancient and contemporary Mongolian samples are examined, two clusters are apparent (figure 4.12). This suggests that Mongolia was inhabited by two ancient morphotypes. Subsamples from the Bronze Age,

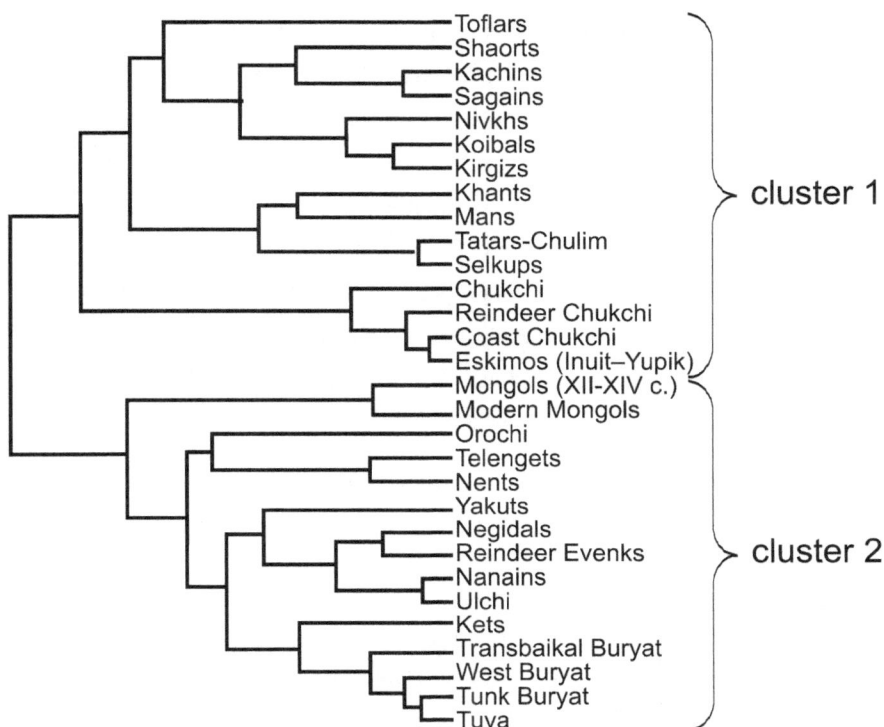

Figure 4.11. Dendrogram showing relationships among medieval and modern Mongolians as well as populations from North Asia.

Xiongnu, and the Early Mongolian, Mongolian, and Modern periods form one cluster, suggesting a close genetic relationship among Neolithic populations from eastern Mongolia, Bronze Age populations (affiliated with the Slab Grave culture) from central and eastern Mongolia, and the Xiongnu, Early Mongolian, Mongolian period, and contemporary populations of Mongolia. Prehistoric populations from western Mongolia belong to a separate cluster, which included the Neolithic population, the Bronze Age population of the Kurgan or Khirigsuur culture, and the Early Iron Age population (Chandman culture).

Populations from these time periods in western Mongolia can be characterized as having predominantly Caucasoid features; this is especially true of the Neolithic population (Tumen 1977, 1978, 1985, 1992; Mamonova 1979). However, in the Bronze and Early Iron Ages there was extensive genetic exchange between local Caucasoid populations and Mongoloid immigrants (affiliated with the Slab Grave culture) from central and eastern Mongolia. In accordance with this migration, the Mongoloid component increased in the local Caucasoid population of western Mongolia. Such genetic exchange

Figure 4.12. Dendrogram showing relationships among ancient and contemporary populations of Mongolia.

probably continued until the end of the Xiongnu period, which again is further supported by archaeological and historical evidence.

According to recent historical and archaeological studies (Tsybektarov 1998; Konovalov 1999), the Xiongnu were not homogeneous either ethnically or linguistically. Based on the results of archaeological studies of the Xiongnu in Mongolia, Turbat (2004) concluded that the Xiongnu culture was formed by means of two-way exchanges between peoples affiliated with the Iron Age Slab Grave culture and the early nomads of northern China, a process that began during the fourth to third century BC (Turbat 2004).

In the course of investigating Xiongnu archaeological monuments, Batsaikhan (2002) noted that, beginning in the third century BC, the movements of Indo-European groups across the territories of Inner Asia progressed in several stages. These migrations not only affected the development of the ethno-culture in Mongolia but also had a significant impact on all Central Asian populations. In addition, migration of groups from northern China to Northeast Asia, which is evident archaeologically, established the Slab Grave cultural complex as it is known from the territory of Mongolia and South Siberia (Batsaikhan 2002).

Conclusions

The chief aim of this study was to explore cranial morphological variation among past and present Mongolian populations and to further compare these same populations with a range of Northeast Asian peoples. Calculated Penrose shape distances and subsequent cluster analysis have demonstrated that human remains from Mongolia dating to the Neolithic, Bronze, and Early Iron Ages, as well as the Xiongnu period, present significant heterogeneity in their morphological traits. During the Neolithic and Early Bronze Age, western Mongolia was inhabited by peoples with Caucasoid or mixed morphological features, while central and eastern Mongolia were occupied by populations with developed Mongoloid traits. The Bronze and Early Iron Age was characterized by human migrations from eastern Mongolia into western Mongolia, southwestern Siberia, and west-central Asia. The western Mongolian populations of the Bronze and Early Iron Ages exhibited more pronounced Mongoloid features than had been seen in earlier times.

Comparative morphological analysis shows that Neolithic, Bronze, and Early Iron Age populations from northern Asia can be divided into several major cranio-morphologically defined clusters. The first cluster includes all known populations from South Siberia and western Mongolia, as well as the Jomon Japanese. The second cluster includes populations from eastern Mongolia and the Lake Baikal region.

The Xiongnu populations of Mongolia were not craniometrically homogeneous. This may be explained by extensive cross-migration of nomadic peoples from the Eurasian steppe (Caucasoid or mixed populations from west to east and Mongoloids from east to west), which occurred in Inner Asia during the Bronze and Early Iron Age, as well as during the Xiongnu period.

Comparative studies of human remains from a range of temporal periods in Mongolia clearly demonstrate specific genetic relationships among Neolithic populations from eastern Mongolia, Bronze Age populations (affiliated with the Slab Grave culture) from central and eastern Mongolia, and Xiongnu, Early Mongolian, and Mongolian period populations, as well as the contemporary peoples of Mongolia.

Acknowledgments

We thank the Asian Research Center (ARC) at the National University of Mongolia and Korea Foundation for Advanced Research (KFAS) for their financial support of this research as part of the Eastern Mongolia 2002–7 project. In the course of this program of archaeological fieldwork, human remains belonging to a wide range of different time periods in Mongolia were unearthed; results of the analysis of all those human remains are included in this chapter. I thank the International Research Exchange Board (IREX) for giving me the opportunity of also studying skeletal collections housed in the National Museum of Natural History, Smithsonian Institution in 1998, as well as at the Russian Academy of Sciences, Anthropological Museum, Saint Petersburg Branch of RAN in 1992.

Literature Cited

Alekseev VP. 1961. Paleoanthropology of Neolithic and Bronze Age period of Altai-Sayan mountain region. In: *Anthropological Collection III*. Moscow: USSR Academy of Sciences. Pp. 107–206.

Alekseev VP. 1966. *Osteometry* (Остеометрия). Moscow: Nauka.

Alekseev VP, Debets GF. 1964. *Craniometry*. Moscow: Nauka.

Alekseev VP, Gokhman II. 1983. *Anthropology Aziatskoi Chaste USSR*. Moscow: Nauka.

Alekseev VP, Gokhman II, Tumen D. 1987. *Paleoanthropology of Central Asia: Archaeology, ethnography and anthropology of Mongolia*. Novosibirsk: Science Press.

Bass WM. 1987. *Human osteology: A laboratory and field manual*. Columbia: Missouri Archaeological Society.

Batsaikhan Z. 2002. *Hunnu (Xiongnu)*. Ulaanbaatar: Printing House of the National University of Mongolia.

Bayar D. 1999. *Altain hun chuluun khushee*. Ulaanbaatar: Press of the Mongolian Academy of Sciences.

Bernshtam AN. 1951. *History of Huns (Ocherk istorii gunnov)*. Leningrad: Leningrad State University.

Brothwell DR. 1965. *Digging Up Bones*. London: Trustees of the British Museum (Natural History).

Davydova AB. 1995. *Ivolginskii archeologicheskii kompleks*. Vol. 1. Saint Petersburg: Archaeological Monuments of Sunnu.

Davydova AB. 1996. *Ivolginskii archeologicheskii kompleks*. Vol. 2. Saint Petersburg: Archaeological Monuments of Sunnu.

Debets GF. 1948. *Paleoanthropologiya USSR*. Moscow: Nauka.

Di Cosmo N. 2002. *Ancient China and its enemies: The rise of nomadic power in East Asian history*. Cambridge: Cambridge University Press.

Dorj D. 1971. *Neolithic of eastern Mongolia* (Неолит Восточной Монголии). Ulaanbaatar: Press of the Mongolian Academy of Sciences.

Dorjsuren T. 1961. Umard Hunnu. *Arkheologiin Sudlal* 1 (5): 13–45. Ulaanbaatar: Press of the Mongolian Academy of Sciences.

Erdenebaatar D. 2002. *Slab Grave and Heregsuur culture of Mongolia*. Ulaanbaatar: Soembo.

Erdenebaatar D, Kovalev AA. 2006. Report of Mongolian-Russian joint archaeological expedition "Central Asian Archaeology." Unpublished. Manuscript Archives of Archaeological Annual Fieldwork Reports housed in the Department of Archaeology, Ulaanbaatar University. Ulaanbaatar, Mongolia.

Erdenebaatar D, Kovalev AA. 2007. Report of Mongolian-Russian joint archaeological expedition "Central Asian Archaeology." *Mongolian Journal of Anthropology, Archaeology and Ethnology* 3 (1) (287): 35–51.

Gumilev LN. 1960. *Xiongnu* (Хунну). Moscow: Nauka.

Ganchinsuren Ch. 2000. Tamsagbulagiin shune chuluun zevsgiin suuringiin on tsagiig dahin avch uzeh ni. *Arkheologiin Sudlal* 20: 5–15. Ulaanbaatar: Press of the Mongolian Academy of Sciences.

Howells WW. 1973. *Cranial variation in man: A study by multivariate analysis of patterns of difference among recent human populations*. Harvard, MA: Harvard University Press.

Ismagulov R. 1970. *Ancient populations of Kazakhstan (Drevnie naselenie Kazakhstana)*. Alma-Ata, Kazakh SSR: Nauka.

Khrisanfova EN, Perevozchikov IV. 1999. *Anthropology* (Антропология). Moscow: Moscow State University Press.

Knusmann R. 1988. *Anthropologie*. Handbuch der verleichenden Biologie des Menschen, vol. 1. Stuttgart: Gustav Fischer.

Konovalov PB. 1999. *Ethnic aspects of Central Asian history: Antiquity and Middle Ages (Ethnicheskie aspekti istorii Central Asia)* (Этнические аспекты истории Центральной Азии). Ulaan-Ude: National Academy of Science.

Kovalev AA, Erdenebaatar D. 2003. Research report of archaeological fieldwork 2002, 2003. Unpublished. Manuscript Archives of Archaeological Annual Fieldwork Reports, housed in the Department of Archaeology, Ulaanbaatar University, Ulaanbaatar, Mongolia.

Kruykov MV, Sofronov MV, Cheboksarov NN. 1978. *Ancient Chinese: The problem of ethnogenesis* (Древние китайцы. Проблемы этногенеза). Moscow: Nauka.

Lahr MM. 1996. *The evolution of modern human diversity: A study of cranial variation*. Cambridge: Cambridge University Press.

Mamonova NN. 1979. Ancient populations of Mongolia based on paleoanthropological data. In: Derevjanko AP, Nacakdorzh Sh, editors. *Archaeology, anthropology, and ethnography of Mongolia* (Археология, этнография и антропология Монголии). Novosibirsk: Nauka.

Namsrainaidan L. 1975. Tamsag Bulgaas Oldson Neolitiin Uein Khunii Bulshnii Tukhai. *Studiya Archaeologii* 10: 6. Ulaanbaatar: Mongolian Academy of Sciences.

Navaan D. 1975. *Dornod Mongoliin Khurel (Bronze Age of eastern Mongolia)*. Ulaanbaatar: Mongolian Academy of Sciences.

Navaan D. 1980. *Ertnii Mongoliin Tuukhiin Dursgaluud (Historical monuments of Mongolia)*. Ulaanbaatar: Printing House of the Ministry of Culture of Mongolia.

Novgorodova EA. 1987. *Ancient culture of Mongolia* (Древняя культура Монголии). Moscow: Nauka.

Novgorodova EA. 1989. *Ancient Mongolia: Problems of chronology and ethnocultural history* (Древняя Монголия: некоторые проблемы хронологии и этнокультурной истории). Moscow: Nauka.

Okladnikov AP. 1963. *Archaeological research in Mongolia, years 1961–1962* (Археологическое исследование в Монголии 1961–1962 гг). Proceedings of Siberian Branch of Russian Academy of Sciences. Social Sciences, vol. 1. Novosibirsk: Russian Academy of Sciences.

Okladnikov AP. 1964. On the question of the earliest history of Mongolia: Early Mongolia. In: *Studia Archeologica Instituti Historiae Academiae Scientiarum Republicae Populi Mongoli*, vol. 3. Ulaanbaatar. Pp. 8–10.

Penrose LS. 1954. Distance, size and shape. *Annals of Eugenics* 18: 337–43.

Perlei H. 1959. *Hyadan Nar, Tednii Mongoltoi Holbogdson Ni*. Tuuhiin Sudlal no. 1. Ulaanbaatar: Mongolian Academy of Sciences.

Roginskii YY. 1978. *Anthropologiya* (Антропология). Moscow: Vysshaija Shkola.

Rykushina GV. 1976. Anthropology of Krasnoyarsk region during Eniolithic and Bronze Age. In: Alekseev VP, editor. *Problems of ethnogenesis and ethnic history of world populations* (Некоторые проблемы этногенеза и этнической истории народов мира). Moscow: Nauka. Pp. 69–81.

Ser-Odjav N. 1956. *Mongol Orni Neolit (Neolithic of Mongolia)*. Proceedings of Mongolian Academy of Sciences, vol. 1. Ulaanbaatar.

Ser-Odjav N. 1964. Arkheologichesoe Issledovanie V Bostochnom Aimage. *Studiya Arkheologii* 3: 8–10. Ulaanbaatar: Press of the Mongolian Academy of Sciences.

Ser-Odjav N. 1977. *Mongolin Ertnii Tuukh*. Ulaanbaatar: Press of the Mongolian Academy of Sciences.

Sukhbaatar G. 1980. *Mongolchuudiin Ertnii Eveg*. Ulaanbaatar: Press of the Mongolian Academy of Sciences.

Tseveendorj D. 1987. Hunnugiin archaeology (Xiongnu archaeology). *Mongoliin Archaeology, Arkheologiin Sudlal* 12: 58–81. Ulaanbaatar: Mongolian Academy of Sciences.

Tseveendorj D. 1993. *Hunnu naryn orshuulgyn dursgal ba ugsaa khamaadahyn zarim asuudal.* Mongolian-Korean Joint Research 2. Seoul.

Tsybektarov AD. 1998. *Culture of slab burials in Mongolia and Zabaikal region* (Культура плиточных могил Монголии и Забайкалья). Ulaan-Ude: Buryat State University Press.

Tumen D. 1976. Paleoanthropology Zapadnoi Mongolii. *Journal of the Study of Archaeology* 7: 7. Ulaanbaatar: Mongolian Academy of Sciences.

Tumen D. 1977. *Nekotorie Voprosi Anthropologicheskogo Issledovaniy Bostochnoi Mongolia*. Reports of the Institute of General and Experimental Biology (Труды Института Обшей и Експериментальной Биологии), vol. 2. Ulaanbaatar: Mongolian Academy of Sciences.

Tumen D. 1978. Nekotorie Voprosi Anthropologicheskogo Issledovaniy Bostochnoi Mongolia (Anthropology of East Mongolia). *Trudi Instituta Obshei I Experimentalnoi Biologii* 2: 39–49.

Tumen D. 1979. Paleoanthropologicheskie nakhodki in Khar-Khorin. *Study of Archaeology* 8: 10.

Tumen D. 1985. *Voprosi etnogeneza mongolob v sveta dannie paleoanthropologii.* Papers of International Congress of Mongolianists (Труды Международного Конгресса Монголоведов). Ulaanbaatar: Mongolian Academy of Sciences.

Tumen D. 1987. Anthropological characteristics of Mongolian Hunnu. In: Derevianko AP, Natsagdorj SH, editors. *Ancient cultures of Mongolia* (Древние культуры Монголии), Novosibirsk: Nauka. Pp. 87–97.

Tumen D. 1992. Anthropology of contemporary populations of Mongolia (Антропология современного населения Монголии) (Anthropologiya Sovermennogo Naseleniya Mongolii). Unpublished Ph.D. thesis, Moscow State University.

Tumen D. 1996. Craniofacial morphology of ancient population from Eastern Mongolia. In: Korea-Mongolian Joint Studies Association, Korea Institute of Anthropology, Dankook University, editor. *Proceedings of the Mongolian-Korean Joint Research Project "Eastern Mongolia."* Vol. 5. Seoul: Hyean Publishing Co. Pp. 263–73.

Tumen D. 2002. Paleoanthropological study of Hunnu from Mongolia. *Scientific Journal of the National University of Mongolia: Archaeology, Anthropology and Ethnology* 187: 13. Ulaanbaatar: Printing House of the National University of Mongolia.

Tumen D. 2003. Craniofacial morphology of human remains from ancient burials of Tsuvraa Mountain in Uguumur area, Khulenbiur sum, Dornod aimag, Mongolia. *Scientific Journal of the National University of Mongolia: Archaeology, Anthropology and Ethnology* 210: 19. Ulaanbaatar: Printing House of the National University of Mongolia.

Tumen D. 2006. Craniofacial comparative study of ancient populations of Mongolia. *Mongolian Journal of Anthropology. Archaeology and Ethnology* 2 (1): 90–108. Ulaanbaatar: Printing House of the National University of Mongolia.

Tumen D. 2007. *Ancient populations of Mongolia*. Toronto Studies in Central and Inner Asia, vol. 8: 51–77. University of Toronto: Asian Institute, Canada.

Turbat Ts. 2004. *Hunnugiin Jiriin Irgediin Bulsh*. Ulaanbaatar.

Volkov VV. 1967. *Bronze and Early Iron Age of northern Mongolia* (Бронзовый и ранний железный век Северной Монголии). Ulaanbaatar: Press of Mongolian Academy of Sciences.

Volkov VV. 1981. *Olennye Stones of Mongolia* (Оленые камни монголии). Ulaanbaatar: Printing House of the National University of Mongolia.

Wu RK, Olsen JW, editors. 1985. *Paleoanthropology and Paleolithic archaeology in the People's Republic of China.* Orlando, FL: Academic Press.

5

A Nonmetric Comparative Study of Past and Contemporary Mongolian and Northeast Asian Crania

ERDENE MYAGMAR

Cranial nonmetric (epigenetic) variation is often employed in analyzing osteological remains at the population level and has successfully been used to evaluate biological affinities among archaeological and modern populations from different regions of the world (Kozintsev 1972; Wenger 1974; Finnegan and Marcsik 1979; Ossenberg 1990; Ishida and Dodo 1992, 1993, 1997; Hanihara et al. 1998; Hanihara and Ishida 2001a–e; Sutter and Mertz 2004). The theoretical basis of any such investigation requires that (1) the traits are heritable (have a genetic basis); (2) populations vary in the frequency of these traits; (3) trait manifestation is not significantly influenced by environmental effects; (4) the traits do not vary significantly with age; (5) the traits do not vary significantly with sex; (6) there is only limited correlation between traits, if any; and (7) the traits are easily defined and assessable, even using fragmentary remains.

The theoretical bases of nonmetric trait analyses have been tested on many sampled populations from Europe, North America, and Northeast Asia. Comparative craniometric studies of ancient Mongolian samples have been conducted (e.g., Tumen 1977, 1985, 1992; Tumen et al. 2002; Tumen and Vanchigdash 2006), while cranial discrete traits of archaeological samples from Mongolia have not yet been investigated. The aim of this chapter is to examine the level and patterning of cranial nonmetric variation in a range of past and contemporary Mongolian samples and compare that to nonmetric cranial variation in other northern and eastern Asian populations. It is hoped that such an analysis will throw light on the origins of the Mongolian peoples and any past interactions (i.e., migrations and assimilations) among the various populations that have occupied the region throughout the prehistoric and historic periods.

Materials and Methods

The primary study sample includes 190 crania, representing a range of prehistoric and historic phases in Mongolia (Neolithic, Bronze Age, Early Iron
Age, Xiongnu, Mongolian period, and modern Mongolian: see table 5.1 for
sample details and figure 5.1 for the sample distribution). These crania are

Table 5.1. Location and brief description of cranial samples from Mongolia

No. on figure 5.1	Site name	Location/province/ region	Historical period/ culture	Dates	Sample size
1.	Norovlin	Bulgan soum, Dornod aimag/eastern Mongolia	Neolithic	10,000–2500 BC	1
2.	Shatar Uul	Bayankhongor aimag/ central Mongolia	Neolithic, Bronze Age, Xiongnu	10,000–2500 BC, 2500–300 BC, 300 BC–AD 200	2, 2, 1
3.	Shuus boom, Aurag	Khentii aimag/eastern Mongolia	Bronze Age/Slab Grave, Mongolian period	2500–300 BC, 1100–1400 BC	5, 8
4.	Urgun shireg	Hyrgas soum, Uvs aimag/ western Mongolia	Bronze Age/ Khirigsuur culture	1300–900 BC	1
5.	Chandman	Ulaangom, Uvs aimag/ western Mongolia	Late Bronze Age/ Early Iron Age, Xiongnu, Modern	900–300 BC, 300 BC–AD 200, 20th century	85, 4, 3
6.	Duulga Uul	Jargaltkhaan soum, Khentii aimag/eastern Mongolia	Xiongnu	300 BC–AD 200	16
7.	Naimaa tolgoi	Erdenemandal soum, Arkhangai aimag/central Mongolia	Xiongnu	300 BC–AD 200	4
8.	Buural Uul	Hongor soum, Selenge aimag/central Mongolia	Xiongnu	300 BC–AD 200	10
9.	Tevsh Uul	Bogd soum, Övörkhangai aimag/central Mongolia	Xiongnu, Mongolian period	300 BC–AD 200, 1100–1400 BC	9, 1
10.	Takhiltin Khotgor	Manhan soum, Khovd aimag	Xiongnu	300 BC–AD 200	3
11.	Tsuvraa, Tahilgat	Hulunbuir soum, Dornod aimag	Mongolian period	1100–1400 BC	17
12.	Tavan tolgoi	Sukhbaatar aimag/ eastern Mongolia	Mongolian period	1100–1400 BC	6
13.	Kharkhorin	Uvurkhangai/ central Mongolia	Mongolian period, Modern	1100–1400 BC, 20th century	6, 3
14.	Renchinlhumbe	Khuvsgul aimag/ central Mongolia	Modern	20th century	3
	Total				190

housed in the Department of Anthropology and Archaeology, National University of Mongolia, Ulaanbaatar. A comparative sample of modern Northeast Asians (Koreans, $n = 93$) housed at the Department of Anatomy, Medical College of Korea University, Seoul, was also assessed for nonmetric traits by the author. To expand the comparative nonmetric database, additional data from southern Siberian and northern, northeastern, and eastern Asian populations (Tagar, Kazakh, Chukchi, Yakut, Evenki, Buriat, Neolithic Baikal, Amur, Sakhalin Ainu, Hokkaido Ainu, Jomon, Doigahama Yayoi, modern Japanese, and northern Chinese) previously reported on by Ishida and Dodo (1992, 1997) were also used (see table 5.2 for sample details).

Of a total of 59 nonmetric traits initially recorded using criteria outlined by Dodo (1974, 1986), Hauser and DeStefano (1989), and Movsesyan and colleagues (1975), 19 traits were subsequently selected for the purpose of assessing biological distance as having high levels of interobserver consistency (Dodo and Ishida 1990) for intersample comparisons. Nonmetric cranial trait frequencies (p) were calculated using the "individual count" method described by Turner and Scott (1977), for which in the case of an individual exhibiting asymmetry in the expression of a given trait, the greatest level of expression is used. Pooled-sex cranial nonmetric trait frequencies for each sample were arcsine-transformed and subsequently used to calculate the mean measure of divergence (MMD). MMD between two populations is calculated as follows (Sjøvold 1973):

$$MMD = \frac{\sum_{i=1}^{r}(\theta_1 - \theta_2)^2 - (1/(n_{1i} + 1/2) + 1/(n_{2i} + 1/2))}{r}$$

Figure 5.1. Geographical locations of the archaeological and modern Mongolian populations sampled in the study (see table 5.1 for key).

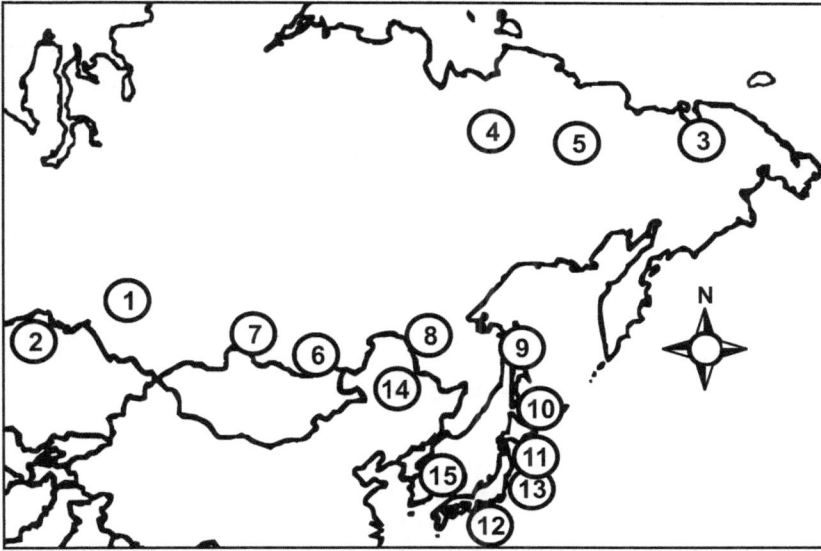

Figure 5.2. Geographical locations of the populations used for comparison (see table 5.2 for key).

Table 5.2. Location and sources of samples of Asian populations used for comparison

No. on figure 5.2	Sample name	Brief information	References
1.	Tagar	Iron Age, southern Siberia (IE–LB; MSU)	Ishida and Dodo 1992
2.	Kazakh	Recent Kazakhs from southern Siberia (IE–LB; MSU)	Ishida and Dodo 1992
3.	Chukchi	Recent Chukchis from the Arctic region of northeastern Siberia (MSU)	Ishida and Dodo 1992
4.	Yakut	Recent Yakuts from northeastern Siberia (MSU)	Ishida and Dodo 1992
5.	Evenki	Evenki (including Even) (MSU)	Ishida and Dodo 1992
6.	Buriat	Recent Buriats from northeastern Siberia (MSU)	Ishida and Dodo 1992
7.	Neolithic Baikal	Neolithic people from around Lake Baikal, northeastern Siberia (IE–LB; MSU)	Ishida and Dodo 1992
8.	Amur	Recent indigenous tribes from Amur River basin: Ulchs, Nanaians, Negidals, and Orochs (MSU)	Ishida and Dodo 1992
9.	Sakhalin Ainu	Recent Ainu from Sakhalin (KTU; IE–LB)	Ishida and Kida 1991
10.	Hokkaido Ainu	Recent Ainu in Hokkaido, Japan (UT)	Ishida and Dodo 1992
11.	Jomon	Neolithic Jomon (UT; NSMT; TU; SMU)	Dodo and Ishida 1990
12.	Doigahama Yayoi	Eneolithic Doigahama Yayoi (KSU)	Dodo and Ishida 1990
13.	Modern Japanese	Recent Japanese from Honshu (CU, TU)	Dodo and Ishida 1987
14.	Northern Chinese	Northern part of China, mainly from Liaoning Prefecture (UT; KTU)	Ishida and Dodo 1993
15.	Modern Koreans	Modern Korean cranial sample (KU)	Erdene 2006

Sources: MSU, Moscow State University; IE–LB, Institute of Ethnography–Leningrad Branch; KTU, Kyoto University; UT, University of Tokyo; NSMT, National Science Museum, Tokyo; TU, Tohoku University, Sendai; SMU, Sapporo Medical University, Sapporo; KSU, Kyushu University, Fukuoka; CU, Chiba University, Chiba; KU, Korea University, Seoul.

where r is the number of traits used in the comparison, θ_1 and θ_2 are the transformed frequencies in radians of the ith trait in the two groups being compared, and n_{1i} and n_{2i} are the numbers of individuals scored for the ith trait in the two groups.

Standard deviations and standardized distances for MMD values are calculated as suggested by Sjøvold (1973). The variance of the MMD is calculated using the following equation:

$$Var_{MMD} = \frac{2}{r^2} \sum_{i=1}^{r} (1/(n_{1i} + 1/2) + 1/(n_{2i} + 1/2))^2$$

Once the variance of the MMD is found, the standard deviation of the MMD is calculated using the following equation:

$$sd_{MMD} = \sqrt{Var_{MMD}}$$

Finally, the standardized MMD is determined by the following equation:

$$St_{MMD} = \frac{MMD}{sd_{MMD}}$$

Standardized distances are considered statistically significant at the 0.05 level if their value is greater than 2. Multidimensional cluster analysis was applied to the MMD matrix to obtain a dendrogram of phylogenetic relationship between populations studied. Statistical calculations of cranial nonmetric trait frequencies were conducted using the SPSS.12 program, and calculations of MMD were performed in the MS Excel program. Cluster analyses applied to the MMD matrices were done by hand, using Ward's (1963) method.

Results

As can be seen in table 5.3, the frequencies of the 19 cranial nonmetric traits in the Mongolian and Korean samples are quite variable. The most commonly occurring traits include "complete supraorbital foramen" and "foramen of Vesalius," with more than 50 percent of the individuals from both of the collective Mongolian and Korean samples manifesting these traits. The highest frequencies occur in the Bronze Age and modern Mongolian samples for supraorbital foramen (0.958 and 0.972, respectively) and in the Neolithic and modern Mongolian samples for foramen of Vesalius (0.917 and 0.972, respectively). The least common traits include metopic suture (0.011–0.086), medial palatine canal (0.006–0.125), pterigospinous foramen (0.015–0.083), and mylohyoid groove closed (0.037–0.152).

The frequencies of frontal groove and jugular foramen bridging are higher in the earlier Mongolian than in the medieval and modern Mongolian samples. The high frequency of tympanic dehiscence in the Mongolian period sample is comparable to that of the Neolithic and unlike that observed in other Mongolian or Korean samples. Frequencies of parietal notch bone, transverse zygomatic suture, and occipito-mastoid ossicle are lower in all of the samples examined in comparison to that of the Neolithic sample. Compared to other samples, the frequency of precondylar tubercle in the modern Mongolian sample is relatively high, as is mylohyoid groove closed in the Xiongnu sample. In general, the results summarized in table 5.3 indicate that the Neolithic Mongolian sample is quite different in terms of the manifestation of nonmetric traits in comparison with all other samples analyzed.

In order to compare the archaeological and modern Mongolian and Korean samples, their standardized MMDs (st-MMD) were calculated based on the 19 nonmetric traits (see table 5.4). Cluster analyses applied to the MMD matrix of cranial nonmetric trait frequencies are given in figure 5.3. The resulting dendrogram reveals one major cluster that encompasses all of the Mongolian samples with a distinct separation between the Mongolian and Korean samples. The Mongolian cluster is further subdivided into two subclusters: the first composed of Bronze Age and Early Iron Age samples and the somewhat more distant Neolithic sample; the second indicating a close relationship between the Xiongnu and Mongolian period samples, with a more distant link to the modern Mongolian sample.

Standardized MMDs (st-MMD) were also calculated, based on the same 19 nonmetric traits, for the other comparative Asian samples (see table 5.5). A cluster analysis based on the st-MMD matrix was carried out for the Mongolian, Korean, and other comparative Asian samples (figure 5.4). The first major division occurs between the Hokkaido Ainu and Jomon on the one hand and, on the other hand, all other samples, which form four major groupings. The first grouping includes two subclusters: (1) Mongolian Neolithic and Tagar, with the Kazakhs slightly more distant; and (2) Yakut and Northern Chinese, closely related, with the Buriats somewhat more distant.

The second grouping contains all of the ancient and modern Mongolian samples as well as modern Koreans, in several subclusters: (1) Bronze and Early Iron Age Mongolians; (2) Xiongnu and Mongolian period individuals; and (3) stand-alone modern Mongolians on the one hand and modern Koreans on the other hand. The third grouping consists of Northeast Asian samples subclustered as (1) Evenki and Neolithic Baikal and (2) somewhat more distant Amur River basin and Chukchi samples. The fourth grouping includes Japanese samples: (1) Sakhalin Ainu and modern Japanese forming a subcluster with (2) a more distant Doigahama Yayoi neighbor.

Table 5.3. Incidence of cranial nonmetric traits recorded in the samples of ancient and modern Mongolian and Korean populations

| | Mongolian samples | | | | | | | | | | | | | Modern Korean sample | |
| | Neolithic period | | Bronze Age | | Early Iron Age | | Xiongnu | | Mongolian period | | Modern | | | |
	Obs/N	P[a]	Obs/N	P[a]	Obs/N	P[a]	Obs/N	P[a]	Obs/N	P[a]	Obs/N	P[a]	Obs/N	P[a]
Metopic suture	0/3	(0.083)	0/7	(0.036)	2/86	0.023	1/45	0.022	3/35	0.086	0/9	(0.028)	1/93	0.011
Frontal groove	0/3	(0.083)	2/7	0.286	23/85	0.271	11/45	0.244	5/34	0.147	1/9	0.111	10/77	0.130
Supraorbital foramen complete	2/3	0.667	6/6	(0.958)	49/84	0.583	29/45	0.644	21/36	0.583	9/9	0.972	35/68	0.515
Transverse zygomatic suture vestige	1/2	0.500	1/5	0.200	7/80	0.088	7/43	0.163	4/25	0.160	2/8	0.250	12/68	0.176
Tympanic dehiscence	1/3	0.333	1/7	0.143	16/85	0.188	9/47	0.191	14/36	0.389	2/9	0.222	9/68	0.132
Parietal notch bone	2/3	0.667	0/6	(0.042)	13/77	0.169	8/45	0.178	5/29	0.172	1/9	0.111	14/67	0.209
Asterionic bone	1/3	0.333	3/6	0.500	18/77	0.234	9/45	0.200	9/30	0.300	1/9	0.111	14/67	0.209
Ossicle at lambda	0/3	(0.083)	0/8	(0.031)	19/82	0.232	5/45	0.111	1/29	0.034	1/9	0.111	7/61	0.115
Occipito-mastoid wormian	1/3	0.333	1/6	0.167	8/71	0.113	3/41	0.073	1/23	0.043	1/9	0.111	8/65	0.123
Biasterionic suture	0/3	(0.083)	0/8	(0.031)	14/81	0.173	6/45	0.133	6/26	0.231	2/9	0.222	5/67	0.075

Trait													
Medial palatine canal	0/2	(0.125)	0/5	(0.050)	5/83	0.060	0/41	(0.006)	0/29	(0.009)	0/9	(0.028)	3/66	0.045
Foramen of Vesalius	3/3	(0.917)	2/4	0.500	67/74	0.905	34/42	0.810	20/25	0.800	9/9	(0.972)	47/68	0,691
Pterigospinous foramen	0/3	(0.083)	0/4	(0.063)	3/73	0.041	1/42	0.024	1/21	0.048	0/9	(0.028)	1/68	0.015
Precondylar tubercle	0/3	(0.083)	0/6	(0.042)	2/72	0.028	2/40	0.050	2/19	0.105	4/8	0.500	6/67	0.090
Hypoglossal canal bridging	1/3	0.333	1/6	0.167	14/77	0.182	10/41	0.244	3/19	0.158	1/9	0.111	16/67	0.239
Posterior condylar canal patent	1/3	0.333	4/5	0.800	59/74	0.797	32/40	0.800	11/18	0.611	6/8	0.750	55/67	0.821
Sagittal sinus groove flexes left	0/3	(0.083)	0/8	(0.031)	15/84	0.179	8/47	0.170	4/29	0.138	0/9	(0.028)	17/69	0.246
Jugular foramen bridging	0/3	(0.083)	1/4	0.250	13/65	0.200	8/35	0.229	1/14	0.071	0/8	(0.031)	8/66	0.121
Mylohyoid groove closed	0/3	(0.083)	0/4	(0.063)	3/74	0.041	5/33	0.152	1/27	0.037	0/3	(0.083)	4/67	0.060

Note: Obs/N = affected/observed.

[a] P is the proportion of any particular trait observed for a given sample size (n). Following Bartlett (1936), where a trait is not observed ($p = 0$) the proportion is calculated as $p = 1/4n$, where n is the sample size. Where a trait is always scored as present ($p = 1$), then the proportion is calculated as $p = 1—(1/4n)$. Proportion values in parentheses have been calculated using Bartlett's adjustment.

Table 5.4. Matrix of st-MMD values for ancient and modern Mongolian and Korean populations

	Neolithic	Bronze Age	Early Iron Age	Xiongnu	Mongolian period	Modern Mongolians	Modern Koreans
				Mongolian populations			
Neolithic		7.13	6.74	8.44	13.29	7.73	9.06
Bronze Age			1.50	7.22	1.94	1.51	1.80
Early Iron Age				3.26	17.64	19.19	26.88
Xiongnu					1.64	11.07	2.73
Mongolian period						3.98	14.73
Modern Mongolians							20.90
Modern Koreans							

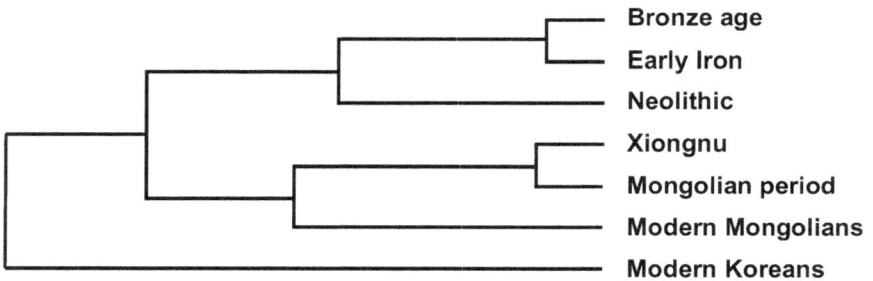

Figure 5.3. Dendrogram of the relationships of ancient and modern Mongolian and Korean populations.

Discussion and Conclusions

The results of this analysis highlight distinct features of the ancient and modern Mongolian samples relative to comparative samples from North, Northeast, and East Asia. While the Mongolian Neolithic sample was found to be more similar to the Central Asian samples, all of the later Mongolian samples cluster within a common biologically related grouping.

Previous craniometric studies of Mongolian samples have suggested that Mongolian period and Modern Mongolians share a genetic heritage with the Xiongnu (e.g., Tumen 1985), with the present cranial nonmetric analysis also supporting this proposal. However, the possible genetic continuity

Table 5.5. Matrix of st-MMD values for archaeological and modern Asian populations

	Neolithic	Bronze Age	Early Iron Age	Xiongnu	Mongolian period	Modern Mongolian	Modern Korean	Chukchi	Yakut	Evenki	Buriat
Neolithic		-7.13	-6.74	-8.44	-13.29	-7.73	-9.06	4.07	-3.01	2.79	2.19
Bronze Age			1.50	-7.22	-1.94	-1.51	-1.80	3.34	5.12	11.74	3.75
Early Iron Age				-3.26	17.64	19.19	26.88	167.52	90.43	157.60	165.87
Xiongnu					1.64	11.07	-2.73	70.01	36.87	81.93	63.51
Mongolian period						3.98	14.73	79.59	21.51	50.23	41.33
Modern Mongolian							20.90	52.11	20.93	39.73	26.88
Modern Korean								100.20	57.61	73.17	117.75
Chukchi									41.34	35.86	42.09
Yakut										27.03	-11.51
Evenki											40.81
Buriat											
Neolithic Baikal											
Tagar											
Kazakh											
Amur											
Sakhalin Ainu											
Hokkaido Ainu											
Jomon											
Doigahama Yayoi											
Modern Japanese											
Northern Chinese											

Table 5.5 Matrix of st-MMD values for archaeological and modern Asian populations (*Continued*)

	Neolithic Baikal	Tagar	Kazakh	Amur	Sakhalin Ainu	Hokkaido Ainu	Jomon	Doigahama Yayoi	Modern Japanese	Northern Chinese
Neolithic	1.85	0.56	-4.56	0.93	-7.64	0.92	6.36	-5.92	-4.70	-5.44
Bronze Age	-4.74	0.57	-3.03	-11.44	6.62	22.56	40.45	4.13	4.66	2.08
Early Iron Age	111.85	65.49	94.50	181.70	170.21	311.53	274.43	160.41	157.15	106.04
Xiongnu	40.72	24.49	25.41	58.80	60.35	137.55	159.71	82.92	64.19	45.64
Mongolian period	47.91	37.10	23.89	47.58	46.58	99.27	101.53	68.81	35.18	24.01
Modern Mongolian	36.48	43.95	29.72	42.50	47.13	67.79	68.03	47.85	38.89	26.93
Modern Korean	28.01	66.22	42.37	69.54	53.82	116.62	178.11	70.50	79.59	66.54
Chukchi	42.18	75.53	48.82	45.34	69.70	113.54	204.58	75.93	91.78	74.89
Yakut	39.59	39.38	3.29	51.45	56.11	147.73	192.85	95.54	23.80	-2.41
Evenki	3.06	113.77	63.26	39.28	39.29	103.71	149.08	60.29	65.07	34.97
Buriat	49.56	82.80	21.55	104.29	123.69	265.22	263.72	144.13	93.67	21.55
Neolithic Baikal		79.27	43.85	11.11	15.92	67.86	123.77	37.08	53.50	36.73
Tagar			8.83	118.82	129.63	301.74	333.62	154.81	111.49	55.44
Kazakh				63.63	76.53	200.12	271.83	105.38	67.72	16.83
Amur					64.42	213.20	330.65	102.65	129.28	107.52
Sakhalin Ainu						53.44	137.51	62.15	49.41	73.21
Hokkaido Ainu							90.48	185.26	206.25	238.41
Jomon								198.96	216.67	230.20
Doigahama Yayoi									74.10	78.81
Modern Japanese										13.91
Northern Chinese										

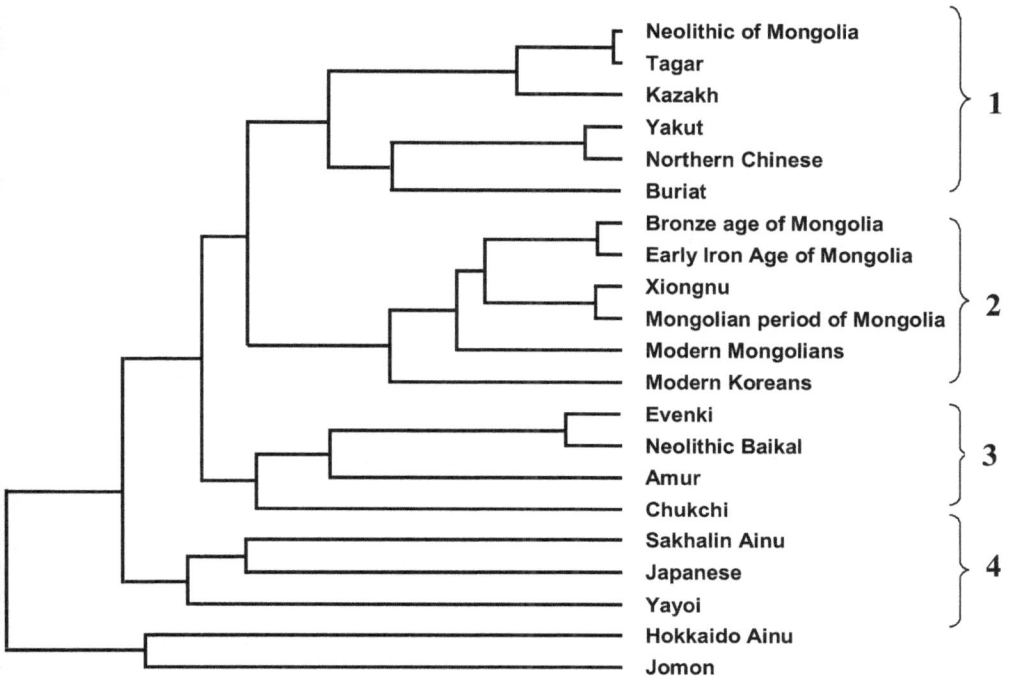

Figure 5.4. Dendrogram of the relationships of ancient and modern Mongolian and Korean populations with North, Northeast, and East Asian populations.

from Bronze Age populations of Central and Eastern Mongolia to Xiongnu
populations of Central Mongolia, hypothesized by several Mongolian (Batsaikhan 2002; Navaan 1975; Turbat 2006) and Western archaeologists (e.g.,
see Wright et al. 2009 and references therein), is not supported by the findings in the present study. While the Central Mongolian Bronze Age and Early
Iron Age samples from Western Mongolia showed clear similarities in the
present study, they, in turn, were both somewhat different from the Xiongnu
and Mongolian period samples.

Why archaeologists have favored a view of genetic continuity between
Bronze Age, Iron Age, and later Xiongnu populations is unclear, but this likely
stems from a long-held implicit and sometimes explicit (e.g., see Wright et
al. 2009: 372) assumption of an ancestor-descendant relationship. The observed apparent genetic discontinuity between Bronze/Iron Age populations and the later Xiongnu is difficult to explain, but the reasons may be
found in high levels of mobility (particularly migration) during the Bronze
Age in the territory of Central Asia on the one hand and an elevated level of
genetic heterogeneity within the Xiongnu population on the other. Finally,
the clustering of modern Koreans with Mongolians in grouping 2 (see figure

5.4) is intriguing. There is little other evidence of a close genetic relationship between Mongolians and Koreans (see also chapter 7), and the pattern seen here requires further investigation.

Acknowledgments

This study was carried out within a larger research project titled "Eastern Mongolia," supported financially by the Asian Research Center, National University of Mongolia and the International Scholar Exchange Fellowship Program from the Korea Foundation for Advanced Studies (KFAS), South Korea. I wish to thank Professor Uhm Chan Sub, Department of Anatomy, College of Medicine of Korea University, South Korea, and the members of his laboratory staff who facilitated and made possible examination of the cranial sample at their department.

Literature Cited

Bartlett MS. 1936. The square root transformation in the analysis of variance. *Journal of the Royal Statistical Society, supplement* 3: 68–78.

Batsaikhan Z. 2002. *Xiongnu*. Ulaanbaatar: Publishing House of the National University of Mongolia.

Dodo Y. 1974. Nonmetrical cranial traits in the Hokkaido Ainu and the northern Japanese of recent times. *Journal of the Anthropological Society of Nippon* 82: 31–51.

Dodo Y. 1986. A population study of the jugular foramen bridging of the human cranium. *American Journal of Physical Anthropology* 69: 15–19.

Dodo Y, Ishida H. 1987. Incidences of nonmetric cranial variants in several population samples from East Asia and North America. *Journal of the Anthropological Society of Nippon* 95: 161–77.

Dodo Y, Ishida H. 1990. Population history of Japan as viewed from cranial nonmetric variation. *Journal of the Anthropological Society of Nippon* 98: 269–87.

Erdene M. 2006. Cranial nonmetric variation of modern Koreans. *Mongolian Journal of Anthropology, Archaeology and Ethnology* 2 (2) (271): 144–64.

Finnegan M, Marcsik A. 1979. A nonmetric examination of the relationships between osteological remains from Hungary representing populations of Avar period. *Acta Biologica Szegediensis* 25: 97–118.

Hanihara T, Ishida H. 2001a. Os incae: Variation in frequency in major human population groups. *Journal of Anatomy* 198: 137–52.

Hanihara T, Ishida H. 2001b. Frequency variations of discrete cranial traits in major human populations. I: Supernumerary ossicle variations. *Journal of Anatomy* 198: 689–706.

Hanihara T, Ishida H. 2001c. Frequency variations of discrete cranial traits in major human populations. II: Hypostotic variations. *Journal of Anatomy* 198: 707–25.

Hanihara T, Ishida H. 2001d. Frequency variations of discrete cranial traits in major human populations. III: Hyperostotic variations. *Journal of Anatomy* 199: 251–72.

Hanihara T, Ishida H. 2001e. Frequency variations of discrete cranial traits in major human populations. IV: Vessel and nerve related variations. *Journal of Anatomy* 199: 273–87.

Hanihara T, Ishida H, Dodo Y. 1998. Os zygomaticum bipartitum: Frequency distribution in major human populations. *Journal of Anatomy* 192: 539–55.

Hauser G, DeStefano GF. 1989. Epigenetic variants of the human skull. Stuttgart: E. Schweizer-bartsche Verlagsbuchhandlung.

Ishida H, Dodo Y. 1992. Differentiation of the Northern Mongoloid: The evidence of cranial nonmetric traits. In: Hanihara K, editor. *Japanese as a Member of the Asian and Pacific Populations*. Kyoto: Nichibunken. Pp. 78–93.

Ishida H, Dodo Y. 1993. Nonmetric cranial variation and the populational affinities of the Pacific peoples. *American Journal of Physical Anthropology* 90: 49–57.

Ishida H, Dodo Y. 1997. Cranial variation in prehistoric human skeletal remains from the Marianas. *American Journal of Physical Anthropology* 104: 399–410.

Ishida H, Kida M. 1991. An anthropological investigation of the Sakhalin Ainu with special reference to nonmetric cranial traits. *Journal of the Anthropological Society of Nippon* 99: 23–32.

Kozintsev AG. 1972. Nonmetrical traits on crania of 1000 BC from Minusinsk Hollow (Nemet-richeskie priznaki na cherepah 1-go tysyacheletiya do n.e. iz Minusinskoi kotloviny). *Arkhiv Anatomii Gistologii I Embriologii* (Leningrad) 62: 53–59.

Kozintsev AG. 1977. *Anthropological component and the origin of people of the Tagar culture* (Антропологический состав и происхождение населения Тагарской культуры). Leningrad: Nauka.

Movsesyan AA, Mamonova NN, Rychkov Yu G. 1975. Program and methods of study of cranial anomalies (Программа и методика исследования аномалии черепа). *Voprosy Antropologii* (Вопросы Антропологии) 51: 127–50.

Navaan D. 1975. *Bronze Age of eastern Mongolia (Dornod Mongoliin Khureliin ue)*. Ulaanbaatar: Mongolian Academy of Sciences.

Ossenberg NS. 1990. Origins and affinities of the native peoples of northwestern North America: The evidence of cranial nonmetric traits. In: Bonnichsen R, Steele DG, editors. *Method and theory for investigating the peopling of the Americas*. Corvallis, OR: Center for the Study of the First Americans. Pp. 79–115.

Sjøvold T. 1973. The occurrence of minor non-metrical variants in the skeleton and their quantitative treatment for population comparisons. *Homo* 24: 204–33.

Sutter RC, Mertz L. 2004. Nonmetric cranial trait variation and prehistoric biocultural change in the Azapa valley, Chile. *American Journal of Physical Anthropology* 123: 130–45.

Tumen D. 1977. *Anthropology of western Mongolia (K antropologii zapadnoi Mongolii)*. Studia Archeologica, Instituti Historiae Academiae Scientiarum, vol. 7, no. 5. Ulaanbaatar. Pp. 39–59.

Tumen D. 1985. Ethnogenesis of Mongolians from the paleoanthropological perspective (Вопросы этногенеза Монгольского народа в свете данных палеоантропологии). Ph.D. dissertation, Moscow State University.

Tumen D. 1992. Ethnogenesis of Xiongnu from the paleoanthropological perspective (Hunnu-chuudiin garal uusliig paleoantropologiin uudnees hundun sudalsan sudalgaanii zarim dun). In: Bira Sh, editor. *Proceedings of the 5th International Congress of Mongolists*, vol. 3. Ulaanbaatar: International Association for Mongol Studies. Pp. 55–59.

Tumen D, Oyungerel B, Uuriintsolmon Ts. 2002. Paleoanthropological study of Xiongnu from Mongolia (Mongolyn Hunnugiin paleoantropologi). *Proceedings of the National University of Mongolia, Ulaanbaatar* 187: 39–54.

Tumen D, Vanchigdash Ch. 2006. Physical characteristics of ancient populations from Mongolia (Mongolyn ertnii nuudelchdiin bie buttsiin ontslog). *Mongolian Journal of Anthropology, Archaeology and Ethnology* 2: 116–43.

Turbat Ts. 2006. The origin of Xiongnu archaeological culture based on funeral rites. *Mongolian Journal of Anthropology, Archaeology and Ethnology* 2: 22–36.

Turner CG II, Scott GR. 1977. Dentition of Easter Island. In: Graber TM, editor. *Orofacial growth and development.* Chicago: Mouton. Pp. 229–50.

Ward JH. 1963. Hierarchical grouping to optimize an objective function. *Journal of the American Statistical Association* 58: 236–44.

Wenger S. 1974. Craniomorphological anomalies in the historical populations of the central Danubian basin. *Annales Historico-Naturales Musei Nationalis Hungarici* 66: 413–27.

Wright J, Honeychurch W, and Amartuvshin C. 2009. The Xiongnu settlements of Egiin Gol, Mongolia. *Antiquity* 83: 372–87.

6

Tuberculosis and Population Movement across the Sea of Japan from the Neolithic Period to the Eneolithic

TAKAO SUZUKI

From prehistory until the present, humankind has been affected by a variety of infectious diseases. Major epidemics have caused the extermination of millions of human beings, at times leading to the downfall and even annihilation of entire nations (Sigerist 1943). The early African origin of the tuberculosis pathogen, *Mycobacterium tuberculosis* (Mostowy and Behr 2005), leprosy, *M. leprae* (Monot et al. 2005), and a number of other infectious agents (e.g., Linz et al. 2007) has now been documented by molecular phylogeny of this and related microorganisms. Thus, tuberculosis and other highly virulent infectious diseases have been a major natural selective factor in human evolution and have deeply influenced human population history and social organization.

Because the progression and spread of tuberculosis infection involves complex interactions between the host's immune system, the pathogen, and the environment, change in one will lead to change in another (Roberts and Buikstra 2003; Wilbur et al. 2008). With respect to the host and environment, factors such as population growth and increased population density, unsanitary living conditions, malnutrition, natural disasters, war, and migration may render humans more vulnerable to tuberculosis, an infection that often leaves specific lesions on the skeleton. It is very important to clarify the relationship between archaeological cases diagnosed as evidencing tuberculosis and the epidemiological factors that accelerated and aggravated the prevalence of tuberculosis, particularly in the early history of the disease. Its mere presence in an individual or a population, without an epidemiological context, is of minor significance in the evaluation of the biological and social implications of the disease (Powell 1991).

This chapter deals with the early prevalence of tuberculosis in Far East Asia from both a paleoepidemiological and a sociological point of view. There is now a substantial consensus (e.g., Brace and Nagai 1982; Turner 1990; Nakahashi 1995; Pietrusewsky 1999; Nakahashi et al. 2002; Yasuda 2002) that during the Eneolithic period,[1] which began around 2600 BC in China, a major influx of people and culture entered the principal Japanese islands by way of the Korean peninsula, resulting from a large-scale movement of human population originating in China. In particular, I would emphasize that evidence of infectious disease, as represented by tuberculosis, can be seen as an indicator of this population movement between China and Korea, as well as across the Sea of Japan to Japan during that time. While the study reported here may be somewhat less detailed than paleopathological syntheses previously developed for other regions, the results and implications presented in this chapter lay a foundation for further work on tuberculosis in the past, not only in Far East Asia but also in the Americas.

Historical Background of the Far East Asian Region

China and Korea

From around the fifth century BC to the third century AD, there was a large-scale migration of people from the Chinese mainland via the Korean peninsula across the Sea of Japan to the Japanese archipelago (see figure 6.1 for a summarized chronology). In China, iron weapons and infantry were first deployed during the Eastern Zhou (周) dynasty (770–221 BC). This period, which generally witnessed a fragmentation of political power in northern China (Tsuruma 1996), has traditionally been divided into the Spring and Autumn period (春秋時代) (770–476 BC) and the Warring States period (戦国時代) (475–221 BC). Rebellion by subordinate kings led to the annexation of smaller states and created huge numbers of refugees, particularly in the north. Finally, with the victory of the Qin (秦) state over its rivals, the first emperor, Qin Shi Huang Di (秦始皇帝), unified China in 221 BC. Subsequently, following a policy of continuous expansion, the Han (漢) dynasty (206 BC–AD 200) asserted sovereignty over vast regions of today's China.

During that same time, the northern peninsula of Korea was under the influence of the Chinese state of Yen (燕), one of a number of small competing polities based in the northern part of China and a notable producer of iron. From about the fourth to the third century BC, bronze and iron products were introduced to the northern part of Korea, accompanying one or more new populations, referred to in historical texts as the Yemaek (濊貊). According to the *Samguk Sagi* (三国史記) (*The History of Three Kingdoms in Korea*), the Yemaek were originally from the northeastern Chinese region of Liaoning (遼寧). These people invaded Korea, founding the Koguryo (高句

Age	China	Korea	Japan
BC 1,500	Shang Dynasty	Comb-Pattern Pottery Culture	Jomon (Cord-marked) Pottery Culture
		Non-Decorated Pottery Culture	
1,000	1027 Western Zhou		
		Songguk-ri Pottery	800
	770 Eastern Zhou Dynasty		(TR*)
500	Spring - Autumn period	(Bronze Age)	
	403	Suseog-ri Pottery	(AMS*)
	Warring States		300
	221 Qin Dynasty.	Nukdo Pottery	Yayoi Culture Itazuke Type II Pot.
	206 Western Han Dynasty	109	Sugu Type I Pottery
		Proto-Three-Kingdom (Iron Age)	Sugu Type II Pottery
0 AD	AD8		
	AD25 Eastern Han Dynasty		
200		Three-Kingdom (AD 313)	Kofun Period (ca. AD 300)

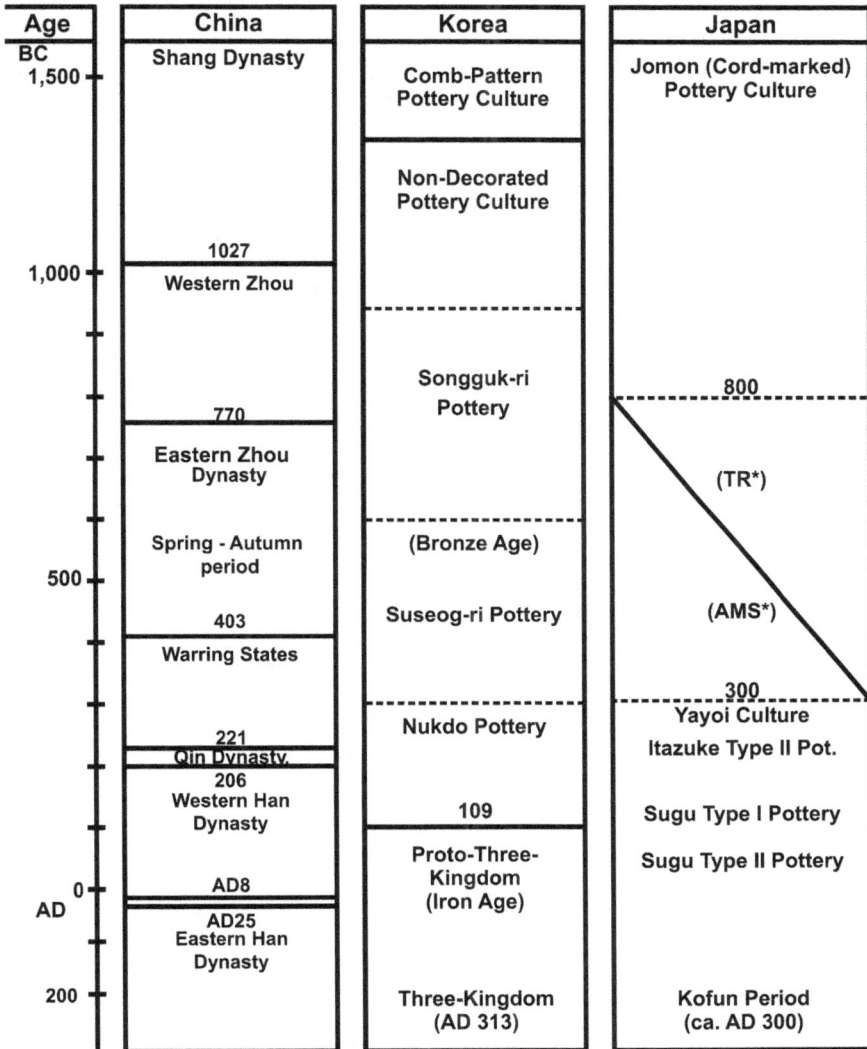

Figure 6.1. Late prehistoric and early historic periods of China, Korea, and Japan. (Note on transition between Yayoi and Jomon: * TR = in accord with traditional ceramic typologies and/or conventional ^{14}C dating; AMS = in accord with more recent ^{14}C dating by means of accelerator mass spectrometry.)

麗) Kingdom, and thus initiating the Korean Historical Age (Riotto 1989). In 108 BC, forces of the Han dynasty conquered the northern peninsula and established three military commands in the region. With the acquisition of new iron-working and stoneware production technology, Korea's Non-decorated Pottery (無文土器) culture developed in the southern peninsula, during this so-called Commandery period (108 BC–AD 313).

Japan

The ultimate origins of the Japanese people are not altogether clear, although finds of Paleolithic stone implements suggest that their ancestors have inhabited the archipelago for more than ten thousand years (Suzuki 1998). Dating of the earliest of the Japanese Neolithic cultures, Jomon, is still somewhat controversial, but Jomon lasted at least several thousand years, ending in about the third century BC (Harunari 1990). The principal subsistence strategies of the Jomon were hunting, fishing, and gathering. The Jomon made many of their utensils of clay, including pottery characterized by cord-marking (縄文). The Jomon often buried their dead under shell mounds, which have tended to protect their skeletal remains from the destructive effects of volcanic and acid soils (Suzuki 1965).

During the Eneolithic period—Yayoi (弥生) (third century BC to third century AD, according to traditional dating), which followed Jomon—a large number of immigrants migrated to the western part of Japan via the Korean peninsula. While the magnitude and timing of this new influx of people is still being debated, most anthropologists (e.g., Nakahashi 1995; Nakahashi and Iizuka 1998; Pietrusewsky 1999; Nakahashi et al. 2002) agree that this new immigrant group displaced and/or assimilated the Jomon hunter-gatherer-fishers. According to Hanihara (1987), using population growth simulation models, the total number of migrants from the Asian continent during the Yayoi period and through the seventh century AD is estimated to have been more than a million.

Hanihara (1987) also asserts that the relative proportions of native Jomon and migrants in the total Japanese population was about 1:9 or 2:8 in early historic times. Immigrants from continental East Asia apparently mixed with the Jomon aboriginals almost immediately upon entering the archipelago in large numbers. It was during this same period that the Japanese mastered the art of wet-rice cultivation, began to use metal implements, and set the fundamental pattern of Japanese tradition and life.

According to the traditional history of Japan, migration from the Korean peninsula continued until around the seventh century AD. From a paleopathological point of view, some new infectious diseases also seem to have been transmitted from the Asian mainland to Japan during that time. Japanese living in the western and central areas were most likely to have been affected by such migration, while Ainu in Hokkaido and Ryukyu Islanders seem to have remained unmixed (Hanihara 1991). Therefore, the influence of the admixture that took place after the Yayoi period is still evident in the western and central parts of Japan. However, the northern (Ainu) and southern (Ryukyu) people largely escaped genetic admixture with the Yayoi im-migrants and, as a consequence, retain many of the physical characteristics of the indigenous Jomon people.

Korea and Japan (the Nukdo Archaeological Site)

Nukdo Island (勒島) is one of the archaeological sites where strong evidence has been found of interchange between Korea and Japan from the end of the Neolithic to the beginning of the Eneolithic. Nukdo Island is a small island off the coast of Sachon (泗川), the most southern part of the Korean peninsula. Excavation at the Nukdo archaeological site, which constitutes the entire is-land, produced an enormous amount of plain, undecorated Mumon pottery (無文土器), identified as the Nukdo type (勒島式) and representative of pottery from the late Non-decorated (or Mumon) Pottery culture of the Ko-rean peninsula (Kyongnam Archaeological Institute 2003, 2006).

A large number of pieces of Sugu I type (須玖I 式) pottery and Sugu II type (須玖II 式) pottery—typical of the northern part of Kyushu, Japan—were also found on Nukdo Island, together with the Nukdo type pottery. Sugu I and Sugu II pottery are representative of the middle Yayoi period, dating from about 100 BC to AD 1. Other finds at Nukdo included Chinese coins made during the Early (Western) Han dynasty (202 BC–AD 8), which extended its territorial administration through the Commandery System to the northern part of the Korean peninsula.

These archaeological materials, particularly the quantity and variety of pottery, suggest that Nukdo was a trade center involved in exchange between the southern part of Korea and the northern part of Kyushu. The skeletal remains of more than 200 individuals were unearthed at Nukdo during field seasons between 1985 and 1999. Numerous fragments of animal bone were also recovered, including the remains of dogs, as well as the scapulae of bo-vids that were cracked and burned while being used for the purposes of divi-nation (Busan University 1989).

Tuberculosis

Oldest Descriptions of Tuberculosis in Far East Asia

Tuberculosis is described in many older medical documents as having been present in China, Korea, and Japan for more than 500 years. In China, the first description of tuberculosis appeared in the famous medical book *Shang Han Za Bing Lun* (傷寒雜病論), or *Essay on Typhoid and Miscellaneous Dis-eases Combined,* a sixteen-volume set, written by Zhang Zhongjing (張仲

景) in AD 210, during the Han dynasty. Zhang Zhongjing, one of the greatest physicians that China ever produced, is often spoken of as the Chinese Hippocrates and is venerated as the Sage of Medicine. Later, this medical textbook was split into two parts that were published separately, as the *Shang Han Lun* (傷寒論), or *Essay on Typhoid,* and the *Jin Kui Yao Lue* (金櫃要略), or *Synopsis of the Golden Chamber.* A detailed description of the sputum and cough probably attributable to pulmonary tuberculosis can be found in the *Jin Kui Yao Lue* (Wong and Wu 1985).

In Japan, the oldest description of tuberculosis was written by Yasuyori Tanba (丹波康頼) in a medical book titled *I Shin Hou* (医心方), or *Essentials of Medical Treatment.* This 30-volume comprehensive textbook of internal medicine was published in AD 984. The symptoms of pulmonary tuberculosis and its treatment are described in volume 13 (Okanishi 1975). Also among the oldest descriptions of the major symptoms of pulmonary tuberculosis—including cough, sputum, and fever—are those contained in two historical textbooks of indigenous medicine in Korea: *Hyang-yak-jip-seong-bang* (郷楽集成方), or *Comprehensive and Indigenous Medical Book,* published in AD 1433; and *Tong-I Bogam* (東医宝鑑), or *East Medical Textbook,* in AD 1610 (Miki 1985).

Paleopathological Evidence of Tuberculosis in Far East Asia

According to a number of previous reviews on the antiquity of tuberculosis in the Old World, there is no evidence of the disease prior to Neolithic times (Steinbock 1976; Ortner and Putschar 1981; Aufderheide and Rodriguez-Martin 1998). The earliest evidence of tuberculosis in Europe comes from a Neolithic grave near Heidelberg, Germany, dated to about 5000 BC (Bartels 1907), and another in Italy dated to about 3500–4000 BC (Formicola et al. 1987; Canci et al. 1996). In Asia, evidence of an early case of possible tuberculosis was found at a prehistoric site in northern Thailand, dated to around 2400–900 BC (Pietrusewsky 1974). Tayles and Buckley (2004) have also suggested tuberculosis as the diagnosis for the cause of spinal lesions found on the remains of a young adult female from the Noen U-Loke site, located near the valley of the Mun River in northeastern Thailand, which has been dated as Iron Age (300 BC–AD 200).

In the Far East, the earliest case of tuberculosis reported so far dates to the late Longshan (龍山) period in China (Pechenkina et al. 2007). Longshan was a Late Neolithic culture that succeeded the Yangshao (仰韶) culture and persisted from about 3000 BC to 2000 BC. It was centered on the central and lower Yellow River (黄河), and Longshan sites are marked by finds of polished gray and black pottery. In much of the lowlands, population increased dramatically during this period. The affected individual (M7) was recovered from a burial unearthed at Meishan, a site in Henan (河南) Province that dates to approximately 2500–2000 BC. The remains exhibit an angular deformity of the spine, resulting from complete resorption of the 9th and partial resorption of the 8th thoracic vertebral bodies, a condition consistent with spinal tuberculosis (figure 6.2; see also Pechenkina et al. 2007: fig. 18.3). In summary, the earliest evidence of tuberculosis can be traced back to approximately 4,000 years ago in the Far East.

Another possible case of early tuberculosis in China is found on the fully preserved cadaver of an older female, discovered in 1972 at Mawangtui (馬王堆), on the eastern outskirts of Changsha (長沙), in Hunan (湖南) Prov-

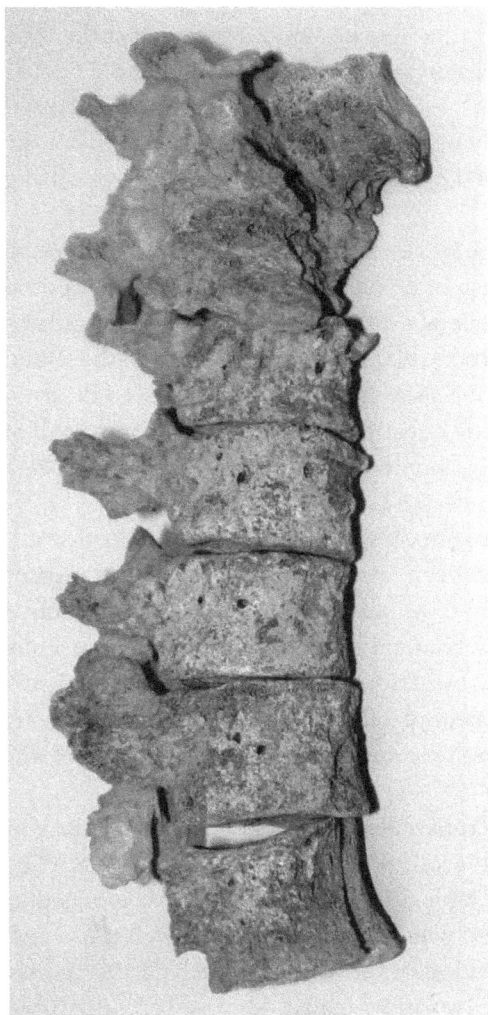

Figure 6.2. Left lateral view of spinal column dating to c. 3000–2000 BC (M7, Meishan site, Henan Province, China), showing collapse and angular deformity around the 9th thoracic vertebra. (Photo by E. Pechenkina)

ince. This woman, estimated to have been over 50 years of age at the time of her death, has been identified as the wife of the chancellor of the Kingdom of Chansha at about 200 BC, during the time of the Western Han dynasty (後漢) (Hunan Medical Institute 1980). Systemic autopsy studies and pathological examination revealed that she suffered from general atherosclerosis, multiple cholelithiasis, and schistosomiasis japonica. Moreover, many calcified foci were identified in the upper lobe and hilum of the left lung, probably indicating the presence of pulmonary tuberculosis.

Evidence of a possible case of early tuberculosis in Korea stems from a skeleton recovered at Nukdo (勒島), which appears to date to sometime between the beginning of the first century BC and the end of the first century AD. The skeleton, now housed at the Kyongnam Archeology Institute (Suzuki et al. 2008), is that of a young adult female (15–20 years old at the time of death), which shows abnormal fusion and destruction at T11 and T12. The last two thoracic and the first lumbar (L1) vertebral bodies had collapsed ventrally, with multiple small and larger confluent cavities localized on the anterior part of the body, all caused by severe pathological changes during life.

Massive resorption and collapse of the body of T12 resulted in marked kyphosis of the thoracolumbar vertebral column (figure 6.3A). The central part of the body of T12 had completely disappeared due to severe inflammatory destruction. The exposed trabecular bone that constituted the lateral pillars of the remaining spongy bone showed active resorptive and destructive changes that occurred during the infectious process. At L1, almost half of the body had disappeared, probably from lytic processes. The collapsed body resulted in a wedge-shape appearance at L1.

The anterior part of the remaining body was most affected by the disease. The whole surface of the body had been eroded by destructive and resorptive changes (figure 6.3B). These observations are consistent with destructive processes of the vertebral body by bilateral or circumferential paraosseous abscessing. In addition, new bone formation was found on the visceral surfaces, resulting in extensive periosteal plaque, consisting of porous fibrous bone, rather than compact bone in the lower left ribs (probably 9th to 12th; see Suzuki et al. 2008: fig. 5).

Nine typical cases of early spinal tuberculosis have been reported to date in Japan (Ogata 1972; Suzuki 1978, 1985, 1988, 1991, 2000; Tashiro 1982; Suzuki and Inoue 2007), as shown in table 6.1. None of these cases belonged to the prehistoric Jomon population, of which a great number of well-preserved skeletons have been studied. The oldest of these cases of spinal tuberculosis discovered so far in Japan include two in which rib lesions were identified

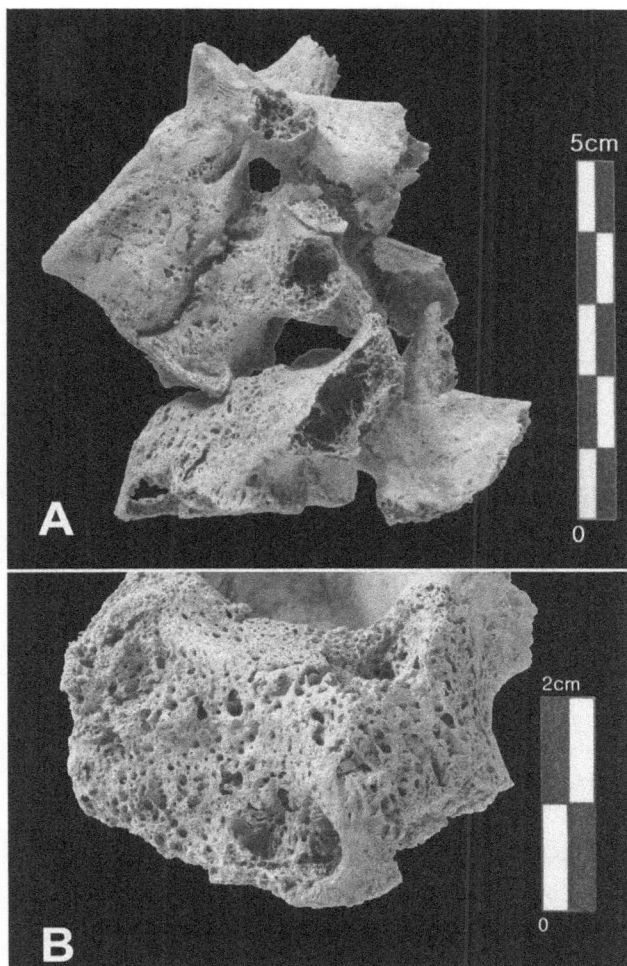

Figure 6.3. *A*, Left lateral view showing collapsed and wedge-shaped T12 fusing with T11 (#117, Nukdo site, Korea); *B*, anterior aspect of the vertebral body of L1 (#117, Nukdo site, Korea) showing multiple small and larger confluent cavities with severe destruction caused by inflammatory processes.

from skeletal remains excavated at the Eneolithic, or Yayoi, Aoyakamijichi site, which faces the Sea of Japan from the southern part of Honshu Island and is dated by means of dendrochronology to between 454 BC and AD 124 (Suzuki and Inoue 2007).

A total of 5323 pieces of human bone, stemming from at least 109 individuals, have been unearthed at the Aoyakamijichi site. Found scattered across a low-lying riverside plain, these remains are thought to be those of massacre victims either left unburied and scattered by scavengers or reburied individually in the aftermath. Apart from the human skeletal remains, numerous fragments of animal bone were also found at the site, including many bovid scapulae bearing divination marks. Many artifacts, including fishhooks, fish spears, and harpoons made of bone, as well as wooden boards with images of

Table 6.1. Paleopathological cases of bone tuberculosis previously reported from Japan

Designation/(Institution)	Period[a]	Sex[b]	Age[c]	Location of lesion	Reference
Shiroyama No. 3 (Nigata University)	Kofun	M	Adult	Spine (lumbar–sacrum)	Ogata 1972
Unoki No. 3 (Tokyo University)	Kofun	F	Mature	Spine (thoracic–lumbar)	Suzuki 1978
Asahidai No. 9 (Nagasaki University)	Kofun	M	Mature	Spine (thoracic–lumbar); ribs	Tashiro 1982
Ainu A-1336 (Tokyo University)	Recent	F	Adult	Sacrum	Suzuki 1985
#325268 (NMNH, Smithsonian)	Recent	M	Adult	Spine (thoracic–lumbar)	Suzuki 1988
Okuma-Ku-2 (Doigahama Anthropology Museum)	Recent	F	Adult	Spine (thoracic)	Suzuki 2000
Ainu A-1453 (Tokyo University)	Recent	M	Adult	Spine (cervical–thoracic)	Suzuki 2000
Aoyakamijichi No. 31711 (Tottori University)	Yayoi	?	Adult	Spine (thoracic)	Suzuki and Inoue 2007
Aoyakamijichi No. 30616 (Tottori University)	Yayoi	?	Adult	Spine (thoracic)	Suzuki and Inoue 2007

[a] Yayoi corresponds to the Eneolithic (c. 300 BC–AD 300); Kofun to the Protohistoric (c. AD 300–700); Recent to the Edo period through Meiji period (AD 1700–1900).
[b] M = male; F = female; ? = indeterminate sex.
[c] Adult = approximately 20–40 years old; mature = approximately 40 or more years old.

sharks on one side and a fleet on the other, have also been recovered there. Such finds suggest that the people inhabiting this site during the Eneolithic Yayoi period were engaged in fishing and rice farming, and furthermore that long-distance commerce to and from the Korean peninsula, including Nukdo Island, was conducted primarily using rudimentary watercraft.

Among the remains recovered at Aoyakamijichi, there were two identified cases of spinal tuberculosis and at least four ribs showing inflammatory changes likely caused by tuberculosis. However, because of the mix of individual bones scattered across the site, it was difficult to ascertain how many individuals were specifically affected by this virulent infectious disease. One possible case of spinal tuberculosis pertained to an apparent adult male (No. 31711) showing block-vertebrae formation, which is very characteristic of spinal tuberculosis. The bodies of T3 to T7 were almost completely destroyed and had collapsed into an irregular bony mass. In spite of this vertebral collapse and the resulting deformity, the diameter of the spinal canal was normal (figure 6.4A; see also Suzuki and Inoue 2007: figs. 2 and 3). At T5, there was a strong angulation of almost 90° forming marked kyphosis.

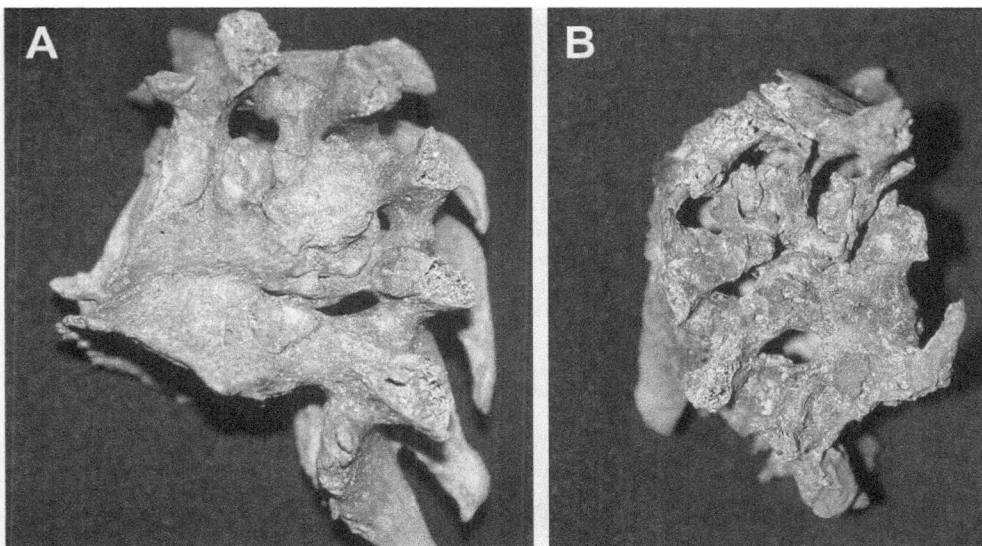

Figure 6.4. *A*, Left lateral view of the vertebral block reveals the upper and the lower terminal plates almost touching because of marked spinal angulation (No. 31711, Aoyakamijichi site, Tottori Prefecture, Japan); *B*, right lateral view showing kyphosis at T8 and fused mass of adjacent vertebral bodies T10 and T11 (No. 30616, Aoyakamijichi site, Tottori Prefecture, Japan).

Another possible case of spinal tuberculosis was found on an adult skeleton (No. 30616), which also showed marked kyphosis, with block-vertebrae formation from T7 to T11 (figure 6.4B). While the bodies of T10 and T11 retained their individual shapes, the bodies of the remaining three thoracic vertebrae had almost disappeared, and their remnants had become joined into a wedge-shaped formation. Gross observation of the inside of the fused vertebral bodies showed a large cavity without trabecular bone structure. At T8 a marked angulation of almost 90° could be seen, forming a marked kyphosis.

These two adult vertebral columns, showing very similar inflammatory changes, with a presumptive diagnosis of spinal tuberculosis, have very marked kyphosis at the middle or lower thoracic vertebrae, with complete destruction and collapse of the vertebral bodies involved and minimal bone regeneration. Some inflammatory bone changes could be found also in one rib (no. 30993). The lesion showed coarse and proliferative changes on the visceral surface of the middle or lower rib. Evidence of three probable cases of spinal tuberculosis has been discovered from sites on Honshu and Kyushu dating to the Protohistoric Kofun period (figure 6.5). Clearly, tuberculosis must have already been prevalent throughout the Japanese archipelago by the Kofun period.

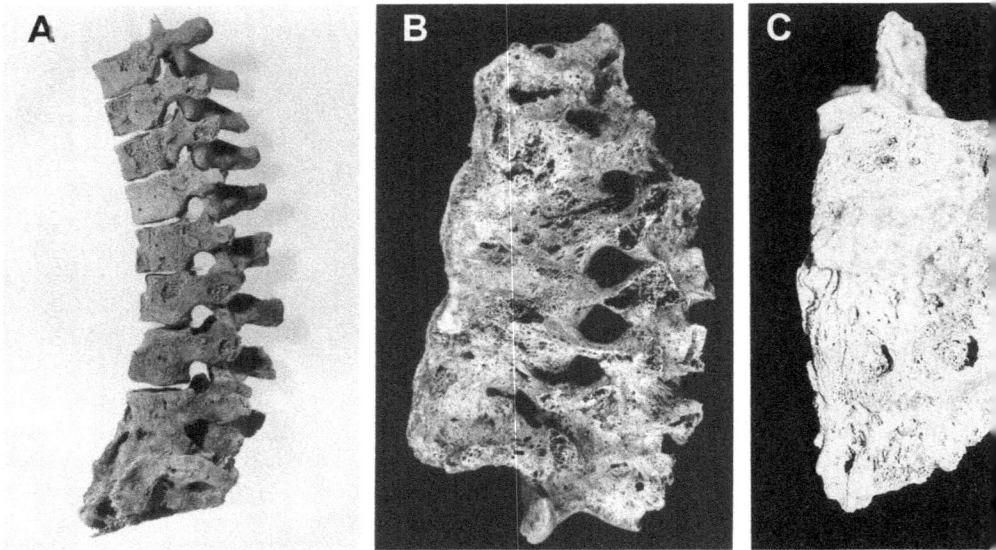

Figure 6.5. Three cases of spinal tuberculosis from the Protohistoric Kofun period in Japan: *A*, Shiroyama-Kofun site, Chiba Prefecture; *B*, Unoki-Kofun site, Tokyo; *C*, Asahidai-Kofun site, Miyazaki Prefecture, Kyushu.

First Transmission of Tuberculosis to Japan

As summarized in the preceding section, evidence of the oldest cases of tuberculosis discovered so far in Japan are found on skeletal remains stemming from the Yayoi and Kofun periods. In contrast, no instance of this disease has been identified in the large number of known well-preserved and carefully studied skeletal remains dating to the prehistoric Jomon period. The skeletal remains of more than ten thousand Jomon period individuals, curated at various institutions in Japan, have been or are presently being studied from diverse perspectives, including the paleopathological and that of the population history of the Japanese. In spite of such intense scrutiny, no case of Jomon spinal tuberculosis has been identified. This strongly suggests that tuberculosis first appeared in Japan during the Eneolithic Yayoi period, probably transmitted by carriers among the large number of immigrants who came to Japan from the Korean peninsula at that time.

There would appear to be at least two alternative explanations as to why no evidence of tuberculosis has been identified from the large number of well-preserved skeletal remains dating to the Jomon period. The first hypothesis attributes the lack of tuberculosis during Jomon to lower population density. Tuberculosis is a density-dependent disease and may have first become established in human population aggregates. In this context, even if tuberculosis had existed during the Jomon period, it might have existed in a very limited area as a local endemic form. Tuberculosis reached epidemic proportions after the Yayoi and Kofun periods, following a rapid increase in population density.

The second hypothesis is more probable and relates to the migration of *Mycobacterium tuberculosis*. As stated previously, a great number of people from the Asian continent migrated to Japan via the Korean peninsula during the Yayoi and Kofun periods. Not only did they introduce various cultural characteristics, including the Chinese writing system, ideology, and religion (Confucianism and Buddhism), as well as agricultural methods and associated technology, but they brought some new infectious diseases, probably including smallpox, measles, and tuberculosis. These new virulent infectious diseases must have been disseminated throughout the country, accompanying a rapid increase of the population in Japan during the Yayoi and Kofun periods.

One of the major reasons for such a rapid increase in the population in Japan at that time was population movement to escape the chaos of wars during the Spring and Autumn period and the Warring States period in China (c. 600 BC–221 BC). China during the Warring States period of the Eastern Zhou dynasty was in such a state of turmoil that migration to safer regions or forced evacuations of strategic areas affected the Chinese population itself, which surely must have had a remarkable effect on neighboring people (Tsuruma 1996). Particularly in the northern part of China, waves of invasion into Korean territory were instigated by the state of Yen at around the end of the fourth and the beginning of the third century BC.

Even after the establishment of both the first empire (Qin, at 221 BC) and the second empire ([Western] Han dynasty, at 202 BC), the Xiongnu menace drove the Han to intervene militarily in Korea in 109 BC, destroying the state of Wiman Choson and establishing the three commanderies of Lelang, Lintun, and Zhenfan (the last of which would persist until AD 313), and later that of Xuantu in Manchuria (Mullie 1969; Riotto 1989). These continuous conflicts and military operations were largely contemporaneous with the movement of people from the northern to southern part of the Korean peninsula, which would have had a great influence on migration from Korea to the Japanese archipelago across the Sea of Japan.

Contemporaneously with an increase in the numbers of immigrants into Japan from the continent during the Eneolithic Yayoi and Protohistoric Kofun periods, people began to (1) domesticate cattle; (2) develop agriculture, leading to sedentism and urbanism; and (3) produce crowded conditions leading to frequent conflicts. There is no evidence of domesticated cattle in Japan during the Jomon period. Bones of domesticated fowl, cattle, and horses have been reported occasionally in Yayoi sites and frequently from the Kofun period (Nishinakagawa 1992). Since *M. bovis* infection in humans is indistinguishable from *M. tuberculosis* in pathogenesis, lesions, and clinical findings, even in modern-day humans (Moda et al. 1996), we cannot specify which species of *Mycobacterium* was responsible for the spinal tuberculosis in the cases presented in this study.

Among the factors influencing the early outbreak and transmission of tuberculosis in this region, rice agriculture deserves particular consideration. In a broader perspective, studies of the prehistory and historical-biological relationships of the peoples of East Asia and Southeast Asia have recently centered on the so-called agricultural colonization model composed of the domestication of rice, the development of agriculture, and the dispersal of languages emanating most likely from southern China (Bellwood 2000; Higham 2001). It has now been established that wild rice (*Oryza rufipogon*) existed in the middle and lower reaches of the Yangtze River in China. Wild rice has the characteristics of a water plant and is either a perennial or an annual grass. "Wild type" wild rice possesses some features of cultivated rice (*Oryza sativa*), which emerged as a result of mutation. The earliest rice cultivation probably began no later than about 7600 cal BP in the Chinese province of Zhejiang, located in the lower reaches of the Yangtze River (揚子江) (Yasuda 2002).

Rice and the art of its cultivation reached Japan both directly from regions south of the Yangtze River in China and from Korea between the fifth and second century BC. The introduction of agricultural practices, including techniques of reclaiming rice paddy fields, irrigation systems, and the transplanting of rice seedlings, as well as harvesting and threshing, marked the beginning of a rice-centered agricultural age in the western part of Japan, which was to develop and eventually bring the hunting-and-gathering culture of the Jomon period to an end. Various customs and rituals associated with rice paddy cultivation were also introduced. Cultural and social changes from Jomon to Yayoi accompanying the development of agriculture led to the development of sedentism, urbanism, and human crowding, all of which are linked to population density–associated infectious diseases, including tuberculosis.

In all probability, tuberculosis, which is a density-dependent infectious disease, was introduced into Japan by waves of immigrants during the Eneolithic Yayoi period. These immigrants came from Korea, probably via Nukdo Island, which was one of the trade centers; cultural exchange between southern Korea and northern Kyushu first began mainly in the western part of Japan, including the area of the Aoyakamijichi site, and spread quickly along with the associated increase in population and urbanization. Various infectious diseases, including tuberculosis and probably including measles and smallpox as well, were also exchanged and transmitted between these two regions at that time. These new infectious diseases were likely fatal to the "virgin" host populations living in a previously infection-free environment. They caused serious damage to the prehistoric Jomon people, resulting in a rapid reduction of the indigenous population.

In general, as pointed out by Cockburn (1963), because the infectious agents that kill the host tend to die off quickly as well, there is a tendency for the infectious agent to become attenuated and survive as a less virulent agent to maintain infection in new hosts. At the same time, the host population usually becomes more resistant to the pathogen, since those who survive acquire more effective immune responses. These changes are termed coevolution of the pathogen and the host. Such a complicated process of change in population immunity results in a change of infection from an acute to a chronic form, the results of which are more commonly detectable on archaeological human skeletal remains (Ortner 1999).

Following the first outbreak of tuberculosis during the Yayoi period, which caused high mortality among the indigenous Jomon population, it is likely that the coevolution process eventually resulted in a high prevalence of tuberculosis in Japan. During the Kofun period, which followed the Yayoi era, tuberculosis was manifested more commonly in a chronic form, whereby the infectious agent survives in the host by causing nonlethal harm.

How and When Did Tuberculosis Spread to the Americas?

Ancient cases of tuberculosis in Far East Asia at around 2200–2000 years BP, probably associated with population movement at that time, raise a question concerning the origin and transmission of tuberculosis to the Americas. Many archaeological and physical anthropological studies estimate that the first migrants from Northeast Asia entered the American continent around 14,000–12,000 years BP across what is now the Bering Strait (Greenberg et al. 1986; Neves and Pucciarelli 1991; Sardi et al. 2005). However, the earliest evidence of tuberculosis in Asia dates to much later than the time of this estimated population movement through Beringia to the Americas. It is also clear that the earliest cases of tuberculosis found in the Old World, including those from Far East Asia, are dated to much earlier in time than the cases in the New World. On the American continents, the earliest recognized cases of tuberculosis date to only approximately 1500 years ago in South America and 1,000 years ago in North America (Roberts and Buikstra 2003). In this context, the dating of the earliest cases of tuberculosis to well after the disappearance of Beringia suggests independent dispersals of this disease in Asia and in the Americas.

However, recent molecular evidence on the ancient origin and progenitor of *M. tuberculosis* suggests that tubercule bacilli were contemporaneous even with early hominids in East Africa and have thus been coevolving with their human hosts much longer than previously thought (Brosch et al. 2002; Guiterrez et al. 2005). From a paleopathological point of view, it seems odd that tuberculosis coevolved over a long time with early human beings, while the earliest evidence of skeletal tuberculosis dates to only the past 10,000 years, and probably much later in the New World, long after the formation of larger sedentary populations. So, what was the likely origin of ancient American tuberculosis? As pointed out by Roberts and Buikstra (2003), the many mysteries that surround the origin and spread of ancient tuberculosis in the New World will doubtless concern medical and anthropological scholarship well into the twenty-first century.

Further research is required to better understand the early occurrence and transmission of tuberculosis in Far East Asia and the Americas. The cases of tuberculosis described here provide evidence for the contemporaneous existence of this disease in both of these regions, are an excellent biological indicator of population movement across the Sea of Japan, and give us additional challenging research material concerning the spread of tuberculosis across the Pacific Ocean.

Note

1. The term *Eneolithic* is used to refer to the transition between the Neolithic and Bronze Age, when metal implements were first introduced and used alongside stone tools.

Literature Cited

Aufderheide AC, Rodriguez-Martin C. 1998. *The Cambridge encyclopedia of human paleopathology.* Cambridge: Cambridge University Press.

Bartels P. 1907. Tuberculose (Wirbelkaries) in Jüngerer Steinzeit (Vertebral tuberculosis in the Neolithic). *Archiv Für Anthropologie* 6: 243–55.

Bellwood P. 2000. Some thoughts on understanding the human colonization of the Pacific. *People and Culture in Oceania* 16: 5–17.

Brace CL, Nagai M. 1982. Japanese tooth size: Past and present. *American Journal of Physical Anthropology* 59: 399–411.

Brosch R, Gordon SV, Marmisse M, Brodin P, Buchrieser C, Eigmeier K, Garnier T, Guiterrez C. 2002. A new evolutionary scenario for the *Mycobacterium tuberculosis* complex. *Proceedings of the National Academy of Sciences* 99: 3684–89.

Busan University Museum. 1989. *Nukdo archeological site*. Busan: Busan University Museum (釜山大学博物館).

Canci A, Minozzi S, Tarli S. 1996. New evidence of tuberculous spondylitis from Neolithic Liguria (Italy). *International Journal of Osteoarchaeology* 6: 497–501.

Cockburn A. 1963. *The evolution and eradication of infectious disease*. Baltimore, MD: Johns Hopkins University Press.

Formicola V, Milanesi Q, Scarshini C. 1987. Evidence of spinal tuberculosis at the beginning of the fourth millennium BC from Arene Candide Cave (Liguria, Italy). *American Journal of Physical Anthropology* 72: 1–6.

Greenberg JM, Turner CG II, Zegura SL. 1986. The settlement of the Americas: Comparison of the linguistic, dental and genetic evidence. *Current Anthropology* 27: 477–97.

Gutierrez MC, Brisse S, Brosch R, Fabre M, Omais B, Marmisse M, Supply P, Vincent V. 2005. Ancient origin and gene mosaicism of the progenitor of *Mycobacterium tuberculosis*. *PLoS Pathogens* 1: e5. doi:10.1371/journal.ppat.0010005.

Hanihara K. 1987. Estimation of the number of early migrants to Japan: A simulative study. *Journal of the Anthropological Society of Nippon* (日本人類学会雑誌) 95: 391–403.

Hanihara K. 1991. Dual structure model for the population history of the Japanese. *Japan Review* 2: 1–33.

Harunari H. 1990. *Yayoi jidai no hajimari (The beginning of the Yayoi period)*. Tokyo: Tokyo University Press.

Higham CFW. 2001. Prehistory, language and human biology: Is there a consensus in East and Southeast Asia? In: Jin L, Seiestad M, Xiao C, editors. *Genetic, linguistic and archeological perspectives on human diversity in Southeast Asia*. Hackensack, NJ: World Scientific. Pp. 3–16.

Hunan Medical Institute. 1980. *Study of an ancient cadaver in Mawangtui Tomb No. 1 of the Han dynasty in Changsha*. Beijing: Editorial Board of the Study of an Ancient Cadaver in Mawangtui Tomb No. 1.

Kyongnam Archeological Institute. 2003. *Nukdo shellmound: A Area site*. Shinju: Kyongnam Archeological Institute.

Kyongnam Archeological Institute. 2006. *Nukdo shellmound (V) archaeology*. Shinju: Kyongnam Archeological Institute.

Linz B, Balloux F, Moodley Y, Manica A, Liu H, Roumagnac P, Falush D, Stamer C, Prugnolle F, van der Merwe SW, Yamaoka Y, Graham DY, Perez-Trallero E, Wadstrom, T, Suerbaum S, Achtman, M. 2007. An African origin for the intimate association between humans and *Helicobacter pylori*. *Nature* 445: 915–18.

Miki S. 1985. *Chronological table of Korean medicine*. Tokyo: Shibunkaku.

Moda G, Daborn CJ, Grange JM, Cosivi O. 1996. Zoonoic importance of *M. bovis*. *Tubercle and Lung Disease* 77: 103–8.

Monot M, Honoré N, Garnier T, Araoz R, Coppée J-Y, Lacroix C, Sow S, Spencer JS, Truman RW, Williams DL, Gelber R, Virmond M, Flageul B, Cho S-N, Ji B, Paniz-Mondolfi A, Convit J, Young S, Fine PE, Rasolofo V, Brennan PJ, Cole ST. 2005. On the origin of leprosy. *Science* 308: 1040–42.

Mostowy S, Behr MA. 2005. The origins and evolution of *Mycobacterium tuberculosis*. *Clinics in Chest Medicine* 26: 207–16.

Mullie JLM. 1969. Les Toung-hou. *Central Asiatic Journal* 12: 241–49.

Nakahashi T. 1995. Temporal craniometric changes from the Jomon to the Modern period in western Japan. *American Journal of Physical Anthropology* 90: 409–25.

Nakahashi T, Iizuka M. 1998. Anthropological study of the transition from the Jomon to the Yayoi period in Northern Kyushu using morphological and paleodemographical features. *Anthropological Science* 106: 31–53.

Nakahashi T, Minchang L, Yamaguchi B. 2002. Anthropological study on the cranial measurements of the human remains from Jiangnan region, China. In: Nakahashi T, Minchang L, editors. *Ancient people in the Jiangnan region, China: Anthropological study on the origin of the Yayoi people in northern Kyushu.* Kyushu: Kyushu University Press. Pp. 17–33.

Neves WA, Pucciarelli HM. 1991. Morphological affinities of the first Americans: An exploratory analysis based on early South American human remains. *Journal of Human Evolution* 21: 261–73.

Nishinakagawa S. 1992. *Origin of cattle and horse in Japan—based on the archeo-zoological material.* Tokyo: Reports for the Grants-in-Aid on Scientific Research of Ministry of Education, Science and Culture.

Ogata T. 1972. Paleopathological studies on the ancient Japanese skeletons. *Niigata Medical Journal* 86: 466–77.

Okanishi J. 1975. *Man and tuberculosis.* Tokyo: Ishiyaku Shuppan.

Ortner DJ. 1999. Paleopathology: Implications for the history and evolution of tuberculosis. In: Pálfi G et al., editors. *Tuberculosis: Past and present.* Szeged: Golden Book and Tuberculosis Foundation. Pp. 255–61.

Ortner DJ, Putschar WGJ. 1981. *Identification of pathological conditions in human skeletal remains.* Washington, DC: Smithsonian Institution Press.

Pechenkina EA, Benfer RA Jr., Ma X. 2007. Diet and health in the Neolithic of the Wei and middle Yellow River basins, northern China. In: Cohen MN, Crane-Kramer GMM, editors. *Ancient health: Skeletal indicators of agricultural and economic intensification.* Gainesville: University Press of Florida. Pp. 255–72.

Pietrusewsky M. 1974. *Non Nok Tha: The human skeletal remains from the 1966 excavations at Non Nok Tha, northeastern Thailand.* University of Otago Studies in Prehistoric Anthropology, vol. 6. Dunedin: University of Otago.

Pietrusewsky M. 1999. Multivariate craniometric investigations of Japanese, Asians, and Pacific Islanders. In: Omoto K, editor. *Interdisciplinary perspectives on the origins of the Japanese.* Proceedings of the 11th International Symposium of the International Research Center for Japanese Studies, Kyoto 1996. Pp. 65–104.

Powell ML. 1991. Endemic treponematosis and tuberculosis in the prehistoric southeastern United States: Biological costs of chronic endemic disease. In: Ortner DJ, Aufderheide AC, editors. *Human paleopathology: Current syntheses and future options.* Washington, DC: Smithsonian Institution Press. Pp. 173–80.

Riotto M. 1989. *The Bronze Age in Korea.* Italian School of East Asian Studies Occasional Papers 1. Kyoto: Istituto Italiano di Cultura.

Roberts CA, Buikstra JE. 2003. *The bioarchaeology of tuberculosis: A global view on a reemerging disease.* Gainesville: University Press of Florida.

Sardi ML, Rozzi FR, Gonzales-Jose R, Pucciarelli HM. 2005. South Amerindian craniofacial morphology: Diversity and implications for American evolution. *American Journal of Physical Anthropology* 128: 747–56.

Sigerist HE. 1943. *Civilization and disease.* Ithaca, NY: Cornell University Press. (Japanese version, Tokyo: Iwanami-Shoten, 1975.)

Steinbock RT. 1976. *Paleopathological diagnosis and interpretation.* Springfield, IL: Charles C. Thomas.

Suzuki H. 1965. *The skeletal remains in Japan.* Tokyo: Iwanami-Shoten.

Suzuki T. 1978. A paleopathological study of the vertebral columns of the Japanese from Jomon to Edo period. *Journal of the Anthropological Society of Nippon* (日本人類学会雑誌) 86: 321–36.

Suzuki T. 1985. Paleopathological diagnosis of bone tuberculosis in the lumbosacral region. *Journal of the Anthropological Society of Nippon* (日本人類学会雑誌) 93: 381–90.

Suzuki T. 1988. Bone pathology found in the Japanese skeletal collection housed in the Smithsonian Institution. In: Nagai Y, editor. *Formation of Japanese people and culture.* Tokyo: Rokkou Shuppan. Pp. 163–74.

Suzuki T. 1991. Paleopathological study on infectious disease in Japan. In: Ortner DJ, Aufderheide AC, editors. *Human paleopathology: Current syntheses and future options.* Washington, DC: Smithsonian Institution Press. Pp. 128–39.

Suzuki T. 1998. Indicator of stress in prehistoric Jomon skeletal remains in Japan. Supplement, *Anthropological Science* (日本人類学会雑誌) 106: S127–S137.

Suzuki T. 2000. Bone tuberculosis in paleopathology: Evidences from Ainu and Ryuku Islanders. *Bone* 14: 487–91.

Suzuki T, Fujita H, Choi JG. 2008. New evidence of tuberculosis from prehistoric Korea-Population movement and early evidence of tuberculosis in Far East Asia. *American Journal of Physical Anthropology* 136: 357–60.

Suzuki T, Inoue T. 2007. Earliest evidence of spinal tuberculosis from the aneolithic Yayoi period in Japan. *International Journal of Osteoarchaeology* 17: 392–402.

Tashiro K. 1982. Paleopathological study on human bone excavated in Kyushu, Japan. *Nagasaki Medical Journal* (長崎医学雑誌) 57: 77–102.

Tayles N, Buckley HR. 2004. Leprosy and tuberculosis in Iron Age Southeast Asia? *American Journal of Physical Anthropology* 125: 239–56.

Tsuruma K. 1996. *An approach to the Qin and Han dynasty.* World History Library 6. Tokyo: Yamakawa.

Turner CG II. 1990. Major features of Sundadonty and Sinodonty, including suggestions about East Asian microevolution, population history, and late Pleistocene relationships with Australian Aboriginals. *American Journal of Physical Anthropology* 82: 295–317.

Wilbur AK, Farnbach AW, Knudson KJ, Buikstra JE. 2008. Diet, tuberculosis, and the paleopathological record. *Current Anthropology* 49: 963–91.

Wong KC, Wu LT. 1985. *History of Chinese medicine: Being a chronicle of medical happenings in China from ancient times to the present period.* Taipei: Southern Materials Center, ROC. Pp. 906.

Yasuda Y. 2002. Origin of pottery and agriculture in East Asia. In: Yasuda Y, editor. *The origins of pottery and agriculture.* Yangtze River Civilization Programme. Singapore: Lustre Press. Pp. 119–42.

7

Biological Connections across the Sea of Japan

A Multivariate Comparison of Ancient and More Modern Crania from Japan, China, Korea, and Southeast Asia

MICHAEL PIETRUSEWSKY

A great many studies in physical anthropology have demonstrated that the Ainu of Japan are living descendants of the prehistoric Jomon (e.g., Brace et al. 1989; Dodo et al. 1998; K. Hanihara 1985, 1998; Howells 1966; Ishida 1996; Matsumura 2001; Mizoguchi 1986; Omoto et al. 1996; Ossenberg 1986; Turner 1976; Yamaguchi 1992). While major agreement has been reached regarding the relationship between Jomon and Ainu, the biological relationship between these two groups and the Ryukyu Islanders from the remote southern region of Japan is less clear. In contrast to earlier studies, several researchers (e.g., Dodo et al. 1998; Doi et al. 1997; Pietrusewsky 1999, 2004) have demonstrated that the Ainu and Jomon are not closely related to Ryukyu Islanders. These same researchers, as well as others (e.g., Omoto and Saitou 1997), have also challenged the more traditional view that the Jomon, Ryukyu Islanders, and Ainu are of Southeast Asian origin (K. Hanihara 1991; Turner 1992a).

There is now major consensus among physical anthropologists that, beginning approximately 2500 years BP at the commencement of the Yayoi period, a major influx of new people (and culture) entered the main Japanese Islands by way of the Korean peninsula, with northern Kyushu and southwestern Honshu as the likely entry points (see figure 7.1). While the magnitude and timing of this new incursion of people are still under debate, most agree that this new migrant group displaced and/or assimilated Jomon hunter-gatherers, a view articulated by Kazuro Hanihara (1991) in the popular dual structure hypothesis. According to this hypothesis, the modern Japanese are an amalgamation of earlier Jomon, whose antecedents arrived in late Pleistocene times from a presumed southern origin, and a later group of immigrants who appeared during the Yayoi period from a more northerly homeland. Also, according to this model, the Ainu and Ryukyu Islanders are viewed as representing the relatively unmixed descendants of the Jomon, people who largely escaped genetic admixture with the later Yayoi migrants and, as a consequence, retain many physical characteristics of these earlier people (K. Hanihara 1986, 1991).

In recent years archaeologists and linguists have advanced the so-called agricultural colonization model (e.g., Bayard 1996; Bellwood 1996, 1997, 2000; Blust 1996; Glover and Higham 1996; Higham 1996, 2001). This model is centered on rice domestication and the development of agriculture for understanding the prehistory and historical-biological relationships of the peoples of East Asia and Southeast Asia. That is, an agriculturally driven demic expansion of peoples and cultures of a more northern origin are seen replacing the earlier indigenous peoples of Southeast Asia (Bellwood 1997).

An opposing model, the population continuity model, most notably advanced by Christy Turner (1987, 1989, 1990), maintains that the present-day

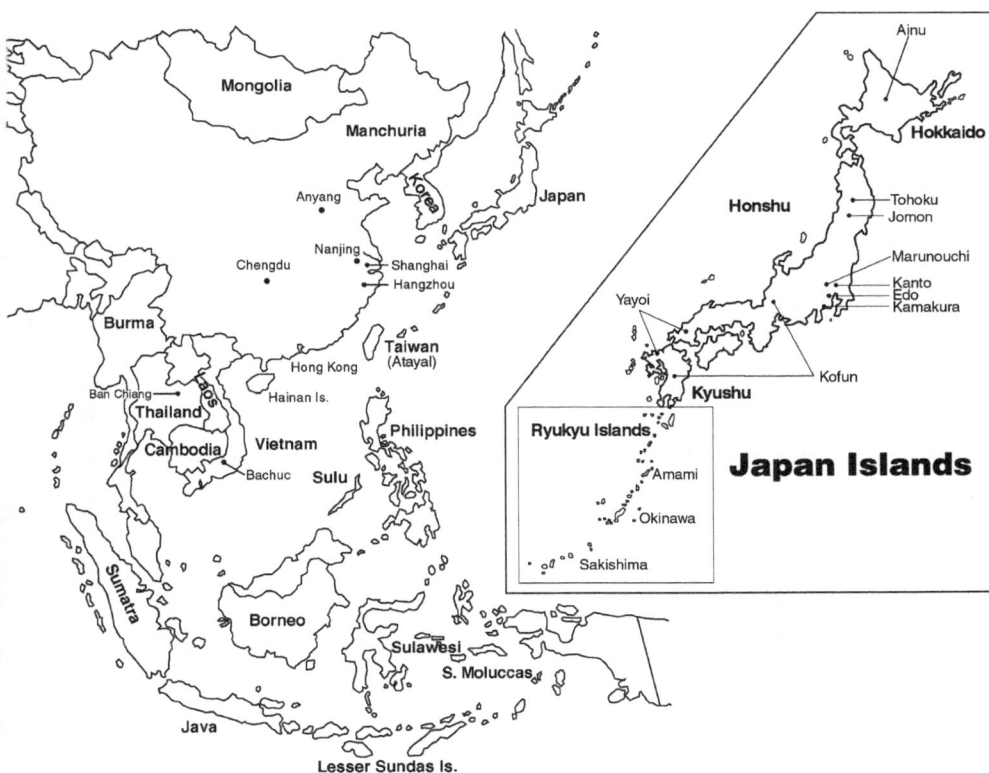

Figure 7.1. Map of East Asia and Southeast Asia showing the locations of the 39 male cranial series used in this analysis.

inhabitants of Southeast Asia evolved from earlier groups living within this region from the late Holocene onward. In this model, Southeast Asia is seen as the ultimate source, rather than the recipient, of a "southern Mongoloid" (Sundadont) population, one that ultimately spread northward to give rise to a "northern Mongoloid" (Sinodont) group.

Studies in physical anthropology, especially those that utilize human skeletal and dental remains, should help in evaluating models of displacement and continuity in East/North Asia and Southeast Asia or should suggest alternative explanations for the biological variability of the region's inhabitants, past and present. The primary focus of this study is to investigate, using craniometric data, the historical-biological relationships of earlier and more recent inhabitants of East/North Asia and Southeast Asia. More specifically, this new multivariate analysis of craniometric data examines cranial variation on both sides of the Sea of Japan, with the expressed goal of understanding the origins of the modern Japanese and their relationship to Jomon, Ainu, and Ryukyu Islanders, and the relationship of these groups to the rest of East Asia. Additionally, this study examines the biological relationships of the inhabitants, prehistoric and modern, of Southeast Asia and East Asia for testing some of the models that have been used to explain the settlement and colonization of these regions.

Crania and Biological Distance Studies

Because of both flawed theory and unrefined methodology, earlier studies in physical anthropology often fell short of reconstructing biological relatedness and human evolution. In recent years, however, anthropology has experienced a resurgence of interest in biological distance studies. While craniometric variation is subject to environmental influences, this category of variability mostly reflects genetic similarity that provides the basis for biological distance studies (Buikstra et al. 1990). Improvements in statistical methods, especially the development of multivariate statistical procedures, and breakthroughs in evolutionary and population biology provide increased objectivity for comparing human groups and measuring biological relationships. As a result, metric data continue to be an important and valuable source of information for examining relatedness between and within populations (see, e.g., Pietrusewsky 2008; Van Vark and Howells 1984). The precision and repeatability of measurement techniques, the generally conservative nature of this category of variation, its direct link with the past, and demonstration that craniometric traits have a genetic component (e.g. Sjøvold, 1984) have all contributed to this renewed interest.

Cranial Series and Methods

Because multivariate statistical procedures do not allow for missing variables, only complete, or nearly complete, male crania are used in the present study. Comparable data for female specimens were not available for all the series and for that reason are not included in this analysis. Given the scale of the present analysis in terms of geography and time, the absence of females should not seriously bias these results. All data sets included in this chapter are listed in table 7.1. A total of 1765 male crania are used in the present study. A map showing the locations of these cranial series is provided as figure 7.1. The majority of the cranial series used in this analysis represent modern and near-modern crania from Northeast and Southeast Asia. A few of the cranial series used represent earlier time periods. Some of these earlier cranial series are described in the following paragraphs.

Ban Chiang, a premetal (Neolithic) to Bronze/Iron Age site located in northeastern Thailand, is dated to approximately 2100 BC to AD 200 (Pietrusewsky and Douglas 2002; White 1986). In addition to yielding distinctive decorative pottery, ornaments, and elaborate burial offerings, the archaeological sequence at Ban Chiang provides early evidence of agriculture and metallurgy, including domesticated rice and early bronze artifacts. Ten of the twelve specimens are from the earliest phases of the Ban Chiang site (EPI–EPV, or 2100–900 BC), and two additional specimens are from the Middle Period (MPVI–MPVII, or 900–300 BC). All specimens are currently located at the University of Hawai'i, Honolulu.

Anyang is a Bronze Age site located in Henan Province, northern China. The Anyang crania are from "sacrificial pits" excavated prior to World War II from Shang dynasty tombs (11th century BC) (Li 1977), and were examined at Academia Sinica, Taipei, in 1983 and 1991. A random selection of 56 adult male crania is used in this analysis.

The cranial series from Japan include prehistoric (Jomon, Yayoi, Kofun), medieval, and modern dissecting room specimens from the twentieth century CE. The Jomon specimens represent the Late (4000–3000 years BP) to the Final Jomon period (c. 3000–2500 years BP in southern Honshu and c. 3000–2300 years BP in northern Honshu) (Habu 2004). The Jomon specimens (no. 36 in table 7.1) used in this analysis derive primarily from two sites located on Honshu Island: Ebishima ($N = 11$), Iwate Prefecture, Tohoku District; and Tsukumo ($N = 12$), Okayama Prefecture, Chugoku District. In addition to these cranial series, others representing the Ainu and Ryukyu Islanders are included. Information on the remaining series from Japan is provided in table 7.1.

Table 7.1. The 39 male cranial series used in the present study

ID	Site[a]	N	Location[b] and number of specimens	Remarks
Mainland Southeast Asia				
1.	Ban Chiang, (BC)	12	UHM-12	10 specimens are from the earliest phases of the Ban Chiang site (EPI–EPV, or 2100–900 BC); 2 are from the Middle Period (MPVI–MPVII, or 900–300 BC)
2.	Vietnam (VTN)	49	HCM-49	Specimens are from Hanoi (Van Dien Cemetery) and Ho Chi Minh City
3.	Bachuc Village (BAC)	51	BAC-51	Victims of the 1978 Khmer Rouge massacre in Bachuc Village in western Angiang Province, Vietnam
4.	Cambodia and Laos (CML)	40	PAR-40	A combined sample of crania from various locations in Cambodia and Laos collected between 1877 and 1920
5.	Thailand (THI)	50	SIR-50	Most of the specimens represent dissecting room cases from Bangkok
6.	Burma (BUR)	16	ZUR-16	The crania in Zurich are from a series (cat. nos. 93–125) of skulls collected in Mandalay, Myanmar (Burma), described in a catalogue dated c. AD 1900
Island Southeast Asia				
7.	Sumatra (SUM)	39	BER-1; BRE-1; DRE-5; LEP-4; PAR-3; ZUR-25	The specimens in Zurich are designated "Battak," specific locations within the island of Sumatra are not known
8.	Java (JAV)	50	BER-1; BLU-8; CHA-9; DRE-1; LEP-24; PAR-7	Crania were collected from several different localities in Java
9.	Borneo (BOR)	34	BER-2; BRE-2; DRE-6; FRE-4; LEP-8; PAR-12	A great many of the specimens are indicated as representing Dayak tribes, some have elaborate decorations
10.	Sulawesi (SLW)	41	BAS-7; BER-10; DRE-4; FRE-7; LEP-5; PAR-8	An exact location is known for many of these specimens
11.	Lesser Sundas Is. (LSN)	61	BAS-5; BER-15; BLU-2; CHA-1; DRE-24; LEP-1; PAR-6; ZUR-7	Crania from Bali (13), Flores (9), Sumba (1), Lomblem (2), Alor (2), Timor (11), Wetar (2), Leti (4), Barbar (1), Tanimbar (13), Kai (2), and Aru (1) Islands of the Lesser Sunda Islands
12.	S. Moluccas Is. (SML)	65	FRE-48; DRE-17	Crania are from Ceram (48) and Buru (17) Islands of the southern Molucca Islands
13.	Sulu (SUL)	38	LEP-1; PAR-37	The specimens in Paris were collected by Montano-Rey c. AD 1900
14.	Philippines (PHL)	28	BER-9; DRE-19	Most specimens are from Luzon Island
North and East Asia				
15.	Shanghai (SHA)	50	SHA-50	The specimens are mostly from post-Qing cemeteries in Shanghai
16.	Hangzhou (HAN)	50	SHA-50	Ancient skeletal remains exhumed in the modern city of Hangzhou, Zhejiang Province, in eastern China
17.	Nanjing (NAN)	49	SHA-49	Ancient remains exhumed from the modern city of Nanjing, Jiangsu Province, in eastern China

ID	Site[a]	N	Location[b] and number of specimens	Remarks
18.	Chengdu (CHE)	53	SHA-10; CHE-43	A majority of these specimens date to the Ch'en dynasty (AD 1796–1908) and are from Chengdu, Sichuan Province, in western China; 10 crania are from Leshan, Lizhong County, Sichuan Province
19.	Hong Kong (HK)	50	HKU-50	Specimens represent individuals who died in Hong Kong between 1978 and 1979
20.	Taiwan Chinese (TAI)	47	TPE-47	Modern Chinese living in Taiwan who trace their immediate origins to Fijian and Guangdong Provinces on the mainland of China
21.	Hainan Island (HAI)	47	TPE-47	Chinese immigrants originally from the Canton region of China who began arriving around 200 BC (Howells 1989: 108); this material was excavated by T. Kawasaki in Haikou City on Hainan Island
22.	Anyang (ANY)	56	TPE-56	Bronze Age (11th century BC) Shang dynasty sacrificial victims excavated at Anyang in northern Henan Province in northern China (Li 1977)
23.	Manchuria (MAN)	50	TKO-50	Many of the specimens are from northeastern China or the region formerly referred to as Manchuria, which today includes Heilongjiang and Jilin Provinces and adjacent northern Korea; many of these specimens are identified as soldiers or cavalrymen who died in battle in the late 19th century
24.	Korea (KOR)	32	KYO-7; SEN-3; TKM-2; TKO-20	Specific locations are known for most of these specimens
25.	Mongolia (MOG)	50	SIM-50	The skulls are identified as coming from Ulaanbaatar (Urga), Mongolia, and were purchased by A. Hrdlička in 1912

Taiwan Aboriginal

ID	Site[a]	N	Location[b] and number of specimens	Remarks
26.	Atayal (ATY)	36	TPE-28; TKM-7; TKO-1	The specimens in Taipei represent slain victims of Atayal, the second largest surviving Aboriginal tribe in Taiwan; the incident took place in 1932, and the specimens were collected by T. Kawasaki in the same year (Howells 1989: 109)

Japan—main islands

ID	Site[a]	N	Location[b] and number of specimens	Remarks
27.	Kanto Japanese (KAN)	50	CHB-50	A dissecting room sample of modern Japanese from the Kanto District of eastern Honshu Island; the majority of the individuals were born during the Meiji period (1868–1911), and most died well before 1940
28.	Tohoku Japanese (TOH)	53	SEN-53	Dissecting room specimens of modern Japanese from the Tohoku District in northern Honshu Island
29.	Kyushu Japanese (KYU)	51	KYU-51	Modern Japanese that derive mostly from Fukuoka Prefecture in Kyushu Island; other specimens are from Yamaguchi, Saga, Nagasaki, and adjoining prefectures

(*continued*)

(*continued*)

ID	Site[a]	N	Location[b] and number of specimens	Remarks
30.	Edo (EDO)	55	NSM-55	The specimens are from the Joshinji (Tokyo) site and date to the Edo period, or approximately the 17th to mid-19th centuries
31.	Kamakura (KAM)	52	NSM-9; TKO-43	Specimens are from the medieval mass burial sites of Zaimokuza and Gokurakuji in the city of Kamakura, victims of a war that occurred in 1333
32.	Marunouchi (MAR)	27	NSM-26; TKO-1	Specimens are from the medieval Muromachi period (1338–1603 AD) and were excavated from 16 temples in Marunouchi, Chiyoda-ku, Tokyo, by H. Suzuki
33.	Kofun (KOF)	62	KYO-5; KYU-53; NSM-4	The Kofun period follows the Yayoi period: the traditional dates for the Kofun Period are the 4th to 6th century AD
34.	Yayoi (YAY)	62	KYU-62	A combined sample of Yayoi specimens from Doigahama (39), Yoshimohama (14), and Nakanohama (2) sites in Yamaguchi Prefecture and from the Koura (7) site in Shimane Prefecture: the dates for the Yayoi period are approximately 300 BC to 300 AD
35.	Ainu (AIN)	50	SAP-18; TKM-5; TKO-27	Remarks: Skeletons collected by Y. Koganei in 1888–89 from abandoned Ainu cemeteries in Hokkaido (Koganei 1893–94)
36.	Jomon (JOM)	51	TKO-16; NSM-19; KYO-15; SAP-1	All specimens represent Late to Final (c. 3,500 yrs. BP to 2,000 yrs. BP) Jomon sites on Honshu Island; the largest series are Ebishima (11) in Iwate Prefecture in Tohoku District and Tsukumo (12) in Okayama Prefecture in the Chugoku District
Ryukyu Islands				
37.	Amami Islands (AMA)	31	KYO-19; KYU-12	Specimens are from Tokunoshima (19) and Yoro Islands (12) of the Amami Islands
38.	Okinawa Island (OKI)	53	KYO-11; KYU-1; TKO-1; GYO-19; KAN 21	Specimens are from Okinawa Island and neighboring Kume Island in the central Ryukyu Islands; 19 are from Gyokusendo Cave, located in southeastern Okinawa (18th century AD), and 21 are two different locations (Yattchi [17] and Hiyajo [4]) on Kume Island, an island located west of Okinawa Island; the remainder are from Okinawa Island
39.	Sakishima Group (SAK)	24	RYU-11; KYU-5; TKO-8	The specimens are from five separate islands in the Sakishima Group of the southern Ryukyu Islands: Hateruma Is. (2); Miyako Is. (6); Iriomote Is. (3); Ishigaki Is. (1); and Yonaguni Is. (12)

[a] Name of cranial series is followed by group abbreviation in parentheses.
[b] AUK = University of Auckland, Auckland, New Zealand
BAC = Bachuc Village, Angiang Province, Vietnam
BAS = Naturhistorisches Museum, Basel
BER = Museum für Naturkunde, Berlin

BLU = Anatomisches Institut, Universität Göttingen, Göttingen
BRE = Über-see Museum, Bremen
CHA = Anatomisches Institut der Chairté, Humboldt Universität, Berlin
CHB = Chiba University School of Medicine, Chiba
CHE = Department of Anatomy, Chengdu College of Traditional Chinese Medicine, Chengdu, PRC
DRE = Museum für Völkerkunde, Dresden
FRE = Institut für Humangenetik u. Anthropologie, Universität Freiburg, Freiburg
GYO = Gyokusendo Cave, Okinawa Island
HCM = Faculty of Medicine, Ho Chi Minh City, Vietnam
HKU = University of Hong Kong, Hong Kong
KAN = Kanegusuku Storage Room, Board of Education Cultural Division, Kanegusuku, Okinawa
KYO = Lab of Physical Anthropology, Faculty of Science, Kyoto University, Kyoto
KYU = Department of Anatomy, Faculty of Medicine, Kyushu University, Fukuoka
LEP = Anatomisches Institut, Karl Marx Universität, Leipzig
NSM = National Science Museum, Tokyo
PAR = Musée de l'Homme, Paris
RYU = University of the Ryukyus, Naha, Okinawa Island
SAM = South Australian Museum, Adelaide
SAP = Department of Anatomy, Sapporo Medical College, Sapporo
SEN = Department of Anatomy, School of Medicine, Tohoku University, Sendai
SHA = Institute of Anthropology, College of Life Sciences, Fudan University, Shanghai
SIM = National Museum of Natural History, Smithsonian Institution, Washington, DC
SIR = Department of Anatomy, Siriraj Hospital, Bangkok
TKM = Medical Museum, University Museum, University of Tokyo, Tokyo
TKO = University Museum, University of Tokyo, Tokyo
TPE = Academia Sinica, Nankang, Taipei
TUB = Institut für Anthropologie und Humangenetik, Universität Tübingen, Tübingen
UHM = University of Hawai'i–Manoa, Honolulu
ZUR = Anthropologisches Institut, Universität Zürich, Zurich

Multivariate Statistical Procedures

In this study, two multivariate statistical procedures, stepwise discriminant function analysis and Mahalanobis' generalized distance statistic (Mahalanobis 1936), were applied to a total of 24 standard cranial measurements (see table 7.2 for the exact measurements used). A more detailed discussion of these methods is provided by Pietrusewsky (2008).

Stepwise Discriminant Function (Canonical) Analysis

The major purpose of discriminant function analysis is to maximize differences between groups by producing a linear array of weighted variables, referred to as discriminant functions or canonical variates, from the original measurements (Tatsuoka 1971). Typically, the first few functions, or canonical variates, account for most of the variation among groups. In this analysis, the original measurements were selected in a stepwise manner such that, at each step, the measurement that adds most to the separation of groups was entered into the discriminant function in advance of others (Dixon and Brown 1979: 711). This procedure allows identification of those variables that are most responsible for the observed differentiation between individuals of the various groups. Interpretations of discriminant functions and the patterns of group separation are based on an inspection of standardized canonical coefficient values.

At the end of the stepping process, each individual specimen is classified into one of the original groups based on the discriminant scores it receives through the calculation of posterior (regular classification) and/or typicality (jackknifed classification) probabilities (Van Vark and Schaafsma 1992: 244–55). Jackknifed classification represents a common cross-validation procedure in multiple discriminant analysis, where cases are classified without using misclassified individuals in computing the classification function. The "correct" and "incorrect" classification results provide a general guide for assessing the homogeneity or heterogeneity of the original series. Another useful feature of this procedure is that it allows group means to be plotted on the first few canonical variates, thus allowing visualization of intergroup relationships. The computer program BMDP-7M (Dixon 1992; Dixon and Brown 1979) is used to perform the stepwise discriminant function analysis, while two-dimensional and three-dimensional plots are made using the SY-GRAPH module of SYSTAT (Wilkinson 1992).

Mahalanobis' Generalized Distance

Mahalanobis' generalized distance, or the sum of squared differences, provides a single quantitative measure of dissimilarity (distance) between groups using several variables while removing the correlation between the variables (Mahalanobis 1936). The significance of these distances is determined using the method of Rao (1952: 245), a procedure recommended by Buranarugsa and Leach (1993: 17).

The average linkage within group clustering algorithm, or Unweighted Pair Group Method Algorithm—UPGMA (Sneath and Sokal 1973), is the clustering procedure used to construct the diagrams of relationship, or dendrograms, using Mahalanobis' distances. This latter algorithm combines clusters so that the average distance among all cases in the resulting cluster is as small as possible and the distance between two clusters is taken to be the average among all possible pairs of cases in the cluster. The NTSYS-PC computer software program is used to construct the dendrograms (Rohlf 1993).

Results

The results of applying stepwise discriminant function analysis and Mahalanobis' generalized distance to 24 cranial measurements recorded in 1765 male crania, the largest number of measurements comparable to all 39 series, are presented.

Results of Stepwise Discriminant Function Analysis

A summary of the measurements (table 7.2) ranked according to the F-values (tests of equality of group means using classical one-way analysis of variance) received in the final step provides an indication of the discriminatory power of the original variables. Among the variables that are ranked highest (i.e., contributing the most to the discrimination produced) in this analysis are nasio-occipital length, nasal height, nasal breadth, and minimum cranial breadth.

Eigenvalues and level of significance (Rao 1952: 323) for the 24 canonical variates are presented in table 7.3. The eigenvalues provide an indication of the proportion of dispersion accounted for by each canonical variate. In this analysis, the first four canonical variates account for 67.6 percent of the total variation. The first 18 eigenvalues are significant at the 1 percent level, indicating significant heterogeneity for these canonical variates.

Canonical coefficients for the first three canonical variates are given in table 7.4. Maximum cranial length, nasio-occipital length, orbital breadth, and cheek height are the most important variables in producing group separation in the first canonical variate. This first variate may, therefore, be defined as a cranial length, orbital breadth, cheek height, and cranial breadth discriminator. Nasal height, nasal breadth, maximum cranial breadth, and alveolar breadth are most responsible for group separation produced in the second canonical variate. Nasio-occipital length, bregma-lambda chord, bifrontal breadth, and nasion-bregma chord are primarily responsible for the discrimination produced in the third canonical variate.

A summary (table 7.5) of the group classification results, regular and jackknifed, indicate that the Mongolia, Southern Moluccas, Atayal, Cambodia/Laos, Ainu, Amami, Chengdu, Okinawa, and Jomon are among the series with the best classification results. The poorest jackknifed classification results are found for the Marunouchi, Burma, Sulawesi, Hangzhou, Nanjing, Sumatra, Edo, and Borneo series. The best classification results accurately classified more than 37 percent of cases, while the poorest results correctly classified less than 12 percent of cases.

Table 7.2. Summary ranking of cranial measurements according to F-values received in the final step of discriminant function analysis (39 male groups, 24 measurements)

Step no.	Measurement[a]	F-value	df_B/df_W[b]	p[c]
1	Nasio-occipital length (M-1d)	17.3	38/1726	*
2	Nasal height (M-55)	15.0	38/1725	*
3	Nasal breadth (M-45)	11.6	38/1724	*
4	Minimum cranial breadth (M-14)	11.4	38/1723	*
5	Basion-bregma (M-17)	8.6	38/1722	*
6	Maximum cranial breadth (M-8)	8.8	38/1721	*
7	Basion-nasion (M-5)	8.4	38/1720	*
8	Cheek height (M-48[4])	6.4	38/1719	*
9	Biorbital breadth (H-EKB)	6.5	38/1718	*
10	Bifrontal breadth (M-43)	11.2	38/1717	*
11	Orbital height (M-52)	6.5	38/1716	*
12	Biauricular breadth (M-116)	5.8	38/1715	*
13	Alveolar breadth (M-61)	4.4	38/1714	*
14	Mastoid height (H-MDL)	4.1	38/1713	*
15	Nasion-bregma chord (M-29)	4.0	38/1712	*
16	Maximum cranial length (M-1)	3.7	38/1711	*
17	Bistephanic breadth (H-STB)	3.4	38/1710	*
18	Maximum frontal breadth (M-10)	5.5	38/1709	*
19	Orbital breadth (M-51a)	3.6	38/1708	*
20	Bimaxillary breadth (M-46)	3.4	38/1707	*
21	Minimum frontal breadth (M-9)	3.1	38/1706	*
22	Bregma-lambda chord (M-30)	2.5	38/1705	*
23	Mastoid width (H-MDB)	1.9	38/1704	*
24	Biasterionic breadth (M-12)	1.7	38/1703	n.s.

[a] M = Martin and Saller 1957; H = Howells 1973. The numeric and alphabetical abbreviations following "M" and "H" refer to the original number or alphabetic code used by the authors for defining these measurements.

[b] df_B/df_W = degrees of freedom between/degrees of freedom within.

[c] * $p \le .01$; n.s. = not significant.

Table 7.3. Eigenvalues, percentage of total dispersion, cumulative percentage of dispersion, and level of significance for 24 canonical variates (39 male groups, 24 measurements)

Canonical variate	Eigenvalue	% dispersion	Cumulative % dispersion	df[a]	p[b]
1	.98038	24.9	24.9	61	*
2	.73004	18.6	43.5	59	*
3	.58702	14.9	58.4	57	*
4	.36214	9.2	67.6	55	*
5	.27073	6.9	74.5	53	*
6	.19383	4.9	79.4	51	*
7	.13096	3.3	82.7	49	*
8	.10662	2.7	85.4	47	*
9	.09333	2.4	87.8	45	*
10	.06877	1.8	89.6	43	*
11	.06029	1.5	91.1	41	*
12	.05642	1.4	92.5	39	*
13	.05130	1.3	93.8	37	*
14	.04911	1.3	95.1	35	*
15	.04228	1.1	96.2	33	*
16	.03770	0.9	97.1	31	*
17	.02989	0.8	97.9	29	*
18	.02409	0.6	98.5	27	*
19	.01756	0.4	98.9	25	n.s.
20	.01447	0.4	99.3	23	n.s.
21	.00892	0.2	99.5	21	n.s.
22	.00798	0.2	99.7	19	n.s.
23	.00579	0.2	99.9	17	n.s.
24	.00480	0.1	100.0	15	n.s.

[a] df = degrees of freedom, calculated as $(p + q - 2)$, $(p + q - 4)$, etc.
[b] * $p \leq .01$ when eigenvalues are tested for significance according to criterion $[N - \frac{1}{2}(p + q)] \log_e (\lambda + 1)$, where N = total number of crania, p = number of variables, q = number of groups, and λ = eigenvalue, all of which are distributed approximately as chi-square (Rao 1952: 323); n.s. = not significant.

Table 7.4. Canonical coefficients of 24 cranial measurements for the first three canonical variates (39 male groups)

	Canonical Variate 1	Canonical Variate 2	Canonical Variate 3
Maximum cranial length (M-1)	-0.31372	0.01035	-0.02270
Nasio-occipital length (M-1d)	0.28735	-0.01681	0.13937
Basion-nasion (M-5)	0.12847	-0.05559	-0.07742
Basion-bregma (M-17)	-0.07854	-0.03174	0.07466
Maximum cranial breadth (M-8)	0.13019	0.12034	0.05770
Maximum frontal breadth (M-10)	-0.05025	0.00638	-0.05737
Minimum frontal breadth (M-9)	0.07170	0.00253	-0.04764
Bistephanic breadth (H-STB)	-0.05557	-0.05145	-0.02248
Biauricular breadth (M-116)	-0.06499	0.00635	-0.02071
Minimum cranial breadth (M-14)	-0.01372	-0.06381	0.04413
Biasterionic breadth (M-12)	0.01045	-0.04694	-0.07036
Nasal height (M-55)	0.05089	-0.18977	-0.04655
Nasal breadth (M-45)	0.04390	-0.15627	0.07553
Orbital height (M-52)	0.08644	0.10678	-0.04107
Orbital breadth (M-51a)	-0.20038	0.04018	0.02666
Alveolar breadth (M-61)	0.06095	0.11385	-0.01639
Mastoid height (H-MDL)	0.02913	0.00145	-0.07384
Mastoid width (H-MDB)	-0.02397	-0.03089	0.04496
Bimaxillary breadth (M-46)	0.05800	-0.01019	0.06213
Bifrontal breadth (M-43)	-0.01586	-0.06565	-0.11891
Biorbital breadth (H-EKB)	-0.05325	0.02251	0.09342
Cheek height (M-48[4])	-0.16919	0.06403	0.08232
Nasion-bregma chord (M-29)	0.00735	0.05967	-0.09890
Bregma-lambda chord (M-30)	0.04268	0.06005	-0.12221

Note: M = Martin and Saller 1957; H = Howells 1973. The numeric and alphabetical abbreviations following "M" and "H" refer to the original number or alphabetic code used by these authors for defining these measurements.

Table 7.5. Classification results (regular and jackknifed) arranged by groups with the best to the poorest results showing the percentage of correctly assigned cases

Regular classification results		Jackknifed classification results	
Group	**%**	**Group**	**%**
Mongolia	80.0	Mongolia	78.0
S. Moluccas	64.6	S. Moluccas	60.0
Chengdu	60.4	Atayal	52.8
Cambodia/Laos	60.0	Cambodia/Laos	45.0
Atayal	58.3	Ainu	42.0
Ainu	58.0	Amami	41.9
Amami	54.8	Chengdu	41.5
Okinawa	52.8	Okinawa	39.6
Bachuc	51.0	Jomon	37.3
Sulu	50.0	Sulu	34.2
Burma	50.0	Bachuc	33.3
Ban Chiang	50.0	Manchuria	30.0
Jomon	45.1	Ban Chiang	25.0
Manchuria	44.0	Anyang	25.0
Taiwan	42.6	Kofun	24.2
Kanto	38.0	Taiwan	23.4
Thailand	36.0	Vietnam	22.4
Anyang	35.7	Thailand	22.0
Vietnam	34.7	Shanghai	22.0
Kofun	33.9	Kanto	22.0
Sakishima	33.3	Java	22.0
Philippines	32.1	Hong Kong	20.0
Java	32.0	Kamakura	19.2
Shanghai	32.0	L. Sundas	18.0
Borneo	29.4	Sakishima	16.7
Hong Kong	28.0	Korea	15.6
L. Sundas	26.2	Tohoku	15.1
Kyushu	25.5	Yayoi	14.5
Kamakura	25.0	Philippines	14.3
Tohoku	24.5	Kyushu	13.7
Yayoi	24.2	Hainan	12.8
Hainan	23.4	Borneo	11.8
Korea	21.9	Edo	10.9
Nanjing	20.4	Sumatra	10.3
Hangzhou	20.0	Nanjing	10.2
Edo	18.2	Hangzhou	8.0
Sumatra	17.9	Sulawesi	7.3
Sulawesi	14.6	Burma	6.2
Marunouchi	11.1	Marunouchi	3.7

The most frequent (first ten) misclassifications for each of the 39 groups are given in table 7.6. Examination of some of the Japanese series reveals that only 9 of the 62 Yayoi specimens, or 14.5 percent of the total, are correctly reclassified to that group. Among the misclassified Yayoi, 6 are reclassified as Kofun, 5 each as Kanto and Jomon, 4 each as Vietnamese and Mongolian, and 3 each as Manchurian and from Ban Chiang. Of the original 62 Kofun crania, 15 are reclassified to that group, while 11 are reassigned to one of the Ryukyu Island series and 5 are reclassified as Jomon, 4 as Kamakura, and 3 each as Yayoi and Marunouchi. Equally low correct classification results (10/52, 19.2 percent) were found for the Kamakura series: 7 of the Kamakura crania are misclassified as one of the Ryukyu Island series, 5 each as Kyushu and Ainu, 4 each as Atayal and Kofun, and 2 as from Anyang. Only 5 Korean specimens are correctly classified as Korean (5/32, 15.6 percent). Of the Korean crania, 4 are reclassified as Hainan, and 2 each are reclassified as from Hong Kong, Atayal, and Tohoku, while 11 are reclassified to one of the Southeast Asian series. In the results shown, 16 of the misclassified specimens from Manchuria are reclassified as Chinese, and 9 are classified as Japanese.

A majority of the Ryukyu crania are misclassified to one of the Ryukyu cranial series or to Korea, Kamakura, Jomon, Ainu, or Yayoi. Of the Jomon specimens, 7 are reclassified as Ainu, 6 as one of the Ryukyu series, and 4 as Yayoi. Of the Ainu specimens, 7 are classified as Jomon, 5 as Kanto, and 2 as Kamakura. Misclassifications among the more modern Japanese series (e.g., Kanto, Edo, Tohoku, Kyushu) are most often to Atayal, Korea, Manchuria, Hainan, and Taiwan.

Only a quarter (14/56) of the Anyang specimens are classified to their original group, while 10 Anyang crania are classified to one of the Ryukyu series, 6 to Hong Kong, and 3 each to Taiwan and Hainan Islands.

The series with the best classification results is Mongolia, with 78 percent correct assignments. As expected, the few misclassified crania are reclassified to one of the Chinese or Japanese series. Very few of the misclassifications among the Southeast Asian crania are to series outside this region. Many of the Hainan crania are misclassified to Taiwan, Anyang, or to one of the Southeast Asian series.

Three separate clusters emerge when the 39 group means are plotted on the first two canonical variates (figure 7.2). The cranial series from mainland and island Southeast Asia form one of these clusters, as seen in the lower left quadrant of this diagram. Four Chinese cranial series anchor a separate group to which Mongolia, Manchuria, and Hong Kong are marginally attracted. The last major cluster includes most of the remaining Chinese cranial series and those from Japan. The cranial series from Korea and Anyang are

Table 7.6. Some of the jackknifed classification results obtained from stepwise discriminant function analysis showing the cases reclassified at the end of the stepping process

Shanghai (50)		Hong Kong (50)		Chengdu (53)		Hangzhou (50)		Nanjing (49)		Taiwan (47)		Hainan (47)		Atayal (36)	
SHA	11	HK	10	CHE	22	SHA	10	HAN	7	TAI	11	HAI	6	ATY	19
HAN	8	HAN	5	NAN	11	HK	7	MAN	5	ANY	6	TAI	5	KOR	2
NAN	6	NAN	5	VTN	3	NAN	5	NAN	5	MAN	3	ANY	4	TOH	2
HK	5	EDO	3	SHA	2	CHE	4	CHE	5	HAI	3	THI	4	KYU	2
CHE	4	VTN	3	HK	2	HAN	4	SHA	5	KAM	3	BC	3	SML	2
KAN	4	AMA	2	MOG	2	MOG	3	YAY	4	THI	2	BUR	2	TAI	1
THI	4	TAI	2	YAY	2	SUM	3	HK	3	OKI	2	BAC	2	HAI	1
CML	1	HAI	1	LSN	1	BOR	3	AMA	2	TOH	2	VTN	2	ANY	1
BC	1	MAN	1	BC	1	BUR	2	KOR	2	CHE	2	JAV	2	KAM	1
OKI	1	BC	1	MAR	1	ANY	2	MOG	2	KOR	1	AMA	2	AIN	1

Manchuria (50)		Anyang (56)		Mongolia (50)		Korea (32)		Kanto (50)		Edo (55)		Kamakura (52)		Kofun (62)	
MAN	15	ANY	14	MOG	39	KOR	5	KAN	11	EDO	6	KAM	10	KOF	15
CHE	4	HK	6	SHA	3	HAI	4	ATY	5	KYU	6	KYU	5	AMA	5
NAN	3	AMA	5	CHE	2	HK	2	TAI	3	KAN	4	AIN	5	JOM	5
ANY	3	SAK	5	HAN	1	ATY	2	TOH	3	ATY	4	SAK	5	KAM	4
EDO	3	TAI	3	HAI	1	TOH	2	AIN	3	MAR	4	ATY	4	YAY	3
KOF	3	HAI	3	YAY	1	SUM	2	JAV	2	HK	2	KOF	4	OKI	3
TOH	3	KYU	3	TOH	1	JAV	2	OKI	2	CHE	2	ANY	2	SAK	3
HK	2	LSN	2	JOM	1	PHL	2	KYU	2	KOR	2	TOH	2	MAR	3

(continued)

(continued)

TAI	2	EDO	2	THI	1	BUR	2	ANY	2	KAM	2	AMA	2	CHE	2
ATY	2	KOR	2	BUR	0	THI	1	HK	2	KOF	2	BOR	2	EDO	2

Yayoi (62)		Tohoku (53)		Kyushu (51)		Ainu (50)		Amami (31)		Jomon (51)		Okinawa (53)		Sakishima (24)	
YAY	9	TOH	8	KYU	7	AIN	21	AMA	13	JOM	19	OKI	21	OKI	5
KOF	6	KYU	5	KAN	7	JOM	7	KAM	3	AIN	7	AMA	7	SAK	4
KAN	5	MAN	5	KOR	4	KAN	5	THI	2	OKI	4	VTN	3	AMA	3
JOM	5	SUM	5	HK	3	EDO	2	YAY	2	YAY	4	JOM	3	SHA	1
VTN	4	KAM	4	ATY	3	KAM	2	AIN	2	SUM	2	KOR	3	TAI	1
MOG	4	KOR	3	KAM	3	TOH	2	OKI	2	BC	2	TAI	2	HAI	1
MAN	3	AIN	3	HAI	2	SUM	2	HAI	1	SAK	2	HAI	2	ANY	1
BC	3	ATY	2	EDO	2	SML	1	ATY	1	KOF	2	EDO	2	KAN	1
TOH	2	KAN	2	KOF	2	LSN	1	MAN	1	KAM	2	SAK	2	KAM	1
AMA	2	KOF	2	TOH	2	MAR	1	TOH	1	KAN	2	BAC	1	KOF	1

Marunouchi (27)		Ban Chiang (12)		Sumatra (39)		Java (50)		Borneo (34)		Sulawesi (41)		L. Sundas (61)		S. Moluccas (65)	
ATY	3	BC	3	BOR	8	JAV	11	BOR	4	CML	6	LSN	11	SML	39
YAY	3	HAI	2	SUM	4	THI	5	SUM	4	SUM	4	BOR	8	LSN	6
HK	2	ATY	1	SML	3	SUL	4	BUR	3	JAV	3	VTN	4	ATY	3
EDO	2	ANY	1	PHL	3	BAC	3	VTN	3	SLW	3	CML	4	BOR	3
KOF	2	AMA	1	BUR	3	SLW	3	SUL	3	SUL	3	HAI	3	SUL	3

JOM 2	OKI 1	CHE 2	SLW 2	HK 2	SLW 2	ATY 3	THI 2	SLW 2
OKI 2	JAV 1	SHA 2	KAM 2	HAI 2	SUM 2	BUR 2	VTN 2	SUM 2
LSN 2	BOR 1	JAV 2	JAV 2	PHL 2	KAN 1	PHL 2	PHL 2	KAN 1
NAN 1	BUR 1	CML 1	BAC 2	CML 2	KAM 1	SUL 2	LSN 2	KAM 1
MAN 1	THI 0	SUL 1	CML 1	BUR 2	KOF 1	JAV 2	BOR 2	KOF 1

Sulu (38)		Philippines (28)		Vietnam (49)		Bachuc (51)		Cam. & Laos (40)		Thailand (50)		Burma (16)	
SUL	13	PHL	4	VTN	11	BAC	17	CML	18	THI	11	BAC	4
SML	8	VTN	3	HK	4	BUR	4	SUL	8	JAV	4	SLW	2
BUR	4	SHA	2	OKI	3	CML	3	BAC	2	SLW	4	BUR	1
BOR	3	MAN	2	ATY	3	HK	3	SML	2	BAC	4	CML	1
AIN	2	BUR	1	KOR	3	JAV	3	JAV	2	KOR	3	SUL	1
JAV	2	CML	1	BC	3	BOR	3	CHE	1	PHL	3	SUM	1
SLW	2	BAC	1	JOM	2	VTN	2	ATY	1	HAN	2	MAR	1
BAC	2	SUL	1	TAI	2	PHL	2	KAN	1	KAN	2	JOM	1
PHL	1	SML	1	SLW	2	SML	2	SUM	1	BC	2	AIN	1
SML	1	SLW	1	SUL	2	SLW	2	SLW	1	SML	2	YAY	1
SLW	1												

Note: Numbers in parentheses represent the number of crania originally assigned to each group. See table 7.1 for explanation of group abbreviations.

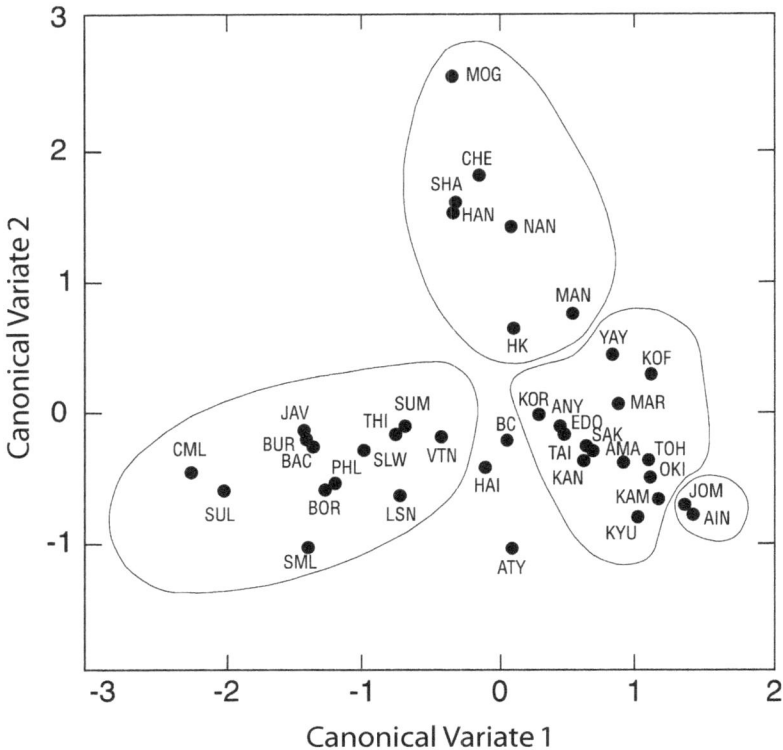

Figure 7.2. Plot of 39 group means on the first two canonical variates using 24 cranial measurements (see table 7.1 for explanation of group abbreviations).

also members of this cluster, while Ban Chiang, Atayal, Jomon, and Ainu are more marginal in their placement. Notably, the cranial series that connect the Northeast Asian (Chinese) and Japanese clusters include Manchuria, Yayoi, Kofun, Korea, and Anyang.

Disregarding the series from Southeast Asia, figure 7.3 emphasizes overlap between cranial samples from mainland Northeast Asia and those from the Japanese archipelago. The group mean for the Yayoi series lies midway between Manchuria and Kofun. Korea, Anyang, and Taiwan Chinese are in close proximity to the cluster that includes most of the Japanese cranial series. Again, Hainan, Atayal, and Mongolia occupy marginal positions in this diagram. The means for Jomon and Ainu form a cluster peripheral to the remaining cranial series from the Japanese archipelago. The plots of these same groups on the first three canonical variates (figures 7.4 and 7.5) give an even clearer representation of these associations. The central placement of Manchuria, Hainan, Korea, and Anyang is seen in both plots. The marginal placement of the Jomon and Ainu series is again apparent.

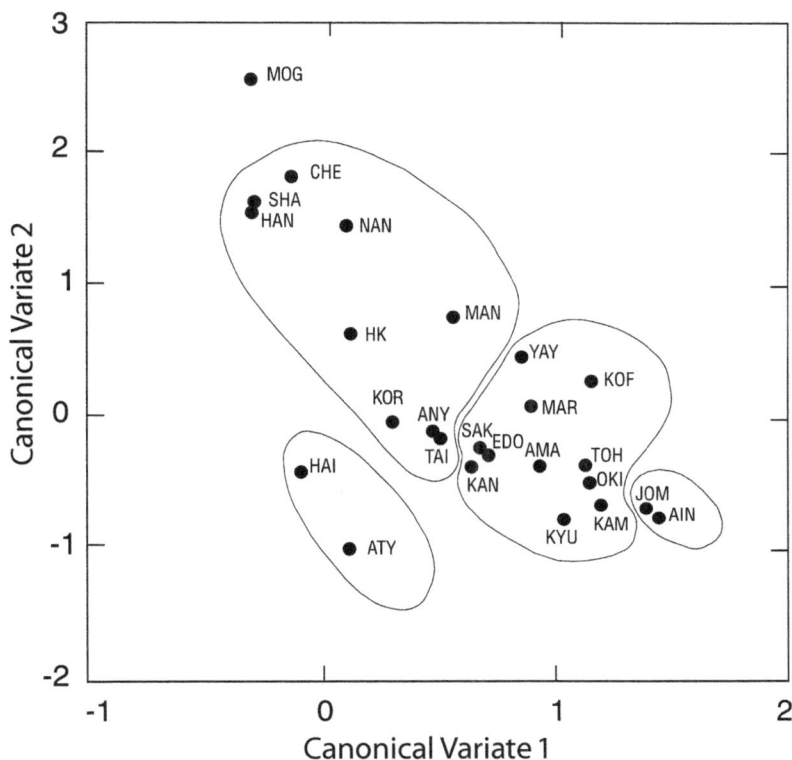

Figure 7.3. Plot of 25 of the 39 group means on the first two canonical variates using 24 cranial measurements (see table 7.1 for explanation of group abbreviations).

Mahalanobis' Generalized Distance Results

Inspection of the ten smallest distances for each of the 39 groups (table 7.7) gives additional information on biological relatedness that is not always evident in the diagrams generated by clustering algorithms. When distance size is used as a measure of similarity, the groups closest to Manchuria are Edo, Nanjing, and Korea. Three more Japanese series (Tohoku, Marunouchi and Kyushu) are among the ten closest groups to Manchuria. Five modern, or nearly modern, cranial series from Japan (Edo, Kyushu, Tohoku, Marunouchi, and Kanto) are among the most similar to Korea. Six cranial series from Japan, including two Ryukyu Island series, are among the groups most similar to Anyang. Four of the cranial series from Japan (Yayoi, Kofun, Marunouchi, and Sakishima) cluster with Mongolia.

The cranial series closest to Yayoi are Kofun and two medieval series (Marunouchi and Kamakura) from Japan. The three Ryukyu Island series, as well as Korea and Jomon, are among the ten closest series to Yayoi. Examining the groups closest to Kofun reveals that Yayoi and the two medieval series

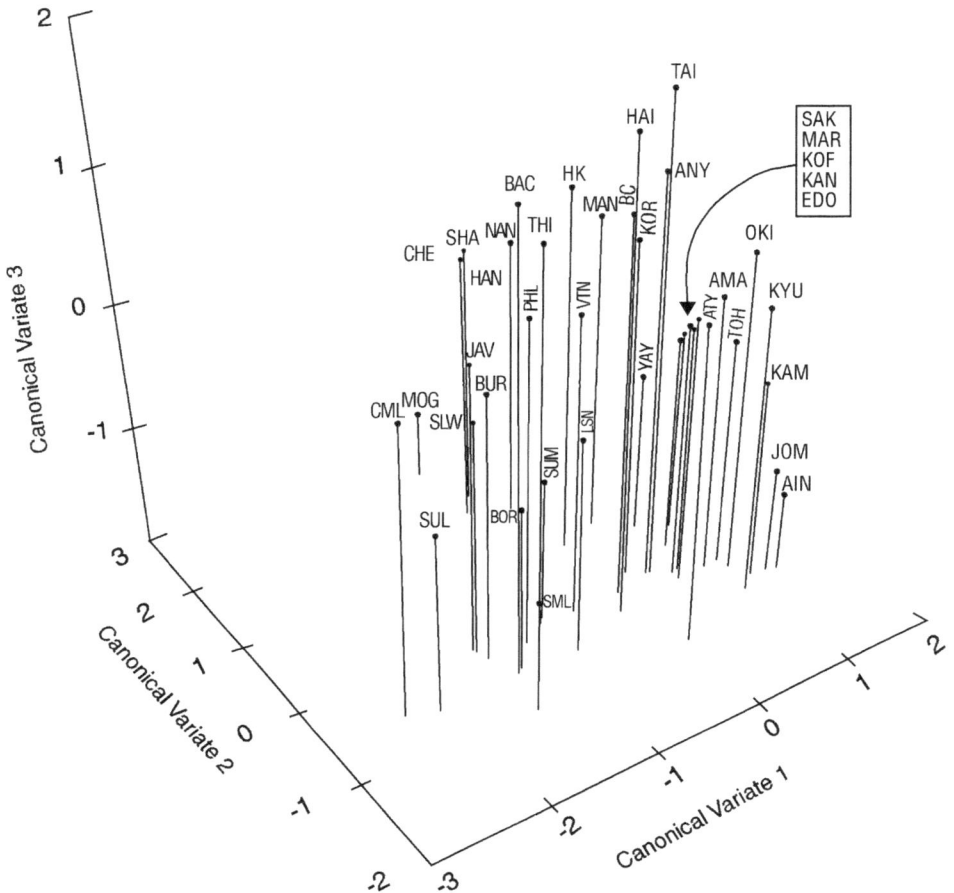

Figure 7.4. Plot of 39 group means on the first three canonical variates using 24 cranial measurements (see table 7.1 for explanation of group abbreviations).

from Japan are associated with the smallest distances, followed by the three Ryukyu Island series. Again, Korea and Jomon are also among the ten closest groups to Kofun. The groups closest to the Kamakura series include another medieval series, Marunouchi, followed by Kyushu, Kofun, Amami, and Yayoi. The Ainu series is among the ten closest series to Kamakura. Further inspection of these distances reveals the biological closeness of the Jomon and Ainu series. The groups next closest to Ainu and Jomon include cranial series from Japan such as Yayoi, Kofun, Kamakura, and Marunouchi. Absent from the ten closest series to either Jomon or Ainu are cranial series from mainland Northeast Asia. Among the groups that are regularly closest to the three Ryukyu Island series are Kamakura, Yayoi, Kofun, and the Marunouchi.

Applying the UPGMA clustering algorithm to the distances for 39 groups

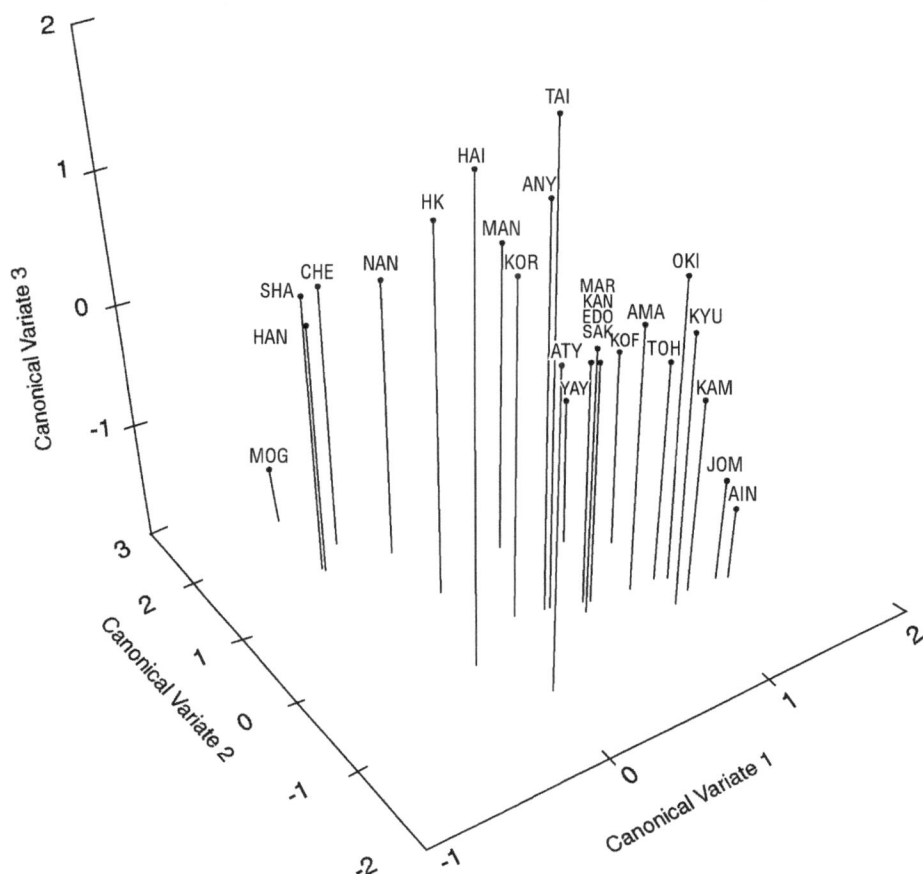

Figure 7.5. Plot of 25 of the 39 group means on the first three canonical variates using 24 cranial measurements (see table 7.1 for explanation of group abbreviations).

results in the dendrogram shown in figure 7.6. The mainly contemporaneous cranial series from mainland and island Southeast Asia occupy one major branch of this diagram. The remaining series representing the Japanese archipelago, China, and Northeast Asia form a second major aggregate grouping. Within this latter grouping, Shanghai, Hangzhou, Nanjing, Hong Kong, and Chengdu unite in a separate branch. Taiwan, Hainan, Korea, Anyang, and Manchuria form another branch, one that unites with the Japanese cranial series. The more modern Japanese cranial series occupy a branch separated from one that includes Kamakura, Kofun, Yayoi, and the Ryukyu Island cranial series. The Ainu and Jomon fall outside the second major branch that contains all the cranial series from North and East Asia. Mongolia and Ban Chiang are the most isolated cranial series in this diagram.

Table 7.7. The smallest Mahalanobis' distances and level of significance for 39 male cranial groups using 24 measurements

Shanghai		Hong Kong		Chengdu		Hangzhou	
HAN	0.537	HAN	2.474 **	NAN	2.583 *	SHA	0.537
NAN	1.961	NAN	2.713 *	HAN	3.775 *	NAN	1.331
HK	2.844 *	SHA	2.844 *	SHA	3.825 *	HK	2.474 **
CHE	3.825 *	ANY	3.886 *	MAN	5.312 *	CHE	3.775 *
MAR	5.157 *	VTN	3.927 *	HK	6.338 *	SUM	4.447 *
SUM	5.230 *	KOR	4.327 *	YAY	6.598 *	MAR	4.878 *
MAN	5.758 *	MAR	4.355 *	MAR	6.734 *	MAN	5.095 *
THI	5.823 *	EDO	4.463 *	VTN	7.082 *	YAY	5.305 *
YAY	5.925 *	HAI	4.530 *	KOR	7.089 *	VTN	5.550 *
KOR	5.997 *	THI	4.766 *	EDO	7.399 *	KOR	5.568 *
Nanjing		**Taiwan**		**Hainan**		**Atayal**	
HAN	1.331	HAI	2.801 *	KOR	2.561	KYU	4.997 *
SHA	1.961	ANY	3.439 **	TAI	2.801 **	EDO	5.200 *
CHE	2.583 *	KOR	3.781 *	ANY	3.107 *	LSN	5.221 *
HK	2.713 *	MAN	5.056 *	THI	3.313 *	KOR	5.281 *
MAN	3.322 *	OKI	5.068 *	BAC	3.615 *	TOH	5.305 *
MAR	3.985 **	SAK	5.157 *	EDO	4.237 *	HAI	5.902 *
EDO	4.670 *	EDO	5.814 *	VTN	4.292 *	SAK	6.058 **
YAY	4.990 *	KYU	5.879 *	HK	4.530 *	MAR	6.543 *
ANY	5.552 *	VTN	5.902 *	KYU	4.672 *	VTN	6.634 *
SUM	5.690 *	HK	5.929 *	PHL	4.760 *	PHL	6.729 *
Manchuria		**Anyang**		**Mongolia**		**Korea**	
EDO	3.125 *	HAI	3.107 *	HAN	8.173 *	EDO	2.041
NAN	3.322 *	KOR	3.327 **	SHA	8.789 *	KYU	2.470
KOR	3.343 **	AMA	3.436 **	CHE	8.968 *	HAI	2.561
TOH	4.106 *	TAI	3.439 *	YAY	9.046 *	TOH	2.890 **
MAR	4.544 *	HK	3.886 *	NAN	10.324 *	MAR	3.070
HK	5.015 *	KYU	4.230 *	KOF	10.947 *	KAN	3.220 **
TAI	5.056 *	MAR	4.306 *	SUM	11.565 *	ANY	3.327 **
ANY	5.086 *	KAM	4.368 *	SLW	12.306 *	MAN	3.343 **
HAN	5.095 *	EDO	4.541 *	MAR	12.903 *	THI	3.509 **
KYU	5.261 *	SAK	4.563 *	SAK	13.829 *	TAI	3.781 **

Kanto		Edo		Kamakura		Kofun	
EDO	2.211 **	KYU	1.177	MAR	2.004	YAY	1.363
TOH	2.447 **	TOH	1.368	KYU	2.423 **	MAR	2.549
KYU	2.476 **	MAR	1.553	KOF	2.682 *	KAM	2.682 *
MAR	2.642	KOR	2.041	AMA	2.747	SAK	3.256 **
KOR	3.220 **	KAN	2.211 **	YAY	2.783 *	AMA	3.339 *
SUM	4.935 *	KAM	3.022 *	SAK	2.853	OKI	3.416 *
THI	5.116 *	SAK	3.087	EDO	3.022 *	EDO	3.693 *
AIN	5.175 *	MAN	3.125 *	TOH	3.411 *	KOR	3.781 *
YAY	5.437 *	YAY	3.226 *	AIN	3.955 *	KYU	4.225 *
KAM	5.595 *	KOF	3.693 *	OKI	4.113 *	JOM	4.276 *

Yayoi		Tohoku		Kyushu		Ainu	
KOF	1.363	EDO	1.368	EDO	1.177	JOM	3.236 *
MAR	1.645	KYU	1.750	TOH	1.750	EDO	3.780 *
KAM	2.783 *	MAR	2.036	MAR	2.131	KAM	3.955 *
SAK	2.890	KAN	2.447 **	KAM	2.423 **	KYU	4.075 *
EDO	3.226 *	KOR	2.890 **	KOR	2.470	TOH	4.189 *
AMA	3.356 *	KAM	3.411 *	KAN	2.476 **	MAR	4.669 *
TOH	3.888 *	YAY	3.888 *	SAK	3.599	YAY	5.095 *
JOM	4.107 *	MAN	4.106 *	AIN	4.075 *	KAN	5.175 *
KOR	4.301 *	AIN	4.189 *	KOF	4.225 *	KOF	6.118 *
OKI	4.521 *	SAK	4.385 **	ANY	4.230 *	SAK	6.545 *

Amami		Jomon		Okinawa		Sakishima	
KAM	2.747	AIN	3.236 *	SAK	2.956	KAM	2.853
KOF	3.339 *	YAY	4.107 *	KOF	3.416 *	MAR	2.874
YAY	3.356 *	MAR	4.139 **	AMA	3.473 **	YAY	2.890
SAK	3.409	KOF	4.276 *	MAR	3.935 **	OKI	2.956
ANY	3.436 **	KAM	4.405 *	KAM	4.113 *	EDO	3.087
OKI	3.473 **	OKI	5.106 *	YAY	4.521 *	KOF	3.256 **
MAR	3.981	EDO	5.696 *	EDO	4.812 *	AMA	3.409
KOR	4.882 **	KYU	5.761 *	VTN	4.857 *	KYU	3.599
EDO	4.937 *	AMA	6.047 *	KYU	4.898 *	KOR	3.816
VTN	5.301 *	TOH	6.183 *	HAI	4.929 *	TOH	4.385 **

(continued)

Marunouchi		Ban Chiang		Sumatra		Java	
EDO	1.553	HAI	5.632	BOR	1.999	SLW	1.998
YAY	1.645	MAR	6.960	LSN	2.061	THI	2.936 *
KAM	2.004	EDO	7.329 **	SLW	2.665	CML	3.103 *
TOH	2.036	LSN	7.460 **	JAV	3.953 *	LSN	3.300 *
KYU	2.131	ANY	7.614 **	MAR	4.070	BOR	3.905 *
KOF	2.549	KOR	7.695	EDO	4.309 *	SUM	3.953 *
KAN	2.642	THI	7.954 **	VTN	4.339 *	PHL	4.168 *
SAK	2.874	VTN	8.102 **	HAN	4.447 *	SUL	4.241 *
KOR	3.070	KYU	8.142 **	PHL	4.836 **	VTN	4.627 *
OKI	3.935 **	HK	8.239 **	KAN	4.935 *	BAC	4.637 *
Borneo		**Sulawesi**		**L. Sundas**		**S. Moluccas**	
LSN	1.648	JAV	1.998	BOR	1.648	LSN	4.774 *
SUM	1.999	CML	2.208	SUM	2.061	BOR	5.141 *
SLW	2.458	BOR	2.458	SLW	2.551 *	SUM	5.966 *
JAV	3.905 *	LSN	2.551 *	PHL	2.932 **	SLW	6.075 *
SUL	4.186 **	SUM	2.665	VTN	3.113 *	SUL	6.758 *
VTN	4.534 *	SUL	2.843	JAV	3.300 *	PHL	7.323 *
PHL	4.779 **	PHL	2.994	EDO	3.735 *	ATY	8.621 *
CML	4.990 *	THI	3.446 *	MAR	4.066 *	CML	9.115 *
SML	5.141 *	VTN	4.346 *	SML	4.774 *	VTN	9.204 *
THI	6.843 *	BAC	4.525 *	KAM	4.783 *	EDO	9.741 *
Sulu		**Philippines**		**Vietnam**		**Bachuc**	
SLW	2.843	VTN	2.000	PHL	2.000	THI	2.919 *
CML	2.908	LSN	2.932 **	LSN	3.113 *	HAI	3.615 *
BOR	4.186 **	SLW	2.994	THI	3.754 *	BUR	4.444
JAV	4.241 *	JAV	4.168 *	KOR	3.809 *	SLW	4.525 *
BUR	5.149	THI	4.256 *	HK	3.927 *	JAV	4.637 *
LSN	5.182 *	KOR	4.648	HAI	4.292 *	VTN	4.825 *
SUM	5.260 *	HAI	4.760 *	SUM	4.339 *	PHL	5.118 *
BAC	6.752 *	BOR	4.779 **	SLW	4.346 *	CML	5.744 *
SML	6.758 *	SUM	4.836 **	EDO	4.381 *	KOR	5.936 *
PHL	6.797 *	HK	4.860 *	BOR	4.534 *	LSN	6.266 *

Cambodia and Laos		Thailand		Burma	
SLW	2.208	BAC	2.919 *	BAC	4.444
SUL	2.908	JAV	2.936 *	THI	4.575
JAV	3.103 *	HAI	3.313 *	SLW	4.803
BOR	4.990 *	SLW	3.446 *	SUL	5.149
THI	5.341 *	KOR	3.509 **	JAV	5.507
LSN	5.534 *	VTN	3.754 *	SUM	5.584
PHL	5.582 *	PHL	4.256 *	CML	5.674
BUR	5.674	BUR	4.575	LSN	7.065 *
BAC	5.744 *	HK	4.766 *	BOR	7.593
SUM	6.232 *	KAN	5.116 *	KAN	7.621 *

Note: Level of significance is defined as the quantity $(n_i \times n_j / n_i + n_j) D^2_{ij}$ that is distributed as chi-square with p degrees of freedom (n_i = sample size of group i; n_j = sample size of group j); D^2_{ij} = square of the generalized distance between groups i and j, and p = number of variables. See table 7.1 for explanation of group abbreviations.

Levels of significance: * distances significant at 1 percent level; ** distances significant at 5 percent level.

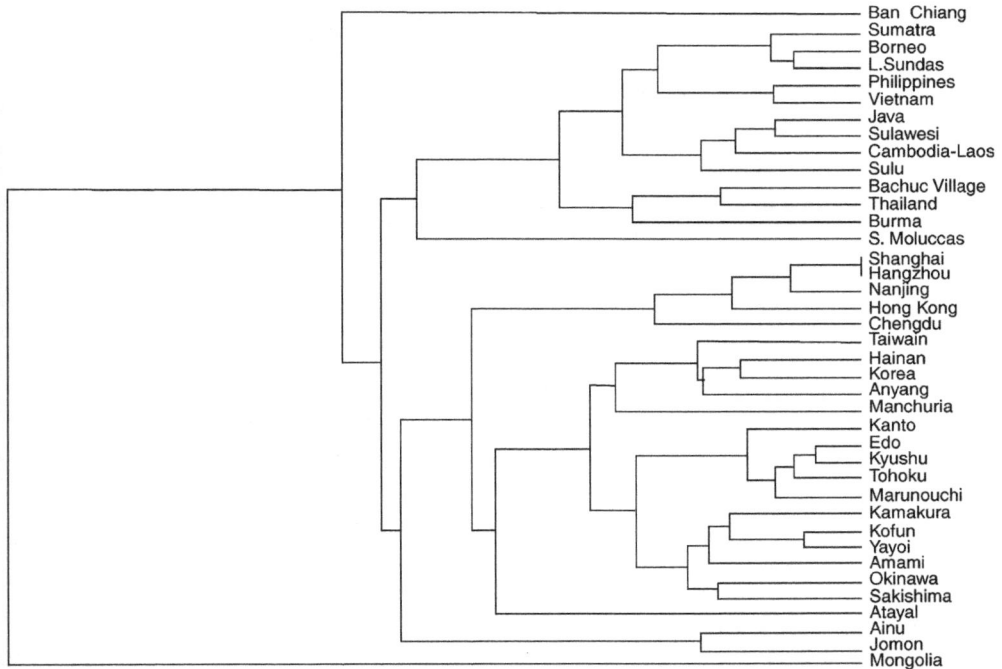

Figure 7.6. Diagram of relationship (dendrogram) based on a cluster analysis (UPGMA) of Mahalanobis' generalized distances using 24 cranial measurements recorded in 39 male groups.

Discussion

Jomon-Ainu Connection

The association between Jomon and modern Ainu people found in the results of this analysis is supported by numerous lines of evidence (e.g., Brace and Hunt 1990; Brace et al. 1989; Dodo 1986; Dodo and Ishida 1990; K. Hanihara 1985, 1991; T. Hanihara 1993; Hanihara et al. 1993; Howells 1966, 1986; Ishida and Kondo 1999; Kozintsev 1990; Matsumura 1989, 2001; Mizoguchi 1986; Omoto et al. 1996; Ossenberg 1986; Pietrusewsky 1996, 2000; Turner 1976, 1987, 1990; Yamaguchi 1992).

Ryukyu Islanders, Jomon, and Ainu

Contrary to previous studies (e.g., Baelz 1911; Newman and Eng 1947; K. Hanihara et al. 1974; Yamaguchi 1992; T. Hanihara 1989, 1991, 1992; Omoto 1992; Matsumura 1995; Omoto and Saitou 1997), the results of the present analysis provide little support for an affinity between the Ryukyu Islanders, Jomon, and the Ainu, a conclusion iterated in earlier work (e.g., Mouri 1988; Pietrusewsky 1994, 1996, 1997, 1999, 2004; Horai et al. 1996; Doi et al. 1997; Dodo et al. 1998). Likewise, the present study finds little evidence for a connection between Jomon, Ainu, and Southeast Asia. Several researchers (e.g., K. Hanihara 1991; Turner 1992a, 1992b) have suggested that Japan's preagricultural Jomon populations (and by association, the Ainu and Ryukyu Islanders, their presumed descendants) derive from people inhabiting in Southeast Asia during the Upper Paleolithic. In addition to a lack of close affinity between the Ryukyu Islanders and the Ainu or Jomon, these results indicate that Jomon, Ainu, Ryukyu Island, and all Japanese series (since Yayoi times) are members of a greater East/Northeast Asian constellation, suggesting a North/East Asian ancestry for these groups. Omoto and Saitou (1997) using genetic data have reached a similar conclusion.

Origin of the Japanese

The results of this analysis demonstrate that the cranial series from the Japanese archipelago fall out into one of three separate groupings. The most isolated group contains the prehistoric Jomon and modern Ainu samples. A second group includes the Ryukyu Islands, Yayoi, Kofun, and Kamakura series. The last group includes Marunouchi and the more modern Japanese cranial series: Edo, Tohoku, Kanto, and Kyushu. With the exception of the Jomon-Ainu grouping, a close biological connection is seen between all cranial series from Japan since Yayoi times.

    This marked differentiation between the Japanese since Yayoi times and the Jomon-Ainu series agrees with the general consensus that a major influx of new people into the Japanese archipelago (that is, via the Korean peninsula) began with the Yayoi (c. 500 BC–AD 300) and Kofun (4th–7th century AD) periods, a view that has been popularized as the "dual structure model" by Kazuro Hanihara (1991). As is evidenced in the diagram of relationship based on distances (figure 7.6), a branch containing Taiwan, Hainan, and more Northeast Asian cranial series, Korea, Bronze-age Chinese from Anyang, and Manchuria is the first to connect to the Japanese series, a view that is consistent with an origin of the Japanese in Northeast Asia beginning in the Yayoi period.

Inspection of the closest distances suggests that Edo, Tohoku, Marunouchi, Kanto, and Kyushu are among the groups with the closest distances to Manchuria, Anyang, and Korea. Korea is closest to several of the Japanese series (e.g., Kanto, Edo, Kofun, Yayoi, Tohoku, and Kyushu). Likewise, closer inspection of the classification results indicates that several of the Yayoi specimens are reclassified as Mongolia and Manchuria (see also chapter 5). Similarly, several of the Manchurian specimens are reclassified as Japanese. The classification results reaffirm the biological connections between Northeast Asia (especially Korea, Manchuria, and Anyang) and the Japanese series (see discussion in chapter 5, which uses nonmetric traits). The Ryukyu Island misclassifications suggest a differentiation of these island inhabitants, who also demonstrate affinities to Hainan Island, Taiwan, and several North Asian series.

When other mainland East and North Asian cranial series are compared, the Japanese cranial series, including Ainu and Jomon, form a major composite grouping that includes cranial series from mainland China, Korea, Manchuria, Taiwan, and Hainan Island. These associations suggest that Northeast Asia is the likely ancestral homeland of the ancient as well as more modern inhabitants of the Japanese and Ryukyu archipelagos.

East/Northeast Asia–Southeast Asian Dichotomy

In addition to aiding our understanding of biological relationships of people on both sides of the Sea of Japan, results of the present analysis provide context for examining some of the current archaeological and linguistic models that attempt to explain the population history of Southeast Asia and East Asia. Bellwood and colleagues (Bellwood 1997, 2005; Diamond and Bellwood 2003) as well as others (e.g., Higham 2001) have emerged as strong supporters of a population displacement model to account for the people who now inhabit Southeast Asia. Advocates of this model maintain that the indigenous inhabitants of Southeast Asia were replaced by migrant people of a more northerly origin, or, to use Bellwood's terminology, "Australo-Melanesians" were replaced by "Mongoloids" (Bellwood 1997). Work in physical anthropology by Matsumura (2001, 2006) and colleagues (Matsumura and Hudson 2005; Matsumura et al. 2001) favors such an interpretation of population history.

An alternative model (population or continuity model) argues that the present-day inhabitants of Southeast Asia evolved within this region from the late Pleistocene onward. The work of Turner (1987, 1989, 1990, 1992a), focusing on dental nonmetric traits and the recognition of two polar dental complexes (Sundadonty for Southeast Asia and Polynesia, and Sinodonty for the inhabitants of East Asia), represents a new and recent variant of this viewpoint. Other work in physical anthropology that supports a continuity model includes that of Bulbeck (1982), Hanihara (1993), Pietrusewsky (2004, 2005, 2006a, 2006b), Pietrusewsky and Douglas (2002), and Pope (1992).

The diagram of relationship based on Mahalanobis' distances (figure 7.6) shows a clear separation between East/North Asian and Southeast Asian cranial series and a clear connection between mainland and island Southeast Asia. Generally, the distances closest to the eastern Chinese (e.g., Shanghai, Hangzhou, and Nanjing) and Northeast Asian (e.g., Manchuria, Korea, and Mongolia) series are from the same regions. The more southerly placed Hainan Island and Taiwan cranial series cluster with samples from Korea, Manchuria, and Anyang. As seen in the dendrogram through an inspection of individual distances, these same five groups are further related to several of the Japanese cranial series. Inspection of the individual distances (table 7.7), although not evident in figure 7.6, reveals that several of the Southeast Asian cranial series (e.g., Sumatra, Vietnam, and Thailand) are among the closest distances to East Asian and Northeast Asian cranial series.

Closer inspection of the jackknifed classification results further reveals that only a few of the East and Northeast Asian specimens reclassify as Southeast Asians. The classifications for Hainan Island are an exception, with 15 of the misclassified Hainan Island crania being assigned to one of the Southeast Asian series.

Although Bachuc, Thailand, and Burma occupy a separate branch, there is no clear separation of mainland and island Southeast Asian series. The Southern Moluccas and Ban Chiang series occupy more marginal positions in this diagram. Inspection of the smallest distances confirms that the series closest to the Southeast Asian series include series from the same region. The exception is the Ban Chiang series, which includes a number of North and East Asian series among its smallest distances.

In summary, the present craniometric results indicate a clear distinction between the inhabitants of East/North Asia and Southeast Asia (mainland and insular). This distinction implies long-term in situ evolution in both regions and argues against displacement to account for the present-day inhabitants of Southeast Asia (see chapter 8 for an alternative position). Finally, studies of classical (e.g., Cavalli-Sfroza et al. 1992; Omoto and Saitou 1997) as well as molecular genetic data (e.g., Su et al. 1999) have demonstrated marked differences between northern and southern Chinese while more recent molecular genetic studies do not support the existence of this genetic distinction (e.g., Ding et al. 2000).

Conclusions

The results of this multivariate craniometric analysis support a number of conclusions regarding the biological relationships of the earlier and more modern inhabitants of East Asia, North Asia, and Southeast Asia. The main conclusions of this analysis are outlined as follows.

1. The prehistoric Jomon and modern Ainu share a close biological relationship, an association that is well removed from the cranial series from Japan beginning during the Yayoi period approximately 2500 years BP.

2. Biological connections between Yayoi and Japanese cranial series with several mainland Northeast Asian cranial series support a major migration of people from the Asian mainland that began during the Yayoi period.

3. The Ryukyu Island cranial series are most similar to the Yayoi, Kofun, and Kamakura cranial series, a connection that suggests an introduction of immigrants from mainland North Asia commencing with the Yayoi period.

4. The Ryukyu Island cranial series are not closely related to either the Jomon or Ainu cranial series.

5. All cranial series from Japan, including modern Japanese, Ryukyu Islanders, Ainu, and Jomon, are members of a greater East Asian/North Asian grouping, their presumed homeland.

6. The marked separation of East/North Asian and Southeast Asian cranial series argues for long-term continuity within regions rather than population intrusion or replacement in Southeast Asia.

7. Possible connections between the premetal inhabitants of Southeast Asia, such as Ban Chiang, Bronze Age Chinese (Anyang), Hainan Island, and modern Ryukyu Island series, are further implied by these results.

Acknowledgments

I wish to thank Rona Ikehara-Quebral for her help with the analysis of data used in this chapter. Rhea Hood and Joey Condit assisted with the construction of the tables. My thanks to Dr. Michele Toomay Douglas for her continued generous advice and comments on earlier versions of this chapter. Ms. Billie Ikeda is responsible for the figures.

Literature Cited

Baelz E von. 1911. Die Riu-Kiu-Insulaner, die Aino und andere kaukasierähnliche Reste in Ostasien. *Korrespondenz-Blatt der Deutchen Gesellschaft für Anthropologie, Ethnologie und Uregeschichte* 42: 187–91.

Bayard DT. 1996. Linguistics, archaeologists, and Austronesian origins: Comparative and sociolinguistic aspects of the Meacham-Bellwood debate. *Bulletin of the Indo-Pacific Prehistory Association* 15: 71–85.

Bellwood P. 1996. Early agriculture and the dispersal of the southern Mongoloids. In: Akazawa T, Szathmáry EJE, editors. *Prehistoric Mongoloid dispersals.* Oxford: Oxford University Press. Pp. 287–302.

Bellwood P. 1997. *Prehistory of the Indo-Malaysian Archipelago.* Rev. ed. Honolulu: University of Hawai'i Press.

Bellwood P. 2000. Some thoughts on understanding the human colonization of the Pacific. *People and Culture in Oceania* 16: 5–17.

Bellwood, P. 2005. *First farmers: The origins of agricultural societies.* Oxford, UK: Blackwell.

Blust R. 1996. Beyond the Austronesian homeland: The Austric hypothesis and its implications for archaeology. In: Goodenough W, editor. *Prehistoric settlement of the Pacific.* Philadelphia: Transactions of the American Philosophical Society. Pp. 117–40.

Brace CL, Brace MC, Leonard WR. 1989. Reflections on the face of Japan: A multivariate craniofacial and odontometric perspective. *American Journal of Physical Anthropology* 78: 93–113.

Brace CL, Hunt KD. 1990. A nonracial craniofacial perspective on human variation: A(ustralia) to Z(uni). *American Journal of Physical Anthropology* 82: 341–60.

Buikstra JE, Frankenberg SR, Konigsberg LW. 1990. Skeletal biological distance studies in American physical anthropology: Recent trends. *American Journal of Physical Anthropology* 82: 1–7.

Fulbeck D. 1982. A re-evaluation of possible evolutionary processes in Southeast Asia since the late Pleistocene. *Bulletin of the Indo-Pacific Prehistory Association* 3: 1–21.

Buranarugsa M, Leach F. 1993. Coordinate geometry of Moriori crania and comparisons with Maori. *Man and Culture in Oceania* 9: 1–43.

Cavalli-Sforza LL, Menozzi P, Piazza A. 1992. Genetic history and geography of Asia. In: Akazawa T, Aoki K, Kimura T, editors. *The evolution and dispersal of modern humans in Asia.* Tokyo: Hokusen-sha. Pp. 613–23.

Diamond J, Bellwood P. 2003. Farmers and their languages: The first expansions. *Science* 300: 597–603.

Ding Y, Wooding S, Harpending HC, Chi H, Li H, Yun-Xin Fu Y, Pang F, Yao Y, Xiang Yu J, Moyzis R, Zhang Y. 2000. Population structure and history in East Asia. *Proceeding of the National Academy of Sciences* (USA) 97: 14003–6.

Dixon WJ, editor. 1992. *BMDP. Statistical Software Manual.* Vol. 1. Berkeley: University of California Press.

Dixon WJ, Brown MB, editors. 1979. *BMDP-79.* Biomedical Computer Programs P-series. Berkeley: University of California Press.

Dodo Y. 1986. Metrical and non-metrical analyses of Jomon crania from eastern Japan. In: Akazawa T, Aikens CM, editors. *Prehistoric hunter-gatherers in Japan.* Tokyo: University of Tokyo. Pp. 137–61.

Dodo Y, Doi N, Kondo O. 1998. Ainu and Ryukyuan cranial nonmetric variation: Evidence which disputes the Ainu-Ryukyu Islands common origin theory. *Anthropological Science* 106: 99–120.

Dodo Y, Ishida H. 1990. Population history of Japan as viewed from cranial nonmetric variation. *Journal of the Anthropological Society of Nippon* 98: 269–87.

Doi N, Dodo Y, Kondo O. 1997. Amami-Okinawans as viewed from cranial measurements. *Anthropological Science* 105: 79.

Glover IC, Higham CFW. 1996. New evidence for early rice cultivation in South, Southeast, and East Asia. In: Harris DR, editor. *The origins and spread of agriculture and pastoralism in Eurasia.* Washington DC: Smithsonian Institution Press. Pp. 413–41.

Habu J. 2004. *Ancient Jomon of Japan.* Cambridge: Cambridge University Press.

Hanihara K. 1985. Origins and affinities of Japanese as viewed from cranial measurements. In: Kirk R, Szathmary E, editors. *Out of Asia: Peopling the Americas and the Pacific.* Canberra: Journal of Pacific History. Pp. 105–12.

Hanihara K. 1986. The origin of the Japanese in relation to other ethnic groups in East Asia. In: Pearson RJ, Barnes GL, Hutterer KL, editors. *Windows on the Japanese past: Studies in archaeology and prehistory.* Ann Arbor: Center for Japanese Studies, University of Michigan. Pp. 75–83.

Hanihara K. 1991. Dual structure model for the population history of Japanese. *Japan Review* 2: 1–33.

Hanihara K. 1998. Reanalysis of local variation in the Ainu crania. *Anthropological Science* 106: 1–15.

Hanihara K, Hanihara T, Koizumi K. 1993. Biological relationships between the Jomon-Ainu and Pacific population groups. *Japan Review* 4: 7–25.

Hanihara K, Masuda T, Tanaka T. 1974. Affinities of dental characteristics in the Okinawa Islanders. *Journal of the Anthropological Society of Nippon* 82: 75–82.

Hanihara T. 1989. Comparative studies of geographically isolated populations in Japan based on dental measurements. *Journal of the Anthropological Society of Nippon* 97: 95–107.

Hanihara T. 1991. Dentition of Nansei Islanders and peopling of the Japanese Archipelago: The basic populations in East Asia IX. *Journal of the Anthropological Society of Nippon* 99: 399–409.

Hanihara T. 1992. Dental and cranial evidence on the affinities of the East Asian and Pacific populations. In: Hanihara K, editor. *Japanese as a member of the Asian and Pacific populations: International Symposium 4.* Kyoto: International Research Center for Japanese Studies. Pp. 119–37.

Hanihara T. 1993. Population prehistory of East Asia and the Pacific as viewed from craniofacial morphology: The basic populations in East Asia VII. *American Journal of Physical Anthropology* 91: 173–87.

Higham CFW. 1996. *The Bronze Age of Southeast Asia.* Cambridge: Cambridge University Press.

Higham CFW. 2001. Prehistory, language and human biology: Is there a consensus in East and Southeast Asia? In: Jin L, Seielstad M, Xiao C, editors. *Genetic, linguistic and archaeological perspectives on human diversity in Southeast Asia.* River Edge, NJ: World Scientific. Pp. 3–16.

Horai S, Marayama K, Hayasaka K, Matsubayashi S, Hattori Y, Fucharoen G, Harihara S, Park KS, Omoto K, Pan I-H. 1996. mtDNA polymorphism in East Asian populations, with special reference to the peopling of Japan. *American Journal of Human Genetics* 59: 579–90.

Howells WW. 1966. *The Jomon population of Japan: A study by discriminant analysis of Japanese and Ainu crania.* Papers of the Peabody Museum of Archaeology and Ethnology, vol. 57, no. 1. Cambridge, MA: Harvard University. Pp. 1–43.

Howells WW. 1973. *Cranial variation in man.* Papers of the Peabody Museum of Archaeology and Ethnology, vol. 67. Cambridge, MA: Harvard University.

Howells WW. 1986. Physical anthropology of the prehistoric Japanese. In: Pearson RF, editor. *Windows on the Japanese past: Studies in archaeology and prehistory.* Ann Arbor: Center for Japanese Studies, University of Michigan. Pp. 85–99.

Howells WW. 1989. *Skull shapes and the map: Craniometric analyses in the dispersion of modern Homo.* Papers of the Peabody Museum of Archaeology and Ethnology, vol. 79. Cambridge, MA: Harvard University.

Ishida H. 1996. Metric and nonmetric cranial variation of the prehistoric Okhotsk people. *Anthropological Science* 104: 233–58.

Ishida H, Kondo O. 1999. Nonmetric cranial variation of the Ainu and neighbouring human populations. *Perspectives on Human Biology* 4: 127–38.

Koganei Y. 1893–94. Beiträge zur physischen anthropologie der Aino. *Mitteilungen der Medizinischen Fakultät der Kaiserlichen Universität (Tokyo)* 2: 1–404.

Kozintsev AG. 1990. Ainu, Japanese, their ancestors and neighbours: Cranioscopic data. *Journal of the Anthropological Society of Nippon* 97: 493–512.

Li C. 1977. *Anyang.* Seattle: University of Washington Press.

Mahalanobis PC. 1936. On the generalized distance in statistics. *Proceedings of the National Institute of Sciences, Calcutta* 2: 49–55.

Martin R, Saller K. 1957. *Lehrbuch der Anthropologie.* Revised 3rd ed. Stuttgart: Gustav Fischer Verlag.

Matsumura H. 1989. Geographical variation of dental measurements in the Jomon population. *Journal of the Anthropological Society of Nippon* 97: 493–512.

Matsumura H. 1995. Dental characteristics affinities of the prehistoric to modern Japanese with the East Asians, American natives and Australo-Melanesians. *Anthropological Science* 103: 235–61.

Matsumura H. 2001. Differentials of Yayoi immigration to Japan as derived from dental metrics. *Homo* 52: 135–56.

Matsumura H. 2006. The population history of Southeast Asia viewed from morphometric analyses of human skeletal and dental remains. In Oxenham MF, Tayles N, editors. *Bioarchaeology of Southeast Asia.* Cambridge: Cambridge University Press. Pp. 33–58.

Matsumura H, Cuong NL, Thuy NK, Anezaki T. 2001. Dental morphology of the early Hoabinhian: The Neolithic Da But and the Metal Age Dong Son cultural people in Vietnam. *Zeitschrift für Morphologie und Anthropologie* 83: 59–73.

Matsumura H, Hudson M. 2005. Dental perspectives on population history of Southeast Asia. *American Journal of Physical Anthropology* 127: 182–209.

Mizoguchi Y. 1986. Contributions of prehistoric Far East populations to the population of modern Japan: A Q-mode path analysis based on cranial measurements. In: Akazawa T, Aikens CM, editors. *Prehistoric hunter-gatherers in Japan.* Tokyo: University of Tokyo. Pp. 107–36.

Mouri T. 1988. Incidence of cranial nonmetric characters in five Jomon populations from west Japan. *Journal of the Anthropological Society of Nippon* 96: 319–37.

Newman MT, Eng RL. 1947. The Ryukyu people. *American Journal of Physical Anthropology* 5: 114–57.

Omoto K. 1992. Some aspects of the genetic composition of the Japanese. In: Hanihara K, editor.

Japanese as a member of the Asian and Pacific populations: International Symposium 4. Kyoto: International Research Center for Japanese Studies. Pp. 139–45.

Omoto K, Hirai M, Harihara S, Misawa S, Washio K, Tokunaga K, Saitou N, Yamazaki K, Du R, Hao L, Yuan Y, Xu J, Jin F, Hu J, Wei X, Li S, Zhao H, Zhang Z, Niu K, Du C, Liu B. 1996. Population genetic studies on national minorities in China. In: Akazawa T, Szathmary EJE, editors. *Prehistoric Mongoloid dispersals.* Oxford: Oxford Science Publications, Oxford University Press. Pp. 137–45.

Omoto K, Saitou N. 1997. Genetic origins of the Japanese: A partial support of the dual structure hypothesis. *American Journal of Physical Anthropology* 102: 437–46.

Ossenberg N. 1986. Isolate conservatism and hybridization in the population history of Japan. The evidence of nonmetric cranial traits. In: Akazawa T, Aikens CM, editors. *Prehistoric hunter-gatherers in Japan.* Tokyo: University of Tokyo. Pp. 199–215.

Pietrusewsky M. 1994. Pacific-Asian relationships: A physical anthropological perspective. *Oceanic Linguistics* 33: 407–30.

Pietrusewsky M. 1996. Multivariate craniometric investigations of Japanese, Asians, and Pacific Islanders. In: Omoto K, editor. *Interdisciplinary perspectives on the origins of the Japanese: International Symposium No. 11-B.* Kyoto: International Research Center for Japanese Studies. Pp. 65–104.

Pietrusewsky M. 1997. The people of Ban Chiang: An early Bronze-Age site in northeast Thailand. *Bulletin of the Indo-Pacific Prehistory Association* 16: 119–48.

Pietrusewsky M. 1999. A multivariate craniometric investigation of the inhabitants of the Ryukyu Islands and comparisons with cranial series from Japan, Asia, and the Pacific. *Anthropological Science* 107: 255–81.

Pietrusewsky M. 2000. Metric analysis of skeletal remains: Methods and applications. In: Katzenberg MA, Saunders SR, editors. *Biological anthropology of the human skeleton.* New York: Wiley-Liss. Pp. 375–415.

Pietrusewsky M. 2004. Multivariate comparisons of female cranial series from the Ryukyu Islands and Japan. *Anthropological Science* 112: 199–211.

Pietrusewsky M. 2005. The physical anthropology of the Pacific, East Asia, and Southeast Asia: A multivariate craniometric analysis. In: Sagart L, Blench R, Sanchez-Mazas A, editors. *The peopling of East Asia: Putting together archaeology, linguistics, and genetics.* London: Routledge-Curzon. Pp. 201–29.

Pietrusewsky M. 2006a. A multivariate craniometric study of the prehistoric and modern inhabitants of Southeast Asia, East Asia, and surrounding regions: A human kaleidoscope? In: Oxenham MR, Tayles N, editors. *Bioarchaeology of Southeast Asia.* Cambridge: Cambridge University Press. Pp. 59–90.

Pietrusewsky M. 2006b. The initial settlement of remote Oceania: The evidence from physical anthropology. In: Simanjuntak T, Pojoh IHE, Hisyam M, editors. *Austronesian diaspora and the ethnogeneses of people in Indonesian Archipelago: Proceedings of the International Symposium.* Jakarta: Indonesian Institute of Sciences, LIPI Press. Pp. 320–47.

Pietrusewsky M. 2008. Metric analysis of skeletal remains: Methods and applications. In: Katzenberg MA, Saunders SR, editors. *Biological anthropology of the human skeleton.* 2nd ed. New York: Wiley-Liss. Pp. 487–532.

Pietrusewsky M, Douglas MT. 2002. *Ban Chiang, a prehistoric site in northeast Thailand. Vol. 1: The human skeletal remains.* University Monograph 111. Philadelphia: University of Pennsylvania Museum of Archaeology and Anthropology.

Pope GG. 1992. Replacement versus regionally continuous models: The paleobehavioral and fossil evidence from East Asia. In: Akazawa T, Aoki K, Kimura T, editors. *The evolution and dispersal of modern humans in Asia.* Tokyo: Hokusen-sha. Pp. 3–14.

Rao RC. 1952. *Advanced statistical methods in biomedical research.* New York: John Wiley.

Rohlf FJ. 1993. *NTSYS-PC: Numerical taxonomy and multivariate analysis system, Version 1.80.* Setauket, NY: Exeter Software.

Sjøvold T. 1984. A report on the heritability of some cranial measurements and non-metric traits. In: Van Vark GN, Howells WW, editors. *Multivariate statistics in physical anthropology.* Dordrecht: D. Reidel. Pp. 223–46.

Sneath PHA, Sokal RR. 1973. *Numerical taxonomy.* San Francisco: WH Freeman.

Su B, Xiao J, Underhill P, Deka R, Zhang W, Akey J, Huang W, Shen D, Lu D, Luo J, Chu J, Tan J, Shen P, Davis R, Cavalli-Sforza L, Chakraborty R, Xiong M, Du R, Oefner P, Chen Z, Jin L. 1999. Y-Chromosome evidence for a northward migration of modern humans into Eastern Asia during the last Ice Age. *American Journal of Human Genetics* 65: 1718–24.

Tatsuoka MM. 1971. *Multivariate analysis: Techniques for educational and psychological research.* New York: John Wiley and Sons.

Turner CG II. 1976. Dental evidence on the origin of the Ainu and Japanese. *Science* 193: 911–13.

Turner CG II. 1987. Late Pleistocene and Holocene population history of East Asia based on dental variation. *American Journal of Physical Anthropology* 73: 305–21.

Turner CG II. 1989. Teeth and prehistory in Asia. *Scientific American* 262: 88–96.

Turner CG II. 1990. Major features of Sundadonty and Sinodonty including suggestions about East Asian microevolution, population history, and late Pleistocene relationships with Australian Aborigines. *American Journal of Physical Anthropology* 82: 295–317.

Turner CG II. 1992a. Sundadonty and Sinodonty in Japan: The dental basis for a dual origin hypothesis for the peopling of the Japanese Islands. In: Hanihara K, editor. *Japanese as a member of the Asian and Pacific populations.* Kyoto: International Research Center for Japanese Studies. Pp. 96–112.

Turner CG II. 1992b. Microevolution of East Asian and European populations: A dental perspective. In: Akazawa T, Aoki K, Kimura T, editors. *The evolution and dispersal of modern humans in Asia.* Tokyo: Hokusen-sha. Pp. 415–38.

Van Vark GN, Howells WW, editors. 1984. *Multivariate statistics in physical anthropology.* Dordrecht: D. Reidel.

Van Vark GN, Schaafsma M. 1992. Advances in the quantitative analysis of skeletal morphology. In: Saunders SR, Katzenberg MA, editors. *Skeletal biology of past peoples: Research methods.* New York: Wiley-Liss. Pp. 225–57.

White J. 1986. A revision of the chronology of Ban Chiang and its implications for the prehistory of northeast Thailand. Ph.D. dissertation, University of Pennsylvania.

Wilkinson L. 1992. *SYSTAT for Windows, Version 5.* Evanston: Systat, Inc.

Yamaguchi B. 1992. Skeletal morphology of the Jomon people. In: Hanihara K, editor. *Japanese as a member of the Asian and Pacific population: International Symposium 4.* Kyoto: International Research Center for Japanese Studies. Pp. 52–63.

8

Population Dispersal
from East Asia into Southeast Asia

Evidence from Cranial and Dental Morphology

HIROFUMI MATSUMURA AND MARC OXENHAM

This chapter addresses the issues of population dispersal from East Asia into Southeast Asia, through prehistoric to modern times, from a bioanthropological perspective based on the analysis of human dental morphology. Given the many studies that discuss the local evolution of indigenous Southeast Asians and include modern southern China as part of Southeast Asia, the precision of geographical terminology is of major importance. We use the distinct designations East and Southeast Asia, with East Asia encompassing modern China, Taiwan, Korea, Japan, Mongolia, and the Russian Far East. Southeast Asia, in contrast, includes modern Myanmar, Thailand, Vietnam, Laos, Cambodia, Malaysia, Singapore, Indonesia, Brunei, and the Philippines. While it may well be argued that the principal geographical origin of the East Asian populations expanding into Southeast Asia lay within the modern borders of China, these people were certainly not Sinitic in the historical or linguistic sense.

Since the early twentieth century, a large number of prehistoric human remains have been discovered in Southeast Asia (see also Oxenham and Tayles 2006; Tayles and Oxenham 2006), enabling scholars to address the issue of the population history of the region with respect to skeletal and dental morphology. In the early stages of this research, a majority of the skeletal remains recovered from the preceramic period were found in cave sites in Malaysia, Indonesia, Laos, Cambodia, and Vietnam. A number of earlier analyses of apparently pre-Neolithic human remains (e.g., Gua Cha, Guar Kepah, and Gua Kerbau in mainland Malaysia and Liang Momer and Liang Toge in Flores), citing dolichocranic skulls with protruding glabellae, massive jaws with relatively large teeth, alveolar prognathism, and long slender limbs, described morphological features akin to recent and living Australian Aborigines or Melanesians (e.g., Evans 1918; Duckworth 1934; Mijsberg 1940; Trevor and Brothwell 1962; Jacob 1967). However, while these assemblages were all associated with pre-Neolithic lithic technologies, such observations were based on quite fragmentary material for the most part and, perhaps as important, lacked reliable dates. Brothwell (1960) examined the late Pleistocene human skull excavated from the West Mouth of the Niah Caves in Sarawak and found that it bore closest similarity to Australian Tasmanians. Remains from the late Pleistocene Tabon caves on Palawan Island in the Philippines were seen by Macintosh (1978) as akin to Australo-Melanesians.

Early theorizing led to the belief that modern Southeast Asian people, originating in North and/or East Asia, arose through a range of north to south migratory processes and subsequent genetic exchange with indigenous populations (van Stein Callenfels 1936; Mijsberg 1940; von Koenigswald 1952; Coon 1962; Jacob 1967; Bellwood 1987, 1989, 1996, 1997; Brace et al. 1991). This model is known as the two layer, the immigration, or in some cases the replacement model for understanding the peopling of Southeast Asia.

Up until now, the immigration hypothesis has gained theoretical support from the fields of historical linguistics and archaeology. The premodern dispersion of the Austronesian and Austroasiatic language families has been specifically linked with the expansion of food-producing populations during the Neolithic period and early Iron Age (Renfrew 1987, 1989, 1992; Bellwood 1991, 1993, 1996, 1997; Bellwood et al. 1992; Hudson 1994, 1999, 2003; Blust 1996a,b; Glover and Higham 1996; Higham 1998, 2001; Bellwood and Renfrew 2002; Diamond and Bellwood 2003). Both linguistic and archaeological considerations suggest that southern China and Taiwan were the ultimate sources of these language and population dispersals.

Furthermore, mtDNA sequences suggest that Taiwan aborigines have temporally deep roots, probably in central or south China (Melton et al. 1998). Other mtDNA analyses, as well as studies based on classic genetic markers (Ballinger et al. 1992; Cavalli-Sforza et al. 1994; Omoto and Saitou 1997; Ding et al. 2000; Tan 2001), have revealed very close biological relationships between Chinese and Southeast Asian samples, a result that may suggest the occurrence of gene flow from north to south across this area. Nonetheless, geneticists have had surprisingly little to say concerning the two layer hypothesis in mainland Southeast Asia, in contrast to the wealth of research on Island Southeast Asia and the Pacific (see recent review in Bellwood et al. 2011).

Despite the long history of the two layer hypothesis, a number of studies have produced results that bring it into question. For instance, Turner's Sundadont/Sinodont dental classification (Turner 1989, 1990, 1992) has resulted in a very different interpretation of Asian population history, often referred to as the regional continuity or local evolution model. His analyses, based on nonmetric dental traits, demonstrated that both early and modern Southeast Asians exhibit the so-called Sundadont dental complex, leading to the conclusion that early Sundadont populations diffused into Northeast Asia and evolved into Sinodont populations. Consequently, he hypothesized that the array of nonmetric Sundadont dental traits possessed by present-day Southeast Asians are the product of long-standing evolutionary continuity, uninterrupted by significant admixture with Sinodont peoples from the north.

Based on multivariate craniometric analyses, Hanihara (1992, 1993a,b,c, 1994, 2006) and Pietrusewsky (1992, 1994, 1996, 1999a,b, 2005, 2006, 2008, 2010) have argued for relatively close affinities between early and modern Southeast Asians, coupled with a distinct dissimilarity to Australo-Melanesians, using their findings as support for regional continuity in Southeast Asian population history. A large-scale genomic survey of nucleotide polymorphisms, conducted by the HUGO Pan-Asian SNP Consortium (2009), also challenges the customary two layer model in supporting a single origin for Southeast Asians.

Nevertheless, some competing dental studies (Kamminga and Wright 1988; Matsumura and Hudson 2005) dispute the validity of a regional continuity model based on Turner's Sinodont/Sundadont concept. In addition, more extensive studies that include new skeletal finds from Thailand, Malaysia, and Vietnam substantiate the two layer hypothesis (Matsumura and Zuraina 1995, 1999; Matsumura and Pookajorn 2005; Matsumura 2006; Matsumura, Oxenham et al. 2008; Matsumura, Yoneda et al. 2008). A recent study by Hanihara (2006), who once rejected the two layer hypothesis, now partially supports this model in a reanalysis using a geographically broad data set.

Debates over the population history of Southeast Asia generally revolve around two main potential issues. The first is whether the early settlers of Southeast Asia were of a different lineage than later, including present-day, populations. In mainland Southeast Asia, early occupants during the pre-Neolithic period are represented by skeletons associated with Hoabinhian material culture (c. 18,000–6,000 years BP [Oxenham et al. 2005]). The Hoabinhian is loosely equivalent to what in Europe would be called the Mesolithic, which was widespread on the mainland of Southeast Asia and southern China during the late Pleistocene and early Holocene (Tan 1976). Revealing the genealogical relationship between such early foragers and later-

period farming populations is crucially important for clarifying our understanding of the population history of the region.

Here, we present the results of an assessment of the biological affinities
of early Southeast Asians, using dental morphological data as a basis of
comparison. Dental morphology is believed to be relatively little affected
by environment and thus genetically conservative through time. Even in
situations where skeletal remains are fragile and fragmentary, teeth are often
well preserved and available for study. Previous comparative analyses using
geographically wide-ranging population samples from Southeast/Northeast
Asia and the circum-Pacific regions demonstrated a significant morphological gap between early Southeast Asians and modern East Asians (Matsumura
and Hudson 2005). We offer the results of a more extensive analysis, using
alternative methods applied to data sets that include newly recorded samples.

These analyses, based on metric and nonmetric dental data, will figure
prominently in elucidating the population lineages of early and recent mainland Southeast Asians. In order to further resolve the aforementioned issue of
the biological affinities of early indigenous populations of Southeast Asia, we
also survey recently discovered skeletal remains from pre- and early Hoabinhian cultural sites using craniometric analysis. The final section of this chapter
introduces key evidence for the initial appearance of immigrants in northern
Vietnam in the form of skeletons recovered from a large mortuary assemblage
at the site of Man Bac (1524–2066 cal BC [Matsumura and Oxenham 2011]).

The Genealogical Affinity of Early Settlers in Southeast Asia: The Dental Morphology

In order to assess the genealogical affinities of mainland Hoabinhian/Neo-
lithic Southeast Asians, comparative population samples encompassing a
wide geographic area and chronological span were selected. The samples
with their associated chronometric dates are given in table 8.1 and table 8.2,
and the localities where the pertinent prehistoric human remains were recovered are shown in figure 8.1. Dental data sets consisting of two different
phenotypic morphological features, more than likely expressed under differing genetic control, were analyzed. The first are metric dental characteristics
represented by mesiodistal and buccolingual crown diameters. The second
includes a battery of nonmetric morphological dental traits, such as shovel-
shaped incisors and accessory cusps (see figure 8.2), recorded using the protocols and criteria outlined by Matsumura (1994).

The data used for outlining population affinities based on dental morphometric analysis included 28 crown diameters (14 mesiodistal and 14 bucco-

Figure 8.1. Locality map of prehistoric human skeletal remains in Southeast/East Asia presented in this chapter. Italicized groups are composite samples from multiregional sites belonging to a similar culture.

lingual diameters), which were taken as the greatest dimensions of crowns; all comparative data are from males. Only male dental crown data were used, because of the generally accepted greater sensitivity of male teeth to ancestral differences and the greater availability of published comparative data on male dentition. Q-mode correlation coefficients (Sneath and Sokal 1973), a procedure that gives indications of likeness in proportions or shape between samples, were computed using the 28 dental metrics. Following that procedure, the neighbor-joining method of Saitou and Nei (1987) was applied to

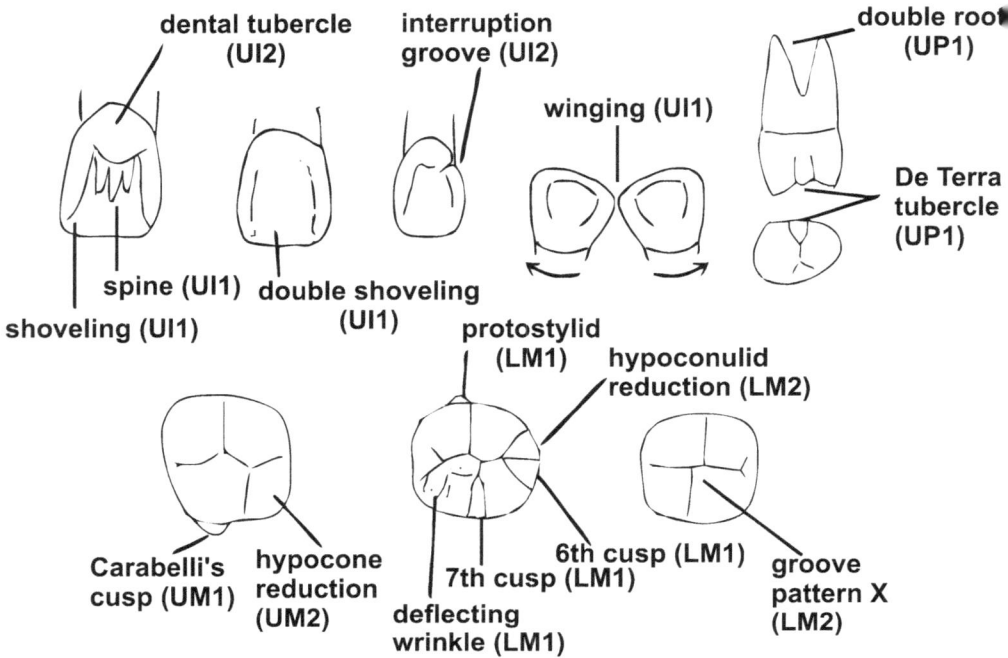

Figure 8.2. Dental traits used in the analysis of nonmetric dental data.

the distance matrix of Q-mode correlation coefficients to aid in the interpretation of intersample phenotypic affinities. This was done using the software package Splits Tree Version 4.0 (Hudson and Bryant 2006).

Figure 8.3 displays sample plotting in tree branching style based on the neighbor-joining method applied to the Q-mode correlation coefficients of the 28 crown diameters. An assemblage of modern East and Southeast Asians occupies the top of the tree, and present-day Southeast Asians are scattered adjacent to the cluster of Northeast/East Asians. The Early Metal Age Dong Son Vietnamese and Neolithic Weidun and Songze from southern China also branched out from this cluster. Interestingly, the Gua Cha Malays and Bac Son, Con Co Ngua, and An Son Vietnamese are distinctively and distantly located (at the bottom of this tree) relative to present-day Southeast Asians. These early mainland Southeast Asian samples, ranging in time from the Hoabinhian to late pre-Neolithic periods, are affiliated with the Australo-Melanesian samples. Among other prehistoric Southeast Asians, the Neolithic to Metal Age Thai specimens represented by Ban Kao and Ban Chiang, as well as early Metal Age Dong Son Vietnamese, show close affinities to present-day Southeast/East Asians, while being very distant from the Hoabinhian/late pre-Neolithic assemblages.

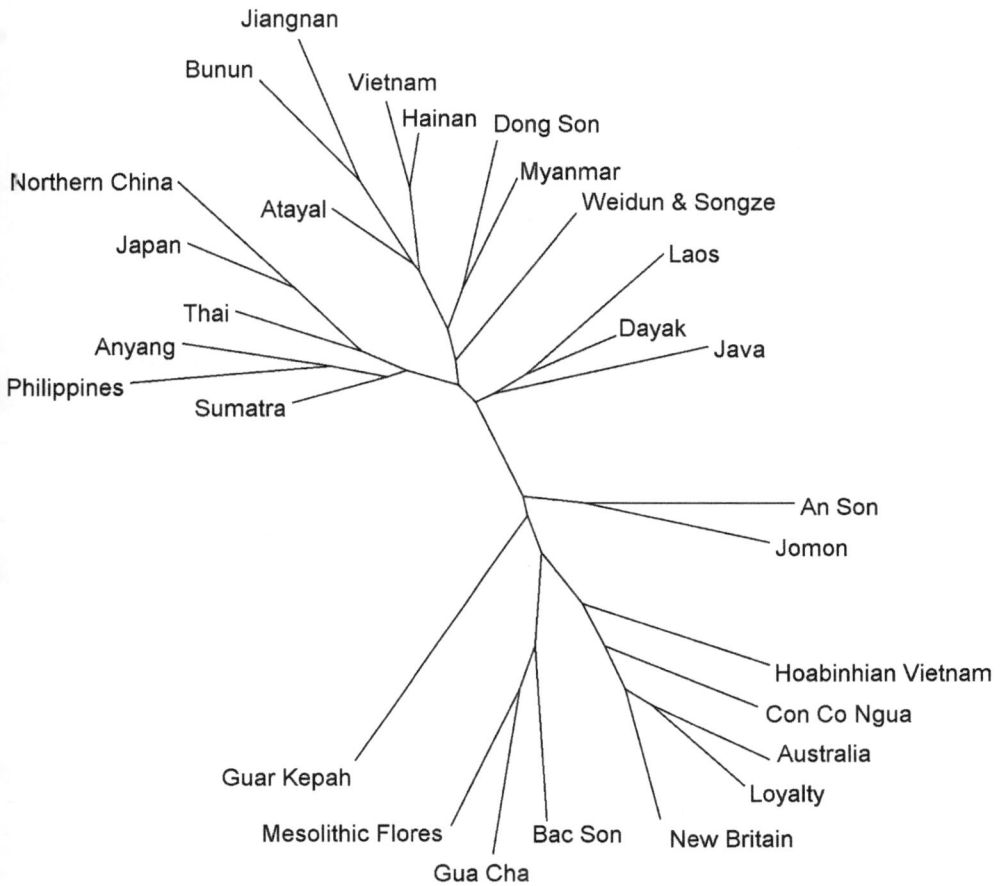

Figure 8.3. Unrooted tree of neighbor joining method applied to Q-mode correlation coefficients, based on 28 dental crown measurements.

Regarding the nonmetric dental traits, Matsumura and Hudson (2005) have argued that shovel-shaped incisors and the De Terra's tubercle in the maxillary first premolar are key traits in distinguishing Northeast and Southeast Asian populations. For this reason, occurrences of these two traits in the comparative samples are represented in figure 8.4 simultaneously. Both traits most frequently appear in Northern Chinese, with their frequency declining toward the south. The close similarity among remains from early Holocene Laos, Vietnam, Malay, and Flores—including Hoabinhian specimens—with Australo-Melanesians, which display low frequencies for both traits, are confirmed in this schema.

To evaluate population affinities based on the nonmetric dental data, C.A.B. Smith's distances (Berry and Berry 1967), often referred to as "mean measure of divergence" values, were computed using presence/absence frequencies

Table 8.1. Comparative prehistoric population samples

Sample	Locality	Period	Remarks[a]	Dental trait data Metrics	n
Liujiang	Guanxi Zhuang Autonomous Region in southern China	Late Pleistocene	—	—	—
Coobool Creek	Coobool Crossing on the Wakool River, Australia	Late Pleistocene (c. 14,000 BP)	—	—	—
Mai Da Nuoc	Site in Thanh Hoa Prov., N. Vietnam	Early Holocene (late Hoabin-hian culture, c. 8000 BP)	A	—	—
Hoabinhian Vietnam	Vietnam	Late Pleistocene–early Holocene (Hoabinhian culture)	B	Matsumura (unpublished)	6
Bac Son	Northern Vietnam	Early Neolithic (Bac Son culture c. 8000–7000 BP)	C	Matsumura and Hudson 2005	8
Con Co Ngua	Site in Than Hoa Prov., N. Vietnam	Middle Neolithic (Da But culture, sample dated to c. 5000 BP)		Matsumura et al. 2001	20
Early Holocene Vietnam and Laos	Vietnam and Laos	Early Holocene including Neolithic	D	—	—
An Son	Site in Long An Prov., S. Vietnam	Late Neolithic (c. 3800 BP)	E	Matsumura (unpublished)	7
Dong Son	Northern Vietnam	Early Metal Age (Dong Son culture, 3000–1700 BP)	F	Matsumura et al. 2001	—
Gua Cha	Site in Kelantan Prov., Malaysia	Hoabinhian-Neolithic (c. 8000–3000 BP)	G	Matsumura and Hudson 2005	9
Guar Kepah	Site in mainland Penang, Malaysia	Early Holocene (Hoabinhian culture)	H	Matsumura and Hudson 2005	11
Mesolithic Flores	Flores Island	Early Holocene (Mesolithic, c. 7000–4000 BP)	I	Matsumura and Pookajorn 2005	5
Early Flores and Malay	Flores Island and Malaysia	Hoabinhian/ Mesolithic-Neolithic	J	—	—
Leang Codong	Site in Sulawesi Island	Early Metal Age	K	—	—
Ban Chiang	Site in Udon Thani Prov., Thailand	Neolithic–Bronze Age (c. 3500–1800 BP)	L	—	—
Weidun and Songze	Site in Jiangsu Prov., S. China	Neolithic (Majiabang culture, c. 7000–5000 BP)	M	Matsumura 2002	48
Anyang	Site in Henang Prov., China	Bronze–Iron Age (c. 3300 BP)	N	Matsumura (unpublished)	60
Jiangnan	Jiangnan Prov., S. China	Zhou–Western Han (2770–1992 BP)	O	Matsumura 2002	14
Jomon	Japan	Neolithic (middle–latest Jomon culture, c. 5000–2300 BP)	P	Matsumura 1989	210
Yayoi	Northern Kyushu and Yamaguchi districts, Japan	Bronze Iron Age (c. 2800–1700 BP)	Nakahashi 1993	—	—

[a] A = Cuong 1986; B = sites of Mai Da Nuoc, Mai Da Dieu, Dong Truong, Du Sang, and Dong Can; C = sites of Pho Binh Gia, Lang Cuom, Lang Bon, and Cua Gi; D = composite sample of groups nos. 1–5; E = Cuong 2006; F = Cuong 1996; G = Sieveking 1954; H = van Stein Callenfels 1936; Mijsberg 1940; I = sites of Liang Momer, Liang Toge, Liang X, Gua Alo, Aimere, Sampung, and Gua Nempong (Jacob 1967); J = composite sample of groups nos. 9–11; K = Verhoeven 1958; Jacob 1967; Bulbeck 2000a,b; L = Gorman and Charoenwongsa 1976; M = Chang 1986; Nakahashi and Li 2002; teeth includes Songze series; N = IHIA and CASS 1982; O = Nakahashi and Li 2002; P = Akazawa and Aikens 1986; Q = Nakahashi 1993.

Cranial measurements

Nonmetrics	n	For comparison with Hang Cho	n	For comparison with Man Bac	n	Storage[b]
—	—	Woo 1959	1	—	—	—
—	—	Brown 1989	9	—	—	—
—	—	—	—	Cuong 1986	1	—
—	—	—	—	—	—	IAH
—	—	—	—	Matsumura (unpublished)	4	MHO
—	—	—	—	Cuong 2003	19	—
Matsumura and Hudson 2005	76	—	—	—	—	—
—	—	—	—	Matsumura (unpublished)	4	LAM
Matsumura et al. 2001	20	Cuong 1996	24	Cuong 2006	9	—
—	—	—	—	Matsumura (unpublished)	1	UCB
—	—	—	—	—	—	—
—	—	—	—	—	—	—
Matsumura and Hudson 2005	52	—	—	—	—	—
Matsumura and Hudson 2005	100	—	—	—	—	—
Matsumura (unpublished)	75	Pietrusewsky and Douglas 2002	28	Pietrusewsky and Douglas 2002; Hanihara 1993a	27	UHW, SAC
Matsumura 2002	111	Nakahashi and Li 2002	3	Nakahashi et al. 2002	29	—
Matsumura (unpublished)	81	—	—	IHIA and CASS 1982	42	AST
—	—	Nakahashi et al. 2002	18	Nakahashi et al. 2002.	18	—
Matsumura 1989	711	Ogata 1981	38	Hanihara 1993a	113	—
—	—	Nakahashi 1989	135	Nakahashi 1993	184	—

Institutions of materials studied by Matsumura for unpublished data. Abbreviations of institutions: AST = Academia Sinica of the Republic of China in Taipei; IAH = Department of Anthropology, Institute of Archaeology, Hanoi; LAM = Long An Museum, Vietnam; MHO = Laboratoire d'Anthropologie Biologique, Musée de l'Homme, Paris; SAC = Princess Maha Chakri Sirindhorn Anthropology Centre, Bangkok; UCB = Department of Biological Anthropology, University of Cambridge; UHW = Department of Anthropology, University of Hawai'i.

Table 8.2. Comparative modern population samples

Sample	Dental trait data				
	Metrics	n	Nonmetrics	n
Vietnam	Matsumura et al. 2011	52	Matsumura et al. 2011	99
Laos	Matsumura et al. 2011	34	—	—
Thai	Matsumura et al. 2011	46	Matsumura 1994	110
Myanmar	Matsumura et al. 2011	30	Matsumura et al. 2011	50
Java	Matsumura and Hudson 2005	45	—	—
Sumatra	Matsumura (unpublished)	24	—	—
Sunda	—	—	Matsumura (unpublished)	119
Dayak (Borneo)	Matsumura and Hudson 2005	42	Matsumura and Hudson 2005	74
Philippines	Matsumura (unpublished)	30	—	—
Atayal	Matsumura (unpublished)	50	Matsumura (unpublished)	79
Bunun	Matsumura (unpublished)	28	Matsumura (unpublished)	45
Hainan	Matsumura (unpublished)	85	Matsumura (unpublished)	128
Taiwan	—	—	—	—
Southern China	—	—	—	—
Northern China	—	—	Matsumura 1994 (early modern)	104
Japan	Matsumura 1994 (early modern)	129	Matsumura 1994 (early modern)	205
Australia	Matsumura and Hudson 2005	63	Matsumura and Hudson 2005	101
Melanesia	—	—	—	—
New Britain	Matsumura and Hudson 2005	95	Matsumura and Hudson 2005	188
Loyalty	Matsumura and Hudson 2005	39	Matsumura and Hudson 2005	62
Tasmania	—	—	—	—
Tolai	—	—	—	—
Negritos	—	—	—	—
Andaman	—	—	—	—

Note: Abbreviations of institutions: BMNH = Department of Paleontology, Natural History Museum, London; MHO = Laboratoire d'Anthropologie Biologique, Musée de l'Homme, Paris; MUB = Department of Anatomy, Faculty of Medicine, Mahidol University, Bangkok; NMP = Department of Archaeology, National Museum of the Philippines, Manila; NTW = Department of Anatomy, National Taiwan University; UCB = Department of Biological Anthropology, University of Cambridge; UMPH = Department of Dental Anatomy, University of Medicine and Pharmacy at Ho Chi Minh City; UTK = University Museum of the University of Tokyo.

[a] Institutions of materials studied by Matsumura for unpublished data.

Cranial measurements

For comparisons with Hang Cho	n	For comparisons with Man Bac	n	Storage[a]
—	—	Cuong 2006	66	MHO, UMPH
—	—	Cuong 2006	17	MHO
—	—	Cuong 2006	28	MUB
—	—	—	—	BMNH
Yokoo 1931	14	—	—	BMNH, UCB
—	—	—	—	BMNH, UCB
—	—	—	—	BMNH, UCB
Yokoo 1931	12	—	—	—
—	—	—	—	NMP, UTK
Howells 1989	38	—	—	NTW
—	—	—	—	NTW
Howells 1989	38	—	—	NTW
—	—	Hanihara 1993a	19	—
—	—	Hanihara 1993a	26	—
—	—	Hanihara 1993a	71	—
Howells 1989 (N. Japan)	32	Hanihara 1993a	140	
Howells 1989	49	Hanihara 1993a	53	BMNH
—	—	Hanihara 1993a	18	—
—	—	—	—	—
—	—	Matsumura (unpublished)	17	MHO
Howells 1989	42	—	—	—
Howells 1989	54	—	—	—
Genet-Varcin 1951	14	—	—	—
Howells 1989	35	—	—	—

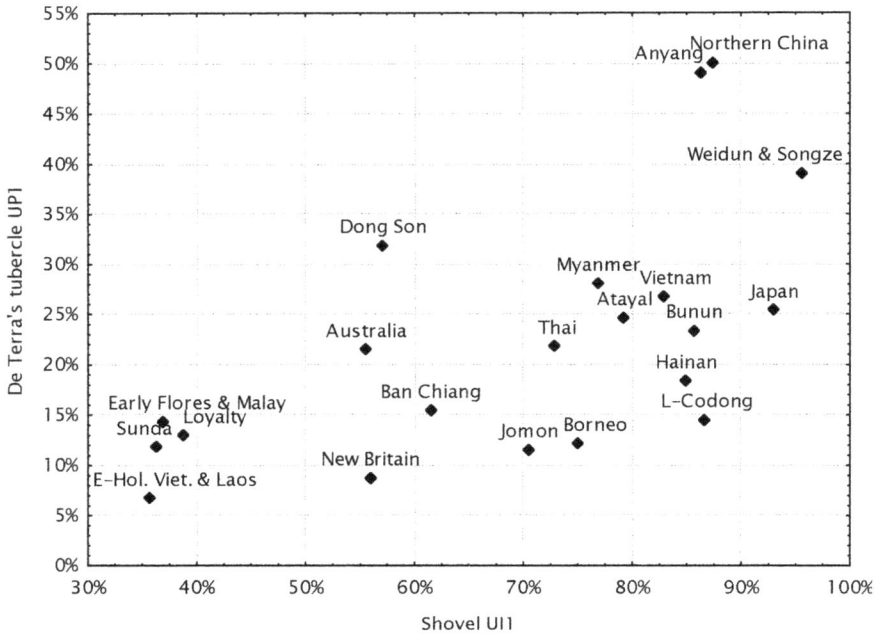

Figure 8.4. Frequencies of shovel-shaped maxillary incisors and De Terra's tubercles in the maxillary first premolars for comparative population samples.

scored for 21 traits. Large sample sizes are required for data comparisons of the nonmetric trait battery, which is based on the frequency of trait presence. Some geographically neighboring ethnic groups with small sample sizes needed to be combined. Based on the nonmetric dental data sets thus summarized, figure 8.5 is an unrooted tree using the neighbor-joining method applied to the computed distance matrix.

Northeast Asians, such as Chinese and Japanese, are clustered together with Taiwanese aborigines and Neolithic Southern Chinese (Weidun and Songze), thus showing their close affinities. The early Metal Age Dong Son Vietnamese are also situated among this array. On the opposite lower side of the tree, early Southeast Asians, represented by the pre-Neolithic Bac Son and Da But composite series and Early Flores and Malay, including Mesolithic/Neolithic specimens from Gua Cha and Guar Kepah, are grouped together with the Loyalty Islanders and Australian Aborigines. Most of the present-day Southeast Asians, as well as those from Ban Chiang, are located in an intermediate position between the two oppositely scattered groups.

This intermediate position of modern Southeast Asians invites two interpretations: (1) they developed through local evolution from early Southeast Asian populations; or (2) they are a hybrid group sharing genetic material of

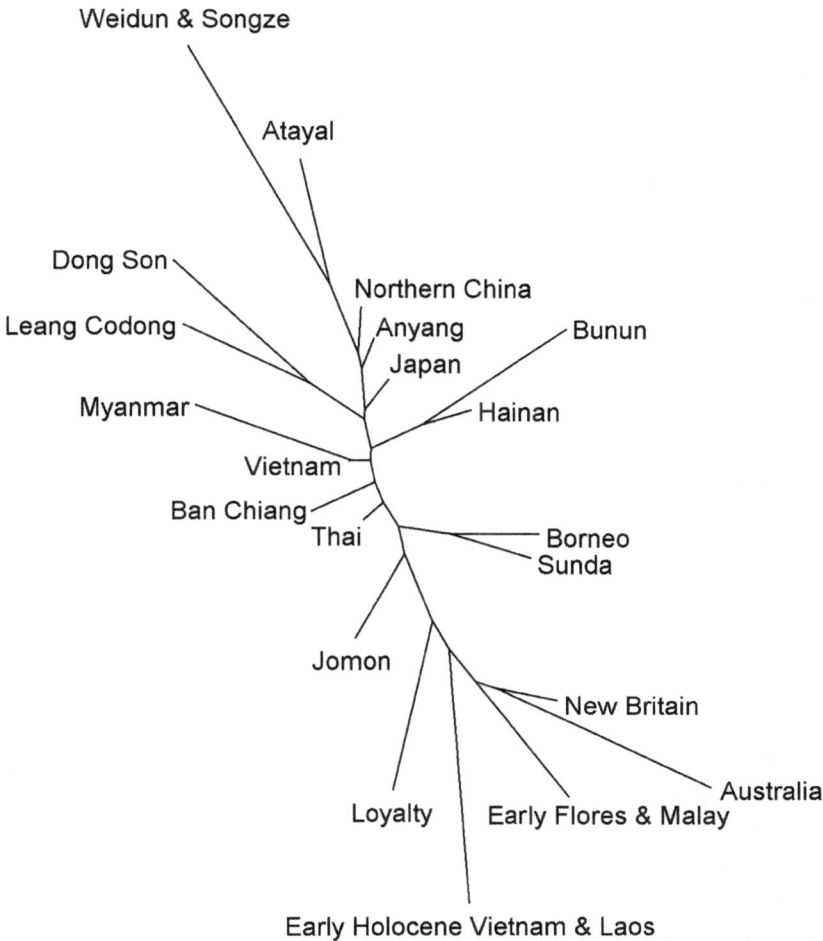

Figure 8.5. Unrooted tree of neighbor joining method applied to Smith's distances, based on 21 nonmetric dental traits.

Northeast Asian immigrants and the descendants of early indigenous Southeast Asians. The results of this dental morphometric study clearly demonstrate that the earliest occupants of the region had Australo-Melanesian affinities. Furthermore, the observed metric and nonmetric dental characteristics, likely expressed under differential genetic control, do not suggest direct genetic continuity between early indigenous and later populations. This study also shows that modern-day Southeast Asians share a suite of features with Northeast/East Asians. These findings taken together support interpretation 2: modern-day Southeast Asians share a common genetic heritage with both early indigenous populations and later Northeast Asian migrants.

Recent Discoveries of Pre- and Early Hoabinhian Skeletons

Although there were numerous earlier discoveries of preceramic period human remains, poor skeletal preservation largely prevented extensive studies assessing the biological affinities of the early occupants of Southeast Asia. However, over the past twenty years, many additional human skeletal remains from the late Pleistocene and early Holocene have been unearthed in various regions of mainland Southeast Asia. As far as the pre- and early Hoabinhian sites (over 10,000 years BP) are concerned, at least three cave sites have produced relatively well-preserved human skeletons that may prove to be extremely important for our understanding of the peopling of this region in the pre-Neolithic period. These include specimens from the cave sites of Moh Khiew in southern Thailand, of Gua Gunung Runtuh in mainland Malaysia, and of the Hang Cho sites in northern Vietnam. With regard to the Moh Khiew and Gua Gunung Runtuh specimens, descriptions and morphometric analyses of their skeletal and dental morphology have been provided elsewhere (Matsumura and Zuraina 1995, 1999; Matsumura and Pookajorn 2005; Matsumura 2006). Therefore, this chapter provides only a summary description of these remains, while discussing in more detail the most recent finding from Hang Cho, which will be one of the keys to further addressing the issue of the peopling of Southeast Asia.

Moh Khiew Cave, located in Krabi Province, southern Thailand, is the site where a late Pleistocene human skeleton was discovered during excavations undertaken in 1990 and 1991 by Surin Pookajorn of Silpakorn University (Pookajorn 1991, 1994). An adult female buried in a flexed position was dated to 25,800+600 years BP. Its preservation and morphology were first described by Choosiri (Pookajorn 1994). Oota and colleagues (2001) analyzed mitochondrial DNA from the skeleton and demonstrated a close similarity with the present-day Semang aborigines of the Malay Peninsula. The Moh Khiew skeleton is currently housed in the Princess Maha Chakri Sirindhorn Anthropology Center in Bangkok, Thailand (see figure 8.6). The facial skeleton is in relatively good condition, although the nasal bones were lost. The mandible is nearly complete, while the postcranial skeleton includes only the upper half of the body. Skeletal preservation has not facilitated clear sex determination. However, preserved elements indicate that the sex of this individual is probably female, while age at death can only be determined as mature adult.

The cave site of Gua Gunung Runtuh, located in Lenggong district of Perakin peninsular Malaysia, was excavated in 1990 and 1991 by a team led by Zuraina Majid of Universiti Sains Malaysia (Zuraina 1994, 2005). Excavation in 1990 revealed a primary burial, dating to 10,000–11,000 years BP, of

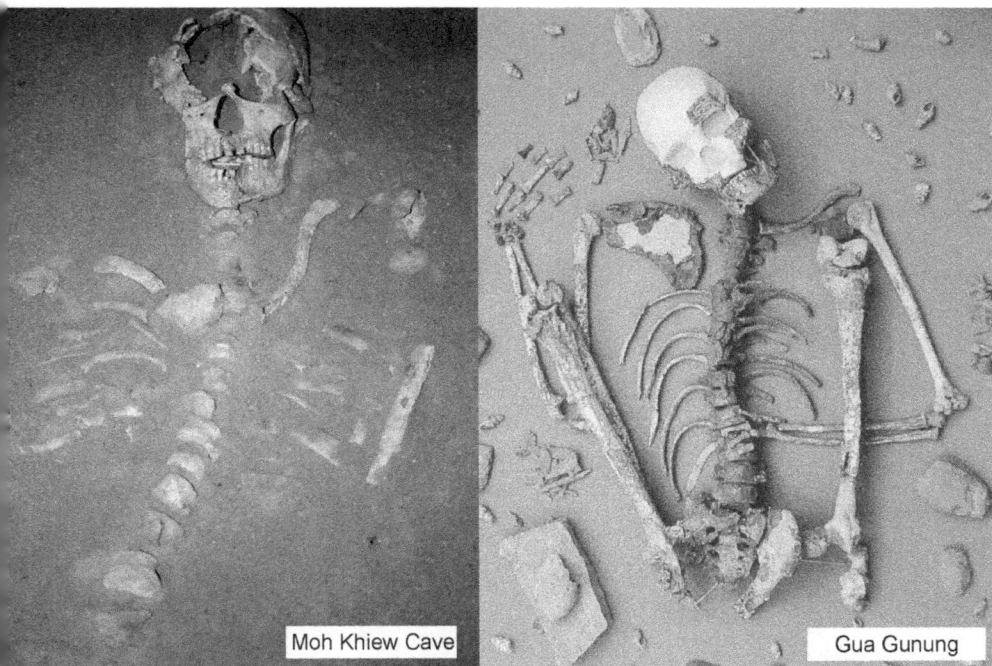

Figure 8.6. Views of the Moh Khiew (*left*) and Gua Gunung (*right*) skeletons.

an adult male in a flexed position. As first described by Jacob and Soepriyo (1994), the Gua Gunung Runtuh individual was well preserved, with the exception of the facial portion of the cranium (figure 8.6). The skeleton was characterized as possessing remarkably slender limbs and massive jaws associated with pronounced prognathism. It is curated at the Center for Archaeological Research Malaysia in the Universiti Sains Malaysia.

More recently, with the cooperation of the excavators, an extensive analysis using cranial and dental measurements recorded for the Moh Khiew and Gua Gunung Runtuh remains was carried out by one of us (HM). Q-mode correlation coefficients and Mahalanobis' generalized distances evaluated the Australo-Melanesian affinities of both specimens, with reference to the late Pleistocene Coobool Creek specimen from Australia (see Matsumura and Zuraina 1999; Matsumura and Pookajorn 2005).

Over the past half century, Vietnamese archaeologists have devoted much of their effort to the study of the Hoabinhian culture; more than 120 Hoabinhian sites have been discovered (Tan 1976). Despite the majority being in limestone caves and rock shelters, which are generally conducive to good preservation of human remains, only a few late Hoabinhian sites, such as Mai Da Nuoc and Mai Da Dieu (Cuong 1986, 2007), have provided well-preserved skeletons. Older skulls dated to the terminal Pleistocene from Don Can (Cuong 2007) and Hang Muoi (Bulbeck et al. 2007) have proved less than ideal for analysis because of incomplete or missing facial skeletons.

A recent excavation project at the cave site of Hang Cho (figure 8.7), located in Luong Son district, Hoa Binh Province, northern Vietnam, revealed a nearly complete skull. This site was first detected by the French archaeologist Colani in the 1920s, and in 1977 a substantial Hoabinhian lithic assemblage was recovered there (Tan 1997; Thuy and Doi 1998). Freshwater shell deposits in the main chamber were dated from 14,100+300 calibrated years BP to 9,710+50 calibrated years BP (Yi et al. 2004).

More recent excavations in 2004 (see Matsumura, Yoneda et al. 2008) recovered a well-preserved flexed female burial lacking lower limbs from in front of the main chamber (figure 8.7). AMS dating provided a calibrated

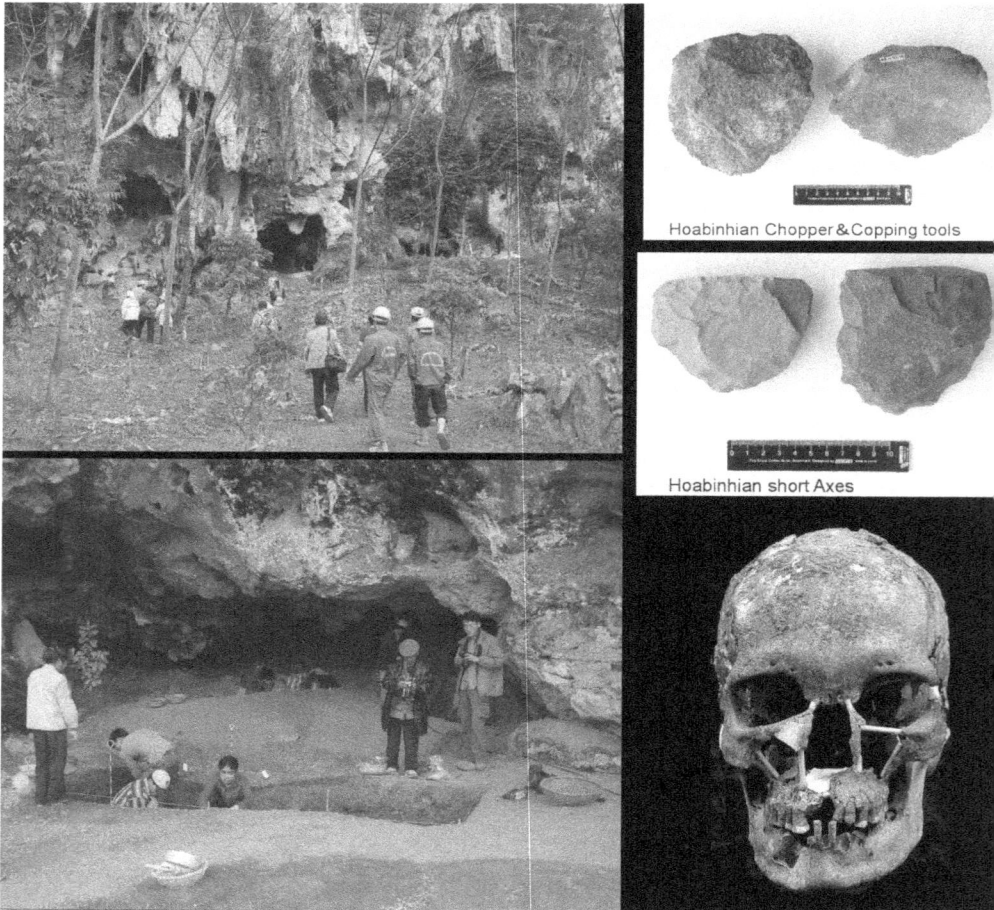

Figure 8.7. Views of the Hang Cho site (*left*), representative stone tools (*upper and middle right*), and skull from the inhumation burial (*lower right*).

result of 10,450+300 years BP for this burial, i.e., terminal Pleistocene. The reconstructed calvarium is dolichocephalic (cranial index 71.9). The glabella protrudes prominently, although the superciliary arches are relatively flat. The facial skeleton is characterized by a low and wide profile (Virchow's index 64.2) and the orbital margins are straight, while the nasal root is slightly concave. The mandible exhibits weak alveolar prognathism, and the mandibular body is relatively small and low.

The biological affinity of the Hang Cho skeleton, based on cranial and dental measurements, was assessed by Matsumura, Yoneda, and colleagues (2008), and figure 8.8 represents the result of a cluster analysis applied to the Q-mode correction coefficients based on nine cranial measurements. Two major clusters are apparent in this dendrogram, in which the late Pleistocene specimens from Liujiang in southern China and Coobool Creek in Australia, along with modern Australian and Tasmanian Aboriginal samples form one major cluster, to which the Hang Cho specimen belongs. The Neolithic Man Bac remains (presented later in this chapter) and early Bronze Age Dong Son specimens, despite being from neighboring regions in northern Vietnam, are clearly separated from the cluster including the Hang Cho specimen. These later period Vietnamese samples belong to another major cluster formed by

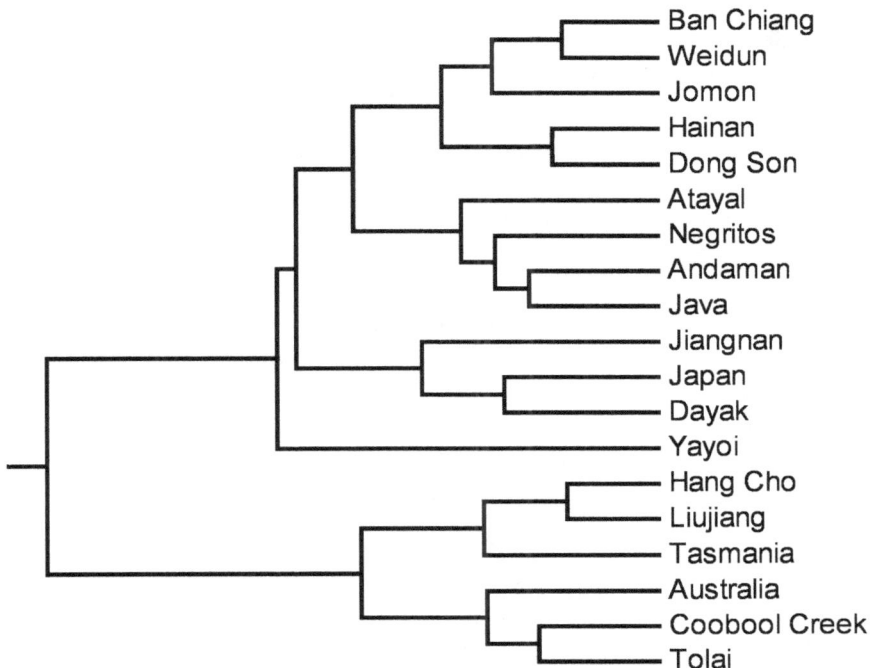

Figure 8.8. Dendrogram of a cluster analysis applied to the distances of Q-mode correlation coefficients, based on nine cranial measurements (females).

the remaining Neolithic to modern samples from Southeast Asia, southern China, and Japan. The Australian affinity of the Hang Cho specimen is reconfirmed in the dendrogram of distance analysis using dental measurements (see Matsumura, Yoneda et al. 2008).

Implications of the Appearance of Initial Immigrants during the Late Neolithic in Vietnam

It has been demonstrated that late Pleistocene and early Holocene settlers of mainland Southeast Asia, represented by Hoabinhian populations, were quite dissimilar from modern populations in the region, while exhibiting close similarities to present-day Australo-Melanesians. These findings strongly support the view that Southeast Asia was initially settled by a common ancestral population of Australo-Melanesians. Furthermore, it is apparent that during the later post-Hoabinhian period, indigenous populations were affected by substantial levels of gene flow from East Asia. In order to further support, or reject, this scenario of the expansion of East Asian populations into Southeast Asia, we focus on the key human remains uncovered from a Neolithic site in northern Vietnam.

The site of Man Bac, located in Yen Mo district, Ninh Binh Province, northern Vietnam, is dated to circa 4000–3500 years BP, although it lacks any evidence for rice farming. In terms of material culture, Man Bac was closely related to the Phung Nguyen culture, which was in turn associated with rice cultivation along the more northerly inland aspect of the Red River delta. In Southeast Asian regional contexts, the overall archaeological evidence suggests that lifeways had much in common with those seen at other contemporaneous sites in Vietnam and Southeast Asia, including animal domestication, land clearance, ceramic manufacture, hunting, marine resource gathering, and trade (Cuong 2001; Hiep and Phung 2004; Matsumura, Oxenham et al. 2008; Oxenham et al. 2008).

Four excavation seasons at Man Bac, between 1999 and 2007, have uncovered over 90 burials, generally in very good condition (figure 8.9). Morphologically, there is substantial intragroup variation, as seen in figure 8.10. Some individuals had very flat faces, while others possessed low, broad faces, with protruding glabella and wide nasal openings. Multivariate analysis based on craniometric data implies the existence of different population lineages at this single site. Figure 8.10 represents the results of a cluster analysis applied to the Q-mode correlation coefficients, based on 10 cranial measurements of male Man Bac individuals and comparative samples. This analysis yields a clear separation within the Man Bac sample. Several Man Bac specimens and early Metal Age Dong Son Vietnamese together form one subcluster, which is connected with one of two main clusters consisting of modern Vietnamese and early Metal Age to modern samples from East/Southeast Asia. Several of the Man Bac individuals branch off from a different major cluster, in which other prehistoric Vietnamese—represented by the Mai Da Nuoc Hoabin-hian specimen and late pre-Neolithic Bac Son and Da But samples—group together as neighbors of the Gua Cha Malaysian Hoabinhian specimen (an individual numbered H12) and Australo-Melanesian samples.

As several Man Bac individuals were clearly separated from the rest of the Man Bac sample, other group average comparisons were made using the two identified Man Bac subsets. Q-mode correlation coefficients were calculated again using the mean values of these two separate Man Bac male groups (Man Bac 1 and Man Bac 2). Figure 8.11 is a dendrogram resulting from a cluster analysis applied to the Q-mode correlation coefficients, based on 16 cranial measurements. An Son, Man Bac 2, Ban Chiang, Yayoi, and Dong Son Vietnamese form a subcluster neighboring another subcluster that includes, among other samples, the Neolithic Weidun from the Yangtze River region and Jiangnan Chinese of the Former Han period. The Jomon sample and

Figure 8.9. Views of the Man Bac site (*left*), inhumation burials (*upper right*), and representative skulls (*lower right*).

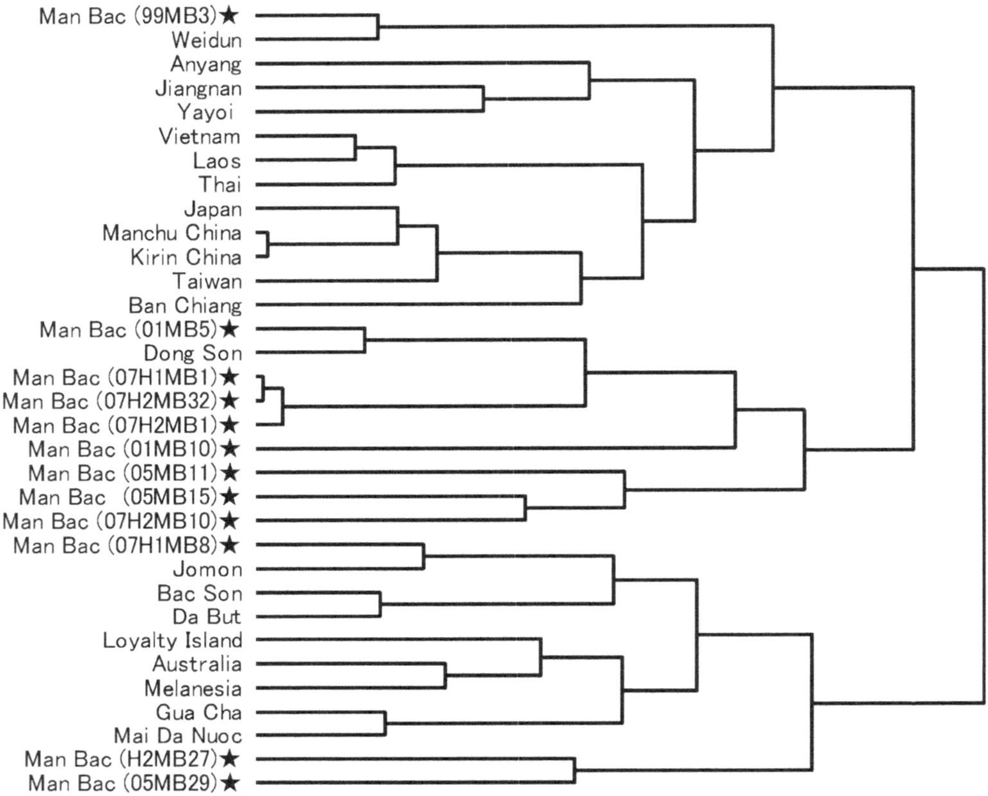

Figure 8.10. Dendrogram of a cluster analysis applied to the distances of Q-mode correlation coefficients for Man Bac individuals and comparative samples, based on 10 cranial measurements (males).

Man Bac 1 are neighbors and branch off from another major cluster, in which other prehistoric Vietnamese, represented by the Mai Da Nuoc Hoabinhian specimen and the Bac Son and Da But samples, are grouped together and neighbor the Gua Cha and Australo-Melanesian samples.

In general, the cranial morphology of the Dong Son sample group (left cranium in figure 8.9) is characterized by relatively narrow faces, flat glabellas, superciliary arches and nasal roots, and round orbits. Some individuals represented by the crania in this figure (right cranium) display robust cranial features, such as a dolichocephalic calvarium, large zygomatic bones, a remarkably prominent glabella and superciliary arches, a concave nasal root, and a low, wide face with a protruding mandible. When the findings of considerable intragroup variation in cranial morphology are taken into account, the Man Bac population appears to have been experiencing a major genetic shift, most likely due to genetic admixture from new immigrants to the region.

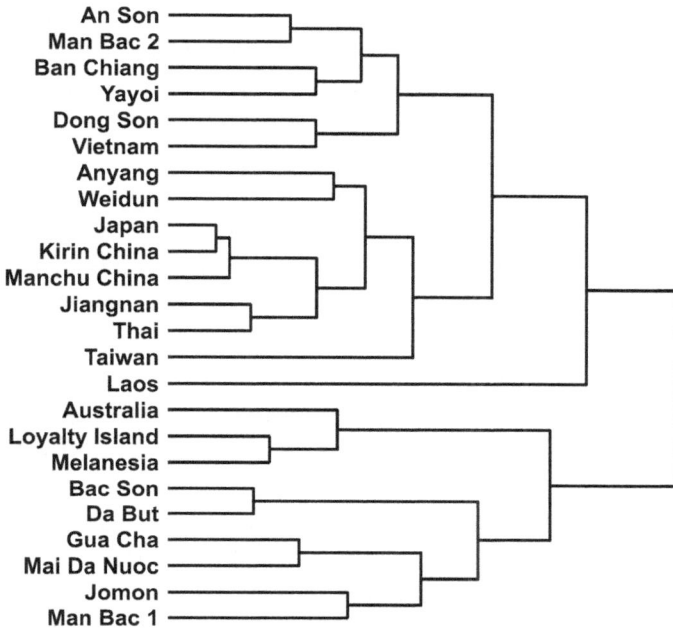

Figure 8.11. Dendrogram of a cluster analysis applied to the distances of Q-mode correlation coefficients for two Man Bac group average samples and comparative samples, based on 16 cranial measurements (males).

Discussion and Conclusions

The late Pleistocene is represented by very few sets of human remains. Niah Cave, Sarawak, has the earliest well-dated modern human remains in Southeast Asia, associated with a radiocarbon date of circa 40,000 years BP (Kennedy 1977; Barker et al. 2007). Tabon Cave on Palawan Island is also a well-known site, and it has produced the oldest human skeletal remains in the Philippines, consisting of a frontal bone and two mandibular fragments and a tibia. The mandibular fragment has been AMS dated to circa 30,000 years BP (Dizon et al. 2002). The Wadjak skulls from central Java in Indonesia (Dubois 1922; Weidenreich 1945; Wolpoff et al. 1984) have long been regarded as late Pleistocene, but AMS dating now indicates that a middle Holocene date (c. 6,500 years BP) may be more appropriate (Storm 1995). Nevertheless, the majority of late Pleistocene human remains, as well as Hoabinhian/Mesolithic material, demonstrate Australo-Melanesian characteristics in their skeletal and dental morphology, with contrary findings arising only when poorly preserved or subadult materials are analyzed.

Recent discoveries from the Moh Khiew, Gua Gunung, and Hang Cho cave sites in mainland Southeast Asia, as reviewed in the current chapter, are notable in terms of their good preservation, including of postcranial elements, along with sound dating that indicates pre- and early Hoabinhian period origins. These skeletons, dating to the late Pleistocene through early Holocene, may represent some of the early indigenous settlers of this region and thus are of crucial importance in addressing the issue under debate here. Skeletal and dental morphometric analysis demonstrates that all of these new specimens share a number of similarities with early Australian or Melanesian samples, suggesting the possibility that the first modern human colonizers of mainland Southeast Asia and the Australian subcontinent were ancestral to modern-day Australo-Melanesian peoples.

The antiquity of this early colonization event is clearer for Australia, where the earliest human occupation dates back to approximately 50,000 years ago (Bowdler 1992). Australian teeth, which are most similar to those of early Southeast Asians, suggest an origin in Sundaland (mainland Southeast Asia, for the most part) for the first Australians. Along with the above-mentioned late Pleistocene and early Holocene samples from Southeast Asia (e.g., Niah, Tabon, Moh Khiew and Gua Gunung Runtuh, and Hang Cho), they can be regarded as descendants of late Pleistocene Sundaland populations, which in turn may share a common ancestry with present-day Australian Aboriginal and Melanesian people. Some cranial and dental traits exhibited by the Pleistocene founding populations in the region were retained, even as late as just prior to the Neolithic period, as represented by the Bac Son and Da But sequences in northern Vietnam.

In mainland Southeast Asia, cases of major population change or large-scale admixture with North/East Asians are especially evident in northern Vietnam. The dental analyses presented in this chapter demonstrate a large morphological gap between the early Metal Age Dong Son people and pre-Neolithic Bac Son and Da But people (isotopic work is currently being carried out to explore this issue further). As mentioned above, Bac Son and Da But populations have generally been regarded as direct lineal descendants of the Hoabinhian settlers of the surrounding region. The close resemblance between the Dong Son people and recent East Asians suggests considerable levels of gene flow facilitated by new immigrants from the northern or eastern peripheral area during the early Metal Age or Neolithic period.

Through the lens of both cranial and dental comparisons presented in this chapter, early Thai people such as at Ban Chiang are not seen to have been directly descended from earlier indigenous Hoabinhian populations, implying the appearance of immigrants before or during the period of occupation of this site. As noted in the introduction, Pietrusewsky (1981, 1982, 1994; Pietrusewsky and Douglas 2002) has used findings from Ban Chiang to argue for regional continuity in Southeast Asia. Recent analysis of mtDNA by Lertrit and colleagues (2008), using human remains from Bronze and Iron Age Noen U-Loke and Ban Lum-Khao, also supports the genetic continuity between these early Thai people and current inhabitants living near these sites. However, these results are, in fact, entirely consistent with and supportive of the two layer immigration hypothesis, with regional continuity being observed only from the Neolithic period of Ban Chiang.

The Ban Chiang assemblage spans a vast period of time (c. 4100 BC–1800 years BP), thus inhibiting precise establishment of the timing of the initial appearance of immigrants. Man Bac had a much shorter temporal span (c. 4,000–3,500 years BP), and evidence recovered there may help resolve the timing of the dispersal of rice farming populations into northern Vietnam. Cranio-morphologically, the Man Bac sample was clearly not a genetically homogeneous group. Some individuals exhibited features thought to have been inherited from earlier indigenous populations, while others had closer affinities to later Dong Son people. This intragroup variation in cranio-morphology suggests an initial appearance of immigrants at Man Bac who were genetically related to populations in the northern peripheral regions, including southern China. Man Bac people may well have been in the process of exchanging genetic material between new settlers and preexisting occupants descended from Hoabinhian and earlier Da But and Bac Son lineages.

As noted at the beginning of this chapter, the two layer model, or immigration hypothesis for understanding the population history of Southeast Asia, is supported by the results of a wide array of archaeological, historical, linguistic, and genetic studies (see chapter 7 for an alternative position). The prehistoric expansion of language families (specifically, the Austronesian and Austro-Asiatic families) can often be linked with the Neolithic dispersal of rice farming populations (Renfrew 1987, 1989, 1992; Bellwood 1991, 1993, 1997; Hudson 1994, 1999, 2003; Higham 1998, 2001; Bellwood and Renfrew 2002; Diamond and Bellwood 2003). A number of recent reviews summarize the archaeological evidence for the spread of this Neolithic horizon into Southeast Asia, beginning in the third millennium BC (Spriggs 1989; Glover and Higham 1996; Bellwood 1997; Bellwood et al. 1992).

From this perspective, as far as the Austro-Asiatic language populations are concerned, analyses of the pertinent skeletal and dental remains support the hypothesis that there was a diffusion of migrants, probably through southern China down the Mekong, Red, and Chao Phraya River valleys, beginning in the time of the Neolithic period (c. 4000–3500 years BP). These migrants exchanged genetic material with the indigenous Australo-Melanesian communities as they diffused through the region. The existence of this north–south migration route is supported by the mtDNA analysis of Ballinger and colleagues (1992), a result that suggests the genetic influence of southern Chinese populations, via Vietnam, on mainland Southeast Asian populations. While Bellwood states that the southward dispersion of populations from China (although people not similar to recent Han Chinese in the historical sense of that term) began in the early Southeast Asian Neolithic period and was associated with rice cultivation, the genetic influence of a northern source seems to have been stronger in the post-Neolithic than during the Neolithic itself.

Acknowledgments

We are grateful to late Professor Surin Pookajorn, Silpakorn University, and to Dato' Professor Zuraina Majid, Universiti Sains Malaysia, for allowing study of excavated skeletal remains from the Moh Khiew and Gua Gunung sites. The authors are also much appreciative of collaborations with Drs. Ha Van Phung, Nguyen Giang Hai, Nguyen Kim Dung, Ve The Long, Nguyen Kim Thuy, and Nguyen Lan Cuong of the Vietnamese Institute of Archaeology and Lam My Dung of Vietnam National University, Hanoi, as well as Professor Peter Bellwood of Australian National University for the Hang Cho and Man Bac excavation projects in Vietnam. For permission to study the comparative cranial and/or dental specimens, thanks are also due to Dr. Bui Phat Diem and Dr. Vuong Thu Hong, Long An Provincial Museum; Dr. Chris Stringer, Department of Palaeontology, Natural History Museum, London; Dr. Gen Suwa, University Museum, University of Tokyo; Dr. Hoang Tu Hung, Faculty of Odonto-Stomatology, University of Medicine and Pharmacy at Ho Chi Minh City; Mr. Korakot Boonlop, Princess Maha Chakri Sirindhorn Anthropology Centre, Bangkok; Dr. Michael Pietrusewsky, Department of Anthropology, University of Hawai'i; Dr. Nguyen Viet, Center for Southeast Asian Prehistory, Hanoi; Dr. Philippe Mennecier, Departement Hommes, Musee de l'Homme, Paris; Dr. Robert Foley, Department of Biological Anthropology, University of Cambridge; Dr. Tsai Hsi-Kue, National Taiwan University, College of Medicine; Dr. Wang Daw-Hwan, IHP, Academia Sinica, Taipei; and Dr. Wilfred Ronquillio, Archeology Division, National Museum of the Philippines.

This research was funded in part by Grant-in-Aid (nos. 15405018, 20370096, 20520666, 22320155, and 23247040) from the Japan Society for the Promotion of Science, by the Toyota Foundation (no. D06-R-0035), and by an Australian Research Council Grant.

Literature Cited

Akazawa T, Aikens CM. 1986. Introduction. In: Akazawa T, Aikens CM, editors. *Prehistoric hunter-gatherers in Japan: New research methods*. University Museum, University of Tokyo, Bulletin no. 27. Pp. ix–x.

Ballinger SW, Schurr TG, Torroni A, Gan YY, Hodge JA, Hassan K, Chen KH, Wallace DC. 1992. Southeast Asian mitochondrial DNA analysis reveals genetic continuity of ancient Mongoloid migrations. *Genetics* 130: 139–52.

Barker G, Barton H, Bird M, Daly P, Datan I, Dykes A, Farr L, Gilbertson D, Harrisson B, Hunt C, Higham T, Kealhofer L, Krigbaum J, Lewis H, McLaren S, Paz V, Pike A, Piper P, Pyatt B, Rabett R, Reynolds R, Rose J, Rushworth G, Stephens M, Stringer C, Thompson G, Turney C. 2007. The human revolution in lowland tropical Southeast Asia: The antiquity and behaviour of anatomically modern humans at Niah Cave (Sarawak, Borneo). *Journal of Human Evolution* 52: 243–61.

Bellwood P. 1987. The prehistory of Island Southeast Asia: A multidisciplinary review of recent research. *Journal of World Prehistory* 1: 171–224.

Bellwood P. 1989. The colonization of the Pacific: Some current hypotheses. In: Hill AVS, Serjeantson SW, editors. *The colonization of the Pacific: A genetic trail*. Oxford, UK: Clarendon Press. Pp. 1–59.

Bellwood P. 1991. The Austronesian dispersal and the origin of languages. *Scientific American* 265: 88–93.

Bellwood P. 1993. An archaeologist's view of language macrofamily relationships. *Bulletin of the Indo-Pacific Prehistory Association* 13: 46–60.

Bellwood P. 1996. Early agriculture and the dispersal of the southern Mongoloids. In: Akazawa T, Szathmàry EJE, editors. *Prehistoric Mongoloid dispersals*. Oxford: Oxford University Press. Pp. 287–302.

Bellwood P. 1997. *Prehistory of the Indo-Malaysian archipelago*. Rev. ed. Honolulu: University of Hawai'i Press.

Bellwood P, Chambers G, Ross M, Hung H. 2011. Are "cultures" inherited? Multidisciplinary perspectives on the origins and migrations of Austronesian-speaking peoples prior to 1000 BC. In: Roberts BW, Linden MV, editors. *Investigating archaeological cultures: Material culture, variability, and transmission*. New York: Springer. Pp. 321–53.

Bellwood P, Gillespie R, Thompson GB, Vogel JS, Ardika IW, Datan I. 1992. New dates for prehistoric Asian rice. *Asian Perspectives* 31: 161–70.

Bellwood P, Renfrew C, editors. 2002. *Examining the farming/language dispersal hypothesis*. Cambridge, UK: McDonald Institute for Archaeological Research.

Berry AC, Berry RJ. 1967. Epigenetic variation in the human cranium. *Journal of Anatomy* 101: 361–79.

Blust RA. 1996a. Austronesian culture history: The window of language. In: Goodenough WH, editor. *Prehistoric settlement of the Pacific*. Philadelphia: American Philosophical Society. Pp. 28–35.

Blust RA. 1996b. Beyond the Austronesian homeland: The Austric hypothesis and its implications for archaeology. In: Goodenough WH, editor. *Prehistoric settlement of the Pacific*. Philadelphia: American Philosophical Society. Pp. 117–40.

Bowdler S. 1992. Homo sapiens in Southeast Asia and the antipodes: Archaeological versus biological interpretations. In: Akazawa T, Aoki K, Kimura T, editors. *The evolution and dispersal of modern humans in Asia*. Tokyo: Hokusensha. Pp. 559–90.

Brace CL, Tracer DP, Hunt KD. 1991. Human craniofacial form and the evidence for the peopling of the Pacific. *Bulletin of the Indo-Pacific Prehistory Association* 12: 247–69.

Brothwell DR. 1960. Upper Pleistocene human skull from Niah Caves. *Sarawak Museum Journal* 9: 323–49.

Brown P. 1989. *Coobool Creek: A morphological and metrical analysis of the crania, mandibles and dentitions of a prehistoric Australian human population.* Terra Australia 13. Canberra: Department of Prehistory, Research School of Pacific Studies, Australian National University.

Bulbeck D. 2000a. Dental morphology at Gua Cha, West Malaysia, and the implications for Sundadonty. *Bulletin of the Indo-Pacific Prehistory Association* 19: 17–41.

Bulbeck D. 2000b. Culture history of the Toalean of south Sulawesi, Indonesia. *Asian Perspectives* 39: 71–108.

Bulbeck D, Oxenham M, Cuong NL, Thuy NK. 2007. Implication of the terminal Pleistocene skull from Hang Muoi, northern Vietnam. *Vietnam Archaeology* 2: 42–52.

Cavalli-Sforza LL, Menozoi P, Piazza A. 1994. *The history and geography of human genes.* Princeton: Princeton University Press.

Chang KC 1986. *The archaeology of ancient China.* 4th ed. New Haven, CT: Yale University Press.

Coon CS. 1962. *The origin of races.* New York: Alfred A. Knopf.

Cuong NL. 1986. Two early Hoabinhian crania from Thanh Hoa province, Vietnam. *Zeitschrift für Morphologie und Anthropologie* 77: 11–17.

Cuong NL. 1996. *Anthropological characteristics of Dong Son population in Vietnam.* Hanoi: Social Sciences Publishing House.

Cuong NL. 2001. About human remains at Man Bac site. *Khao Co Hoc (Vietnamese Archaeology)* 1: 17–46.

Cuong NL. 2003. Ancient human bones in Da But Culture—Thanh Hoa Province. *Khao Co Hoc (Vietnamese Archaeology)* 3: 66–79.

Cuong NL. 2006. About the ancient human bones at An Son (Long An) through the third excavation. *Khao Co Hoc (Vietnamese Archaeology)* 6: 39–51.

Cuong NL. 2007. Paleoanthropology in Vietnam. *Vietnam Archaeology* 2: 23–41.

Diamond J, Bellwood P. 2003. Farmers and their languages: The first expansions. *Science* 300: 597–603.

Ding Y, Wooding S, Harpending HC, Chi H, Li H, Fu Y, Pang J, Yao Y, Yu J, Moyzis R, Zhang Y. 2000. Population structure and history in East Asia. *Proceedings of the National Academy of Sciences* 97: 14003–6.

Dizon E, Détroit F, Sémah F, Falguéres C, Hameau S, Ronquillo W, Cabanis E. 2002. Notes on the morphology and age of the Tabon Cave fossil *Homo sapiens. Current Anthropology* 43: 660–66.

Dubois E. 1922. The proto-Australian fossil man of Wadjak, Java. *Koninklijke Akademie van Wetenschappen te Amsterdam* B23: 1013–51.

Duckworth WLH. 1934. Human remains from rock-shelters and caves in Perak, Pahang and Perlis and from Selinsing. *Journal of Malayan Branch of the Royal Asiatic Society* 12: 149–67.

Evans IHN. 1918. Preliminary report on cave exploration, near Lenggong, upper Perak. *Federation Museums Journal* (Kuala Lumpur) 7: 227–34.

Genet-Varcin E. 1951. *Les Négritos de l'île de Luçon (Philippines).* Paris: Société d'Anthropologie de Paris.

Glover IC, Higham CFW. 1996. New evidence for early rice cultivation in South, Southeast and East Asia. In: Harris DR, editor. *The origins and spread of agriculture and pastoralism in Eurasia.* London: UCL Press. Pp. 413–41.

Gorman CF, Charoenwongsa P. 1976. Ban Chiang: A mosaic of impressions from the first two years. *Expedition* 18: 14–26.

Hanihara T. 1992. Negritos, Australian Aborigines, and the proto-Sundadont dental pattern: The basic populations in East Asia, V. *American Journal of Physical Anthropology* 88: 183–96.

Hanihara T. 1993a. Craniofacial features of Southeast Asians and Jomonese: A reconsideration of their microevolution since the late Pleistocene. *Anthropological Science* 101: 25–46.

Hanihara T. 1993b. Population history of East Asia and the Pacific as viewed from craniofacial morphology: The basic populations in East Asia, IV. *American Journal of Physical Anthropology* 91: 173–87.

Hanihara T. 1993c. Cranial morphological contrasts between Negritos, Australians, and neighbouring populations. *Anthropological Science* 101: 389–404.

Hanihara T. 1994. Craniofacial continuity and discontinuity of Far Easterners in the late Pleistocene and Holocene. *Journal of Human Evolution* 27: 417–41.

Hanihara T. 2006. Interpretation of craniofacial variation and diversification of East and Southeast Asia. In: Oxenham MF, Tayles N, editors. *Bioarchaeology of Southeast Asia*. Cambridge: Cambridge University Press. Pp. 91–111.

Hiep TH, Phung HV. 2004. Man Bac location and its relationship through ceramic data. *Khao Co Hoc (Vietnamese Archaeology)* 6: 13–48.

Higham CFW. 1998. Archaeology, linguistics and the expansion of the East and Southeast Asian Neolithic. In: Blench R, Spriggs M, editors. *Archaeology and language II: Archaeological data and linguistic hypotheses*. London: Routledge. Pp. 103–14.

Higham CFW. 2001. Prehistory, language and human biology: Is there a consensus in East and Southeast Asia? In: Jin L, Seielstad M, Xiao C, editors. *Genetic, linguistic and archaeological perspectives on human diversity in Southeast Asia*. Singapore: World Scientific. Pp. 3–16.

Howells WW. 1989. Skull shapes and the map: Cranio-metric analysis in the dispersion of modern *Homo*. Papers of the Peabody Museum of Archaeology and Ethnology, vol. 79. Cambridge, MA: Harvard University Press.

Hudson MJ. 1994. The linguistic prehistory of Japan: Some archaeological speculations. *Anthropological Science* 102: 231–55.

Hudson MJ. 1999. Japanese and Austronesian: An archaeological perspective on the proposed linguistic links. In: Omoto K, editor. *Interdisciplinary perspectives on the origins of the Japanese*. Kyoto: International Research Center for Japanese Studies. Pp. 267–79.

Hudson MJ. 2003. Agriculture and language change in the Japanese islands. In: Bellwood P, Renfrew C, editors. *Examining the farming/language dispersal hypothesis*. Cambridge, UK: McDonald Institute for Archaeological Research. Pp. 311–18.

Hudson DH, Bryant D. 2006. Application of phylogenetic networks in evolutionary studies. *Molecular Biology and Evolution* 23: 254–67.

HUGO Pan-Asian SNP Consortium. 2009. Mapping human genetic diversity in Asia. *Science* 326: 1541–45.

Institute of History and Institute of Archaeology (IHIA) and Chinese Academy of Social Science (CASS), editors. 1982. *Contributions to the study on human skulls from the Shang sites at Anyang*. Beijing: Cultural Relics Publishing House.

Jacob T. 1967. Some problems pertaining to the racial history of the Indonesian region. Ph.D. dissertation, University of Utrecht.

Jacob T, Soepriyo A. 1994. A preliminary palaeoanthropological study of the Gua Gunung Runtuh human skeleton. In: Zuraina M, editor. *The excavation of Gua Gunung Runtuh and the discovery of the Perak Man in Malaysia. Kuala Lumpur: Department of Museums and Antiquities (Malaysia). Pp. 48–69.

Kamminga J, Wright RVS. 1988. The Upper Cave at Zhoukoudian and the origin of the Mongoloids. *Journal of Human Evolution* 17: 739–67.

Kennedy KAR. 1977. The deep skull of Niah: An assessment of twenty years of speculation concerning its evolutionary significance. *Asian Perspectives* 20: 32–50.

Lertrit P, Poolsuwan S, Thosarat R, Sanpachudayan T, Boonyarit H, Chinpaisal C, Suktitipat B. 2008. Genetic history of Southeast Asian populations as revealed by ancient and modern human mitochondrial DNA analysis. *American Journal of Physical Anthropology* 137: 425–40.

Macintosh NWG. 1978. The Tabon Cave mandible. *Archaeological and Physical Anthropology in Oceania* 13: 143–59.

Matsumura H. 1989. Geographical variation of dental measurements in the Jomon population. *Journal of the Anthropological Society of Nippon* 97: 493–512.

Matsumura H. 1994. Dental characteristics affinities of the prehistoric to modern Japanese with the East Asians, American natives and Australo Melanesians. *Anthropological Science* 103: 235–61.

Matsumura H. 2002. The possible origin of the Yayoi migrants based on the analysis of the dental characteristics. In: Nakahashi T, Li M, editors. *Ancient people in the Jiangnan region, China.* Fukuoka: Kyushu University Press. Pp. 61–72.

Matsumura H. 2006. The population history of Southeast Asia viewed from morphometric analyses of human skeletal and dental remains. In: Oxenham M, Tayles N, editors. *Bioarchaeology of Southeast Asia.* Cambridge: Cambridge University Press. Pp. 33–58.

Matsumura H, Cuong NL, Thuy NK, Anezaki T. 2001. Dental morphology of the early Hoabinhian, the Neolithic Da But and the Metal Age Dong Son Cultural people in Vietnam. *Zeitschrift für Morphologie und Anthropologie* 83: 59–73.

Matsumura H, Domett K, O'Reilly D. 2011. On the origin of Pre-Angkorian peoples: perspectives from cranial and dental affinity of the human remains from Iron Age Phum Snay, Cambodia. *Anthropological Science* 119: 67–79.

Matsumura H, Hudson MJ. 2005. Dental perspectives on the population history of Southeast Asia. *American Journal of Physical Anthropology* 127: 182–209.

Matsumura H, Oxenham MF. 2011. The bioarchaeology of Man Bac: Research methods. In: Oxenham MF, Matsumura H, Nguyen KDD, editors. *Man Bac, the excavation of a Neolithic site in Northern Vietnam: The biology.* Terra Australis 33. Australian National University E Press. Pp. 1–8.

Matsumura H, Oxenham MF, Dodo Y, Domett K, Cuong NL, Thuy NK, Dung K, Hiffer D, Yamagata M. 2008. Morphometric affinity of the late Neolithic human remains from Man Bac, Ninh Binh Province, Vietnam: Key skeletons with which to debate the "Two layer" hypothesis. *Anthropological Science* 116: 135–48.

Matsumura H, Pookajorn S. 2005. Morphometric analysis of the Late Pleistocene human remains from Moh Khiew Cave in Thailand. *HOMO—Journal of Comparative Human Biology* 56: 93–118.

Matsumura H, Yoneda M, Dodo Y, Oxenham MF, Thuy NK, Cuong NL, Dung LM, Long VT, Yamagata M, Sawada J, Shinoda K, Takigawa W. 2008. Terminal Pleistocene human skeleton from Hang Cho cave, northern Vietnam: Implications for the biological affinities of Hoabinhian people. *Anthropological Science* 116: 201–17.

Matsumura H, Zuraina M. 1995. Metrical analysis of the dentition of Perak Man from Gua Gunung Runtuh in Malaysia. *Bulletin of the National Science Museum, Tokyo* 21 (Series D): 1–10.

Matsumura H, Zuraina M. 1999. Metric analyses of the early Holocene human skeleton from Gua Gunung Runtuh in Malaysia. *American Journal of Physical Anthropology* 109: 327–40.

Melton T, Clifford S, Martinson J, Batzer M, Stoneking M. 1998. Genetic evidence for the Proto-Austronesian homeland in Asia: mtDNA and nuclear DNA variation in Taiwanese aboriginal tribes. *American Journal of Human Genetics* 63: 1807–23.

Mijsberg WA. 1940. On a Neolithic Paleo-Melanesian lower jaw found in kitchen midden at Guar Kepah, Province Wellesley, Straits Settlements. In: Chasen FN, Tweedie MWF, editors. *Proceedings of the 3rd Congress of Prehistorians of the Far East.* Singapore: Government Printing Office. Pp. 100–118.

Nakahashi T. 1989. The Yayoi people. In: Nagai M, Nasu T, Kanaseki Y, Sahara M, editors. *Yayoi Bunka no Kenkyu (Research on Yayoi Culture).* Tokyo: Yuzankaku. Pp. 23–51.

Nakahashi T. 1993. Temporal craniometric changes from the Jomon to the modern period in western Japan. *American Journal of Physical Anthropology* 90: 409–25.

Nakahashi T, Li M, editors. 2002. *Ancient people in the Jiangnan region, China.* Fukuoka: Kyushu University Press.

Nakahashi T, Li M, Yamaguchi B. 2002. Anthropological study on the cranial measurements of the human remains from Jiangnan region, China. In: Nakahashi T, Li M, editors. *Ancient people in the Jiangnan region, China.* Fukuoka: Kyushu University Press. Pp. 17–33.

Ogata T. 1981. Geographical variation of the human skeletal morphology of the late Jomon period. In: Ogata T, editor. *The Japanese 1, Anthropology (Jinruigaku-Kouza),* vol. 5. Tokyo: Yuzankaku. Pp. 46–47.

Omoto K, Saitou N. 1997. Genetic origins of the Japanese: A partial support for the dual structure hypothesis. *American Journal of Physical Anthropology* 102: 437–46.

Oota H, Kurosaki K, Pookajorn S, Ishida T, Ueda S. 2001. Genetic study of the Paleolithic and Neolithic Southeast Asians. *Human Biology* 73: 225–31.

Oxenham MF, Matsumura H, Domett K, Nguyen KT, Nguyen KD, Nguyen LC, Huffer D, Muller S. 2008. Health and the experience of childhood in late Neolithic Vietnam. *Asian Perspectives* 47: 190–209.

Oxenham MF, Nguyen KT, Nguyen LC. 2005. Skeletal evidence for the emergence of infectious disease in Bronze and Iron Age northern Vietnam. *American Journal of Physical Anthropology* 126: 359–76.

Oxenham MF, Tayles N. 2006. Synthesizing Southeast Asian population history and health. In: Oxenham MF, Tayles N, editors. *Bioarchaeology of Southeast Asia.* Cambridge: Cambridge University Press. Pp. 335–49.

Pietrusewsky M. 1981. Cranial variation in Early Metal Age Thailand and Southeast Asia studied by multivariate procedures. *Homo* 32: 1–26.

Pietrusewsky M. 1982. The ancient inhabitants of Ban Chiang: The evidence from the human skeletal and dental remains. *Expedition* 24: 42–50.

Pietrusewsky M. 1992. Japan, Asia and the Pacific: A multivariate craniometric investigation. In: Hanihara K, editor. *Japanese as a member of the Asian and Pacific populations.* Kyoto: International Research Center for Japanese Studies. Pp. 9–52.

Pietrusewsky M. 1994. Pacific-Asian relationships: A physical anthropological perspective. *Oceanic Linguistics* 33: 407–29.

Pietrusewsky M. 1996. Multivariate craniometric investigations of Japanese, Asians, and Pacific Islanders. In: Omoto K, editor. *Interdisciplinary perspectives on the origins of the Japanese.* Kyoto: International Research Center for Japanese Studies. Pp. 65–104.

Pietrusewsky M. 1999a. The people of Ban Chiang: An early Bronze site in Northeast Thailand. *Bulletin of the Indo-Pacific Prehistory Association* 16: 119–48.

Pietrusewsky M. 1999b. A multivariate craniometric study of the inhabitants of the Ryukyu Islands and comparison with cranial series from Japan, Asia and the Pacific. *Anthropological Science* 107: 255–81.

Pietrusewsky M. 2005. The physical anthropology of the Pacific, East Asia: A multivariate craniometric analysis. In: Sagart L, Blench R, Sanchez-Mazos A, editors. *The peopling of East Asia: Putting together archaeology, linguistics and genetics.* Abingdon, UK: Routledge Curzon. Pp. 201–29.

Pietrusewsky M. 2006. A multivariate craniometric study of the prehistoric and modern inhabitants of Southeast Asia, East Asia and surrounding regions: A human kaleidoscope? In: Oxenham MF, Tayles N, editors. *Bioarchaeology of Southeast Asia.* Cambridge: Cambridge University Press. Pp. 59–90.

Pietrusewsky M. 2008. Craniometric variation in Southeast Asia and neighboring regions: A multivariate analysis of cranial measurements. *Human Evolution* 23: 49–86.

Pietrusewsky M. 2010. A multivariate analysis of measurements recorded in early and more modern crania from East Asia and Southeast Asia. *Quaternary International* 211: 42–54.

Pietrusewsky M, Douglas MT. 2002. *Ban Chiang, a prehistoric village site in Northeast Thailand I: The human skeletal remains.* Philadelphia: University of Pennsylvania, Museum of Archaeology and Anthropology.

Pookajorn S. 1991. *Preliminary report of excavations at Moh Khiew Cave, Krabi Province, Sakai Cave, Trang Province and ethnoarchaeological research of hunter-gatherer group, so-called Sakai and Semang at Trang Province.* Bangkok: Silpakorn University Press.

Pookajorn S. 1994. *Final report of excavations at Moh Khiew Cave, Krabi Province, Sakai Cave, Trang Province and ethnoarcheological research of hunter-gatherer group, so called Sakai or Semang at Trang Province.* Bangkok: Silpakorn University Press.

Renfrew C. 1987. *Archaeology and language: The puzzle of Indo-European origins.* London: Jonathan Cape.

Renfrew C. 1989. Models of change in language and archaeology. *Transactions of the Philological Society* 87: 103–55.

Renfrew C. 1992. World languages and human dispersals: a minimalist view. In: Hall JA, Jarvie IC, editors. *Transition to modernity: Essays on power, wealth and belief.* Cambridge: Cambridge University Press. Pp. 11–68.

Saitou N, Nei M. 1987. The neighbor-joining method: A new method for reconstructing phylogenetic tree. *Molecular Biology and Evolution* 4: 406–25.

Sieveking GG. 1954. Excavations at Gua Cha, Kelantan, Part 1. *Federation Museums Journal* 1: 75–143.

Sneath PH, Sokal RR. 1973. *Numerical taxonomy.* San Francisco: W. H. Freeman and Co.

Spriggs M. 1989. The dating of the Island Southeast Asian Neolithic: An attempt at chronometric hygiene and linguistic correlation. *Antiquity* 63: 587–613.

Storm P. 1995. *The evolutionary significance of the Wajak Skulls.* Scripta Geologica no. 110. Leiden: Nationaal Natuurhistorisch Museum, Netherlands.

Tan HV. 1976. The Hoabinhian in the context of Vietnam. *Vietnamese Studies* 46: 127–97.

Tan HV. 1997. The Hoabinhian and before. *Bulletin of the Indo-Pacific Prehistory Association* 16: 35–41.

Tan SG. 2001. Genetic relationships among sixteen ethnic groups from Malaysia and Southeast

Asia. In: Jin L, Seielstad M, Xiao C, editors. *Genetic, linguistic and archeological perspectives on human diversity in Southeast Asia.* Singapore: World Scientific. Pp. 83–91.

Tayles N, Oxenham MF. 2006. Southeast Asian bioarchaeology: past and present. In: Oxenham MF, Tayles N, editors. *Bioarchaeology of Southeast Asia.* Cambridge: Cambridge University Press. Pp. 1–30.

Thuy NK, Doi NG. 1998. *Surveying again Cho Cave (Luong Son, Hoa Binh Province), 1997.* Hanoi: Social Sciences Publishing House.

Trevor JC, Brothwell DR. 1962. The human remains of Mesolithic and Neolithic date from Gua Cha, Kelantan. *Federation Museums Journal* 7: 6–22.

Turner CG II. 1989. Teeth and prehistory in Asia. *Scientific American* 260: 70–77.

Turner CG II. 1990. Major features of Sundadonty and Sinodonty, including suggestions about East Asian microevolution, population history and late Pleistocene relationships with Australian Aborigines. *American Journal of Physical Anthropology* 82: 295–317.

Turner CG II. 1992. Microevolution of East Asian and European populations: A dental perspective. In: Akazawa T, Aoki K, Kimura T, editors. *The evolution and dispersal of modern humans in Asia.* Tokyo: Hokusensha. Pp. 415–38.

Van Stein Callenfels PV. 1936. The Melanesoid civilizations of Eastern Asia. *Bulletin of the Raffles Museum* 1 (Series B): 41–51.

Verhoeven TH. 1958. Pleistozane funde in Flores. *Anthropos* 53: 264–65.

Von Koenigswald GHR. 1952. Evidence of a prehistoric Australo-Melanesoid population in Malaya and Indonesia. *Southwestern Journal of Anthropology* 8: 92–96.

Weidenreich F. 1945. *Giant Early Man from Java and South China.* Anthropological Papers of the American Museum of Natural History 40. New York.

Wolpoff MH, Wu X, Thorne AG. 1984. Modern *Homo sapiens* origins: A general theory of hominid evolution involving the fossil evidence from East Asia. In: Smith FH, Spencer F, editors. *The origins of modern humans.* New York: Alan R. Liss. Pp. 411–84.

Woo J. 1959. Human fossils found in Liukiang, Kwangsi, China. *Vertebrata Palasiatica* 3: 108–18.

Yi S, Lee J, Dung LM, Long VT, Thuy NK. 2004. AMS dating of a number of archaeological sites in Vietnam. *Archaeology Journal,* no. 2: 161–74. Hanoi: Social Sciences Publishing House.

Yokoo Y. 1931. Dayak kokkaku no jinruigaku-teki kenkyu. *Journal of the Anthropological Society of Nippon* 46: 339–703.

Zuraina M. 1994. The excavation of Perak Man, an Epi-Palaeolithic burial at Gua Gunung Runtuh. In: Zuraina M, editor. *The excavation of Gua Gunung Runtuh and the discovery of the Perak Man in Malaysia.* Kuala Lumpur: Department of Museums and Antiquities, Malaysia. Pp. 23–47.

Zuraina M, editor. 2005. *The Perak Man and other prehistoric skeletons of Malaysia.* Penang: Penerbit Universiti Sains Malaysia.

Part II

Community Health

9

Conflict and Trauma among Nomadic Pastoralists on China's Northern Frontier

JACQUELINE T. ENG AND ZHANG QUANCHAO

Throughout human history, migration has brought people of differing cultures into contact with one another, creating a necessity for interpersonal negotiation across what are usually parsed as ethnic divisions. Interethnic relationships often involve long-term consequences for all of the participants in such exchanges (Hill 1998). Identifying the specific forms of interaction between or among particular ancient societies, ranging from trade and alliances to warfare and conquest, as well as tracing sociopolitical change resulting from those interactions, has long been of interest to anthropologists. Recently, as investigation of the occurrence and extent of intergroup violence and warfare across a broad sample of ancient societies has been a subject of renewed anthropological attention, questions have arisen as to what might characterize definitive material evidence of those specific activities (Martin and Frayer 1997; Lovell 1997, 2008; Lambert 2002, 2007).

Warfare may be defined broadly as "inter-group armed conflict" (Haas 2001: 331). As seen in that light, warfare may range in scope and frequency from isolated hostile encounters between individuals, through periodic opportunistic raiding, and on to more large-scale combat involving numerous participants over an extended period of time (Lambert 2002: 209). Studies of the evidence for such violence in prehistoric societies, especially among those that were of smaller demographic scale, are hampered by the relatively low archaeological visibility of simple warfare (Milner 1995). Research incorporating osteological analysis of the physical remains of the people themselves can give us a strong, direct line of evidence of past hostile interaction. The skeleton preserves signs of injury and trauma, often being the only surviving indicator of warfare or other violence. The osteological data, when considered in conjunction with other archaeological and historical evidence for conflict, allow us to reconstruct past interaction and behavior (Milner 1995; Vencl 1999; Walker 2001).

Research on ancient China and on the relationships that emerging Chinese states developed with neighboring East Asian societies has benefitted from an early written record. By combining insights derived from study of these historical sources with the results of modern archaeological research into ancient Chinese warfare (e.g., Underhill 1989, 2006), we are now developing a much clearer picture of the forms of conflict that took place on the Central Plains of China, especially during the latter half of the first millennium BC, when agents of expanding Chinese state-level societies increasingly came into contact with mounted nomads on the northern frontier (Di Cosmo 1999). However, previous investigations into the nature of imperial-frontier interaction have often been sinocentric, focused mainly on the policies and motivations of the Chinese. As has been noted, studies of warfare in complex societies have tended to concentrate on the role of armed conflict in the development of political power and/or the state (e.g., Carneiro 1970; D'Altroy 1992; Earle 1997). Actions taken by non-Chinese in response to contact with expansionist Chinese polities and/or the consequences of interaction for non-Chinese have rarely been addressed. This study aims to address that gap.

Work by Barfield (1989, 1991, 2001) and Di Cosmo (1994, 1996, 2002), along with previous research by the first author (Eng 2007), confronts these issues through a focus on nomadic groups and other non-Chinese, as well as by examining synchronic and diachronic diversity in the forms of interaction that played out along the Chinese northern frontier. This chapter further explores these issues through a bioarchaeological study of trauma among people living on China's ancient northern frontier, focusing on four archaeological skeletal collections (Jinggouzi, Lamadong, Nileke, and Yanghai) dating from the Late Bronze Age to the Weijin period (AD 220–439).

We posit that a host of complex interactions occurred as nomads migrated into and out of contested zones near the borders of Chinese expansion, with tensions both between the nomads and the Chinese, and among the nomadic tribes themselves. The following questions are addressed: Were violent interactions mainly a result of tensions between nomads and agents of imperial China, or did intertribal warfare also account for the traumas found within these collections? Which groups were most at risk, and how often did violence lead to death? What was the extent of intergroup violence, both geographically and through time?

In addressing these questions, particular emphasis is given to the Jinggouzi (井沟子) burial sample comprising the remains of a community of migrants who had settled close to what is now Inner Mongolia during the Late Bronze Age. By comparing trauma profiles of Jinggouzi individuals with trauma profiles from samples of other northern frontier regions (Manchuria and Xinjiang), we gain new insights into the nature of conflict and other forms of interaction among nomadic societies in the area, as well as between those societies and imperial China, as all engaged in what Sherratt (2006) has labeled a "Trans-Eurasian Exchange."

The History of Intersocietal Relations on the Northern Frontier

For the purposes of this study, osteological samples were utilized from four sites located in two distinct geographic regions: Manchuria (the northeastern provinces of Heilongjiang, Jilin, and Liaoning) and the Inner Mongolia Autonomous Region in northeastern China; and the northwestern province contiguous with the Xinjiang Uighur Autonomous Region (figure 9.1). Taken together, these two regions roughly correspond with the Asian portion of the vast Eurasian Steppe, also known as the "Northern Zone" or "Inner Asia" (Di Cosmo 2002: 13). The Inner Asian frontier has been defined as a zone of interaction between politically and economically opposing cultures: nomadic pastoralists on the one hand and sedentary Chinese agriculturalists on the other (Lattimore 1940).

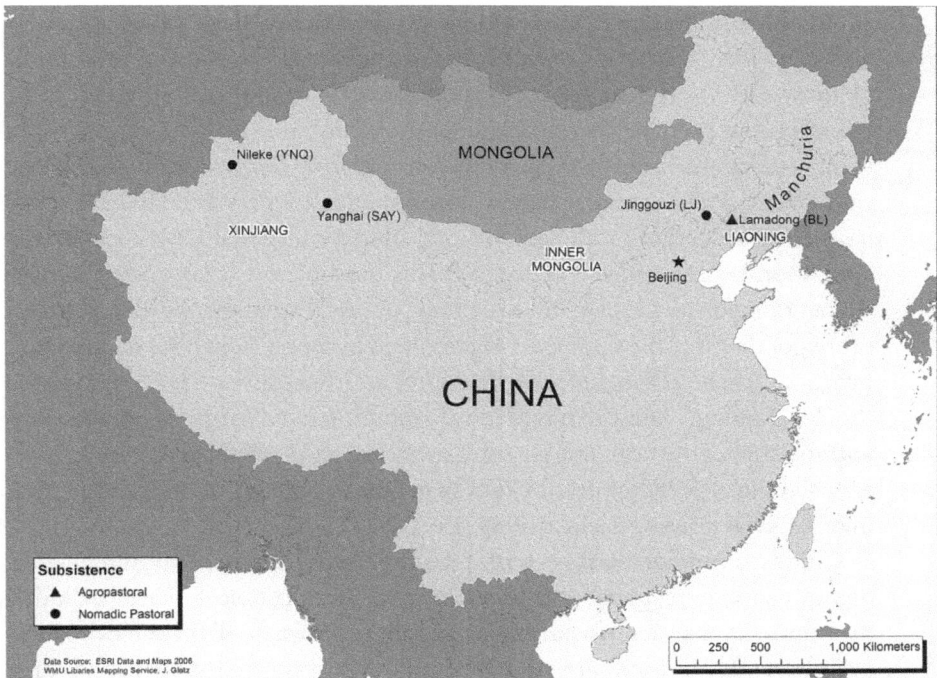

Figure 9.1. Map showing locations of the sites involved in the study. Acronyms refer to the Chinese site names: BL = Lamadong; LJ = Jinggouzi; SAY = Yanghai; YNQ = Nileke.

The populations considered in this study lived during times of major economic, political, and social change in eastern Asia. During the Late Bronze Age and Early Iron Age (circa 1000–200 BC), agrarian states around the fertile Central Plains of China vied with one another for power, while pastoral nomadic societies emerged in the northern steppe zone, spreading from western Asia eastward to the Mongolian steppe by the fourth century BC (Volkov 1995; Shui 2002). As the Chinese empire developed, imperial expansion was seen from within as the spread of its civilizing influence to the outside "barbarians" (Nelson 1995; Underhill 2006), in particular, the nomads occupying the northern frontier.

Historical records from Chinese dynastic courts describe the flow of resources between China and the "tributary" nomadic pastoralists (Yang 1968). These documents, which are available as early as the Han dynasty (206 BC–AD 220), describe the often problematic relations between China and nomads who threatened the borders. From a review of these accounts, a cyclical pattern of imperial-frontier relations may be recognized, within which Chinese imperial policy was usually one of appeasement: enactment of costly peace treaties that provided nomads with direct subsidies, as well as markets supplying them with agricultural products and luxury items (Barfield 1989, 2001).

The historiography of ancient China portrays northern tribes as greedy and aggressive barbarians with a never-ending desire for Chinese goods (Honey 1992). The traditional model of agrarian-nomadic interaction is based on the premise that nomadic pastoralism does not exist outside of a symbiotic relationship with farming communities (Khazanov 1984). In the case of East Asia, nomadic pastoral communities are presumed to have relied heavily upon goods produced and provided by imperial China, especially agricultural comestibles and textiles. This dependence is suggested to have driven nomads to adopt a "trade or raid" political strategy in order to extort more goods from the Chinese (Jagchid and Symons 1989). As a secondary outcome, such relationships with China are thought to have precipitated the development of more hierarchical and militaristic forms of organization within some of the nomadic pastoral societies in the north, as emerging leaders used the redistribution of Chinese goods as a means to underwrite their own political power (Barfield 1989, 1991, 2001).

Chinese imperial relations with foreigners were apparently quite flexible, being shaped in response to a broad array of circumstances. These included the internal dynamics of a particular reigning court, as well the relative political, economic, and military strengths and weaknesses of that dynastic court in relation to the specific nomadic polity in question. Typically, Chinese policy ranged from active military engagement in advance of Chinese expansion and resettlement, to the negotiation of treaties involving trade and marriage alliances (Loewe 1987: 197). It was often risky and logistically impractical for the state to engage in extended military campaigns against mounted nomadic warriors. Even so, when the nomads demanded too much or broke existing treaties, and/or Chinese rulers otherwise wanted to extend their control over people or territory, warfare often ensued.

During the politically fragmented Eastern Zhou period (722–221 BC), policies for interaction with outsiders were influenced by the imperative of the Zhou states to survive and expand, especially when other horse-riding cultures emerged from western Asia and threatened the established northeast Asian states with their own eastward migration. The primary strategy of the Zhou was to attempt conquest; the second was to negotiate peaceful diplomatic relations when conquest was not feasible; the third was to attempt to govern and assimilate foreigners; and the fourth was to use foreigners for military and economic purposes (Di Cosmo 2002: 106).

Thereafter, during the reign of the Han dynasty, in the face of constant pressure from the powerful Xiongnu nomadic confederacy (209 BC–AD 155) of the north, imperial policy readapted to practical concerns about available economic resources and manpower, as well as the immediacy of the nomadic threat. Throughout the long history of interaction on the northern frontier, the nomadic societies involved fluctuated in their status: either as denizens of a "pacified" or wild "barbarian" zone of outsiders or, at times, as conquerors in their own right, as the rulers of part or all of China.

In ancient times, the borders of southern Mongolia (today, Inner Mongolia) and Manchuria (the northeastern provinces) marked the frontier of northern China, a transitional ecological zone that could support either nomadic pastoralists or sedentary farmers. This area served as a gateway through which nomads migrated and Chinese goods flowed; thus, it was an intensely contested area with constantly shifting boundaries. Early Chinese states (and later, the various dynasties of a unified Chinese empire) attempted to control and regulate the movement of people, goods, and ideas through this disputed region by constructing the defensive walls that eventually were incorporated into the Great Wall of China.

Throughout China's imperial history, tribes from along the northern frontier greatly influenced the stability of the unified state. The steppe tribes of Mongolia played a key role in frontier politics, without ever conquering China, except during the brief reign of the Yuan dynasty (AD 1271–1368). Nomadic states rose and fell in accord with their symbiotic relationships with the Chinese imperial dynasties. Manchuria became a breeding ground for tribes establishing foreign dynasties within China proper whenever native dynasties collapsed because of internal rebellion. Barfield (1989, 1991, 2001) suggests that so many of the foreign dynasties emerged from the Manchurian borderlands precisely because that region was inhabited by both Chinese and tribal peoples, providing local rulers with the opportunity to learn how to seamlessly combine Chinese and tribal traditions within a single overarching administrative structure. Whenever imperial China faced the threat of raiding and warfare by mounted forces from beyond the northern frontier, that threat generally came from Mongolia or Manchuria.

Comparing the Northern Frontier Populations

The skeletal remains of ancient pastoralists from Inner Mongolia, recovered at the site of Jinggouzi, were studied in order to gain insight into the living conditions of those peoples inhabiting an economically transitional and politically contested area close to the boundaries of early imperial China. Archaeological evidence suggests that these particular people shifted from an agropastoral to a pastoral nomadic economy during the Late Bronze Age (Wang et al. 2004). Analysis of skeletal remains from the nearby site of Lamadong (喇嘛洞) in the Manchurian province of Liaoning provides insight into the nature of a population in the "pacified zone," whose inhabitants practiced agropastoralism.

In contrast to the situation in Mongolia and Manchuria, the frontier region to the northwest, in modern Xinjiang Province, played a relatively marginal role in China's political history. The ecology of Xinjiang is similar to that of Manchuria, in that parts of the area could support mixed economies. Nevertheless, the similarity did not extend to its peoples' relationships with China, mainly because of geographical constraints on sustained and frequent interaction. China was connected to Xinjiang through the Gansu corridor, around which were a string of oases extending westward from the Ordos desert in Inner Mongolia toward Xinjiang.

These oases were occupied by large numbers of ethnic Chinese, who since the time of the early Han dynasty had been an important element of imperial frontier defense. The Han dynasty rulers sent forces to occupy this region when battling the nomadic Xiongnu confederacy in the first century BC, but China lost control of the area to Uzbek tribes in the second century AD and did not reoccupy the region for another 500 years. Any polity that arose in Xinjiang was separated from central China by a vast distance and arid terrain that prevented mounted campaigns or invasion.

Thus, the far western end of the northern frontier was home to nomads whom the Chinese considered "barbarians," occupying a "wild zone" ostensibly free of Chinese influence for much of the early imperial age. Analysis of the patterns and distribution of traumatic injury among these western pastoral nomads is based on material recovered from two sites in Xinjiang: Nileke (尼勒克) and Yanghai (洋海). These samples provide useful comparisons with those recovered from the eastern sites located in Inner Mongolia and Manchuria, potentially shedding light on differential risk of trauma as a function of proximity to the Chinese heartland.

Materials and Methods

The skeletal series studied here are stored at the Research Center for Frontier Archaeology at Jilin University in the city of Changchun, capital of the northeastern province of Jilin. The human remains of a total of 751 individuals from four different archaeological sites (figure 9.1), including 151 subadults and 600 adults, were analyzed (table 9.1). Most of the collections utilized were limited to cranial remains. The postcranial elements most often curated were large long bones, such as the femur and other limb elements. Thus, much potential information that could have been gleaned from other parts of the skeleton has been lost. Moreover, it is unclear from the pertinent archaeological reports whether the burials that were collected from a given site include the entire available sample or only a cross section of the total. Despite these limitations, many burials within each of the collections were relatively complete, and what was present offered a wealth of information on many variables related to trauma.

The most important skeletal sample considered here came from a Late Bronze Age cemetery (1000–600 BC) located in the Linxi County village of Jinggouzi, near the modern city of Chifeng, in Inner Mongolia. The Jinggouzi site (LJ) was excavated in 2002 and 2003 by archaeologist Wang Lixin and colleagues affiliated with Jilin University, with 100 percent recovery of

Table 9.1. Demographic profiles of the sites analyzed

Site	Region	Economy	Time	Subadult	Adult	M[a]	F[a]	Ind[b]	Total
LJ	Inner Mongolia	Pastoral	1000–600 BC	61	64	29	35	0	125
YNQ	Xinjiang	Pastoral	500–221 BC	9	39	23	16	0	48
SAY	Xinjiang	Pastoral	475 BC–AD 220	32	53	30	23	0	85
BL	Manchuria	Agropastoral	AD 337–410	49	444	229	214	1	493
			Totals:	151	600	311	288	1	751

Note: LJ = Jinggouzi; YNQ = Nileke; SAY = Yanghai; BL = Lamadong.
[a] Adult male and female counts.
[b] Adult of indeterminate sex.

the cemetery (Wang et al. 2004). A total of 59 tombs were found, most of which contained multiple individuals. The sample consisted of a total of 125 individuals, including 61 subadults and 64 adults (29 males and 35 females). The burials were relatively complete and reasonably well preserved.

Animal bones were found among the grave goods in 25 of the 28 tombs encountered during the 2002 excavation season. Many were the remains of domesticated animals, likely the victims of sacrifice. Along with a large collection of weapons made of bronze and/or bone, artifacts associated with animal husbandry and horseback riding were also found among the funerary objects, but nothing directly related to agricultural practices (Wang et al. 2004). One young male was buried with 26 bone arrowheads, bone daggers, and a short bronze sword. These implements suggest that violence was among the preoccupations of at least some of the individuals buried in the cemetery at Jinggouzi.

The specific characteristics of the grave good assemblage have led Wang and colleagues to propose that the individuals buried at Jinggouzi were associated with or descended from persons of the Donghu (Eastern Tu) culture (Wang 2004; Wang et al. 2004; Zhu and Wang 2005). The Donghu (东胡) are described in ancient Chinese written records as a nomadic people or peoples of the northeast. Wang and his colleagues (2004) propose that the people buried at Jinggouzi were new to the area, having migrated southward from Mongolia over a period of several decades and eventually mixed with local farming peoples in what is now Inner Mongolia. Research in the Chifeng region suggests that environmental change during the Bronze Age led to colder, drier conditions that could have precipitated a shift in economic strategies toward increasing reliance on nomadic pastoralism (e.g., Shelach 1994; Linduff et al. 2002).

For the purposes of this study, a skeletal series was also analyzed from each of two other sites left in the archaeological record by nomadic pastoralists, both located in Xinjiang, much farther from ancient imperial China's heartland than is Inner Mongolia. Analysis of the frequency of trauma represented in these two collections offers insight into the patterns of injury among pastoralists who were roughly contemporaneous with those studied from Jinggouzi. The Xinjiang sites stem from time periods when Chinese imperial influence on the region was either minimal or completely absent.

One of these sites, located in Nileke (YNQ), near the Yiling River tributary system, is dated to the Early Iron Age (500–221 BC). Two cemeteries encompassing a total of 55 graves, some of them with stone coffins, were recorded at Nileke. No obvious prestige goods were found. The material associated with the Nileke burials consisted of accoutrements typically found in nonelite graves, such as pottery, knives, or other tools made of wood and iron, along with goat bones, possibly resulting from sacrifice (Liu and Li 2002). The remains of 48 individuals from Nileke were available for analysis, including 9 subadults and 39 adults (23 males and 16 females).

The Yanghai site (SAY), located in the village of Xiacun in Shanshan County, is dated to a range extending from the Warring States period to the Han dynasty (475 BC–AD 220), which makes it somewhat more recent than the Jinggouzi sample. In 2003, the Xinjiang Institute of Cultural Relics and Archaeology and the Turpan Prefectural Bureau of Cultural Relics excavated 510 tombs in three cemeteries at Yanghai. Funerary goods associated with the burials included pottery and implements and other items made of bronze, stone, bone, iron, antler, shell, woven straw, and leather, as well as wool, silk, and cotton (Lu et al. 2004).

Human bone recovered at both Nileke and Yanghai was well enough preserved to indicate that whole burials might have been recoverable. In practice, curation was limited primarily to skulls and secondarily to long bones. The Yanghai collection included the remains of a total of 85 individuals, with 32 subadults and 53 adults (30 males and 23 females).

For comparison, a large collection recovered at the site of Lamadong (BL), or Lama Cave in Beipiao City, Liaoning Province, was also analyzed. This site was home to a more recent agropastoral community, dated to the time of the Weijin period (AD 220–439). The purpose of this particular comparison was to help assess the risk of traumatic injury associated with an agropastoral economic strategy, but in an area fully encompassed by imperial China.

The Liaoning Archaeology Research Center began excavations at the Lamadong cemetery in 1993 as part of an effort to study the Sixteen Kingdoms period (AD 304–439), when much of northern China was ruled by a pastoral ethnic group known as the Xianbei (Zhang and Zhao 2000). The Xianbei apparently originated on the steppes of Mongolia, eventually migrating in the third century AD to northeastern China, where they allied with the Han court against other nomadic groups, including the Xiongnu (Bai 1979).

The Lamadong human skeletal material examined for this study derives mostly from the 1998 excavation season, during which 369 tombs and thousands of cultural artifacts were unearthed (Zhongguo Kaogu Xuehui 1998). Artifacts included both decorative and utilitarian objects, some of iron, mainly in the form of weapons and farm tools. The presence of agricultural tools such as plows and sickles implies that Chinese farming practices had been adopted in the community. Other artifacts included numerous items associated with horseback riding (e.g., iron saddles), as well as helmets. These finds suggest a mixed economy that resulted from a combination of agrarian-based Han Chinese and pastoral influences; the people seemed to have en-gaged in both farming and animal husbandry, as well as military activities (Zhang and Zhao 2000). This Lamadong sample consisted of 493 individu-als, 49 of them subadults and 444 adults (229 males and 214 females, with 1 adult of indeterminate sex).

Osteological analysis was carried out on material from each of the col-lections described above in order to obtain demographic information, along with data on health status, diet, and pathological conditions (see Eng 2007), as well as evidence of trauma, if any. Using a modified scoring system where appropriate, data collection was performed following standardized osteologi-cal protocols codified in *Standards for Data Collection from Human Skeletal Remains* (Buikstra and Ubelaker 1994), in concert with procedures described in *The Backbone of History* (Steckel and Rose 2002), and also outlined in the *Global History of Health Project* (Steckel et al. 2004).

Sliding Mitutoyo calipers were used to record metric data, including the dimensions of traumatic injury. For evidence of trauma, microscopic (loop magnification 16x/64D) and macroscopic examinations were conducted to identify and distinguish between skeletal damage that had resulted from antemortem and perimortem processes, as opposed to taphonomic changes and postmortem damage, in accord with standards previously delineated by several other researchers (Micozzi 1991; Nawrocki 1995; Sauer 1998; Gallo-way 1999a; Lovell 2008). Probable indicators of interpersonal violence that were recorded include fractures of the cranial vault and nasal/facial bones, cutmarks, and embedded projectiles (e.g., Walker 1997; Bridges et al. 2000). These injuries were categorized as resulting from sharp, blunt, or projectile force. Other traumatic injuries recorded include other types of fractures, dis-locations, depressions, and ossified connective tissue, all of which were noted by location, type, and whether evidence of remodeling was present.

Accident-related trauma might be expected to be more prevalent among migratory pastoralists than among farmers, as the former operated in close association with large animals. However, accidents are by definition unex-pected, unusual, and unintended, so the vagaries of chance make predictions of frequency uncertain. An accident can be differentiated from an intention-ally delivered injury based on the uniqueness of the event (e.g., a single injury versus multiple; Judd 2002) and the location of the injury, which may be indicative of chance falls or occupation-related trauma. For the purposes of this study, accidental injuries were defined as those that consisted of single instances of fracture to long bones and did not involve embedded points or impact from a weapon.

While all individual long bones were examined for signs of trauma, counts of the affected limb bones were combined into a catchall "long bone fracture" category, for two reasons. First and foremost, several individuals were represented by only a few long bone elements. Absent a larger sample, more likely to be representative of the population as a whole, interpretation of the results for individual skeletal elements is problematic. Second, long bone fractures, when they did occur, were usually the single recordable instance of trauma for a given individual. In cases where there were multiple injuries on the remains of a single individual, this fact was recorded and construed as potential evidence for interpersonal conflict.

Traumas observed on other elements, such as the ribs and pelves, were also noted whenever found. However, as these bones were not well represented in any of the collections, those observations were withheld from the overall analysis, except when it was obvious to the investigators that a particular injury resulted from violence. Fisher's exact test was used in intrasite and intersite comparisons (when d.f. = 1) and wherever appropriate, chi-square (χ^2) was employed in comparisons of all data (when d.f. > 1), with all tests conducted at the $p = .05$ level of significance.

Age-at-death profiles were divided between the categories of subadult (17 years and younger) and adult, with the latter further subdivided into the narrower categories of young adult (YA, 18–34 years), middle adult (MA, 35–45 years), and old adult (OA, 46+ years); a category of unknown adult (UA, 18+) was used when elements were too fragmentary to confidently estimate age. Although subadults were examined, the results and interpretations presented below focus on injury to adults, who displayed the majority of traumatic lesions.

As sex and age have correlations with trauma (e.g., from the higher likelihood of male injury owing to risky activity by younger males to elder age-related fractures), samples with disproportionate sex ratios or number of older individuals may result in sample bias, so careful attention was paid to the distribution of demographic variables (table 9.2). There are slight differences

Table 9.2. Age and sex profile

Site	N	YA	MA	OA	UA[a]		Male	Female
		(%)	(%)	(%)	(%)		(%)	(%)
Jinggouzi (LJ)	64	64	14	8	14		45	55
Nileke (YNQ)	39	54	28	18	0		59	41
Yanghai (SAY)	53	45	21	26	8		57	43
Lamadong (BL)	443	39	35	9	17		52	48

Note: See text for explanation of age categories.
[a] UA = unknown adult (uncertain age).

in sex ratios in some sites, but the overall distribution is not markedly different among them ($\chi^2 = 2.37$, $[3, N = 599]$ $p = .499$).

Skeletal Evidence of Trauma

Evidence of trauma was found on the remains of some individuals in all four sample groups, described in detail below. There was only a single occurrence of trauma among the remains of subadults from all four sites: an adolescent (age 13–16) from Lamadong, who had a healed fracture of a left metatarsal. Most of those affected were adults, with preserved wounds reflective of both accidental causes and deliberate violence (table 9.3, modified from Eng 2007: table A8.4). The probable cause of a particular trauma was usually diagnosed in accord with the type of injury and its location, as well as by comparison with the results of previous studies of occupational injuries to farmers (Nordstrom et al. 1995; Judd and Roberts 1999) and pastoralists and equestrians (Barber 1973; Björnstig et al. 1991; Bradtmiller 1983; Siebenga et al. 2006; Ball et al. 2007; Havlik 2010; Halser et al. 2011). Findings from previous research describing osteological indicators of violence and warfare in other contexts were also taken into account (Bovee and Owsley 1994; Milner 1995; Lambert 1997; Bridges et al. 2000; Novak 2000).

Long Bone Trauma

As noted earlier, some samples were incomplete (e.g., the Xinjiang collections), making interpretation of the results for trauma in individual long bone elements problematic (table 9.4). In all samples, the larger limb bones of the leg (especially the femur and tibia) had higher representation than did the upper limb bones (humerus, ulna, and radius). This disparity in upper to lower limb ratio was most marked in the Xinjiang samples of Nileke (4:15, i.e., 4 upper to 15 lower limb long bones) and Yanghai (31:62), with less difference in Lamadong (540:784) and Jinggouzi (97:128). Among the pastoral samples, Jinggouzi was evenly split between fractures found in the upper and lower limbs (4/8 found in upper and 4/8 in lower limbs), while Yanghai only had one long bone fracture, found on an ulna, and Nileke had no long bone fractures. In the agropastoral Lamadong sample, 41 percent (9/22) of fractures were found in the upper limb, compared to 59 percent (13/22) found in the lower limb bones. Note, this ratio matches the upper:lower limb ratio of preserved elements (540/1324 = 41 percent vs. 784/1324 = 59 percent), suggesting that as with the results found from Jinggouzi, there was a relatively equal likelihood of suffering injury in either an upper or a lower limb. At all

Table 9.3. Summary of cranial and postcranial trauma

Site	Number	Sex	Age	Bone	Side	Trauma	State
LJ	3A	M	YA	Ulna	R	Parry fx?	Healed
LJ	56A	M	YA	Femur	R	Simple fx	Healed
LJ	46B	M	YA	Ilium	R	Projectile	Perimortem
LJ	49A	M	YA	Humerus	L	Sharp	Healed
LJ	15	M	MA	1) Ulna	L	Parry fx?	Healed
				2) Tibia	L	Simple fx	Healed
LJ	19.02	F	UA	Femur	R	Simple fx	Healed
LJ	18	F	YA	Frontal	L	Sharp	Healed
LJ	31	F	YA	Parietal/ occipital	R	Sharp	Healed
LJ	47B	F	YA	Parietal	L	Blunt fx	Healed
LJ	11A	F	YA	Ulna	L	Parry fx?	Healed
LJ	41A	F	YA	Sacrum	L	Compression	Healing
LJ	36A	F	YA	Ribs (2)	L	Simple fx	Healed
LJ	4	F	MA	Tibia	L	Simple fx	Healed
LJ	17.1	F	OA	Parietal	R	Sharp	Healed
LJ	22B	F	OA	1) Parietal	L	Blunt fx	Healed
				2) Parietal	L	Blunt fx	Healed
				3) Parietal	L	Blunt fx	Healed
YNQ	32	M	YA	Frontal	R	Projectile	Perimortem
YNQ	15A	M	MA	Parietal	R	Blunt fx	Healing
YNQ	31.01	M	MA	Nasal	L	Fracture	Active/nonunion
YNQ	4	M	OA	Parietal	L	Active/slight	Sharp
YNQ	999.03	M	OA	1) Frontal	M	Blunt fx	Healed
				2) Frontal	L	Blunt fx	Healed
				3) Frontal	R	Blunt fx	Healed
				4) Nasal	L	Fracture	Healing
SAY	42.1	M	YA	1) Parietal	R	Blunt fx	Perimortem
				2) Parietal	L	Blunt fx	Perimortem
SAY	42.2	M	YA	1) Parietal	R	Blunt fx	Healed
		M	YA	2) Parietal	L	Projectile	Perimortem
		M	YA	3) Nasal	L	Fracture	Healed
SAY	27.1	M	YA	1) Parietal	R	Sharp	Perimortem
				2) Parietal	L	Sharp	Perimortem
				3) Parietal	L	Sharp	Perimortem
				4) Parietal	L	Sharp	Perimortem
SAY	101.4	M	MA	Zygomatic	L	Fracture	Healed
SAY	48.1	F	MA	Nasal	R	Fracture	Healed
SAY	36.2	F	OA	Parietal	L	Blunt fx	Healed
SAY	101.10	F	OA	Ulna	L	Parry fx?	Nearly healed
BL	258	?	Ad[a]	Metatarsal	?	Fracture	Healed

(continued)

(*continued*)

BL	117	M	YA	Frontal	L	Blunt fx	Healing
BL	371	M	YA	Clavicle	R	Fracture	Well-healed
BL	237	M	YA	1) Humerus	R	Fracture	Healed
				2) Ulna	R	Fracture	Healed
BL	89	M	YA	Tibia	L	Simple fx	Well-healed
BL	280	M	YA	Fibula	R	Simple fx	Active/healing
BL	35	M	YA	Ulna	L	Parry fx?	Well-healed
BL	88	M	YA	Radius	L	Simple fx	Well-healed
BL	11	M	YA	1) Tibia	L	Simple fx	Well-healed
				2) Fibula	L	Simple fx	Well-healed
BL	201.01	M	MA	Parietal	R	Sharp	Perimortem
BL	218	M	MA	Parietal	L	Blunt fx	Healed
BL	315	M	MA	Parietal	R	Blunt fx	Healed
BL	175	M	MA	1) Parietal	R	Blunt fx	Healed
				2) Temporal	R	Sharp	Perimortem
BL	61B	M	MA	Nasal	L	Fracture	Healed
BL	334.01	M	MA	Fibulae	LR	Fracture	Well-healed
BL	45	M	YA	Ulna	L	Parry fx?	Active/healing
BL	164	M	MA	Tibia	L	Simple fx	Well-healed
BL	206.01	M	MA	1) Tibia	L	Simple fx	Active/healing
				2) Fibula	L	Simple fx	Active/healing
BL	369	M	MA	Fibula	L	Simple fx	Active/healing
BL	33	M	MA	Metatarsal 3, 4	R	Fracture	Well-healed
BL	5	M	MA	Ankle	L	Ankylosis	Healed
BL	31.01	M	OA	Femur	R	Fracture	Well-healed
BL	286	M	OA	Ribs (2)	L	Fracture	1) Well-healed
							2) Nonunion
BL	108	M	OA	Tibia	R	Compound fx?	Active/healing
BL	49	M	OA	Metatarsal	?	Fracture	Healed
BL	364	M	UA	1) Nasal	L	Fracture	Healed
				2) Femur	R	Compound fx?	Active/healing
BL	376.01	M	MA	Ulna	L	Parry fx?	Well-healed
BL	270	F	YA	1) Ulna	R	Fracture	Healed
				2) Pubis	LR	Fracture?	Nonunion
BL	233	F	MA	Parietal	L	Blunt fx	Healed
BL	232	F	MA	Humerus	L	Simple fx	Well-healed
BL	375	F	MA	Ulna	L	Parry fx?	Well-healed
BL	102	F	OA	Tibia	L	Simple fx	Healed

Note: See text for site abbreviations and age categories.

[a] Ad = Adolescent: this single instance of subadult injury was not included in the analysis.

Table 9.4. Fractures observed in long bone elements

Bone	LJ		YNQ		SAY		BL	
	Obs./N	%	Obs./N	%	Obs./N	%	Obs./N	%
Humerus	1/32	3.1	0/2	0	0/12	0	2/231	0.9
Ulna	3/32	9.3	0/1	0	1/10	10.0	6/151	4.0
Radius	0/33	0	0/1	0	0/9	0	1/158	0.6
Femur	2/48	4.2	0/8	0	0/36	0	2/316	0.6
Tibia	2/43	4.7	0/5	0	0/17	0	6/307	2.0
Fibula	0/37	0	0/2	0	0/9	0	5/161	3.1
Total	**8/225**	**3.6**	**0/19**	**0**	**1/93**	**1.1**	**22/1324**	**1.7**

sites the most frequently fractured long bone was the ulna, as described in more detail in the discussion below on interpersonal violence.

An assessment was made for the total number of long bones fractured out of the total number of long bones recorded (table 9.4). Among the four sites, Jinggouzi had the highest frequency of fractured long bones (8/225 = 3.6 percent), followed by Lamadong (22/1324 = 1.7 percent) and Yanghai (1/93 = 1.1 percent). No cases of long bone fracture were recorded from the Nileke sample (0/19). A chi-square comparison of these frequencies showed no significant difference among them (χ^2 = 4.49, [3, N = 1,661] p = .213). Such frequencies of long bone fracture are comparable with those reported for a number of different populations in both the Old World and New World, including in a study by Buzon and Richman (2007) on a Nubian New Kingdom population (2.4 percent) and studies summarized by Roberts and Manchester (2005: 98) in their table 5.1 (Lovejoy and Heiple 1981; Bennike 1985; Jurmain 1991, 2001; Alvrus 1996, 1999; Kilgore et al. 1997; Neves et al. 1999; Judd 2000). Frequencies reported from these investigations ranged from 0.8 percent in Denmark (Bennike 1985; a mix of prehistoric and historic samples) to 4.3 percent in Kulubnarti (Kilgore et al. 1997).

Data on traumatic injury were also examined with respect to the number of individuals affected. Although most burials considered in this study did not have complete skeletons, the distribution of trauma across and between the samples can still provide insight into the possible causes of injury, as well as revealing any possible differential rates of injury that may be correlated with age and sex (Roberts and Manchester 2005: 97). In terms of individuals with long bone trauma, including both accidental and deliberate injury across all adult age categories (see "Total %" in table 9.5), the site with the highest percentage of adults showing injury was Jinggouzi (7/57 = 12 percent), followed by the Lamadong site ($18/354 = 5$ percent). Fisher's exact tests comparing the remains from Jinggouzi with those from all other sites showed no significant differences in the frequency of long bone fractures (Nileke, $p = .583$; Yanghai, $p = .139$; Lamadong, $p = .064$). A chi-square comparison of all four sites also revealed no marked difference ($\chi^2 = 6.00$, $[3, N = 457]$ $p = .112$).

Multiple injuries suffered by an individual may indicate violent encounters (Judd 2002). Across all four sites considered, the number of adults who had multiple long bone fractures was not large. There were no examples among the Xinjiang individuals from Nileke or Yanghai. From Jinggouzi, one male had healed fractures of the left ulna and tibia, which may indicate injury from the same event, such as a fall. Five individuals from Lamadong also had multiple injuries that might have resulted from a single incident. One young male suffered trauma to the elbow that fractured both the humerus and the ulna, while two others had fractures to the tibia and fibula at the same proximate location along the shaft. Another male had fractured the ankle at the distal tibia and fibula; one male had fractured both fibulae. Fisher's exact tests comparing the rate of Jinggouzi individuals suffering multiple long bone trauma ($1/64 = 2$ percent) to the rate found for Lamadong ($5/444 = 1$ percent) showed no significant difference between them ($p = .556$).

The age cohort with the highest rate of long bone injury varied across the sites (table 9.5). The highest rates of trauma in the sample from Jinggouzi are in the young adult and middle adult age categories (11 percent and 29

Table 9.5. Long bone trauma in individuals by site and age cohort

Site	YA		MA		OA		UA		Total
	Obs./N	%	Obs./N	%	Obs./N	%	Obs./N	%	
LJ	4/37	11	2/7	29	0/3	0	1/10	11	7/57=12%
YNQ	0/4	0	0/2	0	0/2	0	0/0	0	0/8=0%
SAY	0/16	0	0/9	0	1/9	11	0/4	0	1/38=3%
BL	8/132	6	7/122	6	2/35	6	1/65	2	18/354=5%

Table 9.6. Long bone trauma by site and sex

Site	Male		Female	
	Obs./N	%	Obs./N	%
LJ	4/27	15	3/29	10
YNQ	0/5	0	0/3	0
SAY	0/23	0	1/15	7
BL	14/177	8	4/176	2

percent, respectively). In the collection from Yanghai, the highest rate of long bone trauma was found in the old adult category (11 percent). It should be noted, however, that for Yanghai, this rate stems from only a single instance of long bone fracture found among old adults ($n = 9$). Lamadong has roughly equivalent long bone fractures in all age groups (6 percent). Nileke had no long bone trauma recorded for any of the nine adults with such elements present.

In making comparisons between the sexes in the frequencies of recorded long bone trauma, it was expected that males would have a higher rate of fractures than females owing to differential participation in manual labor and conflict-related activities. This was found to be true for the collections from Jinggouzi and Lamadong, while for the much smaller samples from Xinjiang it was not (table 9.6). Jinggouzi males had a higher proportion of fractures ($4/27 = 15$ percent) than did females from the same site ($3/29 = 10$ percent), although not at a significant level (Fisher's exact $p = .700$), while Lamadong males did have a significantly higher frequency of long bone fractures ($14/177 = 8$ percent) as compared to the females ($4/176 = 2$ percent; $p = .027$). There was no recorded instance of trauma among the five males and three females with long bones from Nileke; there was only a single instance of a long bone fracture recorded from Yanghai, suffered by an old adult female ($1/15$ females compared to $0/23$ in males, Fisher's exact $p = .395$).

Interpersonal Trauma

As has been documented in previous research, signs of deliberate trauma are often manifested as trauma to the head (cranial vault, nasal, and facial bones), as well as wounds from implements and embedded points; adult males are more likely to exhibit these indicators of intentional violence (Walker 1989, 2001; Lambert 1994; Kellner 2002; Lessa and Mendonca de Souza 2004; Jurmain et al. 2009; Torres-Rouff 2011; Brødholt and Holck 2012). Other indicators of nonaccidental injury include fractures of the ulna, which may indicate a "parry fracture" from defensive blocking (Galloway 1999b), and, as mentioned earlier, the presence of repeat injuries in the case of a single individual (Judd 2002).

Data observed for trauma to the head were divided between observations of the cranial vault and nasal fractures. The latter indicates injury to the facial region. While any visible evidence of trauma to other facial bones was also recorded, there was only one instance of a non-nasal facial fracture, to the zygomatic (left side), on the remains of a Yanghai middle adult male. That fracture was included within the nasal fracture count as an indication of a blow directed to the face.

In a comparison of the rates of cranial trauma for all sites, there is a highly significant difference among them ($\chi^2 = 23.1$, $[3, N = 448]$ $p < .001$), with the highest frequency found in the sample from Jinggouzi ($5/29 = 17$ percent, see total in table 9.7). This frequency is significantly greater than that found for the Lamadong remains (Fisher's exact test $p < .001$), which had the lowest recorded rate of evidence for head injury ($6/336 = 2$ percent). The other pastoral sites of Nileke ($4/38 = 11$ percent) and Yanghai ($4/45 = 9$ percent) also had significantly higher frequencies of cranial trauma than did the agropastoral site of Lamadong ($p = .012$ and $p = .021$, respectively), but those rates were not significantly different from the frequency for Jinggouzi ($p = .485$ and $p = .301$, respectively). These results suggest a link between a higher risk of interpersonal violence and the pastoral way of life. In the case of Jinggouzi and Lamadong, these results may also indicate that the risk of violent injury owing to proximity to Chinese borders depended on incorporation within the Chinese polity, with greater risks for Jinggouzi pastoral "outsiders" compared to the people living in the Chinese-controlled area of Lamadong.

Given that warfare is best pursued by the young and fit, it may be expected that within each skeletal series, the remains of younger individuals would evidence higher rates of trauma to the head than do those of older members of the same population. This was found not to be the case in most of the collections studied (table 9.7). Only at the Yanghai site did the young adult group have a higher rate of cranial trauma; at two sites, the highest frequencies were found among the old adult subsamples (Jinggouzi, $2/5 = 40$ percent; Nileke, $2/8 = 25$ percent), while Lamadong had relatively low frequencies of cranial trauma, the highest rate in the middle adult group ($5/136 = 4$ percent). Glen-

Table 9.7. Cranial trauma by site and age cohort

Site	YA		MA		OA		UA		Total
	Obs./N	%	Obs./N	%	Obs./N	%	Obs./N	%	
LJ	3/19	16	0/5	0	2/5	40	0/0	0	5/29=17%
YNQ	1/20	5	1/10	10	2/8	25	0/0	0	4/38=11%
SAY	3/22	14	0/9	0	1/14	7	0/0	0	4/45=9%
BL	1/145	1	5/136	4	0/28	0	0/27	0	6/336=2%

Table 9.8. Nasal trauma by site and age cohort

Site	YA		MA		OA		UA		Total
	Obs./N	%	Obs./N	%	Obs./N	%	Obs./N	%	
LJ	0/14	0	0/4	0	0/3	0	0/0	0	0/21=0%
YNQ	0/20	0	1/10	10	2/6	33	0/0	0	3/36=8%
SAY	1/19	5	1/8	13	0/13	0	0/0	0	2/40=5%
BL	0/65	0	1/55	2	0/14	0	1/4	25	2/138=1%

cross and Sawchuk (2003) have noted that older individuals may display higher rates of fractures owing to their greater accumulated years of exposure to risks; for cranial injuries, which may leave lesions for many years, an injury found in an older adult may have occurred much earlier.

This trend was somewhat repeated in age profiles of the frequency of nasal fractures, although there were relatively few observed nasal fractures, most likely due to the paucity of preserved nasal bones in the studied collections. Where they did appear, it was primarily in middle and old adult subsamples (table 9.8). The lowest frequency of nasal fracturing was recorded from the Lamadong sample (2/138 = 1 percent), while the highest rates were found on the remains of pastoralists from Nileke (3/36 = 8 percent) and Yanghai (2/40 = 5 percent). There were no recorded cases of nasal fracture among the individuals from Jinggouzi. Differences among the sites in their frequencies of nasal trauma were not found to be statistically significant ($\chi^2 = 5.90$, [3, N = 235] $p = .117$).

Another expectation is that males are more at risk for injury than are females within their group, as was the case in rates of long bone trauma for Jinggouzi and Lamadong. Frequencies of recorded cranial trauma followed this expectation in three sites, although the differences between the sexes at each site were not statistically significant (Fisher's exact: Nileke, $p = .124$; Yanghai, $p = .608$; Lamadong, $p = .216$). The sample from Jinggouzi provided the one glaring exception (table 9.9), although the difference between the sexes for rates of cranial trauma at Jinggouzi was also not statistically significant ($p = .126$).

While 28 percent (5/18) of the Jinggouzi females showed evidence of cranial trauma, the majority on the left side and on the parietal (see table 9.3, figure 9.2), not a single instance of cranial trauma was recorded for the Jinggouzi males. The Jinggouzi females had the highest frequency of cranial trauma found among any of the four collections, regardless of sex. This differ-

Table 9.9. Cranial and nasal trauma by site and sex

| Site | Cranial | | | | Nasal | | | |
| | Male | | Female | | Male | | Female | |
	Obs./N	%	Obs./N	%	Obs./N	%	Obs./N	%
LJ	0/11	0	5/18	28	0/9	0	0/12	0
YNQ	4/22	18	0/16	0	3/21	14	0/14	0
SAY	3/23	13	1/22	5	1/22	5	1/20	5
BL	5/174	3	1/162	1	2/68	3	0/70	0

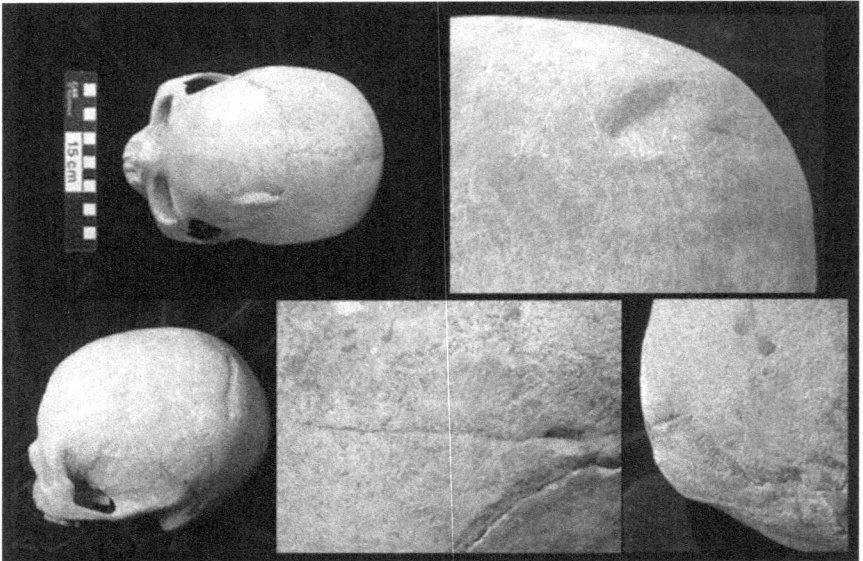

Figure 9.2. Jinggouzi (LJ) females with cranial fractures: (*upper row, left to right*) M18 L frontal, M22B L parietal; (*bottom row, left to right*) M47B L parietal, M17.1 R parietal, M31 R parietal/occipital.

ence was highly significant when comparing the frequencies of cranial trauma among females across the four sites (χ^2 = 39.1, [3, N = 218] p < .001).

There was also a significant difference in the frequencies of cranial trauma among males across the four sites (χ^2 = 12.9, [3, N = 230] p = .005). After the Jinggouzi females, the next two highest rates of cranial trauma came from among the male subgroups of the pastoral populations, at Nileke (4/22 = 18 percent) and Yanghai (3/23 = 13 percent). There was one female victim from Yanghai (1/22 = 5 percent). These frequencies of male cranial trauma were not significantly different from that found for Jinggouzi males. However, the differences were significant when the comparison was made with the Lamadong males (5/174 = 3 percent; Fisher's exact: p = .010 with Nileke; p = .053 with Yanghai). Females in the Lamadong collection had less than a 1 percent (1/162) frequency of cranial trauma.

Nasal fractures are a likely result of face-to-face fist fighting. In his survey of museum collections and archaeological samples of crania from North America, Europe, and Asia, Walker (1997) found a 7 percent frequency (106/1,506) of such fractures, with males, especially older males, more often injured, while Torres-Rouff and Costa Junqueira (2006: 67, table 3) documented rates of facial fractures as high as 17.71 percent in males and 15.38 percent in females of the Late Intermediate Period among a sample from San Pedro de Atacama, Chile. In this study, nasal fractures were not found at such high frequencies, with no observations of nasal fractures within the Jinngouzi sample. Where found, they were more common for males than females within the same populations (table 9.9), but the differences are not statistically significant (Fisher's exact: Nileke, $p = .259$; Yanghai, $p = 1$; Lamadong, $p = .241$). There was only one instance of a female with a nasal fracture among all the sites, a female in the Yanghai sample. Comparison of the male frequencies of nasal fractures across the collections yielded no significant difference ($\chi^2 = 4.90$, $[3, N = 120]$ $p = 0.179$). One individual, an adult male of unknown age from Lamadong, was the only example among the four collections of a person who had both an injury to the head and on the postcrania, as he had a healed nasal fracture and also a healing fracture on his femur.

Researchers have attributed wounds on the left anterior cranium as the result of blows from right-handed attackers in face-to-face fighting (e.g., Tung 2007; Torres-Rouff 2011; Šlaus et al. 2012). Across the samples from all sites, the location of cranio-facial injuries was on the left side in the majority of cases ($20/26 = 77$ percent of all such fractures, including people with multiple wounds), indicating that the blows were delivered by right-handed assailants (table 9.3). One young adult female from Jinggouzi (M31) showed evidence of a blow from a sharp implement on the back of the head, indicating that she had probably been hit while fleeing an assault. The majority of cranial vault injuries were localized on the parietals (Jinggouzi = 4/5, Nileke = 2/4; Yanghai = 4/4; Lamadong = 5/6, for a total of $15/19 = 79$ percent of the cases across all sites). Six individuals had multiple injuries on the cranial vault: an older adult female from Jinggouzi, an older adult male from Nileke (who also had a nasal fracture), three young adult males from Yanghai, and a middle-aged male from Lamadong. Of these, three individuals had injuries to the right and left side of the head: one male from Nileke and two from Yanghai.

When the recorded instances of cranio-facial injury were compared with those of ulnar fractures, both to look for correlations and to discriminate between accidental and deliberate trauma (e.g., Smith 1996), no cases of individuals displaying fractures in both locations were found. The majority of the ulnar fractures that might be considered "parry" fractures (mid- and distal shaft) (Judd 2008) were on the left (7/8 cases across all four sites, with one Jinggouzi male having a right ulna fracture). For the Jinggouzi sample, two of the three cases of such fractures were found on the remains of males (66 percent), along with 75 percent (3/4) of the cases from Lamadong. The lone ulna fracture recorded from the Yanghai sample was on the remains of an older adult female. That fracture may have been the result of a fall, in concert with susceptibility to breakage due to osteoporosis. All other adult remains showing evidence of ulnar trauma were in the young or middle adult categories.

Weapons and Wounds

In order to assess the possible causes of injuries inflicted on several individuals in the overall sample (figure 9.3), it is useful to review some of the weapons and protective gear known to have been used by contemporaneous populations in East Asia. For instance, as described in table 9.3, several individuals had injuries seemingly resulting from assaults with bladed weapons ("sharp," $n = 6/19$ affected crania), some had injuries that resulted from blunt force trauma ($n = 13/19$ in affected crania), and a few had evidence of projectile wounds, with one point found embedded in the right pelvis of a Jinggouzi male (M46B, figure 9.4).

An excellent pictorial and descriptive history of ancient weapons from China and the border areas can be found in *The Ancient Weapons of China* (Hong 1992), from which the following descriptions are drawn.

It has been proposed that the people whose remains were recovered from the cemetery at Jinggouzi were Donghu. The Donghu used bronze weapons, of which the most characteristic was the short *jian* (劍), a double-edged sword with a broad and thick blade, averaging 25–37 cm in length (Hong 1992: 139–40) (figure 9.5). One such weapon was found at Jinggouzi in the

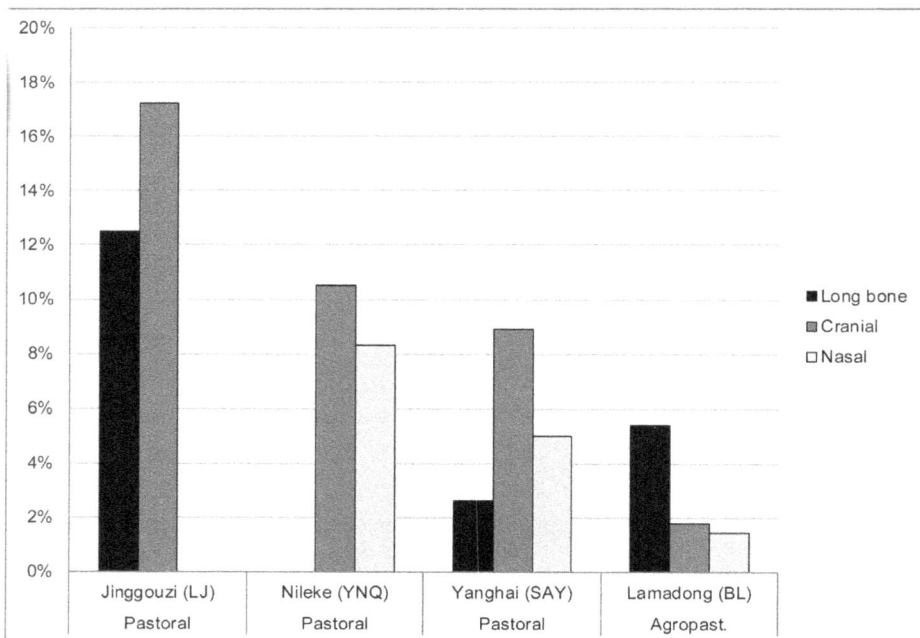

Figure 9.3. Summary of frequencies of trauma found within individuals among the sites.

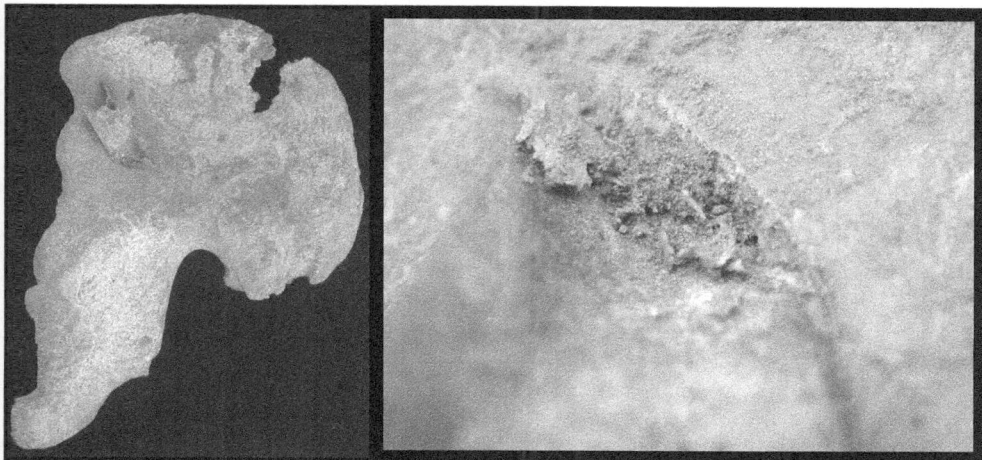

Figure 9.4. Jinggouzi (LJ) male M46B with projectile embedded in right ilium; close-up view to right.

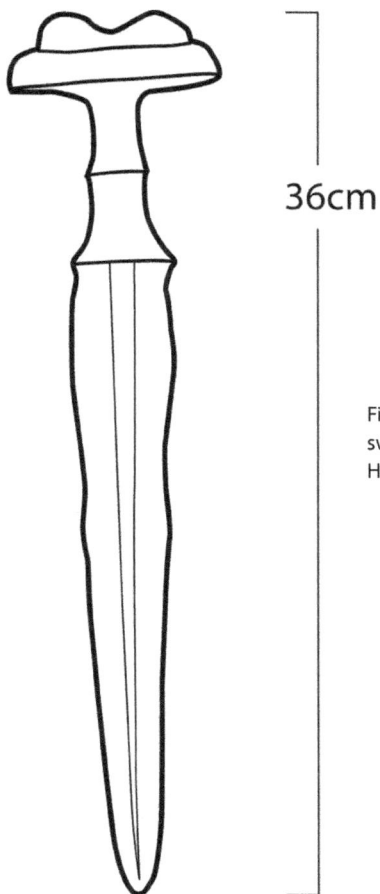

36cm

Figure 9.5. Short bronze *jian* (double-edged sword), adapted by Jenny Eng from fig. 206 in Hong 1992 (p. 142).

burial of a young adult male (M3A) (Wang et al. 2004). This Inner Mongolian population lived in a time contemporaneous with the Eastern Zhou period of the Central Plains, where bronze weapons included the traditional dagger-axe (*ge*, 戈) and spear, as well as the *ji* (戟, halberd); the crossbow and the double-edged sword were also introduced during this time frame (Hong 1992: 90). Excavations elsewhere in Inner Mongolia have produced bronze helmets.

In other parts of China, Eastern Zhou people used leather armor and helmets, along with lacquered leather or wooden shields for protection (Hong 1992: 114–16). There are no distinct differences between either Donghu and Eastern Zhou bronze dagger-axes or short bronze swords, suggesting that the Donghu and bronze cultures of the Central Plains were "closely related" (Hong 1992: 141). Pyramidal bronze arrowheads were also used by the Eastern Zhou, much like the one found embedded in the right ilium of a Jinggouzi male. It is also possible that a similar weapon caused cranial puncture wounds found on the remains of individuals from Xinjiang (figure 9.6).

Intergroup fighting between pastoralists of the Donghu and Xinjiang cultures against the Chinese Eastern Zhou people cannot be implicated with certainty in any of these cases. Given the similarity of weaponry all across the Northern Zone to that of the Eastern Zhou, it is certainly possible that the injuries described were a result of intertribal conflict among nomads. Underhill (2006: 276) has written of an increasing culture of violence during the politically unstable Eastern Zhou period.

The Lamadong people lived during a later time frame, the likewise turbulent Weijin period, which saw both a series of short-lived dynasties and the increased use of mounted cavalry in military engagements (Hong 1992: 230). Bows and crossbows were still in use, while double-edged steel swords and double-edged long spears (*shuo*, 槊) were standard for cavalry. Armor and helmets were made of iron and leather; several burials at Lamadong included iron helmets (Zhongguo Kaogu Xuehui 1998).

The iron horse-rider's helmet was an essential piece of protective gear for cavalrymen; techniques for manufacturing them improved with the intensification of war. They may have offered better protection from cranial trauma than did the earlier leather helmets, which might help explain the relatively low rate of cranial trauma found in the collection from Lamadong. Throughout all periods, the use of protective body armor as well as the inherent vulnerability of the head as a target for lethal blows may account for the higher prevalence of cranio-facial injury overall as compared with other indicators of violence.

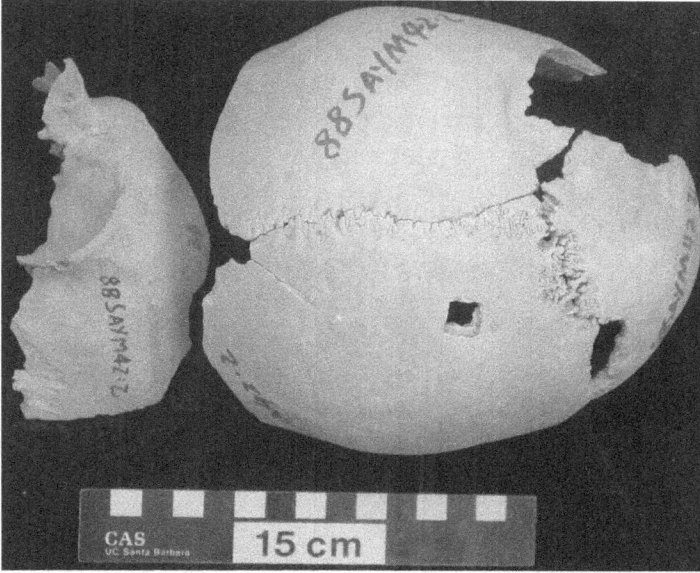

A

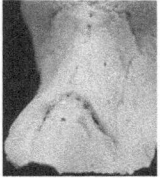

(1)

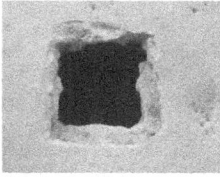

(2)

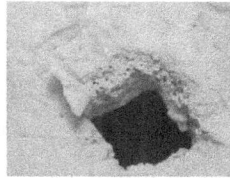

(3)

(4)

B

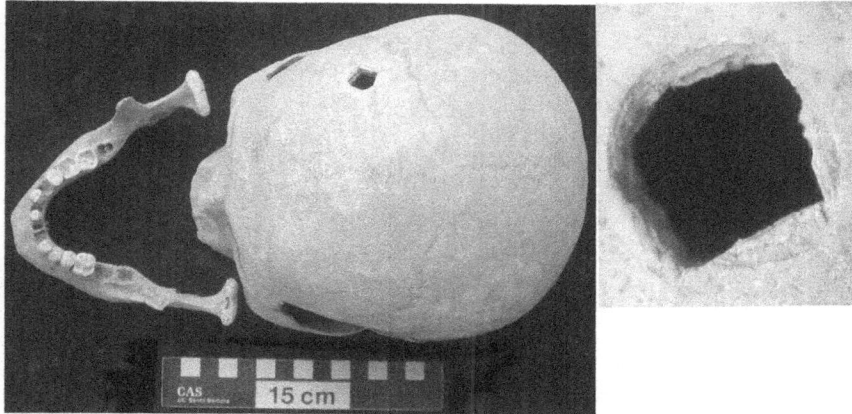

Figure 9.6. Xinjiang crania with trauma: *A*, Yanghai (SAY) male M42.2: (1) nasal fracture; (2) projectile fracture, ectocranial view; (3) projectile fracture, endocranial view; (4) blunt force trauma on posterior right parietal. *B*, Nileke (YNQ) male M32 with projectile wound to right frontal, close-up view to right.

Discussion: Trauma and the Nomadic Lifestyle on the Northern Frontier

The patterns of trauma found among the human remains from each of the four sites give us valuable insight into the types of injuries, and associated impact on health, suffered by nomadic groups from different regions of the northern frontier. The people of Jinggouzi, pastoralists who had recently migrated into the northeast, living close to the Chinese border and yet not part of the state, offer a good basis for comparison with nomadic pastoral groups from Xinjiang, who lived in more distant reaches of the frontier, as well as with those from Lamadong, a border population that had been integrated into the Chinese state.

Were acute traumas more commonplace among the members of migratory pastoral groups? From the higher frequencies of long bone fractures found in the sample from Jinggouzi (both per long bones available and per number of individuals having curated long bones), it appears there may be linkages between the frequency of injury on the one hand and animal husbandry, with or without transhumance, on the other. While the agropastoral Lamadong group had the second highest frequencies of long bone fractures from across all collections, there was only one instance recorded of a long bone fracture in the small combined sample ($n = 112$) of long bones from the Xinjiang collections. These results suggest that, at least with regard to long bone injury, there was no strong correlation between the frequency of injury and risk from specific subsistence-related activities, at least at the sites from which human remains were analyzed here (see Eng 2007 for a larger study of differences according to subsistence).

What about violent conflict and the accounts of violence among nomadic populations? Signs of intentional trauma, as evidenced by wounds to the head, were more commonly found on remains from the Jinggouzi site, followed by the two populations from Xinjiang (who also had the highest rates of nasal fractures), with the least frequent occurrence in the Lamadong sample. These results suggest that nomadic groups had a greater risk of trauma from interpersonal or intergroup violence. However, it must be noted that protective coverings such as the iron helmets found in some Lamadong graves may have afforded some measure of shielding to cranial injury; that may explain their lower percentage of head fractures, though a few individuals in that population, mostly males, did suffer cranial fractures. Most cranial wounds across the sites were inflicted by blunt force. The location of trauma across all sites was predominantly on the left parietal and nasal area, indicative of face-to-face attacks by right-handed assailants.

What type of conflict occurred along the northern frontier, and which subsets of the population were most at risk? Among the nomadic pastoral sites there was evidence of the type of weaponry used, with wounds from projectiles and sharp implements such as swords and axes evident. Whether this was a result of conflict with other nomadic tribes or, possibly in the case of Jinggouzi, a result of disputes with nearby expansive Chinese states is unclear, as there was a high degree of similarity in weaponry among the cultures of the Northern Zone region and with the Chinese Eastern Zhou period. At all sites, males were more likely to have been injured, except in the case of cranial trauma in the Jinggouzi sample, where only females were affected, and at a significantly higher frequency than for the other samples analyzed for the purposes of this study.

Work by other investigators on the high frequency of cranial injuries among women cross-culturally has offered several possible reasons for these findings, including domestic violence, intrasex competition, or domination over a servant/labor class, along with raiding and abduction, particularly in a tribal context (Webb 1995; Martin 1997; Walker 1997; Wilkinson 1997). Jackes (2004) also documented a high rate of interpersonal violence against women in a Neolithic site in central China, which she suggested may have been associated with internal village tensions or conflict with outsiders. Because the wounds found on the remains of Jinggouzi females were antemortem and showed healing, those individuals may have been the victims of intertribal raiding, and the blows were not necessarily meant to kill. One older adult female (M22B) had three healed cranial fractures, indicating survival after several nonlethal blows. Nevertheless, as exemplified in the case of the Jinggouzi male (M46B) with an embedded point, some attacks were meant to kill.

On the remains from all three other sites, more cranio-facial fractures were found among the males, probably indicating that males in general were more frequently involved with interpersonal violence. Most individuals with evidence for any kind of trauma (long bone or head injury) were older adults, except in the Yanghai series. At Yanghai, younger males with cranial wounds suffered perimortem injuries, so they were almost certainly the victims of killing attacks, which fits the normative profile of the young warrior. Ulnar fractures that may have resulted from parrying were found almost exclusively on the remains of males as well, which also implies that participation in interpersonal or intergroup conflict was largely a male activity.

Conclusion

Recent research into warfare in imperial contexts of conquest and coloniza-tion has shown the value of incorporating a bioarchaeological viewpoint in order to help understand the relationships between interacting populations (e.g., Judd 2000, 2006; Kellner 2002; Buzon and Richman 2007; Tung 2007; Murphy et al. 2010; Andrushko and Torres 2011). With archaeological evi-dence of defensive features and weapons, Underhill (2006: 254) has argued for a strong association between the growth of states in China throughout the Bronze Age and a concomitant "increase in the frequency, intensity, and scale of warfare," as well as technological innovations for war. These inter-nal changes within the developing Chinese state and incipient empire were also precipitated by increasing interaction with nomadic groups encountered along the northern frontier (Di Cosmo 1999: 951). As Chinese historical sources document and the divide represented by the Great Wall also attests, tensions were high.

This study has presented osteological evidence of past injury and proof of interpersonal conflict. The analysis of human skeletal remains helps further document the complex relationships between and among groups living along the ancient Chinese northern frontier, especially the risks of interpersonal violence among the members of nomadic pastoral groups, no matter how great their distance from the Chinese core region. It may be that living un-der the aegis of imperial infrastructure, as did the population at Lamadong, provided people relatively greater protection from intentional harm than was afforded the nomadic pastoral occupants of the nearby site of Jinggouzi or distant pastoralists of Nileke and Yanghai in faraway Xinjiang.

Acknowledgments

We thank the editors for the opportunity to contribute to this volume and for their insightful comments; we are grateful for comments by volume reviewers as well. We also thank Professor Zhu Hong, Professor Wang Lixin, and other colleagues at Jilin University for providing the archaeological field materials. The lead author conducted this research with support from the Fulbright-Hays Doctoral Dissertation Research Abroad Program and the University of California Pacific Rim Research Program.

Literature Cited

Alvrus A. 1996. Fracture patterns among the Nubians of Semna South, Sudan. Ph.D. dissertation, Arizona State University.

Alvrus A. 1999. Fracture patterns among the Nubians of Semna South, Sudanese Nubia. *International Journal of Osteoarchaeology* 9: 417–29.

Andrushko VA, Torres EC. 2011. Skeletal evidence for Inca warfare from the Cuzco region of Peru. *American Journal of Physical Anthropology* 146: 361–72.

Bai S. 1979. Xianbei remains in Manchuria and Inner Mongolia: Record of Xianbei remains, part 1. *Chinese Studies in Archaeology* 1: 3–43.

Ball CG, Ball JE, Kirkpatrick AW, Mulloy RH. 2007. Equestrian injuries: Incidence, injury patterns, and risk factors for 10 years of major traumatic injuries. *American Journal of Surgery* 193: 636–40.

Barber HM. 1973. Horse-play: Survey of accidents with horses. *British Medical Journal* 3: 532–34.

Barfield TJ. 1989. *The perilous frontier.* Cambridge, MA: Basil Blackwell.

Barfield TJ. 1991. Inner Asia and cycles of power in China's imperial history. In: Seaman G, Marks D, editors. *Rulers from the steppe: State formation on the Eurasian periphery.* Los Angeles: Ethnographic Press. Pp. 21–62.

Barfield TJ. 2001. The shadow empires: Imperial state formation along the Chinese-nomad frontier. In: Alcock SE, D'Altroy TN, Morrison KD, Sinopoli CM, editors. *Empires.* Cambridge: University Press. Pp. 10–41.

Bennike P. 1985. *Palaeopathology of Danish skeletons: A comparative study of demography, disease and injury.* Copenhagen: Akademisk Forlag.

Björnstig U, Eriksson A, Örnehult L. 1991. Injuries caused by animals. *Injury* 22: 295–98.

Bovee DL, Owsley DW. 1994. Evidence of warfare at the Heerwald site. In: Owsley DW, Jantz RL, editors. *Skeletal biology in the Great Plains: Migration, warfare, health, and subsistence.* Washington, DC: Smithsonian Institution Press. Pp. 355–62.

Bradtmiller B. 1983. The effect of horseback riding on Arikara arthritis patterns. Paper presented at the 82nd Annual Meeting of the American Anthropological Association, Chicago, Illinois.

Bridges PS, Jacobi KP, Powell ML. 2000. Warfare-related trauma in the late prehistory of Alabama. In: Lambert PM, editor. *Bioarchaeological studies of life in the age of agriculture.* Tuscaloosa: University of Alabama Press. Pp. 35–62.

Brødholt ET, Holck P. 2012. Skeletal trauma in the burials from the royal church of St. Mary in medieval Oslo. *International Journal of Osteoarchaeology* 22: 201–18.

Buikstra JE, Ubelaker DH. 1994. *Standards for data collection from human skeletal remains.* Fayetteville: Arkansas Archaeological Survey.

Buzon MR, Richman R. 2007. Traumatic injuries and imperialism: The effects of Egyptian colonial strategies at Tombos in Upper Nubia. *American Journal of Physical Anthropology* 133: 783–91.

Carneiro RL. 1970. A theory on the origins of the state. *Science* 169: 733–38.

D'Altroy TN. 1992. *Provincial power in the Inka empire.* Washington, DC: Smithsonian Institution Press.

Di Cosmo N. 1994. Ancient Inner Asian nomads: Their economic basis and its significance in Chinese history. *Journal of Asian Studies* 53: 1092–1126.

Di Cosmo N. 1996. Ancient Xinjiang between Central Asia and China: The nomadic factor. *Anthropology and Archeology of Eurasia* 34: 87–101.

Di Cosmo N. 1999. The northern frontier in pre-imperial China. In: Loewe M, Shaughnessy EL, editors. *The Cambridge history of ancient China: From the origins of civilization to 221 BC.* Cambridge: Cambridge University Press. Pp. 885–966.

Di Cosmo N. 2002. *Ancient China and its enemies.* Cambridge: Cambridge University Press.

Earle TC. 1997. *How chiefs come to power.* Palo Alto: Stanford University Press.

Eng JT. 2007. Nomadic pastoralists and the Chinese empire: A bioarchaeological study of China's northern frontier. Ph.D. dissertation, University of California, Santa Barbara.

Galloway A. 1999a. The biomechanics of fracture production. In: Galloway A, editor. *Broken bones: Anthropological analysis of blunt force trauma.* Springfield, IL: Charles C. Thomas. Pp. 35–62.

Galloway A. 1999b. Fracture patterns and skeletal morphology: The upper extremity. In: Galloway A, editor. *Broken bones: Anthropological analysis of blunt force trauma.* Springfield, IL: Charles C. Thomas. Pp. 113–59.

Glencross B, Sawchuk L. 2003. The person-years construct: Ageing and the prevalence of health related phenomena from skeletal samples. *International Journal of Osteoarchaeology* 13: 369–74.

Haas J. 2001. Warfare and the evolution of culture. In: Feinman G, Price D, editors. *Archaeology at the millennium: A sourcebook.* New York: Kluwer Academic/Plenum. Pp. 329–50.

Halser RM, Gysslar L, Benneker L, Martinolli L, Schötzau A, Zimmermann H, Exadaktylos AK. 2011. Protective and risk factors in amateur equestrians and description of injury patterns: A retrospective data analysis and a case-control survey. *Journal of Trauma Management and Outcomes* 5: 1–8.

Havlik HS. 2010. Equestrian sport-related injuries: A review of current literature. *Current Sports Medicine Reports* 9: 299–302.

Hill JD. 1998. Violent encounters: Ethnogenesis and ethnocide in long-term contact situations. In: Cusick JG, editor. *Studies in culture contact: Interaction, culture change, and archaeology.* Carbondale, IL: Center for Archaeological Investigations.

Honey DB. 1992. *Stripping off felt and fur: An essay on nomadic Sinification.* Bloomington: Research Institute for Inner Asian Studies, Indiana University.

Hong Y, editor. 1992. *Weapons in ancient China.* New York: Science Press.

Jackes MK. 2004. Osteological evidence for Mesolithic and Neolithic violence: Problems of interpretation. In: Roksandic M, editor. *Violent interactions in the Mesolithic: Evidence and meaning.* Oxford, UK: Archaeopress. Pp. 23–39.

Jagchid S, Symons VJ. 1989. *Peace, war, and trade along the Great Wall: Nomadic-Chinese interaction through two millennia.* Bloomington: Indiana University Press.

Judd MA. 2000. Trauma and interpersonal violence in ancient Nubia during the Kerma period (ca. 2500–1500 BC). Ph.D. dissertation, University of Alberta.

Judd MA. 2002. Ancient injury recidivism: An example from the Kerma period of ancient Nubia. *International Journal of Osteoarchaeology* 12: 89–106.

Judd MA. 2006. Continuity of interpersonal violence between Nubian communities. *American Journal of Physical Anthropology* 131: 324–33.

Judd MA. 2008. The parry problem. *Journal of Archaeological Science* 35: 1658–66.

Judd MA, Roberts CA. 1999. Fracture trauma in a medieval British farming village. *American Journal of Physical Anthropology* 109: 229–43.

Jurmain RD. 1991. Paleoepidemiology of trauma in a prehistoric central Californian population. In: Ortner DJ, Aufderheide AC, editors. *Human paleopathology: Current syntheses and future options.* Washington, DC: Smithsonian Institution Press. Pp. 241–48.

Jurmain RD. 2001. Paleoepidemiological patterns of trauma in a prehistoric population from central California. *American Journal of Physical Anthropology* 115: 18–23.

Jurmain RD, Bartelink EJ, Leventhal A, Bellifemine V, Nechayev I, Atwood M, DiGiuseppe D. 2009. Paleoepidemiological patterns of interpersonal aggression in a prehistoric Central California population from CA-ALA-329. *American Journal of Physical Anthropology* 139: 462–73.

Kellner CM. 2002. Coping with environmental and social challenges in prehistoric Peru: Bioar-chaeological analyses of Nasca populations. Ph.D. dissertation, University of California, Santa Barbara.

Khazanov AM. 1984. *Nomads and the outside world.* Cambridge: Cambridge University Press.

Kilgore L, Jurmain RD, VanGerven D. 1997. Palaeoepidemiological patterns of trauma in a medi-eval Nubian skeletal population. *International Journal of Osteoarchaeology* 7: 1103–14.

Lambert PM. 1994. War and peace on the western front: A study of violent conflict and its cor-relates in prehistoric hunter-gatherer societies of Southern California. Ph.D. dissertation, Uni-versity of California, Santa Barbara.

Lambert PM. 1997. Patterns of violence in prehistoric hunter-gatherer societies of coastal South-ern California. In: Martin DL, Frayer DW, editors. *Troubled times: Violence and warfare in the past.* Amsterdam: Gordon and Breach. Pp. 77–109.

Lambert PM. 2002. The archaeology of war: A North American perspective. *Journal of Archaeo-logical Research* 10: 207–41.

Lambert PM. 2007. The osteological evidence of indigenous warfare in North America. In: Chacon RJ, Mendoza RG, editors. *North American indigenous warfare and ritual violence.* Tuc-son: University of Arizona Press. Pp. 202–21.

Lattimore O. 1940. Inner Asian frontiers of China. New York: American Geographical Society.

Lessa A, Mendonca de Souza S. 2004. Violence in the Atacama Desert during Tiwanaku period: Social tension? *International Journal of Osteoarchaeology* 14: 374–88.

Linduff KM, Drennan RD, Shelach G. 2002. Early complex societies in NE China: The Chifeng International Collaborative Archaeological Research Project. *Journal of Field Archaeology* 29: 45–73.

Liu X, Li S. 2002. Xinjiang Yili He liu yu kaogu faxian (Archaeological discovery at Yili River basin, Xinjiang). *Xiyu Yanjiu* (西域研究) 1: 109–10.

Loewe M. 1987. The Former Han dynasty. In: Twitchett D, Loewe M, editors. *Cambridge history of China.* Vol. 1: *Ch'in to Han Empires, 221 B.C.–A.D. 220.* Cambridge: Cambridge University Press. Pp. 103–222.

Lovejoy CO, Heiple KG. 1981. The analysis of fractures in skeletal populations with an example from the Libben site. *American Journal of Physical Anthropology* 55: 529–41.

Lovell NC. 1997. Trauma analysis in paleopathology. *Yearbook of Physical Anthropology* 40: 139–70.

Lovell NC. 2008. Analysis and interpretation of skeletal trauma. In: Katzenberg MA, Saunders SR, editors. *Biological anthropology of the human skeleton.* Hoboken, NJ: Wiley-Liss. Pp. 341–86.

Lu E, Zhang Y, Zu L, Xu D. 2004. Xinjiang Shanshan Xian Yanghai mudi de kaogu xin shouhuo (New archaeological results of Yanghai cemeteries in Shanshan County, Xinjiang). *Kaogu* (考古) 5: 387–91.

Martin DL. 1997. Violence against women in the La Plata River valley (A.D. 1000–1300). In: Martin DL, Frayer DW, editors. *Troubled times: Violence and warfare in the past.* Amsterdam: Gordon and Breach. Pp. 45–75.

Martin DL, Frayer DW, editors. 1997. *Troubled times: Violence and warfare in the past.* Amsterdam: Gordon and Breach.

Micozzi MS. 1991. *Postmortem change in human and animal remains.* Springfield, IL: Charles C. Thomas.

Milner GR. 1995. An osteological perspective on prehistoric warfare. In: Beck LA, editor. *Re-gional approaches to mortuary analysis.* New York: Plenum. Pp. 221–44.

Murphy MS, Gaither C, Goycochea E, Verano JW, Cock G. 2010. Violence and weapon-related trauma at Puruchuco-Huaquerones, Peru. *American Journal of Physical Anthropology* 142: 636–49.

Nawrocki SP. 1995. Taphonomic processes in historic cemeteries. In: Grauer AL, editor. *Bodies of evidence.* New York: Wiley-Liss. Pp. 49–66.

Nelson SM. 1995. Introduction: the archaeology of northeast China: Beyond the Great Wall. In: Nelson SM, editor. *The archaeology of northeast China: Beyond the Great Wall.* New York: Routledge. Pp. 1–20.

Neves WA, Barros AM, Costa MA. 1999. Incidence and distribution of postcranial fractures in the prehistoric population of San Pedro de Atacama, northern Chile. *American Journal of Physical Anthropology* 109: 253–58.

Nordstrom DL, Layde PM, Olson KA, Stueland D, Brand L, Follen M. 1995. Incidence of farm-work-related acute injury in a defined injury. *American Journal of Industrial Medicine* 28: 551–64.

Novak SA. 2000. Battle-related trauma. In: Fiorato V, Boylston A, Knüsel C, editors. *Blood red roses: The archaeology of a mass grave from the Battle of Towton AD 1461.* Oxford, UK: Oxbow Books. Pp. 90–102.

Roberts CA, Manchester K. 2005. *The archaeology of disease.* Ithaca, NY: Cornell University Press.

Sauer NJ. 1998. The timing of injuries and manner of death: Distinguishing among antemortem, perimortem and postmortem trauma. In: Reichs KJ, editor. *Forensic osteology.* Springfield, IL: Charles C. Thomas. Pp. 321–32.

Shelach G. 1994. Early Bronze Age cultures in North China. *Asian Perspectives* 33: 261–92.

Sherratt A. 2006. The Trans-Eurasian exchange: The prehistory of Chinese relations with the West. In: Mair VH, editor. *Contact and exchange in the ancient World.* Honolulu: University of Hawai'i Press.

Shui T. 2002. Cong Xiao Heishi gou de faxian kan qima minzhu wenhua yinsu xiang dongfang tuo zhan (On the process of horse riding cultural factors spreading to the east: A view from the findings in Xiao Heishigou). *Research of China's Frontier Archaeology* (边疆考古研究) 1: 263–68.

Siebenga J, Segers MJM, Elzinga MJ, Bakker FC, Haarman HJTM, Patka P. 2006. Spine fractures caused by horse riding. *European Spine Journal* 15: 465–71.

Šlaus M, Novak M, Bedić Ž, Strinović D. 2012. Bone fractures as indicators of intentional violence in the eastern Adriatic from the antique to the late medieval period (2nd–16th century AD). *American Journal of Physical Anthropology* 149: 26–38.

Smith MO. 1996. "Parry" fractures and female-directed interpersonal violence: Implications from the Late Archaic period of west Tennessee. *International Journal of Osteoarchaeology* 6: 84–91.

Steckel RH, Larsen C, Sciulli PW, Walker PL. 2004. *The Global History of Health Project: Data collection codebook.* Cleveland, OH: Global History of Health Project.

Steckel RH, Rose JC, editors. 2002. *The backbone of history: Health and nutrition in the Western Hemisphere.* New York: Cambridge University Press.

Torres-Rouff C. 2011. Hiding inequality beneath prosperity: Patterns of cranial injury in middle period San Pedro de Atacama, Northern Chile. *American Journal of Physical Anthropology* 146: 28–37.

Torres-Rouff C, Costa Junqueira MA. 2006. Interpersonal violence in prehistoric San Pedro de Atacama, Chile: Behavioral implications of environmental stress. *American Journal of Physical Anthropology* 130: 60–70.

Tung TA. 2007. Trauma and violence in the Wari Empire of the Peruvian Andes: Warfare, raids, and ritual fights. *American Journal of Physical Anthropology* 133: 941–56.

Underhill AP. 1989. Warfare during the Chinese Neolithic period: A review of the evidence. In: Tkaczuk DC, Vivian BC, editors. *Cultures in conflict: Current archaeological perspectives*. Calgary: Archaeological Association of the University of Calgary. Pp. 229–40.

Underhill AP. 2006. Warfare and the development of states in China. In: Arkush EN, Allen MW, editors. *The archaeology of warfare*. Gainesville: University Press of Florida. Pp. 253–85.

Vencl S. 1999. Stone Age warfare. In: Carmann J, Harding A, editors. *Ancient warfare: Archaeological perspectives*. Phoenix Mill, UK: Sutton Publishing. Pp. 57–72.

Volkov VV. 1995. Early nomads of Mongolia. In: Davis-Kimball J, Bashilov VA, Yablonski LT, editors. *Nomads of the Eurasian steppes in the Early Iron Age*. Berkeley, CA: Zinat Press. Pp. 317–33.

Walker PL. 1989. Cranial injuries as evidence of violence in prehistoric Southern California. *American Journal of Physical Anthropology* 80: 313–23.

Walker PL. 1997. Wife beating, boxing, and broken noses: Skeletal evidence for the cultural patterning of violence. In: Martin DL, Frayer DW, editors. *Troubled times: Violence and warfare in the past*. Amsterdam: Gordon and Breach. Pp. 145–75.

Walker PL. 2001. A bioarchaeological perspective on the history of violence. *Annual Review of Anthropology* 30: 573–96.

Wang L. 2004. Tan xun Donghu yi cun di yige xin xiansuo (A new clue for exploring the remains of Donghu). *Research of China's Frontier Archaeology* (边疆考古研究) 2: 84–95.

Wang L, Ta L, Zhang Y. 2004. 2002 Nian Nei Menggu Linxixian Jinggouzi yi zhi xiqu mu zang fajue jiyao (Excavation of the tombs of the western group at the Jinggouzi site in Linxi County of Inner Mongolia, 2002). *Archaeology and Cultural Relics* (考古与文物) 1: 6–19.

Webb S. 1995. *Paleopathology of aboriginal Australians: Health and disease across a hunter-gatherer continent*. Cambridge: Cambridge University Press.

Wilkinson RG. 1997. Violence against women: Raiding and abduction in prehistoric Michigan. In: Martin DL, Frayer DW, editors. *Troubled times: Violence and warfare in the past*. Amsterdam: Gordon and Breach. Pp. 21–43.

Yang L. 1968. Historical notes on the Chinese world order. In: Fairbank JK, editor. *The Chinese world order: Traditional China's foreign relations*. Cambridge, MA: Harvard University Press. p 20–33.

Zhang K, Zhao Z. 2000. Piao han du te de qima minzhu wenhua (The specific culture of a horse-riding ethnic minority). *Xin Chutu Wenwu* (新出土文物): 11–13.

Zhongguo Kaogu Xuehui. 1998. Beipiaoshi Lamadong San Yan mudi (Beipiao City Lama Cave cemetery of Three Yan dynasties). *Zhongguo Kaoguxue Nianjian* (中国考古年鉴) 3: 154–55.

Zhu Y, Wang L. 2005. Xilamulun heliu yu xian qin shiqi wenhua yi cun de bian nian yu puxi yanjiu (Research on chronology and pedigree of cultures at Xilamulun River region before Qin dynasty). *Research of China's Frontier Archaeology* (边疆考古研究) 4: 52–69.

10

Stresses of Life

A Preliminary Study of Degenerative Joint Disease
and Dental Health among Ancient Populations of Inner Asia

MICHELLE L. MACHICEK AND JEREMY J. BEACH

The steppelands of Inner Asia encompass an extensive range of environmentally and culturally diverse settings. From the very earliest periods of human habitation until the present day, the communities of this region have been influenced by both local and regional variation in ecology and sociopolitical circumstances. The designation "Inner Asia" as it is utilized here refers to the modern-day expanses of southern Siberia, Mongolia, Inner Mongolia, Manchuria, Xinjiang, and Tibet (Lattimore 1940). This study takes a bioarchaeological approach aimed at providing a greater understanding of the populations that inhabited this region in the distant past. Given the paucity of studies examining the paleohealth of this region we considered it important to provide data and supporting discussion of two separate data sets: (1) Iron Age Mongolian and Inner Mongolian (c. 3rd century BC to 2nd century AD) samples through which degenerative joint disease (DJD) can be investigated; and (2) a much later Mongol Period (13th century AD) sample representing a series of sites throughout Mongolia for which oral and physiological health will be examined.

Ideally, a complete dental/physiological health and DJD analysis for both temporal periods would allow an investigation into health trends over time. However, work is ongoing and at this stage we can provide only DJD data for the Iron Age and dental/physiological health data for the Mongolian period; as such, we cannot provide any comparisons between the two temporal periods in this study. Figure 10.1 provides a macro-regional view of the study area and the main site locations discussed throughout this chapter.

The primary purpose of this assessment is to illustrate the applicability

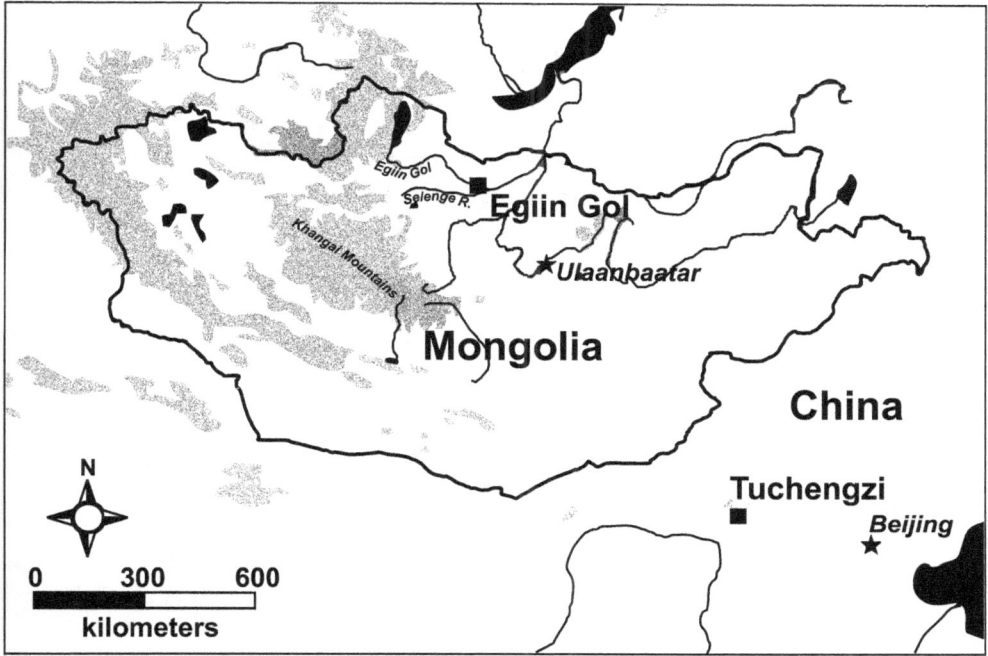

Figure 10.1. Macroregional view of the study region and locations of the two major sites discussed: Egiin Gol Valley (north-central Mongolia) and Tuchengzi (土城子) (Inner Mongolia).

of paleopathological methods to these particular populations and to highlight two possible ways of looking at general health in populations spanning a broad swath of geographic space and time. The distinct temporal horizons in question were characterized by dynamic political and social transformations that took place across the region. The rise of two major nomadic polities during these periods, the Xiongnu (匈奴) of the Iron Age and the well-known Mongol Empire of the thirteenth century AD, was likely accompanied by changes in subsistence regimes and trade economy, as well as increasing mobility and social interaction between populations (Di Cosmo 1994; Rösch et al. 2005; Honeychurch and Amartuvshin 2006, 2007; Erdenebat and Pohl 2009; Shiraishi 2009). A greater understanding of those processes has been steadily developing through increasing numbers of archaeological and anthropological investigations that have been carried out in Mongolia during the past decade (e.g., Erdenebaatar 2000; Turbat et al. 2003; Honeychurch and Amartuvshin 2007; Tseveendorj et al. 2007; Wright et al. 2007; Polosmak et al. 2008; Fitzhugh et al. 2009; Amartuvshin and Honeychurch 2010).

Within the sphere of bioarchaeological research many inquiries have been devoted to examining similarities and variation in paleopathological conditions between hunter-gatherer and agriculturalist populations from a range of archaeological contexts (e.g., Cohen and Armelagos 1984; Goodman et al. 1984; Bridges 1991; Eshed et al. 2006; Eshed et al. 2010). By contrast, fewer studies have focused on DJD and dental pathology in the nomadic pastoralist, seminomadic, and mixed-economy groups of Mongolia and Inner Mongolia. Through this study, we aim to demonstrate what can be discerned from a preliminary assessment of just two of the conditions commonly found on the skeleton in both archaeological and modern human contexts. This in turn provides a starting point for future comparative research of both neighboring populations and more extensive investigations at these particular sites.

Degenerative Joint Disease among Iron Age (c. 3rd Century BC to 2nd Century AD) Populations from Mongolia and Inner Mongolia

A multitude of studies of degenerative joint disease have previously been carried out on samples spanning a wide range of geographic and temporal settings (e.g., Tainter 1980; Bridges 1991; Waldron 1995; Hukuda et al. 2000; Lieverse et al. 2007; Eshed et al. 2010). These inquiries have principally been carried out in order to address questions concerning modes of expression of DJD, as well as how DJD is related to subsistence strategies and cultural practices, along with the effects of age and habitual activities. In a review by Larsen (1995) of biological changes occurring in the human skeleton as a result of the adoption of agriculture, he points out that results of studies examining DJD differentiation between hunter-gatherer populations and agriculturalists have been highly variable. In some cases, the sample remains of hunter-gather populations have shown evidence of a greater prevalence of the condition as compared to the sample remains of some agriculturalist populations, while in other cases no significant difference could be found between such groups (Weiss and Jurmain 2007). A consensus has emerged that there is no specific overall pattern of joint disease that can definitively be related solely to subsistence practices on a worldwide basis. More conclusive patterns emerge when comparisons are confined to more specific geographic settings and temporal frameworks. Additionally, investigations of workload stress and division of labor based on sex—and when possible, social position in society—have yielded far more promising results.

Materials and Methods

DJD was assessed on two samples of human skeletal remains from Inner Asia dating to approximately the first millennium BC. Figure 10.1 indicates the site locations of these samples.

Table 10.1. Sample sex and age composition for DJD analysis

Age group[a]	Males	Females	Total
Mongolia			
Young–middle adults	18	11	29
Older adults	4	6	10
Inner Mongolia			
All adults	29	19	48
Total			87

[a] Age groups: young–middle = 17–45; older = 45+.

The first sample set comprises 39 adult individuals (the majority young to middle aged), 17 females and 22 males, excavated from Xiongnu (匈奴) contexts in Mongolia (see table 10.1). The term *Xiongnu* is derived from ancient Chinese texts that describe a confederation of nomadic groups that banded together and would eventually control a vast portion of the Central Asian steppes (Watson 1993). The designation of the Xiongnu period encompasses a time frame from approximately the third century BC to the second century AD and coincides with archaeological and historical evidence for the existence of this polity in Mongolia (Honeychurch and Amartuvshin 2006). The use of the term *Xiongnu* in this study is intended to denote the general time frame and archaeological context from which these individuals were recovered; it is not intended to apply ethnic or biological identities to these individuals.

The majority of the sample (*n* = 22) was excavated from the Egiin Gol Valley, located in north-central Mongolia along the Egiin Gol and Selenge river system (49°27'N, 103°28'E; see figure 10.1) (Turbat et al. 2003). The remaining individuals were excavated from burial contexts in the vicinity. It has been asserted that during this period nomadic pastoralism had become the major form of subsistence throughout much of Central Asia (Shishlina and Hiebert 1998; van Geel et al. 2004). Nevertheless, archaeological evidence interpreted by means of ethnographic analogy has been used to suggest that a multiresource type of subsistence was practiced in the Egiin Gol Valley during that time. In addition to pastoralism, individuals inhabiting this area were likely to have engaged to some degree in hunting, gathering, fishing, and small-scale agriculture to supplement their diets (Honeychurch and Amartuvshin 2007). This conclusion is further supported by the presence of archaeological faunal samples that included the remains of both wild and domesticated animals, as well as paleobotanical remains recovered from flotation samples that were identified as bread-wheat and barley (Turbat et al. 2003; Honeychurch 2004; Honeychurch and Amartuvshin 2007).

The second sample set consists of 48 adult individuals (more refined age estimation data are not available), 19 females and 29 males, excavated from the site of Tuchengzi (土城子), located in Helinge'er County in Inner Mongolia (see table 10.1 and figure 10.1). Tuchengzi is a multiperiod site, with contexts spanning a time frame from approximately 500 BC to the Yuan dynasty (1271–1368 AD). Only individuals excavated from contexts attributed to the beginning of the Warring States Period (c. 475 BC) through the end of the Han dynasty (220 AD) were included in this study. Archaeological excavations at the site have revealed evidence of long-term habitation, including roof tiles, a surrounding wall, and agricultural tools, as well as the remains of nonpastoral domesticated animals, such as pig and chicken (Nei 1989). From the archaeological evidence, Tuchengzi may be construed as an agricultural settlement. However, because of the location of this site, it is possible that an extensive degree of interaction took place between this more sedentary population and mobile-pastoralist groups in the region (Nei 1989). This could have provided access to commonly herded pastoralist resources of the region, such as sheep and goats.

For each of these two skeletal assemblages, the presence and severity of DJD was determined based on specific characteristics indicative of the condition, including the presence and severity of lipping, porosity, and eburnation on the joint surfaces (Roberts and Manchester 2005: 137). One criterion was sufficient for a joint to merit a score denoting the presence of DJD. The shoulder, elbow, hip, and knee joints were assessed on each skeletal individual for both the presence and the severity of DJD. The recording of the expression and severity of the condition was based on a scale following Bridges (1991): 0 = no trace; 1 = trace or minimal; 2 = minor; 3 = moderate; 4 = severe.

A score of 1 (trace or minimal) was recorded when one or more of the criteria were only just discernible on the joint surface. A score of 4 (severe) was assigned when the joint surface in question was extensively modified over the entire articular surface. Figure 10.2 illustrates an example of a severe case of bilateral DJD of the knee joints in an adult male individual from the site of Tuchengzi in Inner Mongolia.

Specific joint surfaces were examined and scored individually, also following the standard devised by Bridges (1991). For the shoulder joint, two surfaces were examined: the glenoid fossa of the scapula and the proximal articular surface of the humerus. Four surfaces were examined for the elbows: the trochlea and capitulum of the distal humerus, and the corresponding articular surfaces of the proximal radius and the proximal ulna, including the

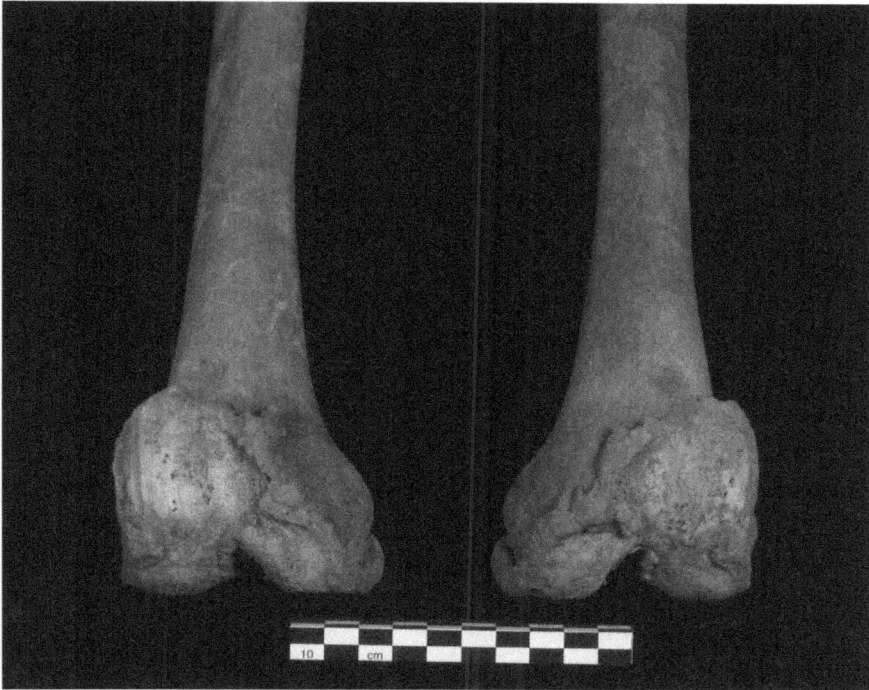

Figure 10.2. Example of severe case of bilateral degenerative joint disease in the distal femurs of an adult male from the site of Tuchengzi (土城子) (Inner Mongolia). Note extensive lipping, porosity, and eburnation on the articular surfaces.

radial notch on the proximal ulna. The acetabulum and proximal femur were examined for the hip joints. For the knee joints, the distal femur and proximal tibia were assessed. These synovial joints were chosen to allow for examination of joints that encompass a wide range of motion. The lack of vertebral elements in either of the skeletal collections available for study did not allow for spinal joint disease to be assessed.

The arthritis scores recorded on each individual were combined into a DJD index. This index is calculated as the sum of DJD scores divided by the sum of joint surfaces scored; it is averaged for groups of individuals in categories based on either age or sex. The index is a true rate of prevalence, which takes into account the number of joint surfaces scored, rather than simply noting presence/absence of DJD markers for each individual. Thus, even relatively incomplete skeletons can be included in the analysis. It is fully recognized that examination of complete skeletons is the ideal approach to diagnosis of specific types of joint disease, as well as for obtaining an accurate picture of the condition. This is particularly the case when one wishes to establish the presence of rheumatoid, psoriatic, or gouty arthritis (Rogers

2000). However, because of the fragmentary and incomplete nature of many of these skeletons, the selected procedure based on an index of all joint surfaces scored was considered most appropriate.

Finally, it is important to acknowledge that DJD is highly correlated with age, in that one would expect an increase in the frequency of DJD with increasing age at death. While data are available on the age composition of the Xiongnu sample, such information is unfortunately lacking for the Tuchengzi assemblage. Any differences in the patterning and frequency of DJD between each of these samples may be due to potential age structure differences in each sample, and this needs to be considered in the subsequent discussion of the results.

Results

Illustrations of the results of the assessment of DJD in the samples can be seen in figures 10.3 and 10.4 (below). As noted above, it is very likely that subsistence regimes for the sampled individuals, particularly those from Egiin Gol, were quite complex during the time frame in question. Therefore, the two samples are identified by geographic location, in order to avoid labeling one group as specifically pastoralist and the other agriculturalist.

Figure 10.3 illustrates differences in the expression of DJD found between male individuals from the two sample sets. A higher degree of DJD can be seen at all joint locations for males from Inner Mongolia, although expression at the elbow joint was roughly similar. Two-tailed t-tests specifying unequal variances found no statistical significance for the differences between results for all joint locations ($t = 1.06$, $p = .329$, df = 6). According to the average index for males from both sample groups, the joint location most commonly affected by DJD was the hip, followed by successively decreasing frequencies for the shoulder, knee, and elbow.

Figure 10.4 displays the results of the DJD index for adult females from the two samples. Overall, the average index of the condition is higher at all anatomical locations for females from Inner Mongolia with the exception of the knee, for which the values are similar for both regions. However, two-tailed t-tests specifying unequal variances showed no statistical significance between indices for the two samples at all joint locations ($t = 2.17$, $p = .0731$, df = 6).

Based on the arthritis index, females from the Mongolian sample experienced a greater degree of DJD in the lower limbs, at the hip and knee joints, than in the upper limbs. This is in slight contrast to the females from Inner Mongolia, who experienced a higher degree of DJD in the upper limb joints. At all joint locations from both samples, males evidenced a greater degree of

DJD (Males)
▣Mongolia ☐Inner Mongolia

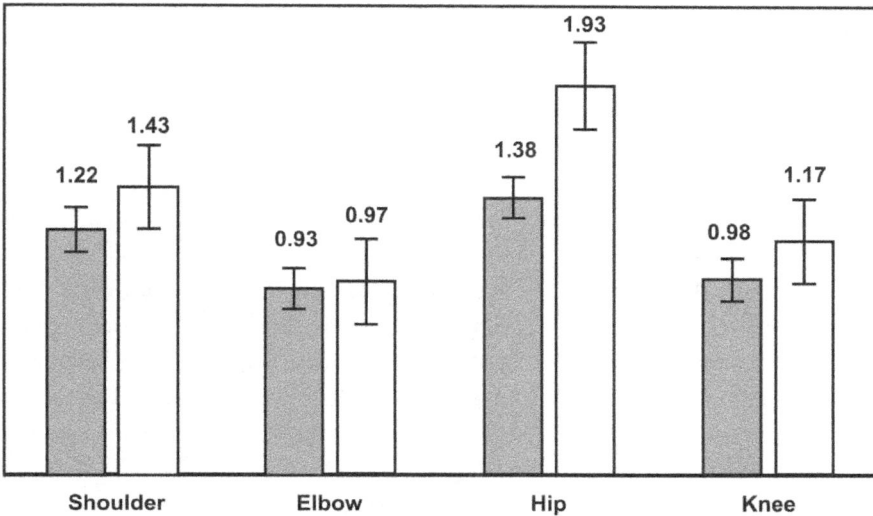

Figure 10.3. Comparative degenerative joint disease index of adult males from the two sample sets from Mongolia and Inner Mongolia. Index was calculated by SAS/NJS = average DJD score, where NJS = number of joint surfaces and SAS = sum of arthritis scores. Error bars indicate standard error.

DJD (Females)
▣Mongolia ☐Inner Mongolia

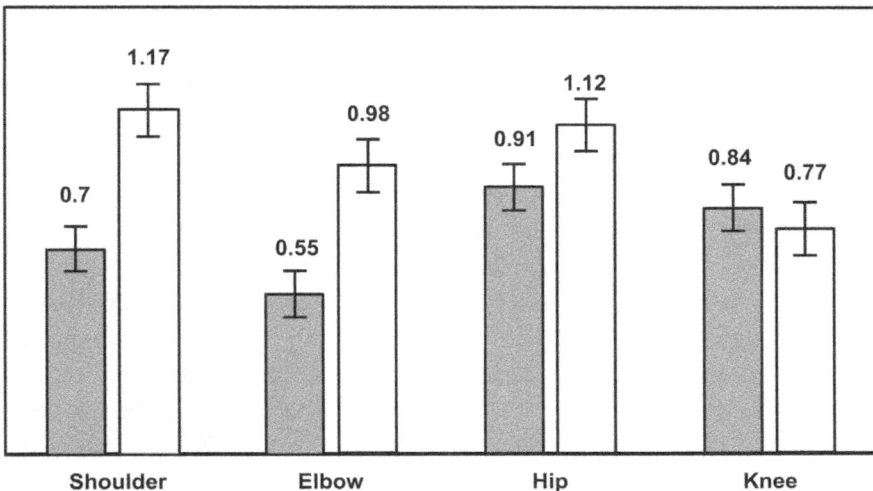

Figure 10.4. Comparative degenerative joint disease index of adult females from the two sample sets from Mongolia and Inner Mongolia. Index was calculated by SAS/NJS = average DJD score, where NJS = number of joint surfaces and SAS = sum of arthritis scores. Error bars indicate standard error.

DJD than did females, with the exception of the females from Inner Mongolia, for whom a slightly higher score was recorded at the elbow than for males from Inner Mongolia. Interestingly, two-tailed t-tests applied to the DJD results for males and females from Mongolia found the differences to be statistically significant ($t = 2.86, p = .0289$, df = 6), while those between males and females from Inner Mongolia were not ($t = 1.61, p = .1225$, df = 6).

Discussion

Degenerative joint disease can be employed as a useful indicator of lifestyle-associated stresses, as its pattern, severity, and progression are affected by the daily routine. Additionally, the patterning and prevalence of the condition may be influenced by adaptive responses to environmental pressures and access to resources, affecting levels of mobility within populations. The results described above allow for a number of observations to be made. However, it should be pointed out that the objective here is not to recognize the specific activities or "occupations" of individuals (as advised in Waldron 1994; Knüsel 2000) but rather to illustrate general patterns relating to differentiation in workload or physiological stresses that can be discerned from this initial assessment.

As mentioned previously, DJD is an age-progressive condition. Before discussing factors that may be contributing to the pattern and frequency of DJD observed in these samples it should be noted that 18.2 percent of the Mongolian male sample was composed of older individuals, compared with 35.3 percent of females. The younger age of the Mongolian male sample would indicate that any observed higher frequency of DJD by joint is related to factors other than age. Unfortunately, the same cannot be said for any comparisons involving the Inner Mongolian sample, where the underlying age structure of the sample is unknown. In light of this, the behaviorally oriented hypotheses developed in the following discussion need to be treated with caution.

Overall, in modern populations, degenerative joint disease appears to be typically more common in females than males. Higher rates of DJD among females have been suggested to be related to modern-day levels of obesity/higher body mass index, which more adversely affects the smaller joint surfaces of females through increased mechanical loading at articular locations (Weiss and Jurmain 2007: 441). Other possible etiological factors include hormonal influences, nutrition, and genetics (Larsen 1997; Weiss and Jurmain 2007). However, to date, information from previous studies of DJD suggests that in prehistoric populations the condition was often more predominant among males (discussed in Larsen 1997).

The higher degree of the condition at the hip joints among males, particularly those from Inner Mongolia, may represent a more substantial degree of physiological stress affecting this joint location than was experienced by females in the same community. This may have been a result of habitual movements or activities, workload strain, or extensive locomotor activities placing greater stress on the lower limbs. The overall higher degree of the condition at all joint locations among males from Inner Mongolia may indicate a greater degree of workload and physiological stress affecting this group.

At the same time, these results may reflect that a lower degree of physical strain was habitually being placed on the body on a long-term basis among the males from Mongolia. It is worthy of mention here that the majority of individuals excavated from the Xiongnu burials in Mongolia should probably be understood as having been members of an elevated level of the social pyramid, based on the quality and quantity of the associated burial goods and the nature of burial construction (Crubezy et al. 1996; Murail et al. 2000). These individuals are derived from what can be considered as, at minimum, local elite burial contexts. This is supported by the wealth of grave inclusions that have been recovered from these burials, which, despite having been looted in antiquity, contained items such as gold jewelry, silk textiles, imported Chinese lacquer-ware, weaponry, horse-riding paraphernalia, and an extensive range of faunal material (Turbat et al. 2003). This faunal material included, in some cases, numerous horse, sheep, and goat crania that were often placed in a northern niche at the bottom of an extensive shaft grave (Turbat et al. 2003).

In contrast, the individuals excavated from Tuchengzi were recovered from burial contexts that may suggest lesser social standing (Nei 1989). Mortuary offerings in these burials were modest by comparison and typically included ceramics, examples of weaponry, and a more limited range of faunal material (Nei 1989). Therefore, it seems likely that the differences found between these two samples in the expression of DJD for both males and females also reflect differences in the respective workloads of persons of unequal social status.

A greater degree of diversity can be seen in the expression of DJD between the female individuals from the two samples. The higher prevalence of the condition at the upper limb joints (shoulder and elbow) for Inner Mongolian females may indicate some type of habitual activity having been carried out by these individuals that differed from habitual anatomical movements having been carried out by the females from Mongolia. The higher degree of expression of DJD at the lower limb sites for females from Mongolia possibly reflects a greater emphasis on certain habitual activities affecting the lower limb, such as prolonged horseback riding or traversing long distances on foot.

The overall higher degree of DJD among males from both samples as compared with females can be attributable to both biological and cultural factors. The etiology of joint disease is commonly understood to be multifactorial (Larsen 1997; Rogers 2000; Roberts and Manchester 2005); other factors that may affect the expression of DJD include age, sex, weight, environment, and genetic predisposition, as mentioned above. However, habitual anatomical movement is also widely acknowledged to be a primary contributor to the expression of DJD on the human skeleton. As has been pointed out by Waldron (1994), given that we do not find evidence of the condition at fixed joint locations, specific habitual or frequent anatomical movements are likely to be among the primary causes of DJD. With that in mind, it can be surmised that the average index of DJD presented in this study represents evidence of some degree of differentiation in specific habitual anatomical movements and/or variations in physical workload among the groups of individuals represented by the two samples.

Dental Health in the Mongol Period (13th Century AD)

Studies of dental health have been applied to a vast and varied range of archaeological skeletal material (e.g., Lukacs 1992; Littleton and Frohlich 1993; Sakashita et al. 1997; Eshed et al. 2006; Temple and Larsen 2007). Questions that have been addressed through dental analysis and the assessment of dental health are informative with regard to the quality of human life during the past in many ways. Linear enamel hypoplasia can indicate periods of stress affecting individuals during their formative growth years (Hillson 1979). Additionally, dental analysis may be used to examine standards of oral hygiene, the overall state of the immune system, food processing techniques, extradietary use of the teeth, and dietary composition (Hillson 1979, 1996).

Materials and Methods

The Mongol period of Mongolia spanned the time range from approximately the thirteenth to fourteenth century AD. Encompassed within this period was the well-known emergence and reign of Chinggis Khan. It has been widely asserted that during this period nomadic pastoralism was the primary form of subsistence and way of life throughout Mongolia (Morgan 2007; Fitzhugh et al. 2009). Nevertheless, variation in both the nature and the complexity of subsistence, economic, statecraft, and funerary practices across both space and time during the Mongol period has been emphasized by some scholars (Rogers et al. 2005; Rösch et al. 2005; Crubezy et al. 2006; Erdenebat 2009). While historical accounts of the Mongol period often reflect considerable bias, much has been written about the subsistence economy of the peoples inhabiting the steppes of Central Asia at that time.

Friar William of Rubruck, a traveller to the Yuan Court, writing in the mid-thirteenth century, described the Mongols' reliance on meat and dairy products but also mentioned hunting and fishing, as well as the incorporation of millet into the nomads' diet (Rockhill 1900). Accounts such as his reinforce awareness of the caution one must take when attempting to assess the effects of subsistence practices on human skeletons from the past. It is important to recognize the often-complex nature of human choice and adaptation when it comes to accessing the resources available for dietary consumption. In addition, extensive archaeological excavations at the site of the Mongol capital of Kharakhorum have also begun to reveal significant evidence for past lifeways during this period (Erdenebat and Pohl 2009). For instance, paleobotanical research at this site has identified several types of grains and seeds that provide evidence for the long-distance importation of a variety of vegetable products and spices (Rösch et al. 2005).

Dental assessment was carried out on the remains of 26 individuals (see table 10.2) excavated from Mongol period mixed-regional contexts in Mongolia. A total of 308 teeth were examined and scored. Sex determination was limited to adult skeletal remains. The distribution between sexes among the adults was nearly equal, including 9 males (41 percent) and 11 females (50 percent). The sex of 2 individuals (9 percent) was indeterminate. Preservation of the sample meant that age assessment was limited to distinguishing between adults and subadults. Individuals with mixed dentition (i.e., the presence of both adult and deciduous teeth) were placed within the subadult category. Age distribution favored adult individuals, with a total of 22 (84.6 percent). The dental remains of only 4 (15.4 percent) subadults were analyzed.

Table 10.2. Sample sex and age composition for dental pathology analysis

Mongolia multisites (Mongol period)

Age and sex category	Number of individuals
Subadults	4
Males	9
Females	11
Indeterminate adults	2
Total adults	22
Total sample	**26**

A range of conditions related to the health of the oral cavity were recorded (caries, periodontal disease, antemortem tooth loss, dental calculus, periapical abscesses, and hypercementosis) in addition to a physiological stress indictor (enamel hypoplasia) and a specific congenital disease signature (congenital syphilis), following Pindborg (1970) and Hillson (1996). These particular traits were chosen because of their relative prevalence as paleopathological dental conditions.

Periodontal disease is usually manifested osteologically through the resorption of alveolar bone around the root structures of the teeth. Any noticeable recession of the bony structure around the roots that could be accurately measured with calipers was scored as the presence of periodontal disease. The amount of root exposure was measured from the cementoenamel junction to the point where the alveolar bone had resorbed. It should also be noted that careful attention was paid to the alveolar bone to make sure it was truly evidencing osteological resorption, rather than the effects of extrinsic taphonomic factors.

The alveolar crypts of teeth lost antemortem go through a process of osteological resorption. Alveolar crypts that were not fully resorbed were closely inspected for signs of osteological remodelling. This examination was carried out in order to differentiate between teeth that had truly been lost prior to the death of the individual and teeth that had been lost posthumously.

All observed pathological conditions were recorded on the basis of gross examination, and their prevalence was noted for each individual (e.g., two carious lesions, one linear enamel hypoplasia, etc.). Dental calculus deposits were scored according to the standards described by Brothwell (1981).

Results

Oral Health

Table 10.3 presents the number and percentages of individuals exhibiting each of the previously listed conditions. The disease that least affected the population was dental caries; not a single carious lesion was noted in the entire sample. The other dental condition with a very low frequency was hypercementosis, with only one individual displaying this pathology. Conversely, the most frequent pathological condition found was dental calculus, present on 73 percent of the sample elements. Various degrees of dental calculus expression were observed, including seven individuals (27 percent) scored as having no calculus on any tooth at all. Only two individuals (8 percent) had at least one tooth scored as having the maximum calculus expression of 3; the majority of teeth scored either a 1 or 2, expressing minimum or medium

Table 10.3. Mongol period: frequency of oral conditions by individual

Condition	No. of individuals affected	% of sample
Oral health		
Caries	0	0
Dental calculus	19	73
Antemortem tooth loss	14	54
Periodontal disease	9	35
Abscesses	8	31
Hypercementosis	1	4
Physiological health		
Enamel hypoplasia	9	35
Congenital disease		
Congenital syphilis	1	4

calculus, respectively. The combined total of specimens scored as either a 1 or 2 was 156, or 51 percent of all the sample teeth.

Periodontal disease affected 35 percent of individuals, with average root exposure due to this condition measuring 2.9 mm, while the maximum amount of root exposure observed was 5.7 mm. Periapical abscesses occurred in 31 percent of individuals, while antemortem tooth loss occurred in 54 percent of individuals.

Physiological Health and Congenital Disease

Enamel hypoplasia affected 35 percent of individuals in the sample, with 36 linear separate enamel hypoplastic events observed. As for evidence of congenital disease, one individual was observed to display signs of congenital syphilis. The dental evidence used to support this hypothesis was found in two forms. First, crowns were misshapen overall and associated with a notch along the incisal edge. Both of these traits are indicative of Hutchinson's Incisors, a syndrome that often is correlated with congenital syphilis (Aufderheide and Rodríguez-Martín 1998). A malformation of the occlusal surface of the molars, commonly known as mulberry molars, found on the remains of the same individual also is strongly correlated with congenital syphilis (Aufderheide and Rodríguez-Martín 1998). Taken in conjunction, these pathological conditions affecting this particular individual's dentition suggest the presence of congenital syphilis.

Discussion

The results of this preliminary analysis of dental health allow for a number of observations. Overall, the most striking feature noted is the prominence of dental calculus across the sample. Accumulation of dental plaque and subsequent mineralization can be linked to such factors as poor oral hygiene or specific dietary composition, as well as the relative mineral content of saliva, which may create an appropriate surface for plaque retention (Hillson 1979). Poor oral hygiene could also be reflected by some of the other conditions found in the course of this study. One of those could be the degree of antemortem tooth loss; over half of the sample individuals apparently lost at least one tooth prior to death.

Approximately one-third of the sample individuals also exhibited either alveolar bone resorption associated with periodontal disease or periapical abscesses, or in some cases, both. These pathologies may also be linked to the poor dental health of an individual. Moreover, although sample size is small, the complete absence of carious lesions may indicate that the diet was low in sugars. The presence of abscesses suggests that the immune systems of the individuals evidencing this condition were compromised, which would have made them more susceptible to infection and disease, thus affecting their overall state of health and well-being.

Dental health aside, the evidence of linear enamel hypoplasia alludes to early childhood stressors or poor health that interrupted the process of amelogenesis, thus causing malformation of a tooth's crown. While this does not necessarily reflect the health of the individual at the time of death, at least not in adult samples, it does suggest that at least one period of high stress occurred within the individual's life span. Finally, the apparent presence of evidence for congenital syphilis on the remains of one individual allows us to suggest that the disease was present in Mongolia at the time of the Mongol period.

Conclusions

This preliminary assessment of common pathological conditions has shed light on a number of important aspects of the health of past populations from Mongolia and Inner Mongolia, allowing us to generate a more nuanced diagnosis of differences in the community health and lifeways of these distinct groups. In particular, the results described above give us a glimpse into the ordinary ailments and conditions that would have affected the lives of the sampled individuals. Degenerative joint disease would have undoubtedly been detrimental to the quality of life of individuals in past populations, just as is the case today. The results of assessment of DJD in the Iron Age sample also serve to highlight the complex etiology of the condition and reaffirm that multiple causal factors must be taken into account. Nevertheless, even at this early stage of analysis, certain patterned differences between the populations inhabiting two discrete environments during a limited time frame are evident. Furthermore, this analysis of the prevalence of DJD in each of the sample populations shows that certain habitual motor behaviors may have differentially affected particular subgroups of individuals variously engaged in mixed-subsistence economies.

The dental aspect of this study, which looked at the later Mongol period, serves as yet another indication of the effects of a pastoralist diet and its association with dental health. Moreover, evidence for the presence of congenital disease and stress in early childhood, as well as the overall state of immune system, has been uncovered. What has also been demonstrated in the course of this study is the need for greater sensitivity to awareness of the complexity of past subsistence practices. This consideration must be operationalized before any more definitive statements can be made concerning either the specific causes of DJD or overall dental health in the disparate populations of Inner and Outer Mongolia during the Mongol period.

While this assessment is based on the analysis of preliminary results, and DJD and oral/physiological health is examined in temporally distinct samples, our intention is to highlight some of the heretofore relatively underutilized ways in which it is possible to examine aspects of health in past populations. Our investigation has been carried out with the aim of providing a framework for future comprehensive and comparative studies (e.g., see Machicek 2011). Further research that holistically considers evidence gained from archaeological, osteological, and chemical analyses will undoubtedly produce even more profound understandings of the everyday lives of the peoples of Inner Asia during the past.

Acknowledgments

The authors would like to acknowledge a number of individuals and institutions for their kind support and for generously facilitating our research. We would like to thank Dr. Tumen Dashtseveg and the Department of Anthropology at the National University of Mongolia, Wei Dong at Jilin University, Center for Chinese Frontier Archaeology, and Chunag Amartuvshin at the Institute of Archaeology, Mongolian Academy of Sciences. We would also like to acknowledge the kind support and assistance of the directors, staff, students, and volunteers of the Baga Gazaryn Chuluu Archaeological Project in Mongolia. This research has been kindly supported by the Council of American Overseas Research Centers (National Museum of Natural History, Smithsonian Institution) and the Wenner-Gren Foundation.

Literature Cited

Amartuvshin CH, Honeychurch W. 2010. *Dundgobi aimagt hiisen arkheologiin sudalgaa: Baga Gazaryn Chuluu.* Ulaanbaatar: Mongolian Academy of Sciences.

Aufderheide AC, Rodríguez-Martín C. 1998. *The Cambridge encyclopaedia of human paleopathology.* Cambridge: Cambridge University Press.

Bridges P. 1991. Degenerative joint disease in hunter-gatherers and agriculturalists from the southeastern United States. *American Journal of Physical Anthropology* 85: 379–91.

Brothwell DR. 1981. *Digging Up bones.* 3rd ed. Ithaca, NY: Cornell University Press.

Cohen MN, Armelagos GJ. 1984. *Paleopathology at the origins of agriculture.* New York: Academic Press.

Crubezy E, Ricaut FX, Martin H, Erdenebaatar S, Coqueugnot H, Maureille B, Giscard PH. 2006. Inhumation and cremation in medieval Mongolia: Analysis and analogy. *Antiquity* 80: 894–905.

Crubezy E, Verdier JP, Maureille B, Erdenebaatar D, Batsaikhan Z, Giscard PH, Martin H. 1996. Pratiques funéraires et sacrifices d'animaux en Mongolie à la période proto-historique: Du perçu au signifié; A propos d'une sépulture Xiongnu de la vallée d'Egyin Gol (Région péri-Baïkal). *Paléorient* 22: 89–107.

Di Cosmo N. 1994. Ancient Inner Asian nomads: Their economic basis and its significance in Chinese history. *Journal of Asian Studies* 53: 1092–1126.

Erdenebaatar D. 2000. Bulgan Aimagiin Khutag-Ondor sumyn Khantai bagiin nutag Egiin Go-lyn khondiid yavuulsan etnografiin ekspeditsiin sudalgaany tailan. Field report. Ulaanbaatar: Department of Archaeology and Ethnology, Ulaanbaatar University.

Erdenebat U. 2009. Cave burials of Mongolia. In: Fitzhugh W, Rossabi M, Honeychurch W, editors. *Genghis Khan and the Mongol Empire.* Washington, DC: Arctic Studies Center, Smithsonian Institution. P. 259.

Erdenebat U, Pohl E. 2009. The crossroads in Khara Khorum: Excavations at the center of the Mongol Empire. In: Fitzhugh W, Rossabi M, Honeychurch W, editors. *Genghis Khan and the Mongol Empire.* Washington, DC: Arctic Studies Center, Smithsonian Institution. Pp. 137–45.

Eshed V, Gopher A, Hershkovitz I. 2006. Tooth wear and dental pathology at the advent of agriculture: New evidence from the Levant. *American Journal of Physical Anthropology* 130: 145–59.

Eshed V, Gopher A, Pinhasi R, Hershkovitz I. 2010. Paleopathology and the origin of agriculture in the Levant. *American Journal of Physical Anthropology* 143: 121–33.

Fitzhugh W, Rossabi M, Honeychurch W, editors. 2009. *Genghis Khan and the Mongol Empire.* Washington, DC: Arctic Studies Center, Smithsonian Institution.

Goodman AH, Lallo J, Armelagos GJ, Rose JC. 1984. Health changes at Dickson Mounds, IL (A.D. 950–1300). In: Cohen MN, Armelagos GJ, editors. *Paleopathology at the origins of agriculture.* New York: Academic Press. Pp. 271–305.

Hillson S. 1979. Diet and dental disease. *World Archaeology* 11: 147–62.

Hillson SW. 1996. *Dental anthropology.* Cambridge: Cambridge University Press.

Honeychurch W. 2004. Inner Asian warriors and khans: A regional spatial analysis of nomadic political organization and interaction. Ph.D. dissertation, University of Michigan.

Honeychurch WH, Amartuvshin CH. 2006. States on horseback: The rise of Inner Asian confederations and empires. In: Stark M, editor. *Archaeology of Asia.* Cambridge, MA: Blackwell. Pp. 255–78.

Honeychurch W, Amartuvshin C. 2007. Hinterlands, urban centers, and mobile settings: The "new" Old World archaeology from the Eurasian steppe. *Asian Perspectives* 46: 36–64.

Fukuda S, Inoue K, Ushiyama T, Saruhashi Y, Iwasaki A, Huang J, Mayeda A, Nakai M, Xiang

L, Zhao Q. 2000. Spinal degenerative lesions and spinal ligamentous ossifications in ancient Chinese populations of the Yellow River civilization. *International Journal of Osteoarchaeology* 10: 108–24.

Knüsel C. 2000. Bone adaptation and its relationship to physical activity in the past. In: Cox M, Mays S, editors. *Human osteology in archaeology and forensic science*. London: Greenwich Medical Media. Pp. 381–402.

Larsen CS. 1995. Biological changes in human populations with agriculture. *Annual Review of Anthropology* 24: 185–213.

Larsen CS. 1997. *Bioarchaeology: Interpreting behaviour from the human skeleton*. Cambridge: Cambridge University Press.

Lattimore O. 1940. *Inner Asian frontiers of China*. New York: Oxford University Press.

Lieverse AR, Weber AW, Bazaliiskiy VI, Goriunova IO, Savel'ev NA. 2007. Osteoarthritis in Siberia's Cis-Baikal: Skeletal indicators of hunter-gatherer adaptation and cultural change. *American Journal of Physical Anthropology* 132: 1–16.

Littleton J, Frohlich B. 1993. Fish-eaters and farmers: Dental pathology in the Arabian Gulf. *American Journal of Physical Anthropology* 92: 427–47.

Lukacs JR. 1992. Dental paleopathology and the agricultural intensification in South Asia: New evidence from Bronze Age Harappa. *American Journal of Physical Anthropology* 87: 133–50.

Machicek ML. 2011. Reconstructing diet, health and activity patterns in early nomadic pastoralist communities of Inner Asia. Ph.D. dissertation, University of Sheffield.

Morgan DO. 2007. *The Mongols*. Oxford: Basil Blackwell.

Murail P, Crubezy E, Martin H, Haye L, Bruzek J, Giscard PH, Turbat T, Erdenebaatar D. 2000. The man, the woman and the hyoid bone: From archaeology to the burial practices of the Xiongnu people (Egyin Gol Valley, Mongolia). *Antiquity* 74: 531–36.

Nei M. 1989. Nei Menggu Helinge'er xian Tuchengzi Gucheng fajue baogao. *Kaoguxue jikan* 6: 175–203.

Pindborg JJ. 1970. *Pathology of the dental hard tissues*. Philadelphia: W. B. Saunders.

Polosmak NV, Bogdanov ES, Tseveendorj D, Erdene-Ochir N. 2008. The burial construction of Noin Ula Mound 20, Mongolia. *Archaeology, Ethnology and Anthropology of Eurasia* 34: 77–87.

Roberts C, Manchester K. 2005. *The archaeology of disease*. 3rd ed. Ithaca, NY: Cornell University Press.

Rockhill WW. 1900. The journey of William of Rubruck to the eastern parts of the world, 1253–55 as narrated by himself, with two accounts of the earlier journey of John of Pian de Carpine. London: Printed for the Hakluyt Society.

Rogers J. 2000. The palaeopathology of joint disease. In: Cox M, Mays S, editors. *Human osteology in archaeology and forensic science*. London: Greenwich Medical Media. Pp. 163–182.

Rogers DJ, Erdenebat U, Gallon M. 2005. Urban centers and the emergence of empires in eastern Inner Asia. *Antiquity* 79: 801–18.

Rösch M, Fischer F, Maerkle T. 2005. Human diet and land use in the time of the khans—Archaeological research in the capital of the Mongolian Empire, QaraQorum, Mongolia. *Arkheologiin Sudlal* 23: 174–89.

Sakashita R, Masakazu I, Naohiko I, Qifeng P, Hong Z. 1997. Dental disease in the Chinese Yin-Shang period with respect to relationships between citizens and slaves. *American Journal of Physical Anthropology* 103: 401–8.

Shiraishi N. 2009. Searching for Genghis: Excavations of the ruins at Avraga. In: Fitzhugh W, Rossabi M, Honeychurch W, editors. *Genghis Khan and the Mongol Empire*. Washington, DC: Arctic Studies Center, Smithsonian Institution. Pp. 132–35.

Shishlina NI, Hiebert FT. 1998. The steppe and the sown: Interaction between Bronze Age Eurasian nomads and agriculturalists. In: Mair V, editor. *The Bronze and Early Iron Age peoples of eastern Central Asia*. Washington, DC: Institute for the Study of Man and University of Pennsylvania Museum Publications. Pp. 222–37.

Tainter JA. 1980. Behavior and status in a Middle Woodland mortuary population from the Illinois Valley. *American Antiquity* 45: 308–13.

Temple DH, Larsen CS. 2007. Dental caries prevalence as evidence for agriculture and subsistence variation during the Yayoi period in prehistoric Japan: Biocultural interpretations of an economy in transition. *American Journal of Physical Anthropology* 134: 501–12.

Tseveendorj D, Polosmak N, Batbold N, Erdene-Ochir N, Tsengel M. 2007. Noyon uulyn Hunnugiin Yazguurtny 20-r bulshny sudalgaa. *Arkheologiin Sudlal* 24: 288–304.

Turbat T, Amartuvshin C, Erdenebat U. 2003. *Egiin Golyn sav nutag dakh' arkheologiin Dursgaluud*. Ulaanbaatar: Mongolian State Pedagogical University.

Van Geel B, Bokovenko NA, Burova ND, Chugunov KV, Dergachev VA, Dirksen VG, Kulkova M, Nagler A, Parzinger H, van der Plicht J, Vasiliev SS, Zaitseva GI. 2004. Climate change and the expansion of the Scythian culture after 850 BC: A hypothesis. *Journal of Archaeological Science* 31: 1735–42.

Waldron T. 1994. *Counting the dead: The epidemiology of skeletal populations*. New York: John Wiley and Sons.

Waldron T. 1995. Changes in the distribution of osteoarthritis over historical time. *International Journal of Osteoarchaeology* 5: 385–89.

Watson B. 1993. *Records of the Grand Historian of China: Han Dynasty II*. New York: Columbia University Press.

Weiss E, Jurmain R. 2007. Osteoarthritis revisited: A contemporary review of aetiology. *International Journal of Osteoarchaeology* 17: 437–50.

Wright J, Honeychurch W, Amartuvshin C. 2007. Initial findings of the Baga Gazaryn Chuluu archaeological survey (2003–6). Antiquity 081: Project Gallery. http://antiquity.ac.uk/projgall/wright/index.html.

11

Dental Wear and Oral Health as Indicators of Diet among the Early Qin People

A Case Study from the Xishan Site, Gansu Province

WEI MIAO, WANG TAO, ZHAO CONGCANG,
LIU WU, AND WANG CHANGSUI

Through a comprehensive analysis of oral health and dental wear, this chapter aims to reconstruct the subsistence practices of the Qin (秦) people during the Bronze Age, as well as some aspects of their habitual behavior involving teeth, in order to better understand the development of Qin culture. The Qin people played a crucial role in the rise of imperial China and its unification in 221 BC. Consequently, the origin of the Qin people, their degree of reliance on cereal agriculture and animal herding, and their relations to nomadic groups in northwestern China have long been debated.

In the history of China, the term *Qin* has three meanings: it signifies the Qin people, the state of Qin, and the Qin dynasty (Yong 2000; Tian 2009). By the time the Qin dynasty (221–206 BC) established the first truly imperial state in Chinese history, the Qin people had already long played an important role in a process of multiethnic integration that took place during the preceding Warring States period dominated by the Eastern Zhou (東周) dynasty (450–221 BC) (Niu 1996). Sima Qian (司馬遷), a prominent historian of the Han (漢) dynasty, provided an epic account of the Qin ascent to power in his *Shi Ji: Qin Ben Ji* (史记秦本纪; *Records of the Grand Scribe: Imperial Biographies of Qin*). He wrote that the ancestors of the Qin people, or Zhongyu (中潏), lived in the far west and protected the western boundary of the late Yin (殷) dynasty (also known as the Shang [商] dynasty).

During the middle of the Western Zhou period, Feizi (非子), who excelled at the breeding of horses and other herding animals, lived in Quanqiu (near modern Tianshui, Gansu Province). The local people recommended

Feizi to King Xiao of the Zhou dynasty, and Feizi was appointed to breed horses for the royal family in the area between the Xi (西) River and the Wei (渭) River. He was very successful. As a result "lands were granted to him by the king as a vassal state whose capital is Qin" (near Qinting, Qingshui County, Gansu Province). Nevertheless, the full details of the relatively sudden emergence of Qin as a powerful vassal state are rather unclear (Wang 2007).

The origin of the Qin people has been the subject of a lengthy debate, initially based on the interpretation of the ancient textual sources and more recently based on archaeological evidence. During the first half of the twentieth century, two different views, which were named the West theory and the East theory (Niu 1996), emerged on the issue. The East theory was developed by Wei Juxie (1934), who proposed that the Qin people originated in Shandong Province, which seems very unlikely based on more recent archaeological discoveries. The proponents of the West theory linked Qin origins to nomadic and seminomadic tribes in what is now Gansu Province.

Meng Wentong (1940) wrote that the Qin people originated among the western Rong, while Wang Guowei (1956) stated that the ancestors of the Qin were descendants of both the Rong and the Di tribe. Given a synthesis of the historical sources and newer evidence based on studies of material culture, it now seems most likely that the Qin were linked to a succession of Bronze Age archaeological cultures in the Tianshui region of Gansu Province (Gong and Hu 1990; Yong 2000; Zhang 2001). Both the relationship of the Qin people to the Rong tribes and the basis of their subsistence regime await further confirmation. In any case, beginning in the Spring and Autumn period (770–450 BC), the Qin began a territorial expansion, which accelerated during the Warring States period (450–221 BC), as lands and people ruled by other vassals of the Zhou eventually came under the control of the Qin emperor, principally by means of conquest (Yong 2000).

In order to further explore the development of the Qin culture, as well as to resolve other issues about the earliest Qin people, a project entitled "Survey and Excavation of the Cities, Tombs, and Early Culture of the Qin Dynasty" was initiated in 2004. The principal operational goal of this project is to conduct a thorough investigation of the archaeological sites distributed around the drainage of the western Hanshui (汉水) (figure 11.1).

Since 2004, the archaeological team has thoroughly surveyed the drainages of the western Hanshui, located in Lixian (礼县) County, as well as the Niutou River (牛头), located in Tianshui (天水), Chingshuixian (清水县) County. Ninety-eight sites were recorded in Lixian County, among which about 70 were newly discovered. Of the 47 Zhou dynasty (1045–256 BC)

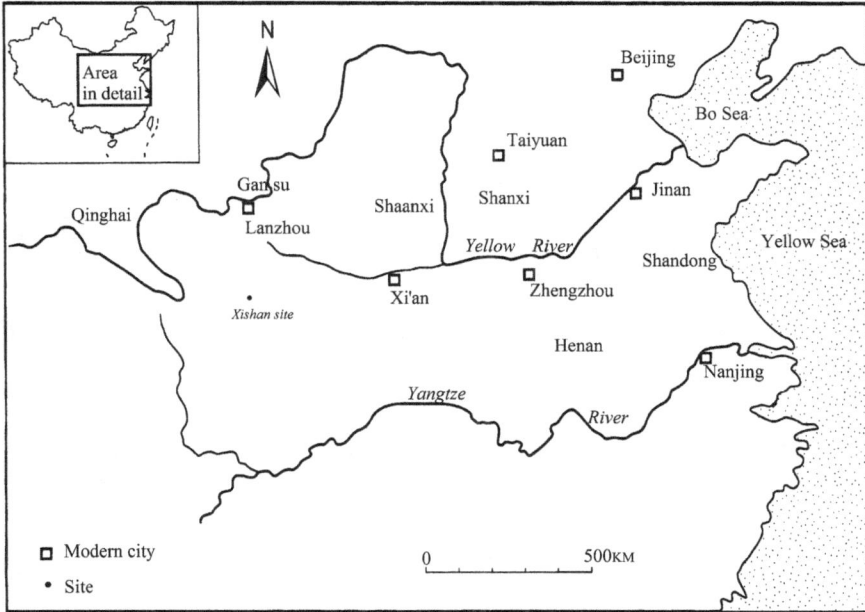

Figure 11.1. Location of the Xishan archaeological site in Lixian County.

sites encountered, 38 were found to contain cultural elements that date to the Zhou-Qin transition. This survey also provides valuable resources useful in resolving issues such as the geographic importance of the early Qin capital, Xiquanqiu (西犬丘), the formation of Qin culture, and the Qin-Rong relationship.

Excavation of the Xishan (西山) site in Lixian County was part of the 2005 project season. The total area uncovered was approximately 2000 m². Discoveries included large numbers of refuse pits containing animal bone, ash pits, fire pits, pottery kilns, human burials, house poles, rammed earth walls, and other structural remnants, from both the prehistoric and the Zhou dynastic periods. These finds provide firsthand evidence that enables us to better understand settlement patterns and the cultural context, including the origins and probable significance of the "semiflexed" style of human burial (figure 11.2). At Xishan, "belt-shaped" terracotta drainpipes (带陶水管道) were incorporated into rammed-earth walls and other structures. This labor-intensive practice suggests that Xishan was an important community—perhaps a central place for the Qin people during the Western and Eastern Zhou periods—that may have played a critical role in the development of early Qin culture.

The same discoveries also provide potential new insights into the socio-economic patterns or political economy of the early Qin people. Archaeo-

Figure 11.2. An example of a flexed human burial from Xishan.

logical finds, in concert with written records, have long been the traditional sources of information for understanding ancient socioeconomic behavior. The specifics of early Qin economic practices—whether they led a nomadic, agricultural, or some other way of life—are still being actively argued. In recent decades, the development of a bioarchaeological approach to studying archaeological human remains has been rapid and fruitful. Bioarchaeology has now begun to play a crucial role in answering some of these more general archaeological questions.

Teeth are a significant component of human skeletal remains, recording information on human survival, environment, diet, culture, and behavior. Parameters of oral health, the distribution of caries lesions, antemortem tooth loss, and intensity and pattern of dental wear are all closely related to dietary practices and food processing techniques (Turner 1979; Larsen et al. 1991; Lukacs 1992; Littleton and Frohlich 1993). The development of mandibular and maxillary exostoses is likely related in part to mechanical loads on the masticatory apparatus (Pechenkina and Benfer 2002). Unique wear patterns can be produced by exposing teeth to nonfood particles introduced through chewing grit-laden foods and by using the teeth to perform nondietary tasks (Molnar 1972; Larsen 1985; Lukacs and Pastor 1988, 1990).

This study focuses on dental wear, unique wear patterns, caries, and antemortem tooth loss, as well as evidence of maxillary and mandibular exostosis preserved on the remains of early Qin individuals from the Xishan site. In combination with results from earlier research on paleodiet (Wei et al. 2009) this study aims to examine the subsistence regime of the early Qin people from a fresh perspective. Using the results of these observations in comparison with those found on samples from elsewhere in China and beyond, the objective is to achieve a better understanding of the state of oral health, behavioral patterns, and dietary structure of the early Qin people.

Materials and Methods

The research reported on in this chapter was carried out on a sample of 24 early Qin human skeletal individuals (13 females, 8 males, 3 subadults) excavated from contexts at Xishan dated to the Eastern and Western Zhou periods. Teeth that were examined included those still attached to the maxilla and mandible, as well as some isolated teeth. The age at death of juvenile and younger individuals was evaluated primarily from tooth eruption, with the emergence of ossification centers on the limbs and epiphyseal union providing additional information. Estimation of the age at death of skeletal adults was based on comprehensive analysis of morphological changes in the pubic symphysis and fusion of the cranial sutures (Todd 1920; Zhang 1982, 1986; Lovejoy et al. 1985; Meindl et al. 1985).

For the purposes of this study, sex determination was based on the pertinent characteristics of the pelvis and the skull, following procedures recommended for the identification of East Asian skeletal remains (Wu et al. 1982; Sun and Qu 1986). In order to limit the bias associated with age-related wear, the sample specimens utilized for wear analysis were the teeth of young to middle-aged adults. Table 11.1 lists the specific teeth used in this study.

The presence and degree of development of carious lesions was assessed following the recommendations of Buikstra and Ubelaker (1994). A dental probe was used to examine presence and degree of extension of carious damage. Only those lesions that admitted a dental probe were recorded as present, which excludes simple discolorations and small pits from the total count.

Table 11.1. Dental specimens used in the present study

| | Isolated teeth | | Teeth in place | | |
	Maxillary	Mandibular	Maxillary	Mandibular	Total
	97	91	83	93	
Total	188		176		364

Such a conservative approach produces lower frequencies of carious lesions than following the recommendation of Hillson (2001) that all discolored spots of enamel are recorded as early stages of carious disease. However, this approach makes our data compatible with those reported for other skeletal collections from East Asia. Antemortem tooth loss was recorded only where complete obliteration of a dental socket was found. Thus, whenever an edentulous dental socket was still present, a tooth was judged to be missing postmortem, even if the socket displayed considerable degenerative changes.

Results

Dental Wear

Food is a basic element for survival. As masticatory organs, the teeth are responsible for processing food and helping to determine nutritional intake. Hence, patterns of wear and the coarseness of food are directly linked (Benfer and Edwards 1991). During normal mastication, human teeth are subject to wear by food particles and through contact with the adjacent teeth. This process leads to slow and progressive wear on tooth enamel, dentine, and even the dental roots. It is clear that dental wear is caused by a combination of the two mechanisms; the wear rate is controlled by tooth hardness, food categories, masticatory habits, and the strength of the masticatory musculature (Scott and Turner 1988).

There are a variety of dental wear scales specifically designed for different research purposes and samples (e.g., Scott 1979; Smith 1984). Smith (1984) scaled degree of wear into a series of eight categories that can be used to evaluate the differences in wear patterns between foragers and agriculturalists. In China, Liu and colleagues (2005) used this same scale to compare the wear patterns of Bronze Age and early Iron Age residents of the northwestern frontier and the Central Plains, in the context of their respective subsistence patterns.

In the present study, Smith's eight-level scale is used to compare wear levels among individuals and thereby to infer the dietary structure and subsistence behavior of the early Qin people buried at Xishan. An average wear level (AWL) was calculated for each tooth type. The frequency of each wear score was calculated in terms of a proportion from all observable teeth, and the overall level of wear for each tooth type was determined by means of a weighted average. In other words: AWL = Σ (proportion of teeth with each wear score multiplied by its associated wear score according to Scott [1979]).

Results show that, in terms of the Smith (1984) protocol, average wear scores for the early Qin dental remains examined from Xishan were close to 3. Table 11.2 shows average dental wear for each tooth type. In addition, four indices were computed to compare wear levels between the anterior and posterior teeth: upper central incisor/upper first molar (I^1/M^1) = 3.9/3.5 = 1.11; lower central incisor/lower first molar (I_1/M_1) = 3.2/4.3 = 0.74; the sum of upper anterior teeth/sum of upper molars $(I^{1-2}C/M^{1-3})$ = 10.9/8.1 = 1.35; sum of lower anterior teeth/sum of lower molars $(I_{1-2}C/M_{1-3})$ = 9.4/9.6 = 0.98 (figure 11.3). These are the same indices employed by Liu and colleagues (2005), allowing us to directly compare dental wear rates in the Xishan series to those described previously for skeletal series from other places in northern and central China. As can be seen from figure 11.3 and tables 11.2 and 11.3, Xishan dentitions are characterized by overall low wear of the posterior teeth and heavy wear of the anterior teeth relative to the posterior teeth.

Comparing molar wear rates among three ancient populations from the Huabei area, He Jianing and colleagues (2007) hypothesized that populations whose subsistence depended heavily on meat would have lower wear rates of the posterior teeth than those relying on other types of food. They

Table 11.2. Average tooth wear as determined in the present study

Tooth type	I1	I2	C	P1	P2	M1	M2	M3
Maxillary	3.9	3.5	3.5	3.2	2.4	3.5	3.3	1.3
Mandibular	3.2	3.3	2.9	2.5	2.6	4.3	3.3	2.0

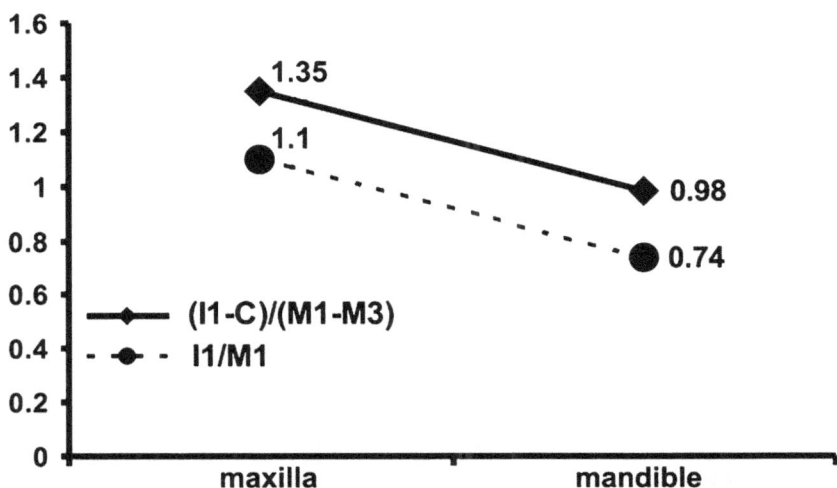

Figure 11.3. Dental wear indices for upper and lower human dentitions from the Xishan collection.

also suggested that the particular chewing patterns used to process different categories of foodstuffs are the key factors affecting the rate of wear. Processing meat using the teeth involves tearing actions, which requires more vertical movement of the lower jaw, whereas chewing fibrous plant foods requires lateral excursion of the jaw as the principal action, involving more horizontal movement. In addition, nondietary particles introduced by using grinding stones and other food-processing devices make plant foods more abrasive, which would tend to increase the rate of tooth wear. From an energetics point of view, greater quantities of the nutritionally inferior plant foods need to be consumed—and thus chewed—in order to satisfy one's energy requirements, which also tends to escalate the rate of dental wear.

Moreover, different tooth types are responsible for different chewing functions: incisors are for cutting, canines are for piercing and tearing, and molars are mainly for grinding. Belcastro and colleagues (2007) demonstrated that excessive wear on the posterior teeth is often due to increased consumption of fibrous foodstuffs that require extensive chewing, while populations with higher meat consumption would tend to have higher wear levels on the anterior teeth and more apparent differences in the levels of wear between anterior and posterior teeth, as compared with those relying less on meat. This trend was corroborated by research on collections from multiple geographical areas and with diverse diets (Belcastro et al. 2007).

Liu and colleagues (2005) compared dental samples from seven different sites in Xinjiang (Inner Mongolia), Henan, and Shaanxi (table 11.3). They found that human dental remains from the Neolithic archaeological sites of Youyao (游邀) and Xiawanggang (下王岗), located on the Central Plains of China, as well as the Xinjiang dentitions, all showed higher rates of wear on the anterior teeth, both in absolute terms and as compared to molars. Among the samples from those sites, the remains from Xinjiang evidenced the most distinct differences between anterior and posterior teeth in rates of wear. For the remains from Xishan reported here, overall wear levels were most similar to those previously determined for the Xinjiang samples; the severity of differential wear at Xishan was apparently even higher than at Xinjiang (table 11.3).

As documented archaeologically, the three Xinjiang sites—Yingpan (营盘), Qiongkeke (穷克科), and Yanghai (洋海)—date to the Bronze and Early Iron Age. The people living there relied principally on a combination of animal husbandry and millet agriculture for their subsistence. At the Neolithic sites in Central China (Youyao and Xiawanggang), a mixed subsistence regime apparently was also followed (Liu et al. 2005). Therefore, it seems likely that the people buried at Xishan may have pursued a similar

Table 11.3. Average tooth wear at Xishan and other sites

Sites	I1	I2	C	P1	P2	M1	M2	M3	Source
Maxillary									
Xishan	3.9	3.5	3.5	3.2	2.4	3.5	3.3	1.3	This study
Xinjiang	4.4	3.8	3.8	3.7	4.3	5.3	3.8	2.5	Liu Wu et al. 2005
Inner Mongolia Shuiquan	3.9	3.6	3.6	3.9	3.9	5.9	4.7	3.0	Liu Wu et al. 2005
Inner Mongolia Yinniugou	3.1	3.0	3.8	3.6	3.8	5.1	4.3	3.5	Liu Wu et al. 2005
Shaanxi Youyao	3.1	3.6	4.3	4.5	4.5	5.0	3.5	2.5	Liu Wu et al. 2005
Henan Xiawanggang	3.5	3.1	3.6	3.3	3.5	4.6	3.4	2.5	Liu Wu et al. 2005
Mandibular									
Xishan	3.2	3.3	2.9	2.5	2.6	4.3	3.3	2.0	
Xinjiang	4.1	3.9	4.0	3.6	3.6	5.0	4.0	3.1	
Inner Mongolia Shuiquan	3.8	3.8	3.1	4.0	3.9	5.4	4.5	3.1	
Inner Mongolia Yinniugou	3.2	3.4	3.5	3.5	3.3	5.0	4.5	2.7	
Shaanxi Youyao	4.1	3.9	4.1	4.4	4.0	5.1	4.6	2.6	
Henan Xiawanggang	3.7	3.5	3.8	3.2	3.4	4.5	4.0	2.7	

mix of subsistence strategies, with a considerable proportion of meat in their diet.

To judge from the sum of these observations, it seems likely that a distinct dietary regimen explains lower average wear on the posterior teeth of the people buried at Xishan than the averages determined previously on samples from elsewhere in East Asia. However, it should be noted that small sample size and the age distribution of the sample are possible sources of bias in the results. Furthermore, a high rate of antemortem tooth loss (AMTL) was found for the Xishan sample (31.82 percent by individual count, mainly molars). Severe and traumatic wear can lead to early tooth loss. Therefore, the high proportion of AMTL observed in the Xishan collection could have resulted in the underestimation of actual wear.

Special Wear Patterns

During examination of the Xishan sample, a few teeth were noted as having special or unusual wear patterns. These patterns predominantly affected the lingual enamel of the maxillary anterior teeth and sometimes extended to the exposed dentine. Interestingly, the mandibular teeth whose maxillary counterparts exhibit special wear patterns do not show similar patterns, so there is considerable incongruence between the occluding surfaces. This type of wear has been designated as "lingual surface wear of (the) maxillary anterior teeth (LSAMAT)" by Turner and Cheuiche Machado (1983); it is a pattern observed frequently on the dentitions of prehistoric Native Americans. Turner and Cheuiche Machado (1983) suggest that this pattern may be associated with processing or consuming coarse and/or fibrous foods (e.g., peeling cassava roots with the upper anterior teeth). In research on Chinese Neolithic diet and health, Pechenkina and colleagues (2002) observed LSA-MAT on dental remains from Jiangzhai. Large areas of minor wear around the lingual cementoenamel junction (CEJ) on upper central incisors, lateral incisors, and canines were also found, but without matching wear on the lower counterparts.

Liu and colleagues (2005) reported similar patterns of wear on teeth from Bronze Age–Iron Age sites in Xinjiang, Inner Mongolia, and Shaanxi, with the wear most frequent on sample dentitions from Xinjiang and Inner Mongolia. In addition to wear on anterior teeth, some posterior teeth from this sample assemblage show excessive lingual wear. Liu and colleagues (2005) propose that these patterns could have been created by habitually using the teeth as tools and/or for chewing tough food or nonfood items.

The Xishan teeth with special wear patterns often also display enamel chipping, which occurred mainly around the occlusal edge of the dental crown. Rounding of the edges around the chipped areas indicate that these were formed antemortem. Dental chipping can be caused by chewing on grit incorporated with food through processing with grinding stones, by accidents, and by activities such as cracking nuts or breaking bones to get at the marrow using the teeth. Prior research suggests that such chipping on the anterior teeth is often associated with accidents (Belcastro et al. 2007). Lingual chipping is probably caused by chewing damage, while buccal and multiple surface chipping is more likely to be a result of using the teeth as tools. Grit and other contaminants of some foodstuffs are generally responsible for a high frequency of chipping on the posterior teeth.

The unusual lingual wear patterns found on the sample Xishan remains are dissimilar from those reported by Pechenkina and colleagues (2002) and Liu and colleagues (2005). The Xishan patterns are closer to those described for the prehistoric Inuit by Turner and Cadien (1969), who reported chipping damage that covered most of the lingual side of the upper anterior teeth, or by Wallace (1973), who studied anterior enamel chipping on the teeth of australopithecines, concluding that such damage was mostly pressure-induced during the mastication of meat. Zhang Yinyun (1989) found that severe anterior wear on early *Homo sapiens* from Chaohu, Anhui Province, was probably caused by nonfood-related chewing activities (using the teeth as tools) and/or gnawing at muscles and tendons still attached to bone.

For the people buried at Xishan, the special wear patterns and chipping probably resulted from using the teeth for detaching meat from bones with a scraping motion and peeling plant roots, or else resulted from chewing or grinding tough foodstuffs. Irregular patterning on the lingual surfaces and the wear curvature across adjacent teeth are more suggestive of the use of teeth to scrape bones but might also have resulted from performing nondietary tasks with the teeth (figures 11.4 and 11.5). That such wear patterns have more generally been associated with meat preparation lends additional weight to the inference that people living at Xishan consumed a great deal of meat.

In addition to these wear patterns, we found a few marks that resemble traces of "tooth-picking" behavior (figure 11.6). "Tooth-picking" marks have been found on the dentitions of people from many different cultures, both across time and worldwide. Bermudez de Castro and colleagues (1997) studied interproximal wear on dental samples from mid-Pleistocene Spain. They proposed that the grooving they observed might be an indicator of the use of an ancient "toothpick" made of a fibrous substance. Another possible cause of the grooving may have been the habitual grinding of coarse foodstuffs in the mouth.

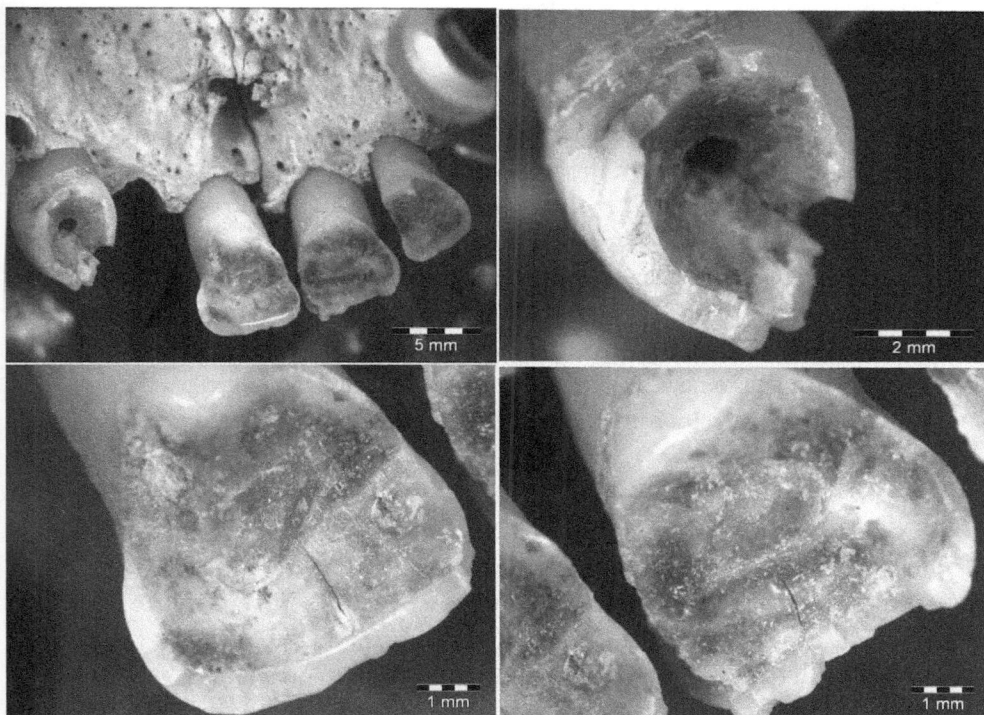

Figure 11.4. Occlusal wear grooves and enamel chipping on the maxillary anterior teeth from Xishan.

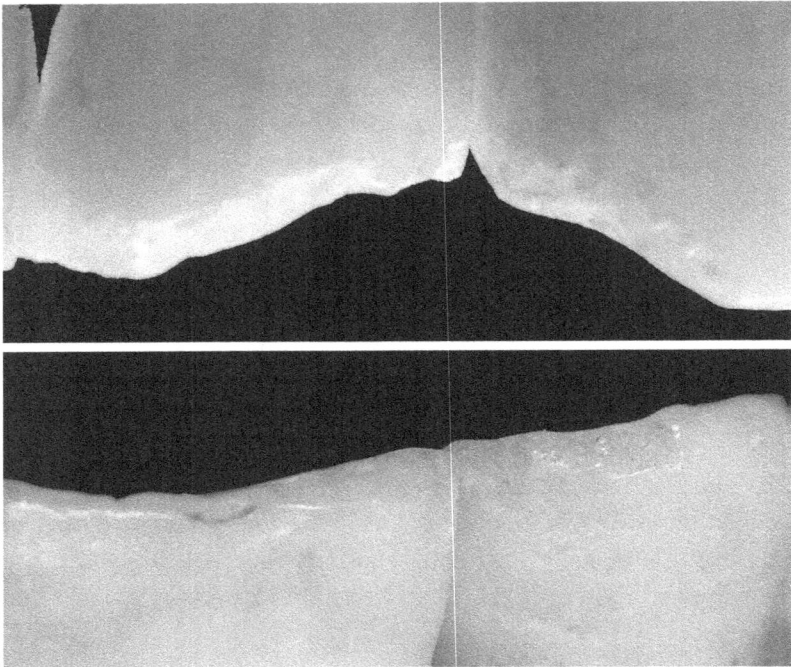

Figure 11.5. An example from Xishan of enamel chipping and wear incongruence between the maxillary and mandibular anterior teeth.

Among the dental remains of Xishan individuals that were examined for the purposes of this study, the upper second molar of M1028 shows interproximal grooving on the medial neck. The pattern is in no way similar to "tooth-picking" marks—a groove of the same depth and width on both the lingual and buccal surfaces—found on Upper Yin period teeth from Anyang, in Hui County, Henan Province (Mao and Yan 1959). The one Xishan tooth possibly showing such grooving also was affected by a severe cariotic lesion that destroyed the neck and crown on the distal side, which makes it impossible to definitively identify this as a "tooth-picking" mark.

Caries

In total, 364 teeth derived from 22 individuals were scored for caries (the teeth of two individuals among the total sample of 24 from Xishan were not preserved). Of these, 39 teeth (10.71 percent by tooth count) derived from 12 individuals (54.55 percent of individuals) were found to be carious. Because many teeth had fallen out antemortem, the actual frequencies of carious lesions at Xishan may have been higher. When categorized according to their derivation from either the upper or the lower jaws, 21 maxillary teeth were

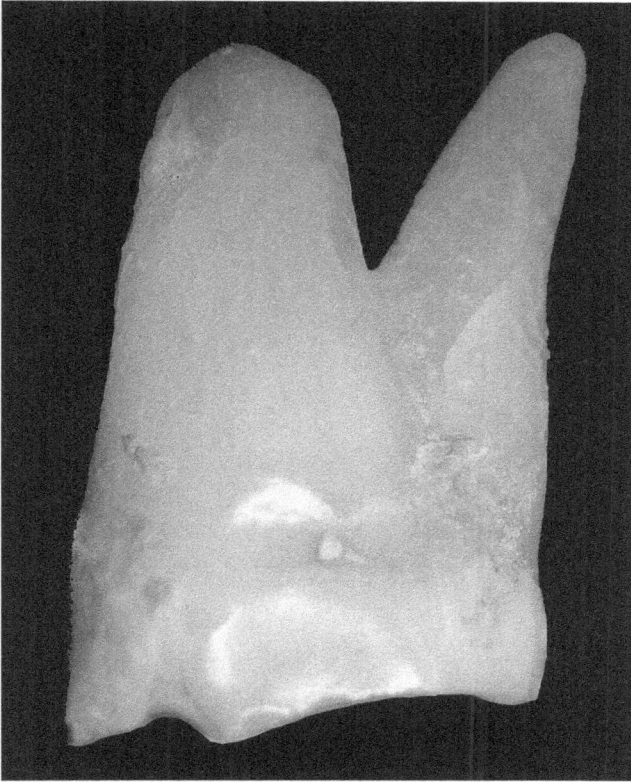

Figure 11.6. An example from Xishan of an interproximal groove on a maxillary second molar.

affected by caries (53.85 percent of carious teeth), as were 18 mandibular teeth (43.24 percent).

Caries prevalence was found to be 9.84 percent for males and 12.44 percent for females. A χ^2 test shows no significant difference between males and females from Xishan in the prevalence of caries. As expected, there was a strong association between caries frequency and age at death, so that young adults had a caries frequency of only 1 percent, while 8.19 percent of middle-aged adults and 25.26 percent of older adults were affected. The difference in caries frequencies between older adults and young adults was found to be statistically significant ($p < .01$), as was the difference between older adults and middle-aged adults ($p < .05$). Such association between caries prevalence and age at death of an individual has been observed repeatedly in research on dental pathology in past populations (e.g., Wasterlain et al. 2009).

The overwhelming majority of carious lesions were found on the second molars. Of 39 carious teeth, the frequencies for each tooth type were as follows: 2.56 percent of central incisors (1/39); 5.13 percent of lateral incisors (2/39); 7.69 percent of canines (3/39); 10.26 percent of first premolars

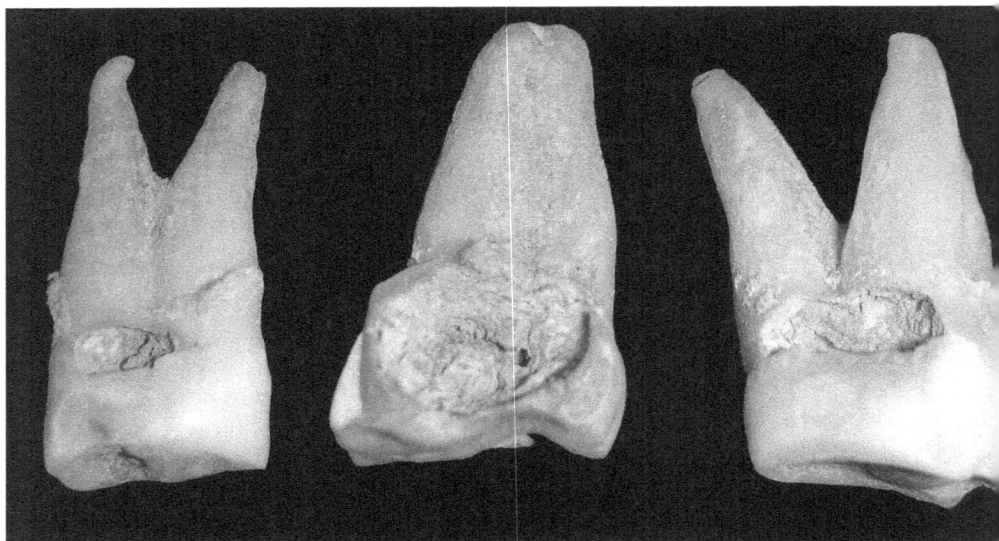

Figure 11.7. Teeth from Xishan affected by interproximal caries. Note severe development of these lesions, which tend to penetrate the pulp chamber.

(4/39); 5.13 percent of second premolars (2/39); 15.38 percent of first molars (6/39); 41.03 percent of second molars (16/39); and 12.82 percent of third molars (5/39). As for location, most carious lesions were found on interproximal surfaces (64.10 percent [figure 11.7]), followed by occlusal surfaces (17.95 percent), the neck of a tooth (15.38 percent), and buccal surfaces (2.56 percent).

Previous studies have shown that increasing frequencies of carious lesions are generally found as subsistence moves from a focus on nomadic hunting and gathering to settled agriculture, primarily because of the high percentage of water-soluble carbohydrates in domesticated grains (Turner 1979: Larsen 1995), although there are notable exceptions (Tayles et al. 2000). In contrast, nomadic people, who rely more on animal food products and the fibrous portions of plants—which are lacking in water-soluble carbohydrates—tend to suffer fewer carious lesions (Turner 1979).

From China, previously reported caries frequencies for past populations span a wide range of subsistence patterns. A comparative study by He Jianing (何嘉宁; 2004) demonstrated that the frequency of caries may be tightly linked to both the economic and the cultural characteristics of a given population. Following an earlier study by Turner (1979) on correspondence between subsistence strategy and caries frequency, He divided ancient Chinese populations into four groups, according to the specific economic strategy each pursued: "an incipient agricultural society"; "a relatively well-developed agricultural society"; "a nomadic society"; and "an agricultural and animal husbandry society."

Caries has been seen most frequently on the dental remains of individuals from the relatively well-developed agricultural societies (4.3–14.8 percent, average = 9.2 percent) and most rarely found on the remains of individuals from nomadic societies (0.2–0.9 percent). Incipient agricultural societies were found to have caries frequencies ranging from 1.2 percent to 8.3 percent (average = 5 percent), while a much wider range of frequencies (0.5–10.7 percent) was observed across the whole set of agricultural and animal husbandry societies (average = 6 percent). Among this group, societies with frequencies at the lower end of the spectrum fell within the range of nomadic societies, while those with higher frequencies reached the levels of the well-developed agricultural societies.

For the individuals buried at Xishan, the prevalence of caries was determined to be 10.7 percent, which is the same as that of the Maoqinggang people in northern China, who practiced both agriculture and animal husbandry. This frequency also lands Xishan within the range of well-developed agricultural groups (Inoue et al. 1997). Stable isotope analysis of seven collagen bone samples from Xishan human remains (Wei et al. 2009) yielded $\delta^{13}C$ values ranging from -14.09‰ to -7.56‰, suggesting that C4 plants, in this case most likely millets, were the primary caloric source for the human diet, although their specific contribution relative to C3 plants and C3-derived animal products varied considerably from person to person.

The wide range of $\delta^{15}N$ values determined for these samples—from 7.67‰ to 10.75‰—indicates considerable interindividual variation in terms of animal product consumption at Xishan (Wei et al. 2009). Although the range of $\delta^{15}N$ values overlaps considerably with that documented for millet farmers from Yangshao sites (7.3–9.18‰ [Pechenkina et al. 2005]), higher maximum $\delta^{15}N$ values at Xishan suggest that the proportion of animal products in the diet of at least some Xishan individuals was considerable. Taken together, caries prevalence and stable isotope analysis suggest that the Xishan people practiced a form of mixed subsistence, in which the agricultural production of plant foods and animal husbandry were the main foci.

Comparing the caries frequencies found for males and females among the Xishan dental remains revealed no significant difference between the sexes. Older adults exhibited a far higher prevalence of caries than did either young or middle-aged adults. This is a reasonable pattern, since increasing age generally leads to the absorption of alveolar tissues, the exposure of dental roots, aggregation of cariogenic bacteria, and, as a result, an increased incidence of carious lesions.

Second molars were found to be the most affected tooth type in the Xishan sample. This pattern has previously been observed for hunter-gatherers and peoples with mixed subsistence regimes, while being vastly different from the typical pattern for agriculturalists.

In an agricultural population relying heavily on grain foodstuffs, high levels of consumption of carbohydrates, which are extremely cariogenic, tend to erode the first molars most frequently, especially as these are the first permanent teeth erupted. In a population with a mixed form of subsistence, for whom the most common foodstuffs are often very coarse, the first permanent molars tend to be worn down quickly and are therefore somewhat less likely to manifest caries. The area most frequently affected by caries in such populations is the interproximal surface on the tooth neck, as was found to be the case for the sample from Xishan.

With a slow rate of occlusal wear experienced by agriculturalists that depend on cooked cereals, carious lesions often develop at crown fissures on the occlusal surface. In the case of Xishan, where coarse foodstuffs rapidly wore away these features on the occlusal surface and exposed dentine and pulp chambers, caries frequency was depressed at those loci. In addition, severe interproximal wear altered the original contact between adjacent teeth and enlarged the gaps between them. Such gaps trap meat and plant fibers, favoring bacterial proliferation and increasing the chances of carious lesions developing on the interproximal surface of the tooth neck (Wang and Zeng 2004).

Antemortem Tooth Loss (AMTL)

Antemortem tooth loss in preindustrial populations has usually been associated with one or the other of two principal causes. One is the extraction or ablation of otherwise healthy teeth for cultural reasons, whether ceremonial, customary, or aesthetic (Han and Pan 1982; Pietrusewsky and Douglas 1993). As intentional removal/ablation tends to occur in a patterned way, such behavior can be tracked by detailed studies in a specific geographical area of the tooth types affected, the age at which teeth were lost, and/or the social identities of the individuals affected. The other cause of antemortem tooth loss is degeneration of the dental tissues induced by wear or trauma and/or infection penetrating deep into the tooth or affecting periodontal tissues, which may result in alveolar recession, widening of the dental socket, and eventual loosening of a tooth (reviewed in Lukacs 2007). Distinguishing between these causes is difficult but can be tackled by assessing infection- or trauma-related changes in the residual ridges.

Among the Xishan individuals represented by dental remains, 7 out of 22 show evidence of AMTL (31.82 percent), generally affecting the posterior dentition—molars, in particular—in an asymmetrical or unpatterned way. An individual from burial M1012 was elderly and completely edentulous in both jaws, probably as a result of old age. For M1011, both upper central incisors and one lateral incisor were apparently lost antemortem. Three molars and one upper central incisor were lost antemortem by M1024. Evidence of such heavy loss of the anterior teeth is unusual in a preindustrial skeletal collection and suggests that at least some people at Xishan used their anterior teeth to excess, as corroborated by heavy wear (figure 11.7).

In addition to the contribution of aging, severe wear, severe calculus accretion, and caries leading to progression of periodontal disease and periapical abscesses may all have been operative as causes of AMTL at Xishan. AMTL is closely correlated with rates of caries infection (Belcastro et al. 2007). As reported by Cohen and Armelagos (1984), studies of the dental health profiles of many Western populations indicate that the prevalence of both caries and AMTL increased markedly with the transition to agriculture. All individuals from Xishan with AMTL considered in this study were affected by caries, with the apparent exception of M1024 and M1012 (for which caries could not be scored, because all teeth were lost antemortem). High frequencies of both caries and AMTL at Xishan suggest that the people buried there routinely consumed a diet fairly rich in carbohydrates, in addition to meat.

Notwithstanding the deleterious effect of caries, severe dental wear is also linked to AMTL. According to Liu and colleagues (2005), the prevalence of AMTL among the more hunting-and-gathering-oriented Xinjiang and Inner Mongolian populations studied was 33.6 percent and 30.0 percent, respectively. These rates are much higher than those reported from sites in Central China, such as Xiawanggang (11.5 percent) or Youyao (8.1 percent). In the same study, Liu and colleagues also found that AMTL in the Xinjiang and Inner Mongolian samples involved a significant number of incisors. Both AMTL prevalence (31.82 percent by individual count) and patterns of incisor loss at Xishan were found to be similar to those found for the Xinjiang and Inner Mongolian samples. These converging lines of evidence suggest that the people buried at Xishan may have had subsistence and living environments similar to those at Xinjiang and in Inner Mongolia. Frequent loss of incisors may have been due to breakage during heavy chewing of tough foodstuffs or other items, and/or biting down on food frozen in the course of harsh winters.

Maxillary Exostosis and Mandibular Torus

Maxillary and mandibular exostosis can be distinguished as mandibular torus lingually and maxillary exostosis buccally; both may be categorized as
slight, mild, or severe exostosis. This condition is a gauge of chewing force.
The threshold model of exostosis development suggests that propensity to
develop this trait is inherited yet requires mechanical loads on the chewing
apparatus to reach a certain threshold level for the trait to develop (Eggen
1989; Hauser and De Stefano 1989; Haugen 1992; Seah 1995). A number
of skeletal studies confirm this model of exostosis development for human
populations that subsisted on a variety of diets (Suzuki and Sakai 1960; Pechenkina et al. 2002; Liu et al. 2005; Ihunwo and Phukubye 2006).

The results of prior studies on human skeletal collections from Shaanxi
(Pechenkina et al. 2002) have suggested that the severity and prevalence of
maxillary exostosis decreases as food coarseness decreases, following a trajectory from heavy reliance on wild plants and wild animal protein to a dietary
focus on softer agricultural products and the use of domesticated animals to
provide meat. In that study, the authors observed that exostoses were common at Beiliu and Shijia (Yangshao) but were not found in the chronologically later Kangjia and Xicun collections.

In reporting on studies of human remains from sites in Xinjiang, Inner
Mongolia, and Central China during the Bronze Age–Iron Age, Liu and colleagues (2005, 2010) pointed out that when evidence of mild-to-severe exostosis appeared on human dental remains from Xinjiang and Inner Mongolia,
it was most often associated with severe dental wear. This wear resulted in
the loss of contact between adjacent teeth, mechanical damage to individual
teeth, and the accumulation of calculus, all of which may stimulate the alveolar process and trigger continuous exostosis formation.

Qin individuals from the Xishan site whose remains were used in this
study exhibited little sign of either maxillary exostosis or mandibular torus.
This finding indicates that at Xishan the human jaw may have needed to sus-
tain only a relatively limited chewing force. However, the lack of distinct exostosis in the Xishan collection might be explained by the small number of
skeletons examined. Even so, the mechanical demands on the jaws of Xishan
individuals appear to have been fairly low, possibly because they ate foods
with a fairly high caloric content that did not require prolonged chewing and/
or were more highly processed than the foods consumed by Bronze Age–Iron
Age people from Xinjiang and Inner Mongolia. Differences in the genetic
backgrounds of the people represented by the Xishan collections and the
populations examined by Pechenkina and colleagues (2002) and Liu and
colleagues (2005) might also account for the difference.

Discussion and Conclusions

By means of observations and comparisons of a suite of dental pathologies—wear, special wear patterns, caries, AMTL, and maxillary exostosis/
mandibular torus—recorded on the remains of early Qin people recovered at
the Xishan site in Gansu Province, the following conclusions may be drawn.

1. The average wear level of the Xishan sample, according to the protocol developed by Smith (1984), was found to be 3. The average wear
   level for each tooth type at Xishan was close to that found for human
   dental remains from Neolithic sites on the northern frontier and in
   Central China.
2. In terms of wear patterns, many individuals exhibited evidence of
   lingual surface wear on the maxillary anterior teeth, accompanied by
   chipping on the lingual enamel. This specialized wear and chipping
   pattern may have been associated with nonmasticatory activities,
   such as using the teeth as tools.
3. The prevalence of caries among the sample individuals whose remains were recovered at the Xishan site was 10.7 percent. No significant difference in the rates of caries was found between males and
   females. As for age at death, older adults had a significantly higher
   rate of caries than did middle-aged adults, while middle-aged adults
   had significantly higher rates of caries than did young adults. With
   regard to tooth types, second molars were found to exhibit the greatest prevalence of caries, followed by first molars, and third molars;
   incisors had the lowest rate. With regard to the location of carious
   lesions, most appeared on interproximal surfaces, followed in order
   by occlusal surfaces, the neck of the tooth, and buccal surfaces.
4. The prevalence of AMTL was found to be 31.82 percent by individual
   count, mainly on posterior teeth (molars in particular), with no apparent patterning or symmetry.
5. Well-developed maxillary exostoses or mandibular torii were not
   found on either maxillae or mandibles from Xishan.

Overall, the specific dental pathologies and patterns exhibited by the remains of people buried at Xishan, including dental wear, caries (in particular, the distribution among tooth types and location of the lesions), and
AMTL—mainly of the anterior teeth—suggest that animal protein was an
important element of the human diet at Xishan. Nevertheless, high frequencies of both AMTL and caries suggest that carbohydrates were also a major
component of the diet, while the rarity of exostosis points to a relatively light

masticatory load on the human jaw. A nonmasticatory function for human teeth at Xishan is inferred based on specialized wear patterns and associated chipping of the tooth enamel. Among the remains of all the individuals studied, only one exhibited interproximal grooving on a molar that bore a resemblance to the kind of marks left by frequent "tooth-picking."

In summary, studies of dental wear and dental pathologies are informative for our understanding of issues related to the behavior and survival of past populations. Based on the data from Xishan, it appears most likely that the people buried at Xishan practiced a mixed subsistence regimen, resulting in a diet that included both meat and agriculturally derived plant foods. This conclusion agrees with the results of analysis of bone chemistry (Wei et al. 2009), analysis of the pertinent historical literature (Wang 2007), and reconstructions of the paleoenvironment (Zhou 2002). Future analysis of zooarchaeological and paleobotanical evidence from Xishan will further test our hypothesis regarding Qin subsistence. In a synthesis of all available evidence, it is clear that the early Qin people deployed a suite of strategies in which plant cultivation was combined with animal husbandry to create an extremely effective subsistence regime.

Note

Chapter translated by Liu Chinhsin from Chinese.

Literature Cited

Belcastro G, Rastelli E, Mariotti V, Consiglio C, Facchini F, Bonfiglioli B. 2007. Continuity or discontinuity of the life-style in central Italy during the Roman Imperial Age–Early Middle Ages transition: Diet, health, and behavior. *American Journal of Physical Anthropology* 132: 381–94.

Benfer RA, Edwards DS. 1991. The principle axis method for measuring rate and amount of dental wear: Estimating juvenile or adult tooth wear from unaged adult teeth. In: Kelley MA, Larsen CS, editors. *Advances in dental anthropology.* New York: Wiley-Liss. Pp. 325–40.

Bermudez de Castro JM, Arsuaga JL, Perez PJ. 1997. Interproximal grooving in the Atapuerca-SH hominid dentitions. *American Journal of Physical Anthropology* 102: 369–76.

Buikstra JE, Ubelaker DH. 1994. *Standards for data collection from human skeletal remains.* Arkansas Archaeological Research Survey Series 44. Fayetteville.

Cohen MN, Armelagos GJ, editors. 1984. *Paleopathology at the origins of agriculture.* New York: Academic Press.

Eggen S. 1989. Torus mandibularis: An estimation of the degree of genetic determination. *Acta Odontologica Scandinavica* 47: 409–15.

Eggen S. 1992. Correlated characteristics of the jaws: Association between torus mandibularis and marginal alveolar bone height. *Acta Odontologica Scandinavica* 50: 1–6.

Gong Q, Hu L. 1990. Archaeology of Qin material culture. *Journal of Museum and Archaeology* (文博) 5: 19–29.

Han K, Pan Q. 1982. Late Neolithic human skeletons from Hedang site, Foshan, Guangdong. *Acta Anthropologica Sinica* (人类学学报) 1: 42–51.

Haugen LK. 1992. Palatine and mandibular tori: A morphologic study in the current Norwegian population. *Acta Odontologica Scandinavica* 50: 65–77.

Hauser G, De Stefano GF. 1989. *Epigenetic variants of the human skull.* Stuttgart: Schweizerbart.

He J. 2004. *Tooth decay in the ancient populations of northern China and cultural implications. Acta Anthropologica Sinica* (人类学学报) 23: 61–70.

He J, Tao S, Shang M. 2007. A comparative study on the molar attrition rates in Taosi, Shangma and Yanqing ancient populations. *Acta Anthropologica Sinica* (人类学学报) 26: 116–24.

Hillson S. 2001. Recording dental caries in archaeological human remains. *International Journal of Osteoarchaeology* 11: 249–89

Ihunwo AO, Phukubye P. 2006. The frequency and anatomical features of torus mandibularis in a black South African population. *HOMO—Journal of Comparative Human Biology* 57: 253–62.

Inoue N, Pan Q, Sakashita R, Kamegai T. 1997. *Tooth and facial morphology of ancient Chinese skulls.* Tokyo: Therapeia Publishing.

Larsen CS. 1985. Dental modifications and tool use in the western Great Basin. *American Journal of Physical Anthropology* 67: 393–402.

Larsen CS. 1995. Biological changes in human populations with agriculture. *Annual Review of Anthropology* 24: 185–213.

Larsen CS, Shavit R, Griffins MC. 1991. Dental caries evidence for dietary change: An archaeological context. In: Kelley MA, Larsen CS, editors. *Advances in dental anthropology.* New York: Wiley-Liss. Pp. 179–202.

Littleton J, Frohlich B. 1993. Fish-eaters and farmers: Dental pathology in the Arabian Gulf. *American Journal of Physical Anthropology* 92: 427–47.

Liu W, Zhang Q, Wu X, Zhu H. 2005. The tooth wear and health condition of the Bronze–Iron Ages populations in Xinjiang and Inner Mongolia. *Acta Anthropologica Sinica* (人类学学报) 24: 32–53.

Liu W, Zhang Q, Wu X, Zhu H. 2010. Tooth wear and dental pathology of the Bronze–Iron Age people in Xinjiang, Northwest China: Implications for their diet and lifestyle. *HOMO—Journal of Comparative Human Biology* 61: 102–16.

Lovejoy CO, Meindl RS, Mensforth RP, Barton TJ. 1985. Multifactorial determination of skeletal age at death: A method and blind tests of its accuracy. *American Journal of Physical Anthropology* 68: 1–14.

Lukacs JR. 1992. Dental paleopathology and agricultural intensification in South Asia: New evidence from Bronze Age Harappa. *American Journal of Physical Anthropology* 87: 133–50.

Lukacs JR. 2007. Dental trauma and antemortem tooth loss in prehistoric Canary Islanders: Prevalence and contributing factors. *International Journal of Osteoarchaeology* 17: 157–73.

Lukacs JR, Pastor RF. 1988. Activity-induced patterns of dental abrasion in prehistoric Pakistan: Evidence from Mehrgarh and Harappa. *American Journal of Physical Anthropology* 76: 377–98.

Lukacs JR, Pastor RF. 1990. Activity-induced patterns of dental abrasion in prehistoric Pakistan. In: Taddei M, editor. *South Asian archaeology.* Naples: Instituto Universitario Oriental. Pp. 79–110.

Mao X, Yan Y. 1959. Report on Shang human dentitions from Huixian, Anhui Province. *Vertebrate Paleontology and Paleoanthropology* (古脊椎动物与古人类) 1: 165–72.

Meindl RS, Lovejoy OC, Mensforth RP, Walker RA. 1985. A revised method of age determination using the os pubis, with a review and tests of accuracy of other current methods of pubic symphyseal aging. *American Journal of Physical Anthropology* 68: 29–45.

Meng W. 1940. *Qin society.* Collected Papers of History Studies (史学季刊) 1.

Molnar S. 1972. Tooth wear and culture: A survey of tooth functions among some prehistoric populations. *Current Anthropology* 13: 511–26.

Niu S. 1996. Cultural tradition and the agricultural development of Qin. *Kaogu* (考古) 41: 233–42.

Pechenkina EA, Benfer RA Jr. 2002. The role of occlusal stress and gingival infection in the formation of exostosis on mandible and maxilla from Neolithic China. *Homo* 53: 112–30.

Pechenkina EA, Benfer RA Jr., Wang Z. 2002. Diet and health changes with the intensification of millet agriculture at the end of the Chinese Neolithic. *American Journal of Physical Anthropology* 117: 15–36.

Pechenkina EA, Ambrose SH, Ma X, Benfer RA Jr. 2005. Reconstructing northern Chinese Neolithic subsistence practices by isotopic analysis. *Journal of Archaeological Science* 32: 1176–89.

Pietrusewsky M, Douglas MT. 1993. Tooth ablation in old Hawai'i. *Journal of the Polynesian Society* 102: 255–72.

Scott EC. 1979. Dental wear scoring technique. *American Journal of Physical Anthropology* 51: 213–18.

Scott R, Turner C. 1988. Dental anthropology. *Annual Review of Anthropology* 17: 99–126.

Seah, YH. 1995. Torus palatinus and torus mandibularis: A review of the literature. *Australian Dental Journal* 40: 318–21.

Smith H. 1984. Patterns of molar wear in hunter-gatherers and agriculturalists. *American Journal of Physical Anthropology* 63: 39–56.

Sun S, Qu Y. 1986. The measurements and sexual diagnosis of the greater sciatic notch in Chinese. *Acta Anthropologica Sinica* (人类学学报) 5: 368–71.

Suzuki M, Sakai T. 1960. A familial study of torus palatinus and torus mandibularis. *American Journal of Physical Anthropology* 18: 263–72.

Tayles N, Domett K, Nelsen K. 2000. Agriculture and dental caries? The case of rice in prehistoric Southeast Asia. *World Archaeology* 32: 68–83.

Tian Y. 2009. On the founding of the Qin state. *Journal of Tianshui Normal University* (天水师范学院学报) 29: 56–58.

Todd TW. 1920. Age changes in the pubic bone. I: The white male pubis. *American Journal of Physical Anthropology* 3: 285–334.

Turner CG II. 1979. Dental anthropological indications of agriculture among the Jomon people of central Japan. X: Peopling of the Pacific. *American Journal of Physical Anthropology* 51: 619–36.

Turner CG II, Cadien JD. 1969. Dental chipping in Aleut, Eskimos and Indians. *American Journal of Physical Anthropology* 31: 303–10.

Turner CG II, Cheuiche Machado LM. 1983. A new dental wear pattern and evidence for high carbohydrate consumption in a Brazilian Archaic skeletal population. *American Journal of Physical Anthropology* 61: 125–30.

Wallace JA. 1973. Tooth chipping in the Australopithecines. *Nature* 244: 117–18.

Wang G. 1956. *View of Tang Ji Li: Research on the Qin capital* (观堂集林-秦都邑考). Beijing: China Publishing House.

Wang W, Zeng X. 2004. Pathology of ancient human teeth in China. *Chinese Journal of Orthodontics* (口腔正畸學) 11: 41–43.

Wang Z. 2007. Research on early Qin culture (早期秦文化研究). Ph.D. dissertation, Xibei University.

Wasterlain SN, Hillson S, Cunha E. 2009. Dental caries in a Portuguese identified skeletal sample from the late 19th and early 20th centuries. *American Journal of Physical Anthropology* 140: 64–79.

Wei J. 1934. *Origins of Chinese nationalities.* Ancient History Research, vol. 3 (古史研究). Shanghai: Shanghai Commercial Press.

Wei M, Wang T, Wang CS, Zhao CC, Chen L. 2009. Diet and oral hygiene of the people in early Qin dynasty from the Xishan site, Gansu Province. *Acta Anthropologica Sinica* (人类学学报) 28: 45–56.

Wu X, Shao X, Wang H. 1982. Sex differences and sex determination of the innominate bone of modern Han nationality. *Acta Anthropologica Sinica* (人类学学报) 1: 118–31.

Yong J. 2000. On the formation of Qin culture and its characteristics. *Journal of Tianshui Normal University* (天水师范学院学) 20: 54–58.

Zhang T. 2001. Brief discussion on the issues of early Qin cultural relics in Li County and other areas (禮縣等地所見早期秦文化遺存有關問題芻論). *Relics and Museology* (文博) 3: 67–74.

Zhang Y. 1989. Tooth wear in early *Homo sapiens* from Chaohu and the hypothesis of use of anterior teeth as tools. *Acta Anthropologica Sinica* (人类学学报) 8: 314–19.

Zhang Z. 1982. A preliminary study of estimation of age by morphological changes in the pubic symphysis. *Acta Anthropologica Sinica* (人类学学报) 1: 132–36.

Zhang Z. 1986. A further study on the relationship between morphologic features of pubic symphysis and age estimation. *Acta Anthropologica Sinica* (人类学学报) 5: 130–37.

Zhou K. 2002. Ancient civilization and environment of the Central Plains. In: Zhou K, editor. *Pollen analysis and environmental archaeology* (花粉分析与环境考古). Beijing: Xueyuan Press. Pp. 145–54.

12

Yangshao Oral Health from West to East

Effects of Increasing Complexity and Contacts with Neighbors

KATE PECHENKINA, MA XIAOLIN, FAN WENQUAN,
WEI DONG, AND ZHANG QUANCHAO

Human teeth are routinely exposed to and affected by a wide range of substances, including water and other liquids; food and nonfood particles incorporated into food during processing and cooking (Wallace 1975; Schollmeyer and Turner 2004; Lev-Tov Chattah and Smith 2006; Watson 2008); saliva and regurgitated food, as during vomiting (Lukacs and Largaespada 2006); hygiene-related objects and pastes (Ubelaker et al. 1969; Formicola 1988; Lukacs and Pastor 1988; Turner 1988; Formicola 1991); the edges of cups and plates, eating utensils, and smoking pipes and other devices for delivering recreational substances (Corruccini et al. 1982), as well as the substances themselves (Langsjoen 1996; Indriati and Buikstra 2001). Animal and plant materials that might be processed using the teeth (Larsen 1985), along with an array of tools clenched between the teeth to aid in a task or out of habit (Molnar 1972), all may affect the tooth surfaces. Of this broad array of factors, it is variation in food composition and more specifically the presence of water-soluble carbohydrates and sucrose that result in the most distinctive suites of oral pathology markers and most strongly affect rates of caries development and antemortem tooth loss (Turner 1979; Lukacs 1992; Littleton and Frohlich 1993; Nelson et al. 1999; Pechenkina et al. 2002; Papathanasiou 2005; Eshed et al. 2006; Temple and Larsen 2007; Lanfranco and Eggers 2010). However, oral indicators unrelated to caries show less clear relationships to any specific dietary regimen, and their progression at least partially depends on other extrinsic factors, as well as on intrinsic development of other pathological conditions in the mouth (Hillson 2001: 268–69).

In this chapter we examine variation in oral health in three skeletal collections, derived from the Xipo (西坡), Guanjia (关家), and Xishan (西

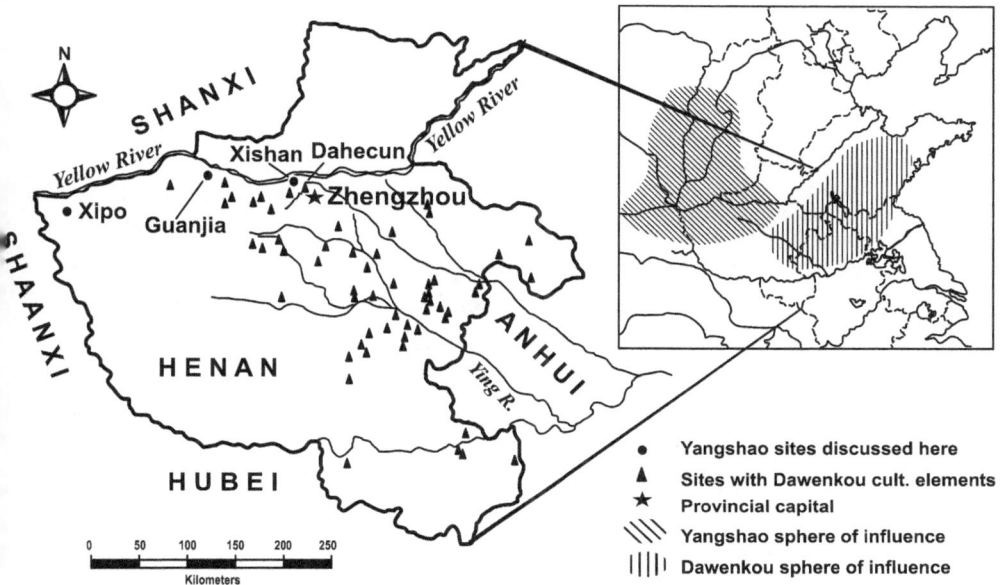

Figure 12.1. Archaeological sites in Henan Province. Map shows the locations of the three Yangshao sites providing skeletal collections for this study: Xipo, Guanjia, and Xishan. The distribution of archaeological sites with Dawenkou cultural elements (marked by triangles) is based on Zhang 2003. The approximate area of Dawenkou influence and its expansion into northern Anhui and eastern Henan is based on Yan and Xia 2001.

山) Middle/Late Yangshao (仰韶) archaeological sites. These collections represent communities with similar millet-based diets, allowing us to evaluate observed differences in oral health and dental wear in relation to the consequences of local population density and variation in the specific degree of social stratification, as well as the likelihood of opportunities to interact with affiliates of the Dawenkou cultural entity, who had begun to encroach on Yangshao territory from the east. All three collections in our study are dated to between 4000 and 3000 BC, and their locations of origin are spread along the Yellow River and its tributaries from west to east in Henan Province, China (figure 12.1). Notwithstanding this essential commonality, they also represent communities that likely interacted with their natural surroundings and neighboring settlements in a very different manner, as they differed greatly in size and geographic location. Xipo was a large settlement located deep within the considerable extent of the Yangshao territory, while Guanjia was a much smaller farming settlement to the east. Xishan, the easternmost of the three sites, was located in close proximity to settlements that display Dawenkou cultural elements as part of their archaeological record (figure 12.1).

The Yangshao Cultural Entity and Its Neighbors

In brief, Yangshao (仰韶) can be characterized as a Middle Neolithic cultural entity that developed and flourished from approximately the fifth to the third millennium BC along the middle and upper reaches of the Yellow River, along the Fen and Wei Rivers, and along smaller tributaries of these rivers on the Loess Plateau (黄土高原) and Central Plains (中原). Yangshao is best known for its black-on-red painted pottery with zoomorphic, anthropomorphic, and later geometric and floral/abstract motifs, although most Yangshao pottery was undecorated ware produced by coiling (An 1959; Ma 1987; Yan 1992; Ren and Wu 1999). In accord with changing ceramic styles and settlement patterns, the total duration of Yangshao is commonly divided into three sequential phases: Early, or Banpo (c. 5000–4000 BC), Middle, or Miaodigou (4000–3500 BC), and Late, sometimes referred to as Xiwang (3500–3000 BC), although local chronologies vary somewhat from these ranges (Dai 1998; Zhang and Qiao 1992).

The skeletal collections examined in this study come from burial grounds that date to the Middle and Late phases of Yangshao. During this time frame, the number and size of settlements increased, and settlement hierarchies had already been established in some areas (Dai 1998; Su 1999). To the east of Yangshao, within the territory of present-day Shandong, another prominent Neolithic cultural manifestation, Dawenkou (大汶口) (4300–2400 BC), is recognized on the basis of its distinctive ceramic tradition (Wu 1982, 1987; Chang 1986: 159–60), as well as elaborate burial practices linked to status hierarchy and gender differences (Underhill 2000; Fung 2002). The degree of political integration within the Yangshao and Dawenkou territories has not been well documented. Peterson and colleagues (2010) argue that during the fourth millennium BC, settlement patterns for all of the major Neolithic traditions in northern and northeastern China could be loosely characterized as representing chiefdom-like societies. Starting at about 3300–3200 BC, Dawenkou culture began to spread westward into the territory of northern Anhui and farther upstream along the shores of the Ying and Jialu rivers into eastern Henan (Yan and Xia 2001; Zhang 2003). He Deliang (2007) notes that this westward expansion of Dawenkou led to cultural cross-fertilization and the formation of a unique amalgamated culture. Eventually, both Yangshao and Dawenkou were succeeded by Late Neolithic Longshan (龙山) (Liu 2009).

The subsistence practices of both Yangshao and Dawenkou typically focused on millet farming and pig tending (Yan 1992; Yuan and Flad 2002; Bellwood 2005: 124). Yangshao farmers also grew small quantities of both wet and dry rice (Yan 1982; An 1988; Wang et al. 1998; Wei et al. 2001); their other cultivated plants included leaf mustard and Chinese cabbage. Domesticated dogs and chickens were present in Yangshao communities (Wang 1985; Ren 1996), while fishing, hunting, and foraging for wild plant foods were pursued to various degrees.

There was an apparent decline in wild resource exploitation toward the Middle to Late phases of Yangshao (Yuan and Flad 2002). Analysis of stable isotope signatures in animal and human bone samples from Xipo (Pechenkina et al. 2005; Gong 2007) shows that millets were an overwhelmingly prevalent component of the local human diet, albeit with minor sex-based differences in terms of specifics: male averages of $\delta^{15}N$ = 8.8‰ and $\delta^{13}C$ = -9.08‰ (N = 5) and female averages of $\delta^{15}N$ = 9.5‰ and $\delta^{13}C$ = -9.38‰ (N = 4) (based on Gong 2007: 162–63, and our sex assessment). For Dawenkou, a mixed diet with substantial contributions from animal products and C3 plants has been documented by stable isotope analysis of human collagen samples from the Xigongqiao (西公桥) site in Shandong ($\delta^{15}N$ ranging from 5.31‰ to 10.44‰ and $\delta^{13}C$ ranging from -23.79‰ to -12.88‰ [N = 18]) (Hu et al. 2005). Hu and colleagues (2005) note that the relative contribution of millet to the human diet at Xigongqiao increased during the later phase of site occupation.

Because caries development and related oral pathologies are strongly affected by the proportion of water-soluble carbohydrates in foodstuffs, given the assumption of reliance on millet agriculture at Xipo, Guanjia, and Xishan, we would expect to find similar overall rates of these dental pathologies, typical of farming communities. Notwithstanding the similarities in diet between people of the three Yangshao sites, we would expect to find considerable variation with regard to oral pathologies that are less affected by the proportion of carbohydrates in food. The three Yangshao sites in our study differed considerably in terms of settlement size, archaeological evidence for social complexity, and proximity to the settlements of Dawenkou neighbors. Therefore, we suspect that these populations probably interacted with their surrounding environments in differing ways, likely engaged in different cooking and oral hygiene practices, and may have employed their teeth for craftwork and other tasks that differed as well.

We examined a wide range of oral health parameters, including the frequency and distribution of carious lesions, antemortem tooth loss, periapical abscesses, calculus accretion, periodontal disease, the occurrence of enamel chipping, and traumatic pulp exposure and dental fractures, as well as specific types of dental wear in all three of the Yangshao skeletal series. Our intent was to determine to what degree factors other than dietary composition—namely, differences in food preparation techniques, oral hygiene practices, and craft-related activities—may have affected oral health among several communities with generally similar subsistence bases. Because the three collections represent populations all relying on a diet with a similar carbohydrate and protein content, we would expect them to manifest similar rates of caries infection and related pathologies but to differ with respect to other oral parameters.

Archaeological Background

Xipo is located in the upper Sha River valley, in the western corner of Henan. It is a 40 ha site, representing a very large settlement with a notable degree of social stratification and hypothesized to have functioned as a regional center (Ma et al. 2005, 2006). Among the structures encountered at Xipo, there is a three-tier size hierarchy. Some larger buildings were quite substantial, evidencing labor-intensive construction. Of these, building F105 measured 516 m^2 and has been interpreted as a gathering place for the surrounding region, used for ritual activities or other public functions (Ma 2003: 100; Liu 2004).

The Xipo cemetery is located approximately 130 to 150 meters south of the residential area of the site. Thirty-four burials excavated at Xipo were generally similar in design. Single interments were made in rectangular graves. The corpse was placed in a supine position, as was typical for Middle/Late Yangshao burials, with the arms alongside of the body and the head facing due west or northwest; in only one case, the head was facing south. Size of the burials varied from slightly larger than minimally sufficient to place the body in the grave to considerably more expansive interments, with accessory pits for grave goods (e.g., M27 measured 5.03 m long and 3.36 m wide). Burials also differed considerably with respect to the number and quality of grave goods (Guojia Wenwuju 2005).

The most common burial goods were ceramic vessels of several types, including *hu* (壺) and *gui* (簋), as well as bowls and cups. Stone objects included axes, scrapers, and a spindle whorl. A spoon, a ring, and a hairpin were among the bone artifacts that were placed in a few burials. Probably of greater symbolic significance were jade objects, including jade axes, or *yue* (鉞), which were found in six burials at Xipo (Ma et al. 2005, 2006).

In contrast, Guanjia was a small-scale farming settlement (Fan 2000), which may have facilitated more effective exploitation of wild resources than at Xipo. Burials at Guanjia were minimal in extent, affording no evidence of social elaboration or differentiation and having only small personal adornments as occasional grave goods. Guanjia was also located more on the outskirts of the Yangshao territory, although no sites with identifiable foreign cultural elements have been encountered in the vicinity.

Xishan was a large Yangshao settlement surrounded by a rammed earth wall and a moat (Sun 2001). As at Xipo, one large structure at Xishan (F84) might have functioned as a community building of some sort (Liu 2004: 93–94). Its location on the easternmost edge of the documented Yangshao territory and the proximity of settlements evidencing Dawenkou cultural elements, such as Dahecun (大河村) (Zhang 2003), very likely created a distinct socioecological niche for the people living at Xishan. The occupation at Xishan generally coincided with the time of Dawenkou territorial expansion. Therefore, the people living at Xishan might have found themselves in a fairly precarious position with respect to their Yangshao and Dawenkou neighbors.

Methods

Dentitions were examined visually and with a 10x magnifying glass for nine oral parameters, including carious lesions, periapical lesions, antemortem tooth loss, calculus accretion, periodontal disease, root hypercementosis, patterns of dental wear, enamel chipping, and tooth fractures. In cases where teeth were still tightly fixed in the dental sockets, so that their roots could not be examined directly, X-ray images were obtained to evaluate the development of circum-root pathologies.

Caries was evaluated by visual observation using a magnifying glass. A dental probe was used to assess the depth of necrotic areas and the progression of caries into the pulp chamber, enabling the application of a caries correction factor (Lukacs 1995). Shallow necrotic pits in the dental enamel, less than 2 mm in depth, were noted as incipient caries but are not included in computed caries rates reported in this chapter. Following the recommendations of Buikstra and Ubelaker (1994), carious lesions were classified, according their location, as originating on either the occlusal, interproximal, or smooth surface of the crown, at the cementoenamel junction, on the root, as multifocal, or as large lesions involving more than one dental surface. Noncarious traumatic pulp exposure due to rapid wear or trauma was also recorded. Antemortem tooth loss was recorded based on remodeling of the dental sockets. Empty sockets retaining sharp margins and showing minimal remodeling were considered as evidence of postdepositional, rather than antemortem, tooth loss.

Fenestrated periapical lesions, also known as periapical abscesses, were recorded according to location as opening on the buccal or lingual aspect of the jaw or into a paranasal sinus. Some periapical lesions that had not fenestrated before death were nevertheless visible because of the fragmentary nature of the skeletal remains or on X-rays. In order to maintain consistency with other publications, these were not taken into account in analysis and therefore are not discussed in this chapter. Consequently, the actual frequency of periapical abscesses was probably somewhat higher than reported here (Lukacs 1989).

Calculus accretion was classified as absent, mild, forming a thin belt around the crown, moderate, or severe, according to the protocol of Hillson (1979). Periodontal disease was recorded following Clarke and colleagues (1986), based on alteration in the morphology of the alveolar crest and interdental septa. The necessary criteria for a skeletal individual to be diagnosed with periodontal disease included a porous appearance, uneven alveolar margin and septa, horizontal bone loss, and intrabony pockets. In and of itself, horizontal bone loss alone was not a sufficient criterion, even if the distance from the cementoenamel junction to the alveolar crest exceeded 2 mm. Root hypercementosis, excessive cementum deposited on the dental root of a tooth (Lukacs 1981), resulting in an abnormally thick root with an uneven texture, was evaluated visually and from the X-rays.

Teeth were also examined for the presence of unusual wear patterns. Following the descriptions of specific dental wear types reported in the bioarchaeological literature, we examined the dentition for the presence of interproximal grooves (IPG), lingual surface attrition of the maxillary teeth (LSAMAT), and heavy wear and labial rounding of the lower anterior teeth (HWLAT), as well as enamel chipping (ECh) and dental fractures (DFr) (Molnar 1972; Turner and Cheuiche Machado 1983; Formicola 1988; Lukacs and Pastor 1988; Milner and Larsen 1991; Lukacs 2007; Scott and Winn 2010). To distinguish these unusual patterns of wear from postmortem or postdepositional damage we carefully examined the edges of wear facets with a magnifying glass, because such damage manifests itself by very sharp and jagged edges, as well as by an abrupt change of color.

In order to test the effects of sample demographics on the distribution of oral pathology indicators, sex and age were evaluated for each skeletal individual. Preference was given to techniques of age and sex assessment that were developed or have been tested with human skeletons from East Asian populations (Zhang 1986; Sakaue 2006). Wherever possible, pelvic morphology was used to assign sex. Overall skeletal robusticity, muscle marking, and the size and shape of the skull were also considered (Bass 1987; Buikstra and Ubelaker 1994). Age was estimated based on metamorphosis of the auricular surface, the pubic symphysis (Lovejoy et al. 1985; Meindl et al, 1985; Sakaue 2006), and, whenever they were available for examination, the sternal rib ends (Işcan et al. 1984; Işcan 1991), as well as on ectocranial and palatal suture obliteration (Mann et al. 1991). The demographic composition of the analyzed collections is summarized in table 12.1.

Table 12.1. Sex and age composition of the skeletal samples analyzed

Group	Xipo	Guanjia	Xishan
Sex			
Males	21	24	36
Females	11	17	50
Unknown	0	3	22
Age			
10–19	3	8	22
20–29	1	7	23
30–39	8	14	8
40–49	15	10	33
50+	5	5	22
Total	**32**	**44**	**108**

Results: Distribution of Oral Indicators in the Middle/Late Yangshao Collections

Tables 12.2, 12.3, and 12.4 summarize the distribution of oral and alveolar pathologies for the three collections in our study. Where appropriate, we provide the frequencies of specific oral indicators per tooth, as well as per individual (ind.). When pathology frequency is provided per tooth, the total percentage is given both as a crude total based on all teeth present and as a proportion corrected total, wherein different classes of teeth are weighted, so that their relative contribution to the total percentage corresponds to that in the dental formula of *Homo sapiens* (i.e., 2 incisors per 1 canine, per 2 premolars, per 3 molars). Statistically significant differences with less than .05 probability values are boldfaced.

Because many dental and alveolar pathologies are affected by the age of an individual and/or show sex-related differences, to test whether or not intersite differences were affected by the demographic composition of a specific collection we employed general linear models (table 12.5). In our design, age at death, the midpoint of the estimated range, was used as a covariate, so that the effect of age was linearly removed. Sex and site affinities were used as grouping factors to test to what degree sex, site, and/or interaction between the two factors determined the differences among the sites that are highlighted in tables 12.2–12.4. The results of general linear model analysis are summarized in table 12.5; differences and covariances with *p* values less than .05 are shown in boldface. Skeletons judged to be of indeterminate sex were not included in the analysis presented in table 12.5. This mode of analysis requires continuous variables, so only those oral indicators that could be represented as a number

Table 12.2. Carious lesions and antemortem tooth loss in the Middle/Late Yangshao collections

	Xipo		Guanjia	
	Obs./N	%	Obs./N	%
Caries				
Molars	46/205	22.4	103/352	29.3
Premolars	13/175	7.4	28/271	10.3
Canines	2/92	2.2	14/140	10.0
Incisors	0/142	0	22/251	8.8
Total	61/614	9.9	167/1014	16.5
Proportion corrected total %		10.5		17.0
Corrected caries %				
Molars	104/300	34.7	151/455	33.3
Premolars	31/221	14.2	43/311	13.8
Canines	5/108	4.7	17/153	11.2
Incisors	15/207	7.1	32/309	10.4
Total	155/836	18.6	243/1228	19.8
Weighted total %		18.9		19.9
Ind. affected				
Molars	20/30	66.7	32/44	72.7
Premolars	6/32	18.8	10/41	24.4
Canines	2/32	6.25	8/43	18.6
Incisors	0/31	0	10/43	23.3
Total	20/30	66.7	30/41	73.2
Antemortem tooth loss				
Molars	78/300	26.0	65/455	14.3
Premolars	24/221	10.9	23/311	7.4
Canines	4/108	3.7	4/153	2.6
Incisors	21/207	10.1	15/309	4.9
Total	127/836	15.2	107/1228	8.71
Proportion corrected total %		15.5		8.75
Ind. with lost teeth				
Molars	21/31	67.7	19/44	43.2
Premolars	11/32	34.4	11/42	26.2
Canines	3/32	9.4	3/43	6.98
Incisors	9/32	28.1	8/43	18.6
Total	22/31	71	20/42	47.6

Xishan		Level of significance	
Obs./N	%	χ^2	p (2 df)
186/792	23.5	5.10	.078
70/556	12.6	3.81	.149
23/275	8.4	5.17	.075
38/414	9.2	**13.88**	**.001**
317/2037	15.6	**14.64**	**.001**
	15.3		
292/984	29.7	3.51	.172
102.5/686	14.9	0.24	.888
33/353	9.3	3.42	.181
86/672	12.7	5.20	.074
513/2695	19.0	0.55	.760
	19.2		
60/108	55.6	4.29	.117
34/99	34.3	3.42	.181
19/105	18.1	2.81	.246
20/106	18.9	**7.91**	**.019**
58/99	58.6	2.82	.244
120/984	12.2	**34.47**	**.000**
26/686	3.8	**16.29**	**.000**
5/353	1.4	2.33	.312
36/672	5.4	**7.44**	**.024**
187/2695	6.9	**53.92**	**.000**
	7.04		
42/108	38.9	**8.17**	**.017**
14/105	33.3	**8.02**	**.018**
3/106	2.83	2.71	.258
19/105	18.1	1.61	.447
50/105	47.6	5.59	.061

Table 12.3. Calculus accretion and bone manifestations of periodontal disease in the Middle/Late Yangshao collections

	Xipo		Guanjia		Xishan		Level of significance	
	Obs./N	%	Obs./N	%	Obs./N	%	χ^2	p (2 df)
Calculus accretion								
Teeth affected								
Mod+sev	36/614	5.9	176/1,014	17.4	183/2,037	8.98	67.88	.000
Total	162/614	26.4	354/1,014	34.9	876/2,037	43.0	60.93	.000
Ind. affected	19/30	63.3	24/41	58.5	79/99	79.8	7.75	.021
Periapical abscesses								
Lesions/skull	95/30		42/42		97/105			
Affected ind.	20/30	66.7	17/42	40.5	38/105	36.2	8.95	.011
Periodontal disease and related pathologies								
Ind. affected								
Root exposure	23/31	74.2	24/42	57.1	92/99	92.9	16.6	.0002
Alveolar pockets	6/31	19.4	2/42	4.76	9/99	9.1	4.998	.0821
Uneven alveolar margin	23/31	74.2	23/42	54.8	83/99	83.8	9.214	.0099
Mod+sev	7/31	22.6	6/42	14.3	28/99	28.3	2.584	.2747
Total	23/31	74.2	23/42	54.8	86/99	86.9	11.74	.0028
Root hypercementosis	11/31	35.5	5/42	11.9	22/99	22.2	6.405	.04

Table 12.4. Special types of wear and dental traumas in the Middle/Late Yangshao collections

	Xipo			Guanjia			Xishan			Level of significance	
	Obs.	N	%	Obs.	N	%	Obs.	N	%	χ^2	p (2 df)
Affected per individual											
LSAMAT	2	22	9.1	2	31	6.5	6	64	9.4	0.24	.887
HWLAT	5	25	20.0	0	34	0.0	9	59	15.3	**6.8**	**.0332**
IPG	6	28	21.4	4	42	9.5	6	99	6.1	**6.01**	**.049**
TPE	3	30	10.0	10	42	23.8	12	99	12.1	3.35	.145
ECh	6	30	20.0	7	42	16.7	49	99	49.5	**17.91**	**.0001**
Dent. Fracture	6	30	20.0	3	42	7.1	11	99	11.1	2.879	.237
Affected per tooth											
IPG	14	614	2.28	4	1,014	0.39	9	2,037	0.44	**24.4**	**.0000**
TPE	6	614	0.98	35	1,014	3.45	21	2,037	1.03	**34.03**	**.0000**
ECh	25	614	4.07	9	1,014	0.88	113	2,037	5.55	**29.62**	**.0000**
Dent. Fracture	7	614	1.14	10	1,014	0.98	19	2,037	0.93	0.388	.8235

Table 12.5. Effects of age at death, sex, and recovery at a specific site on the distribution of oral health indicators

	Age (1 df)		Sex (1 df)		Site (2 df)		Sex × site (2 df)		N
	F	p	F	p	F	p	F	p	
Caries:									
Molars	16.71	**.000**	3.10	.080	2.93	.057	0.97	.382	157
Premolars	20.99	**.000**	14.60	**.000**	1.74	.180	1.86	.160	158
Canines	21.24	**.000**	1.57	.213	3.96	**.021**	0.94	.392	159
Incisors	12.15	**.001**	6.20	**.014**	5.31	**.006**	1.05	.353	158
Caries total	36.09	**.000**	8.68	**.004**	4.01	**.020**	1.73	.180	154
AMTL:									
Molars	39.78	**.000**	9.51	**.002**	5.16	**.007**	1.69	.187	158
Premolars	19.92	**.000**	3.64	.058	3.72	**.026**	1.29	.279	159
Canines	6.37	**.013**	0.05	.825	0.63	.533	0.35	.704	159
Incisors	8.47	**.004**	0.09	.762	0.28	.758	0.38	.683	158
AMTL total	37.28	**.000**	5.72	**.018**	4.61	**.011**	1.13	.327	157
Other dental health indicators:									
Calculus	13.69	**.000**	4.84	**.009**	8.19	**.005**	0.71	.494	154
Abscesses	9.40	**.003**	0.54	.463	4.57	**.012**	0.12	.889	157
Periodontal	6.39	**.013**	3.32	.071	6.31	**.002**	3.51	**.033**	154
Wear and trauma:									
IPG	2.54	.113	0.50	.482	6.49	**.002**	2.16	.119	152
TPE	10.39	**.002**	2.54	.083	3.21	**.043**	0.97	.327	154
ECh	1.86	.175	4.94	**.028**	5.49	**.005**	1.48	.231	154
Dent. Fracture	4.38	.038	4.46	**.037**	0.64	.527	0.52	.595	154

of affected teeth/alveoli were considered. As is clear from the results offered in tables 12.2, 12.3, 12.4, and 12.5, despite a presumed similarity in dietary compositions across the three sites, analysis of the pertinent skeletal collections reveals very different patterns of oral pathology among them.

Caries Infection

The most critical impediment to accurate assessment of caries rates in the skeletal collections analyzed was a high frequency of postdepositional tooth loss. In the Xishan collection alone, 304 teeth (13 percent) were lost postdepositionally. Rates of postdepositional tooth loss were somewhat lower for Guanjia and Xipo, with 106 teeth (9.5 percent) lost and 27 (4.2 percent) lost, respectively. Because of the impossibility of accurately assessing the caries frequency for teeth that were lost after the death of the individual, we are forced to assume that it was the same as among the teeth that were still in place. However, this approach likely underestimates actual caries frequencies, as caries infection is commonly associated with the loosening of the dental socket, thus making postdepositional tooth loss more likely. While cleaning the dental sets we found that some teeth with particularly large carious lesions disintegrated upon contact. Although we kept track of such teeth, we have to assume that additional carious teeth were lost during excavation for the same reason. Consequently, the actual frequencies of caries infection must have been at least slightly higher than we estimate here.

As expected, there was little difference among the three series in the rate of caries (table 12.2). Statistically significant differences among the three collections were found for the anterior teeth only, as a result of higher anterior caries rates for Guanjia and Xipo (table 12.5). Although caries frequency appears to have been significantly lower for Xipo than in the two other collections ($\chi^2 = 14.64$; $p = .001$, 3 df) when pooled across all teeth, that difference is likely due to high antemortem tooth loss resulting from the more advanced caries evident at Xipo. This suggestion is supported primarily by the very high frequency of antemortem tooth loss found in the Xipo collection (127/836 teeth, or 15 percent, were lost before death in this series). It is also supported by a high ratio of dental pulp exposure due to caries in the Xipo series (70 percent) as compared to the incidence of pulp chambers exposed as a result of trauma, as well as a high frequency of periapical abscesses that destroyed the dental sockets (95 lesions per 30 skulls [table 12.2]). Consequently, once caries frequencies are adjusted to account for antemortem tooth loss using Lukacs' caries correction factor (Lukacs 1995), as well as for differing representation of molars, premolars, canines, and incisors, as suggested by Erdal and Duyar (1999), the total frequencies of carious teeth in all three samples

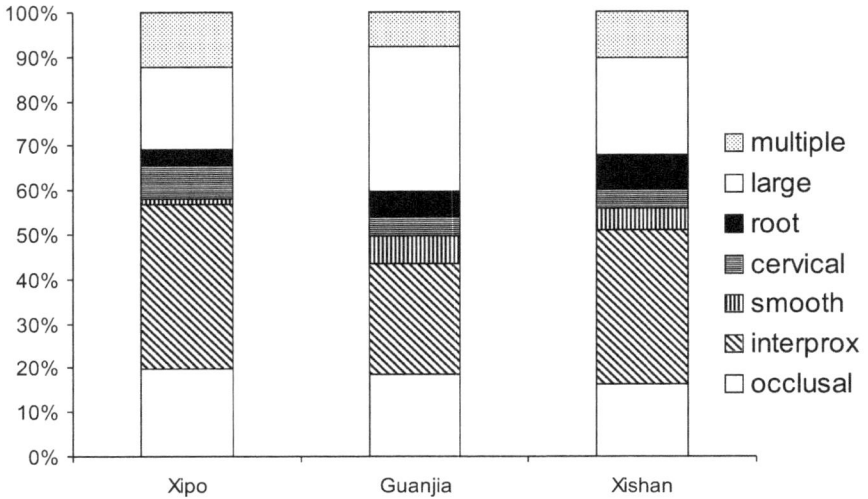

Figure 12.2. The distribution of carious lesions across dental surfaces for the Xipo, Guanjia, and Xishan collections.

become very similar (18.9 percent for Xipo, 19.9 percent for Guanjia, and 19.2 percent for Xishan), obliterating the statistical significance of this difference ($\chi^2 = 0.55$; $p = .760$, 3 df, n.s.).

The distribution of carious lesions across dental surfaces was also similar in all three series (figure 12.2). An overwhelming plurality of such lesions were found in the interproximal spaces (42.2 percent for Xipo, 27.0 percent for Guanjia, and 38.8 percent for Xishan), followed by occlusal caries, generally representing about half as many lesions as interproximal caries (i.e., 22.5 percent, 20.2 percent, and 18.0 percent for Xipo, Guanjia, and Xishan, respectively). Carious lesions on smooth labial/buccal/lingual surfaces, at the cementoenamel junction, or on the root were fairly infrequent. This pattern corroborates a recent observation by Lanfranco and Eggers (2010) about South American maize farmers: extraocclusal caries are more frequent in agriculture-dependent groups. Large lesions that affected more than one dental surface and thus could not be classified according to their location were most common for Guanjia (35.4 percent). Such lesions were least frequent in the Xipo series (21.1 percent), again probably because of high antemortem tooth loss, specifically of teeth with large carious lesions.

Antemortem Tooth Loss and Intentional Tooth Removal

With regard to antemortem tooth loss, statistically significant differences among the collections were found for all classes of teeth, except the canines (tables 12.2, 12.5). As mentioned above, antemortem tooth loss was most frequent in the Xipo series for all classes of teeth, with 26 percent of molars, 11 percent of premolars, 4 percent of canines, and 10 percent of incisors lost before death. These frequencies were approximately twice those found for the collections from Guanjia and Xishan. Caries was probably the major contributor to this tooth loss, as carious lesions exposing pulp chambers and leading to periapical abscesses were very frequent on the remaining teeth, exceeding the incidence of pulp exposure due to trauma and rapid wear. Given that an overwhelming majority of the Xipo individuals whose remains were examined died after the age of 40, their carious lesions often had had enough time to progress to a stage leading to the loss of multiple teeth. That being said, when the effect of age was removed by regression, statistically significant differences were still found between the Xipo series and the other two collections in the antemortem loss of molars and premolars (table 12.5).

Intentional tooth removal/ablation also needs to be considered as a possible contributing factor to AMTL in these Chinese collections, as intentional removal of specific teeth has been documented for Chinese skeletal collections from as early as 6500 years ago (Han and Pan 1982; Han and Nakahashi 1996). Bioarchaeological research has detected a well-established pattern of ritual tooth ablation, involving the removal of upper lateral incisors, as documented in Neolithic collections from Shandong and northern Jiangsu. This practice was apparently typical of the Dawenkou culture, eventually spreading, likely as far as Japan (Han and Nakahashi 1996). In skeletal collections from Japan, the intentional removal of teeth is less systematic, affecting not only upper lateral incisors but also various upper and lower anterior teeth (Doi and Tanaka 1988; Takenaka et al. 2001).

The recognition of intentional tooth removal for ritual or hygienic/medical reasons is complicated for two reasons. First, when a complete luxation of the gomphosis is achieved, the residual dental socket heals quickly and adjacent teeth shift, so that it becomes impossible to establish whether the tooth was intentionally removed, was lost due to caries or trauma, or was never there. However, when a residual root is still present in a dental socket, one can suspect either intentional ablation or trauma leading to tooth fracture. Second, even in cases of bilaterally missing teeth that seem to suggest ritual tooth removal, this may be confused with congenital bilateral agenesis. Agenesis of the third molars is widespread and is particularly common in Eskimo (Pedersen 1949) and East Asian populations (Brothwell 1963; Turner 1990: 301). Agenesis of the upper lateral incisors is also present in modern human populations at a frequency of about 1 percent (Meskin and Gorlin 1963; Garib et al. 2010) and is likely inherited as an autosomal dominant allele with variable penetrance and expressivity (Burzynski and Escobar 1983).

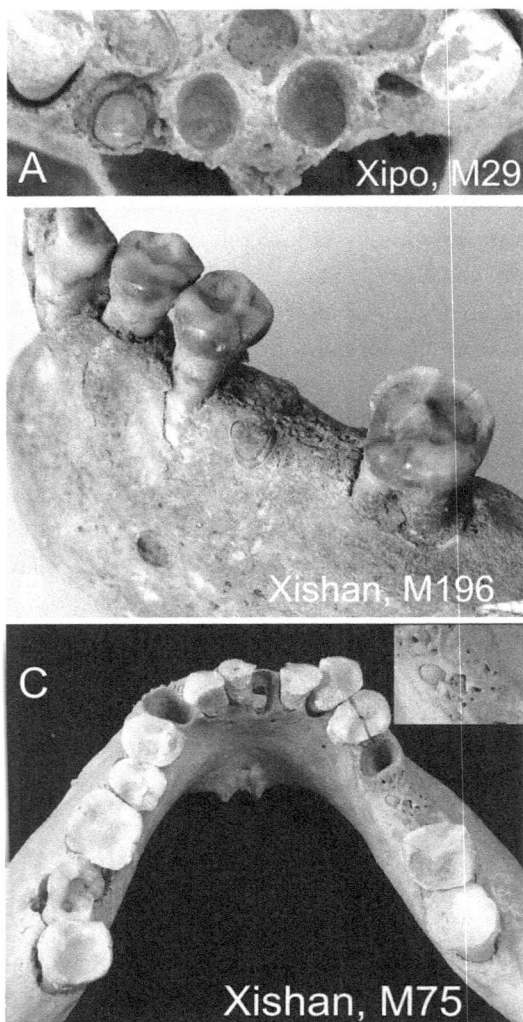

Figure 12.3. Cases of tooth ablation from Xipo and Xishan. *A*, Maxilla of Xipo M29, showing broken root of left lateral incisor, associated with a small periodontal pocket. *B*, Mandible of Xishan M196, showing a root-peg of the first left molar. *C*, Mandible of Xishan M75, showing root fragments of the first right molar.

In some Asian populations this allelic variant has been encountered at a particularly high rate. For instance, Nelsen and colleagues (2001) documented a 79 percent frequency of congenital agenesis of the upper lateral incisors in the Noen U-Loke skeletal collection from Thailand.

A fairly convincing case of intentional upper lateral incisor ablation was found on the skull from Xipo burial M29 (figure 12.3A), where a stub of the root of the upper left incisor is still present in the dental socket. The margin of the surrounding alveolus was partially remodeled, forming a small pocket around the root. The upper right incisor was apparently also removed, as suggested by a partially remodeled corresponding dental socket.

Several possible examples of tooth ablation were found in the Xishan collection. These we divide into two types that merit separate discussion. The first type includes dental sockets that still retain the pegs of roots (figure 12.3B–C), while the second type refers to dental sets that are missing teeth in a specific pattern, that is, the lateral incisors. There are three examples of the first type in the Xishan series, all involving molar teeth. A female mandible from burial M196 retains a root-peg of the left M_1 in the dental socket, suggesting that the tooth was filed down or broken off, whether intentionally or by accident. The mandible of this individual is also missing the wisdom tooth on the same side, while all other teeth are present. Carious infection was fairly well developed on this mandible, with 11 teeth affected by carious lesions. The female mandible from burial M75 is missing the first molar on the right side (figure 12.3C), while all of the other teeth, both upper and lower, were present at the time of death. The left second molar from the same mandible has a traumatically fractured crown that resulted in exposure of the pulp chamber. Carious infection was also well developed on this dentition, affecting four of the posterior teeth. Finally, a female mandible from burial M10 retains a stub of the right M_2, the crown of which was either broken off or filed down. No other teeth were lost antemortem, but carious infection of the posterior dentition was considerable, affecting eight teeth.

There are 11 possible cases of the second type—patterned tooth removal—in the Xishan collection, all of which merit discussion, given possible alternative explanations. Individuals from burials M65, M72, M82:2, T5033, and H1556 were missing both upper lateral incisors and had small gaps between the first incisors and the canines. However, there are no root traces in the dental sockets. If these lateral incisors were removed intentionally, sufficient time passed thereafter for the dental sockets to be fully remodeled, so that it is now impossible to verify that the teeth had been there in the first place (figure 12.4A–B). Additional possible cases of lateral incisor removal come from burials M91, which is missing the right I^2, and from M94:2, missing the left I^2; unfortunately, the opposite sides of both maxillae were destroyed postdepositionally, which prevents us from being able to verify or affirm the absence of the opposing lateral incisors. Evidence of bilateral agenesis or removal of the lower I_2 was found on the mandible from another female burial (M128). In this case, congenital agenesis seems by far a more likely explanation than ablation, as this mandible suffered severe crowding of the anterior teeth and there were no gaps between the respective canines and first incisors.

The most convincing case of patterned incisor removal was found on the cranium from burial M77, thanks in part to the procedure having been botched (figure 12.4C). In this instance there is a sharp and narrow root-peg protruding from the dental socket of the right I^2, indicating that the crown

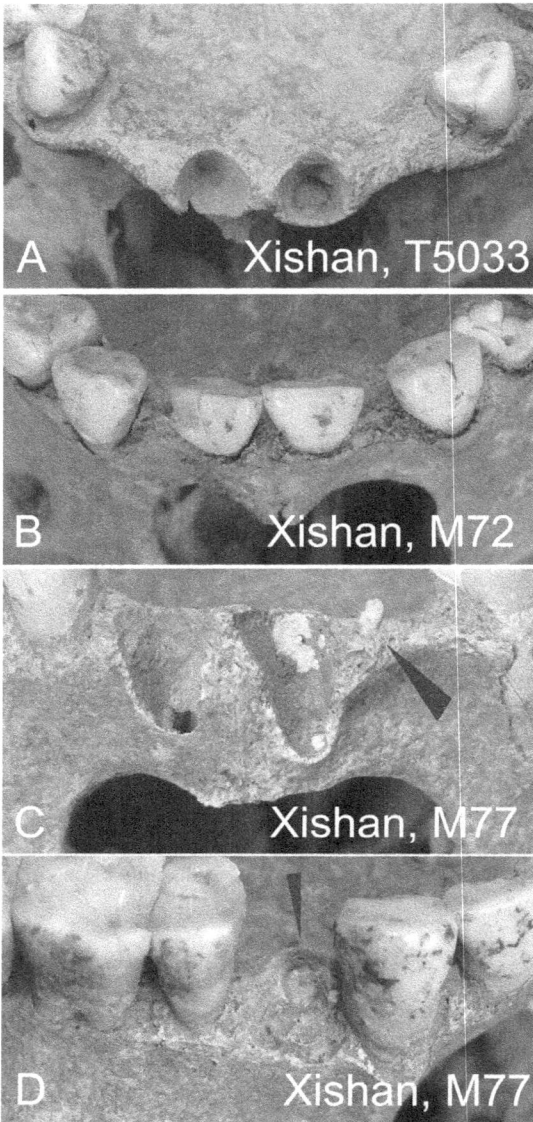

Figure 12.4. Likely cases of intentional tooth removal from Xishan. A, Xishan T5033, bilateral removal or agenesis of maxillary second incisors. B, Xishan M72, bilateral removal or agenesis of maxillary second incisors. C, Xishan M77, root fragment of maxillary right lateral incisor. D, Xishan M77, root fragment of maxillary left third premolar.

of this tooth was either ground down or knocked off. On the left side of the same maxilla, I^2 was left untouched, while the crown of P^3 was ground down to below the cementoenamel junction (figure 12.4D); the root-peg remained in the dental socket, surrounded by a small periodontal pocket.

Calculus Accretion and Periodontal Disease

Bacterial plaque, represented in skeletal collections by its mineralized form, calculus, is an agent capable of instigating and exacerbating alveolar recession and inflammation of the periodontal tissues (Hillson 1979; Lieverse 1999). Thus, tight positive correlation between the amount of calculus and evidence of periodontal disease is expected. Indeed, as seen in table 12.3, the lowest rates of both calculus accretion and periodontal disease were found in the Guanjia collection (58.5 percent and 54.8 percent, respectively), while the Xishan and Xipo collections both had much higher rates. The frequencies of these pathologies were slightly higher in the Xishan series (79.8 percent and 86.9 percent of individuals affected, respectively) than for Xipo (63.3 percent and 74.2 percent).

In the Xipo collection, there is a peculiar discordance between the number of teeth affected by calculus, which was fairly low at 162 out of 614 teeth (26 percent), and a relatively high number of individuals affected by calculus and periodontal disease (see above). We attribute this to high postdepositional loss of calculus from this particular series, as some of the Xipo skeletons were exposed to weathering for several days after being unearthed. In this respect, the frequency of calculus per individual rather than per tooth is more indicative of the actual rates of calculus accretion for Xipo, because given random postdepositional loss of calculus, it is likely that traces will still remain on at least some of the teeth of an affected individual.

With regard to the specific indicators of periodontal disease, including periodontal pockets and alveolar recession, along with an uneven and hyperporous alveolar margin, all appear tightly correlated (table 12.3). However, there were some interesting differences between the three Yangshao collections. Of the three indicators, alveolar pockets were most common in the Xipo collection (6/31 individuals, or 20 percent), while in the Xishan collection, periodontal disease was usually expressed as alveolar recession and an uneven alveolar margin.

Hypercementosis of the dental root has a mixed and somewhat uncertain etiology. It is commonly associated with periodontal disease, as inflammation of the periodontal ligament can lead to excessive cement deposition on the root. Additional factors that may exacerbate hypercementosis development include starvation interrupted by seasonal rehabilitation and vitamin C deficiency (Corruccini et al. 1987), as well as the application of excessive pressure during mastication or activity-related tooth use, leading to microfractures inside the root (Leider and Garbarino 1987). Root hypercementosis was most common in the Xipo series (11/31 individuals), where it was largely associated with periodontal pockets. There was a somewhat lesser incidence of this pathology at Xishan (22/99 affected individuals). The close association of hypercementosis with the markers of periodontal disease supports the likelihood of a cause and effect relationship between these two oral conditions in the Middle/Late Yangshao populations represented in this study.

Dental Wear and Traumas

The three Middle/Late Yangshao series examined for this study manifest an array of specific patterns of tooth wear, including lingual surface attrition of the anterior maxillary teeth (LSAMAT), heavy wear of the lower anterior teeth (HWLAT) (figure 12.5A–C), interproximal grooves (IPG) (figure 12.6A–C), traumatic pulp exposure (TPE) due to rapid wear of a particular tooth, enamel

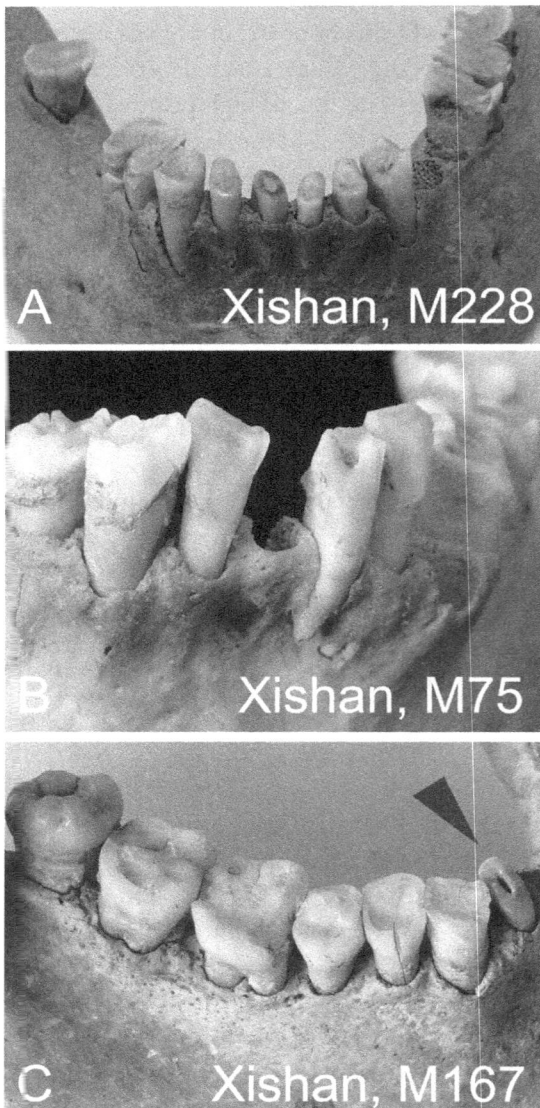

Figure 12.5. Heavy wear of the lower anterior teeth at Xishan. A, Mandible of Xishan M228, showing anterior teeth worn below CEJ and crowns of posterior teeth worn with a strong buccal tilt. B, Xishan M75, heavy wear of lower anterior teeth with a strong labial tilt. C, Mandible of Xishan M167, lateral left incisor heavily worn with a strong labial tilt; note traumatic pulp exposure (other incisors from this specimen were lost postdepositionally).

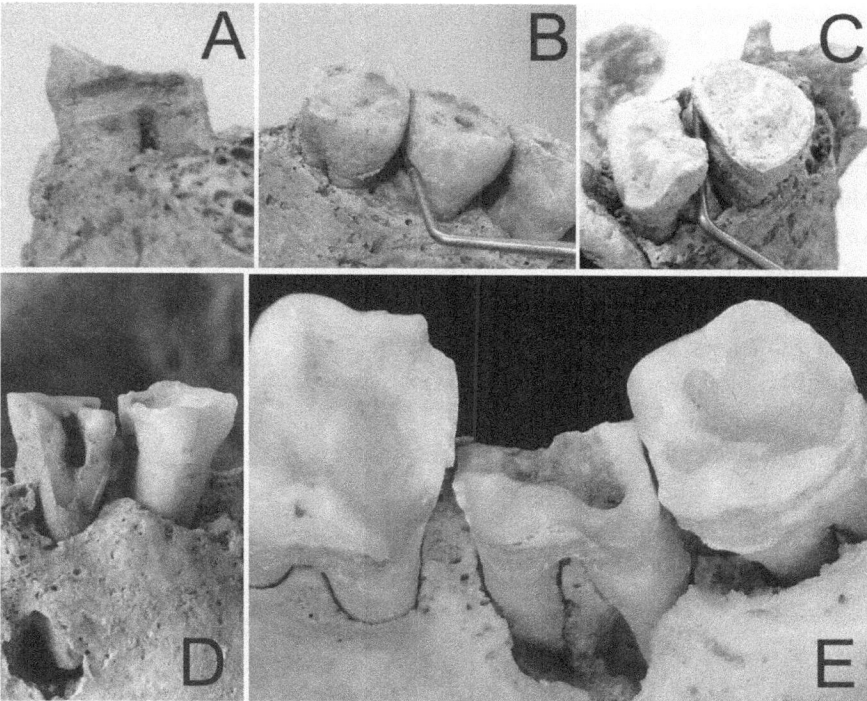

Figure 12.6. Interproximal grooves on Xipo maxillary teeth: *A*, Xipo M26; *B*, Xipo M7; *C*, Xipo M23. Traumatic injuries to the dental crowns: *D*, trauma of the upper third right premolar leading to a traumatic pulp exposure in the maxilla of Xishan M167; *E*, trauma of the crown of the lower left second molar in mandible of Xishan M75 mandible.

chipping (ECh), and fractures of the dental crowns (DFr) (figure 12.6D–E). Unequal distribution of these indicators across the three collections (table 12.4) suggests that mechanical loadings exerted on the teeth—their direction, strength, and the materials applied to produce them—differed considerably among the human communities they represent.

LSAMAT was present at a low frequency in all three skeletal series examined, and no statistically significant difference was found among them in that respect (table 12.4, $\chi^2 = 0.24$, $p = .89$, n.s.). We previously documented a low frequency of this type of crown wear in an Early Yangshao collection from Jiangzhai (Pechenkina et al. 2002: fig. 6). Similar wear patterns have also been reported for skeletal collections from Colorado and the U.S. Virgin Islands, Brazil, and Panama, as well as for historic Senegalese, primarily attributed to the use of the maxillary teeth in scraping/peeling sugary plants, such as sugar cane and manioc (Turner and Cheuiche Machado 1983; Irish and Turner 1987, 1997; Larsen et al. 1998). Chemical erosion of dental surfaces through exposure to the acidic and sugary juices of these plants results in wear patches with a polished appearance. Because plant matter is apparently pressed against the superior teeth using the hands and tongue, the lower teeth are uninvolved and develop no corresponding wear facets.

In this respect, the etiology of LSAMAT in northern China remains unclear. There is very little evidence that tubers or fleshy fruit were commonly used as food either on the Central Plains or in northeastern China during the Neolithic (Crawford et al. 2005; Lee et al. 2007). The strong development of LSAMAT facets on the incisors of an elderly female from Xipo burial M14 suggests that such wear was produced by fairly abrasive materials, perhaps as a result of processing plant fibers for weaving. In the three Middle/ Late Yangshao skeletal collections examined, all but one of the recognized cases of LSAMAT was on a dentition attributed to a male individual, with the sole exception being the elderly female from Xipo burial M14. Nevertheless, considering the small number of cases observed, it would be unjustifiable to ascribe this pattern to gender-related task differences, despite the uneven distribution of such wear between the two sexes.

Unlike with LSAMAT, HWLAT was most common in the Xipo collection, being found on 5 out of 25 intact mandibles. There were 9 cases out of 59 mandibles from Xishan, and HWLAT was completely absent from the Guanjia series ($\chi^2 = 6.80$, $p = .033$, sig.). Although we did not observe this type of wear in earlier Yangshao collections (Pechenkina et al. 2002), there was one recognized case of such wear (see Pechenkina et al. 2009: fig. 3A) on a mandible from Burial M363 at the Peiligang (7000–5800 BC) site of Jiahu in central Henan (for a site description, see Li et al. 2003; Zhang et al. 2004). Outside of China, this pattern of wear is widely documented in skeletal series from communities of Inuits, Australian Aborigines, and Bushmen, among others (Merbs 1968; Lous 1970; Wallace 1975; Hinton 1981; Richards 1990). Factors proposed to have caused this wear differ partly in relation to its specific shape. They include use of the teeth for processing fibers or animal skins, for scraping blubber, a result of shifting mastication to the anterior teeth following either the loss of posterior teeth or hypersensitivity due to infection in the distal portion of the mouth, as well as the so-called stuff-and-cut method of meat eating (reviewed in Molnar 1972).

In the Middle/Late Yangshao skeletal collections we examined, this type of wear was often found on mandibles with a number of missing posterior teeth. Nevertheless, those molars that remained always retained considerable crown height and were worn to a lesser degree than the anterior dentition. Where the upper teeth were preserved, they showed matching severe wear of the dental enamel. Examination of teeth with such wear from Xishan using SEM revealed deep parallel grooves, suggesting that highly abrasive materials, probably plant fibers, were pulled downward while being clenched

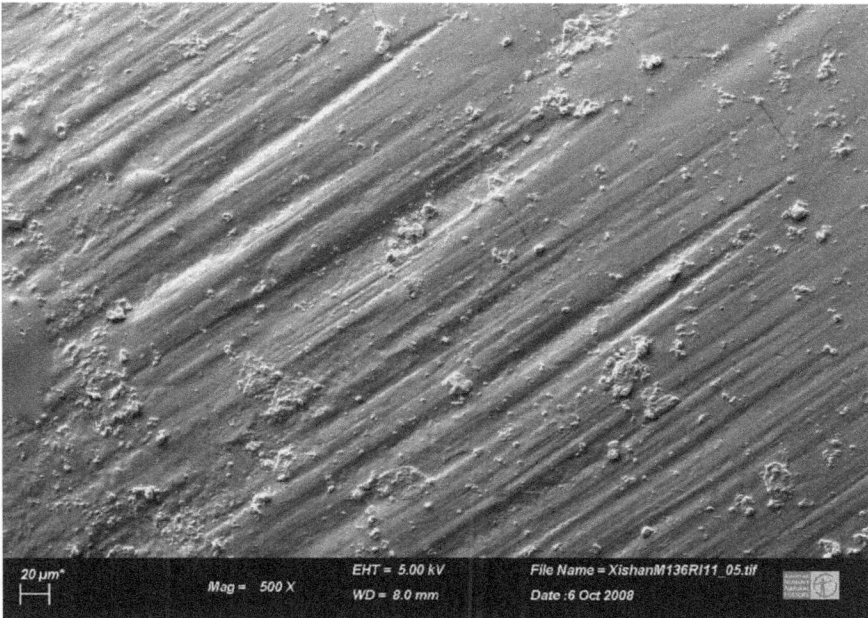

Figure 12.7. Xishan M136, wear-grooves on the lingual surface of the upper right first incisor. SEM image courtesy of Rachel Shoichet.

between the teeth (figure 12.7). In the Xishan series, HWLAT was more or less equally distributed between the sexes, with three cases found on female dental sets, one in the case of an individual of indeterminate sex, and five occurring among males. All such cases were found on the remains of individuals with an estimated age at death of 40 years and older.

The recognized cases of HWLAT in the Xishan series were often quite severe, having been associated with dental fractures and traumatic pulp exposure. For instance, in the dental set from burial M167 (male, 45+), wear was so severe that it led to traumatic pulp exposure on the right I_2, which had developed a strong labial tilt of the crown; the first incisor was lost, probably because of the same wear. The buccal aspect of the right P^3 of the same individual was fractured, resulting in a fully exposed pulp chamber. In the case of a dentition from Xishan burial M228 (female, 50+), wear of the lower teeth, while severe, did not result in a labial tilt. The same dentition had a posterior tooth with a fractured crown, while the upper anterior teeth showed pronounced wear with a labial tilt that likely resulted in an open bite.

In the Xipo collection, all recognized cases of HWLAT occurred on male individuals, perhaps not surprising, as this series consists predominantly of male skeletons. Unlike for Xishan, some of the Xipo cases of HWLAT were found on the remains of relatively younger individuals, with ages at death of

30 to 40 years. Cases of anterior wear from Xipo seem to have been milder, while the crowns of lower teeth had little, if any, labial tilt. In four instances, this wear was associated with the loss of several posterior teeth, suggesting a shift of mastication to the anterior teeth due to pain as a possible explanation. When the differences in the degree of expression between the HWLAT cases from Xipo and Xishan are considered, it seems that the specific mode of tooth use leading to development of this pattern of wear differed between the two communities. Unfortunately, poor preservation of dental enamel in the Xipo collection made SEM analysis of the pertinent specimens impossible.

Interproximal grooves (IPGs) were most common in the Xipo collection. The differences in frequency among the collections with regard to IPG is statistically significant, both when the number of affected individuals ($\chi^2 = 6.01$, $p = .049$, sig.) and when the number of grooves per individual ($\chi^2 = 24.4$, $p = .000$, sig.) are compared (table 12.4). Analysis of trait association with age at death and sex revealed no statistically significant differences (table 12.5). Interproximal grooves in the Xipo collection all occurred between the upper posterior teeth. Half of these (7/14) were associated with interproximal caries. One case was associated with severe occlusal caries penetrating deep into the dental root. In another instance, a surrounding discoloration suggests that the caries might have been removed by probing. These grooves always showed a medial tilt, in some instances very distinct, and were found on both the left and right sides of the mouth.

Interproximal grooves have previously been documented in skeletal collections from throughout the world (e.g., Brace 1975; Berryman et al. 1979; Frayer and Russell 1987; Lukacs and Pastor 1988; Formicola 1991; Frayer 1991). Their development is most typically attributed to tooth picking or probing, whether because of irritation from carious infection and/or habitually (Ubelaker et al. 1969; Formicola 1988; Lukacs and Pastor 1988; Turner 1988; Formicola 1991). Pulling animal sinew or plant fibers between the teeth (Brown and Molnar 1990), chemical erosion, and the effect of grit particles passing through the interproximal spaces between the teeth (Brothwell 1963; Wallace 1975) have also been named as possible explanatory factors.

Formicola (1991) proposed that interproximal grooves induced by habitual probing typically develop on the maxillary teeth, have a clear tilt, and impinge on the mesial and distal aspects of two adjacent teeth. Thus, the Xipo IPGs clearly conform to the pattern expected for habitual or infection incited probing. However, oral infections in general and, more specifically, interproximal caries were present in the Xishan and Guanjia collections at frequencies similar to those found for Xipo. Nevertheless, IPGs were considerably less common at either site than at Xipo. Therefore, cultural differences between Xipo and the other two communities with regard to oral hygiene can be suspected.

Enamel chipping was documented in all three of the Yangshao skeletal collections considered here, affecting individual dentitions at low to moderate frequencies in comparison to the occurrence of this indicator in skeletal collections representing past human populations from outside of China (Turner and Cadien 1969; Emerson et al. 1983; Milner 1984; Bonfiglioli et al. 2004; Consiglio 2008; Scott and Winn 2010). Overall, enamel chipping was most frequent at Xishan with regard to both the number of individuals having at least one affected tooth (49/99 [49.5 percent]) and the number of teeth affected (113/2,037 [5.6 percent]), followed by Xipo (6/30 [20.0 percent] and 25/614 [4.1 percent], respectively). The frequency of this pathology in the Guanjia collection was low (7/42 [16.7 percent] and 9/1,014 [0.9 percent]), and it affected only one or two teeth per dental set (table 12.4).

The distribution of enamel chipping among different teeth was strikingly different between the Xipo and Xishan collections (figure 12.8). At Xipo, the posterior teeth, particularly premolars, were most commonly affected (12/175), while only 1 out of 142 incisors exhibited chipped enamel. A similar pattern of the distribution of enamel chipping, albeit at a much higher frequency, has been described for Inuit populations relying on a hard and grit-laden diet (Scott and Winn 2010). At Xishan, enamel chipping was "anterior-dominant," affecting incisors at the highest frequency (37/414). Such a pattern of enamel chipping has been described for cranial series from Norway and Spain dating to between the eleventh and sixteenth centuries (Scott and Winn 2010). However, unlike in the European cases, the chipping of anterior teeth at Xishan occurred almost exclusively on maxillary dentitions.

Lukacs and Hemphill (1990), analyzing dentitions from Neolithic Mehrgarh in Pakistan (9,000–4,500 years ago), attributed a similar pattern of dental traumas observed on anterior maxillary teeth to the use of the teeth as tools. In the Xishan collection, five dental sets with all maxillary incisors affected and one set with enamel chipping concentrated on the left portion of the anterior maxilla seem to fit a pattern suggestive of using the teeth for nonmasticatory tasks. As at Xipo, wherever individual posterior teeth were chipped on other dental sets from Xishan, that condition is likely best explained by accidental traumas due to grit in the diet.

Interestingly, instances of enamel chipping showed no clear association with fractures of dental crowns. Such fractures, although uncommon, predominantly affected posterior teeth in dental sets with heavy crown wear and often occurred on dentitions that also had teeth suffering traumatic pulp exposure. At both Xishan and Xipo, but not at Guanjia, traumatic pulp ex-

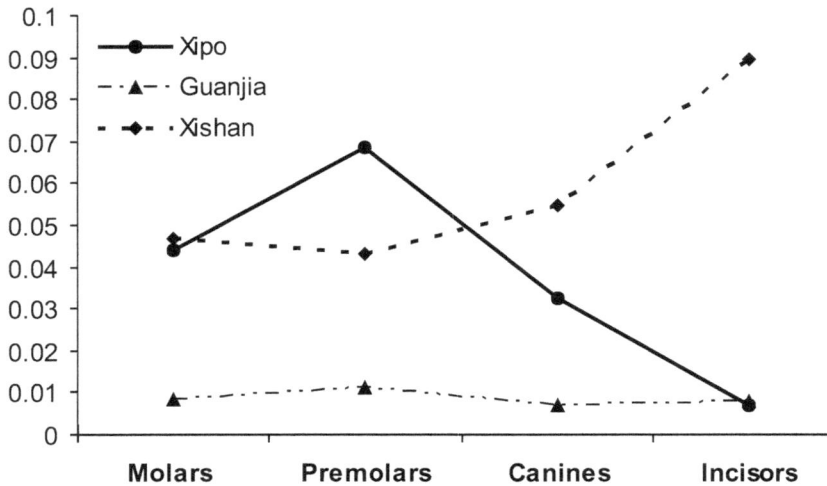

Figure 12.8. The distribution of enamel chipping among incisors, canines, premolars, and molars across the Guanjia, Xipo, and Xishan collections.

posure and crown fractures display statistically significant Spearman Rank Order correlation (R = 0.68, 29 df for Xipo and R = 0.56, 98 df for Xishan) and tended to occur on dentitions with very heavy posterior wear. Crown fractures occurring on anterior teeth affected dental sets with heavy wear of the lower teeth, as described above.

Discussion

The assumption of a simplistic relationship between caries frequency and the proportion of carbohydrates in the diet has been challenged several times (Tayles et al. 2000; Temple and Larsen 2007; Tayles et al. 2009). However, because the presence of sucrose in the oral cavity appears to be the only necessary and sufficient requirement for proliferation of the cariogenic *Streptococcus mutans* (Tayles et al. 2000; Paes Leme et al. 2006; see Pechenkina et al. chapter 18, this volume, for a more detailed discussion), it is not surprising that populations with a similar proportions of sucrose in the diet show similar rates of carious lesions. In this respect, all three collections in our study appear to be remarkably similar with respect to the development of caries, as well as the prevalence of its development on the posterior teeth, followed by the interproximal and then occlusal spaces.

On a global scale, the frequency of carious lesions per tooth in all three samples appears to be fairly high yet falls below the rates reported for some communities dependent on maize as a primary calorie source (Turner 1978;

Larsen et al. 1991; Schollmeyer and Turner 2004; Pechenkina, Vradenburg et al. 2007) or later Chinese series from millet/wheat/barley subsistence groups (Pechenkina et al., chapter 18). Evoking the classical study by Christy Turner II (1979), the caries frequencies in our study (10.5–17.0 percent of affected teeth) fall slightly above the upper end of the range reported for communities with mixed economies (0.4–10.3 percent) and toward the middle of the range for groups dependent on agriculture (2.1–26.9 percent).

In other aspects of oral health, the dentitions from the three Middle/Late Yangshao collections in our study show marked differences. The frequency of antemortem tooth loss was slightly affected by intentional tooth ablation, especially in the series from Xishan, a site located in proximity to Dawenkou settlements, where the practice was apparently widespread (e.g., Yan Yan 1972). However, as discussed above, such instances in Yangshao were very infrequent. Beyond a cariogenic diet, which should have equally favored caries-related tooth loss at all three sites, tooth loss at Xipo and to some extent at Xishan was enhanced by traumatic injuries to the dental crowns, due to either task-related tooth use or interpersonal violence. Elsewhere (Pechenkina, Benfer et al. 2007), based on the frequent occurrence of healed forearm fractures of the parrying type, we have proposed that there was a high rate of interpersonal violence in the Xipo community, possibly recreational in nature. In some instances, the loss of anterior teeth in that series could be ascribed to the effects of a blow with an anterior-posterior thrust direction. In other cases, the presence of root-pegs in the dental sockets and correspondence between atypical wear types at Xipo and Xishan indicate tooth loss due to unusual traumatic forces applied to the dental surfaces. Use of the teeth in nondietary tasks at Xipo and Xishan likely also explains elevated rates of periodontal disease and its various manifestations at these two settlements. Such tooth use could introduce abrasive particles into the oral cavity, adversely affecting gingival tissue, as well as exerting pressure on the periodontal ligament, causing damage and thus provoking an inflammatory response (Costa 1980; Clarke et al. 1986).

The Guanjia collection, representing the residents of a very small settlement well within the boundaries of the Yangshao sphere of influence, displays the least evidence of unusual patterns of wear or dental trauma. The generally lesser amount of wear and traumatic damage to the dental surfaces observed on dentitions from this site suggests consumption of a suite of fairly well-processed, possibly monotonous, food substances. At both Xipo and Xishan, traumatic changes in teeth were quite frequent, yet the distribution of their types differed greatly between the two collections. Interproximal grooves were particularly common in the Xipo collection, and we have tentatively suggested that this type of wear might reflect an oral hygiene practice specific to the site. In the Xishan series, the anterior teeth were the most frequently affected by various types of traumatic wear.

These included enamel chipping of multiple teeth and—in one case—deep, unilateral wear grooves, suggesting that some type of fiber was pulled forward and down while clenched between the front teeth. Heavy wear of the lower teeth, coincident with labial rounding and LSAMAT, also suggests that the front teeth were used for a wide range of specialized nondietary tasks at Xishan. Perhaps the high frequencies of unusual wear and dental traumas found in the collection from Xishan were a consequence of increased opportunities for trade and exchange of goods and ideas with Dawenkou neighbors, favoring development of specialized crafts, some of which might have required using the teeth in novel ways. A more complete understanding of the archaeological contexts along with further evaluation of Dawenkou patterns of tooth wear are necessary prerequisites to validating this suggestion. The Xipo collection had the highest frequency of heavily worn lower front teeth. Furthermore, the manner of their wear—flat—was quite different from that found at Xishan, suggesting yet a different type of task-related tooth use.

Conclusions

In line with expectations based on the largely millet-based diet of Middle/Late Yangshao farmers, caries frequencies and distribution showed considerable consistency across the three assemblages studied. While the Guanjia series, representing a smaller settlement, evidenced a slightly lower rate of caries development, as also expected, that result was not statistically significant.

Indicators of dental disease that are less affected by the presence of carbohydrates in food items—including antemortem tooth loss, development of periodontal disease, calculus accretion, and periapical abscesses—differed considerably across the three collections, most likely in relation to differing tasks that were performed with the aid of the teeth and perhaps also because of differing attitudes toward intentional ablation, as well as differing frequencies of interpersonal violence, differing perspectives on oral hygiene, and probably differing approaches to food processing and food preparation.

The Xishan assemblage, derived from a site located in the contact area between the Yangshao and Dawenkou cultural territories, displayed the greatest variation in task-related wear and dental trauma. This diversity of tooth wear may proceed from there having been a greater variety of tasks performed with the teeth at Xishan, in line with He Deliang's (2007) supposition that populations resident in the Dawenkou-Yangshao contact area benefited from cultural exchange. Evidence for probable tooth ablation of various kinds was also recorded in the Xishan series, only some of which accord with the typical Dawenkou pattern of upper lateral incisor removal. One cranium from Xipo also gave evidence for the removal of a lateral incisor, suggesting at least the possibility that this practice penetrated deeper into Yangshao territory.

Literature Cited

An Z. 1959. Discussion of Neolithic culture in the Yellow River valley. *Kaogu* (考古) 10: 559–65.

An Z. 1988. Chinese prehistoric agriculture. *Kaogu* (考古) 4: 375–84.

Bass WM. 1987. *Human osteology: A laboratory and field manual.* Columbia: Missouri Archaeological Society.

Bellwood P. 2005. *First farmers: The origins of agricultural societies.* Malden, MA: Blackwell.

Berryman HE, Owsley DW, Henderson AM. 1979. Non-carious interproximal grooves in Arikara Indian dentitions. *American Journal of Physical Anthropology* 50: 209–12.

Bonfiglioli B, Mariotti V, Facchini F, Belcastro MG, Condemi S. 2004. Masticatory and non-masticatory dental modifications in the Epipalaeolithic necropolis of Taforalt (Morocco). *International Journal of Osteoarchaeology* 14: 448–56.

Brace CL. 1975. Comment on "Did La Ferrassie I use his teeth as tools." *Current Anthropology* 16: 396–97.

Brown T, Molnar S. 1990. Interproximal grooving and task activity in Australia. *American Journal of Physical Anthropology* 81: 545–53.

Brothwell DR. 1963. The macroscopic dental pathology of some earlier populations. In: Brothwell DR, editor. *Dental anthropology.* Oxford, UK: Pergamon Press. Pp. 271–88.

Buikstra JE, Ubelaker DH, editors. 1994. *Standards for data collection from human skeletal remains: Proceedings of a seminar at the Field Museum of Natural History.* Arkansas Archaeological Survey Research Series no. 44. Fayetteville.

Burzynski NJ, Escobar VH. 1983. Classification and genetics of numeric anomalies of dentition. *Birth Defects Original Article Series* 19: 95–106.

Chang KC. 1986. *The archaeology of ancient China.* 4th ed. New Haven, CT: Yale University Press.

Clarke NG, Carey SE, Srikandi W, Hirsch RS, Leppard PI. 1986. Periodontal disease in ancient populations. *American Journal of Physical Anthropology* 71: 173–83.

Consiglio C. 2008. Non masticatory dental lesions in the study of biology and behaviour of ancient populations: The contribution of the stereomicroscopy and scanning electron microscopy. Ph.D. dissertation, University of Bologna.

Corruccini RS, Handler JS, Mutaw RJ, Lange FW. 1982. Osteology of a slave burial population from Barbados, West Indies. *American Journal of Physical Anthropology* 59: 443–59.

Corruccini RS, Jacobi KP, Handler JS, Aufderheide AC. 1987. Implications of tooth root hypercementosis in a Barbados slave skeletal collection. *American Journal of Physical Anthropology* 74: 179–84.

Costa RL Jr. 1980. Age, sex and antemortem loss of teeth in prehistoric Eskimo samples from Point Hope and Kodiak Island, Alaska. *American Journal of Physical Anthropology* 53: 579–87.

Crawford GW, Underhill A, Zhao Z, Lee GA, Feinman G, Nicholas L, Luan F, Yu H, Fang H, Cai F. 2005. Late Neolithic plant remains from northern China: Preliminary results from Liangchengzhen, Shandong. *Current Anthropology* 46: 309–17.

Dai X. 1998. The development of the Neolithic cultures in the middle reaches of the Yellow River. *Kaogu Xuebao* (考古研究所) 4: 389–418.

Doi N, Tanaka Y. 1988. Ritual tooth ablation in the Kofun period. In: Nagai Masafumi Taikan

Kinen Ronbunshu Kankokai. *The genesis of the Japanese population and culture*. Tokyo: Rokko. Pp. 197–215.

Emerson TE, Milner GR, Jackson DK. 1983. *The Florence Street site*. Urbana: University of Illinois Press.

Erdal YS, Duyar I. 1999. A new correction procedure for calibrating dental caries frequency. *American Journal of Physical Anthropology* 108: 237–40.

Eshed V, Gopher A, Hershkovitz I. 2006. Tooth wear and dental pathology at the advent of agriculture: New evidence from the Levant. *American Journal of Physical Anthropology* 30: 145–59.

Fan W. 2000. Guanjia yizhi fajue huo zhongyao chengguo (A fruitful excavation at the Guanjia site). *Zhongguo Wenwubao* (中国文物报), Beijing, February 13.

Formicola V. 1988. Interproximal grooving of teeth: Additional evidence and interpretation. *Current Anthropology* 29: 663–71.

Formicola V. 1991. Interproximal grooving: Different appearances, different etiologies. *American Journal of Physical Anthropology* 86: 85–86.

Frayer DW. 1991. On the etiology of interproximal grooves. *American Journal of Physical Anthropology* 85: 299–304.

Frayer DW, Russell MD. 1987. Artificial grooves on the Krapina Neanderthal teeth. *American Journal of Physical Anthropology* 74: 393–405.

Fung C. 2002. The drinks are on us: Ritual, social status, and practice in Dawenkou burials, North China. *Journal of East Asian Archaeology* 2: 67–92.

Garib DG, Alencar BM, Pereira Lauris JR, Baccetti T. 2010. Agenesis of maxillary lateral incisors and associated dental anomalies. *American Journal of Orthodontics* and *Dentofacial Orthopedics* 137: 732–33.

Gong JZ. 2007. Inequalities in diet and health during the intensification of agriculture in Neolithic China. Honors B.A. thesis, Harvard University.

Guojia Wenwuju (State Administration of Cultural Heritage). 2005. Middle Yangshao cemetery and moat at the Xipo site in Lingbao, Henan. In: *2005 Zhongguo Zhongyao Kaogu Faxian (Major Archaeological Discoveries in China in 2005)*. Beijing: Cultural Relics Publishing House.

Han K, Nakahashi T. 1996. A comparative study of ritual tooth ablation in ancient China and Japan. *Anthropological Science* 104: 43–64.

Han K, Pan Q. 1982. Late Neolithic human skeletons from Hedang site, Foshan, Guangdong. *Acta Anthropologica Sinica* (人类学学报) 1: 42–51.

He D. 2007. Reexamination of the origin of civilization in Haidai area and the Central Plains. *Cultural Relics of Central Plains* (中原文物) 6: 22–38.

Hillson SW. 1979. Diet and dental disease. *World Archaeology* 11: 147–62.

Hillson S. 2001. Recording dental caries in archaeological human remains. *International Journal of Osteoarchaeology* 11: 249–89.

Hinton RJ. 1981. Form and patterning of anterior tooth wear among aboriginal human groups. *American Journal of Physical Anthropology* 54: 555–64.

Indriati E, Buikstra JE. 2001. Coca chewing in prehistoric coastal Peru: Dental evidence. *American Journal of Physical Anthropology* 114: 242–57.

Hu Y, He D, Dong Y, Wang Ch, Gao M, Lan Y. 2005. Stable isotopic analysis on human bones in Xigongqiao site, Tengzhou, Shangdong. *Quaternary Sciences* (第四纪研究) 25: 561–7.

Irish JD, Turner CG II. 1987. More lingual surface irritation of the maxillary anterior teeth in American Indians: Prehistoric Panamanians. *American Journal of Physical Anthropology* 73: 209–13.

Irish JD, Turner CG II. 1997. Brief communication: First evidence of LSAMAT in non-Native

Americans; Historic Senegalese from West Africa. *American Journal of Physical Anthropology* 102: 141–46.

Işcan MY. 1991. The aging process in the rib: An analysis of sex- and race-related morphological variation. *American Journal of Human Biology* 3: 617–23.

Işcan MY, Loth SR, Wright RK. 1984. Metamorphosis of the sternal rib end: A new method to estimate age at death in white males. *American Journal of Physical Anthropology* 65: 147–56.

Lanfranco LP, Eggers S. 2010. The usefulness of caries frequency, depth, and location in determining cariogenicity and past subsistence: A test on early and later agriculturalists from the Peruvian coast. *American Journal of Physical Anthropology* 143: 75–91.

Langsjoen OM. 1996. Dental effects of diet and coca-leaf chewing on two prehistoric cultures of northern Chile. *American Journal of Physical Anthropology* 101: 475–89.

Larsen CS. 1985. Dental modifications and tool use in the western Great Basin. *American Journal of Physical Anthropology* 67: 393–402.

Larsen CS, Shavit R, Griffins MC. 1991. Dental caries evidence for dietary change: An archaeological context. In: Kelley MA, Larsen CS, editors. *Advances in dental anthropology*. New York: Wiley-Liss. Pp. 179–202.

Larsen CS, Teaford MF, Sandford MK. 1998. Teeth as tools at Tutu: Extramasticatory behavior in prehistoric St. Thomas, U.S. Virgin Islands. In: Lukacs JR, editor. *Human dental development, morphology, and pathology: A tribute to A. A. Dahlberg*. University of Oregon Anthropological Papers. Eugene. Pp. 401–20.

Lee G, Crawford G, Chen X. 2007. Plants and people from the Early Neolithic to Shang periods in North China. *Proceedings of the National Academy of Sciences* 104: 1087–92.

Leider AS, Garbarino VE. 1987. Generalized hypercementosis. *Oral Surgery, Oral Medicine, Oral Pathology, Oral Radiology and Endodontology* 63: 375–80.

Lev-Tov Chattah N, Smith P. 2006. Variation in occlusal dental wear of two Chalcolithic populations in the southern Levant. *American Journal of Physical Anthropology* 130: 471–79.

Li X, Harbottle G, Zhang Z, Wang C. 2003. The earliest writing? Sign use in the seventh millennium BC at Jiahu, Henan Province, China. *Antiquity* 77: 31–44.

Lieverse AR. 1999. Diet and the aetiology of dental calculus. *International Journal of Osteoarchaeology* 9: 219–32.

Littleton J, Frohlich B. 1993. Fish-eaters and farmers: Dental pathology in the Arabian Gulf. *American Journal of Physical Anthropology* 92: 427–47.

Liu L. 2004. *The Chinese Neolithic: Trajectories of early states*. Cambridge: Cambridge University Press.

Liu L. 2009. State emergence in early China. *Annual Review of Anthropology* 38: 217–32.

Lous I. 1970. The dental system as a tool. *Dental Abstracts* 15: 457–58.

Lovejoy CO, Meindl RS, Mensforth RP, Barton TJ. 1985. Multifactorial determination of skeletal age at death: A method and blind tests of its accuracy. *American Journal of Physical Anthropology* 68: 1–14.

Lukacs JR. 1981. Dental pathology and nutritional patterns of South Asian megalith-builders: The evidence from Iron Age Mahurjhari. *Proceedings of the American Philosophical Society* 125: 220–37.

Lukacs JR. 1989. Dental paleopathology: Methods for reconstructing health status and dietary patterns in prehistory. In: Iscan Y, Kennedy KAR, editors. *Reconstructing life from the skeleton*. New York: Alan R. Liss. Pp. 261–86.

Lukacs JR. 1992. Dental paleopathology and agricultural intensification in South Asia: New evidence from Bronze Age Harappa. *American Journal of Physical Anthropology* 87: 133–50.

Lukacs JR. 1995. The "caries correction factor": A new method of calibrating dental caries rates to compensate for antemortem loss of teeth. *International Journal of Osteoarchaeology* 5: 151–56.

Lukacs JR. 2007. Dental trauma and antemortem tooth loss in prehistoric Canary Islanders: Prevalence and contributing factors. *International Journal of Osteoarchaeology* 17: 157–73.

Lukacs JR, Hemphill BE. 1990. Traumatic injuries of prehistoric teeth: New evidence from Baluchistan and Punjab Provinces, Pakistan. *Anthropologischer Anzeiger* 48: 351–63.

Lukacs JR, Largaespada LL. 2006. Explaining sex differences in dental caries prevalence: Saliva, hormones, and "life-history" etiologies. *American Journal of Human Biology* 18: 540–55.

Lukacs JR, Pastor RF. 1988. Activity-induced patterns of dental abrasion in prehistoric Pakistan: Evidence from Mehrgarh and Harappa. *American Journal of Physical Anthropology* 76: 377–98.

Ma H. 1987. Survey of Wei River valley Neolithic sites, Shanxi, China. *Kaogu* (考古) 1987: 769–72, 859.

Ma X. 2003. Emergent social complexity in the Yangshao culture: Analyses of settlement patterns and faunal remains from Lingbao, western Henan, China. Ph.D. dissertation, La Trobe University, Australia.

Ma X, Li X, Yang H. 2005. *A great breakthrough in the fifth excavation at Xipo in Lingbao, Henan.* Zhongguo Wenwubao 26. Zhengzhou: Henan Provincial Institute of Cultural Relics and Archaeology.

Ma X, Li X, Yang H. 2006. A study of jade articles from the Yangshao cultural cemetery at Xipo in Lingbao. *Zhongyuan Wenwu* 3: 72–76.

Mann RW, Jantz RL, Bass WM, Willey PS. 1991. Maxillary suture obliteration: A visual method for estimating skeletal age. *Journal of Forensic Sciences* 36: 781–91.

Meindl RS, Lovejoy OC, Mensforth RP, Walker RA. 1985. A revised method of age determination using the os pubis, with a review and tests of accuracy of other current methods of pubic symphyseal aging. *American Journal of Physical Anthropology* 68: 29–45.

Merbs CF. 1968. Anterior tooth loss in Arctic populations. *Southwestern Journal of Anthropology* 24: 20–32.

Meskin LH, Gorlin RJ. 1963. Agenesis and peg-shaped permanent maxillary lateral incisors. *Journal of Dental Research* 42: 1476–79.

Milner GR. 1984. Dental caries in the permanent dentition of a Mississippian period population from the American Midwest. *Collegium Antropologicum* 8: 77–91.

Milner GR, Larsen CS. 1991. Teeth as artifacts of human behavior: intentional mutilation and accidental modification. In: Kelley MA, Larsen CS, editors. *Advances in dental anthropology.* New York: Wiley-Liss. Pp. 357–78.

Molnar S. 1972. Tooth wear and culture: A survey of tooth functions among some prehistoric populations. *Current Anthropology* 13: 511–26.

Nelson GC, Lukacs JR, Yule P. 1999. Dates, caries, and early tooth loss during the Iron Age of Oman. *American Journal of Physical Anthropology* 108: 333–43.

Nelsen K, Tayles N, Domett K. 2001. Missing lateral incisors in Iron Age South-East Asians as possible indicators of dental agenesis. *Archives of Oral Biology* 46: 963–71.

Paes Leme AF, Koo H, Bellato CM, Bedi G, Cury JA. 2006. The role of sucrose in cariogenic dental biofilm formation: New insight. *Journal of Dental Research* 85: 878–87.

Papathanasiou A. 2005. Health status of the Neolithic population of Alepotrypa Cave, Greece. *American Journal of Physical Anthropology* 126: 377–90.

Pechenkina EA, Ambrose SH, Ma X, Benfer RA Jr. 2005. Reconstructing northern Chinese Neolithic subsistence practices by isotopic analysis. *Journal of Archaeological Science* 32: 1176–89.

Pechenkina EA, Benfer RA Jr., Ma X. 2007. Diet and health in the Neolithic of the Wei and Yellow

River basins, northern China. In: Cohen MN, Crane-Kramer GMM, editors. *Ancient health: Skeletal indicators of agricultural and economic intensification.* Gainesville: University Press of Florida. Pp. 255–72.

Pechenkina EA, Benfer RA Jr., Zhijun W. 2002. Diet and health changes with the intensification of millet agriculture at the end of Chinese Neolithic. *American Journal of Physical Anthropology* 117: 15–36.

Pechenkina EA, Ma X, Eng J, Shoichet R, Wei D, Zhang Q, Li X, Fan W, Zhu H. 2009. Reconstructing behavior in ancient China from human skeletal remains. *SAA Archaeological Record* 9: 14, 36–39.

Pechenkina EA, Vradenburg JA, Benfer RA Jr., Farnum JF. 2007. Skeletal biology of the central Peruvian coast: Consequences of changing population density and progressive dependence on maize agriculture. In: Cohen MN, Crane-Kramer GMM, editors. *Ancient health: Skeletal indicators of agricultural and economic intensification.* Gainesville: University Press of Florida. Pp. 93–112.

Pedersen PO. 1949. *The East Greenland Eskimo dentition, numerical variations and anatomy.* Meddelelser om Grönland, vol. 142, no. 3. Copenhagen: Biance Lunos Bogtrykken.

Peterson CE, Lu X, Drennan RD, Zhu D. 2010. Hongshan chiefly communities in Neolithic Northeastern China. *Proceedings of the National Academy of Sciences* 107: 5756–61.

Ren S. 1996. Several major achievements in early Neolithic China ca. 5000 BC. *Kaogu* (考古) 6: 37–49.

Ren S, Wu Y. 1999. Fifty years of Neolithic archaeology in China. *Kaogu* (考古) 9: 11–22.

Richards LC. 1990. Tooth wear and temporomandibular joint change in Australian aboriginal populations. *American Journal of Physical Anthropology* 82: 377–84.

Sakaue K. 2006. Application of the Suchey-Brooks system of pubic age estimation to recent Japanese skeletal material. *Anthropological Science* 114: 59–64.

Schollmeyer KG, Turner CG II. 2004. Dental caries, prehistoric diet, and the Pithouse to Pueblo transition in southwestern Colorado. *American Antiquity* 69: 569–82.

Scott GR, Winn JR. 2010. Dental chipping: Contrasting patterns of microtrauma in Inuit and European populations. *International Journal of Osteoarchaeology* 21: 723–31.

Su B. 1999. *New research on the origins of Chinese civilization.* Beijing: Sanlian Press.

Sun G. 2001. Discovery and research on Yangshao culture in Henan. *Cultural Relics of Central Plains* (中原文物) 5: 41–52.

Takenaka M, Mine K, Tsuchimochi K, Shimada K. 2001. Tooth removal during ritual ablation in the Jomon period. *Bulletin of the Indo-Pacific Prehistory Association* 21: 49–52.

Tayles N, Domett K, Halcrow S. 2009. Can dental caries be interpreted as evidence of farming? The Asian experience. *Frontiers of Oral Biology* 13: 162–66.

Tayles N, Domett K, Nelsen K. 2000. Agriculture and dental Caries? The case of rice in prehistoric Southeast Asia. *World Archaeology* 32: 68–83.

Temple DH, Larsen CS. 2007. Dental caries prevalence as evidence for agriculture and subsistence variation during the Yayoi period in prehistoric Japan: Biocultural interpretations of an economy in transition. *American Journal of Physical Anthropology* 134: 501–12.

Turner CG II. 1978. Dental caries and early Ecuadorian agriculture. *American Antiquity* 43: 694–97.

Turner CG II. 1979. Dental anthropological indications of agriculture among the Jomon people of central Japan: X. peopling of the Pacific. *American Journal of Physical Anthropology* 51: 619–36.

Turner CG II. 1988. Interproximal grooving of teeth: Additional evidence and interpretation. *Current Anthropology* 29: 664–65.

Turner CG II. 1990. Major features of Sundadonty and Sinodonty, including suggestions about

East Asian microevolution, population history, and Late Pleistocene relationships with Australian Aboriginals. *American Journal of Physical Anthropology* 82: 295–317.

Turner CG II, Cadien JD. 1969. Dental chipping in Aleuts, Eskimos and Indians. *American Journal of Physical Anthropology* 31: 303–10.

Turner CG II, Cheuiche Machado LM. 1983. A new dental wear pattern and evidence for high carbohydrate consumption in a Brazilian Archaic skeletal population. *American Journal of Physical Anthropology* 61: 125–30.

Ubelaker DH, Phenice TW, Bass WM. 1969. Artificial interproximal grooving of the teeth in American Indians. *American Journal of Physical Anthropology* 30: 145–49.

Underhill AP. 2000. An analysis of mortuary ritual at the Dawenkou site, Shandong, China. *Journal of East Asian Archaeology* 2: 93–127.

Wallace JA. 1975. Did La Ferrassie I use his teeth as a tool? *Current Anthropology* 16: 393–401.

Wang J. 1985. The earliest agriculture in Henan Province and surroundings according to Peiligang site tools. *Nongye Kaogu* (农业考古) 2: 81–85.

Wang X, Sun C, Zhang J. 1998. Status and prospect of research on the origin of Chinese cultivated rice (*Oryza sativa* L.). *Nongye Kaogu* (农业考古) 1: 11–20.

Watson JT. 2008. Changes in food processing and occlusal dental wear during the early agricultural period in northwest Mexico. *American Journal of Physical Anthropology* 135: 92–99.

Wei X, Kong Z, Liu C. 2001. The finding and importance of rice remains from the Yangshao cultural site of Nanjiakou in Sanmenxian. *Nongye Kaogu* (农业考古) 3: 77–79.

Wu R. 1982. Lun Dawenkou wenhua de leixing yu fenqi (On the types and periodization of the Dawenkou culture). *Kaogu Xuebao* (考古学报) 3: 261–82.

Wu R. 1987. Shilun Dawenkou wenhua de san chu mudi (A discussion of three cemeteries of the Dawenkou culture). *Kaogu Xuebao* (考古学报) 3: 275–92.

Wu X, Shao X, Wang H. 1982. Sex differences and sex determination of the innominate bone of modern Han nationality. *Acta Anthropologica Sinica* (人类学学报) 1: 118–20.

Yan W. 1982. Origin of rice cultivation in China. *Nongye Kaogu* (农业考古) 1: 19–31.

Yan Y. 1972. Research report on Neolithic human skeletons of Dawenkou Culture. *Kaogu Xuebao* (考古学报) 1: 91–122.

Yan W. 1992. Origins of agriculture and animal husbandry in China. In: Aikens CM, Rhee SN, editors. *Pacific Northeast Asia in prehistory.* Pullman: Washington State University Press. Pp. 113–23.

Yan X, Xia C. 2001. On the periodization and character of the Dawenkou culture in northern Anhui and eastern Henan. *Huaxia Archaeology* (华夏考古) 3: 36–51, 86.

Yuan J, Flad RK. 2002. Pig domestication in ancient China. *Antiquity* 76: 724–32.

Zhang J, Xiao X, Lee YK. 2004. The early development of music: Analysis of the Jiahu bone flutes. *Antiquity* 78: 769–79.

Zhang X. 2003. A brief analysis of Dawenkou cultural elements in the area south of Yellow River. *Huaxia Archaeology* (华夏考古) 4: 39–70.

Zhang Z. 1986. A further study on the relationship between morphologic features of pubic symphyses and age estimation. *Acta Anthropologica Sinica* (人类学学报) 5: 130–37.

Zhang Z, Qiao L. 1992. Study of the Hougang I culture. *Kaogu Xuebao* (考古学报) 3: 261–80.

13

Life on the Frontier

The Paleopathology of Human Remains from
the Chinese Early Imperial Taojiazhai Mortuary Site

ZHANG JINGLEI

This chapter presents data and analysis of the skeletal biology of a set of human remains recovered from the early imperial period Taojiazhai (陶家寨) cemetery, located in Qinghai Province, on the frontier between the Loess Plateau and the Qinghai-Tibet Plain. To the east were the farming communities of the Central Plains of China. To the north and northwest was Xinjiang (新疆), a region populated by nomadic pastoralists and agropastoralists, once partially controlled by the Xiongnu (匈奴) polity. When Qinghai was constituted as a buffer zone between steppe nomads and the farming populations of early imperial China by the Han dynasty (汉朝) (206 BC–AD 220), it was the scene of ongoing political turmoil based in a struggle for control over territory and resources. Considering the precarious location of the source population for the Taojiazhai collection, this chapter recruits skeletal pathology to explore to what extent people buried at Taojiazhai were involved in violent confrontations, as well as to assess the general epidemiological profile of the area and the relative contribution of different subsistence practices to the local diet.

Historical records (Cui et al. 1999) and anthropological research indicate that during the rule of the Qin and Han dynasties the area around the city of Xining was largely occupied by the Qiang (羌) (Han et al. 2005; Li et al. 2009). Xiongnu nomadic tribes, active to the northwest of Qinghai, were a constant threat to the northern borders of a newly unified imperial China. Xiongnu tribes of the Ordos steppe region were first mentioned in the chronicles of the Qin dynasty, when construction of the Great Wall was instigated during the rule of Qin Shi Huang Di (秦始皇帝), ostensibly to protect against their frequent invasions. Despite these efforts, Han dynasty records indicate that the Xiongnu continued to be a constant problem for the Han court, with raids breaching the Great Wall defenses and frequent demands for tribute (Cui et al. 1999). Regarding this perpetual struggle, Sima Qian, a prominent historian of the Han dynasty, wrote circa 109–91 BC, "The Son of Heaven has set out to punish the Xiongnu. In my humble opinion, every worthy man should be willing to fight to the death to defend the borders, and every person with wealth ought to contribute to the expense. If this were done, then the Xiongnu could be wiped out!" (Watson 1993: 73).

In 121 BC, during the early years of the reign of Emperor Wu of the Western Han dynasty, General Huo Qubing (霍去病), also known as the Piaoji General, was dispatched to fight the Xiongnu. His troops succeeded in subjugating a number of their tribes and established four counties in Hexi. At about the same time, to strengthen the imperial border and enforce the Immigrating Frontier Area Policy, the Western Han government sent a large number of people into the region to build a military fort called Xipingting. Starting in 111 BC, Han Chinese increasingly moved into Qinghai, especially into the eastern part of the province, mixing with the local residents. Thus, the peoples of Qinghai were gradually brought under Han rule.

In 61 BC, during the rule of Emperor Xuan, General Zhao Chongguo was ordered to deploy his troops to open up "wasteland" in Qinghai for the cultivation of farm crops. After defeating a Xianling-Qiang force led by Yang Yu, General Zhao set up the "Jincheng Prefecture." Thereafter, the Western Han government created seven counties in the area ruled by Jincheng: Linqiang (now part of Huangyuan County); Anyi (now part of Pinan County); Poqiang (now part of Ledu County); Yunwu (now part of Minhe County); Haomen (now part of Yongdeng County, in Gansu Province); Yunjie (now part of the Honggu District of Lanzhou City in Gansu Province); and Heguan (now part of Guide County). During the Jin dynasty, Han migration into the area increased dramatically, and evidence of Han impact on material culture in the Qinghai area from that time forward is overwhelming (Cui et al. 1999).

The Burial Context and Assemblage

The Taojiazhai cemetery is located in Qinghai Province, north of the provincial capital of Xining (西宁), in the upper/middle reaches of the Huang (湟) River valley (figure 13.1). The eastern boundary of the cemetery runs along the Beichuan River, while to the west it is flanked by Daye Mountain. A central point within the known area of the cemetery is located at coordinates 35°41.348' N and 101°44.443' E, 2,330 meters above sea level (Xu 1984). The

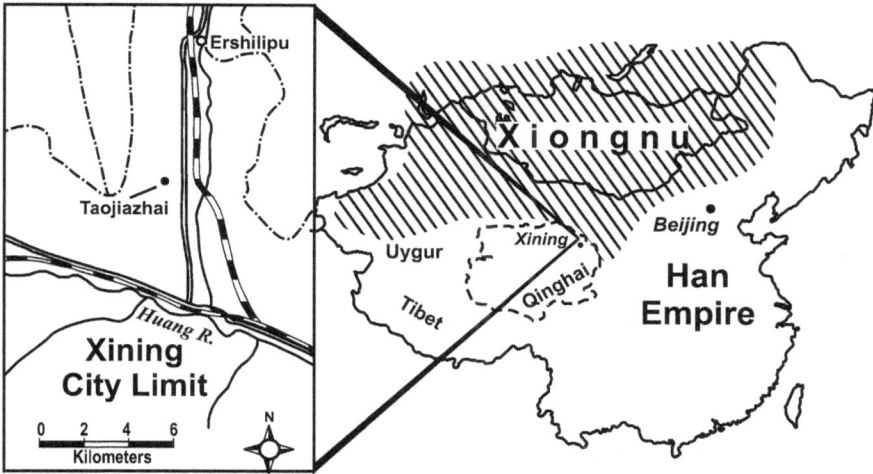

Figure 13.1. Map showing the location of the Taojiazhai archaeological site in Qinghai Province, in relation to the modern capital, the Xiongnu polity, and the core of the Han empire.

human skeletons discussed in this chapter were recovered during rescue excavations carried out between 2002 and 2005 (Qinghai Provincial Institute of Cultural Relics and Archaeology 2007). All human skeletal remains excavated from Taojiazhai are curated at the Anthropology Center of Jilin University, in Changchun.

Based on stylistic analysis of the associated funerary objects and tomb construction, the human remains recovered from Taojiazhai date to early imperial times, spanning the Han (汉) (206 BC–AD 220) to Jin (晋) (AD 265–420) dynasties. Burials were found mainly in large-scale clusters, with the individual interments made in wooden coffins and incorporating numerous funerary offerings. These clusters are generally interpreted as having corresponded to family groups.

The purpose of this chapter is to add to the existing corpus of skeletal evidence on human health and morbidity during early imperial times in China, as well as to highlight some comparisons with published data on other human skeletal collections dating to the period immediately after the original unification of China under centralized rule. Considering the specific historical context of the Taojiazhai assemblage, particular attention has been given to the distribution of traumatic injury and degenerative joint disease, which are construed as possible evidence of extreme physicality and aggressive interpersonal encounters, as well as to the prevalence of chronic infections that probably spread into the area via routes of extralocal contact. The long bone lengths of adult individuals and the frequency of porotic hyperostosis have been assessed to test whether or not the somewhat precarious geopolitical

Table 13.1. Age at death distribution estimated for human remains from the Taojiazhai site

Age group	Males (%)	Females (%)	Indeterminate (%)	Total (%)
0–2	0 (0.00)	0 (0.00)	7 (23.33)	7 (2.07)
3–6	1 (0.63)	1 (0.68)	6 (20.00)	8 (2.37)
7–14	5 (3.13)	0 (0.00)	15 (50.00)	20 (5.92)
15–24	15 (9.38)	25 (16.89)	2 (6.67)	42 (12.43)
25–34	44 (27.50)	45 (30.41)	0 (0.00)	89 (26.33)
35–54	92 (57.50)	66 (44.59)	0 (0.00)	158 (46.75)
55+	3 (1.88)	11 (7.43)	0 (0.00)	14 (4.14)
Total	160 (100.00)	148 (100.00)	30 (100.00)	338 (100.00)

circumstances that pertained to the Qinghai area during early imperial times had any particularly adverse consequences for general community health. In the description of pathological conditions, the present study adheres to standards established by Chen Shixian (1980), Pi Xin (2000), and Donald Ortner (2003).

The remains of a total of 378 individuals were recovered from burials at Taojiazhai, of which 175 were identified as male and 167 as female; the remainder were of indeterminate sex. An overwhelming majority of the interments were those of adults, indicating that the recovered assemblage does not accurately reflect age-specific mortality. Of the 338 skeletons that were sufficiently complete that the age at death of the individual could be confidently determined, only 7 were the remains of persons less than 3 years of age; 28 belonged to children between 3 and 14 years of age, 42 were of young adults (15–24 years old), 89 were assessed to have been between 25 and 34 years of age, 158 were of older adults of 35 to 54 years of age, and 14 were assigned ages of greater than 55 years (table 13.1). Female skeletons were overrepresented in the young adult category (25 females vs. 15 males). This skewing is likely explained by the high mortality of young females during childbirth, as proposed for some skeletal assemblages from an earlier time frame, where a similar age distribution was observed (Shang 2002).

Traumatic Injury

For the purposes of this study, fractures are defined as the complete or partial discontinuity of bone tissue caused by a force that exceeded the capacity of this tissue to accommodate strain. Fractures were classified as complete or partial, simple, multiple, and depressed or compressed; as antemortem (healed) or perimortem (no evidence of healing); as caused by application of sharp or blunt force; and as either direct or indirect (Lovell 1997).

Given the relatively large number of individuals represented in the collection, only a small proportion of the remains show evidence of traumatic injury. Of 378 complete skeletons, only 24, or 6.35 percent, had one or more bones affected by fractures. Three skeletons displayed multiple injuries on bones from different parts of the skeleton. For instance, one skeleton (M32:1) had a depressed fracture of the frontal bone (figure 13.2A), fractures of the ulna and radius, and fractured ribs. Fractures of the mandible, tibia, and fibula were observed on the remains of another individual (M22:1). A number of the fractures seen in the series from Taojiazhai affected the facial skeleton and cranium in a manner suggesting the results of violent interpersonal confrontation.

Rib fractures were the most frequent, found on the remains of eight individuals. Because ribs were often too poorly preserved to permit accurate

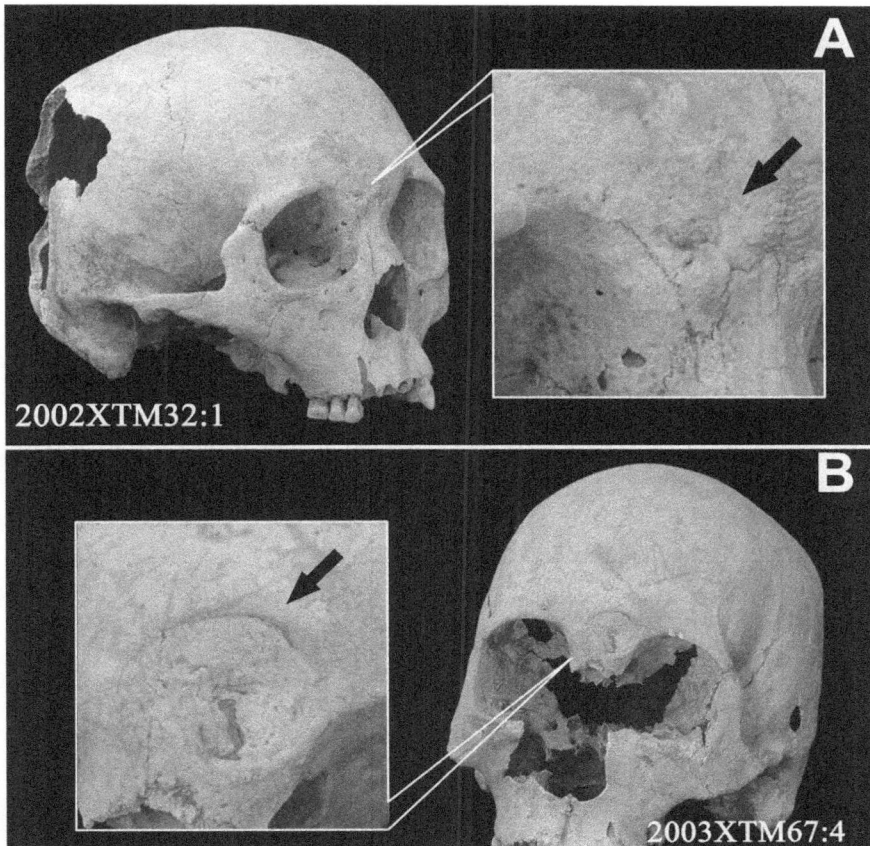

Figure 13.2. Examples of blunt force traumas, probably inflicted during face-to-face confrontation. A, Cranium from M32:1, with a healed depressed injury of the frontal bone. B, Cranium from M67:4, with a depressed healed depressed blunt force trauma of the frontal bone.

evaluation of their pathology, the actual number and proportion of these frac-tures could have been even greater. Apart from the ribs, postcranial bones affected by traumatic injuries included the clavicle ($n = 1$), sternum ($n = 1$), scapula ($n = 2$), humerus ($n = 1$), ulna ($n = 2$), radius ($n = 2$), tibia ($n = 2$), and fibula ($n = 1$). Healed cranial fractures were observed on frontal ($n = 2$), nasal ($n = 2$), parietal ($n = 1$), and zygomatic ($n = 1$) bones; evidence of peri-mortem sharp force traumas was found on an occipital bone and extending onto a parietal, as well as on maxillae. Two traumas of the mandible were also recorded. More detailed descriptions of these injuries follow below.

Depressed Fractures

Depressed fractures are frequently inflicted on the cranial bones using a large blunt object. Blunt force applied at low velocity or with a weak thrust often results in a spherical depression with a smooth surface. Application of greater force or delivery at a higher velocity results in cone-shaped fractures, with distinct fragments surrounded by a ringlike fracture line. Of 343 adult crania present, 3 in the Taojiazhai collection displayed depressed fractures (0.875 percent). These include a wound imposed on the parietal bone (M24:11) and two fractures of the frontal sinus between the eyebrows (M32:1 and M67:4 [figure 13.2A,B]); one is more toward the left and the other more toward the right.

The cranium of an older male individual (M24:1), having an estimated age at death of over 50 years, displays an oblong fracture of the right parietal in the area directly above the lambdoid suture. The depressed area is smooth, measuring approximately 60 mm along the major axis and 26 mm along the lesser axis; it is surrounded by a barely discernible fracture line. The fracture was very well healed, suggesting that the person survived for a long time af-ter suffering the injury. On the cranium of M32:1 (a male individual 30–40 years of age at death), a depressed area is located on the medial aspect of the right superciliary arch, directly above the nasal bone and impacting the fron-tal sinus (figure 13.2A). The fracture is small and deep, conical in shape, and clearly demarcated by a fracture line. As in the preceding case, the fracture was very well healed. In the case of a female with an estimated age of around 30 years at death (M67:4), the wound is located between the two supercili-ary arches and slightly to the left; its left aspect involved the frontal sinus. The total area affected was larger than in the preceding case, almost circular, with a 19 mm diameter. The depression is shallow, surrounded by a clearly visible fracture line. This fracture was also well healed.

The three depressed fractures likely resulted from violent face-to-face con-frontations involving blunt objects. In the case of one male skeleton (M24:1), the location of the fracture suggests a right-handed attack on a fleeing victim, whereas in the other two cases fractures were inflicted when the opponent was facing the victim. Although the patterning of these injuries indicates that these probably resulted from violent confrontations, the frequency of such injuries at Taojiazhai was considerably less than found for other communities where substantial person-to-person violence has been diagnosed by means of bioarchaeological research (e.g., Standen and Arriaza 2000; Judd 2004; Buzon and Richman 2007; Tung 2007; earlier studies reviewed in Larsen 1997: 119–51). The low incidence of healed depressed cranial injuries in the sample does not necessarily imply the limited involvement of individuals buried at Taojiazhai in violent encounters. Instead, it may suggest that such confrontations often led to death, as indicated by the evidence of perimortem trauma described below, as well as evidence for use of sharp metal weapons that may kill an individual, with or without leaving marks on the skeleton.

Compression Fractures

Compression fractures principally affect the vertebrae and can occur under two different circumstances: jumping or falling from a height and/or carrying a heavy load on one's back. In the latter case, compression is often exacerbated by the osteopenia of old age. There is only one case of such a fracture in the Taojiazhai series. An adult male skeleton (M6:3) had compression fractures of four vertebrae, including the 11th and 12th thoracic vertebrae, as well as the 1st and 2nd lumbar vertebrae (figure 13.3). The centrum of each of these

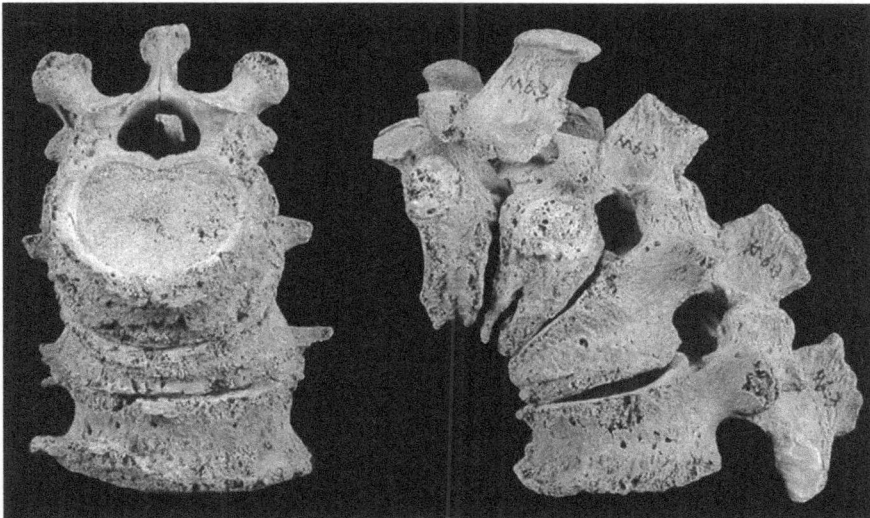

Figure 13.3. Compression fractures of the lower thoracic vertebrae that led to an angular deformity of the spine of a male individual (M6:3).

four vertebrae assumed a wedge shape, resulting in an angular deformity of the vertebral column. The anterior aspects of these vertebrae were drastically shortened, forming an inward fold or cleft. Schmorl's nodes were evident in the superior aspect of the body of T11. Such a fracture likely proceeded from mechanical stress due to carrying heavy loads and was furthered by the old age osteopenia suffered by this individual.

A similar compression fracture in the lower thoracic area is frequently associated in the literature with tuberculosis infection, but in this particular case the morphology of the fracture does not appear to be typical of tuberculosis. In cases of tuberculous spondylolysis, bone fracture usually affects a single vertebra and is associated with a large resorptive lesion of the centrum. The Taojiazhai individual in question suffered the compression of several centrums, and there is no evidence of resorptive lesions. In addition, the presence of Schmorl's nodes on other vertebrae suggests that the vertebral column of this individual was frequently subjected to significant compressive force, probably due to carrying heavy loads.

Linear Bone Fractures

Linear bone fractures can be caused by a sharp force applied directly or by indirect stress; they can be either simple, with a single line of fracture, or multiple. In the Taojiazhai skeletal collection, there are many examples of linear bone fractures, affecting both cranial and postcranial bones, as listed in table 13.2. The facial fractures included a fracture of the left zygomatic/maxilla bones (M89:5) and two cases of nasal bone fractures. All these fractures were well healed. The line of the first fracture proceeded across the inferior portion of the maxillozygomatic suture. Postdepositional damage precluded evaluation of the extent of the fracture line on the zygomatic bone. It appears that the maxilla and zygomatic became slightly misaligned during healing. The nasal fractures affected the inferior portions of both nasal bones. On the cranium of M26:5, the fracture was more or less symmetrical, while on M20:4, the right nasal bone was more affected than the left.

In addition to the three facial fractures, an elderly female (M22:1) had a mandibular fracture that resulted in misalignment of the chin. This fracture was very well healed, so the precise location of the fracture line is difficult to assess. Nevertheless, there appear to have been multiple lines of fracture, and the central portion of the mandible was completely separated, most likely from a sharp anteroposterior blow. The same skeleton also carries evidence of healed fractures on the distal third of the right tibia and fibula. The line of fracture proceeded in an oblique direction. As a consequence of misalignment and cicatrization, a large callus formed around the fracture.

Table 13.2. Linear bone fractures in the Taojiazhai series

Fractured bone	Burial	Sex	Age
Nasal	M26:5	F	50+
Nasal	M20:4	M	50–55
Zygomatic	M89:5	M	40–45
Mandible	M22:1	F	55+
Clavicle	M70:2	M	35–45
Sternum	M70:2	M	35–45
Scapula	M20:4	M	50–55
	M24:10	F	50+
Humerus	M24:6	M	50+
Ulna	M6	F?	adult
	M32:1	M	30–40
Radius	M52:1	M	45–50
	M32:1	M	30–40
Tibia	M22:1	F	55+
	M32:2	F	40–50
Fibula	M22:1	F	55+
Ribs			
One rib	M7:2	F	20–30
Two ribs	M9:1	F	55+
Two ribs	M11:2	M	45–50
Three ribs	M22:2	F	55+
Five ribs	M24:2	M	45–50
One rib	M32:1	M	30–40
One rib	M52:7	F	50+
Five ribs	M70:2	M	35–45

One male skeleton (M70:2) exhibited evidence of a fracture of the left clavicle and of the body of the sternum, as well as of five ribs. The fragments of the clavicle healed in an incorrect orientation, preserving a superoposterior shift of the medial portion of the clavicle relative to its lateral portion, which probably occurred as a result of contraction of the sternocleidomastoid muscle at the time of fracture. The line of fracture is still clearly visible, because of the partial nonunion of the clavicular body; the line proceeds at a sharp angle to the main axes of the body and runs through its middle, dividing the clavicle into roughly equal parts. Consequently, this fracture can be tentatively interpreted as having been caused by an indirect force from extending the arm to break a fall, as opposed to direct force applied by a weapon. The sternum of the same individual was fractured along the middle of the body. The fractured area is surrounded by a thick layer of oppositional bone and multiple spurs.

There are two cases of scapula fracture in the Taojiazhai collection (M20:4 and M24:10), both of them simple linear fractures that were well healed. The

injury suffered by one of these individuals (M20:4) was somewhat more serious, affecting the lateral aspect of the scapula below the glenoid fossa and
associated with a slight misalignment of the separated fragments.

Altogether, the remains of five individuals in the Taojiazhai collection
showed evidence of long bone fractures. A left ulna from burial cluster M6
displays an oblique linear fracture, located at about midshaft, likely a parry
fracture. Cicatrization had occurred, with a slight misalignment giving the
bone a curved outline. A very high frequency of such parry fractures has been
reported for a Neolithic collection from the Central Plains (Pechenkina et
al. 2007); based on a virtual absence of cranial injuries in this collection, the
authors inferred that they resulted from frequent face-to-face confrontation
for display or ritualistic purposes. The Taojiazhai example of a parry fracture
came from a multiple burial and the remains were commingled, so ascertaining to which particular individual this ulna belonged is difficult.

As previously mentioned, the distal portion of the right ankle of M22:1
was fractured. Individual M32:1 had fractures in the distal third of both left
forearm bones. The fracture line on this radius is horizontal, while on the
ulna, it proceeded in an oblique direction and was accompanied by misalignment of the two diaphyseal fragments. The tibia of individual M32:2 was broken at about midshaft. Although the fracture occurred antemortem, the two
fragments of the diaphysis did not unite during cicatrization; there are clear
signs of atrophy and shortening of this bone from misuse. Finally, the right
radius of skeleton M52:1 had fractured a few centimeters below the midshaft
and healed in a misaligned orientation.

Cut and Chop Marks

Among the Taojiazhai skeletons, there were also several cases of bones with
perimortem cut-marks. These cut-marks were likely inflicted by a sharp metal
instrument and represent fairly deep and narrow wounds to the bone surface.
Cut-marks were observed on the left scapula of an individual from cluster
M7, a multiple burial with commingled remains. The association of this scapula with any of the other bones in this burial cluster is unclear, so assessing the
sex or age of this individual was impossible. The cut-marks were located on
the medial aspect of the superior angle and proceeded in an oblique direction.

In the case of a chop, a fragment of bone is separated completely from the
rest of the bone as a consequence of application of force using a sharp tool
or weapon. A single chop-mark was clearly visible on the posterior portion
of the skull of a male adolescent (M9:7). The injury began on the left side of
the occipital bone, crossing the nuchal lines and extending onto the left parietal. Two ribs of skeleton M32:1 displayed chop-marks. These wounds were

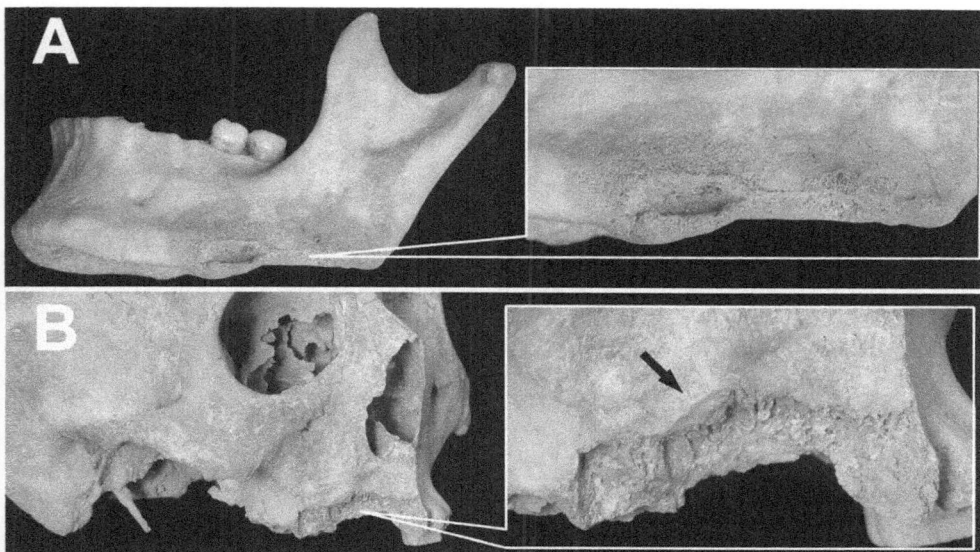

Figure 13.4. Sharp traumas inflicted by a sword or a large knife. *A*, Deep cut on the inferior portion of the left side of the mandible of a male (M9:3); note reactive bone around the wound. *B*, Maxilla of male M9:8; part of the right maxilla was cut off completely.

located at about the middle of each rib and penetrated roughly through half of each rib's thickness. However, there were no wounds or cut-marks on the neighboring ribs.

Two skeletons from burial M9—M9:3 (figure 13.4A) and M9:8 (figure 13.4B)—evidenced wounds inflicted by a sword or a large knife. The mandible of a 35–45-year-old male (M9:3) suffered a deep cut on the inferior portion of the left side of the body, below the second and the third molars. The oblique direction of the wound suggests that the person likely dodged sideways, which caused the weapon to slip along the mandible. There is evidence of the healing process around the wound. However, the healing of the wound is slight, suggesting that the person died soon after the attack, even though he survived the violent encounter itself. In the case of M9:8, also a male around 40 years of age, part of the right maxilla was cut off completely. This wound proceeded along the alveolar process and resulted in the removal of the alveoli bearing the incisors. No evidence of healing was present, suggesting that the wound was inflicted around the time of death.

Gross Skeletal Pathology

Evidence of a wide array of gross pathological changes was found on the skeletons from the Taojiazhai collection. Some of these changes can be linked to specific or nonspecific infectious agents, chronic degenerative or autoimmune conditions, or congenital malformations. In some cases multiple etiologies are possible and a specific underlying cause cannot be pinpointed with any degree of certainty.

Skeletal Changes Related to Degenerative Conditions

Hazardous lifestyles in the Taojiazhai community are implicated by the number and specific characteristics of the traumatic injuries found. This conclusion is also supported by evidence of a range of degenerative conditions affecting joint surfaces, many of which were likely induced by either minor trauma or significant continuing mechanical stress on the respective surface. Cases of degenerative osteoarthropathy manifested as osteophyte formation, hyperporosity, and erosion, as well as eburnation and partial or complete ankylosis. Table 13.3 lists specific cases evidencing severe development of degenerative joint disease. In the case of articular surfaces involved in the formation of synovial joints, severe osteoarthropathy was diagnosed when the surfaces involved displayed osteophyte formation, changes of the surface outline, as well as eburnation and/or severe erosion.

Table 13.3. Cases of severe degenerative osteoarthropathy at Taojiazhai

Burial	Sex	Age	Affected elements and location
M2:3	M	50+	Proximal epiphysis of right femur
M2:6	F	35–40	Distal facies articularis of right fibula
M6:3	M	50+	All facies articularis involved in elbow and shin joints; lower thoracic and upper lumbar vertebrae
M9:2	M	40–45	Superior and inferior facies articularis of vertebrae
M11	M	50+	Facies articularis of right foot
M12:5	M	40–50	Occipital condyle facies articularis
M24:3	F	40–50	Right occipital condyle facies articularis
M30:1	M	35–45	Facies articularis of left foot
M32:2	F	40–50	Facies articularis of axis, especially on the left side
M16:1	M	45–50	Distal radioulnar articulation
M26:8	M	45–50	Costal foveae of thoracic vertebrae and articular surfaces of ribs 1–6
M43:3	M	45–50	Temporomandibular joint
M60:2	M	23–28	Glenoid fossa of right scapula
M60:5	M	40–45	Elbow facies articularis
M61:6	M	50–55	Temporomandibular joint
M62:3	M	25–30	Elbow facies articularis
M66:1	F	50–55	Distal ulna facies articularis; temporomandibular joint, left side
M77:2	F	50+	Right elbow facies articularis
M84:2	F	45–50	Glenoid fossa of right scapula; temporomandibular joint
M89:1	F	35–40	Temporomandibular joint

As can be seen from table 13.3, severe osteoarthropathies predominantly affected older individuals, although in two cases they developed in males with an estimated age at death of less than 30 years. No specific association between the joints affected and the sex of the individuals was noted. Temporomandibular joints often displayed severe degenerative changes, usually in association with tooth loss in older individuals. Elbow joint surfaces also were often affected, while the shoulders and knees were affected less often. Although most of the osteoarthropathies developed bilaterally, when asymmetric development occurred, it was more pronounced on the right side.

Whereas the hip joint in general was not frequently affected, the degenerative changes in the right hip of skeleton from M2:3 were particularly severe. The femoral head of this individual was flattened and displayed clear dystrophic changes typical of coxarthrosis, including a rough topology of the cortical bone and a small area of erosion. These changes also extended onto the femoral neck of this individual. There was an additional articular facet on the anterior surface of the femoral neck that displayed strong degenerative changes (figure 13.5). Interestingly, such facets have been described for skeletal collections derived from ancient communities that engaged in horseback riding, thus being referred to as "rider's facet" (Buzhilova 2008: 117). This sug-

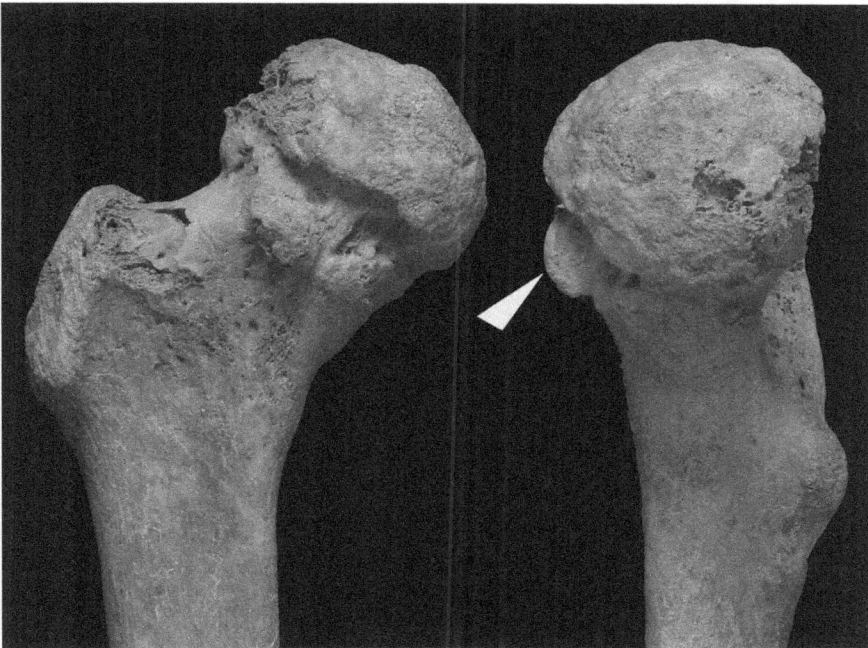

Figure 13.5. Coxarthrosis of the right femur of M2:3. The white arrow points at an extra articular facet on the anterior portion of the femoral neck. This facet is also evident on the anterior view.

gests that the pathological changes in the right hip of M2:3 may have been related to habitual riding.

Given the evidence of joint ossification, fusion, and entheses, several specific types of spondyloarthropathies, as well as possible diffuse idiopathic skeletal hyperostosis (DISH), could be diagnosed in the Taojiazhai collection, following criteria developed by Arriaza (1993) based on the clinical literature. Four skeletons displayed unilateral or bilateral sacroiliac fusion. One male with an estimated age at death of over 50 years (M34:1) suffered continuous fusion extending from the ninth thoracic to the second lumbar vertebra on the right side. Sacroiliac fusion is not typical for DISH and is more likely to occur in some spondyloarthropathies. Nevertheless, the "dripping candle wax" (Aufderheide and Rodriguez-Martin 1998: 98) appearance of this particular vertebral column calcification seems to be most consistent with DISH. Alternative diagnoses of ankylosing spondylitis or psoriatic arthritis are less likely, as in the first case the vertebral fusion is usually symmetrical, while in the second it is bulkier in appearance. As has been shown by several paleopathological studies, DISH was not uncommon in past populations and occurred at a frequency similar to that in the present day (Zhang 1995; Vidal 2000; Oxenham et al. 2006).

The skeleton of a 35–40-year-old male (M28:1) displays complete fusion of the sacroiliac joint on both sides, although traces of the line of fusion are still visible in places. The smooth trabecular bridging proceeding from ilium to sacrum may be indicative of ankylosing spondylitis (Arriaza 1993), although no intervertebral fusion had taken place. Thus, an early stage of ankylosing spondylitis, before the disease affected the vertebral column, can be proposed. Unilateral fusion of the sacroiliac joint was also found on the skeleton of a male 45–50 years of age at death (M24:2). In this case, the fusion of the sacroiliac joint occurred on the left side only. The line of fusion is still visible, and there is none of the smooth bridging characteristic of ankylosing spondylitis. Because the same skeleton evidenced healed fractures of four ribs (table 13.2), it seems reasonable to tentatively attribute sacroiliac fusion in this case to the same traumatic injury that led to the rib fractures. In the case of an elderly (40+) female (M59:2), sacroiliac fusion occurred on the right side in the superior portion of the articulation only. The fusion was continuous and smooth, yet no other parts of the skeleton display the fusion expected to result from spondyloarthropathies. While this pathology might represent an initial state of one of the spondyloarthropathies, it is impossible to narrow the diagnosis any further.

Fusion of several vertebrae together was also found on a number of skeletons. With the exception of the case of individual M34:1, discussed above, these usually involved only two to four vertebrae and are most easily explained as resulting from the progression of age-related degenerative changes in the spine. One particularly severe case involving the lower thoracic and upper lumbar vertebrae was found on the remains of an elderly male (M6:3), already discussed above in connection with compression fracture of these vertebrae.

Of particular interest are the degenerative changes observed in the foot bones of a male skeleton of about 40 years of age at death (M2:4) (figure 13.6). The metatarsals and phalanges of this individual evidence small focal resorptive lesions, predominantly affecting the distal epiphyses, which led to bilateral thinning and deformity of the distal ends. Prominent proliferative changes in the area immediately adjacent to the articular surfaces are also found on the first metatarsals. The distal phalanges were particularly affected, displaying atrophy associated with thinning and shape distortion. These changes were more prominent on the right foot. The articular surfaces of the other synovial joints of this individual show minimal degenerative changes. Such polyarthritic changes principally affecting the smaller articulations of the hands and feet may be consistent with rheumatoid arthritis, an autoimmune inflammatory condition that typically progresses from the smallest joints of the hands and feet in a more or less symmetrical pattern. While phalangeal changes are also typical of psoriatic arthritis, these would tend to be more asymmetric in their distribution. Poor preservation of the hand bones in this case prevents further evaluation of lesions in the upper extremities.

Cases of rheumatoid arthritis described from archaeological skeletons are fairly rare. A single convincing case was documented on a male skeleton from the Final Jomon period in Japan (1400–400 years BC) (Inoue et al. 1999).

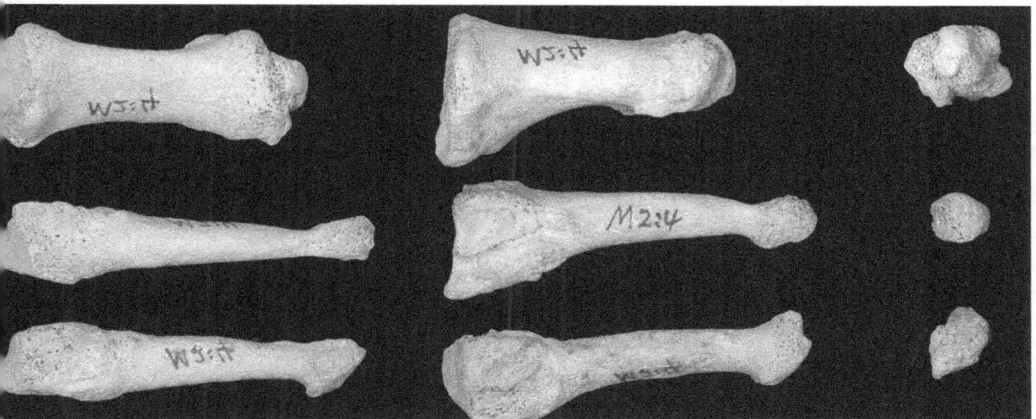

Figure 13.6. Metatarsals and phalanges of the right foot of M2:4, representing a possible case of rheumatoid arthritis.

In European populations, a relatively early case was described by Klepinger (1979) for a Hellenistic skeleton dated to 330–210 BC. In this instance, there were bony spurs in the calcaneus and reactive bone throughout the skeleton, conditions that do not pertain to individual M2:4 from Taojiazhai. A number of possible Roman and medieval cases of rheumatoid arthritis have also been described in the literature (Hacking et al. 1994; Blondiaux et al. 1997). Recently, a possible case of severe rheumatoid arthritis was described on a female skeleton from Korea dated to around AD 1760 (Kim et al. 2001). Considering the difficulty of diagnosing rheumatoid arthritis from ancient skeletal remains and given the small number of such skeletons with well-preserved hand and foot bones, we can only suggest that this condition was present in early East Asia.

Pyogenic Pathological Changes

A single incidence of pyogenic osteomyelitis was found in the Taojiazhai collection, on the skeleton of a young female with an estimated age of between 20 and 23 years at death (M33:1). Only one bone was affected, the right femur, which suffered exuberant development of infection-induced lesions—including periostosis, bone necrosis, and cloacae—that showed little evidence of healing (figure 13.7A). A proliferative lesion with a very roughly woven morphology affected the distal one-third portion of the diathesis, reaching its greatest thickness on the medial and especially posterior aspect of the femur. The unilateral and localized nature of this lesion suggests that the underlying infection was likely introduced through an open injury to the soft tissue, but that did not directly affect the bone. The presence of cloacae surrounded by active proliferative lesions, as well as the extreme roughness of the newly formed bone, implicates an acute infectious process. We can extrapolate that it led to the death of this individual before any considerable healing or remodeling could take place.

Another interesting case of infection-related change was presented on the cranium of a middle-aged female (M35:1). The bones of the cranial vault, particularly the frontal and the right parietal, display clusters of resorptive lesions on both the ectocranial and the endocranial aspect (figure 13.7B). As in the previous instance, a lack of evidence of healing suggests that the underlying cause of the lesions eventually led to the death of this individual. The mosaic appearance of these lesions resembles the effects of caries sicca, although not in its most typical form; there is little evidence of bone sclerosis or healing. Therefore, this case may be tentatively linked to an acquired treponemal infection,[1] possibly syphilis.

The origin of treponematosis in general and venereal syphilis more specifically has been vociferously debated for some time and is still a controversial

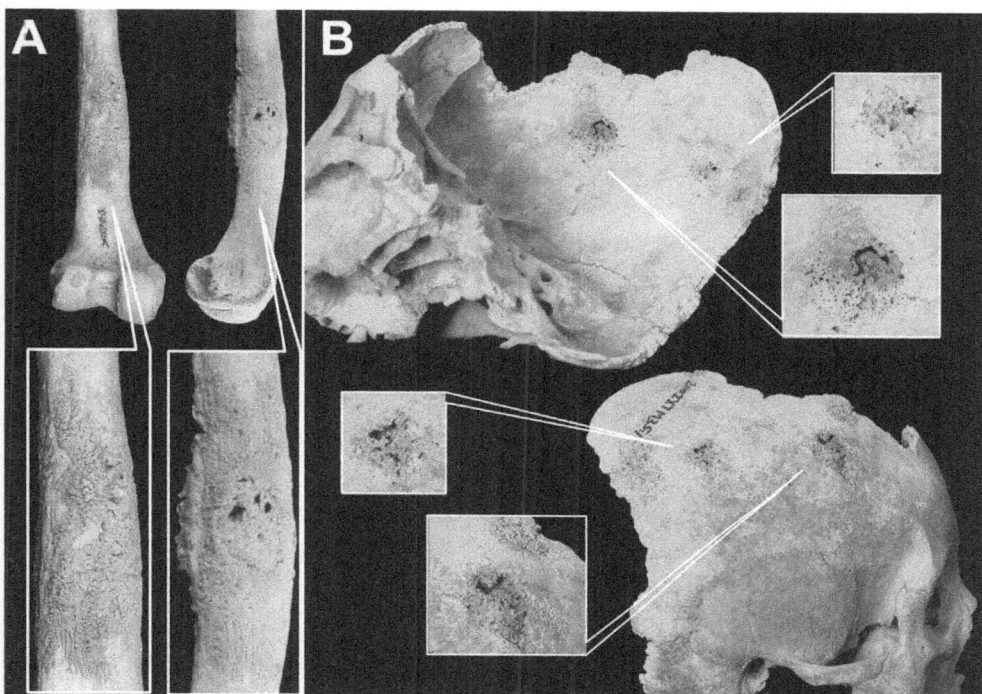

Figure 13.7. Evidence of systemic infection on two skeletons from Taojiazhai. *A*, Pyogenic osteomyelitis of the right femur of M33:1. *B*, Resorptive lesions on the cranial vault of M35:1.

subject (Hudson 1965; Baker and Armelagos 1988; Baker 2005). The results of recent studies of the molecular phylogeny of different *Treponema pallidum* strains (Harper et al. 2007; Mulligan et al. 2008) are somewhat inconclusive, although these seemingly point toward a New World origin for the venereal form. Several early cases of treponemal infection in Asia have been tentatively diagnosed, based on skeletal evidence from Eneolithic and Iron Age India (Vasulu 1993; Rao et al. 1996).

In China, cranial lesions resembling the present case were described by Zhang Zhenbiao (1994) on a skeleton from Fujiang Province dated to the Song dynasty (AD 960–1279). Two even earlier possible cases of treponematosis are reported from northeastern Qinghai Province, stemming from a study of human remains recovered at a number of Bronze Age archaeological sites located in the vicinity of Xining (Kayue culture) (500 BC–AD 150) (Suzuki et al. 2005). The investigators based this conclusion on the bilateral distribution of periosteal lesions and on their plaque-like nodular appearance on distal femora, which investigators interpreted as consistent with endemic syphilis, while also considering alternative diagnoses, including primary osteogenic osteosarcoma, pyogenic osteomyelitis, and Paget's disease. Suzuki and colleagues (2005) therefore proposed that treponemal infection must have reached China via the Silk Road by approximately 1000 BC. The case of individual M35:1 from Taojiazhai seems to support that argument. However, a review of documented skeletal evidence of treponemal infection from Japan suggests that this infectious disease did not reach Honshu until AD 1510, rapidly leading to an epidemic (Suzuki 1991). For now, possible diagnoses of early treponemal infection from Qinghai are fairly tentative, as none of the skeletons show changes in both the cranium and postcrania.

Oral Health

Dental caries is arguably the most common disease observed in the mouth. It starts from the dental surface; when untreated, it progresses inside the tooth, possibly into the pulp chamber, eventually leading to tooth loss. Multiple types of dental caries may be specified, depending on which tooth surface is affected, including occlusal caries that affects the chewing surface of a tooth, interproximal caries that develops between two adjacent teeth, buccal/labial caries on the smooth surface of a tooth, cervical caries that progresses from the area of cementoenamel junction, root caries, and belt caries that surrounds the dental crown. No evidence of the latter two types of caries was encountered in the Taojiazhai skeletal series.

Among the 79 adult crania in the Taojiazhai collection that could be usefully examined for this parameter, caries was relatively common, with 18, or 23 percent, of those individuals evidencing carious lesions. Rates of caries incidence were somewhat different for males (9, or 19.6 percent; $N = 46$) and females (9, or 28 percent; $N = 33$). When caries frequencies were computed for individual teeth, females also appear to have had a somewhat greater incidence of caries than did males: 23, or 8.5 percent ($N = 268$), versus 23, or 5.6 percent ($N = 410$). However, that difference was not statistically significant ($\chi^2 = 2.26, p = .132$, 1 df, n.s.).

When individuals who had lost at least one tooth are counted, antemortem tooth loss was also fairly high at Taojiazhai (38, or 48 percent; $N = 79$), more or less equally affecting males and females (22 [or 47.8 percent] vs. 16 [or 48.4 percent], respectively). Among individuals with an estimated age at death of under 50, tooth loss was generally limited to one or two teeth per dental set. However, in older individuals, massive tooth loss had occurred, likely as a consequence of progressing caries, as well as periodontal infection. Several crania of older individuals had complete or nearly complete tooth loss. For instance, one female (M34:3) with an estimated age at death of over 50 was completely edentulous. All dental sockets were completely remodeled and obliterated, indicating that she survived for some time after her last tooth was lost. Likewise, another female (M73:1) had a completely edentulous mandible. One male (M62:2) retained just a few teeth.

Caries and antemortem tooth loss frequencies found in the Taojiazhai collection appear to be fairly modest when compared to those observed in other series reported in this volume (chapters 11, 12, and 18) and considerably less than those found in populations with a well-established millet-based diet (chapter 12). Nevertheless, these frequencies are fairly high when compared to those observed in populations with foraging- or herding-based economies, suggesting the presence of water-soluble carbohydrates that promote caries in the Taojiazhai diet (Han 1985). Therefore, people at Taojiazhai likely practiced mixed subsistence that combined animal husbandry with cereal agriculture.

Conclusions

The Taojiazhai skeletal assemblage represents a population that occupied a frontier zone established as buffer between the Xiaongnu polity and the farming communities of the Han and Jin dynasties. This analysis of the human skeletal remains recovered from Taojiazhai confirms the perilous nature of life on that frontier.

1. Cranial injuries and cut-marks, albeit not very frequent, are best explained by interpersonal violence, some inflicted by metal weapons, clearly with the purpose of killing the individual. Several fractures of nasal bones and depressed fractures of the frontal bone produced by heavy blunt objects suggest face-to-face confrontation. Postcranial injuries could be related to violent encounters, as well as to accidents of daily life that may have involved horseback riding.

2. There is one case of systemic infection with a pattern of lesions suggesting treponemal infection, which could have been introduced to the area via contact with the outside populations.

3. A fairly high proportion of carious teeth and considerable antemortem tooth loss suggests a diet rich in carbohydrates, with likely reliance on a mixed diet derived from cereal agriculture combined with substantial animal husbandry.

Notes

Chapter translated from Chinese by Kate Pechenkina.

1. Lack of the mandatory postcranial involvement that accords with chronic treponemal infection casts serious doubt on this possible diagnosis. Clustered resorptive lesions of the cranial vault can be caused by a number of other infectious processes including, but not limited to, mycobacterial infections.

Literature Cited

Arriaza BT. 1993. Seronegative spondyloarthropathies and diffuse idiopathic skeletal hyperostosis in ancient northern Chile. *American Journal of Physical Anthropology* 91: 263–78.

Aufderheide AC, Rodriguez-Martin C. 1998. *The Cambridge encyclopedia of human paleopathology.* Cambridge: Cambridge University Press.

Baker BJ. 2005. Patterns of pre- and post-Columbian treponematosis in the northeastern United States. In: Powell ML, Cook DC, editors. *The myth of syphilis: The natural history of treponematosis in North America.* Gainesville: University Press of Florida. Pp. 119–44.

Baker B, Armelagos GJ. 1988. Origin and antiquity of syphilis: A dilemma in paleopathological diagnosis and interpretation. *Current Anthropology* 29: 703–37.

Blondiaux J, Cotten A, Fontaine C, Hänni C, Bera A, Flipo R-M. 1997. Two Roman and Medieval cases of symmetrical erosive polyarthropathy from Normandy: Anatomico-pathological and radiological evidence for rheumatoid arthritis. *International Journal of Osteoarchaeology* 7: 451–66.

Buzhilova AP. 2008. On the question regarding how widespread the tradition of horseback riding was: Analysis of anthropological sources. *Opus: Interdisciplinary Research in Archaeology* (Opus междисциплинарные исследования в археологии) 6: 110–20.

Buzon MR, Richman R. 2007. Traumatic injuries and imperialism: The effects of Egyptian colonial strategies at Tombos in Upper Nubia. *American Journal of Physical Anthropology* 133: 783–79.

Chen S. 1980. *Medical examiner osteology* (法医骨学). Beijing: Populace Publishing House.

Cui Y, Zhang D, Du C. 1999. *Qinghai general history.* Xining: Qinghai People's Publishing Agency.

Hacking P, Allen T, Rogers J. 1994. Rheumatoid arthritis in a medieval skeleton. *International Journal of Osteology* 4: 251–55.

Han K. 1985. Skeleton anthropology appraisal to archaeology research function. *Archaeology and Cultural Relics* (考古与文物) 3: 50–55.

Han K, Tan J, Zhang F. 2005. *Research on ancient indigenous races of northwestern region of China: Ancient times resident race research* (中国西北地区古代居民种族研究). Fudan: Fudan University Publishing House.

Harper KN, Ocampo PS, Steiner BM, George RW, Silverman MS, Bolotin S, Pillay A, Saunders, NJ, Armelagos GJ. 2007. On the origin of the treponematoses: A phylogenetic approach. *PLoS Neglected Tropical Diseases* 2: e148.

Hudson EH. 1965. Treponematosis in perspective. *Bulletin of the World Health Organization* 32: 735–48.

Inoue K, Hukuda S, Nakai M, Katayama K, Huang J. 1999. Erosive peripheral polyarthritis in ancient Japanese skeletons: A possible case of rheumatoid arthritis. *International Journal of Osteoarchaeology* 9: 1–7.

Judd MA. 2004. Trauma in the city of Kerma: Ancient versus modern injury patterns. *International Journal of Osteoarchaeology* 14: 34–51.

Kim DK, Lee IS, Kim WL, Lee JS, Koh BJ, Kim MJ, Youn MY, Shin MH, Kim YS, Lee SS, Oh CS, Shin DH. 2001. Possible rheumatoid arthritis found in the human skeleton collected from the tomb of Joseon dynasty, Korea, dating back to the 1700s AD. *International Journal of Osteoarchaeology* 21: 136–49.

Klepinger, LL. 1979. Paleopathologic evidence for the evolution of rheumatoid arthritis. *American Journal of Physical Anthropology* 50: 119–22.

Larsen CS. 1997. *Bioarchaeology: Interpreting behavior from the human skeleton.* Cambridge: Cambridge University Press.

Li S, Zhao Y, Gao S, Zhou H. 2009. Analysis of ancient mtDNA based on Taojiazhai tomb M5 individuals. *Progress in Natural Science* (自然科学进展) 19: 1159–63.

Lovell N. 1997. Trauma analysis in paleopathology. *Yearbook of Physical Anthropology* 40: 139–70.

Mulligan CJ, Norris SJ, Lukehart SA. 2008. Molecular studies in *Treponema pallidum* evolution: Toward clarity? *PLoS Neglected Tropical Diseases* 2: e184.

Ortner DJ. 2003. *Identification of pathological conditions in human skeletal remains.* 2nd ed. San Diego, CA: Academic Press.

Oxenham MF, Matsumura H, Nishimoto T. 2006. Diffuse idiopathic skeletal hyperostosis in late Jomon Hokkaido, Japan. *International Journal of Osteoarchaeology* 16: 34–46.

Pechenkina EA, Benfer RA Jr., Ma X. 2007. Diet and health in the Neolithic of the Wei and middle Yellow River basins, northern China. In: Cohen MN, Crane-Kramer GMM, editors. *Ancient health: Skeletal indicators of agricultural and economic intensification.* Gainesville: University Press of Florida. Pp. 255–72.

Pi X. 2000. *Oral cavity dissection physiology* (口腔解剖生理学). 4th ed. Beijing: People's Medical Publishing House.

Qinghai Provincial Institute of Cultural Relics and Archaeology. 2007. Report on Qinghai Province Xining Taojiazhai Han burials excavated in 2002. *Antiquities of East Asia* (东亚古物) B: 311–50. Nanjing: Nanjing Normal University Museum of Cultural Relics.

Rao VV, Vasulu TS, Rector Babu AD. 1996. Possible paleopathological evidence of treponematosis from a Megalithic site at Agripalle, India. *American Journal of Physical Anthropology* 100: 49–55.

Shang H. 2002. *Research on human skeletons of Neolithic age from Guangrao, Shandong* (山东广饶新石器时代人骨及其与中国早期全新世人类之间关系的研究). Beijing: Chinese Academy of Science.

Standen VG, Arriaza BT. 2000. Trauma in the preceramic coastal populations of northern Chile: Violence or occupational hazards? *American Journal of Physical Anthropology* 112: 239–49.

Suzuki T. 1991. Paleopathological study of infectious diseases in Japan. In: Ortner DJ, Aufderheide AC, editors. *Human paleopathology: Current syntheses and future options.* Washington, DC: Smithsonian Institution Press. Pp. 128–39.

Suzuki T, Matsushita T, Han K. 2005. On the possible case of treponematosis from the Bronze Age in China. *Anthropological Science* 113: 253–58.

Tung TA. 2007. Trauma and violence in the Wari empire of the Peruvian Andes: Warfare, raids, and ritual fights. *American Journal of Physical Anthropology* 133: 941–95.

Vasulu TS. 1993. The origin and antiquity of syphilis (treponematosis), in Southeast Asia. *Human Evolution* 8: 229–33.

Vidal P. 2000. A paleoepidemiologic study of diffuse idiopathic skeletal hyperostosis. *Joint Bone Spine* 67: 210–14.

Watson B. 1993. *Records of the Grand Historian, by Sima Qian.* Translated by Burton Watson. Hong Kong: Chinese University of Hong Kong.

Xu S. 1984. Report on the excavation of Xining Taojiazhai Han burials. *Qinghai Archaeology Society Bulletin* (青海考古学会会刊) 6: 34.

Zhang Z. 1994. The skeletal evidence of human leprosy and syphilis in ancient China. *Acta Anthropologica Sinica* (人类学学报) 13: 294–99.

Zhang Z. 1995. The skeletal evidence of the ankylosing spondylitis in ancient China. *Acta Anthropologica Sinica* (人类学学报) 14: 110–17.

14

Bioarchaeological Perspectives on Systemic Stress during the Agricultural Transition in Prehistoric Japan

DANIEL H. TEMPLE AND CLARK SPENCER LARSEN

The purpose of this chapter is to document and interpret patterns of systemic stress during the agricultural transition in prehistoric Japan. Patterns of stress during the agricultural transition in this region have been explored by earlier research that generally relied on singular skeletal indicators of stress and disease (Sanui 1960; Inoue et al. 1986; Oyamada et al. 1996; Todaka et al. 2003; Suzuki and Inoue 2007; Suzuki et al. 2008). This chapter uses multiple skeletal indicators of diet and physiological stress to examine whether similar trends (i.e., little change in health profiles) are identifiable in Jomon populations from prehistoric Japan following the transition to a wet-rice economy circa 4000 through 2300 BP.

The agricultural transition was a crucial period in human prehistory once thought to act as a beacon of modernity—ushering in numerous technological developments. Bioarchaeological research has, however, questioned the extent to which modern humans benefited from the transition to food-producing economies (Cohen and Armelagos 1984; Larsen 1987, 1995, 2002, 2006; Cohen and Crane-Kramer 2007). Numerous studies report increased frequencies of linear enamel hypoplasia (LEH) defects and porotic hyperostosis among skeletal samples from the early agricultural periods of the Western Hemisphere, Europe, and Southwest Asia (El-Najjar et al. 1976; Cook 1980; Larsen 1983; Kennedy 1984; Rose et al. 1991; Larsen et al. 2002). Spikes in periostitis frequencies in Africa (Armelagos 1969; Armelagos et al. 1984; Martin et al. 1984), the Western Hemisphere (Lallo et al. 1978; Ubelaker 1984; Powell 1988; Larsen and Harn 1994), and Vietnam (Oxenham et al. 2005) are also observed. These trends reflect dietary reliance on nutritionally inadequate cultigens and population aggregation (Larsen 1987, 1995, 2002, 2006).

Bioarchaeological studies of systemic stress in Southeast and East Asia provide mixed support for general models of increased stress during the agricultural transition. In particular, these studies find little change in dental caries, LEH defect, cribra orbitalia, or periostitis prevalence following the transition to wet-rice agriculture (Oxenham et al. 2002; Pietrusewsky and Douglas 2002a,b; Douglas and Pietrusewsky 2007; Domett and Tayles 2007). Factors such as the gradual adoption of intensive agriculture, low cariogenecity of rice, and stasis in chronic infectious disease are all offered as explanatory factors for these trends. This chapter attempts to assess whether similar trends are identifiable in prehistoric Japan following the transition to a wet-rice economy, using multiple skeletal indicators of diet and stress.

Biocultural Context

Jomon

Jomon period (16,000–2300 BP in eastern Japan) cultures were part of a 13,000-year foraging tradition in the Japanese islands (Imamura 1996a). Jomon foragers were the descendants of Pleistocene nomads who migrated to Japan around 20,000 BP and subsumed preexisting "knife-blade" cultures (Kobayashi 2005). These later groups were associated with a "microblade" technology that first appeared in Hokkaido, likely in relation to the expansion of cultural networks from eastern Siberia (Imamura 1996a; Kobayashi 2005). Microblade Paleolithic industries diversified from Hokkaido into Tohoku around 14,000 BP, evolved into the Mikoshiba tradition, and formed the basis for the earliest spread of Jomon culture (Imamura 1996a).

One set of hypotheses surrounding the earliest migrations to the Japanese islands suggest that the ancestors of Jomon people migrated from Sundaland (Turner 1990; Hanihara 1991). Hypotheses predicting that Pleistocene foragers migrated to Japan from this region are associated with a dental morphological complex observed in Jomon people that is shared with the early inhabitants of Sundaland (Turner 1990, 1992; Matsumura and Hudson 2005). Multivariate analyses of cranial and dental measurements also find similarities between the Paleolithic foragers of Japan, Jomon people, and individuals from this region (Hanihara 1991; Baba et al. 1998).

Other multivariate analyses of cranial and dental traits suggest a Northeast Asian point of origin for the Pleistocene ancestors of Jomon foragers (Pietrusewsky 1999, 2005; Seguchi et al. 2007; Hanihara and Ishida 2009; and others). Cold-derived body size among Jomon foragers and the Pleistocene occupants of the Japanese islands suggest that this region was initially populated by foragers from a colder environment such as Northeast/Central Asia (Temple et al. 2008). Analysis of classic loci and Y chromosomes derived from the Ainu suggest a Northeast/Central Asian point of origin for the ancestors of Jomon people dating to approximately 20,000 BP (Omoto and Saitou 1997; Hammer et al. 2006). More recently, ancient DNA analysis of Jomon period skeletal remains from Hokkaido indicate that the Pleistocene ancestors of Jomon people migrated to the Japanese islands from Northeast Asia (Adachi et al. 2009).

There is some disagreement regarding the use of the term *forager* to describe the subsistence economies of Jomon people due to the domestication of numerous cultigens and possible modification of the landscape to manage plant foods (Underhill and Habu 2006; Imamura 2006). It is, however, important to point out that the term *forager* does not describe a static subsistence framework. In fact, many "foraging" societies domesticate considerable numbers of plant species and express variation in mobility and social complexity (Binford 1981; Harris 1989; Smith 2000). In this sense, Jomon people are best associated with complex foraging behavior, in which production and care of plant domesticates is noted, but food procurement still remains the primary mode of subsistence activity.

Broad reliance on cariogenic cultigens is reported during the Jomon period, despite variation in resource availability (Turner 1979; Fujita 1995; Todaka et al. 2003; Temple 2007a). Spikes in carious tooth frequencies are observed following climatic oscillations around 4300 BP, indicating a shift in diet across eastern and western Japan (Fujita 1995; Temple 2007a). Dietary changes among prehistoric Jomon people are related to the ubiquitous exploitation of a cariogenic food source such as taro or yams and resulted in elevated caries prevalence among Late/Final compared to Middle Jomon people (Turner 1979; Fujita 1995; Todaka et al. 2003; Temple 2007a), with exceptions reported on Hokkaido Island (Oxenham and Matsumura 2008). Increased consumption of these products did not precipitate agricultural economies per se, as the types of energy expenditure, social organization, and caries prevalence expected in agricultural economies are not observed until the subsequent Yayoi period (Sanui 1960; Inoue et al. 1986; Imamura 1996a,b; Oyamada et al. 1996; Tsude 2001; Todaka et al. 2003; Temple and Larsen 2007).

Yayoi

Migrations from continental Asia during the Yayoi period (c. 2500 BP) introduced wet-rice agriculture to the Japanese islands (Imamura 1996a,b; Hudson 1999; Tsude 2001). These migrations are indicated by variation in cranial and dental size and shape between Jomon and Yayoi people due to gene flow, with some replacement (Brace and Nagai 1982; Mizoguchi 1986; Hanihara 1991;

Turner 1992; Nakahashi 1993a; Pietrusewsky 1999, 2005). Yayoi period (2500 to 1700 BP) agriculturalists were the descendants of people from modern-day Korea or northern China who migrated to Japan and interbred to varying degrees with indigenous Jomon foragers around 2500 BP (Brace and Nagai 1982; Hanihara 1991; Nakahashi 1993a; Omoto and Saitou 1997; Pietrusewsky 1999, 2005; Hammer et al. 2006).

The earliest dates for migrant arrival correspond with the earliest dates for wet-rice production in northern Kyushu and southern Honshu Island, specifically, those obtained from the Doigahama, Itatzuke, and Notame sites (Imamura 1996b). Tool types and irrigation systems that closely resemble those found at farming sites from southern China and Korea also suggest that wet-rice agriculture was brought to Japan by migrant people (Tsude 2001). For example, the paddy field excavated at the Itatzuke site is remarkably similar to wet-rice fields found in southern China and North Korea circa 6000 BP (Tsude 2001).

Significant energy expended on the care of domesticated plants is recorded during the Yayoi period in the form of large-scale agricultural ecosystems based on wet-rice farming (Imamura 1996b; Hudson 1999; Tsude 2001). General variation in cranial morphology between historic Japanese compared to Yayoi people suggests in situ behaviorally related changes in morphology after the arrival of these migrants to the Japanese islands (Mizoguchi 1986).

Samples

Bioarchaeological data were collected from approximately 400 individuals from eight Jomon period sites (figure 14.1; table 14.1). These sites are dated from the Middle (5000 to 4000 BP) through Final Jomon period (3300 to 2500 BP). All Jomon sites are located in the eastern and western regions of Honshu Island. This study also collected data from approximately 521 individuals recovered from six Yayoi period archaeological sites dated from approximately 2500 to 1700 BP (table 14.1; figure 14.1). Sites from which the Yayoi skeletal samples were recovered are located on northern Kyushu, southwestern Honshu, and Tanegashima Islands. Sites were chosen in association with large sample sizes and geographic distribution.

Methods

Basic Osteological Protocols

Sex was determined in adults using morphological features of the os pubis and greater sciatic notch. Morphological features for sex determination were

Figure 14.1. Map of Japan illustrating approximate locations of the sites used in this study. Yayoi period sites are listed with letters: (A) Hirota; (B) Torinomine; (C) Kanenokuma; (D) Nagaoka; (E) Doigahama; (F) Koura. Jomon period sites are listed with numbers: (1) Yosekura; (2) Tsukumo; (3) Inariyama; (4) Yoshigo; (5) Hobi; (6) Nakazuma; (7) Kitamura; (8) Ota.

scored using standard osteological methods (Buikstra and Ubelaker 1994). Age was estimated on the basis of long bone epiphyseal fusion, tooth development/eruption stages, and tooth wear scores obtained from premolar and molar teeth. All features were scored according to standard osteological methods (Buikstra and Ubelaker 1994).

Dental Caries

Dental caries is an infectious condition characterized by the demineralization of enamel by the waste products of oral bacteria following fermentation of food particles (Hillson 1996; Larsen 1997). Carious lesions were identified based on stages of enamel demineralization that ranged from destruction of entire tooth crowns to pinprick-sized lesions characterized by darkened enamel. Caries prevalence was calculated as the total number of teeth with at

Table 14.1. Samples utilized in this study

Sites	Dates	Location	Collection
Yayoi period			
Doigahama	2500–1900 BP	Southern Honshu	Univ. Kyushu[a]
Koura	1900–1700 BP	Southern Honshu	Univ. Kyushu[a]
Kanenokuma	2100–1900 BP	Northern Kyushu	Univ. Kyushu[a]
Nagaoka	2100–1900 BP	Northern Kyushu	Univ. Kyushu[a]
Torinomine	2100–1700 BP	Tanegashima Island	Univ. Kyushu[a]
Hirota	2100–1700 BP	Tanegashima Island	Univ. Kyushu[a]
Jomon period			
Hobi	3000–2300 BP	Eastern Honshu	Univ. Tokyo[b]
Inariyama	4000–2300 BP	Eastern Honshu	Univ. Kyoto[c]
Yoshigo	4000–2300 BP	Eastern Honshu	Univ. Kyoto[c]
Nakazuma	4000–3000 BP	Eastern Honshu	Toride[d]
Ota	5000–4000 BP	Western Honshu	Univ. Kyoto[c]
Tsukumo	4000–2300 BP	Western Honshu	Univ. Kyoto[c]
Kitamura	5000–3000 BP	Inland Honshu	Nagano[e]
Yosekura	4000–3000 BP	Western Honshu	Univ. Tokyo[b]

[a] School of Basic Human Structures, University of Kyushu.
[b] University Museum, University of Tokyo.
[c] Laboratory of Physical Anthropology, University of Kyoto.
[d] Toride Maizo Bunkazai.
[e] Nagano Historical Society.

least one carious lesion divided by the total number of teeth observed. Caries prevalence was compared between two age groups: subadults (age <15 years) and adults (age >15 years).

These percentages may be biased by unequal numbers of anterior or molariform tooth preservation. That is, molariform teeth are more likely to develop carious lesions than are teeth in the anterior dentition. As a result, percentages of observed teeth and teeth with carious lesions were evaluated to ensure a normal distribution. Percentages of observed tooth types among the Yayoi period samples were approximately equal to those of a normally distributed sample (Temple and Larsen 2007). However, percentages of observed tooth types among the Late to Final Jomon period differed from the expected distribution (Temple and Larsen 2007). Expected frequencies of teeth and carious teeth were calculated for the Late to Final Jomon period sample to eliminate the potential for errors associated with over- or under-sampling teeth from a specific section of the jaw, using methods described by Temple and Larsen (2007). Dental caries prevalence for the Jomon sample was then calculated as the expected number of carious teeth divided by the total number of expected teeth.

Linear Enamel Hypoplasia (LEH)

Enamel hypoplasia is a pathological condition characterized by horizontal furrows that form on teeth in response to the disruption of enamel forming cells following systemic perturbation (Goodman and Rose 1991). Enamel hypoplasia frequency provides useful insights into systemic stress prevalence in prehistoric people (Goodman et al. 1991; Lukacs et al. 2001; Floyd and Littleton 2006; Temple 2008).

LEH defect presence was determined by macroscopic observation aided by the use of a magnifying glass (10x), natural fluorescent lighting, and a 100-watt Toshiba desk lamp. Identification of LEH defects follow Skinner and colleagues (1995) and Guatelli-Steinberg (2003), where adjacent perikymata were compared to possible LEH defects to prevent confusing normal variation in tooth morphology with disrupted enamel production.

LEH prevalence is reported using overall and antimeric calculations. These frequencies were calculated using the following methods: the number of anterior, permanent teeth with at least one LEH defect was divided by the total number of observed anterior, permanent teeth (overall prevalence). LEH defect prevalence on maxillary first incisor (MxFI) and mandibular canine (MaC) tooth antimeres were calculated. MxFI and MaC teeth were selected because these teeth appear to be the most susceptible to LEH defect formation (Goodman and Armelagos 1985). Prevalence of antimeric teeth with LEH defects was calculated as the numbers of mandibular canine (MaC) and maxillary first incisor (MxFI) antimeres with at least one observable LEH defect on *both* teeth divided by the total number of observed MaC and MxFI antimeres respectively. Individual frequencies have been reported by Temple (2010) and omitted here because these frequencies were biased.

Cribra Orbitalia (CO)

Cribra orbitalia is associated with the formation of sieve-like lesions accompanied by abnormal diploic inflammation on the orbital roof. This condition is related to nutritional stressors such as iron deficiency anemia, megaloblastic anemia, scurvy, rickets, and trachoma (Stuart-Macadam 1985; Schultz 2001; Wapler et al. 2004; Walker et al. 2009).

CO lesions were identified using a 10x magnifying lens under florescent lighting and a 100-watt desk lamp. CO was identified as sieve-like lesions on the orbital roof. The presence of marrow hyperplasia through the orbital cortex and/or remodeling on the borders of sieve-like lesions helped differentiate this condition from postmortem damage. CO was scored following methods reported by Steckel and colleagues (2002) and described by Temple (2007b). Prevalence of this condition was compared as the total number of individuals with at least one orbital roof with evidence of CO divided by the total number of individuals with at least one orbital roof. CO prevalence was calculated separately for two age groups: subadults (age <15 years) and adults (age >15 years).

Periostitis

Periostitis is a nonspecific indicator of infectious disease and is character-ized by long rugged spicules of woven bone with porous surfaces that are raised above the bony cortex (Ortner 2003). Periosteal reactions also occur in response to trauma; bilateral distribution of lesions helps differentiate peri-ostitis arising from infectious disease (Ortner 2003). Because this study ad-dresses systemic perturbation, only individuals with both observable tibiae are included. Periostitis prevalence was calculated as the number of individu-als with bilaterally distributed periosteal reaction on the tibiae divided by the total number of individuals with two intact tibiae. Intact tibiae preserve approximately ¾ of tibial length. Frequency of periostitis was calculated separately for three age groups: subadults (age <15 years), young adults (age 15–23 years), and older adults (age >23 years).

Results and Discussion

Dental Caries and Dietary Variation

Summary statistics for carious tooth frequencies compared between the Jomon and Yayoi samples are listed in table 14.2. The Yayoi period people from northern Kyushu/southern Honshu (NK/SH) in Age Group 1 had sig-nificantly greater overall carious tooth frequencies than did those from the Jomon period (G = 2.8; $p < .05$; df = 1). Tanegashima Island people from

Table 14.2. Percentages of carious teeth compared between Jomon and Yayoi samples

Group	Ant.		Pre.		Mol.		Total	
	N	% C	N	% C	N	% C	N	% C
Age Group 1								
NK/SH Yayoi	109	2.8	91	3.3	121	18.1	321	8.7
Tanegashima Yayoi	40	—	29	—	50	10.0	119	4.2
Late to Final Jomon	160.1	1.3	106.8	5.2	160.1	18.8	427	6.5
Age Group 2								
NK/SH Yayoi	613	6.9	494	5.1	618	19.1	1,725	10.7
Tanegashima Yayoi	282	0.07	245	4.4	327	18.3	854	8.3
Late to Final Jomon	604.2	3.1	402.8	3.4	604.2	14.1	1,611.2	9.8

Note: N = number of teeth in a tooth group (Ant. = anterior teeth; Pre. = premolar teeth; Mol. = molar teeth); % C = percentage of carious teeth.

the Yayoi period in Age Group 1 did not have statistically significantly different frequencies of carious teeth when compared to foragers from the Jomon period.

The Yayoi period people from NK/SH in Age Group 2 likewise had significantly greater carious tooth frequencies than did those from the Jomon period ($G = 6.7$; $p < .01$; $df = 1$). Statistically significant differences in carious tooth frequencies between the Tanegashima Island people from the Yayoi period compared to foragers from the Jomon period were not observed in the Age Group 2. Total carious tooth frequencies did not differ between males and females from the Yayoi period in Age Group 1 (table 14.3). However, the total frequency of carious teeth among females from the Yayoi period was statistically significantly ($p < .001$) greater than males in Age Group 2.

The generally greater frequency of carious teeth among the prehistoric people from the Yayoi period when compared to foragers from the Jomon period is consistent with an agriculturally dependent economy. This finding is supported by a greater degree of social complexity, population density, and archaeological evidence for human reliance on cultigens during the Yayoi period (Koyama 1978; Imamura 1996a,b; Tsude 2001; Mizoguchi 2002, 2003).

Rises in carious tooth frequencies following the introduction of wet-rice

Table 14.3. Sex-specific percentages of carious teeth during the Yayoi period

Group	Ant.		Pre.		Mol.		Total	
	N	% C	N	% C	N	% C	N	% C
Age Group 1								
NK/SH males	83	—	66	3.0	97	15.4	246	6.9
NK/SH females	42	—	28	3.5	41	17.1	111	7.2
Tanegashima Island males	42	—	30	—	41	—	113	—
Tanegashima Island females	—	—	—	—	—	—	—	—
Total males	125	—	96	2.1	138	10.9	359	7.8
Total females	69	—	50	2.0	70	10.0	189	6.9
Age Group 2								
NK/SH males	214	4.2	161	5.6	189	17.9	564	9.2
NK/SH females	161	7.5	124	10.4	124	33.9	409	16.7
Tanegashima Island males	49	—	40	1.6	46	19.2	135	3.7
Tanegashima Island females	27	—	22	7.1	29	17.6	78	6.4
Total males	263	3.4	201	5.0	235	18.3	699	8.2
Total females	161	7.5	124	12.1	124	38.7	409	16.6

Note: N = number of teeth in a tooth group (Ant = anterior teeth; Pre = premolar teeth; Mol = molar teeth); % C = percentage of carious teeth.

economies in prehistoric Japan contrast with previous findings from Southeast Asia (Oxenham 2000; Tayles et al. 2000; Pietrusewsky and Douglas 2002a,b). Rice contains significant levels of starch (Arens 1999). Starch molecules require considerable time before clearance from the oral cavity by saliva (Firestone et al. 1982; Arens 1999). In this sense, rice is a cariogenic product. It is, however, possible that the wet rice consumed by prehistoric people of Thailand and Vietnam was less refined than the wet rice consumed in prehistoric Japan—wet-rice agriculture was introduced to the Japanese islands some 1,000 years after its spread across the Asian continent (Imamura 1996a,b; Tsude 2001).

Malocclusion is associated with greater caries burdens because food particles are often trapped between maloccluded teeth and exposed to oral bacteria for greater periods of time. In Yayoi period Japan, malocclusion prevalence increased significantly compared to the Jomon period and may also have contributed to the greater caries prevalence among these agricultural people (Inoue et al. 1986; Temple and Larsen 2007).

The similar frequency of carious teeth between the Jomon and Yayoi from Tanegashima Island (TI) likely represents dietary continuity between the two groups. Studies of tooth size and shape among living and prehistoric people from TI suggest that the residents of this region are closely related to Jomon people (Suzuki 1992; Matsumura 1995). This indicates that gene flow from continental Asia to TI was muted during the Yayoi period. It is, by extension, possible that the introduction of an economic base from continental Asia such as wet-rice agriculture was also minimized on TI. In particular, only slight reductions in tooth attrition are noted between Jomon and Yayoi period groups from TI (Todaka et al. 2003).

Significantly greater frequencies of carious teeth were observed in Yayoi period females compared to males. The sexual division of labor in many traditional agricultural and horticultural societies is associated with differential access to meat versus plant products and subsequently observed carious teeth (e.g., Walker and Hewlett 1990). These differences are also observed in bioarchaeological studies where sex-based variation in carious tooth frequencies is attributed to greater consumption of meat by men and greater plant consumption among women (Larsen 1983; Larsen et al. 1991; Kelley et al. 1991; Lukacs and Pal 1993; Lukacs 1996). Similar results are reported among agricultural people from select sites in Vietnam and Thailand (Oxenham 2000; Tayles et al. 2000).

Recent reviews of the clinical literature suggest that female reproductive physiology in association with life history may influence caries prevalence between the sexes (Lukacs and Largaespada 2006; Lukacs 2008). Two major findings associated with salivary buffering capacity support this hypothesis: (1) salivary buffering capacity is greatly reduced in association with pregnancy and hormone fluctuations during development; and (2) pregnancy is associated with a reduction in the antimicrobial properties of saliva (Lukacs and Largaespada 2006). Enhanced differences in caries prevalence between the sexes in many agricultural and industrial groups are observed following fertility spikes (Lukacs 2008).

Variation in sex-specific caries prevalence is observed in southern Honshu but not northern Kyushu (Oyamada et al. 1996; Temple and Larsen 2007). Both regions experienced exponential population growth following the agricultural transition (Koyama 1978; Hanihara 1987). If reproductive ecology were a primary contributor to variation in caries prevalence between the sexes during the Yayoi period, then similar variation in caries prevalence should be noted between males and females from southern Honshu and northern Kyushu.

In addition, stable isotope studies of Yayoi period skeletal remains from the Koura site found evidence for greater consumption of marine products by males, while females consumed greater amounts of terrestrial plant foods (Chisholm et al. 1992). Furthermore, greater population growth rates are observed in northern Kyushu compared to southwestern Honshu during the Initial Yayoi period (Nakahashi 1993b; Nakahashi and Iizuka 1998). If reproductive ecology were a primary contributor to variation in caries prevalence between the sexes during the Yayoi period, then significant differences in caries prevalence should also be noted between the sexes in northern Kyushu. This suggests that differences in caries prevalence between males and females of the Yayoi period primarily reflect dietary variation, possibly in concert with a sexual division of labor.

Linear Enamel Hypoplasia (LEH) and Systemic Stress

Overall prevalence of teeth with at least one observable LEH defect is significantly greater among eastern ($G = 6.9$; $p < .05$) and western ($G = 95.6$; $p < .001$) Jomon foragers compared to Yayoi agriculturalists (table 14.4).

No significant differences are observed in MxFI antimeres affected by LEH defects between the eastern Jomon and Yayoi samples ($G = 3.2$), while significantly greater frequencies of MxFI antimeres affected by LEH defects are observed among western Jomon compared to Yayoi groups ($G = 5.5$; $p < .05$) (table 14.5). No significant difference in MaC antimeres affected by LEH defects are observed between the eastern Jomon and Yayoi samples ($G = 0.644$). Significantly greater frequencies of MaC antimeres are affected by LEH defects among western Jomon compared to Yayoi people ($G = 7.8$; $p < .05$) (table 14.5).

Table 14.4. Distribution of enamel hypoplasia between Jomon and Yayoi samples

Group	Teeth N	LEH %
NK/SH Yayoi	965	30.2
Tanegashima Island Yayoi	402	53.5
Eastern Jomon	559	36.8
Western Jomon	165	57.0

Table 14.5. Percentage of antimeric tooth pairs expressing LEH defects on both teeth

Group	MxFI antimeres[a] N	LEH[b] %	(Y:) p<	MaC antimeres[c] N	LEH[b] %	(Y:) p<
Yayoi (Y)	77	35.1	—	76	34.2	—
Eastern Jomon (EJ)	47	21.2	n.s.[d]	23	56.5	n.s.[d]
Western Jomon (WJ)	28	60.7	.05	39	61.5	.01

[a] Number of maxillary first incisor antimeres.
[b] Percentage of antimeres expressing LEH defects.
[c] Number of mandibular canine antimeres.
[d] Does not reflect a statistically significant result compared to Yayoi samples.

Significantly greater frequencies of teeth (antimeric and overall) with LEH defects were observed among western Jomon compared to Yayoi people. Western/inland Jomon people consumed foods that were available in a seasonal capacity (Akazawa and Aikens 1986; Akazawa 1999) and experienced greater stress prevalence as a consequence (Shigehara 1994; Temple 2007b). In contrast, Yayoi people were agriculturally dependent, relying on a predictable and renewable source of food (Imamura 1996a,b). It is, therefore, likely that the variation in enamel hypoplasia prevalence observed between the western/inland Jomon and NK/SH Yayoi is associated with resource stability. Yayoi people relied on dietary products with greater availability and predictability than those chosen by the western Jomon.

Similar frequencies of teeth with LEH defects were observed between eastern Jomon and Yayoi people. Jomon foragers from eastern Japan relied upon combinations of food that was annually available, including maritime resources, terrestrial mammals, and various plant products (Akazawa 1999). Yayoi people relied heavily on wet-rice agriculture with the continued consumption of marine resources (Chisholm et al. 1992; Chisholm and Koike 1999). Here, Jomon and Yayoi groups likely relied on different staple foods but were both active participants in economies characterized by renewable, stable food sources.

Increased stress levels among the TI Yayoi compared to the eastern Jomon and NK/SH Yayoi is associated with population density and environment. Enamel growth is sensitive to infectious disease. Experimental studies of sheep demonstrate that artificially induced parasite infection is related to a greater risk of enamel hypoplasia (Suckling and Thurley 1984; Suckling et al. 1986). Parasite loads are particularly heavy among maritime foragers, for whom the contamination of water supplies and the consumption of improperly cooked fish facilitate outbreaks of infectious disease (Walker 2006). This process is well documented in coastal environments such as Guam and the Channel Islands, where elevated frequencies of enamel hypoplasia are observed among prehistoric coastal foragers in response to infectious disease prevalence (Walker and Lambert 1989; Lambert 1993; Stodder 1997).

Prehistoric Yayoi people from Tanegashima Island consumed significant amounts of maritime resources (Chisholm et al. 1992; Chisholm and Koike 1999) and likely experienced a large population spike following the agricultural transition (Koyama 1978). It is, therefore, possible that the densely packed island environment occupied by TI Yayoi cultures fostered greater levels of infection. These infectious diseases are associated with the elevated level of enamel hypoplasia observed among TI Yayoi groups.

Cribra Orbitalia (CO) and Infection

Table 14.6 lists the summary statistics for cribra orbitalia prevalence between Jomon and Yayoi samples. Cribra orbitalia frequencies were not statistically significantly different between Middle to Final Jomon foragers and Yayoi agriculturalists between the ages of 0 and 15 years or those greater than 15 years old.

Cranial porosity is described among maritime foragers from the California coast (Walker 1986) and densely populated desert agriculturalists (Walker 1985). These lesions are, in maritime/populous environments, associated

Table 14.6. Distribution of cribra orbitalia between Jomon and Yayoi samples

Group	IndividualsN	Porotic%
Age Group 1		
Jomon	24	51.5
Yayoi	33	50.0
Age Group 2		
Jomon	209	9.9
Yayoi	111	8.6

Note: Tanegashima Island sample not included.

with systemic stress stemming from parasitic infection, prolonged weaning due to poor resource availability, and diarrhea caused by the use of contaminated water supplies (Walker 1985, 1986).

Jomon and Yayoi people occupied coastal, populous environments and consumed maritime resources (Koyama 1978; Imamura 1996a; Chisholm and Koike 1999). Whipworms are observed in coprolites from the Jomon period Sannai Maruyama site (Matsui et al. 2003). Both whipworms and roundworms are found in coprolites recovered from the moat alongside the Ikegami-Sone Yayoi site (Matsui et al. 2003). These findings suggest that the patterns of CO observed between Jomon and Yayoi people were associated with parasite infection, particularly *Ascaris* and *Trichuris* genera. The environment and distribution of Jomon and Yayoi people suggest that infection by parasites such as *Schistosoma japonica, Diphyllobothrium* sp., and *Ascaris* sp. may also have contributed to the patterning of CO reported by this study (Temple 2010).

It is also important to consider trachoma as a possible contributor to these lesions (Wapler et al. 2004; Walker et al. 2009). Trachoma is an infectious disease of the eye caused by direct contact with the bacteria *Clamidia trachomitis* (Wright et al. 2008). Elevated frequencies of trachoma are reported in dense populations lacking access to sanitary bathing and drinking facilities, particularly those where young people lack access to clean water for proper facial cleansing (Wright et al. 2008).

Access to sanitary bathing and drinking facilities were a major environmental hazard for prehistoric coastal communities, particularly those with dense populations (Walker 2006). Both Jomon and Yayoi people occupied regions of high population density and were likely crowded in many communities (Koyama 1978). Poor sanitation among these groups is indicated by reports of fecal material within water sources around settlements (Matsui et al. 2003). In this sense, both Jomon and Yayoi people occupied environments where trachoma infection was a likely environmental hazard and a contributor to the CO lesions observed by this study.

Chronic Systemic Infection

Summary statistics for periostitis frequencies are listed in table 14.7. No statistically significant differences were observed in periostitis frequencies between Jomon and Yayoi subadults (0–15 years) or young adults (15–23 years). The small sample sizes from which data were collected in the younger age groups is most likely associated with this result. Eastern Jomon adults (23+ years) had statistically significantly greater frequencies of periostitis than did the Yayoi (G = 8.03) in the same age group. A statistically signifi-

Table 14.7. Distribution of periostitis between Jomon and Yayoi samples

Group	No. of individuals	Periostitis	
		N	%
Age Group 1			
Yayoi	10	—	—
Eastern Jomon	28	4	14.3
Western Jomon	2	—	—
Age Group 2			
Yayoi	11	—	—
Eastern Jomon	17	2	11.8
Western Jomon	11	1	9.1
Age Group 3			
Yayoi	110	3	2.7
Eastern Jomon	125	12	9.6
Western Jomon	44	1	2.3
Pooled groups			
Yayoi	131	3	2.3
Eastern Jomon	170	18	10.6
Western Jomon	57	2	3.5

Note: Tanegashima Island sample not included.

cantly greater frequency of periostitis was also observed among the Jomon compared to the Yayoi samples when the three age groups were pooled.

The significant decrease in periostitis frequency from the Jomon to Yayoi period was unexpected given the increase in population density recorded during this time (Koyama 1978; Hanihara 1987) and the likely introduction of tuberculosis bacilli to the Japanese islands by migrants from continental Asia (Suzuki and Inoue 2007; Suzuki et al. 2008). Stasis in the frequency of infectious disease is reported for many early agricultural communities in Southeast Asia (Pietrusewsky and Douglas 2002a,b; Domett and Tayles 2007). Greater diversity in the specific diseases identified in human skeletal remains is, however, observed following the agricultural transition in Vietnam, possibly because of greater exposure to animal vectors and population migration/colonization (Oxenham et al. 2005).

A similar trend is observed in Japan. Here, nonspecific and specific indicators of chronic infectious disease decline between the Jomon and Yayoi periods. The earliest skeletal case of tuberculosis is, however, reported in one Early Yayoi period skeleton (Suzuki et al. 2008) and is attributable to population movement into Japan from the Korean peninsula (Suzuki et al. 2008; Suzuki, this volume). Given the correspondence between migrant arrival and early cases of tuberculosis, population movement into Japan likely increased the *diversity* but not *frequency* of infectious disease during the agricultural transition. It is, however, important to point out that a greater prevalence of nonspecific and specific indicators of chronic infection are observed during the subsequent Kofun and Medieval periods (Suzuki 1996; Suzuki and Inoue 2007; Suzuki et al. 2008). This suggests that chronic infection increased in frequency following centralized political authority and intensive agricultural practices.

Conclusions

The transition to agriculture in prehistoric Japan is associated with a variety of changes within the biocultural landscape. Migrant groups from Northeast Asia introduced wet-rice agriculture and biologically and culturally subsumed the majority of indigenous Jomon people. Following this transition, there is a precipitous increase in carious tooth prevalence. Increases in carious teeth are likely associated with the introduction of a starch-heavy dietary staple in the form of wet rice and rises in malocclusion. Sex-specific differences in caries prevalence are also observed. Based on demographic and isotopic analyses, these differences are primarily attributable to dietary differences between males and females.

Reduction in enamel hypoplasia is observed between western/inland Jomon and Yayoi people. This trend is associated with the introduction of a predictable, renewable food source in the form of wet-rice agriculture. Few differences are observed in enamel hypoplasia between eastern Jomon and Yayoi people. These findings likely reflect the fact that both groups were active participants in economies reliant upon predictable, renewable food sources.

Similar frequencies of cribra orbitalia are observed between Jomon and Yayoi subadults and adults. These patterns likely reflect similar exposure to parasites and infectious bacteria. Similar exposure to such pathogens suggests little variation in living conditions between the two groups.

Finally, periostitis frequencies decline following the transition to agriculture in prehistoric Japan. Declines in periostitis prevalence suggest that chronic infectious disease reduced during the Yayoi period. Despite such declines, evidence for tuberculosis in Early Yayoi period skeletal remains (Suzuki et al. 2008) indicate a trend toward greater diversity in infectious disease burdens, likely a consequence of population movement into the Japanese islands (Suzuki et al. 2008; Suzuki, this volume). A rise in infectious disease prevalence during subsequent historic periods argues that lifestyles associated with the agricultural transition (i.e., migration and sedentism) likely exacerbated the infectious disease load once certain aggregation/density thresholds were met.

The results of this study are important to understanding the biological impact of wet-rice farming within the global context of agricultural economies for several reasons. First, the results suggest that increases in dental caries prevalence are linked to the consumption of carbohydrate-heavy foods, including those with elevated starch composition. Japan does, however, represent the first location where increased cariogenesis in response to wet-rice agriculture is observed. This implies that food processing and preparation may play a role in activating the cariogenic, starch-based component of wet rice. This pattern differs from the uniform increase in caries prevalence in regions where sucrose-rich plant foods such as maize were adopted as primary nutritional staples.

Second, decreases in nutritional stress among the Yayoi compared to Jomon people argue that the biological impact of agriculture was not uniform: some communities experienced reduced disruptions in nutritional homeostasis. It is, however, important to point out that the improvement in nutritional status during the agricultural transition in prehistoric Japan is linked to the continued procurement of animal-source foods and the adoption of a mature form of agricultural production. Many regions that experienced increases in nutritional stress prevalence utilized newly adopted subsistence technologies and primarily consumed nutritionally inadequate plant foods.

Finally, two major findings regarding infectious disease and the global contextualization of the agricultural transition in prehistoric Japan are also important to point out. First, similar prevalence of cribra orbitalia suggests little change in lifestyle between Jomon and Yayoi people. This process is attributed to the continuation, rather than adoption, of dense, sedentary lifestyles among Yayoi communities. This differs from communities where the agricultural transition resulted in a more abrupt pattern of population aggregation and subsequent exposure to parasites. Second, while evidence for chronic systemic infection declined, bioarchaeological evidence for the diversification of infectious disease is reported. Greater diversity in infectious disease is consistent with the introduction of new pathogens by migrant people (Yayoi) and continued dense, sedentary lifestyles.

Acknowledgments

Grant sponsors: Wenner-Gren Foundation for Anthropological Research; Office of International Affairs, Ohio State University.

Literature Cited

Adachi N, Shinoda K, Umetsu K, Matsumura H. 2009. Mitochondrial DNA analysis of Jomon skeletons from the Funadomari site, Hokkaido, and its implication for the origins of Native Americans. *American Journal of Physical Anthropology* 138: 255–65.

Akazawa T. 1999. Regional variation in Jomon hunting-fishing-gathering societies. In: Omoto K, editor. *Interdisciplinary perspectives on the origins of the Japanese.* Kyoto: International Research Center for Japanese Studies. Pp. 223–31.

Akazawa T, Aikens CM. 1986. Introduction. In: Akazawa T, Aikens CM, editors. *Prehistoric hunter-gatherers in Japan: New research methods.* University Museum, University of Tokyo, Bulletin no. 27. Pp. ix–x.

Arens U. 1999. *Oral health: diet and other factors.* Amsterdam: Elsevier.

Armelagos GJ. 1969. Disease in ancient Nubia. *Science* 163: 255–59.

Armelagos GJ. 1990. Health and disease in prehistoric populations in transition. In: Swedlund AC, Armelagos GJ, editors. *Disease in populations in transition.* New York: Bergin and Garvey. Pp. 127–44.

Armelagos GJ, Van Gerven DP, Martin DL, Huss-Ashmore R. 1984. Effects of nutritional change on the skeletal biology of northeast African (Sudanese Nubian) populations. In: Clark JD, Brandt SA, editors. *From hunters to farmers: The causes and consequences of food production in Africa.* Berkeley: University of California Press. Pp. 132–46.

Baba H, Narasalo S, Ohyama S. 1998. Minatogawa hominid fossils and the evolution of Late Pleistocene humans in East Asia. *Anthropological Science* 106S: 27–45.

Binford LR. 1981. Willow smoke and dogs' tails: Hunter-gatherer settlement systems and archaeological site formation. *American Antiquity* 45: 4–20.

Brace CL, Nagai M. 1982. Japanese tooth size: Past and present. *American Journal of Physical Anthropology* 59: 399–411.

Buikstra JE, Ubelaker DH. 1994. *Standards for data collection from human skeletal remains.* Arkansas Archaeological Research Survey Series no. 44. Fayetteville.

Chisholm B, Koike H. 1999. Reconstructing prehistoric Japanese diet using stable isotopic analysis. In: Omoto K, editor. *Interdisciplinary perspectives on the origins of the Japanese.* Kyoto: International Research Center for Japanese Studies. Pp. 199–222.

Chisholm B, Koike H, Nakai N. 1992. Carbon isotopic determination of paleodiet in Japan: Marine versus terrestrial resources. In: Aikens CM, Nai Rhee S, editors. *Pacific Northeast Asia in prehistory: Hunter-fisher-gatherers, farmers, and sociopolitical elites.* Pullman: Washington State University Press. Pp. 69–74.

Cohen MN, Armelagos GJ. 1984. *Paleopathology at the origins of agriculture.* Orlando, FL: Academic Press.

Cohen MN, Crane-Kramer GMM, editors. 2007. *Ancient health: Skeletal indicators of agricultural and economic intensification.* Gainesville: University Press of Florida.

Cook DC. 1980. Subsistence base and health in the prehistoric Illinois Valley: Evidence from the human skeleton. *Medical Anthropology* 3: 109–24.

Domett K, Tayles N. 2007. Population health from the Bronze to the Iron Age in the Mun River Valley, northeastern Thailand. In: Cohen MN, Crane-Kramer GMM, editors. *Ancient health: Skeletal indicators of agricultural and economic intensification.* Gainesville: University Press of Florida. Pp. 286–99.

Douglas MT, Pietrusewsky M. 2007. Biological consequences of sedentism: Agricultural intensification in northeast Thailand. In: Cohen MN, Crane-Kramer GMM, editors. *Ancient health:*

skeletal indicators of agricultural and economic intensification. Gainesville: University Press of Florida. Pp. 300–319.

El-Najjar MY, Ryan DJ, Turner CG, Lozoff B. 1976. The etiology of porotic hyperostosis among prehistoric and historic Anasazi Indians of southwestern United States. *American Journal of Physical Anthropology* 44: 477–87.

Firestone AR, Schmid R, Muhlemann HR. 1982. Cariogenic effects of cooked wheat starch alone or with sucrose and frequency controlled feedings in rats. *Archives of Oral Biology* 27: 759–63.

Floyd B, Littleton J. 2006. Linear enamel hypoplasia and growth in an Australian Aboriginal community: Not so small, but not so healthy either. *Annals of Human Biology* 33: 424–43.

Fujita H. 1995. Geographical and chronological differences in dental caries in the Neolithic Jomon period of Japan. *Anthropological Science* 103: 23–37.

Goodman AH, Armelagos GJ. 1985. Factors influencing the distribution of enamel hypoplasias within the human permanent dentition. *American Journal of Physical Anthropology* 68: 479–93.

Goodman AH, Martinez C, Chavez A. 1991. Nutritional supplementation and the development of linear enamel hypoplasias in children from Tezonteopan, Mexico. *American Journal of Clinical Nutrition* 53: 773–81.

Goodman AH, Rose JC. 1991. Dental enamel hypoplasias as indicators of nutritional status. In: Kelley MA, Larsen CS, editors. *Advances in dental anthropology.* New York: Wiley-Liss. Pp. 279–93.

Guatelli-Steinberg D. 2003. Macroscopic and microscopic analyses of linear enamel hypoplasia in Plio-Pleistocene South African hominins with respect to aspects of enamel development and morphology. *American Journal of Physical Anthropology* 120: 309–22.

Hammer MF, Karafet TM, Park H, Omoto K, Harihara S, Stoneking M, Horai S. 2006. Dual origins of the Japanese: Common ground for hunter-gatherer and farmer Y-chromosomes. *Journal of Human Genetics* 51: 47–58.

Hanihara K. 1987. Estimation of number of early migrants to Japan: A simulative study. *Journal of the Anthropological Society of Nippon* 56: 391–403.

Hanihara K. 1991. Dual structure model for the population history of the Japanese. *Japan Review* 2: 1–33.

Hanihara T, Ishida H. 2009. Regional differences in craniofacial diversity and the population history of Jomon Japan. *American Journal of Physical Anthropology* 139: 311–22.

Harris DR. 1989. An evolutionary continuum of people-plant interaction. In: Harris DR, Hillman GC, editors. *Foraging and farming: The evolution of plant exploitation.* London: Unwin Hyman. Pp. 11–26.

Hillson SW. 1996. *Dental anthropology.* Cambridge: Cambridge University Press.

Hillson SW. 2001. Recording dental caries in archaeological human remains. *International Journal of Osteoarchaeology* 11: 249–89.

Hudson MJ. 1999. *Ruins of identity: Ethnogenesis in the Japanese islands.* Honolulu: University of Hawai'i Press.

Imamura K. 1996a. *Prehistoric Japan: New perspectives on insular East Asia.* Honolulu: University of Hawai'i Press.

Imamura K. 1996b. Jomon and Yayoi: The transition to agriculture in Japanese prehistory. In: Harris DR, editor. *The origins and spread of agriculture and pastoralism in Eurasia.* Washington, DC: Smithsonian Institution Press. Pp. 442–64.

Imamura K. 2006. Archaeological theory and Japanese methodology: A review of Junko Habu's "Ancient Jomon of Japan." *Anthropological Science* 114: 223–29.

Inoue N, Ito G, Kamegai T. 1986. Dental pathology of hunter-gatherers and early farmers in prehistoric Japan. In: Akazawa T, Aikens CM, editors. *Prehistoric hunter-gatherers in Japan: New research methods.* University Museum, University of Tokyo Bulletin 27. Tokyo. Pp. 163–98.

Kelley MA, Levesque DR, Weidl E. 1991. Contrasting patterns of dental disease in five early northern Chilean groups. In: Kelley MA, Larsen CS, editors. *Advances in dental anthropology.* New York: Wiley-Liss. Pp. 179–202.

Kennedy KAR. 1984. Growth, nutrition, and pathology in changing paleodemographic settings in South Asia. In: Cohen MN, Armelagos GJ, editors. Paleopathology at the origins of agriculture. Orlando, FL: Academic Press. Pp. 169–92.

Kobayashi T. 2005. *Jomon reflections: Forager life and culture in the prehistoric Japanese archipelago.* Oxford, UK: Oxbow Books.

Koyama S. 1978. Jomon subsistence and population. *Senri Ethnological Studies* 2: 1–65.

Lallo J, Armelagos GJ, Rose JC. 1978. Paleoepidemiology of infectious disease in the Dickson Mounds population. *Medical College of Virginia Quarterly* 14: 17–23.

Lambert PM. 1993. Health in prehistoric populations of the Santa Barbara Channel Islands. *American Antiquity* 58: 509–22.

Larsen CS. 1983. Behavioural implications of temporal change in cariogenesis. *Journal of Archaeological Science* 10: 1–8.

Larsen CS. 1987. Bioarchaeological interpretations of subsistence economy and behavior from human skeletal remains. In: Schiffer MB, editor. *Advances in archaeological method and theory.* New York: Academic Press. Pp. 339–445.

Larsen CS. 1995. Biological changes in human populations with agriculture. *Annual Review of Anthropology* 24: 185–213.

Larsen CS. 1997. *Bioarchaeology: interpreting behavior from the human skeleton.* Cambridge: Cambridge University Press.

Larsen CS. 2002. Post-Pleistocene human evolution: Bioarchaeology of the agricultural transition. In: Ungar PS, Teaford MF, editors. *Human diet: Its origin and evolution.* Westport, CT: Bergin and Garvey. Pp. 19–35.

Larsen CS. 2003. Animal source foods and human health during evolution. *Journal of Nutrition* 133: 3893S–3897S.

Larsen CS. 2006. The agricultural revolution as environmental catastrophe: Implications for health and lifestyle in the Holocene. *Quaternary International* 150: 12–20.

Larsen CS, Crosby AW, Griffin MC, Hutchinson DL, Ruff CB, Russell KF, Schoeninger MJ, Sering LE, Simpson SW, Takács JL, Teaford MF. 2002. A biohistory of health and behavior in the Georgia Bight: The agricultural transition and the impact of European contact. In: Steckel RH, Rose JC, editors. *The backbone of history: Health and nutrition in the Western Hemisphere.* Cambridge: Cambridge University Press. Pp. 406–39.

Larsen CS, Harn DE. 1994. Health in transition: Disease and nutrition in the Georgia Bight. In: Sobolik K, editor. *Paleonutrition: The diet and health of prehistoric Americans.* Center for Archaeological Investigations, Occasional Papers 22. Carbondale: Southern Illinois University at Carbondale. Pp. 222–34.

Larsen CS, Shavit R, Griffin MC. 1991. Dental caries as evidence for dietary change: An archaeological context. In: Kelley MA, Larsen CS, editors. *Advances in dental anthropology.* New York: Wiley-Liss. Pp. 179–92.

Lukacs JR. 1996. Sex differences in dental caries with the origin of agriculture in South Asia. *Current Anthropology* 37: 147–53.

Lukacs JR. 2008. Fertility and agriculture accentuate sex differences in dental caries rates. *Current Anthropology* 49: 901–14.

Lukacs JR, Largaespada L. 2006. Explaining sex differences in dental caries prevalence: Saliva, hormones, and life-history etiologies. *American Journal of Human Biology* 18: 540–55.

Lukacs JR, Pal JN. 1993. Mesolithic subsistence in northern India: Inferences from dental pathology and odontometry. *Current Anthropology* 34: 745–65.

Lukacs JR, Walimbe SR, Floyd B. 2001. Epidemiology of enamel hypoplasia in deciduous teeth: Explaining variation in prevalence in western India. *American Journal of Human Biology* 13: 788–807.

Martin DL, Armelagos GJ, Goodman GJ, Van Gerven DP. 1984. The effects of socioeconomic change in prehistoric Africa: Sudanese Nubia as a case study. In: Cohen MN, Armelagos GJ, editors. *Paleopathology at the origins of agriculture*. Orlando, FL: Academic Press. Pp. 193–214.

Matsui A, Kanehara M, Kanehara M. 2003. Palaeoparasitology in Japan: Discovery of toilet features. *Memórias do Instituto Oswaldo Cruz* 98 (Suppl. 1): 127–36.

Matsumura H. 1995. A microevolutional history of the Japanese people as viewed from dental characteristics. *Anthropological Science* 102: 93–118.

Matsumura H, Hudson M. 2005. Dental perspectives on the population history of Southeast Asia. *American Journal of Physical Anthropology* 127: 182–209.

Mizoguchi K. 2002. *Archaeological history of Japan: 30,000 BCE to AD 700*. Philadelphia: University of Pennsylvania Press.

Mizoguchi K. 2003. Time and genealogical consciousness in the mortuary practices of the Yayoi period, Japan. *Journal of East Asian Archaeology* 3: 173–97.

Mizoguchi Y. 1986. Contributions of prehistoric Far East populations to the population of modern Japan: A Q-mode path analysis based on cranial measurements. In: Aikens CM, Akazawa T, editors. *Prehistoric hunter-gatherers in Japan: New research methods*. University Museum, University of Tokyo Bulletin 27. Tokyo. Pp. 107–36.

Nakahashi T. 1993a. Temporal craniometric changes from the Jomon to the Modern period in western Japan. *American Journal of Physical Anthropology* 90: 409–25.

Nakahashi T. 1993b. Explosive increase of Yayoi population estimated from the number of graves. *Gen Nihonjin Asahi One Theme Magazine* 14: 30–46.

Nakahashi T, Iizuka M. 1998. Anthropological study of the transition from the Jomon to the Yayoi periods in Northern Kyushu using morphological and paleodemographical features. *Anthropological Science* 106: 31–53.

Omoto K, Saitou N. 1997. Genetic origins of the Japanese: A partial support for the dual structure hypothesis. *American Journal of Physical Anthropology* 102: 437–46.

Ortner DJ. 2003. *Identification of pathological conditions in human skeletal remains*. Amsterdam: Academic Press.

Oxenham MF. 2000. Health and behavior during the Mid-Holocene and Metal period of northern Viet Nam. Ph.D. dissertation, Northern Territory University.

Oxenham MF, Matsumura H. 2008. Oral and physiological paleohealth in cold-adapted peoples: Northeast Asia, Hokkaido. *American Journal of Physical Anthropology* 135: 64–74.

Oxenham MF, Nguyen KT, Nguyen LC. 2005. Skeletal evidence for the emergence of infectious disease in Bronze Age and Iron Age northern Vietnam. *American Journal of Physical Anthropology* 126: 359–76.

Oxenham MF, Nguyen LC, Nguyen KT. 2002. Oral health in northern Viet Nam: Neolithic through Metal periods. *Bulletin of the Indo-Pacific Prehistory Association* 22: 121–34.

Oyamada J, Manabe Y, Kitagawa Y, Rokutanda A. 1996. Dental morbid condition of hunter-gatherers on Okinawa Island during the middle period of the prehistoric shell midden culture and of agriculturalists in northern Kyushu during the Yayoi period. *Anthropological Science* 104: 261–80.

Pietrusewsky M. 1999. Multivariate craniometric investigations of Japanese, Asians, and Pacific Islanders. In: Omoto K, editor. *Interdisciplinary perspectives on the origins of the Japanese*. Kyoto: International Research Center for Japanese Studies. Pp. 65–104.

Pietrusewsky M. 2005. The physical anthropology of the Pacific, East Asia and Southeast Asia: A multivariate craniometric analysis. In: Sagart L, Blench R, Sanchez-Mazas A, editors. *The peopling of East Asia: Putting together archaeology, linguistics and genetics*. London: Routledge-Curzon. Pp. 201–29.

Pietrusewsky M, Toomey-Douglas M. 2002a. *Ban Chiang: A prehistoric village site in northeast Thailand*. Vol. 1: *The human skeletal remains*. Philadelphia: University of Pennsylvania Press.

Pietrusewsky M, Toomey-Douglas M. 2002b. Intensification of agriculture at Ban Chiang: Is there evidence from the skeletons? *Asian Perspectives* 40: 157–78.

Powell ML. 1988. *Health and status in prehistory: A case study from Moundville*. Washington, DC: Smithsonian Institution Press.

Rose JC, Marks MK, Tieszen LL. 1991. Bioarchaeology and subsistence in the central and lower portions of the Mississippi Valley. In: Powell ML, Bridges PS, Mires AMW, editors. *What mean these bones? Studies in southeastern bioarchaeology*. Tuscaloosa: University of Alabama Press. Pp. 7–21.

Sanui Y. 1960. Anthropological researches on the teeth of the prehistoric Yayoi-ancients excavated from the Doigahama site, Yamaguchi Prefecture. *Journal of the Anthropological Society of Nippon* 3: 861–64.

Schultz M. 2001. Paleohistopathology of bone: A new approach to the study of ancient diseases. *Yearbook of Physical Anthropology* 44: 106–47.

Seguchi N, Umeda H, Nelson AR, Brace CL. 2007. Population movement into the Japanese archipelago during antiquity: A craniofacial and odontometric perspective [abstract]. *American Journal of Physical Anthropology Supplement* 44: 213.

Shigehara N. 1994. Human skeletal remains of the Middle to Late Jomon period excavated from the inland Kitamura site, Nagano Prefecture. *Anthropological Science* 102: 321–44.

Skinner MF, Dupras TL, Moya-Sola S. 1995. Periodicity of enamel hypoplasia among Miocene *Dryopithecus* from Spain. *Journal of Paleopathology Monograph Series* 7: 197–222.

Smith BD. 2000. Low level food production. *Journal of Archaeological Research* 9: 1–43.

Steckel RH, Sciulli PW, Rose JC. 2002. A health index from skeletal remains. In: Steckel RH, Rose JC, editors. *The backbone of history: Health and nutrition in the Western Hemisphere*. Cambridge: Cambridge University Press. Pp. 61–93.

Stodder ALW. 1997. Subadult stress, morbidity, and longevity in Latte period populations on Guam, Mariana Islands. *American Journal of Physical Anthropology* 104: 363–80.

Stuart-Macadam P. 1985. Porotic hyperostosis: representative of a childhood condition. *American Journal of Physical Anthropology* 66: 391–98.

Suckling G, Eliot DC, Thurley DC. 1986. The macroscopic appearance and associated histological changes in the enamel organ of hypoplastic lesions of sheep incisor teeth resulting from induced parasitism. *Archives of Oral Biology* 31: 427–39.

Suckling G, Thurley DC. 1984. Developmental defects of enamel: Factors influencing their macroscopic appearance. In: Fearnhead RW, Suga S, editors. *Tooth enamel IV*. New York: Elsevier Science Publishers. Pp. 357–62.

Suzuki A. 1992. Tooth crown affinities among five populations from Akita, Tsushima, Okinawa, in Japan and Middle Taiwan. *Journal of the Anthropological Society of Nippon* 100: 171–82.

Suzuki T. 1991. Paleopathological study on infectious diseases in Japan. In: Aufderheide AC, Ortner DJ, editors. *Human paleopathology: Current syntheses and future options.* Washington, DC: Smithsonian Institution Press. Pp. 128–39.

Suzuki T. 1996. Indicators of stress in prehistoric Jomon skeletal remains from Japan. *Anthropological Science* 106: 127–37.

Suzuki T, Inoue T. 2007. Earliest evidence of spinal tuberculosis from the Aneolithic Yayoi period in Japan. *International Journal of Osteoarchaeology* 17: 392–402.

Suzuki T, Inoue T, Choi JG. 2008. Brief communication: New evidence of tuberculosis from Korea—Population movement and evidence of tuberculosis in Far East Asia. *American Journal of Physical Anthropology* 136: 357–60.

Tayles N, Domett K, Nelsen K. 2000. Agriculture and dental caries? The case of rice in prehistoric Southeast Asia. *World Archaeology* 32: 68–83.

Temple DH. 2007a. Dietary variation and stress among prehistoric Jomon foragers from Japan. *American Journal of Physical Anthropology* 133: 1035–46.

Temple DH. 2007b. Human biological variation during the agricultural transition in prehistoric Japan. Ph.D. dissertation, Ohio State University.

Temple DH. 2008. What can stature variation reveal about environmental differences between prehistoric Jomon foragers? Understanding the impact of systemic stress on developmental stability. *American Journal of Human Biology* 20: 431–39.

Temple DH. 2010. Patterns of systemic stress during the agricultural transition in prehistoric Japan. *American Journal of Physical Anthropology* 142: 112–24.

Temple DH, Auerbach BM, Nakatsukasa M, Sciulli PW, Larsen CS. 2008. Variation in limb proportions between Jomon foragers and Yayoi agriculturalists from prehistoric Japan. *American Journal of Physical Anthropology* 137: 164–74.

Temple DH, Larsen CS. 2007. Dental caries prevalence as evidence for agriculture and subsistence variation during the Yayoi period in prehistoric Japan: Biocultural interpretations of an economy in transition. *American Journal of Physical Anthropology* 134: 501–12.

Todaka Y, Oyamada J, Manabe Y, Kitagawa Y, Kato K, Rokutanada A. 2003. The relationship between immigration and the prevalence of dental caries in the Yayoi people. *Anthropological Science* 111: 265–92.

Tsude H. 2001. Yayoi farmers reconsidered: New perspectives on agricultural development in East Asia. *Bulletin of the Indo-Pacific Prehistory Association* 5: 53–59.

Turner CG II. 1979. Dental anthropological indications of agriculture among the Jomon people of central Japan. X. Peopling of the Pacific. *American Journal of Physical Anthropology* 51: 619–36.

Turner CG II. 1990. Major features of Sundadonty and Sinodonty, including suggestions about East Asian microevolution, population history, and Late Pleistocene relationships with Australian Aboriginals. *American Journal of Physical Anthropology* 82: 295–317.

Turner CG II. 1992. Sundadonty and Sinodonty in Japan: the dental basis for a dual origin hypothesis for the peopling of the Japanese islands. In: Hanihara K, editor. *Japanese as a member of the Asian-Pacific populations.* Kyoto: International Research Center for Japanese Studies. Pp. 97–111.

Ubelaker DH. 1984. Prehistoric human biology of Ecuador: Possible temporal trends and cultural correlations. In: Cohen MN, Armelagos GJ, editors. *Paleopathology at the origins of agriculture.* Orlando, FL: Academic Press. Pp. 491–513.

Underhill A, Habu J. 2006. Early communities in East Asia: Economic and sociopolitical organization at the local and regional levels. In: Stark MT, editor. *Archaeology of East Asia*. London: Blackwell Publishing. Pp. 121–48.

Walker PL. 1985. Anemia among prehistoric Indians of the American Southwest. In: Merbs CF, Miller RJ, editors. *Health and disease in the prehistoric Southwest*. Arizona State University Anthropological Research Papers 34. Tempe. Pp. 139–64.

Walker PL. 1986. Porotic hyperostosis in a marine-dependant California Indian population. *American Journal of Physical Anthropology* 69: 345–54.

Walker PL. 2006. A paleopathological perspective on coastal adaptations [abstract]. *American Journal of Physical Anthropology Supplement* 42: 183.

Walker PL, Bathurst RR, Richman R, Gjerdrum T, Andrushko VA. 2009. The causes of porotic hyperostosis and cribra orbitalia: A reappraisal of the iron-deficiency anemia hypothesis. *American Journal of Physical Anthropology* 139: 109–25.

Walker PL, Hewlett BS. 1990. Dental health, diet, and social status among central African foragers and farmers. *American Anthropologist* 92: 383–98.

Walker PL, Lambert P. 1989. Skeletal evidence for stress during a period of culture change in prehistoric California. *Journal of Paleopathology Monograph Series* 1: 207–12.

Wapler U, Crubézy E, Schultz M. 2004. Is cribra orbitalia synonymous with anemia? Analysis and interpretation of cranial pathology in Sudan. *American Journal of Physical Anthropology* 123: 333–39.

Wright HR, Turner A, Taylor HR. 2008. Trachoma. *Lancet* 371: 1945–54.

15

Change in the Linear Growth of Long Bones with the Adoption of Wet-Rice Agriculture in Japan

KENJI OKAZAKI

In an effort to demonstrate how changes in living conditions have affected body development, especially with the beginning of agriculture, the growth patterns of ancient Japanese populations were investigated using samples of juvenile skeletons from time frames ranging from the prehistoric Middle–Final Jomon (縄文) (c. 4000 –500/400 BC) to the early Modern periods (AD 1900–1950). Population health and levels of environmental stress experienced by ancient peoples have previously been assessed based on examination of skeletal remains excavated at sites in many different parts of the world. Some of the parameters considered in evaluating human well-being in the past include mean life expectancy, the frequency and severity of bone lesions indicative of systemic infection, and evidence of growth disruption. In the case of Japan, such studies have been relatively few in number, especially with regard to the Yayoi (弥生) period (c. 500/400 BC–AD 250/300), which is the time when agriculture first made a significant contribution to human subsistence in the archipelago. In this chapter, changes in community health and well-being through time in Japan are evaluated by comparing the average limb length of juvenile samples dating to each of four different prehistoric and historical periods. Dental eruption/formation was used for estimating the age at the death of juvenile samples.

Growth studies using older skeletal materials have been conducted in the context of a plethora of available information about the growth patterns of modern people. Modern children growing up in varied environments in many different countries have been measured to determine how environmental factors affect patterns of growth in height. For instance, children brought up in the impoverished living conditions typical of many developing nations (suffering, among other things, from poor nutrition, diarrhea, and infectious disease) are usually found to be relatively short as compared with children from more affluent backgrounds (Eveleth and Tanner 1990; Bogin 1999). These differences in height are most pronounced during childhood, while growth trajectories at puberty are more similar.

Although growth at all stages of development is controlled by an interaction between genetic inheritance and environmental conditions (Johnston et al. 1976; Martorell et al. 1977; Frisancho et al. 1980; Bogin 1999), these results suggest the possibility that growth patterns are more sensitive to environmental factors before puberty and that genetic influences on growth are expressed more strongly during adolescence. Studies of the growth trajectories of ancient peoples, such as that initiated by Johnston (1962), have demonstrated that growth in limb length is sensitive to environmental stress in the same way as height (Stloukal and Hanakova 1978; Hummert and Gerven 1983; Molleson 1989; Hoppa 1992; Saunders et al. 1993; Miles and Bulman 1994; Steyn and Henneberg 1996). In particular, studies of the subadult remains of native North Americans have shown that growth retardation increased markedly with the spread of maize agriculture and also after initial European contact and subsequent colonial expansion (Cook 1984; Goodman et al. 1984; Jantz and Owsley 1984a,b; Mensforth 1985; Lovejoy et al. 1990).

Well-preserved ancient juvenile skeletal remains are rarely recovered in Japan, largely because of the acidic soils typical of the archipelago. Studies of juvenile growth among prehistoric and early historic populations have also lagged somewhat behind in Japan because of a traditional focus in Japanese physical anthropology on "the origin of the Japanese" (i.e., the genealogical relationship between the Jomon and Yayoi peoples). It is conventionally believed that adult skeletons are the most appropriate source of information on this theme, because their morphological features are fully developed. However, in this study, emphasis is placed on how the change in living conditions that accompanied the introduction of wet-rice agriculture at the Jomon/ Yayoi transition affected trajectories of human growth in Japan, with the expectation of developing a more nuanced understanding of the circumstances of human life during that period.

Change in the trajectory of growth in femur length between Yayoi and the early Modern period has already been reported in an earlier paper (Okazaki 2004). In the present study, a group of Jomon skeletal individuals are added to the overall sample; measurements have also been taken in each case on the lengths of five other limb bones. The intention is to use growth suppression as a proxy measure for comparing overall health among Jomon, Yayoi, Muromachi (室町), and early Modern populations, as well as to evaluate how the effects of a switch from foraging to food production in Japan compare with findings made previously in the case of native North Americans, who underwent a similar transition.

Materials and Methods

Samples

The subadult skeletal samples used in this study—derived from the Neolithic Jomon, the Eneolithic Yayoi, the Medieval Muromachi, and the early Modern periods in Japan—are listed in table 15.1. The Jomon skeletal remains considered were excavated mainly in the part of the Japanese archipelago extending east from Yamaguchi Prefecture (山口県); most belong to the Middle–Final Jomon period (c. 4000–500/400 BC). Their distinctive morphological features separate them from later Japanese (Yamaguchi 1980, 1982; Dodo 1982). Archaeological evidence indicates that the Jomon people engaged mainly in gathering, hunting, and fishing. Yayoi (c. 500/400 BC–AD 250/300) skeletal remains were excavated in northern Kyushu and the Yamaguchi region (figure 15.1); they largely represent immigrants from the Asian mainland and their descendants (Kanaseki et al. 1960; Yamaguchi 1982; Hanihara 1984; Dodo 1987; Mizoguchi 1988; Nakahashi and Nagai 1989a; Hanihara 1991; Kim et al. 1993; Nakahashi 1993a; Yamaguchi and Huang 1995; DSAM/SPI 2000; Nakahashi and Li 2002). Most archaeologists accept that the Yayoi people either brought or received knowledge of wet-rice agriculture from the Asian mainland. The medieval Muromachi skeletal remains considered in this study were excavated at the Yoshimohama (吉母浜) site in Yamaguchi Prefecture (c. AD 1400–1600). They have morphological features in common with medieval people in other parts of Japan (Nakahashi and Nagai 1985). The early modern skeletal remains are those of individuals whose bodies were dissected at medical schools from late in the Meiji (AD 1868–1912) to the beginning of the Showa period (AD 1926–1989).

Juvenile skeletal materials excavated from different sites have been pooled together as a group in the cases of both the Jomon and the Yayoi periods; the total number of juvenile skeletons available is insufficient to make useful comparisons of differences in growth patterns between the remains from individual archaeological sites. The Yayoi skeletal samples were excavated from sites relatively close to one another, while those from the Jomon period came from a much wider swath of the Japanese archipelago. A study of regional differences during Jomon awaits the availability of a considerably larger sample.

For the purposes of this analysis, comparisons were also made with the morphological characteristics of prehistoric Native American subadult skeletons recovered at the Libben site (Lovejoy et al. 1990), as well as modern

Table 15.1. Materials used in this study

Sample name	Period/region	Developmental stage	Number of individuals[b]				Collection[c]
			Male	Female	Unknown	Total	
Jomon	Neolithic Jomon (9000 BC–500/400 BC)	Infancy (0–1 yr)	—	—	4	4	SMU, TUM, NUMD
	Hokkaido, Honshu	Childhood I (1–6 yrs)	—	—	35	35	UMT, NMNS, PAKU
	Shikoku, Kyushu	Childhood II (6–12 yrs)	—	—	26	26	KUM
		Adolescence (12–20 yrs)	1	1	10	12	KUM
		Total	1	1	75	77	
Yayoi	Eneolithic Yayoi (500/400 BC–AD 250/300)	Infancy (0–1 yr)	—	—	3	3	
	Northern Kyushu	Childhood I (1–6 yrs)	1	4	6	11	KUM
	Yamaguchi	Childhood II (6–12 yrs)	4	3	2	9	ECC
		Adolescence (12–20 yrs)	3	1	1	5	
		Total	8	8	12	28	
Muromachi	Medieval Muromachi (AD 1400–1600)	Infancy (0–1 yr)	—	—	9	9	
		Childhood I (1–6 yrs)	—	—	12	12	
	Yamaguchi	Childhood II (6–12 yrs)	1	—	2	3	KUM
		Adolescence (12–20 yrs)	2	2	0	4	
		Total	3	2	23	28	
Modern	Early Modern (AD 1900–AD 1950)	Infancy (0–1 yr)	—	—	1	1	
		Childhood I (1–6 yrs)	1	5	1	7	TUM, UMT, PAKU
	Tohoku, Kanto, Kinki	Childhood II (6–12 yrs)	5	7	—	12	KUM
	Kyushu	Adolescence (12–20 yrs)	5	5	—	10	
		Total	11	17	2	30	

[a] About 95 percent of the Jomon specimens are derived from the Middle–Final Jomon period (4000–500/400 BC).

[b] For information about sex determination for the Yayoi childhood individuals, see Okazaki 2005. The sex of the modern individuals was determined by means of archival documentation. The age of individuals was estimated by the criteria of dental eruption/formation.

[c] ECC = Educational Committee of Chikushino City; KUM = Kyushu University Museum; NMNS = National Museum of Nature and Science; NUMD = Niigata University Graduate School of Medical and Dental Science; PAKU = Laboratory of Physical Anthropology, Kyoto University; SMU = Sapporo Medical University; TUM = Tohoku University School of Medicine; UMT = University Museum, University of Tokyo.

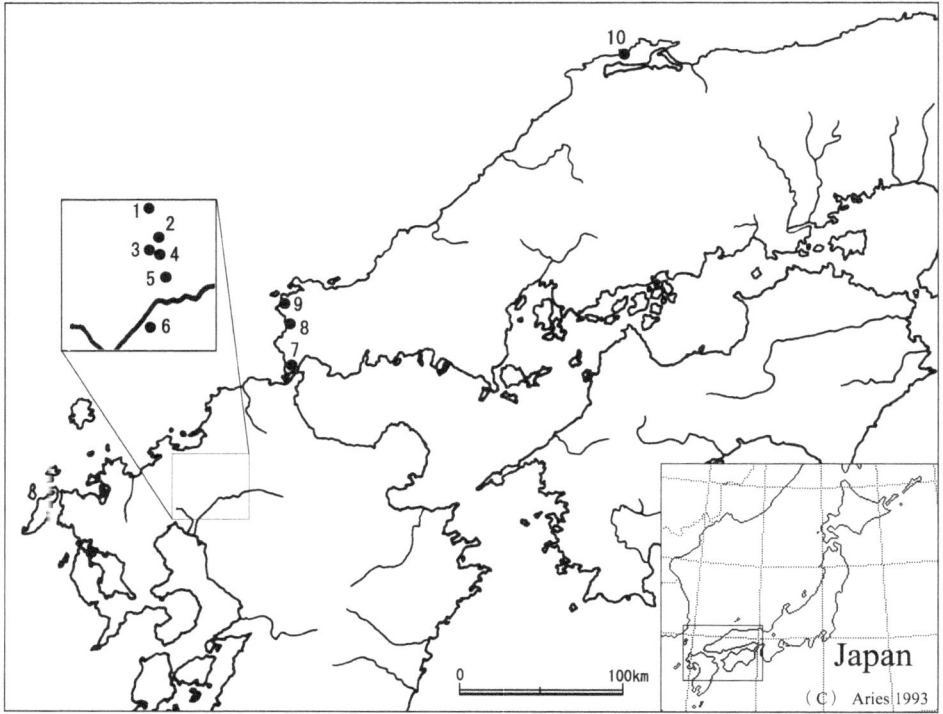

Figure 15.1. Location map of the excavation sites: (1) Kanenokuma; (2) Yoshigaura; (3) Dojoyama; (4) Nagaoka; (5) Kuma-Nishioda; (6) Tsukazakihigashihara; (7) Yoshimohama; (8) Nakanohama; (9) Doigahama; (10) Koura.

Euro-Americans from the Child Research Council growth study in the city of Denver (Maresh 1955). The Libben site is located in the Great Black Swamp of northern Ohio and dates to the late Woodland period (c. AD 800–1100). Archaeological analysis indicates that people living at Libben consumed maize, although it was not the main dietary staple (Lovejoy et al. 1990). Data on the modern Euro-Americans (c. AD 1930–1950) were collected using radiological measurements and are therefore slightly overstated, by a factor of 1.0–1.5 percent. Nevertheless, when considering ratios of subadult to adult long bone length, this technical difference between radiological and direct anatomical measurements would be inconsequential.

Age Determination

Age at the time of death of each subadult skeleton was estimated using the standard put forth by Smith (1991), itself based on a study by Moorrees and colleagues (1963a,b) of both the deciduous and permanent teeth of a sample composed of Euro-American children. This standard was adjusted to match the profile of Japanese subadults by referring to the method of Lovejoy and colleagues (1990). First, we calculated the difference between Euro-American children (Moorrees et al. 1963a,b) and Japanese children (Kaneda 1957) in the ages given at the stage when all but M3 formation is complete. It was found that the tooth formation of Japanese children is delayed by an average of 0.0458 years per year as compared with Euro-American children (e.g., a Euro-American 5-year-old would be equivalent in tooth development to a Japanese child of 5 + 5*0.0458 years of age). Therefore, the standard set forth by Smith (1991) was modified using a sliding scale based on this progressive discrepancy.

We tested the efficacy of this method of age determination using the early modern subadult skeletons, for which records of birth and death or an otherwise documented age at death were available (table 15.2). As viewed in the context of individuals for whom sex was correctly determined, incorrectly determined, or indeterminate, it was found that none of these conditions made a significant difference in estimated error (5 of 18 individuals had a smaller error when correctly identified as to sex). This suggests that sex differences in rates of tooth formation were not the main factor affecting estimated error in this study. In addition, a negative estimated error signifies that estimated age is greater than true age. Individuals for whom age was overestimated age were relatively few (4/18). This result seems to lend support to the validity of modifying the age standard used in this study to more accurately reflect the growth rates of Japanese children. Finally, estimated error converged at 0.5 years until about 8 years old but thereafter increased with age; it rose to a maximum of over two years after the middle teens, when most adult teeth are completely formed and only the third molar can be used for further age determination. The importance of this relatively large estimated error for the teenage years is minimized because of the focus in this study on growth before adolescence, thought to be more sensitive to environmental influences, as mentioned above.

Calculating Growth

For the purposes of this study, measured long bone length corresponds to diaphyseal length, because many of the available subadult skeletal remains lack their epiphyses. Sample sizes were insufficient to allow determination of precise growth curves, so regression curves were utilized to model trajectories of change relative to age. Linear, quadratic, or cubic regression formulae yielding the highest statistically significant correlation coefficient (R) were generally selected, although formulae with lower R were chosen if the difference was less than 0.03. The reason for this is to exclude curves that—unlike

Table 15.2. Dental ages assigned to the early modern subadult skeletons of known chronological age

Sample no.	Sex	True age	Outcome of sex determination	Number of teeth	Dental age			
					Mean	S D	CV	Error[a]
Kyushu Univ. no. 5585	Male	0.57	Correct sex	3	0.71	0.17	23.8	-0.14
			Sex unknown	3	0.70	0.20	28.5	-0.13
			Incorrect sex	3	0.68	0.23	33.4	-0.11
Tokyo Univ. no. 3031	Female	1.17	Correct sex	2	0.95	0.15	15.7	0.23
			Sex unknown	2	0.97	0.18	19.0	0.20
			Incorrect sex	2	2.00	0.22	22.0	0.18
Tokyo Univ. no. 398	Female	1.17	Correct sex	1	1.10	—	—	0.07
			Sex unknown	1	1.10	—	—	0.07
			Incorrect sex	1	1.10	—	—	0.07
Tokyo Univ. no. 390	Male	1.25	Correct sex	2	1.18	0.26	22.3	0.08
			Sex unknown	2	1.18	0.26	22.3	0.08
			Incorrect sex	2	1.18	0.26	22.3	0.08
Tokyo Univ. no. 3035	Female	1.75	Correct sex	1	2.35	—	—	-0.60
			Sex unknown	1	2.35	—	—	-0.60
			Incorrect sex	1	2.35	—	—	-0.60
Tokyo Univ. no. 3061	Female	2.33	Correct sex	1	2.17	—	—	0.16
			Sex unknown	1	2.17	—	—	0.16
			Incorrect sex	1	2.17	—	—	0.16

Specimen	Sex		Category					
Kyushu Univ. no. 5525	Female	3.22	Correct sex	5	2.30	0.40	17.2	0.92
			Sex unknown	5	2.35	0.37	15.8	0.87
			Incorrect sex	5	2.39	0.35	14.6	0.83
Kyushu Univ. no. 4667	Male	3.72	Correct sex	3	3.21	0.52	16.2	0.51
			Sex unknown	3	3.19	0.56	17.4	0.53
			Incorrect sex	3	3.17	0.60	18.8	0.55
Kyushu Univ. no. 4666	Female	5.87	Correct sex	7	5.56	0.42	7.5	0.31
			Sex unknown	6	5.79	0.32	5.5	0.08
			Incorrect sex	6	5.93	0.32	5.4	-0.06
Kyushu Univ. no. 679	Female	5.94	Correct sex	5	5.46	0.57	10.4	0.48
			Sex unknown	4	5.66	0.58	10.2	0.28
			Incorrect sex	4	5.75	0.58	10.0	0.19
Tokyo Univ. no. 3062	Female	6.75	Correct sex	1	6.80	—	—	-0.05
			Sex unknown	1	6.85	—	—	-0.10
			Incorrect sex	1	6.90	—	—	-0.15
Kyushu Univ. no. 831	Male	7.33	Correct sex	5	6.73	0.59	8.7	0.60
			Sex unknown	5	6.59	0.53	8.0	0.74
			Incorrect sex	5	6.44	0.49	7.6	0.89
Tokyo Univ. no. 3066	Female	8.50	Correct sex	2	6.38	0.44	6.9	2.12
			Sex unknown	2	6.54	0.45	6.8	1.97
			Incorrect sex	2	6.70	0.45	6.7	1.81

(continued)

(continued)

Kyushu Univ. no. 5541	Female	12.89	Correct sex	3	11.61	0.89	7.7	1.28
			Sex unknown	3	11.80	0.61	5.2	1.09
			Incorrect sex	3	11.99	0.32	2.7	0.90
Kyushu Univ. no. 5519	Male	13.65	Correct sex	1	12.86	—	—	0.79
			Sex unknown	1	12.60	—	—	1.05
			Incorrect sex	1	12.34	—	—	1.31
Kyushu Univ. no. 753	Female	15.05	Correct sex	2	12.45	1.34	10.7	2.61
			Sex unknown	2	12.73	1.44	11.3	2.32
			Incorrect sex	2	13.02	1.56	11.9	2.03
Kyushu Univ. no. 5255	Male	18.26	Correct sex	1	19.97	—	—	-1.71
			Sex unknown	1	20.18	—	—	-1.92
			Incorrect sex	1	20.39	—	—	-2.13
Kyushu Univ. no. 5538	Male	18.98	Correct sex	1	15.12	—	—	3.86
			Sex unknown	1	15.22	—	—	3.76
			Incorrect sex	1	15.33	—	—	3.65

[a] True age minus dental age.

true growth trajectories—are overly complex and probably stem from an unequal distribution of individuals among the age cohorts.

"Degree-of-attained-growth," defined as the length of a subadult long bone divided by the average length of the corresponding adult long bone from a sample group of the same population, is a measure of growth rate, calculated in order to detect growth suppression. It must be noted that degree-of-attained-growth theoretically cannot reach 100 percent, because, unlike the case of adult long bones, the measurable length of subadult long bones excludes the epiphyses. Differences between groups in the adjusted mean values determined for the degree-of-attained-growth index were scrutinized for statistical significance using ANCOVA (StatSoft Inc. 1996), with chronological age (covariate) and groups (classified data) as parameters. The ages of the individuals considered in this analysis by means of ANCOVA were restricted to a range of 1–10 years. This is because growth during this age range is relatively sensitive to environmental stress and because limiting the analysis to this age range produced smaller differences between the sexes and yielded more accurate estimated ages (table 15.2). In addition, the number of individuals 0–1 years of age available for examination varied widely across the groups.

Results

Table 15.3 shows the mean length and degree-of-attained-growth values determined for six long bones within each age class (from birth to 12 years old). It is obvious that the sample size for each age class was insufficient to support a separate statistical analysis. Therefore, adjusted mean degree-of-attained-growth values were determined for the ages of 1–10 years using ANCOVA, as mentioned above. In terms of general tendencies, figures 15.2–7 show an immediate sharp rise from birth to an age of 1–2 years for most groups and elements, followed by a relatively slower rate of increase from the age of 2–3 years up to about 10 years old. Differences among groups were found to be greater after about 10–12 years of age. Specific trends for each of the individual measured elements are described below in greater detail.

Humerus

Figure 15.2 shows that degree-of-attained-growth values for the humerus increased with age among all Japanese groups considered, as well as for prehistoric Native Americans from the Libben site. It should be noted that—unlike in the case of the Japanese data produced in the present study—only average values by age class were available for the Libben data. All of the Japanese

Table 15.3. Mean diaphyseal lengths, ratio to adult length achieved, and sample size

Age[a]	Groups	Humerus			Ulna			Radius			Femur			Tibia			Fibula		
		mm	%	N	mm	%	N	mm	%	N	mm	%	N	mm	%	N	mm	%	N
0.5	Jomon	63	23	2	61	26	2	54	25	2	74	18	2	69	21	3	62	19	1
	Yayoi	83	28	3	79	32	1	66	29	3	102	24	3	88	26	2	86	26	1
	Muromachi	75	27	7	66	28	5	60	28	5	97	24	6	76	23	3	71	22	4
	Modern	73	26	1	63	28	1	56	26	1	90	23	1	75	24	1	71	23	1
1.5	Jomon	104	38	6	95	40	5	84	38	4	141	35	5	116	35	5	113	35	3
	Yayoi	106	36	3	95	39	1	85	37	1	140	33	3	108	32	2	—	—	0
	Muromachi	113	40	3	—	—	0	81	37	4	138	35	4	104	31	2	105	33	1
	Modern	93	33	6	79	34	6	70	33	6	117	30	6	97	31	6	94	30	6
2.5	Jomon	119	43	8	105	44	6	92	42	7	158	39	8	130	39	8	137	43	4
	Yayoi	124	42	2	106	43	2	96	42	2	159	38	3	134	39	3	132	39	2
	Muromachi	130	46	3	103	44	1	96	44	2	160	40	1	137	41	2	—	—	0
	Modern	129	46	1	102	45	1	92	43	1	164	42	1	134	43	1	—	—	0
3.5	Jomon	125	45	3	107	45	2	95	43	2	168	42	4	137	41	3	141	44	2
	Yayoi	—	—	0	—	—	0	—	—	0	170	41	2	—	—	0	—	—	0
	Muromachi	134	47	1	114	49	1	—	—	0	191	48	1	153	46	1	150	47	1
	Modern	—	—	0	—	—	0	—	—	0	—	—	0	—	—	0	—	—	0

Size	Period																		
4.5	Jomon	139	50	5	125	53	1	108	49	4	198	49	4	160	48	5	159	50	1
	Yayoi	128	44	1	—	—	0	—	—	0	—	—	0	—	—	0	—	—	0
	Muromachi	—	—	0	—	—	0	—	—	0	179	45	1	—	—	0	—	—	0
	Modern	—	—	0	—	—	0	—	—	0	—	—	0	—	—	0	—	—	0
5.5	Jomon	157	57	6	140	59	3	120	55	4	221	55	3	174	52	6	194	60	2
	Yayoi	166	56	1	—	—	0	131	58	1	230	55	1	190	56	1	184	55	1
	Muromachi	135	48	1	118	50	1	107	49	1	198	50	1	163	49	1	159	50	1
	Modern	—	—	0	—	—	0	—	—	0	—	—	0	—	—	0	—	—	0
6.5	Jomon	157	57	4	138	58	1	126	58	2	230	57	4	187	56	2	215	—	0
	Yayoi	184	63	1	165	67	1	148	65	1	243	58	2	218	64	1	184	64	1
	Muromachi	159	56	1	140	59	2	127	58	2	230	58	2	184	56	1	181	58	1
	Modern	158	56	3	127	56	3	117	55	2	214	54	4	173	55	3	170	58	1
7.5	Jomon	162	59	2	146	62	2	132	60	2	217	54	2	175	53	2	170	53	1
	Yayoi	193	66	1	—	—	0	—	—	0	—	—	0	236	69	1	—	—	0
	Muromachi	—	—	0	—	—	0	—	—	0	—	—	0	—	—	0	—	—	0
	Modern	163	57	1	126	55	1	115	54	1	225	57	1	170	54	1	173	56	1
8.5	Jomon	162	59	2	152	64	2	127	58	3	233	58	3	187	56	3	—	—	0
	Yayoi	—	—	0	—	—	0	—	—	0	285	68	1	—	—	0	—	—	0
	Muromachi	—	—	0	—	—	0	—	—	0	—	—	0	—	—	0	—	—	0
	Modern	178	63	1	141	62	1	127	60	1	249	63	1	188	60	1	193	62	1

(continued)

(continued)

9.5	Jomon	186	67	4	164	70	2	146	67	3	270	67	5	218	65	5	220	68	2
	Yayoi	—	—	0	—	—	0	—	—	0	282	67	1	237	69	2	—	—	0
	Muromachi	—	—	0	—	—	0	—	—	0	—	—	0	—	—	0	—	—	0
	Modern	203	71	1	160	70	1	146	69	1	278	70	1	224	71	1	222	71	1
10.5	Jomon	195	71	2	166	70	1	156	71	2	288	72	3	230	69	1	223	69	1
	Yayoi	218	74	1	183	74	1	—	—	0	310	74	1	—	—	0	242	72	1
	Muromachi	—	—	0	—	—	0	—	—	0	—	—	0	—	—	0	—	—	0
	Modern	196	69	3	154	68	3	140	66	3	279	71	3	219	69	3	218	70	3
11.5	Jomon	206	75	2	—	—	0	174	79	2	285	71	2	244	73	4	234	73	2
	Yayoi	205	70	1	—	—	0	152	67	0	288	69	1	235	69	2	—	—	0
	Muromachi	—	—	0	—	—	0	—	—	0	238	60	1	—	—	0	—	—	0
	Modern	193	68	2	156	69	2	138	65	2	269	68	2	210	66	2	211	68	2

[a] Age indicates the midpoint of a one-year-long age class.

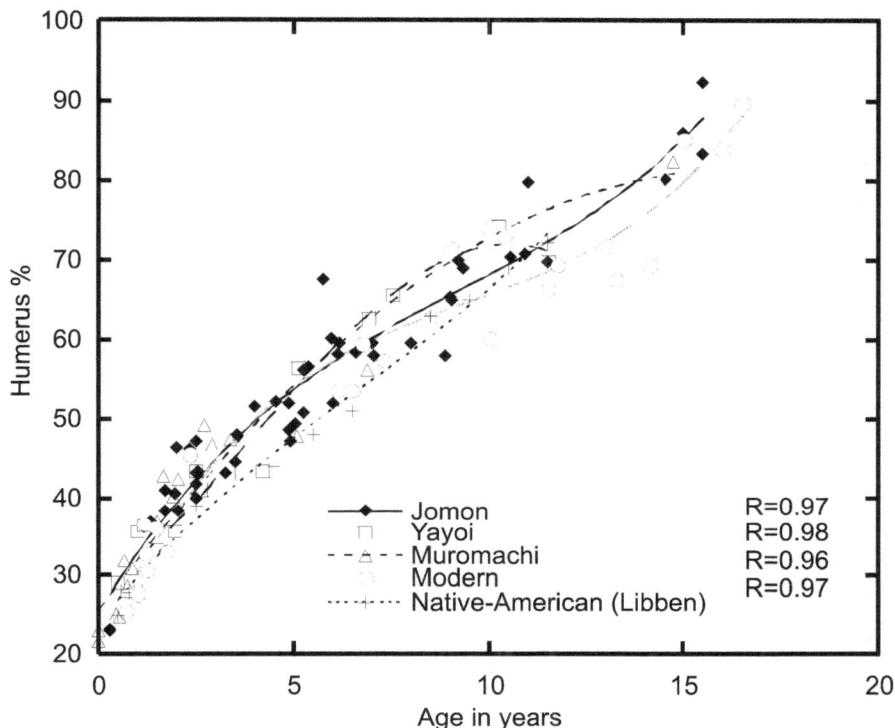

Figure 15.2. Ratios of the percentage of adult length of the humerus by age in years.

groups showed higher degree-of-attained-growth values up to about the age of 10 years than those determined for the Libben group. Focusing on the differences among the Japanese groups, the Yayoi (cubic equation, df = 13, R = .984, p < .001) and the Muromachi (quadratic equation, df = 16, R = .962, p < .001) groups were found to have elevated values for the humerus in comparison with the Jomon (cubic equation, df = 49, R = .969, p < .001) and the modern groups (cubic equation, df = 24, R = .975, p < .001) after the age of about 6 years of age. Table 15.4 shows the results of statistical examination of the humerus. The adjusted mean of the Jomon sample (47.9 percent) was significantly higher than that of the Modern sample (45.2 percent) (p = .012), while the Muromachi sample (48.6 percent) yielded a greater mean than the Jomon sample (p = .017).

Radius

Figure 15.3 shows degree-of-attained-growth curves for the radius in the same way. The degree-of-attained-growth curve for the Modern sample (quadratic equation, df = 27, R = .971, p < .001) is below that of all the other groups up

Table 15.4. Group differences in degree of attained growth of the upper limb bones

Limb bone	Neolithic Jomon	Eneolithic Yayoi	Medieval Muromachi	Early Modern
Humerus				
Adjusted mean	47.9	47.6	48.6	45.2
Jomon	—			
Yayoi	0.096	—		
Muromachi	0.017*	—	—	
Modern	0.012*	0.992	—	—
Radius				
Adjusted mean	47.0	50.0	47.3	44.5
Jomon	—			
Yayoi	—	—		
Muromachi	0.005**	0.207	—	
Modern	0.001**	0.182	1.000	—
Ulna				
Adjusted mean	50.6	51.2	49.8	46.6
Jomon	—			
Yayoi	0.431	—		
Muromachi	0.986	0.273	—	
Modern	0.004**	0.957	0.057	—

Note: Multiple comparison (modified HSD test) of main effect by ANCOVA.
$^*p < 5\%$
$^{**}p < 1\%$

until at least 10 years of age. The Jomon sample (quadratic equation, df = 47, R = .973, p < .001) produced elevated degree-of-attained-growth values for the radius as compared with those determined for the Libben sample until the age of about 10 years. The Yayoi sample (cubic equation, df = 11, R = .992, p < .001) and the Muromachi sample (quadratic equation, df = 16, R = .979, p < .001) also seem to have achieved higher degree-of-attained-growth values for the radius as compared with those determined for the Libben sample up until at least an approximate age of 7 years. However, it should be noted that sample sizes for both groups were relatively small. Table 15.4 indicates that the adjusted mean for the Jomon sample (47.0 percent) was significantly higher than that of the Modern sample (44.5 percent) (p = .001), while the adjusted mean for the Muromachi sample (47.3 percent) was greater than that of the Jomon sample (p = .005) for the radius.

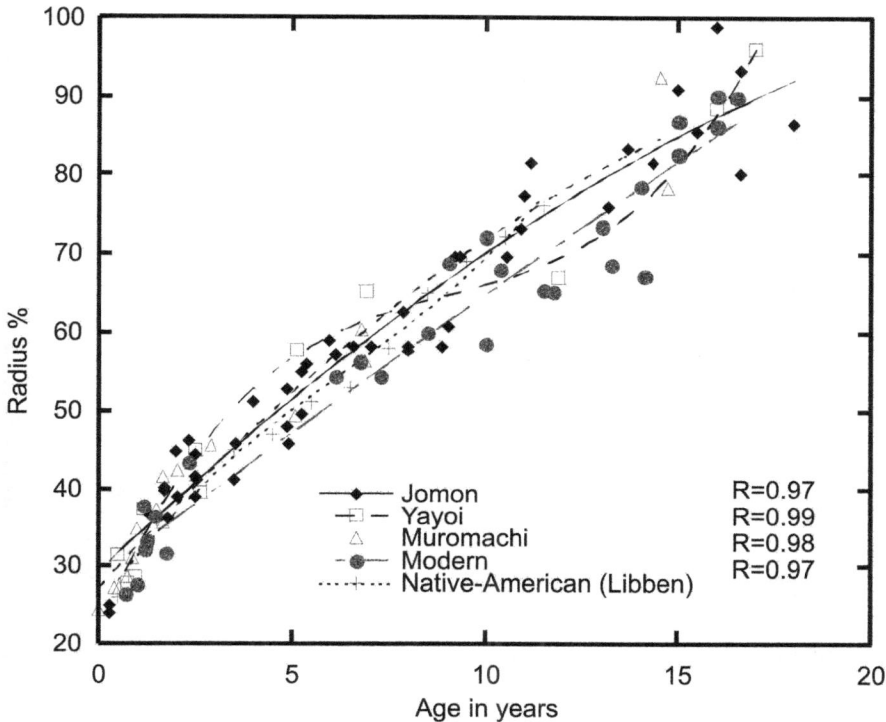

Figure 15.3. Ratios of the percentage of adult length of the radius by age in years.

Ulna

Figure 15.4 shows degree-of-attained-growth curves for the ulna. The Modern sample (quadratic equation, df = 26, R = .968, p < .001) produced the lowest means for the ulna among all the groups considered in this study. The degree-of-attained-growth curve for this element determined from the Yayoi sample (quadratic equation, df = 6, R = .992, p < .001) was elevated in comparison with those for both the Modern sample and the Muromachi sample (quadratic equation, df = 10, R = .986, p < .001), as well as for the Libben sample. The number of the individuals in both the Yayoi and the Muromachi samples is too small to evaluate the significance of the respective differences. Table 15.4 indicates that the adjusted mean for the Jomon sample (50.6 percent) was significantly higher than that of the Modern sample (46.6 percent) (p = .004) for the ulna.

Femur

Figure 15.5 shows degree-of-attained-growth curves for the femur. All of the Japanese groups produced elevated degree-of-attained-growth values for the

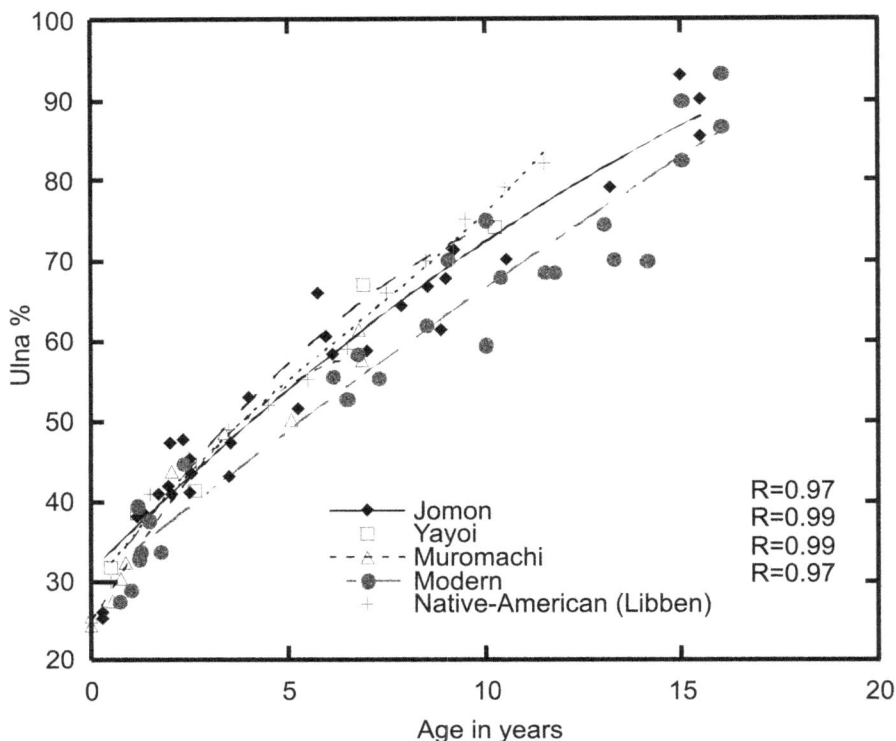

Figure 15.4. Ratios of the percentage of adult length of the ulna by age in years.

femur as compared with those determined for the Libben sample, although they reached much the same level at about the age of 10 years. Overall, the degree-of-attained-growth for this element as determined from the Yayoi sample (cubic equation, df = 20, R = .989, p < .001) was greater than that for the Jomon (quadratic equation, df = 53, R = .972, p < .001), the Muromachi (quadratic equation, df = 20, R = .970, p < .001), and the Modern sample (quadratic equation, df = 30, R = .970, p = .001) from between 4–5 years of age up until about 11–12 years old. Table 15.5 illustrates that the adjusted mean for the Muromachi sample (46.8 percent) was significantly greater than that for the Jomon sample (46.0 percent) (p = .003) for the femur.

Tibia

Figure 15.6 shows degree-of-attained-growth curves for the tibia. The Yayoi group (cubic equation, df = 19, R = .990, p < .001) produced higher values as compared with the other groups from 3–4 years old up to about 10 years of age. The Libben sample yielded a curve for the tibia similar to those determined for both the Jomon sample (quadratic equation, df = 55, R = .966, p < .001)

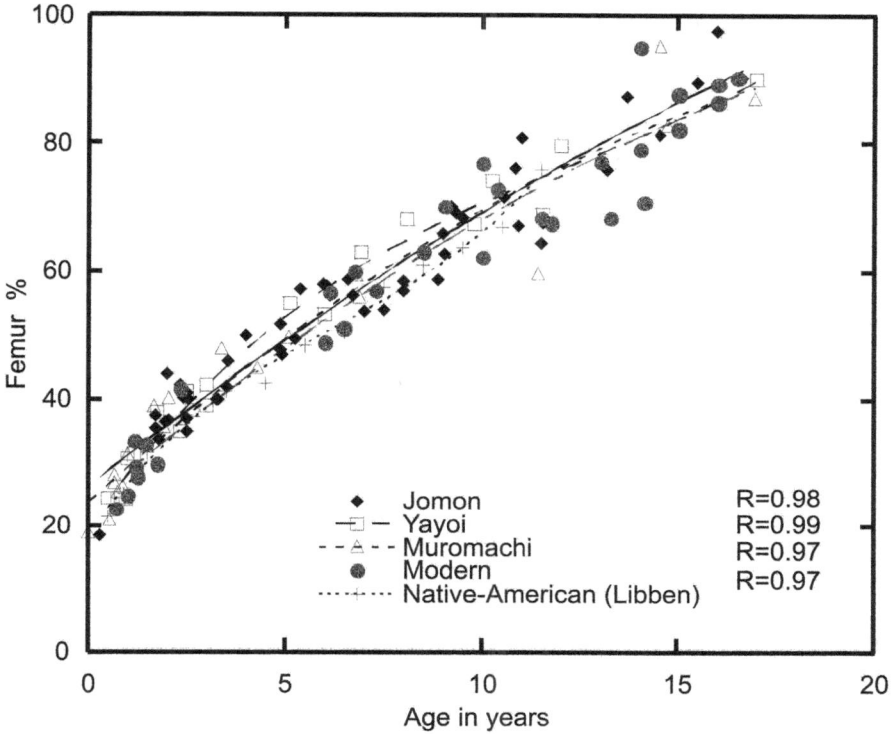

Figure 15.5. Ratios of the percentage of adult length of the femur by age in years.

and the Modern sample (quadratic equation, df = 29, R = .964, p < .001) but surpassed both groups after the age of about 9–10 years. Due to small sample size, a degree-of-attained-growth curve for this element was difficult to determine reliably from the Muromachi sample (quadratic equation, df = 12, R = .989, p < .001). Table 15.5 indicates that the adjusted mean of the Yayoi sample (44.7 percent) was the lowest among all the Japanese groups, while that of the Muromachi sample (46.6 percent) was greater than that of the Jomon sample (45.5 percent) (p = .042), with the Yayoi sample (48.7 percent) even higher than the Muromachi (p = .001) for the tibia.

Fibula

Figure 15.7 shows degree-of-attained-growth curves for the fibula. The Libben sample yielded the lowest values, while the Yayoi sample (cubic equation, df = 5, R = .998, p < .001) gave the highest among the groups considered in this study. However, the relatively small total number of fibulae available for examination makes it impossible to evaluate the significance of the group differences. Table 15.5 does show that the adjusted mean determined for the

Table 15.5. Group differences in degree of attained growth of the lower limb bones

Limb bone	Neolithic Jomon	Eneolithic Yayoi	Medieval Muromachi	Early Modern
Femur				
Adjusted mean	46.0	46.7	46.8	44.3
Jomon	—			
Yayoi	0.156	—		
Muromachi	0.003**	0.314	—	
Modern	—	0.655	0.889	—
Tibia				
Adjusted mean	45.5	48.7	46.6	44.7
Jomon	—			
Yayoi	—	—		
Muromachi	0.042*	0.001**	—	
Modern	0.075	0.003**	0.807	—
Fibula				
Adjusted mean	47.9	48.8	46.5	44.0
Jomon	—			
Yayoi	0.972	—		
Muromachi	0.940	0.748	—	
Modern	0.017*	0.089	0.476	—

Note: Multiple comparison (modified HSD test) of the main effect by ANCOVA.
* $p < 5\%$
** $p < 1\%$

Jomon sample (47.9 percent) was significantly larger than that of the Modern group (44.0 percent) ($p = .017$) for the fibula.

Discussion

Reliability of Group Comparisons of the Degree-of-Attained-Growth Curves in This Study

Previous studies have repeatedly demonstrated that the growth rates of long bones are sensitive indicators of environmental stress (e.g., Johnston and Zimmer 1989; Saunders 1992; Saunders and Hoppa 1993), although certain technical issues that affect the interpretation of analyses based on skeletal samples have yet to be fully resolved. The most serious problem is in determining the magnitude of errors resulting from the use of different ageing standards. For example, Merchant and Ubelaker (1977) have shown that the growth curves produced by using two different methods of age determination on a single

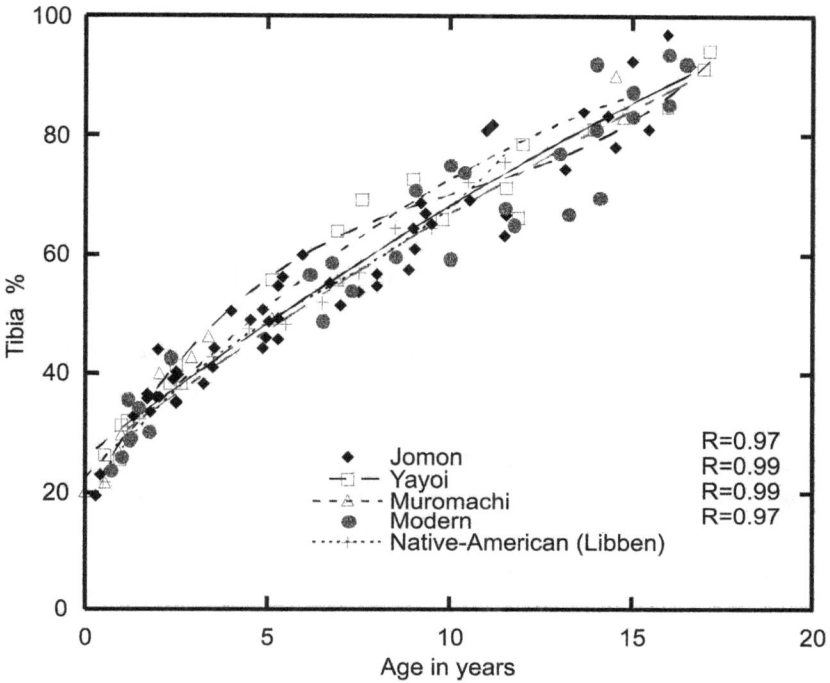

Figure 15.6. Ratios of the percentage of adult length of the tibia by age in years.

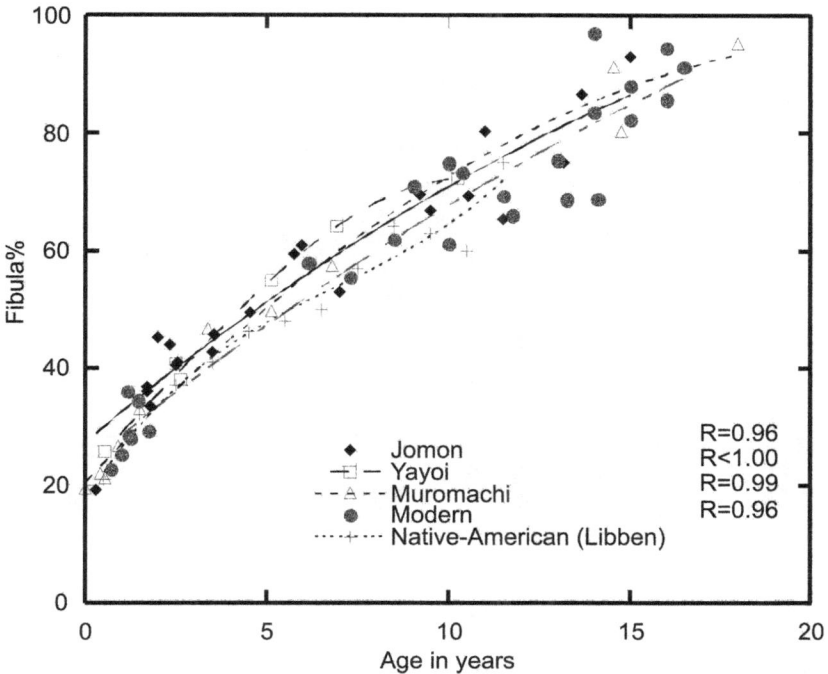

Figure 15.7. Ratios of the percentage of adult length of the fibula by age in years.

388   Kenji Okazaki

sample differ to much the same degree as do those of different groups. However, this issue is not a serious problem in terms of the study reported here,
because of the use of a unified standard for ageing the Japanese sample groups.

The standard originally employed in order to determine the age of the
members of the sample group from the Libben site used for comparison in
this study was adjusted to be advanced in relation to a previously established
standard for Euro-Americans (Lovejoy et al. 1990), while the standard used
to determine the ages of members of the Japanese samples has been adjusted
to be delayed in relation to that same standard. Therefore, a finding that the
members of those Japanese groups generally attained a higher degree of
growth on average than did members of the Libben group in the same age
ranges probably cannot result from systematic errors that may be ascribed
to systematic differences between the ageing methods. The health and living
conditions experienced by members of the Japanese groups may have been
superior to those experienced by Native Americans at the Libben site, where
many individuals were found to carry evidence of infection, in the form of a
periosteal reaction (Lovejoy et al. 1990).

Results of this analysis indicate that the Yayoi had the highest degree-

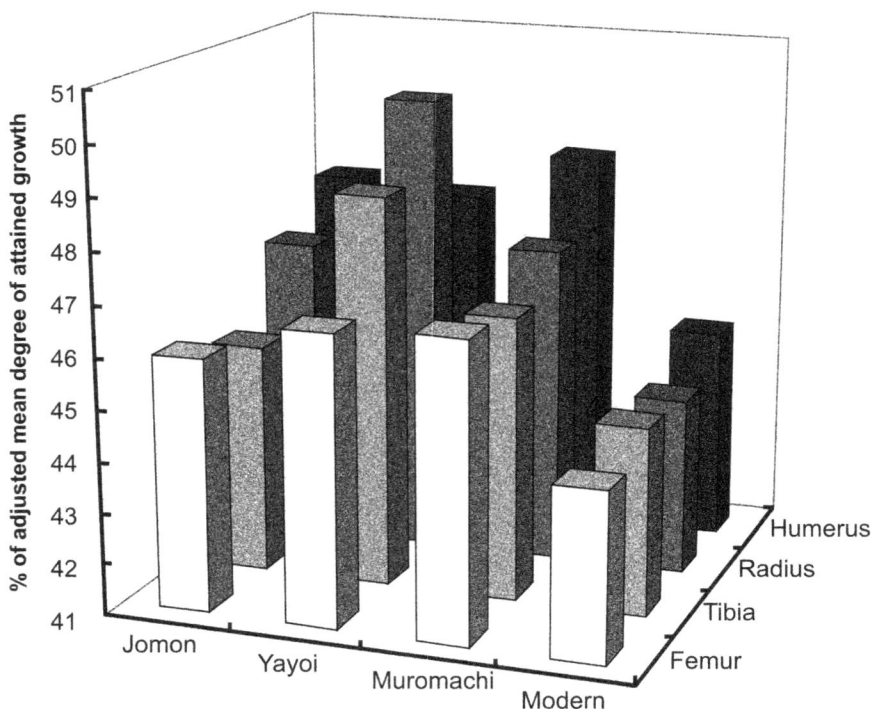

Figure 15.8. Comparison of adjusted means of degree of attained growth for the upper and lower
limbs among the Japanese groups considered in this study.

of-attained-growth values for most elements of the extremities among the groups considered in this study, while those of the Modern sample was lowest, apart from the values determined for the Libben sample (figures 15.2–7). Adjusted means for degree-of-attained-growth on all long bones, apart from the humerus and femur, were also highest for the Yayoi, while the Modern sample scored the lowest for all elements of the extremities (tables 15.4, 15.5). This tendency is illustrated in figure 15.8, based on the adjusted means of the degree-of-attained-growth for the humerus, radius, femur, and tibia for all Japanese groups.

The conditions underlying the unexpected result that environmental stress apparently had a more profound negative impact on the growth of early Modern Japanese than on any of the more ancient groups considered in this study bear some further examination. The early Modern sample was made up of individuals dissected at medical schools. According to what has been preserved of their medical records, many were thought to have suffered from chronic disease (e.g., tuberculosis) and/or to have lived out their lives in socioeconomically deprived circumstances (Fukushima 1988).

In order to determine to what degree growing up in these relatively unhealthy conditions may have biased the results of comparison with the ancient Japanese samples, other comparative data were brought to bear as a form of control. As it was not possible to access any similar data for Japan, a sample of modern Euro-Americans from mid-twentieth-century Denver (Maresh 1955) was selected for this purpose. Table 15.6 shows the adjusted mean values determined for degree-of-attained growth of the femur during the age range of 1–10 years old for all groups considered in this study. On average, the modern Euro-American sample yielded the highest degree-of-attained growth values, while the Libben sample produced the lowest. This result lends some support to the possibility that the health status of the members of the Japanese Modern sample utilized in this study did indeed bias the outcome. It seems likely that the results given in table 15.6 are largely explained by the inherent bias toward chronic poor health of the individuals making up the early Modern Japanese sample.

Table 15.6. Comparison of degree of attained growth in the femur among Japanese and American groups

	Jomon	Yayoi	Muromachi	Modern	Native American (Libben site)	Euro-American (Denver)
Adjusted average	47.6	48.4	48.6	46.0	44.2	49.2

Sources: Libben site: Lovejoy et al. 1990; Denver: Maresh 1955.

Secular Change in Health from the Jomon Period to the Yayoi Period

There was almost surely an indigenous horticultural tradition in Japan dating back to sometime during the Jomon period, based on small-scale cultivation of dry rice, chestnut, and soybeans, as well as a few tubers and some root crops (e.g., Watanabe 1975; Yamazaki 1978; Nishida 1981; Sasaki 1991). It is generally agreed that wet-rice agriculture (which, given sufficient labor inputs, can yield enough calories to maintain significantly larger human populations) began in Japan during the Yayoi period, along with the cultivation of several other exotic domesticated plants (i.e., millet, barnyard grass, and adzuki bean). Agricultural intensification has long been understood to have had important consequences for early human societies, but its precise trajectory in Japan is not yet fully understood. Here, the focus is on the way that agricultural intensification impacted the human body in Japan.

Unlike in some other cases of the introduction and spread of agriculture, such as that of North America, no evidence of a decline in overall health was found between the Jomon and Yayoi periods in Japan. On the contrary, average mean degree-of-attained growth values for all limb bones, except the humerus, were higher for the Yayoi sample than for the Jomon, although differences between the groups were not significant (figures 15.2–8, tables 15.4, 15.5). A possible explanation of why secular change in the growth trajectory of the humerus was different from that evidenced by the other limb bones may be that it is the result of the effect of differences in growth timing among the various parts of the extremities. Growth disruption is most pronounced for the rapidly growing long bones of the lower extremities (Tanner 1978).

It is not all that surprising to find that the Jomon people, whose main occupations seem to have been gathering-hunting-fishing, were generally no more and perhaps a little bit less healthy than their wet-rice-agriculture-dependent successors of the Yayoi period. This conclusion is also supported by the results of an examination of stress markers on bones and teeth. There was no apparent general increase in the frequencies of enamel hypoplasias, Harris lines, or cribra orbitalia between the Jomon and Yayoi periods in the north Kyushu–Yamaguchi region, although Harris line frequency at one of the Yayoi sites (Koura [古浦]) was notably elevated (Koga 2002, 2003). A similar lack of trend in the frequencies of enamel hypoplasia and cribra orbitalia is supported by data collected on Jomon skeletal remains from eastern Japan (Temple 2007). In addition, paleodemographic analysis has demonstrated that people had slightly greater mean life expectancy during the Yayoi and Muromachi periods than during the Jomon (Kobayashi 1967; Nakahashi and Nagai 1989b).

This finding differs considerably from the standard model of the effects of agricultural adoption and/or intensification that has been developed on the basis of studying skeletal samples from prehistoric North America and Nubia (Cohen and Armelagos 1984). Given a decrease through time in mean degree-of-attained-growth values, as well as increases in the frequencies of various stress markers and nonspecific periosteal reactions, several different groups of prehistoric Native Americans are thought to have suffered an overall decline in community health coincident with the spread of corn-based agriculture after AD 800–1000 (Cook 1984; Goodman et al. 1984). The most likely explanation is that the living conditions that followed the adoption and intensification of agriculture prompted a general deterioration in hygiene with increasing sedentism, as well as a decline in the availability of protein (Cohen and Armelagos 1984; Larsen 1995).

The reasons for the apparent difference between the general North American and Japanese cases in the ways in which the adoption of agriculture and agricultural intensification affected community health are not hard to imagine. Many previous studies have demonstrated varying trajectories in community health conditions among different groups of prehistoric Native Americans (Cook 1984; Goodman et al. 1984; Milner 1991; Steckel and Rose 2002; Steckel 2005). It is apparent that even in North America, the adoption of agriculture did not always lead directly to an overall decline in human health status; health change is a result of interplay among multiple specific factors (Jackes et al. 1997; Larsen 1997; Lambert 2000).

Hodges (1987) compared the frequencies of several stress markers between groups from Oaxaca, Mexico, thought to have respectively pursued a nonintensive agricultural strategy (1400–500 BC) and an intensive agricultural strategy (500 BC–AD 1400). No evidence for a general decline in community health coincident with agricultural intensification was found. Hodges (1987) suggests that this difference from the more general North American case is explained by a long and gradual period of agricultural development in Oaxaca, which afforded indigenous societies the opportunity to maintain a diversified diet based on a complementary suite of cultigens (maize, beans, and squash) as well as wild foods (acorns, nopal, tuna, maguey, and hackberries). The slow pace of this development also restrained drastic population growth and held down population density, decreasing the risk of creating a poor hygienic environment. This gradual process of subsistence change afforded the means of keeping a balance among dietary quantity, dietary quality, and population size, all of which are important concerns related to health (Cassidy 1984).

This gradual process of agricultural development described for Oaxaca is partly analogous with the Japanese case. Terasawa and Terasawa (1981) analyzed the species distribution of plant remains excavated at sites of the Yayoi period. Unexpectedly, their results indicated that the quantity of acorns—one of staple foods of the preceding Jomon period—was greater than that of rice. They proposed that during the Yayoi period, people continued to consume large quantities of acorns, because wet-rice agriculture was still too unstable and risky to rely on. Komoto (1986) estimated the amount of energy obtained from rice during Yayoi as less than one-third of total caloric requirements. Unpolished rice also contains considerable protein and a variety of other important dietary elements (vitamin B_1, vitamin E, and magnesium) as compared with corn.

The specific circumstances of the Jomon period indicate that the process of agricultural development during the time leading up to Yayoi was also relatively gradual. Based on a study of changes in cookware, Yamazaki (1978, 1983) has pointed out the likelihood that sedentism was already well under way during the Jomon period, supported by an abundance of wild plants and other foods, as well as small-scale horticulture. It is thought that the Yayoi people merely added wet-rice agriculture and cultivation of a few exogenous food plants to the diverse adaptations inherited from the former period (Terasawa and Terasawa 1981; Komoto 1991; Fujio 1993). Moreover, a relatively vast land with low population density became available for wet-rice agriculturalists (Koyama and Sugito 1984), which may have allowed them to achieve substantial population growth without immediately creating food shortages.

Evidence from the Kuma-Nishioda (隈・西小田) site, utilized in a paleodemographic study based on number of graves (Nakahashi 1993b), suggests a process of abrupt population growth (more than 1 percent per year) from early to the middle of the Yayoi period (figure 15.1). There is also evidence from the large number of sites concentrated around nearby Chikushino and Ogori, where an increase in the number of villages during the Yayoi period suggests steep population growth and eventually a high population density (Tanaka 1991). According to evidence for the timing of the spread of wet-rice agriculture, immigrant Yayoi people, whose physical characteristics were similar to those of contemporaneous peoples native to the Asian mainland, dispersed from northern Kyushu and the Yamaguchi region eastward at least as far as the Kanto region (e.g., Nakahashi 1993a; Matsumura 1998).

In the Japanese case, these immigrants and their descendants were people who had already mastered the pertinent agricultural technology and might also have had immunity to infectious diseases originating from domesticated animals and spread in sedentary contexts on the Asian mainland. The process of immigration seems to have been quite gradual, because the cultural factors expressed by archaeological evidence do not show anything like complete replacement between the Jomon and Yayoi periods (Tanaka 1991). Nevertheless, once the immigrants were in place, a steep increase in the rate of population growth prompted relatively rapid diffusion eastward across environments that were advantageous for wet-rice agriculture (Nakahashi and Iizuka 1998; Iizuka and Nakahashi 2002). These circumstances appear to have been quite suitable for supporting a process of agricultural intensification, without causing a concomitant degeneration in human health. This trajectory contrasts markedly with the general North American case, in which at least some long-time hunter-gatherers altered their subsistence regimes fairly rapidly with the adoption of corn agriculture.

Conclusions

The growth patterns of six long bones were determined using samples of subadult skeletal remains from the Jomon, Yayoi, Medieval Muromachi, and early Modern period in Japan. The results of comparison among these groups showed that the early Modern Japanese individuals had suffered the most serious disruption of growth. Unfortunately, this finding seems to be due, at least in part, to selection bias, as the available specimens proved to be overwhelmingly the remains of persons who suffered from chronic disease (e.g., tuberculosis). An increase in skeletal evidence for growth suppression with the adoption of intensive agricultural practices, like that found in previous studies of the remains of prehistoric native North Americans, was not evident for the Jomon to Yayoi transition, which is the time when wet-rice agriculture was introduced to Japan. This finding could be partly caused by the gradual adaption of wet-rice farming during the Yayoi period and the already sedentary behaviors of the Jomon populations.

Acknowledgments

For their helpful comments I am greatly indebted to Dr. Takahiro Nakahashi, Dr. Yoshiyuki Tanaka, and Dr. Hiroko Koike of Kyushu University; Dr. Osamu Kondo of the University of Tokyo; and Dr. Masaru Iizuka of Kyushu Dental College. I express my gratitude to the following for facilitating my investigation of materials in their care: Dr. Gen Murakami and Dr. Hirofumi Matsumura of Sapporo Medical College; Dr. Yukio Dodo, Dr. Wataru Takigawa, and Dr. Fumiko Saeki of Tohoku University; Dr. Katsuji Kumaki of Niigata University; Dr. Hisao Baba and Dr. Yuji Mizoguchi of the National

Science Museum, Tokyo; Dr. Gen Suwa, Dr. Aiko Sasou and Dr. Souichiro Mizushima of the University of Tokyo; Dr. Kazumichi Katayama, Dr. Masato Nakatsukasa, Dr. Naomichi Ogiwara, and Dr. Saori Fujisawa of Kyoto University; and Dr. Keiichi Kusaba of the Educational Committee of Chikushino City. Finally, I thank Dr. Ekaterina Pechenkina and Daniel Temple for their invitation to contribute to this volume, as well as an anonymous reviewer for very precise suggestions on how to improve the manuscript.

Literature Cited

Bogin B. 1999. *Patterns of human growth*. 2nd ed. Cambridge: Cambridge University Press.

Cassidy CM. 1984. Skeletal evidence for prehistoric subsistence adaptation in the central Ohio River valley. In: Cohen MN, Armelagos GJ, editors. *Paleopathology at the origins of agriculture*. New York: Academic Press. Pp. 307–45.

Cohen MN, Armelagos GJ, editors. 1984. *Paleopathology at the origins of agriculture*. Academic Press, New York.

Cook DC. 1984. Subsistence and health in the lower Illinois valley: Osteological evidence. In: Cohen MN, Armelagos GJ, editors. *Paleopathology at the origins of agriculture*. New York: Academic Press. Pp. 235–69.

Dodo Y. 1982. A metrical analysis of Jomon crania from the Tohoku district. *Journal of the Anthropological Society of Nippon* (人類学雑誌) 90 (Suppl.): 119–28.

Dodo Y. 1987. Supraorbital foramen and hypoglossal canal bridging: The two most suggestive nonmetric cranial traits in discriminating major racial groupings of man. *Journal of the Anthropological Society of Nippon* 95: 19–35.

DSAM/SPI (Doigahama Site Anthropological Museum and Shandong Provincial Institute of Cultural Relics and Archaeology) 2000. *Searching in the continent for the root of the immigrant Yayoi people*. The Report of the Joint Research between Japan and China (日中共同研究報告) 1. Yamaguchi and Shangdong.

Eveleth PB, Tanner JM. 1990. *Worldwide variation in human growth*. 2nd ed. Cambridge: Cambridge University Press.

Frisancho AR, Guire K, Babler W, Borken G, Way A. 1980. Nutritional influence on childhood development and genetic control of adolescent growth of Quechuas and Mestizos from the Peruvian Lowlands. *American Journal of Physical Anthropology* 52: 367–75.

Fujio S. 1993. Secular change from the Jomon to the Yayoi period viewed from occupations. *Bulletin of the National Museum of Japanese History* (国立歴史民俗博物館研究報告) 48: 1–66.

Fukushima K. 1988. On the lesions of bones of Yayoi people in southwest Japan. *Fukuoka Acta Medica* (福岡医学雑誌) 79: 227–48.

Goodman AH, Lallo J, Armelagos GJ, Rose JC. 1984. Health changes at Dickson Mounds, Illinois (A.D. 950–1300). In: Cohen MN, Armelagos GJ, editors. *Paleopathology at the origins of agriculture*. New York: Academic Press. Pp. 271–305.

Hanihara K. 1984. Origins and affinities of Japanese viewed from cranial measurements. *Acta Anthropogenetica* 8: 149–58.

Hanihara K. 1991. Dual structure model for the population history of the Japanese. *Japan Review* 2: 1–33.

Hodges DC. 1987. Health and agricultural intensification in the prehistoric valley of Oaxaca, Mexico. *American Journal of Physical Anthropology* 73: 323–32.

Hoppa RD. 1992. Evaluating human skeletal growth: An Anglo-Saxon example. *International Journal of Osteoarchaeology* 2: 275–88.

Hummert JR, Van Gerven DP. 1983. Skeletal growth in a medieval population from Sudanese Nubia. *American Journal of Physical Anthropology* 60: 471–78.

Iizuka M, Nakahashi T. 2002. A population genetic study on the transition from Jomon people to Yayoi people. *Genes and Genetic Systems* 77: 287–300.

Jackes M, Lubell D, Meiklejohn C. 1997. Healthy but mortal: Human biology and the first farmers of Western Europe. *Antiquity* 71: 639–58.

Jantz RL, Owsley DW. 1984a. Long bone growth variation among Arikara skeletal populations. *American Journal of Physical Anthropology* 63: 13–20.

Jantz RL, Owsley DW. 1984b. Temporal changes in limb proportionality among skeletal samples of Arikara Indians. *Annals of Human Biology* 11: 157–63.

Johnston FE. 1962. Growth of the long bones of infants and young children at Indian Knoll. *American Journal of Physical Anthropology* 20: 249–54.

Johnston FE, Wainer H, Thissen D, MacVean R. 1976. Hereditary and environmental determinants of growth in height in a longitudinal sample of children and youth of Guatemalan and European ancestry. *American Journal of Physical Anthropology* 44: 469–76.

Johnston FE, Zimmer LO. 1989. Assessment of growth and age in the immature skeleton. In: Iscan MY, Kennedy KAR, editors. *Reconstruction of life from the skeleton.* New York: Alan R. Liss. Pp. 11–21.

Kanaseki T, Nagai M, Sano H. 1960. Craniological studies of the Yayoi-period ancients, excavated at the Doigahama site, Yamaguchi prefecture. *Jinruigaku Kenkyu* (人類学研究) 7 (Suppl.): 1–36.

Kaneda Y. 1957. A study about the age of permanent teeth formation, Japan. *Shikageppou* (歯科月報) 31: 167–72.

Kim JJ, Ogata T, Mine K, Takenaka M, Sakuma M, Seo YN. 1993. Human skeletal remains from the Yeanri site, Kimhae. *Archaeological Research Report of the University Museum, Pusan National University* (釜山大学校博物館遺蹟調査報告) 15: 281–334.

Kobayashi K. 1967. Trend in the length of life based on human skeletons from prehistoric to modern times in Japan. *Journal of the Faculty of Science, University of Tokyo, Section V: Anthropology* 3: 107–62.

Koga H. 2002. Stress-markers in the ancient people of western Japan 1: Harris's lines. *Anthropological Science* (Japanese Series) 110: 71–87.

Koga H. 2003. Stress-markers in the ancient people of western Japan 2: Cribra orbitalia, enamel hypoplasia and the relationship between three stress markers containing Harris' lines. *Anthropological Science* (Japanese Series) 111: 51–67.

Komoto M. 1986. Foods of the Yayoi people. *Archaeology Quarterly* (季刊考古学) 14: 29–33.

Komoto M. 1991. The spread of agriculture at the Yayoi period. *Archaeology Quarterly* (季刊考古学) 37: 29–33.

Koyama S, Sugito S. 1984. A study of Jomon population: Computer simulation analysis. *Bulletin of the National Museum of Ethnology* (国立民族学博物館研究報告) 19: 1–39.

Lambert PM. 2000. *Bioarchaeological studies of life in the age of agriculture.* Tuscaloosa: University of Alabama Press.

Larsen CS. 1995. Biological changes in human populations with agriculture. *Annual Review of Anthropology* 24: 185–213.

Larsen CS. 1997. *Bioarchaeology: Interpreting behavior from the human skeleton.* Cambridge: Cambridge University Press.

Lovejoy CO, Russell KF, Harrison ML. 1990. Long bone growth velocity in the Libben population. *American Journal of Human Biology* 2: 533–41.

Maresh MM. 1955. Linear growth of long bones of extremities from infancy through adolescence. *American Journal of Diseases of Children* 89: 725–42.

Martorell R, Yarbrough C, Lechtig A, Delgado H, Klein RE. 1977. Genetic-environmental interactions in physical growth. *Acta Paediatrica Scandinavica* 66: 579–84.

Matsumura H. 1998. Discriminant method by tooth crown diameters between the native and migrant types of the Eneolithic Yayoi Japanese. *Memoirs of the National Science Museum* 30: 199–210.

Mensforth RP. 1985. Relative tibia long bone growth in the Libben and Bt-5 prehistoric skeletal populations. *American Journal of Physical Anthropology* 68: 247–62.

Merchant VL, Ubelaker DH. 1977. Skeletal growth of the protohistoric Arikara. *American Journal of Physical Anthropology* 46: 61–72.

Miles AEW, Bulman JS. 1994. Growth curves of immature bones from a Scottish island population of sixteenth to mid-nineteenth century: Limb-bone diaphyses and some bones of the hand and foot. *International Journal of Osteoarchaeology* 4: 121–36.

Milner GR. 1991. Health and cultural change in the late prehistoric American Bottom, Illinois. In: Powell ML, Bridges PS, Wagner Mires AM, editors. *What mean these bones?: Studies in southeastern bioarchaeology.* Tuscaloosa: University of Alabama Press. Pp. 52–70.

Mizoguchi Y. 1988. Affinities of the protohistoric Kofun people of Japan with pre- and protohistoric Asian populations. *Journal of the Anthropological Society of Nippon* 96: 71–109.

Molleson T. 1989. Social implications of mortality patterns of juveniles from Poundbury Camp, Romano-British Cemetery. *Anthropologischer Anzeiger* 47: 27–38.

Moorrees CFA, Fanning EA, Hunt EE. 1963a. Age variation of formation stages for ten permanent teeth. *Journal of Dental Research* 42: 1490–1502.

Moorrees CFA, Fanning EA, Hunt EE. 1963b. Formation and resorption of three deciduous teeth in children. *American Journal of Physical Anthropology* 21: 205–13.

Nakahashi T. 1993a. Temporal craniometric changes from the Jomon to the Modern period in western Japan. *American Journal of Physical Anthropology* 90: 409–25.

Nakahashi T. 1993b. Explosive increase of Yayoi population estimated from the number of graves. In: Kawai N, editor. *Gen-Nihonjin, Asahi One Theme Magazine* (原日本人,朝日ワンテーマ マガジン) 14. Tokyo: Asahi Shinbunsya. Pp. 30–46.

Nakahashi T, Iizuka M. 1998. Anthropological study of the transition from the Jomon to the Yayoi periods in northern Kyushu using morphological and paleodemographical features. *Anthropological Science* 106: 31–53.

Nakahashi T, Li M. 2002. *Ancient people in the Jiangnan region, China: Anthropological study on the origin of the Yayoi people in northern Kyushu.* Fukuoka: Kyushu University Press.

Nakahashi T, Nagai M. 1985. The skeletons excavated from the Yoshinohama site, Shimonoseki, Yamaguchi. In: Educational Committee of Shimonoseki City, editors. *The Yoshinohama site* (吉母浜遺跡). Shimonoseki. Pp. 154–225.

Nakahashi T, Nagai M. 1989a. The physical features of the Yayoi people. In: Nagai M, Nasu T, Kanaseki H, Sahara MA, editors. *Study of the Yayoi culture.* Vol. 1: *The Yayoi people and their environment* (弥生文化の研究－1: 弥生人とその環境). Tokyo: Yuzankaku. Pp. 129–46.

Nakahashi T, Nagai M. 1989b. The life span of the Yayoi people. In: Nagai M, Nasu T, Kanaseki H, Sahara MA, editors. *Study of the Yayoi culture.* Vol. 1: *The Yayoi people and their environment* (弥生文化の研究—1: 弥生人とその環境). Tokyo: Yuzankaku. Pp. 76–95.

Nishida M. 1981. Man-plant relationships in the Jomon Period and the emergence of food production. *Bulletin of the National Museum of Ethnology* (国立民族学博物館研究報告) 6: 234–55.

Okazaki K. 2004. A morphological study on the growth patterns of ancient people in the northern Kyushu-Yamaguchi region, Japan. *Anthropological Science* 112: 219–34.

Okazaki K. 2005. Sex assessment of subadult skeletons based on tooth crown measurements: An examination on the interpopulational variation of sex differences and an application to excavated skeletons. *Anthropological Science* (Japanese Series) 113: 139–59.

Sasaki K. 1991. *The creation of the Japanese history* (日本史誕生). Tokyo: Shuei Publisher.

Saunders SR. 1992. Subadult skeletons and growth related studies. In: Saunders SR, Katzenberg MA, editors. *Skeletal biology of past peoples: Research methods.* New York: Wiley-Liss. Pp. 1–20.

Saunders SR, Hoppa RD. 1993. Growth Deficit in survivors and non-survivors: Biological mortality bias in subadult skeletal samples. *Yearbook of Physical Anthropology* 36: 127–51.

Saunders S, Hoppa R, Southern R. 1993. Diaphyseal Growth in a nineteenth century skeletal sample of subadults from St Thomas' church, Belleville, Ontario. *International Journal of Osteoarchaeology* 3: 265–81.

Smith BH. 1991. Standards of human tooth formation and dental age assessment. In: Kelley MA, Larsen CS, editors. *Advances in dental anthropology.* New York: Wiley-Liss. Pp. 143–68.

StatSoft Inc. 1996. *STATISTICA, a user's manual* (STATISTICA, ユーザーズマニュアル). Tokyo: StatSoft Japan.

Steckel RH. 2005. Health and nutrition in pre-Columbian America: The skeletal evidence. *Journal of Interdisciplinary History* 36: 1–32.

Steckel RH, Rose JC. 2002. Patterns of health in the Western Hemisphere. In: Steckel RH, Rose JC, editors. *The backbone of history: Health and nutrition in the Western Hemisphere.* Cambridge: Cambridge University Press. Pp. 563–79.

Steyn M, Henneberg M. 1996. Skeletal growth of children from the Iron Age site at K2 (South Africa). *American Journal of Physical Anthropology* 100: 389–96.

Stloukal VM, Hanakova HP. 1978. The length of long bones in ancient Slavonic populations: With particular consideration to the questions of growth. *Homo Beiheft* 29: 53–69.

Tanaka Y. 1991. A re-examination of so-called the "immigration hypothesis" (torai-setsu). In: Association of the Project on Professor Yokoyama Kouichi's Retirement Ceremony, editors. *Formation of the early Yayoi Culture in Japan* (日本における初期弥生文化の成立). Fukuoka: Bunken Publisher. Pp. 482–505.

Tanner JM. 1978. *Fetus into man.* Cambridge, MA: Harvard University Press.

Temple DH. 2007. Human biological variation during the agricultural transition in prehistoric Japan. Ph.D. dissertation, Ohio State University.

Terasawa K, Terasawa T. 1981. The basic study about vegetable foods at the Yayoi period: The beginning of cultivation. *Koukogaku-Ronko* (考古学論攷) 5: 1–129.

Watanabe M. 1975. *The report of the excavation at the Kuwagaishimo site in Maitsuru city, Kyoto* (京都府舞鶴市桑飼下遺跡発掘調査報告書). Maitsuru: Educational Committee of Maitsuru City.

Yamaguchi B. 1980. A study on the facial flatness of the Jomon crania. *Bulletin of the National Science Museum, Series D* 6: 21–28.

Yamaguchi B. 1982. A review of the osteological characteristics of the Jomon population in prehistoric Japan. *Journal of the Anthropological Society of Nippon* 90: 77–90.

Yamaguchi B, Huang X. 1995. *Studies on the human skeletal remains from Jiangnan, China.* National Science Museum Monographs no. 10. Tokyo: National Museum of Nature and Science.

Yamazaki S. 1978. The present circumstance of the discussion about agriculture at the Jomon period. *Rekishi Kouron* (歴史公論) 4: 106–12.

Yamazaki S. 1983. Agriculture in western Japan at the Later and Final Jomon periods. In: Kato S, Kobayashi T, Fujimoto T, editors. *Study of the Jomon culture.* Vol. 2: *Occupations* (縄文文化 の研究—2: 生業). Tokyo: Yuzankaku. Pp. 267–81.

16

Trauma and Infectious Disease in Northern Japan

Okhotsk and Jomon

MARC OXENHAM, HIROFUMI MATSUMURA,
AND ALLISON DRAKE

The cold of the Far North has been characterized as a screen serving in past times to prevent the flow of many pathological germs along with the movements of their human hosts. . . . Apparently the cold screen explains why at the time of the first European contact the Indians lacked many disease entities common to the Old World, and hence were so vulnerable to the diseases introduced by the Europeans and their African slaves.

Stewart 1960: 265

Stewart was writing more than 50 years ago in order to pose a mechanism to explain the perceived lack of disease in the New World prior to European contact. Influential in developing the notion of a relatively disease-free pre-European-contact New World was Ashburn's (1947) thesis for good initial contact indigenous population health in the ethnohistorical records, coupled with the devastating effects of European-introduced diseases (e.g., typhus, smallpox, and measles, to name a few) on these same people. Stewart's (1960) hypothesis was that the northern climate, being very different from that in which humans originally evolved, was able to cold-filter out a number of disease agents (Merbs 1992), particularly considering the slow speed, measured in generations, at which early migrants probably travelled (Araujo et al. 1988). More recently Crawford (1998) noted the importance of the cold screen hypothesis with respect to parasite life cycles outside of the human body and other pathogens that are not closely related to their human hosts. Newman (1976) and Merbs (1992) have also provided support for the view that the cold screen hypothesis is still relevant in explaining disease flow into the Americas from Asia.

What is missing from the discussion are data on infectious disease loads in cold-adapted Northeast Asian populations in the past. Given that far northern Japan extends into the subarctic zone and skeletal samples are available for this region, it might be expected that the evidence for infectious disease would be limited because of an analogous cold screen effect. The purpose of this study is to (1) examine the evidence for infectious disease and trauma in Hokkaido, Japan; (2) compare these findings to other subarctic and arctic samples from Alaska; and (3) explore the implications of the observed patterning and frequency of infectious disease and debilitating traumatic lesions in cold-adapted marine foraging communities in Northeast Asia.

Methods and Materials

The skeletal samples used in this study derive from a number of Jomon and Okhotsk sites on Hokkaido and Rebun Island, Japan. Because sample sizes from individual Jomon and Okhotsk sites are small for the most part, an aggregated Jomon and Okhotsk sample form the analytical units used in this study. Listed sample sizes are indicative only; refer to the section on sample preservation below. The earliest sample (Initial Jomon, ~8000–5100 years BP, n = 3 individuals) is from Midorimachi, while the Middle Jomon (5100–4050 years BP, n = 13) is sampled at Kitakogane and Kotan-Onsen. Five sites represent the late Jomon (4050–3000 years BP, n = 32): Funadomari, Takasago, Irie, Usujiri, and Tenneru. One site, Misawa, falls into the Final Jomon (3000–2400 years BP, n = 1). The five sampled Epi-Jomon sites (2400–1400 years BP, n = 13) comprise Onkoromanai, Rebunge, Minami-Usu, Bozuyama, and Chatsu 4. The aggregated Okhotsk (AD 550–1200) sample is composed of individuals from seven sites: Ohmisaki (n = 19), Hamanaka 2 and 1 (n = 4), Oshonai (n = 3), Utoro-Jinjayama (n = 6), Menashidomari (n = 1), Pirikatai (n = 2), and Tomiiso (n = 2).

A range of other studies that have assessed paleohealth indicators in subarctic and arctic samples from the North American continent serve as appropriate (see Oxenham and Matsumura 2007) comparisons for the subarctic Hokkaido material. These comparative samples include Keenleyside's (1998) early Aleuts (3000–500 years BP, n = 65) and Eskimo (1,450–100 years BP, n = 128) as well as a late Aleut sample (14th–18th century AD, n = 227) (Keenleyside 2003). A study by Guatelli-Steinberg and colleagues (2004), using a composite sample of Inuits from Point Hope Alaska (500 BC–AD 1700, n = 21), provided another data set on enamel hypoplasia.

Summarizing Hokkaido skeletal preservation and determining actual individual sample sizes are difficult because of the curatorial methods employed (separate storage of each body element by type). Sample preservation is presented in two ways: (1) preservation of each element expressed as a percentage of the minimum number of individuals (MNI) determined for each particular element; and (2) preservation of each element expressed as a percentage of the overall MNI for the sample in question. For example, using the former method there are 25 humeri with 100 percent preservation in the Okhotsk sample where the MNI based on humeri alone is 31 (25 humeri/62 expected humeri [MNI × 2] gives a preservation figure of 40.3 percent for complete humeri). However, using the latter method, the MNI for the entire sample regardless of which element is assessed is 39 based on the preservation of cranial material. When this figure is used, the expected number of humeri is 78 (MNI of 39 × 2) with a resulting preservation figure of 32.1 percent (25 complete humeri/78 expected humeri). The first method provides information on how well particular skeletal elements are preserved with reference to themselves; for instance, while there are fewer Okhotsk tibiae preserved than expected (MNI of 28) compared to femora (MNI of 35), some 32.1 percent of tibiae are 100 percent preserved, as compared to 24.3 percent of femora. The second method allows an assessment of the preservation of each skeletal element with regard to the entire skeleton: the greater MNI for Okhotsk femora as compared to tibiae indicates better overall preservation of the femur in this sample.

Data concerning enamel hypoplasia and cribra orbitalia are summarized from previous publications in order to provide a generalized health context in which to interpret evidence for infectious disease and trauma in the samples under consideration. Methodological protocols for the identification and recording of these physiological stress indicators have been provided by Oxenham and colleagues (Oxenham et al. 2006; Oxenham and Matsumura 2007).

Only the evidence for healed lesions of a traumatic etiology are examined in this study, because of difficulties in identifying perimortem events for which bone in deceased individuals can react to postmortem trauma in the same manner as a living individual for several months after death (Weiberg and Wescott 2008). Protocols for recording and interpreting healed traumatic lesions followed Lovell (1997). Nontraumatic lesions were recorded following advice given by Buikstra and Ubelaker (1994).

Results

Preservation

Figure 16.1 summarizes the preservation of the Hokkaido samples by way of the minimum number of individuals (MNI) as calculated by each element

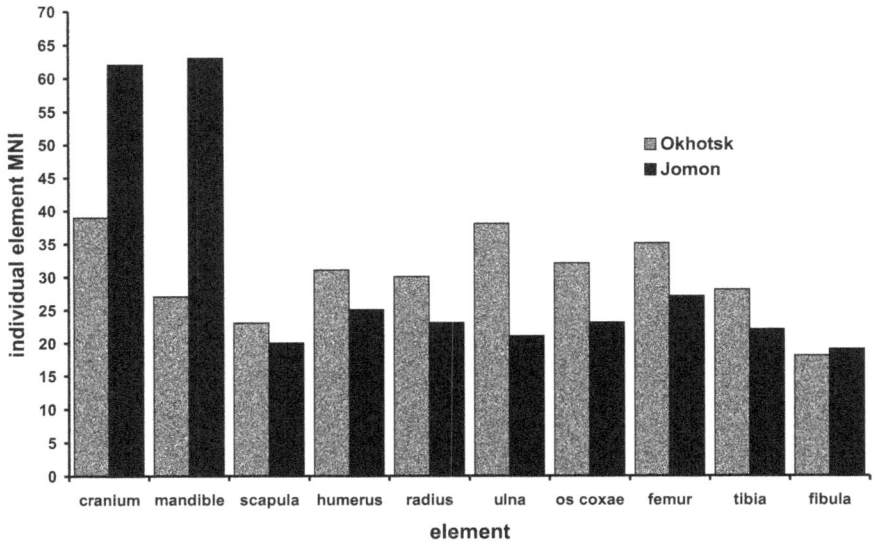

Figure 16.1. Hokkaido element preservation represented as a proportion of element-specific MNIs.

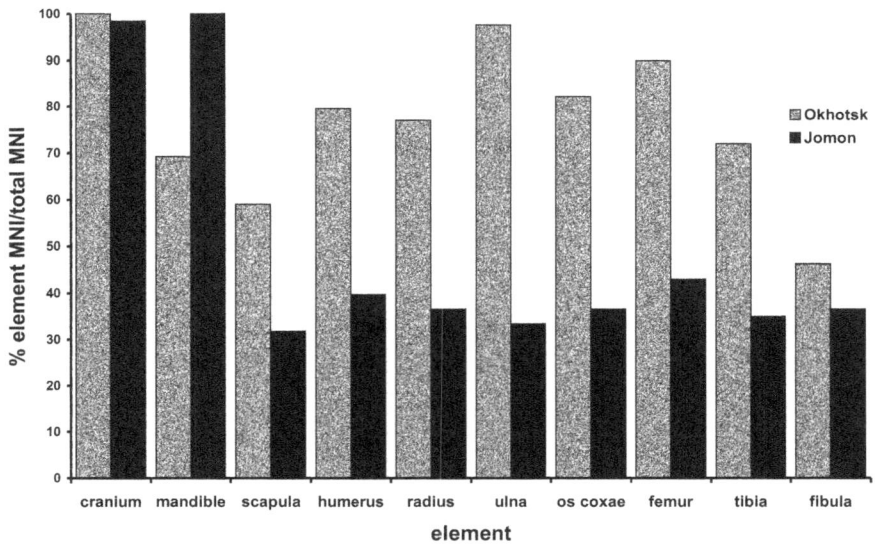

Figure 16.2. Hokkaido element preservation as a proportion of individual skeletal element MNIs in relation to the total (most common element) MNI.

separately. The maximum MNI for the Jomon sample is 63 individuals based on the mandible, while the maximum MNI for the Okhotsk sample is 39 based on the cranium. Figure 16.2 summarizes preservation as a percentage of individual skeletal element MNIs in relation to the total (most common element) MNI. There is much better representation of cranial (including man-

Table 16.1. Adult oral pathology and physiological health summary: Hokkaido and Alaskan samples

Sample	Site	CO	C LEH	I LEH	CI LEH	Reference
Jomon	Hokkaido	25/58 (43.1)	39/134 (29.1)	30/227 (13.2)	69/331 (20.8)	1
Okhotsk	Hokkaido	23/37 (62.2)	15/75 (20.0)	10/101 (9.9)	25/176 (14.2)	1
Aleuts	Aleutian Is. (early)	2/54 (3.7)	2/83 (2.4)	0/64 (0.0)	2/147 (1.4)	2
Aleuts	Aleutian Is. (late)	51/221 (23.1)	8/186 (4.3)	1/205 (0.5)	9/391 (2.3)	3
Eskimo	Pt. Hope/Pt. Barrow, Alaska	10/118 (8.5)	41/180 (22.8)	26/209 (12.4)	67/389 (17.2)	2
Inuit	Point Hope, Alaska	32/111 (28.8)				4

References: 1 = Oxenham and Matsumura 2007 (and unpublished data); 2 = Keenleyside 1998; 3 = Keenleyside 2003; 4 = Guatelli-Steinberg et al. 2004.
Note: Comparative data calculated as affected/n, with percentage in parentheses. Empty cell indicates that appropriate comparative data are not available from literature.
Abbreviations: CO = cribra orbitalia; LEH = linear enamel hypoplasia; C = canine; I = incisor; CI = canine and incisor combined.

dibular) remains in the Jomon sample, with most postcranial representation rather low, falling between 30 percent and 40 percent of cranial preservation. There is much better relative representation of Okhotsk elements, and while cranial preservation is highest, many postcranial elements such as the ulna (94.7 percent), femur (89.7 percent) and os coxae (82.1 percent) are almost as well represented as the crania.

Cribra Orbitalia (CO) and Linear Enamel Hypoplasia (LEH)

Table 16.1 summarizes physiological health (cribra orbitalia and enamel hypoplasia) for the Hokkaido and Alaskan samples. The frequency of cribra orbitalia is very high in comparison to the early Aleut and Eskimo samples, although the late Aleut sample shows elevated levels of cribra orbitalia. LEH, considering the combined incisor and canine data, is elevated in comparison to the Aleut samples and similar to the limited data for Alaska. The small sample reported on by Guatelli-Steinberg and colleagues (2004) shows unusually elevated levels of LEH, even in comparison to other samples from the same region and time.

Trauma and Infectious Disease

Table 16.2 presents data for Hokkaido (for two levels of preservation) on the frequency, both by skeletal element and by individual (based on MNI), of trauma and evidence of infectious disease. When the results for any level of preservation are examined, the frequency of infectious lesions in the Okhotsk sample increases in a cephalocaudal direction with no cases of cranial infection, from a low of 1.7 percent of skeletal elements or 3.2 percent MNI (based on the humerus) showing upper appendicular lesions to a high of 8.7 percent of elements or 17.1 percent MNI (based on the femur) displaying lower appendicular lesions. A similar pattern is evident for the Jomon sample, again with no signs of cranial infection, from a low of 2.2 percent skeletal elements or 4.0 percent MNI (based on the humerus) showing upper appendicular lesions to a high of 4.9 percent elements or 9.1 percent MNI (based on the tibia this time) displaying lower appendicular lesions. While the distribution of infectious lesions is similar between the two Hokkaido samples, the Okhotsk sample consistently, with the exception of the humerus, shows higher frequencies of infectious lesions measured by both skeletal element and MNI (see table 16.2 and figure 16.3), albeit not to a statistically significant degree.

While the evidence for infectious disease is nonspecific for the most part, three individuals in the Okhotsk sample display signs of osteomyelitis. Specimen OMK237a (figure 16.4) is represented by the distal half of a left humerus (no other bones associated with this individual are known to be preserved). The bone, which is extremely friable and fragile, displays evidence for osteoarthritis in the form of well-circumscribed capitulum porosity, trochlea marginal osteophytosis and enthesophytic development in the olecranon fossa. While the cortical bone of the shaft is extremely porous, the anteromedial

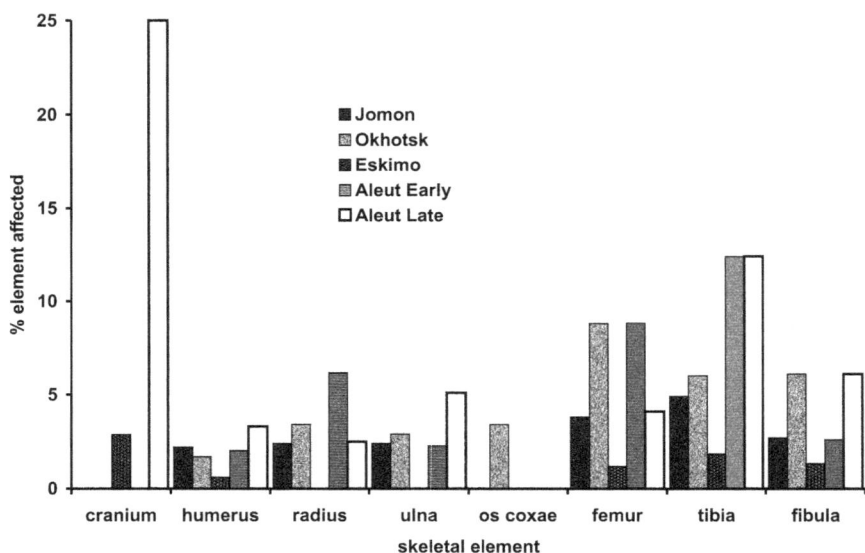

Figure 16.3. Frequency of infectious disease by element for Hokkaido and Alaskan samples.

Table 16.2. Frequency of trauma and infectious disease by skeletal element and MNI in the Hokkaido Jomon and Okhotsk samples

| | Okhotsk | | | | | | | Jomon | | | | | | |
| | Observed | | Affected | | Frequency % | | | Observed | | Affected | | Frequency % | | |
Bone	n	MNI	Infection	Trauma	Infection A/n (A/MNI)	Trauma A/n (A/MNI)		n	MNI	Infection	Trauma	Infection A/n (A/MNI)	Trauma A/n (A/MNI)
Cranium	39	39	0	0	0(0)	0(0)		62	62	0	0	0(0)	0(0)
Mandible	27	27	0	0	0(0)	0(0)		63	63	0	0	0(0)	0(0)
Humerus[a]	35	19	1	0	2.3(5.3)	0(0)		37	19	0	0	0(0)	0(0)
Humerus[b]	59	31	1	0	1.7(3.2)	0(0)		45	25	1	0	2.2(4.0)	0(0)
Radius[a]	25	14	2	0	8.0(14.3)	0(0)		29	16	0	0	0(0)	0(0)
Radius[b]	58	30	2	0	3.4(6.7)	0(0)		42	23	1	0	2.4(4.3)	0(0)
Ulna[a]	29	16	2	0	6.9(12.5)	0(0)		31	17	1	1	3.2(5.9)	3.2(5.9)
Ulna[b]	64	38	2	0	3.1(5.3)	0(0)		42	21	1	1	2.4(4.8)	2.4(4.8)
Os coxae[a]	26	16	2	0	7.7(12.5)	0(0)		21	11	0	0	0(0)	0(0)
Os coxae[b]	58	32	2	0	3.4(6.3)	0(0)		46	23	0	0	0(0)	0(0)
Femur[a]	39	22	3	2	7.7(13.6)	5.1(9.1)		41	21	2	0	4.9(9.5)	0(0)
Femur[b]	69	35	6	2	8.7(17.1)	2.9(5.7)		53	27	2	0	3.8(7.4)	0(0)
Tibia[a]	29	17	2	0	6.7(11.8)	0(0)		31	16	1	0	3.2(6.3)	0(0)
Tibia[b]	50	28	3	1	6.0(10.7)	2.0(3.6)		41	22	2	0	4.9(9.1)	0(0)
Fibula[a]	10	8	2	0	20.0(25.0)	0(0)		32	16	0	0	0(0)	0(0)
Fibula[b]	33	18	2	0	6.1(11.1)	0(0)		37	19	1	0	2.7(5.3)	0(0)

Note: No statistically significant differences between the two samples using Fisher Exact tests.

Abbreviations: n = number of observed elements; MNI = minimum number of individuals observed in the sample, based on most common side; Affected = number of elements affected by traumatic or infectious lesions; A/*n* = proportion of observed (*n*) elements affected (A) with a lesion; A/MNI = proportion of observed MNI affected with a lesion.

[a] Only observed elements >50% preserved.
[b] Any observed element that can be sided.

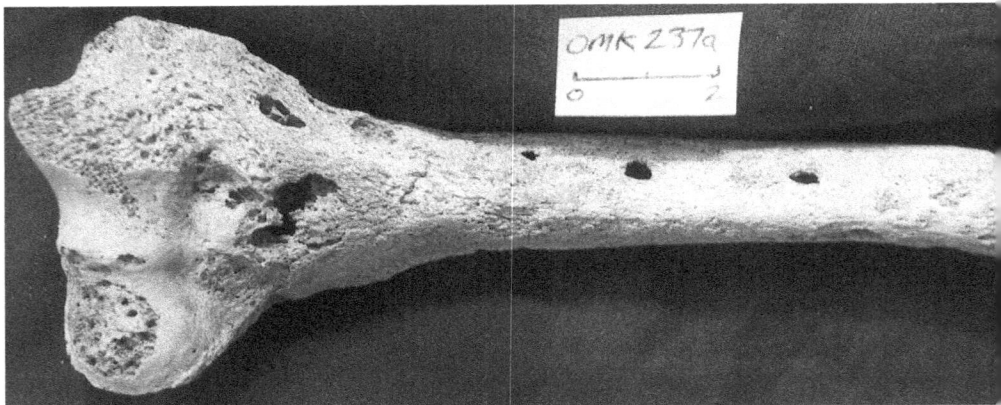

Figure 16.4. Example of osteomyelitis in the left humerus of an Okhotsk individual (specimen OMK237a). Note also area of circumscribed porosity on the capitulum.

aspect of the shaft (particularly more proximally) displays periostitis. The anteromedial aspect presents with two clusters of three lytic lesions or cloacae (first cluster 2–5 mm in diameter; second cluster 3–7 mm in diameter), while several confluent cloacae (an area approximately 13 mm in diameter) are situated on the anterior aspect of the metaphysis, just superior to the coronoid fossa.

Specimen OMK431a is represented by a complete right and left femur only. The right femur displays lesions consistent with osteomyelitis (figure 16.5). With the exception of the lateral aspect of the condyles and the proximal portion superior to the base of the lesser trochanter, the bone is extremely porous and presents scattered periosteal deposits particularly in the distal metaphyseal area (posteriorly and anteriorly), along the distal third of the linea aspera and especially large deposits along the midshaft medial to the linea aspera. On the posterior aspect of the diaphysis a large oval lesion (22 mm long and 8 mm wide) with remodelled edges extends laterally to the linea aspera and is fringed by small subperiosteal bone deposits at its proximal end and along its lateral border. A smaller lytic lesion (8 × 5 mm), also associated with subperiosteal new bone, presents just distal to this. On the anterior aspect of the diaphysis, directly opposite the two posterior lesions, a large confluent lesion (39 mm long and 19 mm wide) opening into the medulla presents with a sequestrum. A further separate small oval lesion (8 × 4 mm) presents just distally and slightly laterally (still on the anterior aspect of diaphysis) to this lesion and also includes a small section of necrotic bone and an area that communicates with the medulla.

The final instance of osteomyelitis (OMK457a) is seen in a small section of femoral diaphysis 89 mm long with a maximum diameter of 34.5 mm (figure

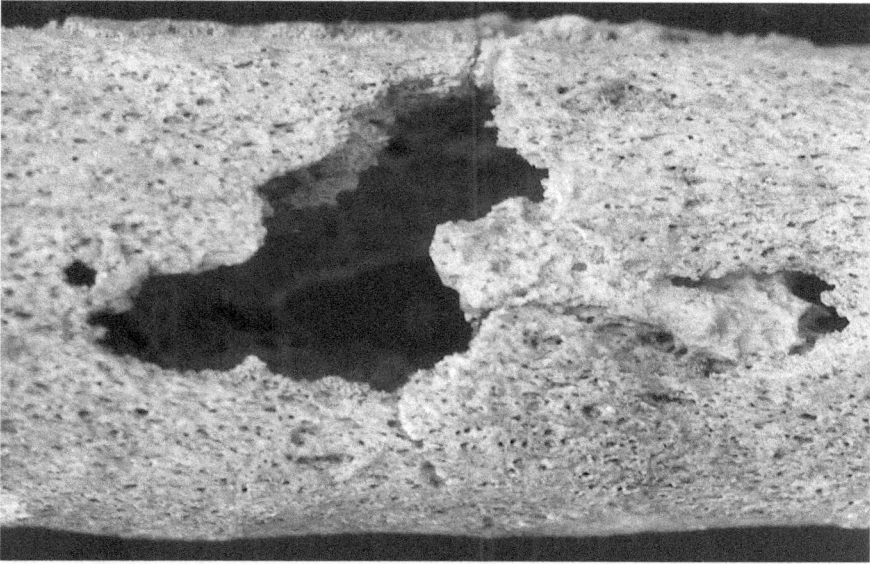

Figure 16.5. Close-up of extensive osteolytic and osteoblastic lesions in a right femur (specimen OMK431a). Note cloaca and sequestrum to right in photo.

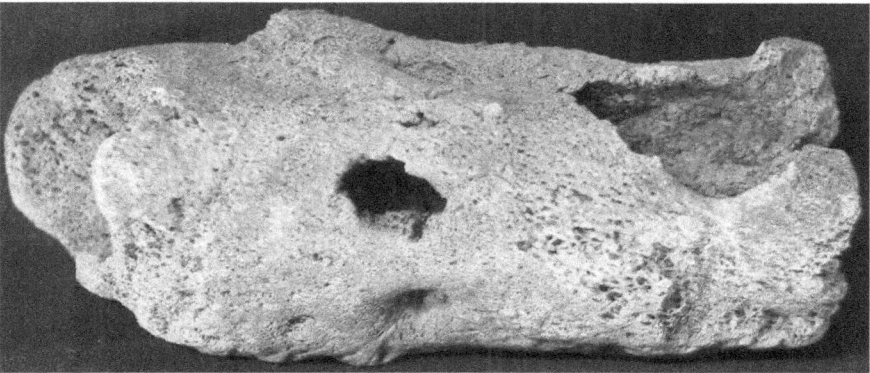

Figure 16.6. Massive osteoblastic (including endosteal) and osteolytic lesions in a short section of femoral diaphysis (OMK457a).

16.6). Extensive osteoblastic and osteolytic modification of this small section precludes identification of side or orientation. One end of the diaphysis (hereafter called A) presents with complete infilling of the medullary cavity with dense trabecular bone. The opposite end (B) is open with one side having a very thin cortical wall (~4.5 mm thick) and the opposite side having a cortical diameter of 15 mm. The thickened side of the shaft displays extensive and continuous remodelled subperiosteal bone deposits. The thin side of the shaft displays three well-circumscribed cloacae running around this side of the shaft at the same height and all communicating with the medulla. Toward bone end A there is a large opening extending about a third (31 mm) the length of the shaft and merging with the end of the shaft. Of the three cloacae, number one (the smallest) is 6 mm in diameter with bevelled sides that slope into the cortical bone; the next (central) lesion is oval (11 × 8 mm) with a combination of smooth and sharp edges; the third lesion is also oval (11 × 8 mm) and has uniformly smooth edges.

Figure 16.1 also includes comparative data on infectious lesions by skeletal element for the Aleut and Eskimo samples of Keenleyside (1998, 2003). The Eskimos display very low levels of infectious disease in general (separate Alaskan data were not reported for the os coxae) although they do follow the general pattern seen for Hokkaido with the upper appendicular skeleton being less affected than the lower. The Eskimo samples display cranial lesions, albeit at a low frequency (2.9 percent). The early and late Aleut assemblages also display a similar pattern to Hokkaido, with relatively lower levels of upper appendicular infection and the highest levels of infection in the lower appendicular skeleton peaking in the tibia (12.4 percent) for both samples. The late Aleut sample stands out in having an extremely high frequency of cranial infection (25 percent).

Keenleyside (2003) suggests that 9/51 (17.6 percent) of the instances of cranial infection in the late Aleut sample are likely due to venereal syphilis. Keenleyside (2003) also indicates that there is one possible case of tuberculosis in the late Aleut sample, with no instances of specific infectious disease noted for the earlier pre-European contact sample. While not strictly diagnosed by way of appendicular lesions, the Jomon sample includes two examples of diffuse idiopathic skeletal hyperostosis (see Oxenham and Matsumura 2007).

Regarding evidence of trauma, table 16.2 indicates that traumatic lesions were uncommon in the Hokkaido samples. Neither Jomon nor Okhotsk demonstrated cranial trauma, while the only traumatic lesions in the Okhotsk were lower appendicular, with 2.9 percent of all assessable femora (5.7 percent of MNI) and 2.0 percent of tibiae (3.6 percent of MNI) showing healed trauma. Only one instance of healed trauma in an ulna (2.4 percent of assessable ulnae, 4.8 percent of MNI) was observed for the Jomon assemblage.

Figure 16.7 includes comparative data on traumatic lesions by skeletal element for the Aleut and Eskimo samples of Keenleyside (1998, 2003) and this study (note that comparative Alaskan data were not available for the os coxae). The frequency of appendicular lesions is low in all samples examined here, and there is no clear pattern with respect to the distribution of healed traumatic lesions. The most obvious difference between the Hokkaido and

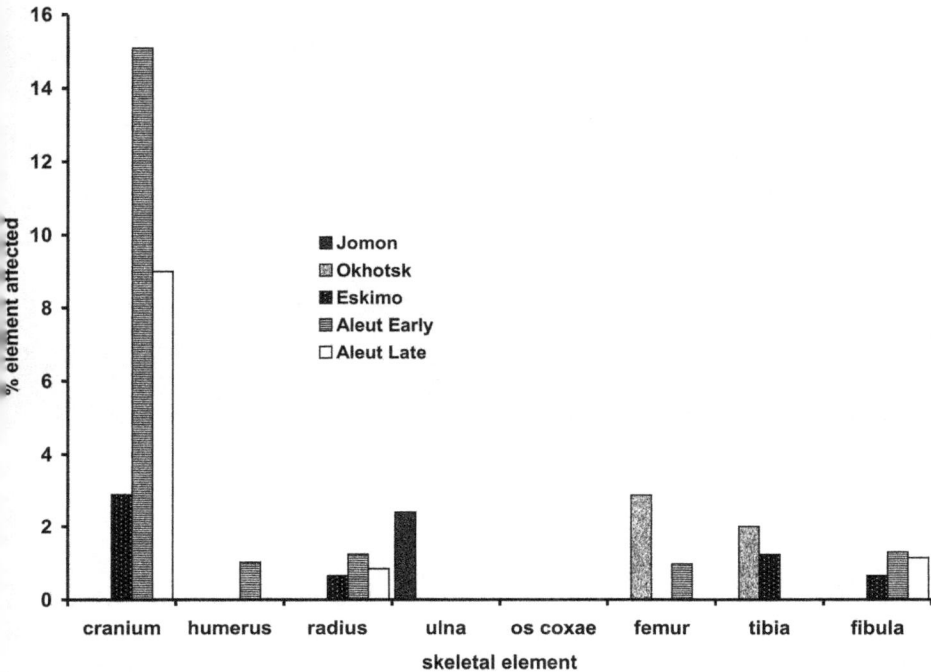

Figure 16.7. Frequency of traumatic lesions by element for Hokkaido and Alaskan samples.

Alaskan samples is the evidence for cranial trauma in Alaska: 15.1 percent of the early Aleut, 9.0 percent of the late Aleut, and 2.9 percent of the Eskimo samples displayed evidence for cranial trauma.

The most severe form of healed trauma in the Hokkaido sample occurred in an Okhotsk (probable) male (OMK429a), represented by left and right femora only (figure 16.8). Both femora are complete, with the exception of the head in the right pathological specimen. The right femur displays a healed fracture at the base of the femoral neck following the intertrochanteric line anteriorly and intertrochanteric crest posteriorly. The entire site of the fracture is well remodelled with no apparent callus. Some scattered porosity of the healed fracture site, especially superiorly, is evident where there is evidence of slightly raised sclerotic bone that shows signs of eburnation. This likely represents some form of postreparative articulation with either the acetabulum or the detached femoral head and/or neck. The lesser trochanter, while similar in size to the left femur, displays slight enthesophytic development on the anteroinferior aspect. The preserved medial condyle shows no sign of osteoarthritis while the lateral condyle is completely lost postmortem. The left femur is free of any signs of osteoarthritis or other pathology.

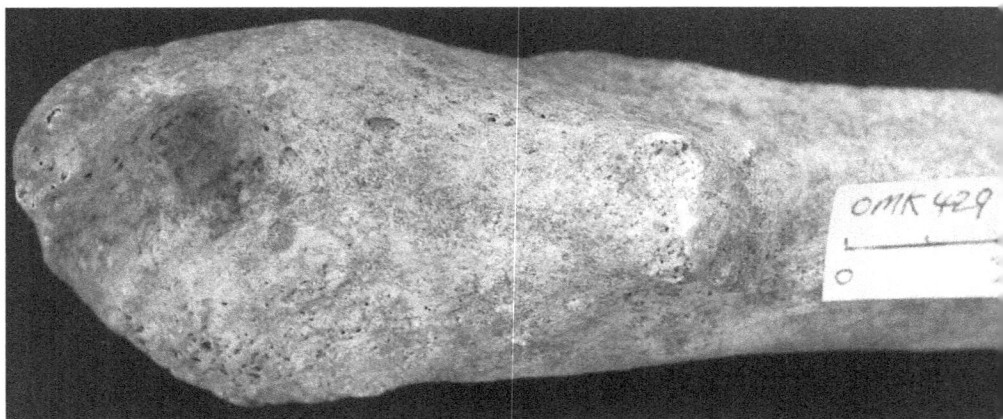

Figure 16.8. Okhotsk male (?) right femur displaying a healed Perthes fracture (OMK429a). Proximal end with medial view.

Discussion

Infectious disease was clearly present in subarctic Japanese populations in the past. Furthermore, with the exception of the cranium, the frequency and pat- terning of infectious lesions were somewhat similar to that seen in subarctic and arctic Alaska, particularly among the Aleuts. A review of the more robust literature on precontact- and contact-period Alaskan health will provide a context in which to explore the nature and perhaps underlying reasons for the evidence and frequency of infectious disease in the far north of Japan.

Prior to historic-period contact, indigenous Alaskans have been character- ized as having been in fairly good health (Shephard and Rode 1996), not- withstanding evidence for a number of minor disorders and skeletal evidence suggesting an average age of 23 years (Shephard and Rode 1996). Precontact infections in the region include cystic and alveolar hydatid disease, trichino- sis, amoebiasis, rabies, botulism, and brucellosis (Shephard and Rode 1996). Gastrointestinal infections do not appear to have been common, although the presence of diarrheal disease in general is implicated by the use of tra- ditional medicines to treat such maladies (Fortuine 1989). Evidence for ear and respiratory infections remains unclear, but otitis media is suggested to have occurred, as well as possible cases of lobar pneumonia and bronchi- tis (Fortuine 1989; Zimmerman et al. 1981; Zimmerman and Aufderheide 1984). The issue of tuberculosis is intriguing, with historical evidence for the presence of this disease in contact-period Aleuts (Fortuine 1989), as well as skeletal lesions consistent with the pulmonary form in a contact-period Aleut sample (Keenleyside 2003).

Survival and maintenance of tubercle bacilli have long been thought to be associated with elevated population size and density. Tuberculosis is generally thought to thrive in situations of poverty and overcrowding, with its origins associated with increasing population density, sedentism, and intensified agricultural activities despite its presence in animal populations much earlier (Roberts and Buikstra 2003). Its airborne transmission, with the tubercle bacilli able to remain suspended in a closed space for long periods, is correlated, among other factors, with crowding (Rieder 1999). However, population density in and of itself has little impact on the maintenance of tuberculosis in a population. Tuberculosis can be maintained in small isolated communities (Daniel 2000), and infection is related to close contact rather than a large number of susceptible individuals. For instance, Farer (1979) argues that because tuberculosis is not a highly infectious disease, prolonged or frequent association is needed in order for the infection to be transmitted, with the greatest hazard to those individuals who are in the same environment as the infected. Although tuberculosis may require crowd conditions to evolve, the argument has been made that it can persist in smaller populations (Black 1975). Indeed, El-Najjar (1979) has used such reasoning to argue that *M. tuberculosis* could have survived the so-called cold screen of Beringia. Clearly, both tuberculosis and venereal syphilis could have been maintained, after an external introduction at least, in a subarctic environment.

Many of the Alaskan and northern Japanese skeletal samples assessed for infectious disease derive from marine-intensive foraging communities. Thompson and colleagues (2006) note that naturally occurring marine mammals can be infected with a range of pathogens transmittable to humans including *Mycobacterium* (various species) and *Brucella* species. Fish and crabs, particularly when handled/processed, pose further potential infectious threats by way of such microorganisms as *Erysipelothrix rhusopathiae* and *Mycoplasma phocacerebrale* (causes seal finger) (Thompson et al. 2006). Indeed, parasites would appear to have been a significant health concern, with past Alaskan populations known to have harbored *Ancylostomatidae* (hookworm) (Bouchet et al. 1999), *Ascaris* (a nematode), and *Diphyllobothrium* (tapeworm) (Bouchet et al. 2001), in addition to *Echinococcus granulosus* (hydatid worm) (Ortner and Putschar 1981), *Trichinella spiralis* (pork worm) (Zimmerman and Aufderheide 1984), and *Cryptocotyle lingua* (fish nematode) (Zimmerman and Smith 1975).

El Molto and colleagues (2000) argue for the presence of yaws in a small ($n = 16$) precontact (1,300–1,900 years BP) Aleut sample based on the presence and distribution of periosteal lesions. The same authors suggest a high frequency of venereal syphilis in a later (including the contact period) sample of 431 individuals from Point Hope, Alaska. The finding of syphilis, at least, at

Point Hope is consistent with the work of Keenleyside (2003), who suggested that the appearance of venereal syphilis in the Aleutians was coincidental with initial European contact. The epidemiology of yaws and the nonspecific nature of the periosteal lesions reported on by El Moto and colleagues (2000) make for a less than convincing case for yaws in the precontact Aleutians.

Keenleyside (1998), while acknowledging the complexity of the results for infectious disease, attributed the higher frequency of infectious lesions in the Aleut sample to lifestyle: crowded longhouse-style accommodation and poor hygiene; and soft tissue trauma-associated infections in Aleut males. In a subsequent paper (Keenleyside 2003), in which early and late (contact period) Aleut samples were analyzed, a marked increase in cranial infections was attributed to an increase in infectious disease in the contact period. While crowded housing is again posited as a contributing variable, introduced venereal syphilis is seen as an important factor. If all late-period Aleut crania are considered, then 9/204 (4.4 percent) of all individuals displayed cranial indications of venereal syphilis. Presumably a significant proportion of the evidence for appendicular infectious lesions is associated with venereal syphilis as well. Given that venereal syphilis generally only manifests skeletally in 10 to 12 percent of individuals with the disease (Roberts and Manchester 1995), it was clearly at epidemic levels in the Aleutians during the initial European-contact phase.

Despite the predictions of the cold screen hypothesis, there is and was considerable potential for relatively high infectious disease loads in subarctic and arctic populations. Based on the Alaskan evidence, the seemingly elevated level and patterning of infectious lesions in the Okhotsk sample, including at least three cases of severe chronic osteomyelitis, is arguably not unexpected for a population operating within a cold environmental zone. Further, both the Okhotsk and the Jomon of Hokkaido appear to have been physiologically compromised, as subadults at least, given the relatively high frequency of cribra orbitalia and enamel hypoplasia for subarctic populations. While the etiology of cribra orbitalia is complex (see Stuart-Macadam 1985; Ortner et al. 1999; Wapler et al. 2004) and probably multifactorial, the high frequency in the Hokkaido samples suggests a degree of depressed immunocompetence that may have facilitated elevated levels of infectious disease, particularly in the case of the Okhotsk.

However, the observation that the Point Barrow/Point Hope Eskimo samples displayed very low levels of evident infectious disease while exhibiting elevated levels of enamel hypoplasia, especially for the small sample analyzed by Guatelli-Steinberg and colleagues (2004), is somewhat counterintuitive. It is possible that the more northerly Point Barrow and Point Hope populations, while being physiologically compromised, did not share the same opportunities for encountering the pathogens associated with chronic infectious disease as did their more southerly Aleutian and Hokkaido (especially Okhotsk) neighbors.

The apparent emphasis on marine foraging (see Oxenham and Matsumura 2007) would have exposed the Okhotsk to contact with a range of marine mammals and fishes and thus the potential for infection either through the ingestion of infected marine mammal products or more directly by way of traumatic inoculation of pathogens. The Okhotsk have also been described as "the only known intrusive culture [in Japan] that remained separate from the other groups for a long period" (Hudson 2004: 290). It is believed that they originated in the Amur River basin in what is now the eastern Russian seaboard, from where they tracked down through Sakhalin Island and finally into northern and eastern Hokkaido (Hudson 2004). Their less-than-sedentary history and a subsistence economy heavily influenced by marked seasonal variations would presumably have been likely stressors associated with the development of cribra orbitalia and enamel hypoplasia, as well as facilitating the intergroup contact necessary for the exchange of infectious pathogens. While Hudson (2004) paints a complex and fluid picture of Okhotsk subsistence, settlement, mobility, and demography, the lack of absolute dates for the skeletal samples assessed in this study does not allow the evidence for Okhotsk—or for that matter Jomon—paleohealth to inform these issues specifically.

Finally, while the level of trauma is not high in the Hokkaido samples, the case of the Perthes fracture suggests that Okhotsk people, at least, were at risk of serious and debilitating injury. The examples of chronic osteomyelitis, in addition to serious healed trauma, indicate that community members with long-term poor health and/or disability were accommodated in this harsh environment. Whether this reflects on community attitudes in terms of care and compassion or survival of the disabled despite indifference is impossible to assess for the time being. What does seem certain, however, is that subarctic populations in the far north of Japan are comparable to their Alaskan counterparts in showing evidence for considerable levels of infectious disease despite the arguably ameliorating effects of a cold screening of many pathogenic organisms.

Fortuine (1989) has extensively reviewed an enormous corpus of ethnohistoric accounts of indigenous Alaskans suffering appalling types and levels of debilitating trauma and chronic infectious disease. Death and traumatic injury through misadventure, directly related to the nature of the environment and the types of subsistence activities engaged in, appears to have been very common in precontact Alaska (Fortuine 1989). While accounts of abuse and ridicule of the sick and deformed exist, there is also extensive evidence for the accommodation and care of such individuals in the early ethnohistoric accounts (Fortuine 1989). There is no reason to believe that a similar situation did not exist in the far north of Japan in the past.

Whether or not a sophisticated health-care system existed within the small, cold-adapted foraging communities of northern Japan, there would certainly have been onerous economic costs in terms of lost labor (through death and/ or disability of both a temporary and a permanent nature) and redirection of resources into caring for such individuals. Despite the fact that the injured, sick, and seriously disabled could have contributed to the community in ways other than generally expected of an able-bodied individual (see Dettwyler 1991 for a discussion of this issue), their input in a strictly economic sense may not have outweighed their inability to engage in the broader range of activities necessary for survival, thus causing a net drain on the community. Finally, it is clear that cold-adapted East Asian samples should be compared to cold-adapted samples globally and not to more southerly East Asians.

Conclusions

This paper set out to assess skeletal samples from the far north of Japan for signs of infectious disease and traumatic injury. It was argued that a suitable comparison is other cold-adapted peoples, and a series of Alaskan samples were used to this end. The patterning and frequency of infectious disease and trauma were discussed in the context of the subsistence and environments these people operated in.

It was shown that despite the arguably ameliorating effect of a cold filter reducing the number of viable pathogens, infectious disease was clearly an important and debilitating factor in cold-adapted peoples in the past generally. The Okhotsk, in particular, were seen to have experienced elevated levels of chronic and highly debilitating infectious disease. Both the Jomon and the Okhotsk samples also experienced the highest levels of cribra orbitalia and a quite elevated frequency of linear enamel hypoplasia relative to other cold-adapted populations. While evidence of cranial trauma was lacking in the Japanese samples (which may indicate a lack of interpersonal violence), the frequency and patterning of postcranial trauma, while low, were comparable to the Aleutian samples from Alaska. The Okhotsk pattern may be indicative of the dangers of their environment, specifically, a focus on large marine mammal hunting. The presence of individuals with chronic infections and debilitating trauma in northern Japan would suggest that these people were accommodated at some level. Whether this accommodation was influenced by compassion or indifference, there would have clearly been economic implications.

Literature Cited

Araujo A, Ferriera LF, Confalonieri U, Chame M. 1988. Hookworms and the peopling of America. *Cadernos de Saude Publica* 2: 226–33.

Ashburn, PM. 1947. *The ranks of death: A medical history of the conquest of America.* New York: Coward-McCann.

Black FL. 1975. Infectious disease in primitive societies. *Science* 187: 515–18.

Bouchet F, Lefèvre C, West D, Corbett D. 1999. First paleoparasitological analysis of a midden in the Aleutian Island (Alaska): Results and limits. *Journal of Parasitology* 85: 369–72.

Bouchet F, West D, Lefèvre C, Corbett D. 2001. Identification of parasitoses in a child burial from Adak Island (Central Aleutian Islands, Alaska). *Comptes-rendus de l'Académie des Sciences de Paris* 324: 123–27.

Buikstra JE, Ubelaker DH, editors. 1994. *Standards for data collection from human skeletal remains.* Arkansas Archaeological Survey Research Series no. 44. Fayetteville.

Crawford MH. 1998. *The origins of Native Americans: Evidence from anthropological genetics.* Cambridge: Cambridge University Press.

Daniel TM. 2000. The origins and precolonial epidemiology of tuberculosis in the Americas: Can we figure them out? *International Journal of Tuberculosis and Lung Disease* 4: 395–400.

Dettwyler KA. 1991. Can paleopathology provide evidence for "compassion"? *American Journal of Physical Anthropology* 84: 374–84.

El Moto J, Rothschild BM, Woods R, Rothschild C. 2000. Unique aspects of West Coast treponematoses. *Chungará* (Arica) 32: 157–65.

El-Najjar M. 1979. Human treponematosis and tuberculosis: Evidence from the New World. *American Journal of Physical Anthropology* 51: 599–618.

Farer LS. 1979. Mycobacterium tuberculosis: Epidemiology and treatment. In: Madell GL, Douglas RG Jr., Bennett JE, editors. *Principles and practice of infectious diseases.* New York: John Wiley and Sons. Pp. 1905–1925.

Fortuine R. 1989. *Chills and fever: Health and disease in the early history of Alaska.* Fairbanks: University of Alaska Press.

Guatelli-Steinberg D, Larsen CS, Hutchinson DL. 2004. Prevalence and the duration of linear enamel hypoplasia: A comparative study of Neandertals and Inuit foragers. *Journal of Human Evolution* 47: 65–84.

Hudson MJ. 2004. The perverse realities of change: World system incorporation and the Okhotsk culture in Hokkaido. *Journal of Anthropological Archaeology* 23: 290–308.

Keenleyside A. 1998. Skeletal evidence of health and disease in pre-contact Alaskan Eskimos and Aleuts. *American Journal of Physical Anthropology* 107: 51–70.

Keenleyside A. 2003. Changing patterns of health and disease among the Aleuts. *Arctic Anthropology* 40: 48–69.

Lovell NC. 1997. Trauma analysis in paleopathology. *American Journal of Physical Anthropology* 40: 139–70.

Merbs CF. 1992. A New World of infectious disease. *Yearbook of Physical Anthropology* 35: 3–42.

Newman MT. 1976. Aboriginal New World epidemiology and medical care, and the impact of Old World disease imports. *American Journal of Physical Anthropology* 45: 667–72.

Ortner DJ, Kimmerle EH, Diez M. 1999. Probable evidence of scurvy in subadults from archeological sites in Peru. *American Journal of Physical Anthropology* 108: 321–31.

Ortner DJ, Putschar WGJ. 1981. *Identification of pathological conditions in human skeletal remains.* Washington, DC: Smithsonian Institution Press.

Oxenham MF, Matsumura H. 2007. Oral and physiological paleohealth in cold adapted peoples: Northeast Asia, Hokkaido. *American Journal of Physical Anthropology* 135: 64–74.

Oxenham MF, Matsumura H, Nishimoto T. 2006. Diffuse idiopathic skeletal hyperostosis in Late Jomon Hokkaido, Japan. *International Journal of Osteoarchaeology* 16: 34–46.

Rieder HL. 1999. *Epidemiologic basis of tuberculosis control.* Paris: International Union against Tuberculosis and Lung Disease.

Roberts CA, Buikstra JE. 2003. *The bioarchaeology of tuberculosis: A global view on a reemerging disease.* Gainesville: University Press of Florida.

Roberts C, Manchester K. 1995. *The archaeology of disease.* Ithaca, NY: Cornell University Press.

Shephard RJ, Rode A. 1996. *The health consequences of "modernization": Evidence from circumpolar peoples.* Cambridge: Cambridge University Press.

Stewart TD. 1960. A physical anthropologist's view of the peopling of the New World. *Southwestern Journal of Anthropology* 16: 259–73.

Stuart-Macadam PL. 1985. Porotic hyperostosis: representative of a childhood condition. *American Journal of Physical Anthropology* 6: 391–98.

Thompson JR, Marcelino LA, Polz MF. 2006. Diversity, sources, and detection of human bacterial pathogens in marine environments. In: Belkin S, Colwell RR, editors. *Oceans and health: Pathogens in the marine environment.* New York: Springer. Pp. 29–68.

Wapler U, Crubézy E, Schultz M. 2004. Is cribra orbitalia synonymous with anemia? Analysis and interpretation of cranial pathology in Sudan. *American Journal of Physical Anthropology* 123: 333–39.

Wieberg DAM, Wescott DJ. 2008. Estimating the timing of long bone fractures: Correlation between the postmortem interval, bone moisture content, and blunt force trauma fracture characteristics. *Journal of Forensic Sciences* 53: 1028–34.

Zimmerman MR, Aufderheide AC. 1984. The frozen family of Utqiagvik: The autopsy findings. *Arctic Anthropology* 21: 53–64.

Zimmerman MR, Smith GS. 1975. A probable case of accidental inhumation of 1,600 years ago. *Bulletin of the New York Academy of Medicine* 51: 828–37.

Zimmerman MR, Trinkaus E, LeMay M, Aufderheide AC, Reyman TA, Marrocco GR, Ortel RW, Benitez JT, Laughlin WS, Horne PD, Schultes RE, Coughlin EA. 1981. The paleopathology of an Aleutian mummy. *Archives of Pathology and Laboratory Medicine* 105: 638–41.

17

A Paleohealth Assessment of the Shih-san-hang Site from Iron Age Taiwan

LIU CHINHSIN, JOHN KRIGBAUM,
TSANG CHENGHWA, AND LIU YICHANG

The assessment of disease from excavated human skeletal remains and inference of health status, in concert with consideration of archaeological context
from which they were recovered, can reveal useful and sometimes unantici-
pated details about past human lifeways. Extensive archaeological work on
Taiwan over the past few decades has uncovered a long sequence of prehistoric human occupation. Numerous sites have been discovered, and many of
them are well studied. Nevertheless, only limited bioarchaeological analysis
has been conducted on human remains from Taiwanese sites.

The goal of this chapter is to characterize the health status of an Iron Age
population at the Shih-san-hang site in northern Taiwan with respect to its
broad-spectrum foraging subsistence practices and the site's transitional nature in Taiwanese prehistory. The site is unique in its temporal span, length
of occupation, evidence of iron-working, diverse artifact distribution, wide
range of abundant faunal remains, and well-preserved human burials. Taiwan
played a critical role in the Austronesian diaspora, as well as the evolution and
transmission of its languages (Bellwood et al. 1995; Bellwood 2001, 2006;
Hung et al. 2007). Results of this paleopathological analysis are interpreted
within a biocultural framework and compared with data from temporally and
geographically relevant East Asian sites, placing the Shih-san-hang community into a larger regional context.

The Archaeological Context of Prehistoric Taiwan
and the Shih-san-hang Site

The prehistory of Taiwan is generally divided into five major periods: Late
Paleolithic to Early Neolithic (c. >15000–5000 BP); Middle Neolithic

(c. 4500–3500 BP); Late Neolithic (c. 3500–2000 BP); and Iron Age (c. 2000–800 BP). Han acculturation followed the Iron Age and represents the beginning of the historic period (Liu 1992; see Chen 2000 for a detailed review). It is noteworthy that scholars note the absence of the Bronze Age in Taiwanese prehistory that is otherwise common throughout East and Southeast Asia (e.g., Imamura 1996; Higham 2004; Chang et al. 2005). This may be attributed to the lack of locally sourced essential metal ores, such as zinc and lead, which prevented the formation of bronze alloy.

Interaction between coastal mainland China and people on Taiwan began long before the start of the Iron Age in Taiwan. Evidence for iron-working in southeastern mainland China has been dated to circa 2700 BP. It is postulated that iron-working techniques in the mainland were transmitted and adopted by the people in Taiwan via contact, thus bypassing the Bronze Age period (Chen 2000; Tsang and Liu 2001b).

Five contemporaneous but geographically discrete Taiwanese Iron Age cultural traditions have been identified: the Shih-san-hang culture (northern and north-coastal), Fan-zih-yuan culture (midwestern), Niao-song culture (southwestern), Guei-shan culture (southernmost), and Jing-pu culture (eastern and east-coastal) (Liu 1992; Chen 2000; Tsang 2000). Each of these Iron Age cultures varies by location and has a distinct assemblage of material culture, based on typological characteristics of the recovered ceramics and lithic tools. The diversity of the cultural landscape in a moderately sized island like Taiwan during prehistoric and protohistoric times suggests a complexity of prehistoric sociocultural structure and the possible existence of multiple lines of interaction among the population groups inhabiting the island.

Located on the northwest coast of Taiwan, near the southern bank of the Damsui River estuary (25'10" N; 121'24" E) (figure 17.1), the Shih-san-hang site was situated on a sand dune, approximately 5 m above sea level and about 200 m away from the present coastline. The site was first discovered in the 1950s, and five intensive salvage excavations were carried out between 1990 and 1992 that yielded thick cultural deposits, including the burial features that are the principal focus of this study. With a total area estimated at 60,000 m², of which 7,000 m² were excavated, Shih-san-hang is considered the "type site" of the Shih-san-hang culture. The chronology of the Shih-san-hang culture is further subdivided into the Early (2000–1000 years BP) and Late periods (1,000 years BP to the time of Han acculturation) (Liu 1995). Calibrated radiocarbon dates indicate that the Shih-san-hang site was occupied between 2000 and 500 years BP, with peak activity between circa 1800 and 800 years BP (Liu 1995; Tsang and Liu 2001a), or during the final prehistoric period on northern Taiwan, just prior to Han acculturation.

Figure 17.1. Location of the Shih-san-hang site.

The Shih-san-hang site is renowned for the abundance of iron-smelting by-products (slag), iron artifacts recovered, and an iron workshop. This evidence suggests that the Shih-san-hang people were actively engaged in iron metallurgy and producing iron tools for subsistence and possibly for defensive purposes (Liu 1992; Tsang 2000; Tsang and Liu 2001b). The composition of the iron includes mineral elements extracted from beach sand, employed in the smelting process to purify the final products. This iron smelting technique is believed to have been a local innovation (Chen 2000). Unfortunately, the iron objects recovered from the site were too oxidized and fragmented to infer their original shapes and functions.

The large quantities of recovered marine faunal remains and fishing-related artifacts suggest that marine resources constituted a major portion of the Shih-san-hang human diet. Somewhat equally abundant are the recovered remains of terrestrial fauna. A wide range of species have been identified, including forest deer, the Formosan barking deer (*Muntiacus reevesii*), chickens, and various other bird species. It is very likely that these terrestrial animals were acquired through hunting (Chang 1993). Nevertheless, analysis of pig mandibles from the site (Lin 1997) suggests that the inhabitants were in the process of domesticating wild boar. Hunting, however, would have been a logical way to procure local fauna.

Botanical remains were not as well preserved as the faunal ones. Traces of rice grains and rice-chaff-tempered pottery were recovered, although the degree to which people may have depended on rice for dietary purposes is not yet clear (Tsang and Liu 2001a,b). Based on their analysis of the archaeological findings, in concert with the prevalence of particular dental pathologies, Pietrusewsky and Tsang (2003) suggest that the people of Shih-san-hang had a mixed diet. Based on the ecological and archaeological findings, subsistence of the Shih-san-hang people appears to be best categorized as broad-spectrum foraging of both terrestrial and marine food resources.

Two hundred ninety-one burial units were recovered from Shih-san-hang, constituting the second-largest human skeletal assemblage found on Taiwan to date. Previous studies on subsets of the Shih-san-hang skeletal assemblage frequently gave recognition to the existence of costo-clavicular grooves on adult skeletons, suggesting habitual heavy use of the upper arms (Chang 1993). Artifacts of nonlocal origins, such as porcelain and coins dated to the Tang and Sung dynasties from mainland China, were commonly associated with human burials (Liu 1992; Tsang 2000; Tsang and Liu 2001b). Such "exotic" artifacts, considered alongside the occupation-related markers on human skeletal remains, has suggested to some scholars that frequent canoeing and/or paddling may have been an important part of daily life for the Shih-san-hang people (Chang 1993). Taken together, the cultural and biological evidence suggests routine engagement in seafaring by the inhabitants of Shih-san-hang, likely as participants in well-orchestrated exchange networks connecting them to contemporaneous groups throughout the island, as well as with people from coastal mainland China and/or the neighboring Pacific islands (Liu 1995; Tsang and Liu 2001b).

The results of cranio-morphometric analysis of Shih-san-hang skeletons by Chang and Pietrusewsky suggest shared biological features among the Babuza, Pazeh, and Shih-san-hang populations (Chang 1993; Pietrusewsky and Chang 2003; $N = 17$ and 13, respectively, males only). The first two groups are identified as plains aborigines who once lived in the central part of western coastal Taiwan. Furthermore, the cranial morphology of the skeletal series from Shih-san-hang shows less affinity with the Atayal (geographically the nearest mountain aborigine group to Shih-san-hang) than with other aboriginal groups on the island. In fact, the cranio-morphometric profile of the Atayal sample is more distinct from that of the Shih-san-hang series than from the profile of a Polynesian/Micronesian sample. In other words, the people buried at Shih-san-hang evidently had close biological affiliations with aborigines from the central-northern Taiwanese plains and most likely were genetically linked to Austronesians from Polynesia as well (Chang 1993; Pietrusewsky and Chang 2003).

That the sociocultural development of prehistoric Taiwan does not involve the Bronze Age places the Iron Age, the period when Shih-san-hang was principally occupied, as the critical period to witness the transition from prehistory to protohistory. The Iron Age not only marked the emergence of a higher quality and more effective tool assemblage suitable for diverse agricultural and hunting activities in Taiwan, but also witnessed population growth, intensified population interaction, and the rapid development of social complexity. The importance of a transitional period in Southeast Asian prehistory is well documented (e.g., Higham 2004). These societies were often well adapted to their landscape, as well as being highly diverse within and among groups insofar as subsistence, diet, labor, and craft production were concerned. Combining the rare advantages of large site size, abundant artifact recovery, and well-preserved skeletal remains, the Shih-san-hang site is well suited for exploring the dynamic nature of such a transitional period and its associated effects on human biology and lifeways.

Materials and Methods

All recovered human skeletal individuals from Shih-san-hang site were included in this study. Table 17.1 outlines the demographic distribution of the sample. The criteria and methods of sex and age identification recommended by Buikstra and Ubelaker (1994) were followed. Selected parameters of skeletal health, including oral health (caries, antemortem tooth loss, abscessing, calculus), nonspecific stress indicators (linear enamel hypoplasia, porotic hyperostosis/cribra orbitalia), trauma, and evidence of infectious diseases were scored. Detailed evaluation and scoring methods for these conditions have been explicated by Liu (2005). A biocultural framework was adopted for interpretation of the results (Goodman and Armelagos 1989).

Because the details of the Shih-san-hang site sequence are still being refined, all human skeletal remains from the site were construed as a single population in this study. The bias in the results due to the long time span represented at Shih-san-hang, as well as the possibility of conflating the disparate health profiles of individuals born of different cultural traditions from the Early and Late Shih-san-hang cultural periods, is acknowledged. The approach followed in this research builds on previous bioarchaeological analyses by Chang (1993) and Pietrusewsky and Tsang (2003), which were each based on different subsets of the total curated adult skeletons from Shih-san-hang.

Table 17.1. Demography of the Shih-san-hang skeletal assemblage

Age group[a]	Male N	Male %	Female N	Female %	? sex[b] N	? sex[b] %	Total N	Total %
Subadult	3	0.9	1	0.3	74	24.2	78	25.4
Young adult	34	11.1	37	12.1	19	6.2	90	29.4
Middle adult	19	6.2	14	4.6	3	0.9	36	11.7
Old adult	2	0.7	3	0.9	0	0.0	5	1.6
? age A	9	2.9	2	0.7	20	6.5	31	10.1
? age	0	0.0	0	0.0	66	21.6	66	21.6
Total	67	21.8	57	18.6	182	59.4	306	100.0

[a] Subadult = 0–20 years; young adult = 21–35 years; middle adult = 36–50 years; old adult = 50 years and older; ? age A = unknown-age adult; ? age = age unknown.
[b] ? sex = unknown sex.

Table 17.2. Site summary of comparative samples used in this study

Site	Country	Period	Dates	References
Shih-san-hang	Taiwan	Iron Age	2000–500 BP	Current study
Eastern Japan	Japan	Late–Final Jomon	4000–2400 BP	Temple 2007
Western/Inland Japan	Japan	Middle–Final Jomon	5000–2300 BP	Temple 2007
Southern Honshu	Japan	Early–Late Yayoi	2500–1700 BP	Temple and Larsen 2007
Northern Kyushu	Japan	Middle Yayoi	2100–1900 BP	Temple and Larsen 2007
Tanegashima Island	Japan	Middle–Late Yayoi	2100–1700 BP	Temple and Larsen 2007
Hokkaido Jomon	Japan	Jomon	5100–1400 BP	Oxenham and Matsumura 2008
Hokkaido Jomon[a]	Japan	Jomon	5100–2400 BP	Oxenham and Matsumura 2008
Hokkaido Okhotsk	Japan	Kofun–Muromachi	1500–600 BP	Oxenham and Matsumura 2008
Beiliu	China	Early Yangshao	6570–6210 BP	Pechenkina et al. 2007
Jiangzhai I	China	Early Yangshao	6180–5465 BP	Pechenkina et al. 2007
Jiangzhai II	China	Early Yangshao	5200–4,590 BP	Pechenkina et al. 2007
Shijia	China	Early Yangshao	5200–4800 BP	Pechenkina et al. 2007
Guanjia	China	Middle Yangshao	6000–5500 BP	Pechenkina et al. 2007
Xipo	China	Middle Yangshao	6000–5500 BP	Pechenkina et al. 2007
Meishan	China	Late Longshan	4500–4000 BP	Pechenkina et al. 2007
Mengzhuang	China	Late Longshan	4500–4000 BP	Pechenkina et al. 2007
Kangjia	China	Han Dynasty	2200–1800 BP	Pechenkina et al. 2007
Xicun	China	Western Zhou	3000–2720 BP	Pechenkina et al. 2007

Note: Eastern Japan includes Inariyama, Hobi, Nakazuma, and Yoshigo; Western/Inland Japan includes Kitamura, Ota, Tsukumo, and Yosekura; Southern Honshu includes Doigahama and Koura; Northern Kyushu includes Kanenokuma and Nagaoka; Tanegashima Island includes Torinominae and Hirota.
[a] Excludes Epi-Jomon sample.

The prevalence of each oral health condition and nonspecific stress marker was assessed both by element count (tooth, socket/locus, cranial bone) and per individual. Because not all recovered individuals from Shih-san-hang have all dental and skeletal elements preserved, prevalence by element counts provides a more accurate assessment of health and well-being. When the rates of oral and skeletal health indicators are compared among populations, it is important to keep in mind the potential bias that a specific demographic profile may cause. As seen in table 17.1, young adults make up the majority of the Shih-san-hang skeletal assemblage, while the distribution of identifiable males and females is fairly similar (22 percent and 19 percent, respectively). In paleodemographic profiles, it is not uncommon to encounter sites with younger individuals well represented, while adults 40 years and older are rare, as short longevity and low life expectancy are characteristics of prehistoric populations (Waldron 1994; Hoppa and Vaupel 2002).

Although it would have been ideal to compare the results from the Shih-san-hang assemblage to those from similar studies on other populations from Taiwan to control for local environmental and cultural factors, large-scale paleopathological studies on human skeletal remains from Taiwan are unfortunately rare. Therefore, results from a number of studies on other East Asian populations were used to place the Shih-san-hang data in broader regional and temporal contexts (table 17.2).

Oral Health

Dental Caries

Dental caries is an infectious disease caused by the acids produced by bacterial fermentation of carbohydrates on the dental surfaces, leading to demineralization of dental enamel (Larsen 1997: 65). The frequency of carious teeth in populations with varied subsistence regimes is widely used as a proxy for assessing the contribution of carbohydrate-rich foods to the human diet (Turner 1979; Hillson 1996). A general worldwide trend has been found between the development and intensification of agriculture and the increased prevalence of caries (Turner 1979; Cohen and Armelagos 1984; Larsen 1997; Cohen and Crane-Kramer 2007).

For the Shih-san-hang people, the prevalence of caries on both deciduous and permanent teeth was very low by tooth count (2.4 percent and 0.7 percent, respectively [table 17.3]). The "corrected caries rate" (Lukacs 1995) was not used, because of an extremely low incidence of caries-induced pulp cavity exposure (1/41) and very limited antemortem tooth loss (see below). Only three subadults (3.9 percent by individual count) and nine adults (5.6 percent; 5 males and 4 females) were affected by caries.

Table 17.3. Prevalence of oral health indicators and LEH at the Shih-san-hang site

Tooth count[a]

Pathology	Posterior teeth			Anterior teeth			Total		
	N	Obs.	%	N	Obs.	%	N	Obs.	%
Caries	19	1,866	0.1	0	1,005	0	19	2,871	0.7
AMTL	41	2,111	1.9	6	1,349	0.4	47	3,460	1.4
Abscessing	4	1,866	0.2	1	1,005	0	5	2,871	0.2
Calculus	386	1,866	20.7	273	1,005	27.2	659	2,871	23.0
LEH	194	1,808	10.7	289	844	34.2	483	2,652	18.2

Individual count[b]

Pathology	Age group[c]					Sex			Total	
	SA	YA	MA	OA	UID	Male	Female	UID[d]	N	%[e]
Caries	1	6	2	1	0	5	4	1	10	3.3
AMTL	0	6	7	4	0	6	11	0	17	5.6
Abscessing	0	0	3	1	0	2	2	0	4	1.3
Calculus	7	36	19	1	2	30	28	7	65	21.2
LEH	24	58	16	4	0	29	37	36	102	33.3

Note: N = number of teeth/loci affected; Obs. = number of teeth/loci observed.
[a] Permanent teeth only.
[b] Number of individuals affected.
[c] Age groups: SA = subadult; YA = young adult; MA = middle adult; OA = old adult; UID = unidentified age.
[d] Unidentified sex.
[e] Number of individuals affected divided by total number of Shih-San-Hang individuals (306), for descriptive and comparative purposes only (see text).

Most of the carious lesions found were located on the occlusal or buccal surface of a tooth. All but one of the identified lesions were found on posterior teeth, and the third molar was the most affected tooth type. Although dental caries is an age-dependent pathology, adults in all age categories were found to be affected. In fact, six of the nine affected individuals were classified as young adults (21–35 years old). Given that young adults constitute the major portion of the assemblage, this outcome may be a result of demographic skewing in the Shih-san-hang sample.

Notwithstanding this possible bias, heavy dental attrition was likely a contributing factor to the low prevalence of dental caries at Shih-san-hang. While dentin exposure on first molars in subadults was not systematically scored, this condition was quite common. Smith's (1984) tooth wear stage five and above on anterior teeth and premolars and Scott's (1979) wear score seven and above on molars were evident on the teeth of almost all adult individuals. Dental attrition removes caries-prone loci such as cuspal fissures early in life, preventing cariogenic substances from building up in occlusal crevices, initiating an infection.

The prevalence of carious lesions among the Shih-san-hang individuals was found to be low both by tooth count and per individual. When compared with the other East Asian assemblages listed in table 17.4, Shih-san-hang individuals represented the least affected population. The prevalence of dental caries at Shih-san-hang falls within the hunter-gatherer range delineated in Turner's (1979) widely cited work on the correlation between the prevalence of dental caries and subsistence practices.

As for other East Asian samples, subsistence regimes ranged from hunting and gathering on the part of the Jomon people of Japan and early Neolithic Chinese to somewhat developed rice/millet agriculture and animal husbandry practiced by those from the later periods of Japanese and Chinese prehistory. Caries prevalence varied widely among these populations. For Japan, the increased incidence of carious teeth during and after the Jomon-Yayoi transition has been interpreted as a consequence of dietary change, specifically, in the direction of heavier reliance on starchy root and tuber plants (Temple 2007; Temple and Larsen 2007).

In the case of Chinese populations, the very high prevalence of caries toward the end of Yangshao and at the beginning of the Longshan period probably resulted from increasing consumption of cariogenic foodstuffs. Stable isotope ratio analysis by Pechenkina and colleagues (2005) reveals that millet constituted 75–85 percent of the diet during the Early Yangshao period and increased to about 90 percent during Middle Yangshao. Less animal protein was consumed during the later part of Early Yangshao. The effects of increasing reliance on millet during the Yangshao and Longshan periods corresponded with an increase in the prevalence of caries.

With respect to Shih-san-hang, its coastal location, the large numbers of fishing-related artifacts recovered, and the substantial amount of marine shell/fish remains are all indicative of a fishing community. A marine-focused diet is possibly linked to increased fluoride levels and therefore may be cariostatic (Oxenham and Matsumura 2008: 70). Other protein sources at Shih-san-hang would have supplemented people's diet, including terrestrial wild and semidomesticated animals, as evidenced by processing marks found on the excavated bones (Lin 1997).

It has yet to be determined whether the rice grains recovered at the site were of a domesticated or a wild variety. There is little doubt that people living and dying at the Shih-san-hang site had a mixed diet, but the animal protein/plant food ratio is also undetermined. Low caries prevalence at Shih-san-hang could have been linked to significant consumption of animal protein, resulting in a caries profile suggestive of a traditional hunting and gathering subsistence.

Table 17.4. Summary of oral health and LEH in the Shih-san-hang and East Asian assemblages

Sample	Caries		Antemortem tooth loss	
	Individual (%)	Tooth (%)	Individual (%)	Tooth (%)
Shih-san-hang[a]	9/306 (3)	19/2871 (1)	17/306 (6)	47/3460 (1)
Eastern Japan	261/2542 (10)			
Western/Inland Japan	137/2327 (6)			
Southern Honshu	313/1904 (16)[c]			
Northern Kyushu	159/1334 (12)[d]			
Tanegashima Island	130/1340 (10)[e]			
Hokkaido Jomon[f]	—(23)	—(3)	—(48)	—(8)
Hokkaido Jomon[f,h]	—(18)	—(3)	—(51)	—(8)
Hokkaido Okhotsk[f]	—(14)	—(2)	—(43)	—(5)
Beiliu	2/7 (29)[i]		7/7 (100)	
Jiangzhai I	2/13 (15)[i]		2/13 (17)	
Jiangzhai II	1/17 (6)[i]		2/17 (12)	
Shijia	6/28 (21)[i]		17/28 (61)	
Guanjia	18/24 (75)[i]		11/24 (46)	
Xipo	15/19 (79)[i]		12/19 (63)	
Meishan	5/7 (71)[i]		2/7 (29)	
Mengzhuang	3/6 (50)[i]		0/5 (0)	
Kangjia	8/13 (62)[i]		10/77 (13)	
Xicun	1/23 (4)[i]		4/23 (17)	

[a] For purposes of comparison, Shih-san-hang dental pathology prevalences shown here are derived from observations on permanent teeth only. All individuals with permanent teeth are included.

[b] Only mandibular canines and maxillary central incisors are observed (Temple 2007).

[c] Doigahama and Koura combined (Temple 2007: table 2).

[d] Kanenokuma and Nagaoka combined (Temple 2007: table 2).

[e] Torinominae and Hirota combined (Temple 2007: table 2).

[f] The LEH prevalence is reported in bar graphs in Oxenham and Matsumura 2008, and the exact numbers cannot be accurately derived. Anterior teeth only are used. See text for comparison and discussion.

[g] Prevalence of "alveolar defects" in Oxenham and Matsumura 2008: table 3 is used.

[h] Hokkaido Jomon excluding the epi-Jomon sample.

[i] Caries on posterior teeth only. Number of individuals affected is derived from Pechenkina et al. 2007: table 18.3.

[j] Number of teeth affected is derived from Pechenkina et al. 2007: table 18.6.

[k] Adults and nonadults combined.

Abscessing		Calculus		LEH	
Individual (%)	Tooth (%)	Individual (%)	Tooth (%)	Individual (%)	Locus (%)
4/306 (1)	5/2871 (0)	65/306 (21)	659/2871 (23)	102/306 (33)	483/2652 (18)
				78/164 (48)[b]	206/559 (37)
				79/122 (64.8)[b]	281/495 (57)[b]
—(37)[g]	—(3)				
—(38)[g]					
—(40)[g]					
0/7 (0)		3/7 (43)			
1/11 (9)		10/13 (77)			8/14 (57)[j]
0/20 (0)		6/17 (35)			3/11 (27)[j]
1/21 (4)		13/28 (46)			2/22 (9)[j]
9/24 (38)		13/21 (62)			16/20 (80)[k]
9/19 (47)		8/19 (42)			4/12 (33)[j]
2/7 (29)		4/7 (57)			4/8 (50)[k]
0/5 (0)		5/6 (83)			4/4 (100)[j]
4/13 (31)		3/13 (23)			8/10 (80)[j]
0/23 (0)		0/23 (0)			—

The nutritional characteristics of rice and its mode of preparation may also have been contributing factors to this outcome. In prehistoric Southeast Asia, wet rice was widely consumed. Contrary to trends found in the New World, there is no clear increase in caries prevalence as a result of either initial agricultural development or later agricultural intensification in Southeast Asia (Tayles et al. 2000; Domett 2001; Oxenham et al. 2002; Pietrusewsky and Douglas 2002). It has been suggested that as compared with maize in the Americas, rice contains less sugar and therefore is less likely to produce large numbers of carious lesions, even when consumed as a staple food. To further delineate the Shih-san-hang human diet, we are conducting a light stable isotope ratio analysis on human and animal bones (results forthcoming).

Antemortem Tooth Loss

The causes of antemortem tooth loss (AMTL) can be multifactorial, and distinct etiological processes are usually involved. The final and most severe stage of periodontal disease, dental attrition, dental caries, exposed pulp cavity, abscessing, or trauma (including intentional ablation) is the loss of the affected tooth or teeth (Lieverse et al. 2007; Lukacs 2007). AMTL is the most age-progressive dental pathology, in that the rate of AMTL almost invariably increases with age. The prevalence of AMTL at Shih-san-hang was calculated using the total number of tooth sockets/loci preserved divided by the number of sockets/loci showing signs of alveolar remodeling and/or healing.

At Shih-san-hang, 1.4 percent of the teeth originally in alveolar sockets/loci were lost antemortem (47/3460 [table 17.3]). Most of the affected sockets/loci show evidence of alveolar resorption. Mandibular posterior teeth were affected most frequently. When counted by individual, 17 adults (11 females, 6 males; 5.6 percent, 17/306) suffered at least one instance of AMTL. Of the affected individuals, 11 were older than 35 years at death and the other 6 were young adults. It is noteworthy that the affected younger adults tended to have only one instance of AMTL, while older individuals tended to have suffered the loss of multiple teeth (maximum: 8). This finding is congruent with the age-progressive nature of AMTL, but it is also evident that the onset of the pathological processes resulting in AMTL began relatively early in life.

As compared with the other East Asian assemblages, the frequency of AMTL at Shih-san-hang was extremely low, among the lowest recorded for the East Asian sites considered (table 17.4). This finding accords well with the low prevalence of carious lesions at Shih-san-hang.

Dental Abscesses

Dental abscessing, or periapical abscess, is a bony lesion (or chronic cyst; Oxenham et al. 2006) where a portion of the alveolar process is perforated because of pus accumulation caused by bacterial infection of and/or near the apex of dental roots. With the alveoli being affected and eroded below the normal height of the alveolar process, the abscessed teeth are likely to be lost antemortem. For Shih-san-hang, no abscesses were found on deciduous teeth, and its prevalence was extremely low on the permanent dentition (0.2 percent by tooth count [table 17.3]). When counted by individual, 1.3 percent (4/306) of the sample population was affected, equally distributed among the sexes. Individuals having abscessed teeth were not young adults; all were more than 35 years old and usually manifested other dental pathologies.

The prevalence of dental abscess per individual in the comparative East Asian samples ranges widely, from none to moderately high (table 17.4). The rate of abscess recorded for Shih-san-hang was the second lowest among all sites considered. Considering the low frequencies of dental caries and AMTL found at Shih-san-hang, a minimal incidence of abscesses was expected.

Dental Calculus

Calculus is mineralized plaque deposited on the nonocclusal enamel surfaces of a tooth. Individuals with a protein-rich diet exhibit less calculus formation (Greene et al. 2005). To control for taphonomic processes that may have dislodged mild calculus, in this study only teeth with moderate and severe calculus deposition were scored. Among all deciduous teeth examined, only one from the Shih-san-hang site exhibited calculus. The overall prevalence of calculus on permanent teeth was 23.0 percent by tooth count. For Shih-san-hang adults, the maxillary dentition exhibited a higher rate of calculus accretion (28.1 percent) than did the mandibular dentition (17.7 percent) (table 17.3).

When categorized by tooth groups, the anterior teeth were affected more often (27.2 percent) than the posterior teeth (20.6 percent). A total of 65 individuals were found to have calculus accretion. Of these, 30 were males (9.8 percent, 30/306), 28 were females (9.2 percent, 28/306), and 7 were of indeterminate sex (2.3 percent, 7/306). The distribution of calculus accretion between the sexes suggests no appreciable differences in protein consumption between males and females. Young adults had the highest frequency of calculus (36/65), followed by middle adults (19/65) and old adults (1/65). Subadults with permanent teeth also were affected; 7 of the 65 were younger than 20 years old at death. The demographic distribution observed suggests that dental calculus buildup at Shih-san-hang started early in life. However, similar to dental caries and AMTL, dental calculus is age-progressive, as it represents the lifelong accumulation of plaque. Therefore, the possibility of demographic bias due to the predominance of the young adults at Shih-san-hang should not be overlooked.

The rate of calculus accretion among the individuals buried at Shih-san-hang was the second lowest among those from all East Asian sites considered (table 17.4). By individual count, it was closest to the rate determined for the Kangjia site (Han dynasty, China). The nature of calculus formation on their dental remains suggests that the Shih-san-hang people may have consumed greater amounts of protein than did most of the other East Asian populations considered. However, heavy attrition may also contribute to the removal of plaque before calculus is formed. Nevertheless, the people of Shih-san-hang may have had better overall dental hygiene than other comparative populations.

Nonspecific Stress: Linear Enamel Hypoplasia

Linear enamel hypoplasia (LEH) is a linear lesion of reduced enamel thickness induced by physiological perturbation (stress) and/or localized dental trauma during enamel formation (Goodman and Rose 1990). The underlying etiology of LEH varies widely and is difficult to pinpoint. Even so, with the aid of archaeological context, the nonspecific nature of LEH lends itself to drawing inferences about both the general life history of individuals and the overall well-being of past populations. Enamel is formed in utero and during early childhood; it does not remodel once formed. Hence, the characteristics and prevalence of LEH across a range of demographic parameters and tooth categories are excellent proxies of stress and health status during the early stages of individual human development.

For the individuals from Shih-san-hang, at least one instance of LEH was found on 0.8 percent (2/266) of the deciduous teeth and 18.2 percent (483/2652) of the permanent teeth (table 17.3). A total of 102 individuals (29 adult males, 37 adult females, 24 subadults, 12 of unknown sex) with at least one observable permanent dentition had one or more hypoplastic teeth. Of the 75 individuals with at least one pair of anterior teeth preserved, 63 (20.6 percent, 63/306) exhibited signs of systemic stress during enamel formation. The most frequently affected tooth type was the mandibular canine (55.7 percent), followed by the maxillary canine and incisors, and the mandibular lateral incisor. The anterior teeth exhibited higher average LEH counts per tooth than did the posterior teeth, with canines particularly affected. More than 50 percent of individuals identified as having LEH on the canines had two or more hypoplastic lines on this tooth type.

Overall, anterior teeth (34.2 percent) from Shih-san-hang showed a significantly higher prevalence of LEH than did posterior teeth (10.7 percent). The pattern for Shih-san-hang is in accord with numerous observations on samples worldwide (e.g., Goodman et al. 1980; Keenleyside 1994; Wright 1997; Domett 2001; Lukacs et al. 2001). Crown geometry and enamel deposition schedule are possible factors producing lower thresholds for evidence of growth disturbances to appear on anterior teeth (Goodman and Rose 1990; Hillson and Bond 1997). The rarity of LEH on deciduous teeth from Shih-san-hang may be indicative of good maternal health that buffered the fetus from physiological stress. In addition, structural mechanisms such as thin layering and rapid deposition of deciduous enamel could also be plausible explanations (Hillson 1996).

LEH was significantly more common on teeth belonging to Shih-san-hang females (20.5 percent vs. 16.7 percent for males, $p < .05$ [table 17.5]); the difference is even greater for anterior teeth (41.2 percent for females, 27.6 percent for males, $p = .00$). In terms of average LEH count per observed tooth, it was more evident on the anterior teeth of females than on those of males. The average LEH count on female mandibular canines (1.18 LEH/tooth) was significantly higher than the corresponding rate for males (0.68 LEH/tooth, p

< .05). Interestingly, the reverse distribution (higher average LEH count per tooth among males and lower average LEH count per tooth among females) was observed on the posterior teeth.

The prevalence of LEH also varied across age groups at Shih-san-hang. By a small margin, subadults were affected most frequently (20.9 percent [table 17.5]), followed by young adults (19.5 percent), old adults (17.1 percent), and middle adults (10.0 percent). Teeth with more than one-third of the original crown height worn away were not scored for LEH, to control for dental attrition. However, buccal abrasion might have erased some shallower LEH lesions from teeth of older individuals, which could have contributed to the apparent lower prevalence of LEH among middle and old adults from Shih-san-hang.

Many previous studies have determined that individuals with LEH (i.e., early childhood stress) tend to have shorter life spans as compared with LEH-free individuals (Rose et al. 1978; Cook and Buikstra 1979; Goodman and Armelagos 1988; Duray 1996; Katzenberg et al. 1996; Wood 1996; Slaus 2000). With

Table 17.5. Prevalence of LEH by demographic parameters (tooth count) at the Shih-san-hang site

Sex

	Male			Female		
	N	Obs.	%	N	Obs.	%
Anterior	86	312	27.6	131	318	41.2
Posterior	87	721	12.1	71	668	10.6
Total	173	1,033	16.7	202	986	20.5

Age group

	Subadult			Young adult			Middle adult			Old adult		
	N	Obs.	%	N	Obs.	%	N	Obs.	%	N	Obs.	%
Total	112	537	20.9	314	1,612	19.5	43	432	10.0	6	35	17.1

Longevity

	Subadult and young adult			Middle adult and old adult		
	N	Obs.	%	N	Obs.	%
Total	426	2,149	19.8	49	467	10.5

Maturity

	Subadult			Adult		
	N	Obs.	%	N	Obs.	%
Total	112	537	20.9	371	2,103	17.6

Note: N = number of teeth affected; Obs. = number of teeth observed.

the abrasion factor in mind, rates of LEH were compared between younger (≤35 years) and older (>35 years) individuals to investigate the relationship between LEH and longevity at Shih-san-hang. The results show that those who died at younger ages were significantly more often affected with LEH than were those who lived longer (19.8 percent and 10.0 percent, respectively, p = .00). In addition, for most tooth types, on average, those who died as subadults had higher LEH counts per tooth than those who survived until adulthood. Intriguingly, among the five individuals with evidence of four separate LEH episodes on their respective canines (the highest number of LEH incidents per tooth found in the Shih-san-hang assemblage and indicative of recurring stress events) four of these individuals survived into young adulthood.

LEH is not only a sign of stress but also an indicator of recovery. An individual only shows evidence of LEH after surviving a stress episode, with enamel secretion resumed normal (Palubeckaite 2001). Therefore, it is inferred that individuals with multiple episodes of LEH on one or more teeth had survived a harsh childhood when morbidity was high. This observation also supports the suggestion that early childhood stress could impair the overall strength of the stress-coping mechanism and lower the threshold against stress later in life, resulting in early mortality. Again, the demographic imbalance of having a large number of young adults in the Shih-san-hang sample needs to be noted. Alternatively, that the Shih-san-hang sample, as a death assemblage, is composed mainly of young people could suggest that the Shih-san-hang individuals were frail, possibly because of stress in childhood, and were not able to survive into later adulthood (Wood et al. 1992).

Among studies of other East Asian skeletal assemblages used for comparative purposes here, LEH was mostly scored for anterior teeth only or its prevalence was reported per individual. Therefore, in order to allow appropriate comparisons, the calculation of LEH prevalence from Shih-san-hang was adjusted to match. As shown in tables 17.3 and 17.4, the rate of LEH on anterior teeth from Shih-san-hang (34.2 percent) was lower than that of the Western/Inland Jomon Japanese (56.8 percent), comparable to the Eastern Jomon Japanese (36.9 percent; Temple 2007), and higher than the Hokkaido Jomon Japanese (~15–20 percent; Oxenham and Matsumura 2008). When counted by individual and with all tooth types considered, LEH prevalence at Shih-san-hang (33.3 percent) fell within the wide range of the Chinese Neolithic samples (Pechenkina et al. 2007). Based on these results, it seems plausible that overall stress loads experienced by the Shih-san-hang people during early life were generally moderate.

The nonspecific nature of LEH renders interpretation of its prevalence at the Shih-san-hang site somewhat difficult. Systemic physiological stress is often associated with infection, trauma, and malnutrition (Goodman and Rose 1990). Signs of infectious diseases and injuries on the Shih-san-hang remains were absent in subadults and extremely rare among adults (see the skeletal pathology section below). While the osteological paradox could be a factor (Wood et al. 1992), it is equally plausible to assign infection and trauma as major causes of physiological stress at Shih-san-hang.

Malnutrition could result from famine, seasonal food shortage, an imbalanced diet, or weaning practices (Corruccini et al. 1985; Goodman et al. 1991; Zhou and Corruccini 1998). At Shih-san-hang, a lengthy occupation, abundant evidence of marine and terrestrial food procurement, and a well-watered subtropical and coastal location suggest that famine and seasonal food shortage were unlikely. It seems more probable that the synergetic effects of weaning stress, most likely diarrhea induced by consumption of contaminated non-breastmilk foods and/or water, inadequate supplementary foods, and periodic childhood illness were the principal underlying causes of the prevalent childhood growth perturbation evidenced on many Shih-san-hang skeletons.

The Shih-san-hang people who survived early childhood stress (LEH-affected) tended to live through a healthy adulthood without developing other skeletal pathologies (see below). In accord with the notion that males are more negatively affected by stress than are females, because of better physiological buffering of females (Stini 1985), the significant sexually dimorphic prevalence of LEH on anterior teeth from Shih-san-hang (males higher than females) also supports the inference that overall living conditions at the site were favorable. Sexual dimorphism in LEH prevalence is usually lower in populations with difficult living conditions (Domett and Tayles 2007: 296).

Porotic Hyperostosis/Cribra Orbitalia

Porotic hyperostosis (PH) is a cranial lesion caused by various types of anemia (Stuart-Macadam 1987; but see Ortner et al. 1999 for scurvy; Wapler et al. 2004 for inflammatory disease and rickets). The gross lesion is observed as a spongy or sieve-like area on various parts of the cranium. If an anemic episode is reverted, remodeling begins to heal the bony lesion. Therefore, different stages of the porotic lesion (active, mixed, or healed) are indicative of multiple anemic processes experienced by an individual before the time of death (but see Stuart-Macadam 1985, discussed below).

While congenital anemia such as thalassemia and sickle-cell anemia may produce porotic reactions in certain parts of the world where they are common, porotic hyperostosis resulting from iron-deficiency anemia due to imbalanced diet is far more prevalent worldwide (Stuart-Macadam 1992; Wintrobe 1993). After reevaluating the underlying physiological and structural causes of PH, Walker and colleagues (2009) argued that iron-deficiency anemia should no longer be used as the main etiology of PH. However, Oxenham and Cavill (2010) offer a counter-argument that Walker and colleagues' position is not supported by the literature pertaining to iron-deficiency anemia.

An imbalanced diet, decreased dependence on iron-rich foodstuffs acquired through hunting and gathering, and low iron concentration in plant foods (maize, specifically) are often cited as causes of this phenomenon (e.g., Cohen and Armelagos 1984; Cohen and Crane-Kramer 2007). However, from a physiological perspective, dietary insufficiency cannot be the sole cause of iron-deficiency anemia. Iron metabolism in the human body is virtually a closed system. Approximately 90 percent of the iron needed for the production of new red blood cells is recycled from old red blood cells, which are destroyed by metabolic processes. It follows, therefore, that very little iron needs to be incorporated from the diet (Hoffbrand and Lewis 1981; Stuart-Macadam 1998). Loss of blood, whether due to menstruation, trauma, or chronic internal bleeding, is the usual cause of decreased iron concentration in the blood. Parasitic infection has long been linked to chronic internal blood loss. Research on the prevalence of PH in populations with high parasitic loads has revealed that incidences of iron-deficiency anemia and parasitic infection are positively correlated (Hengen 1971; Walker 1986; Merbs 1992).

Studies conducted among maritime foragers (Walker 1986; Walker et al. 2009) reveal that the porotic lesions (often CO) were as common in these populations as those that relied less on marine subsistence (or were maize-dependent). This finding counters the expectation that since a diet with a marine component tends to be iron-rich and provides sufficient amino acids needed for normal metabolism, its population would have lower prevalence of iron-deficiency anemia manifesting into PH. However, a higher risk of food and water contamination from fish/shellfish-borne bacteria and parasites

Table 17.6. Prevalence of PH by demographic parameters (individual count) at the Shih-san-hang site

Location	Male			Female			Subadult		
	N	Obs.	%	N	Obs.	%	N	Obs.	
Orbit	10	32	31.3	9	34	26.5	8	37	47.1
Vault	2	45	4.4	5	44	11.4	0	32	0
Orbit and vault	1	30	3.3	3	33	9.1	0	15	0
Pooled[a]	11	47	23.4	11	45	24.4	8	36	22.2

Note: N = number of individuals affected; Obs.= number of individuals observed.
[a] Combined location of PH.

is equally associated with seaside dwelling that could also result in chronic blood loss, thus anemia.

For the purpose of this study, the prevalence of PH was determined per individual. The sample was composed only of those individuals with at least one side of the orbital roof or one side of the parietal bones preserved and available for examination (Wright 1994). Accordingly, the total number of such individuals was used as the denominator when calculating PH prevalence. When overall prevalence was considered, regardless of the location of lesions, individuals were eligible for inclusion when either one side of the orbital roof or one side of the parietals was present.

At Shih-san-hang, 126 out of 306 individuals (42 percent) were found to have cranial preservation adequate for inclusion in the subsample used to determine the prevalence of PH (table 17.6). In this group, 29 individuals (23 percent, 29/126; or 9.5 percent of the total individuals) were affected by PH at one or more loci. The vast majority of the lesions were found on the orbital roof (20.6 percent, 26/126; 8.5 percent, 26/306). Seven individuals showed evidence of PH on the vault (5.6 percent, 7/126); only four had lesions on both the vault and orbit. When compared by sex, males and females had similar frequencies of PH (23.4 percent and 24.4 percent, respectively). In general, males tended to have lesions on the orbit, while the cranial bones were affected more often among females; however, the differences observed were not significant.

All porotic lesions on the cranial vault were found to have healed. However, of the 19 individuals of known sex having orbital lesions, all but one of the females had active lesions at the time of death (table 17.7). In contrast, only two males showed evidence of active orbital lesions. While anemia was probably not the cause of death, Shih-san-hang females tended to die while lesions were active, whereas males seem to have lived for a period of time after recovering from anemic episodes. When prevalence of PH is considered by age group (table 17.6), subadults and young adults showed the highest

Young adult			Middle adult			Old adult			All adults			Total		
N	Obs.	%	N	Obs.	%	N	Obs.	%	N	Obs.	%	N	Obs.	%
17	39	43.6	1	20	5.0	0	4	0	18	46	39.1	26	81	32.1
6	47	12.8	1	26	3.8	0	4	0	7	79	8.9	7	111	6.3
4	37	10.1	0	19	0	0	4	0	4	61	6.6	4	76	5.3
19	55	34.9	2	28	7.1	0	4	0	21	68	30.9	29	125	23.2

Table 17.7. Activity stages of orbital lesions from the Shih-san-hang site compared by sex and maturity (individual count)

	Sex			Maturity		
	Females	Males	Total	Subadult	Adult	Total
Active	8	2	10	5	10	15
Healed	1	8	9	3	8	11
Total	9	10	19	8	18	26
% Active	88.9	20.0	47.4	62.5	55.6	57.7

prevalence. Subadults had a slightly higher incidence (47 percent) of orbital lesions than did young adults (44 percent). In contrast, PH evident on the cranial vault was found only on young adults, as no subadult in the sample exhibited a cranial lesion.

Overall, the prevalence of PH among young adults (35 percent) was much higher than among subadults (22 percent). However, no significant difference was found when all affected adults were pooled and compared with affected subadults. While individuals who died younger (≤ 35 years) were affected with PH more often than those who lived longer, the suggestion that PH is a childhood condition (Stuart-Macadam 1985) is not supported by the fact that many subadults had healed lesions, while active lesions were more common among young adults at Shih-san-hang.

When compared with other East Asian assemblages, the prevalence of PH on the orbital roof at Shih-san-hang per individual was much lower than that of the Hokkaido Jomon and Okhotsk people and was similar to that of the Honshu Jomon Japanese (Oxenham and Matsumura 2008). Compared to Chinese samples, the prevalence of PH on the cranial vault among individuals from Shih-san-hang was equally low, higher only than samples in which no case of cranial PH was recorded. As for cribra orbitalia, its prevalence at Shih-san-hang generally fell between the rates for Yangshao (0–33 percent) and Longshan adults (40–50 percent) (Pechenkina et al. 2007).

In the case of Japanese populations, it is suggested that scurvy induced by a lack of vitamin C and high parasitic loads stemming from a marine diet could have contributed to the incidence of orbital lesions (Oxenham and Matsumura 2008). At Shih-san-hang, there is no indication of dependence on agriculturally produced foods from either dental pathology or the archaeological record. Because the Shih-san-hang people probably subsisted heavily on iron-rich marine resources, parasitic infection brought about by contaminated water and marine foods may have increased the frequency of iron-deficiency anemia (Walker 1986). Other plausible causes of PH, such as rickets, scurvy, and inflammation, may be unlikely because Shih-san-hang skeletal remains displayed few, if any, traces of deformity and/or inflammatory reactions (see below).

Skeletal Pathology

Traces of trauma and infectious disease are rare and isolated in the Shih-san-hang human skeletal assemblage. Five adult individuals showed signs of healed injury on the parietal bones, clavicle, and/or limb bones. In some cases, misaligned healing of these injuries resulted in permanent deformation of the limb bones in ways that must have greatly hindered the individual's mobility. In terms of nontrauma-related pathologies, one case of osteomyelitis was found on the proximal right femur of a young female, and a case of possible spinal bifida on the fifth lumbar vertebra was also recorded.

The remains of one middle-age female include a right humerus that is significantly shorter than the corresponding left humerus. The right humeral head and glenoid fossa are completely deformed, causing the latter to be dislocated from the former, yet there is no sign of skeletal fracture. A suite of skeletal and muscle compensations were manifest (a more pronounced deltoid tuberosity on the right side, larger shaft diameter of the left humerus, a robust left clavicle). It is possible that this individual suffered from a congenital deformation of the right shoulder girdle profound enough to affect the performance of daily activities.

Degenerative joint disease on the vertebral column, manifested as osteophytosis, was the most common type of pathology recorded in the Shih-san-hang collection. Eight individuals showed significant development of osteophytes; all were located on the lower thoracic and lumbar vertebrae. Progressive development of osteophytes led to the fusion of up to three vertebral bodies in some individuals, often accompanied by collapsed discs that may have caused kyphosis. The individuals affected with osteophytosis were mostly middle and old adults, which is consonant with the age-progressive nature of this type of joint disease. Moderate to severe osteoarthritis affecting the limb joints was uncommon at Shih-san-hang, with only three cases recorded.

Conclusions

This chapter characterizes the health status of the Shih-san-hang site, an Iron Age population from northern Taiwan, in regard to its broad-spectrum dietary regime and its transitional nature in Taiwanese prehistory. The prevalence of oral health markers and nonspecific stress indicators was assessed and evaluated. Based on the results of our analysis, oral health at Shih-san-hang was very good, with extremely low frequencies of dental caries, AMTL, abscessing, and calculus. Among the East Asian sample series compared here, the Shih-san-hang people were consistently found to be the least affected by dental pathologies. The factors contributing to this likely were a diet based largely on marine sources of protein, in combination with rice and/or root crops (tubers) as the primary source of carbohydrates.

The prevalence of LEH at Shih-san-hang suggests that the people living there had somewhat stressful childhoods. Shih-san-hang females apparently endured more stress during childhood than did males, as indicated by significantly higher rates of LEH and higher average LEH counts per affected tooth. LEH was more frequently evident among subadults and young adults, possibly as the result of an impaired immune system in early childhood (early morbidity). The combined effects of nutritional imbalance, weaning stress, and childhood illness could have been the major causes of childhood physiological perturbation.

Iron-deficiency anemia tended to impact late-stage teenagers and young adults at Shih-san-hang, as indicated by the age distribution of PH. Males and females were at similar risk of anemic stress. Parasitic infection due to coastal habitation and presumed fishing activities could have been the cause. In addition, evidence of skeletal pathology (trauma, infection, congenital skeletal deformation, degenerative joint disease) was rarely found among the Shih-san-hang people. Overall, while a period of stressful childhood may have caused short-term morbidity for some individuals, the people at Shih-san-hang generally led a healthy life well into adulthood.

Archaeological evidence, including artifact types, as well as faunal and floral remains, suggests that marine and terrestrial resources were both routinely incorporated into the human diet at Shih-san-hang. While marine foodstuffs seem to have been higher in proportion, terrestrial hunting, and possibly crop planting, along with incipient animal domestication (pigs, specifically) all were parts of the Shih-san-hang subsistence regime. Broad-spectrum subsistence dispersed the risk of overreliance on one or limited food items.

An expectation that the Shih-san-hang people's indicators of general health and well-being might resemble those of hunter-gatherer groups represented in the comparative samples was borne out in the results of our study. The adverse impacts of specialized diet and/or heavy reliance on a single crop (maize, in particular) on human biology and health reported from many Western Hemisphere sites are not evident at Shih-san-hang. The skeletal health of the people buried at Shih-san-hang, coupled with evidence of iron-working, ceramic production, and an active role in regional interaction/exchange, suggests a population that was well situated in its landscape. The human skeletal data serve as the most direct gauge of people's health in the context of their daily activities, adding to our understanding of the biocultural milieu of the Shih-san-hang site. The long (and successful) occupation of Shih-san-hang and its diverse craft production are testimonials to the dynamic nature of this transitional site.

Acknowledgments

This study was made possible by the permission and personnel support granted by the Division of Archaeology, Institute of History and Philology, Academia Sinica, Taiwan. This chapter is based on a presentation at the 76th Annual Meeting of the American Association of Physical Anthropologists in Philadelphia, Pennsylvania (2007). We thank Dr. Pechenkina for the invitation to include our work in this volume and the editors for their patience throughout the revision process. We are also grateful to the reviewers for their constructive suggestions on multiple drafts of this chapter.

Literature Cited

Bellwood P. 2001. Early agriculturalist population diasporas? Farming, languages, and genes. *Annual Review of Anthropology* 30: 181–207.

Bellwood P. 2006. Asian farming diasporas? Agriculture, languages, and genes in China and Southeast Asia. In: Stark MT, editor. *Archaeology of Asia*. Malden, MA: Blackwell. Pp. 96–118.

Bellwood P, Fox JJ, Tryon D, editors. 1995. *The Austronesians: Historical and comparative perspectives*. Canberra, Australia: ANU E Press.

Buikstra JE, Ubelaker DH. 1994. *Standards for data collection from human skeletal remains*. Fayetteville: Arkansas Archaeological Survey.

Chang C. 1993. A morphological and paleopathological study and comparison of the human skeletal remains recovered from the Shih San Hang site (十三行遺址出土人骨之形態學與病理學分析及其比較研究). M.A. thesis, National Taiwan University.

Chang KC, Xu P, Allan S, Lu L, editors. 2005. *The formation of Chinese civilization: An archaeological perspective*. New Haven, CT: Yale University Press.

Chen KT. 2000. Ancient iron technology of Taiwan. Ph.D. dissertation, Harvard University.

Cohen MN, Armelagos GJ, editors. 1984. *Paleopathology at the origins of agriculture*. New York: Academic Press.

Cohen MN, Crane-Kramer GMM, editors. 2007. *Ancient health: Skeletal indicators of agricultural and economic intensification*. Gainesville: University Press of Florida.

Cook DC, Buikstra JE. 1979. Health and differential survival in prehistoric populations: Prenatal dental defects. *American Journal of Physical Anthropology* 51: 649–64.

Corruccini RS, Handler JS, Jacobi KP. 1985. Chronological distribution of enamel hypoplasias and weaning in a Caribbean slave population. *Human Biology* 57: 699–712.

Domett KM. 2001. *Health in late prehistoric Thailand.* Oxford: Archaeopress.

Domett KM, Tayles N. 2007. Population health from the Bronze to the Iron Age in the Mun River valley, northeastern Thailand. In: Cohen MN, Crane-Kramer GMM, editors. *Ancient health: Skeletal indicators of agricultural and economic intensification.* Gainesville: University Press of Florida. Pp. 286–99.

Duray SM. 1996. Dental indicators of stress and reduced age at death in prehistoric Native Americans. *American Journal of Physical Anthropology* 99: 275–86.

Goodman AH, Armelagos GJ. 1988. Childhood stress and decreased longevity in a prehistoric population. *American Anthropologist* 90: 936–44.

Goodman AH, Armelagos GJ. 1989. Infant and childhood morbidity and mortality risks in archaeological populations. *World Archaeology* 21: 225–43.

Goodman AH, Armelagos GJ, Rose JC. 1980. Enamel hypoplasias as indicators of stress in three prehistoric populations from Illinois. *Human Biology* 52: 515–28.

Goodman AH, Martinez C, Chavez A. 1991. Nutritional supplementation and the development of linear enamel hypoplasias in children from Tezonteopan, Mexico. *American Journal of Clinical Nutrition* 53: 773–81.

Goodman AH, Rose JC. 1990. Assessment of systemic physiological perturbations from dental enamel hypoplasias and associated histological structures. *Yearbook of Physical Anthropology* 33: 59–110.

Greene TR, Kuba CL, Irish JD. 2005. Quantifying calculus: A suggested new approach for recording an important indicator of diet and dental health. *Homo* 56: 119–32.

Hengen OP. 1971. Cribra orbitalia: Pathogenesis and probable etiology. *Homo* 22: 57–76.

Higham CFW. 2004. Mainland Southeast Asia from the Neolithic to the Iron Age. In: Glover I, Bellwood P, editors. *Southeast Asia: From prehistory to history.* London: Routledge Curzon. Pp. 41–67.

Hillson S. 1996. *Dental anthropology.* New York: Cambridge University Press.

Hillson S, Bond S. 1997. Relationship of enamel hypoplasia to the pattern of tooth crown growth: A discussion. *American Journal of Physical Anthropology* 104: 89–103.

Hoffbrand AV, Lewis SM. 1981. *Postgraduate haematology.* London: William Heinemann Medical Books.

Hoppa RD, Vaupel JW, editors. 2002. *Paleodemography: Age distributions from skeletal samples.* Cambridge: Cambridge University Press.

Hung HC, Iizuka Y, Bellwood P, Nguyen KD, Bellina B, Silapanth P, Dizon E, Santiago R, Datan I, Manton JH. 2007. Ancient jades map 3,000 years of prehistoric exchange in Southeast Asia. *Proceedings of the National Academy of Sciences* 104: 19745–50.

Imamura K. 1996. *Prehistoric Japan: New perspectives on Insular East Asia.* Honolulu: University of Hawai'i Press.

Katzenberg MA, Herring DA, Saunders SR. 1996. Weaning and infant mortality: Evaluating the skeletal evidence. *Yearbook of Physical Anthropology* 39: 177–99.

Keenleyside MA. 1994. Skeletal evidence of health and disease in pre- and post-contact Alaskan Eskimos and Aleuts. Ph.D. dissertation, McMaster University.

Larsen CS. 1997. *Bioarchaeology.* Cambridge: Cambridge University Press.

Lieverse AR, Link DW, Bazaliiskiy VI, Goriunova OI, Weber AW. 2007. Dental health indicators of hunter-gatherer adaptation and cultural change in Siberia's Cis-Baikal. *American Journal of Physical Anthropology* 134: 323–39.

Lin H. 1997. Zooarchaeological study of *Sus* mandibles from the Shih-San-Hang site (十三

行遺址出土動物骨骼之初步分析-以豬下顎骨為例). M.A. thesis, National Taiwan University.

Liu C. 2005. Childhood stress of an Iron Age population from Taiwan: Using linear enamel hypoplasia and porotic hyperostosis as stress indicators. M.A. thesis, University of Florida.

Liu Y. 1992. *The archaeological sites of Taiwan* (台灣的考古遺址). Banqiou, Taiwan: Taipei County Cultural Bureau (板橋, 台灣: 台北縣文化局).

Liu Y. 1995. Preliminary study on the relationship between prehistoric cultures and the aborigines (史前文化與原住民關係初步探討). *Taiwan Folkways* (台灣風物) 45: 75–98.

Lukacs JR. 1995. The "caries correction factor": A new method of calibrating dental caries rates to compensate for antemortem loss of teeth. *International Journal of Osteoarchaeology* 5: 151–56.

Lukacs JR. 2007. Dental trauma and antemortem tooth loss in prehistoric Canary Islanders: Prevalence and contributing factors. *International Journal of Osteoarchaeology* 17: 157–73.

Lukacs JR, Nelson GC, Walimbe SR. 2001. Enamel hypoplasia and childhood stress in prehistory: New data from India and Southwest Asia. *Journal of Archaeological Science* 28: 1159–69.

Merbs CF. 1992. A New World of infectious disease. *American Journal of Physical Anthropology* 35: 3–42.

Nelson SM. 2007. *The archaeology of Korea*. Cambridge: Cambridge University Press.

Ortner DJ. 1998. Male-female immune reactivity and its implications for interpreting evidence in human skeletal paleopathology. In: Grauer AL, Stuart-Macadam P, editors. *Sex and gender in paleopathological perspective*. Cambridge: Cambridge University Press. Pp. 79–92.

Ortner DJ, Kimmerle EH, Diez M. 1999. Probable evidence of scurvy in subadults from archeological sites in Peru. *American Journal of Physical Anthropology* 108: 321–31.

Oxenham MF, Cavill I. 2010. Porotic hyperostosis and cribra orbitalia: The erythropoietic response to iron-deficiency anaemia. *Anthropological Science* 118: 199–200.

Oxenham MF, Matsumura H. 2008. Oral and physiological paleohealth in cold adapted peoples: Northeast Asia, Hokkaido. *American Journal of Physical Anthropology* 135: 64–74.

Oxenham MF, Nguyen LC, Nguyen KT. 2002. Oral health in northern Viet Nam: Neolithic through Metal periods. *Bulletin of the Indo-Pacific Prehistory Association* 22: 121–34.

Oxenham M, Nguyen LG, Nguyen KT. 2006. The oral health consequences of the adoption and intensification of agriculture in Southeast Asia. In: Oxenham M, Tayles N, editors. *Bioarchaeology of Southeast Asia*. Cambridge: Cambridge University Press. Pp. 263–89.

Palubeckaite Z. 2001. Patterns of linear enamel hypoplasia in Lithuanian Iron Age population. *Variability and Evolution* 9: 75–87.

Pechenkina EA, Ambrose SH, Ma X, Benfer RA Jr. 2005. Reconstructing northern Chinese Neolithic subsistence practices by isotopic analysis. *Journal of Archaeological Science* 32: 1176–89.

Pechenkina EA, Benfer RA Jr., Ma X. 2007. Diet and health in the Neolithic of the Wei and Middle Yellow River basins, northern China. In: Cohen MN, Crane-Kramer GMM, editors. *Ancient health: Skeletal indicators of agricultural and economic intensification*. Gainesville: University Press of Florida. Pp. 255–72.

Pietrusewsky M, Chang C-F. 2003. Taiwan aborigines and peoples of the Pacific-Asia region: Multivariate craniometric comparisons. *Anthropological Science* 111: 293–332.

Pietrusewsky M, Douglas MT. 2001. Intensification of agriculture at Ban Chiang: Is there evidence from the skeletons? *Asian Perspectives* 40: 157–78.

Pietrusewsky M, Douglas MT. 2002. *Ban Chiang: A prehistoric village site in northeast Thailand.* Vol. 1: *The human skeletal remains*. Philadelphia: University of Pennsylvania Museum of Archaeology and Anthropology.

Pietrusewsky M, Tsang C. 2003. A preliminary assessment of health and disease in human skeletal remains from Shi San Hang: A prehistoric aboriginal site on Taiwan. *Anthropological Science* 111: 203–23.

Rose JC, Armelagos GJ, Lallo JW. 1978. Histological enamel indicator of childhood stress in prehistoric skeletal samples. *American Journal of Physical Anthropology* 49: 511–16.

Scott EC. 1979. Dental wear scoring technique. *American Journal of Physical Anthropology* 51: 213–18.

Slaus M. 2000. Biocultural analysis of sex differences in mortality profiles and stress levels in the late medieval population from Nova Raca, Croatia. *American Journal of Physical Anthropology* 111: 193–209.

Smith BH. 1984. Patterns of molar wear in hunter-gatherers and agriculturalists. *American Journal of Physical Anthropology* 63: 39–56.

Stini WA. 1985. Growth rates and sexual dimorphism in evolutionary perspective. In: Gilbert RI, Mielke JH, editors. *The analysis of prehistoric diets*. Orlando, FL: Academic Press. Pp. 191–222.

Stuart-Macadam P. 1985. Porotic hyperostosis: Representative of a childhood condition. *American Journal of Physical Anthropology* 66: 391–98.

Stuart-Macadam P. 1987. Porotic hyperostosis: New evidence to support the anemia theory. *American Journal of Physical Anthropology* 74: 521–26.

Stuart-Macadam P. 1992. Porotic hyperostosis: A new perspective. *American Journal of Physical Anthropology* 87: 39–47.

Stuart-Macadam P. 1998. Iron deficiency anemia: Exploring the difference. In: Grauer AL, Stuart-Macadam P, editors. *Sex and gender in paleopathological perspective*. Cambridge: Cambridge University Press. Pp. 45–63.

Tayles N, Domett KM, Nelson K. 2000. Agriculture and dental caries? The case of rice in prehistoric Southeast Asia. *World Archaeology* 32: 68–83.

Temple DH. 2007. Dietary variation and stress among prehistoric Jomon foragers from Japan. *American Journal of Physical Anthropology* 133: 1035–46.

Temple DH, Larsen CS. 2007. Dental caries prevalence as evidence for agriculture and subsistence variation during the Yayoi period in prehistoric Japan: Biocultural interpretations of an economy in transition. *American Journal of Physical Anthropology* 134: 501–12.

Tsang C. 2000. Recent advances in the Iron Age archaeology of Taiwan. *Bulletin of the Indo-Pacific Prehistory Association* 20: 153–58.

Tsang C, Liu Y. 2001a. *Projects report of the exhibitions in the Shih-san-hang Museum* (十三行博物館展示內容相關研究計畫報告). Bali, Taiwan: Organization Committee of the Shih-san-hang Museum, Taipei County.

Tsang C, Liu Y. 2001b. *The Shih-san-hang site: Salvage and preliminary research* (十三行遺址搶救與初步研究). Banqiou, Taiwan: Cultural Affairs Bureau of Taipei County Government.

Turner CG II. 1979. Dental anthropological indications of agriculture among the Jomon people of central Japan. X: Peopling of the Pacific. *American Journal of Physical Anthropology* 51: 619–36.

Waldron T. 1994. *Counting the dead: The epidemiology of skeletal populations*. Chichester, UK: John Wiley and Sons.

Walker P. 1986. Porotic hyperostosis in a marine dependent California Indian population. *American Journal of Physical Anthropology* 69: 345–54.

Walker PL, Bathurst RR, Richman R, Gjerdrum T, Andrushko VA. 2009. The causes of porotic hyperostosis and cribra orbitalia: A reappraisal of the iron-deficiency anemia hypothesis. *American Journal of Physical Anthropology* 139: 109–25.

Wapler U, Crubezy E, Schultz M. 2004. Is cribra orbitalia synonymous with anemia? Analysis and interpretation of cranial pathology in Sudan. *American Journal of Physical Anthropology* 123: 333–39.

Wintrobe M. 1993. *Clinical hematology.* Philadelphia: Lea and Febiger.

Wood JW, Milner GR, Harpending HC, Weiss KM. 1992. The osteological paradox: Problems of inferring prehistoric health from skeletal samples. *Current Anthropology* 33: 343–70.

Wood L. 1996. Frequency and chronological distribution of linear enamel hypoplasia in a North American colonial skeletal sample. *American Journal of Physical Anthropology* 100: 247–59.

Wright LE. 1994. The sacrifice of the Earth? Diet, health, and inequality in the Pasion Maya Lowlands. Ph.D. dissertation, University of Chicago.

Wright LE. 1997. Intertooth patterns of hypoplasia expression: Implications for childhood health in the Classic Maya collapse. *American Journal of Physical Anthropology* 102: 233–47.

Zhou LM, Corruccini RS. 1998. Enamel hypoplasias related to famine stress in living Chinese. *American Journal of Human Biology* 10: 723–33.

18

Trajectories of Health in
Early Farming Communities of East Asia

KATE PECHENKINA, MA XIAOLIN, AND FAN WENQUAN

In this chapter we examine the general trends in health that accompanied increasing reliance on millet cultivation and a later shift to wheat/barley agriculture by human communities of the Yellow and Wei River valleys of north-central China. Using data available in the literature, we then compare those trends to synchronous changes previously documented for communities in other parts of East and Southeast Asia with differing environmental constraints and opportunities, where human health was affected by reliance on other cereals and/or animal herding. The number of skeletal indicators related to general health that have been systematically evaluated in a large number of East Asian skeletal series is fairly small. Therefore, this analysis is focused on the three most commonly reported indicators: adult stature, along with frequency of carious lesions, as well as cribra orbitalia and porotic hyperostosis, which are commonly used as proxies for acquired anemia.

All over the world, human morbidity and mortality underwent large-scale changes during the Holocene (Cohen and Armelagos 1984; Larsen 1997; Cohen and Crane-Kramer 2007; Pinhasi and Stock 2011). These changes were driven, at least in part, by human expansion beyond the accustomed boundaries of our environment of evolutionary adaptiveness (as defined by John Bowlby [1969]), as well as by construction of new ecological niches through the domestication of plants and animals (Smith 2007). The rapid population growth that followed this transition in many human communities (Bocquet-Appel and Naji 2006) gives evidence that creation of these new niches was adaptively advantageous for our species. At the same time, by changing their own ecology, human beings altered their caloric intake and the composition of their diets, exposed themselves to novel pathogens and toxins, and also developed new patterns of physical activity and reproduction; human physiology had no previous exposure to these phenomena and was poorly adapted to them, at least initially. This initial maladaptation often resulted in considerable physiological stress, a rise in morbidity, poor oral health, and decreased life expectancy (Cohen and Armelagos 1984; Cohen and Crane-Kramer 2007).

Of all the new strategies first pursued by some Early and Middle Holocene societies, staple dependence on domesticated plants of the family Poaceae—that is, the cereals—might have been the most detrimental for human health (Stini 1971; Turner 1979; Cohen and Armelagos 1984; Goodman and Armelagos 1985; Rose et al. 1991; Larsen 1997; Cohen and Crane-Kramer 2007). These adverse consequences of cereal-focused subsistence can be largely attributed to the dietary inadequacies of staple grains.

Most of the common domesticated cereals are deficient in one or more of the essential amino acids: barley, maize, millets, and wheat are deficient in lysine; buckwheat in leucine; rye in threonine (FAO 1972). None of these foods provide adequate levels of iron. Health problems resulting from low levels of iron are further exacerbated because the iron atoms available from grain tissue generally are not chelated, which prevents their absorption in the human digestive tract. Grains are also deficient in a number of vitamins, including thiamin (B1), riboflavin (B2), and ascorbic acid (C), among others. The inadequacy of cereals as staple dietary sources not only predicts an increase in deficiency-related diseases but would also be expected to increase malnutrition-related stress responses that correlate with immunosuppression due to activation of the hypothalamic-pituitary-adrenal axis, thereby increasing susceptibility to pathogens (Rhen and Cidlowski 2005).

Our principal objective is to evaluate how increasing reliance on cereal agriculture, in concert with the development of animal husbandry, affected community health in various parts of East Asia. Several different early subsistence complexes can be identified in East Asia based on their degree of reliance on particular cereals and domesticated animals (reviewed in chapter 2): maritime sedentary populations with limited horticulture or incipient agriculture, along with arboriculture, as in the Jomon (縄文) tradition of Japan (Crawford 1983, 2008; Chisholm et al. 1992; Matsui 1996; Matsui and Kanehara 2006); wetland rice agriculture, with continued exploitation of marine resources in coastal areas, as in southern China, prehistoric Taiwan, and during Yayoi (弥生) in Japan (Crawford and Lee 2003); a millet/pig agricultural complex with developed horticulture, along with continued hunting and inland fishing, as during Yangshao (仰韶) in the Yellow River basin of northern China (Yan 1992, 2005; Yuan and Flad 2002), where wheat and barley were added to the suite of cultigens after 2000 BC (Zhao 2002; Zhao and He 2006; Lee et al. 2007); and mobile pastoralism, with limited farming of millet and symbiotic ties to sedentary farmers, such as on the Mongolian steppe (Xie 1972; Di Cosmo 1994).

Materials

The core materials for this study are skeletal collections excavated from archaeological sites on the Central Plains of China, found along the Wei and Yellow Rivers, as well as their tributaries, in Henan and Shaanxi Provinces. The Henan/Shaanxi human skeletal remains considered here have been analyzed and in part published previously (Pechenkina et al. 2002; Pechenkina and Benfer 2002; Pechenkina et al. 2005, 2007). These skeletal series span a time frame beginning with the Early Neolithic Peiligang culture (9,000–7,000 years ago) and ending with the Eastern Zhou dynasty, in 221 BC. The most substantial portion of these materials stems from the Early (4900–4000 BC), Middle 4000–3500 BC), and Late (3500–3000 BC) phases of Yangshao culture. Considerably smaller skeletal collections, often totaling only a dozen individuals or less, were available from the Late Neolithic Longshan culture and Early Dynastic Erlitou. The chronologically more recent Xiyasi skeletal series dates to the Eastern Zhou dynasty and totals more than 200 individuals, of which only a small number were analyzed for the purposes of this study. For comparative purposes, we also draw on a number of recently completed theses, as well as recent publications, to compare changes in human health that accompanied the development of each of the aforementioned subsistence strategies in East Asia. The geographic and chronological distribution of the skeletal samples taken into account are summarized in table 18.1 and shown in figure 18.1.

Substantial skeletal collections from the northern frontier zone, encompassing Xinjiang, Inner Mongolia, and Manchuria were analyzed by Jacqueline Eng (2007) and Zhang Jinglei (2008). The pastoral and agropastoral communities of those areas relied on domesticated herbivores, of which sheep were the most economically important (Barfield 1993: 20–21). The drier and colder climate of this region is less favorable to agriculture than that of the Central Plains, favoring reliance on mixed subsistence strategies and the development of exchange networks. Therefore, during the Neolithic and Bronze Ages, this area was characterized by complex interactions between pastoral, agropastoral, and sedentary communities with agriculture-based subsistence (Eng 2007).

Information on the Japanese skeletal series considered in this chapter is derived from the work of Daniel Temple and his colleagues (Temple 2007a,b; Temple 2008). In Japan, prehistoric economies were characterized by a combination of independent plant domestication and imported agricultural ecosystems, along with substantial exploitation of aquatic resources (see other chapters in this volume). Evidence of dry-rice and millet agriculture is reported from Jomon on Honshu and from slightly later on Hokkaido, although no cereal is thought to have assumed a staple role in Japan until sometime thereafter (D'Andrea et al. 1995; Crawford 2006). Other plant resources such as acorn, bottle gourd, chestnut, walnut, and yam apparently were cultivated by Jomon period foragers (Crawford et al. 1976; Imamura 1996a,b; Sato 1999; Habu 2004). Circa 400–300 BC, a flow of immigrants from the Asian mainland introduced intensive wetland rice agriculture and domesticated soybeans into Kyushu, Honshu, and Shikoku, along with a number of technological innovations, marking the beginning of the Yayoi period (Aikens and Higuchi 1982: 187; Imamura 1996a,b; Tsude 2001).

Unfortunately, at present there are few available data on the ancient wet-

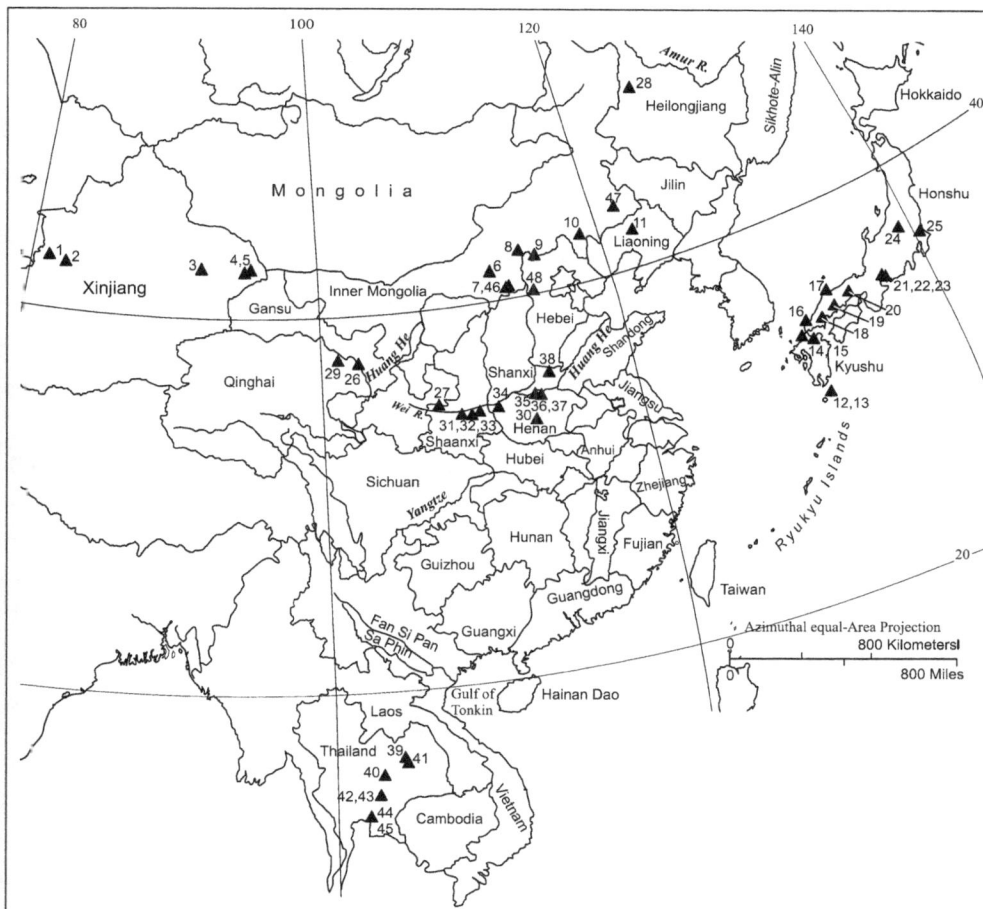

Figure 18.1. Locations of the archaeological sites that produced human skeletal assemblages discussed in this chapter: (1) Dunmaili; (2) Nileke; (3) Yanghai; (4) Hami; (5) Heigouliang; (6) Chengbozi; (7) Miaozigou; (8) Sanmian; (9) Zhenzishan; (10) Jinggouzi; (11) Lamadong. Yayoi period: (12) Hirota; (13) Torinomine; (14) Kanenokuma; (15) Nagaoka; (16) Doigahama; (17) Koura. Jomon period: (18) Yosekura; (19) Tsukumo; (20) Ota; (21) Yoshigo; (22) Hobi; (23) Inariyama; (24) Kitamura; (25) Nakazuma; (26) Shangsunjiazhai; (27) Xicunzhou; (28) Pingyang; (29) Taojiazhai; (30) Jiahu; (31) Jiangzhai; (32) Beiliu; (33) Shijia; (34) Xipo; (35) Guanjia; (36) Meishan; (37) Xiyasi; (38) Mengzhuang; (39) Ban Chiang; (40) Non Nok Tha; (41) Ban Na Di; (42) Noen U-Loke; (43) Ban Lum Khao; (44) Khok Phanom Di; (45) Nong Nor; (46) Yinniugou; (47) Xinglongwa; (48) Jiangjialiang.

Table 18.1. Skeletal collections used in this study

Site/collection	Name in the native writing system	Location	Time period/culture affiliation	Approximate dates	Source
Japan					
Ota	太田	Chugoku	Jomon	3000–2000 BC	Temple 2007, 2008; Temple and Larsen 2007
Yosekura	寄倉	Chugoku	Jomon	2000–1000 BC	"
Yoshigo	吉胡	Tokai	Jomon	1400–400 BC	"
Hobi	保美	Tokai	Jomon	1000–300 BC	"
Tsukumo	津雲	Chugoku	Jomon	1000–300 BC	"
Doigahama	土井ヶ浜	S. Honshu	Yayoi	500 BC–AD 100	"
Kanenokuma	金隈	N. Kyushu	Yayoi	100 BC–AD 100	"
Nagaoka	永岡	N. Kyushu	Yayoi	100 BC–AD 100	"
Koura	古浦	S. Honshu	Yayoi	AD 100–300	"
Northern China, frontier area					
Miaozigou	庙子沟	Inner Mongolia	Miaozigou	3800–3000 BC	Eng 2007
Lamadong	喇嘛洞	Manchuria	Weijin dynasty	AD 337–441	"
Zhenzishan	砧子山	Inner Mongolia	Yuan dynasty	AD 1271–1368	Smith 2005
Xinglongwa	兴隆洼	Inner Mongolia	Xinglongwa	6200–5300 BC	Eng 2007
Dunmaili	敦麦里	Xinjiang	Bronze Age	2000–1000 BC	Li Fajun 2008
Jiangjialiang	姜家梁	Hebei, Yangyuan	Hongshan	c. 3000 BC	Eng 2007
Jinggouzi	井沟子	Inner Mongolia	Warring States	475–221 BC	Zhang 2008
Yinniugou	饮牛沟	Inner Mongolia	Late Bronze Age	475–221 BC	"
Dadianzi	大甸子	Inner Mongolia	Bronze Age	770–221 BC	"
Pingyang	平洋	Heilongjiang	Bronze Age	770–221 BC	"
Jiangjungou	将军沟	Inner Mongolia	Warring States	475–221 BC	"
Taojiazhai	陶家寨	Qinghai	Han and Jin dynasties	206 BC–AD 420	"

Site		Province/Region	Period	Date	Reference
Shangsunjiazhai	上孙家寨	Qinghai		206 BC–AD 220	Zhang 2008
Chengcheng	陕西澄城	Shaanxi		206 BC–AD 220	"
Loess Plateau and Central Plains, China					
Jiahu	賈湖	Henan	Peiligang	7000–5800 BC	Pechenkina et al. 2002, 2007; this study
Beiliu	北劉	Shaanxi	Yangshao	4900–4000 BC	"
Jiangzhai	姜寨	Shaanxi	Yangshao	4900–4000 BC	"
Shijia	史家	Shaanxi	Yangshao	4900–4000 BC	"
Guanjia	关家	Henan	Yangshao	4000–3500 BC	"
Xipo	西坡	Henan	Yangshao	4000–3000 BC	"
Xishan	西山	Henan	Yangshao	4000–3000 BC	"
Meishan	煤山	Henan	Longshan	2500–2000 BC	"
Mengzhuang	孟庄	Henan	Longshan	2500–2000 BC	"
Nanzhai	南寨	Henan	Erlitou	2100–1500 BC	"
Xiyasi	西亚斯	Henan	Eastern Zhou	770–221 BC	"
Xicunzhou	西村周	Shaanxi	Eastern Zhou	475–221 BC	Zhang 2008
Thailand					
Khok Phanom Di	โคกพนมดี	Bang Pakong River area		2000–1500 BC	Tayles 1992 Domett 2001
Ban Chiang	บ้านเชียง	Songkhram drainage		Early: 2100–900 BC; Late: 900 BC–AD 200	Douglas and Pietrusewsky 2007
Ban Lum Khao	บ้านลุมข้าว	Mun River valley	Bronze Age	1000–500 BC	Domett 2001
Non Nok Tha	โนนนกทา	Phu Wiang		Early: 3000–2000 BC; Late: 2100–900 BC	Douglas and Pietrusewsky 2007
Nong Nor	หนองหนองอร	Thailand		1100–500 BC	Domett 2001
Ban Na Di	บ้านนาดี	Thailand		600–400 BC	"
Noen U-Loke	เนินอุโลก	Mun River valley	Iron Age	300 BC–AD 300	Domett and Tayles 2007

land rice agriculture–dependent communities of the Chang Jiang region. Therefore, in order to further represent this mode of subsistence in our study, we employ data on skeletal collections from neighboring Southeast Asia, where wetland agriculture was established by the early Iron Age, albeit in a somewhat different environmental setting from that of Chang Jiang (Tayles et al. 2000; Domett 2001; Oxenham 2006).

Adult Body Height and Sexual Dimorphism

Interpopulation differences in achieved adult stature are determined through a complex interplay between genetic and environmental factors. While some human populations appear genetically predisposed to be taller than others, on the intrapopulation level, stature appears to be a fairly sensitive indicator of chronic stress and malnourishment. In geographical areas where little long-distance migration has occurred and an assumption of genetic continuity between chronologically successive populations is reasonable, changes in the longitudinal growth of children and consequent increases and decreases in the achieved body height of adults have been found to closely mirror a population's nutritional status and levels of physiological stress (Stinson 1985, 2000; Bogin 1999). Lesser adult statures typically reflect chronic malnourishment, a poor diet deficient in one or several essential nutrients, or heavy parasitic loads. While episodes of temporary growth arrest can result from acute disease, trauma, or episodic starvation, the human organism appears to have a great capacity for catch-up growth.

Methods of Estimating Stature in Asian Populations from Skeletal Remains

Long bone measurements and the estimates of stature derived from them are among the most common skeletal data presented in studies of human remains from archaeological contexts (Johnston et al. 1976; Cohen and Armelagos 1984; Larsen 1987). Nevertheless, making informative comparisons of estimates of stature derived from studies carried out by different researchers is far from straightforward. First and foremost, the differing formulae selected by individual researchers to estimate stature complicate any attempt at comparison. Ideally, one would measure stature in situ for individuals buried in the prone position or use Fully's (1956) formula based on the heights of all bones that contribute to the height of an individual: dimensions of the leg bones, height of the calcaneus, the total height of all vertebrae, and the height of the cranium; these approaches have been demonstrated to have the highest precision and accuracy of all available techniques. However, when working with excavated remains, one almost never has the luxury of measuring all of the bones needed to successfully apply Fully's technique. In each of the studies reviewed in this chapter, stature estimates were based on the lengths of one or several long bones, most commonly the femur.

Formulae available for estimating stature from long bone lengths are many and varied (table 18.2). Accuracy of the results obtained will depend on how closely the body proportions of the studied population approach the body proportions of the group used as a basis for development of the selected formula. Selecting any particular one of these equations as a basis for analysis can produce stature estimates with a magnitude of difference beyond the margin of error as compared to others. Furthermore, when long bones other than the femur are used to estimate stature, the error margins of those estimates increase, since there is a lesser correlation of other long bone lengths with stature (Pearson 1899). Consequently, it is difficult to evaluate to what extent differences in stature estimated using differing formulae reflect actual interpopulation variation, as opposed to differences resulting from specific mathematical assumptions.

Leaving aside the argument over which formulae might be best suited for estimating the stature of ancient populations from East Asia, here we use the formulae of Trotter and Gleser (1958) and Pearson (1899) for male and female individuals respectively (table 18.3). We also provide mean maximal

Table 18.2. Formulae for estimating stature from femur length used in East and Southeast Asia

Stature[a]	Source	Basis
Males		
= 1.880F + 81.306	Pearson 1899	Measurement of 50 19th-century French male cadavers
= 2.15F + 72.57 +3.8	Trotter and Gleser 1958	Remains of 98 "Mongoloid" male U.S. military personnel who died in the Korean War
= 2.5F + 54.901	Fuji 1960	Modern Japanese
= 2.4378F + 61.7207 +2.1756	Stevenson 1929	Collection of 48 northern Chinese skeletons
= 1.7289F + 88.132 +5.3885	Sangvichien et al. 1985, n.d.	Thai and Chinese cadavers, 50 males
= 3.66F + 5	Shao 1985	Cadaver study of Chinese
= 2.32F (mm) + 640.21 +3.32 (mm) for middle-aged adults	Chen 1980	Set of age-specific formulae based on cadaver research of Chinese
Females		
= 1.945F + 72.844	Pearson 1899	Measurement of 50 19th-century female French cadavers
= 2.33F + 57.841	Fuji 1960	Modern Japanese
= 2.5815F + 49.2412 +3.0007	Sangvichien et al. 1985, n.d.	Thai and Chinese cadavers, 27 females

[a] All equations are for measurements in centimeters unless specified otherwise.
Note: "F" used in the formulae refers to femur length.

Table 18.3. Stature and femur lengths in the collections studied

Site/collection	Stature			Femur length			Source	Stature formula
	Males (N)	Females (N)	Sex dim.	M	F	Sex dim.		
Japan, Jomon								
Ota	163.1 (5)	154.3 (5)	5.4	43.28	41.38	4.3	Temple 2007a	Fuji 1960
Yosekura	161.0 (5)	145.7 (6)	9.5	42.42	37.72	11.1	"	"
Yoshigo	159.1 (17)	147.5 (11)	7.3	41.69	38.47	7.7	"	"
Hobi	158.0 (6)	149.2 (9)	5.4	41.10	39.20	4.6	"	"
Tsukumo	158.3 (11)	148.4 (9)	6.3	41.35	38.84	6.1	"	"
Eastern Jomon	157.5 (50)	149.0 (45)	5.4				Temple 2008	Fuji 1960
Western Jomon	158.9 (27)	150.2 (14)	5.5				"	"
Middle Jomon	160.8 (11)	152.0 (5)	5.5					"
Late/Final Jomon	156.3 (16)	149.24 (11)	4.5				Temple 2007a	"
All Jomon	157.6	149.7	5				Temple 2007a	"
Yayoi								
Doigahama	166.4 (24)	151.5 (25)	9.0	43.65	40.42	7.4	Temple 2007a	Trotter and Gleser 1958 (M); Pearson 1899 (F)
Kanenokuma	164.1 (5)	149.7 (3)	8.8	42.55	39.50	7.2	"	"
Nagaoka	165.2 (1)			43.1			"	"
Koura	166.1 (9)	149.9 (6)	9.7	43.5	39.62	8.9	"	Stevenson 1929
S. Honshu Yayoi	169.8	159.6	6				"	"
N. Kyushu Yayoi	165.6	158.0	4.6				"	"
Tanegashima Yayoi	153.2	151.9	0.8				"	"
China								
NE; Neolithic (Miaozigou)	170.2 (4)	156.9 (4)	7.8	45.42	43.20	4.9	Eng 2007	Trotter and Gleser 1958 (M); Pearson 1899 (F)

Site / period	Male	Female					Reference	Method
NE; Weijin dynasty (Lamadong)	166.6 (133)	151.4 (141)	9.1	43.72	40.38	7.6	Eng 2007	Trotter and Gleser 1958 (M); Pearson 1899 (F)
NE; Yuan dynasty (Zhenzishan)	166.3 (4)	150.7 (4)	9.4	43.60	40.03	8.2	"	"
NW; Bronze Age	168.2 (5)	153.8 (8)	8.6	44.50	41.61	6.5	"	"
NW; Iron Age	169.5 (46)	153.2 (34)	9.7	45.09	41.29	8.4	"	"
N-central; Bronze Age	165.2 (19)	149.8 (24)	9.3	43.08	39.58	8.1	"	"
N-central; Yuan dynasty	166.4 (6)	149.8 (4)	10	43.66	39.56	9.4	"	"
Nomadic pastoralists, Bronze Age	165.8 (24)	150.8 (32)	9.1	43.37	40.08	7.6	"	"
Nomadic pastoralists, Iron Age	169.5 (46)	153.2 (34)	9.7	45.09	41.29	8.4	"	"
Xinglongwa	167.8 (22)	154.9 (7)	7.7	43.51	42.21	3.0	Smith 2005	"
Jiangjialiang	168.8 (11)	155.5 (6)	7.9	44.80	42.49	5.2	Li Fajun 2004	"
Jinggouzi; Late Bronze Age	166.9	153.1	8.3	43.86	41.26	5.9	Eng 2007	"
Yinniugou; Late Bronze Age	167.7	155.5	7.2	44.23	42.52	3.9	Zhang 2008	"
Dadianzi; Bronze Age	163.3	154.4	5.4	42.19	41.93	0.6	"	"
Pingyang; Bronze Age	165.7	154.8	6.6	43.32	42.14	2.7	"	"
Jiangjungou; Warring States	168.5	153.3	9.0	44.61	41.38	7.2	"	"
Xicunzhou; Zhou	166.8	153.3	8.1	43.83	41.36	5.6	"	"
Taojiazhai (Han and Jin dynasty)	169.3 (128)	152.2 (113)	10.1	45.00	40.78	9.4	"	"
Shangsunjiazhai	168.7	150.9	10.6	44.71	40.13	10.2	"	"
Shanxi Chengcheng	168.7	152.3	9.7	44.70	40.84	8.6	"	"

(continued)

(*continued*)

						Pechenkina et al. 2002, 2007; and this study	Trotter and Gleser 1958 (M); Pearson 1899 (F)
Jiahu	173.7 (32)	156.1 (21)	10.1	47.03	42.81	9.0	Pechenkina et al. 2002, 2007; and this study	Trotter and Gleser 1958 (M); Pearson 1899 (F)
Beiliu	168.9 (4)	152.4 (4)	9.8	44.80	40.88	8.7	"	"
Jiangzhai	169.9 (11)	154.9 (11)	8.8	45.27	42.20	6.8	"	"
Shijia	168.8 (14)	152.6 (10)	9.6	44.77	41.01	8.4	"	"
Guanjia	169.7 (14)	154.5 (9)	9	45.18	41.99	7.1	"	"
Xipo	169.2 (15)	154.5 (6)	8.7	44.93	42.00	6.5	"	"
Meishan	167.6 (5)	148.6 (3)	11.3	44.18	38.96	11.8	"	"
Mengzhuang	166.9 (9)	154.2 (4)	7.6	43.89	41.85	4.7	"	"
Nanzhai	165.6 (4)	149.2 (3)	9.9	43.27	39.27	9.2	"	"
Western Zhou pooled	166.5 (8)	150.1 (6)	9.9	43.70	39.71	9.1	"	"
Xiyasi	170.1 (28)	151.2 (9)	11.1	45.45	39.84	12.3	"	"
Han	165.8 (12)	148.1 (12)	10.7	43.36	38.69	10.8	"	"
Tang	166.7 (5)	151.0 (2)	9.4	43.77	40.20	8.15	"	"
Thailand								
Non Nok Tha Early	164.7 (15)	152.0 (16)	7.7	44.29	39.81	10.1	Douglas and Pietrusewsky 2007	Sangvichien 1985, n.d.
Non Nok Tha Late	166.5 (16)	155.0 (15)	6.9	45.33	40.97	9.6	Domett 2001	"
Khok Phanom Di	162.2 (30)	154.3 (36)	4.9	42.84	40.70	5.0	Douglas and Pietrusewsky 2007	"
Early Ban Chiang	165.4 (17)	153.9 (17)	7.0	44.69	40.54	9.3	Douglas and Pietrusewsky 2007	"
Ban Lum Khao	164.7 (19)	154.7 (25)	6.1	44.29	40.85	7.8	Domett 2001	"
Nong Nor	167.2 (19)	156.1 (14)	6.6	45.73	41.39	9.5	Domett 2001	"
Late Ban Chiang	166.0 (12)	154.4 (7)	7.0	45.04	40.74	9.6	Douglas and Pietrusewsky 2007	"
Ban Na Di	168.0 (17)	155.9 (13)	7.2	46.20	41.32	10.6	Domett 2001	"
Noen U-Loke	169.3 (9)	154.6 (4)	8.7	46.95	40.81	13.1	Domett and Tayles 2007	"

femur lengths to permit interpopulation comparisons that do not rely on any specific assumption about body proportions. Because not all studies reviewed here provided information on the femur lengths of the individuals analyzed (Domett 2001; Domett and Tayles 2007; Zhang 2008), the relevant stature equations were reversed in order to estimate maximal femur length based on the stature estimates reported. This approach does not necessarily produce a precise value for femur length, because other long bones may have been used by the original authors to estimate stature. Nevertheless, assuming that the stature equations used by the respective authors accurately reflect the pertinent body proportions, femur length as estimated from the reversed stature equations should be fairly reliable.

Trends in Adult Stature in Ancient East Asia

Femur lengths and stature estimates for the skeletal series from East and Southeast Asia considered here are summarized in table 18.3. Several interesting trends are suggested in this table. First, a number of geographically defined populations apparently experienced a decline in stature over time, including those from China's Central Plains and on the Chinese northeastern frontier, as well as Japanese during the successive phases of Jomon culture. In other regions, adult body height seems to have increased over time.

Neolithic individuals from China, especially those from the Early and Middle periods of the Neolithic, generally evidence greater stature than do adults from later time periods. This is true for the northeastern area represented by skeletal collections from Liaoning and the western part of Inner Mongolia (Smith 2005; Eng 2007), as well as for collections originating from archaeological sites in the Wei and Yellow River basins (Pechenkina et al. 2002, 2007, this chapter). For the northeastern frontier group, mean statures for male adults from the Neolithic sites of Xinglongwa (6200–5300 BC) and Miaozigou (3800–3000 BC) were estimated at 167.8 cm and 170.2 cm respectively, while corresponding female statures for those collections averaged 154.9 cm and 156.9 cm. These estimates are greater than those for the Beipiao Lamadong collection from the Weijin dynasty (AD 337–441) (166.6 cm for males and 151.4 cm for females), which are themselves greater than the estimated average stature of Yuan dynasty (AD 1271–1368) adults from Zhenzishan (166.3 cm for males and 150.7 cm for females; stature estimates are based on mean femur lengths provided by Smith [2005] and Eng [2007]).

In the Wei/Yellow River area, a decline in adult stature is clearly expressed throughout the succession of Neolithic skeletal series and was especially marked between the Yangshao and Longshan skeletal collections, probably reflecting limitations imposed by greater reliance on millet agriculture. Thus, the average adult stature of a pooled Yangshao sample, incorporating data from Beiliu, Jiangzhai, Shijia, Xipo, and Guanjia individuals, is 169.3 cm for males and 153.9 cm for females. Although Longshan sample sizes are miniscule, both Meishan and Mengzhuang statures are clearly less than those for any of the Yangshao collections analyzed. Mean estimated statures for the pooled Longshan sample are approximately 2 cm less than those for Yangshao: 167.2 cm and 151.8 cm for males and females respectively. A decline in adult stature associated with intensified millet farming is further corroborated by the average statures of individuals from Nanzhai: 165.6 cm for males and 149.2 cm for females. However, chronologically more recent skeletal collections from Western Zhou and Eastern Zhou sites reveal increased sexual dimorphism, with average male statures similar to those estimated for the Yangshao adults, alongside lesser female statures. Average statures estimated from even more recent (Han and Tang) dynastic collections from the same area are all less than those for the Longshan adults: 165.8–166.7 cm for males and 148.1–151.0 cm for females (table 18.3).

For the Japanese archipelago, Ota individuals from Middle Jomon had the greatest average stature of all Jomonese: 163.1 cm for males and 154.3 cm for females (these, as well as stature estimates for other Japanese skeletal collections, are based on individual femur lengths listed in the appendix of Temple's Ph.D. thesis [Temple 2007a]). Slightly lesser stature was found for the Yosekura adults from the early phase of Late Jomon (161.0 cm and 145.7 cm for males and females respectively). Skeletal collections from Late and Final Jomon—Yoshigo, Hobi, and Tsukumo—revealed even lesser statures for males, although statures for females were slightly greater.

Based on measurements of multiple long bones, Temple (2008) estimated average adult stature for Middle Jomon at 160.8 cm for males and 152.0 cm for females, which is almost 4 cm taller than his estimates for Late/Final Jomon (156.3 cm and 149.2 cm for males and females respectively). Nevertheless, Temple (2008) argues that more important differences in stature are observed between geographically defined groups of Jomonese, rather than temporally defined groups. He suggests that for western Japan, greater reliance on cultivated and wild plant resources probably resulted in slightly lesser stature overall, as well as a more pronounced decline in achieved adult stature during Late and Final Jomon (Temple 2008).

Increasing average adult stature over time was evident in studies of skeletons from preagricultural and early agricultural communities in Thailand. Mean adult statures estimated from the later phases of Ban Chiang and Non Nok Tha were generally higher than those from earlier phases at the same sites for both males and females (Douglas and Pietrusewsky 2007) (table

18.3). Individuals from chronologically earlier sites were shorter on average than those from later sites in the same region. For example, in the Bang Pakong River area, the average statures of Khok Phanom Di (2000–1500 BC) adults were the lowest among those estimated for the Thai collections. Adults from the Nong Nor site (1100–500 BC), which is located in the same general vicinity (figure 18.1), were significantly taller (Domett 2001). The same is true for skeletal individuals from archaeological sites located in the proximity of the Mun River. Adults from Ban Lum Khao (1000–500 BC) had average statures of 164.7 cm and 154.7 cm for males and females respectively, while later residents of this area, from the Noen U-Loke site (300 BC–AD 300), had respective average adult statures of 169.3 cm and 154.6 cm.

For Japan, a considerable increase in adult stature apparently took place with the transition to Yayoi. Whereas Jomonese populations tended to be shorter than the Neolithic populations of continental East Asia, during Yayoi, statures in Japan and in northern China converged as a consequence of gene flow from the Asian mainland, which has been documented archaeologically and also on the basis of skeletal remains (Brace and Nagai 1982; Turner 1990; Nakahashi 1995; Pietrusewsky 1999 and this volume; Nakahashi et al. 2002). The overall lesser stature of Jomon people might have been an outcome of microevolutionary processes such as the founder effect or selection imposed by the insular environment of the Japanese archipelago. The first members of our species seem to have arrived in Japan as early as 34,000 years ago (Oda and Keally 1986; Ono et al. 2002) and became isolated from mainland populations when rising ocean levels submerged land bridges between the archipelago and the continent.

Body Height Dimorphism

Male-female body size dimorphism is an important measure that can be estimated from the dimensions of long bones. While there are a variety of approaches to estimating degrees of sexual dimorphism (Holden and Mace 1999), male-female dimorphism is most often calculated as the difference between average male and female statures in a population, expressed as a proportion of average male stature (Molnar 1992). In human populations, this typically ranges between 5 percent and 10 percent.

Relatively greater degrees of sexual dimorphism are found in mammals living in polygenous groups (Trivers 1972; Leutenegger and Kelly, 1977). However, for humans, there seems to be little correspondence between marriage patterns and sexual dimorphism (Holden and Mace 1999; Kanazawa and Novak 2005). An inverse relationship between the degree of sexual dimorphism and women's contribution to subsistence has been documented in a comparative analysis of multiple human communities (Holden and Mace 1999). This relationship between sexual dimorphism and gender roles is probably caused by unequal parental investment in rearing boys and girls, based on their differing economic values. Alternatively, the male vulnerability/female buffering hypothesis (Stini 1985) suggests that the female body is better buffered against environmental stress, perhaps because of selection for performing highly energy demanding reproductive functions. According to this hypothesis, sexual dimorphism is expected to decrease in stressed populations because of a greater degree of suppression of male growth.

Making reliable interpopulation comparisons of degrees of sexual dimorphism based on statures estimated from skeletal collections is confounded by two principal skewing factors. First, possible misidentification of the sex of larger females and smaller males, as well as assigning skeletons with more neutral morphology as indeterminate, can each amplify the apparent degree of sexual dimorphism. Thus, great caution should be used when estimating the degree of sexual dimorphism for collections with partial or commingled skeletal remains. In this study, the estimate for Jiahu was disregarded, since crania and femurs from the site were curated separately and pelves often were not available for sex assessment. Second, sexual dimorphism based on estimated stature is strongly affected by which specific equation was used to estimate stature in the first place. Different equations presume somewhat different body proportions for males and females. Moreover, since the equations used to estimate stature for the two sexes describe nonparallel functions, the same magnitude of long bone length dimorphism can translate into different apparent degrees of stature dimorphism simply because the average bone length upon which statures were estimated is different. In order to circumvent at least the second problem, table 18.3 provides two measures of sexual dimorphism: one based on estimated statures and another based on femur length alone. We focus our discussion on the latter measure.

For several geographical areas in East Asia there was a slight increase in sexual dimorphism over time, especially for populations dating to after 1000 BC. For Japan, levels of sexual dimorphism during Jomon were generally low (a weighted average is 6.9 percent). The Yosekura collection, with a level of dimorphism greater than 11 percent, is an exception, but the sample size is very small. Estimated sexual dimorphism based on femurs from Koura, an AD 100–300 Yayoi site from southern Honshu, is 8.9 percent, greater than that estimated for Early Yayoi Doigahama and Kanenokuma (7.4 percent and 7.2 percent, respectively). For the Chinese northeastern frontier area, the level of sexual dimorphism estimated for Neolithic Miaozigou is only 4.9 percent, much less than for Lamadong of the Weijin dynasty (7.6 percent) or Zhenzishan of the Yuan dynasty (8.2 percent). Slight increases in the degree of sexual dimorphism between the Bronze and the Iron Age are also estimated for the northwestern (Xinjiang Province) and north-central areas (table 18.3).

This trend toward increasing levels of sexual dimorphism over time is validated by data presented on individual sites from northern China in the dissertations of Smith (2005), Eng (2007), and Zhang (2008). The level of dimorphism estimated for the Early Neolithic site of Xinglongwa (8200–7300 BP) is merely 3 percent. For Bronze Age skeletal collections, the level of dimorphism ranges from 0.6 percent at Dadianzi to 5.9 percent at Jinggouzi. In skeletal collections from chronologically later sites, the range of sexual dimorphism is from 5.6 percent to 10.2 percent. This increase in sexual dimorphism for the frontier populations resulted from both an increase in average male statures and a decline in average female long bone lengths.

A trend toward increasing sexual dimorphism is less clearly expressed in the skeletal collections from the Wei and Yellow River valleys, most likely because available skeletal series from the chronologically later sites are very small. Nevertheless, a weighted average of sexual dimorphism levels at all Yangshao sites (7.3 percent) is considerably less than that for the later Dynastic collections (11.7 percent). The magnitude of male/female differences at Yangshao sites is relatively high but more similar to the levels observed in Bronze and Iron Age collections from the frontier part of northern China than to those found for the Neolithic Xinglongwa and Miaozigou series.

Available Southeast Asian skeletal series are generally characterized by high levels of sexual dimorphism but display little change in this indicator over time. The Khok Phanom Di collection appears to be an exception, with 5 percent sexual dimorphism; all other collections examined had male/female stature differences of greater than 9 percent. These levels of sexual dimorphism are similar to those observed for collections from dynastic China but considerably higher than the same measure estimated from the Neolithic and Bronze Age Chinese collections.

Based on these data, we can emphasize several commonalities, as well as a number of interesting exceptions. A marked decline in stature over time was evident only in the areas where millet agriculture was practiced. This primarily refers to populations on the Central Plains of China and in Manchuria, as well as to the western Jomon in Japan during the Late and Final phases of that culture. This decline in stature probably was a consequence of progressively greater reliance on domesticated cereals. However, a slight increase in adult stature occurred on the Chinese Central Plains during the Early Dynastic period, probably as a consequence of slight improvements in nutrition with the spread of wheat and barley production into the area.

An increase in stature over time was found for nomadic pastoralists in the northwest of China, for Japan during the Jomon/Yayoi transition, and for the rice-growing communities of Southeast Asia. In part, increasing stature in Japan and in Thailand can be attributed to gene flow from taller populations, specifically resulting from expansion that accompanied the rise of imperial China. In addition, a broadening of the limited tropical forest resource base in Thailand with the introduction of agriculture might have led to improvement in the nutritional regime of that area. Replacing significant tracts of forest with agricultural fields may have diminished the burden of malaria at the same time.

With the exception of Thailand, degrees of sexual dimorphism increased over time in almost all geographic areas considered in this study. This increase in dimorphism was accomplished largely by declines in female stature, while male stature either increased or stayed the same, which seems to argue against Stini's (1985) female buffering hypothesis. Furthermore, according to Stini (1985), an increase in sexual dimorphism should correspond to an overall amelioration of environmental stress and improvement in community health. Expectations derived from Stini (1985) are the opposite of those stemming from Holden and Mace's (1999) hypothesis relating body size dimorphism to increased disparity in gender roles. In the latter case we would expect an increase in stress markers (discussed below), particularly on female skeletons.

Oral Health

Caries Epidemiology and Diagnosis

The atrocious state of oral health among many subsistence farmers is well documented (Turner 1979; Larsen et al. 1991; Larsen 1997; Schollmeyer and Turner 2004). An increase in the frequency of carious lesions with the transition to farming and as a consequence, high rates of periapical abscesses, along with antemortem tooth loss, have been widely reported for areas where maize was a staple and also to a lesser extent with the transition to wheat/barley and millet farming (Molnar and Molnar 1985; Eshed at al. 2006; Pechenkina et al. 2007). While an increasing focus on rice production does not seem to have resulted in declining oral health in Thailand or Vietnam (Tayles et al. 2000; Oxenham 2006; Domett and Tayles 2007), in Japan there was a notable increase in the rate of carious lesions during the Yayoi period (Temple and Larsen 2007, chapter 14), which coincided with the expansion of wet-rice cultivation.

The adverse consequences of cereal-rich diets for oral health are attributed to the high carbohydrate content of the seeds of all domesticated Poaceae.

Caries is caused by a proliferation of acidogenic bacteria, particularly *Streptococcus mutans* and some species of *Lactobacilli*, which produce lactic acid when fermenting carbohydrates on the dental surface (Fitzgerald and Keyes 1963; Geddes 1994). Lactic acid causes demineralization of the enamel, resulting in irreversible damage to the dental surface. Initiation of caries infection involves attachment of *S. mutans* to the dental surface, which requires the presence of sucrose, a disaccharide of glucose and fructose. When fermenting sucrose, *S. mutans* produces insoluble polysaccharides (glucans) that allow firm attachment of bacteria to the dental surface, as well as to each other (Cury et al. 2000; Shen et al. 2004; Islam et al. 2007). Plaque formed in the absence of sucrose is more mineralized and much less cariogenic, even when concentrations of other carbohydrates are high (Cury et al. 2000; Aires et al. 2006).

While sucrose is necessary for development of this biofilm by *Streptococcus*, high concentrations of water-soluble mono- and disaccharides contribute to the progression of caries by supplying the nutrients necessary for bacterial growth. Consequently, two aspects of the chemical composition of a cereal contribute to its cariogenicity: the concentration of sucrose and the overall concentration of other saccharides, including glucose, fructose, maltose, and raffinose. Considering both of these aspects permits predictions to be made about the relative cariogenicity of different grains.

Sucrose content varies substantially among the staple cereals. Sucrose content is the highest in barley and rye (1.9–2.0 percent and 1.9 percent of dry weight, respectively), followed by maize (0.9–1.9 percent) and foxtail millet (0.9–1.1 percent). Broomcorn millet, wheat, and brown rice have lower sucrose concentrations, with typical ranges of 0.5–0.9 percent, 0.6–0.8 percent, and 0.6–0.7 percent, respectively. Milled rice has a particularly low sucrose content of 0.14 percent (Shelton and Lee 2000). Consequently, based on the availability of sucrose, foxtail millet is expected to be as cariogenic as maize and slightly more cariogenic than broomcorn millet or wheat.

Frequencies of carious lesions and other oral pathologies are reported in the bioarchaeological literature nearly as often as the lengths of long bones. Caries diagnosis based on visual observations generally produces small and insignificant interobserver errors (Rudney et al. 1983). Even so, comparing the frequencies of oral health indicators across publications by different authors is complicated by multiple factors (Wesolowski 2006). The overall frequencies of carious teeth are most often presented as pooled frequencies for all teeth. Because posterior teeth, especially molars, are more susceptible to caries than are anterior teeth (Erdal and Duyar 1999; Hillson 2001)—and because anterior teeth are subject to greater rates of postdepositional loss in some collections—it is not always possible to assess whether reported differences in caries frequencies reflect actual differences in oral health between the populations studied or preservation bias.

Moreover, carious teeth, especially those with large lesions and associated with periapical abscesses, are subject to greater postdepositional loss. Some affected teeth fall apart during recovery and are transformed into tiny fragments, even when extreme care is taken to preserve them. Thus, working with museum-curated collections poses the risk of finding misleadingly low rates of carious lesions, because these samples tend to be biased against teeth with severe lesions. Additional problems arise from demographic differences among skeletal collections.

Here, to maximize the scope of analysis, we compare crude rates of caries on permanent teeth, pooled together for all adult dental sets. Keeping in mind the reservations outlined above, we focus on large-scale changes and repeatability of trends in areas with similar historical subsistence shifts. We limit consideration to adult remains, since subadult dental samples tend to be too small to warrant meaningful comparisons. Wherever possible, caries frequencies are presented by sex. However, because many skeletal collections excavated during the twentieth century are limited to crania, the reliability of recorded sex assessments is highly variable.

Distribution of Carious Lesions in the East Asian Skeletal Collections

The magnitude of differences in the frequencies of carious teeth across skeletal collections from East and Southeast Asia is substantial (tables 18.4 and 18.5). The maximal frequency of carious lesions per tooth (56.3 percent) was recorded for agropastoralists of the frontier area (Eng 2007), but few other samples manifest a carious rate of greater than 20 percent. A number of cranial series from northern China and Southeast Asia, as well as from Jomon Japan, evidenced frequencies of carious lesions very close to 0 percent.

For the Central Plains and adjacent territories of China, fairly low frequencies of carious teeth were found in the skeletal series from Early Yangshao sites: Beiliu (5.6 percent), Jiangzhai (2.6 percent), and Shijia (3.9 percent). In our earlier research (Pechenkina et al. 2002), we proposed that these low frequencies of carious lesions reflect the relatively low cariogenicity of millet as a staple food. However, Middle/Late Yangshao skeletal collections are all characterized by considerably higher caries frequencies: 16.5 percent at Guanjia, 9.9 percent at Xipo, and 15.6 percent at Xishan. The difference between the pooled Early Yangshao and Middle/Late Yangshao series is statistically significant ($\chi^2 = 68.6$, $p < .001$, 1 df).

Because millet was the predominant agricultural crop throughout the

Table 18.4. Frequencies of carious teeth in skeletal collections from East and Southeast Asia

Collection	All adults		
		Carious	
	Obs.	N	%
Japan[a]			
Middle to Late Jomon	1,448	54	3.7
Late to Final Jomon	3,421	322	9.4
S. Honshu Yayoi	1,904	314	16.5
N. Kyushu Yayoi	1,334	159	11.9
Tanegashima Yayoi	1,340	130	9.7
Total Yayoi	4,578	603	13.2
Jomon			
Inariyama	330	18	5.4
Hobi Jomon	416	39	9.4
Nakazuma	615	69	11.2
Yoshigo	1,170	154	13.2
Tsukumo	675	63	9.4
Yosekura	204	18	8.8
Yayoi			
Doigahama	1,417	245	17.3
Koura	487	69	14.1
Kanenokuma	1,006	117	11.6
Nagaoka	328	42	12.8
Torinomine	331	19	5.7
Hirota	1,009	111	11.0
Frontier			
Nomadic Pastoralists[b]	220	60	27.3
Agropastoralists[b]	341	192	56.3
Taojiazhai[c]	678	46	6.8
Central Plains[d]			
Beiliu	89	5	5.6
Jiangzhai	418	11	2.6
Shijia	179	7	3.9
Guanjia	1,014	167	16.5
Xipo	614	61	9.9
Xishan	2,037	317	15.6

(continued)

(continued)

Collection	All adults		
		Carious	
	Obs.	N	%
Meishan	95	22	23.2
Mengzhuang	93	6	6.5
Nanzhai	99	14	14.1
Xiyasi	725	203	28.0
Southeast Asia			
Early Non Nok Tha[e]	666	11	1.7
Late Non Nok Tha[e]	539	22	4.1
Khok Phanom Di[f]	1,282	140	10.9
Early Ban Chiang[e]	534	33	6.2
Late Ban Chiang[e]	560	43	7.7
Nong Nor[f]	1,044	68	6.5
Ban Lum Khao[f]	874	39	4.5
Ban Na Di[f]	516	24	4.7
Noen U-Loke[g]	956	46	4.8
Vietnam[h]			
Da But	944	14	1.5
Ma, Ca Rivers	828	23	2.8
Red River	290	4	1.4

[a] Derived from Temple 2007a; Temple and Larsen 2007 for all Japanese collections.
[b] Based on Eng 2007.
[c] Zhang, this volume.
[d] Based on Pechenkina et al. 2007, and Pechenkina et al. this volume for all Central Plains collections.
[e] Based on Douglas and Pietrusewsky 2007.
[f] Based on Domett 2001.
[g] Based on Domett and Tayles 2007.
[h] From Oxenham 2007 for all Vietnam collections.

duration of both Yangshao and Longshan, factors other than the relative cariogenicity of millet per se must have contributed to an increase in caries frequencies during Middle/Late Yangshao. One possibility is a decline in hunting and foraging activities after Early Yangshao. Shaanxi faunal assemblages dating to Early Yangshao include a high proportion of wild animal bones (Yuan and Flad 2002), while an assemblage from the Middle Yangshao site of Xishan is constituted almost exclusively of domesticated pig bones

Table 18.5. Frequencies of carious teeth for males and females in skeletal collections from East and Southeast Asia

Collection	Males			Females			χ^2	p
		Carious			Carious			
	Obs.	N	%	Obs.	N	%		df=1
Japan								
Total Yayoi	1,058	85	8.1	598	81	13.5	**10.38**	**.0013**
Frontier area								
Nomadic pastoralists	115	24	20.9	105	36	34.3	2.84	.0919
Agropastoralists	173	87	50.3	168	105	62.5	1.44	.2294
Taojiazhai	410	21	5.6	23	268	8.6	2.26	.1324
Central Plains								
Beiliu	43	4	9.3	46	1	2.2	1.90	.1680
Jiangzhai	255	5	2.0	163	6	3.7	1.09	.2975
Shijia	134	5	3.7	45	2	4.4	0.04	.8376
Guanjia	568	65	11.4	446	102	22.9	**29.83**	**.0000**
Xipo	424	43	10.1	190	18	9.5	0.06	.7988
Xishan	695	98	14.1	989	173	17.5	**5.04**	**.0248**
Longshan pooled	106	11	10.4	37	13	35.1	**7.84**	**.0051**
Nanzhai	36	4	11.1	63	10	15.9	0.33	.5682
Xiyasi	556	143	25.7	211	77	36.5	**4.64**	**.0312**
Southeast Asia								
Khok Phanom Di	625	43	6.9	657	96	14.6	**15.98**	**.0001**
Early Non Nok Tha	284	6	2.1	382	5	1.3	0.63	.4288
Early Ban Chiang	310	24	7.7	198	9	4.5	1.80	.1801
Late Non Nok Tha	292	8	2.7	244	6	2.5	0.04	.8433
Nong Nor	527	25	4.7	456	43	9.4	**7.24**	**.0071**
Ban Lum Khao	397	7	1.8	477	32	6.7	**11.42**	**.0007**
Late Ban Chiang	244	21	8.6	316	22	7.0	0.45	.5026
Ban Na Di	147	12	8.2	368	12	3.3	**5.08**	**.0243**
Noen U-Loke	422	19	4.5	382	22	5.8	0.59	.4422
Vietnam								
Da But	445	7	1.6	333	7	2.1	0.29	.5897
Ma, Ca Rivers	435	7	1.6	294	14	4.8	2.37	.1234
Red River	51	0	0	168	3	1.8	0.91	.3409

Note: Boldface numbers indicate significance.
Refer to table 18.4 footnotes for data sources.

(Ma 2005). Larger settlement size and greater population densities during Middle and Late Yangshao could have restricted the productivity of foraging and hunting. In a similar vein, Rose and colleagues (1991) reported that in the lower Mississippi valley, the adverse effects of maize agriculture on dental health were observed only for those settings where settlement patterns limited local foraging activities.

Longshan and Erlitou dental collections available for use in our study were small, ranging from 95 to 99 teeth per series. Based on the rates of carious teeth found in those samples (Meishan, 23.2 percent; Mengzhuang, 6.5 percent; and Nanzhai, 14.1 percent), it appears that caries was at least as common during Longshan and Erlitou as during the Middle Yangshao. A significant increase in the frequency of carious teeth is also documented for the Eastern Zhou series from Xiyasi (28 percent, $\chi^2 = 29.66$, $p < .001$ when compared to the pooled Middle Yangshao sample).

Xiyasi dentitions display considerable differences from earlier series with respect to the distribution of caries among individuals, as well as among different teeth. In the Middle Yangshao collections, a large proportion of individuals had at least one tooth affected by caries, but few had multiple cavities. In the Xiyasi collection, those individuals who suffered from caries had multiple teeth affected in a row. Anterior teeth—incisors and canines—were affected in greater proportion than posterior teeth, unlike in earlier series, where caries was most commonly found on molars. The topography of carious lesions also changed. In all skeletal collections from the Central Plains examined by us, apart from the Xiyasi series, carious lesions predominantly occurred on interproximal and occlusal surfaces of the crown. However, in the Xiyasi series, caries attacked teeth below the cementoenamel junction. This pattern suggests that carious infection at Xiyasi was preceded in many cases by severe periodontal disease, which exposed the dental roots to cariogenic plaque.

In China, changes between the Neolithic and the Early Dynastic in the rate and distribution of carious lesions coincided with at least two documented alterations in the human subsistence regime. Domesticated wheat and barley diffused onto the Central Plains of China during Longshan, likely supplanting the caloric contribution of millets to the human diet during the Shang and Zhou dynasties (Zhao and He 2006; Lee et al. 2007). In addition, according to the paleobotanical record of the Zaojiaoshu (皂角树) site in Henan, dated to 1900–1500 BC (Luoyang Archaeological Team 2002, cited in Lee at al. 2007), early stages of soybean (*Glycine* sp.) domestication are evident from the time of the Shang dynasty.

As explained above, based on sucrose and overall carbohydrate content, wheat and barley are expected to be less cariogenic than foxtail millet. Adhesion and growth of S. *mutans* would be restricted by the smaller quantities of nutrients available for cariogenic bacteria, thereby restraining the progression of caries on surface enamel. Nevertheless, impaction of sticky, glutinous wheat and starchy bean tissues at the gum-line could have led to periodontal disease and the recession of alveolar bone. In addition, unlike small-seeded millets, wheat and barley require extensive grinding. Stone-ground grains would introduce grit particles into the oral cavity, potentially damaging the periodontal tissue and leading to gradual exposure of the dental roots, which are less mineralized than enamel and therefore more susceptible to both demineralization and carious infection.

Our hypothesis that a wheat/barley and legume diet favors the development of carious lesions, specifically on the root and at the cementoenamel junction, is further corroborated by Molnar and Molnar's (1985) analysis of dentitions from Neolithic and Early Metal Age Hungary. That series displayed a pattern of carious infection very similar to what was found in the Xiyasi collection, with a preponderance of caries located on the dental roots and in the area of the cementoenamel junction. During the time frame in question, Eastern European populations also depended primarily on wheat, barley, and various pulses.

Over time, with the development and intensification of agriculture, an increase in caries frequency occurred in Japan, in the frontier area of the Asian mainland, and on the Central Plains of China. For Jomon, there was a significant increase in caries rates between the Middle/Late (3.7 percent) and Late/Final (9.4 percent) pooled series ($\chi^2 = 40.4$, $p < .001$, 1 df). Temple (2007a: 121) attributes this increase to possible changes in subsistence behavior instigated by the climatic instability characteristic of Terminal Jomon. The introduction of wetland rice agriculture during Yayoi led to a further increase in caries rates in some parts of Japan, such as southern Honshu (16.5 percent, $\chi^2 = 45.08$, $p < .001$) and northern Kyushu (11.9 percent, $\chi^2 = 5.36$, $p = .02$), but not on Tanegashima Island (9.7 percent, $\chi^2 = 0.08$, $p = .78$, n.s.), where the transition to wetland rice agriculture seems to have lagged behind (Temple and Larsen 2007).

Overall, caries rates were low in both the Thai and the Vietnamese series (Oxenham 2006; Domett and Tayles 2007), similar to those found for the Middle/Late phases of Jomon in Japan. Tayles and colleagues (2000) attribute low rates of caries in Southeast Asia to the low sucrose content of rice and its consequent low cariogenicity. Contra the argument of Tayles and colleagues (2000), Temple and Larsen (2007) predict that the high starch content of rice would enhance its cariogenicity, by increasing the adhesion of food particles to enamel surfaces. In Japan, consumption of highly processed starchy tubers, such as yam, likely exacerbated problems with oral health by supplying easily fermentable carbohydrates to oral bacteria (Temple 2007a: 173).

An alternative explanation of low caries rates specific to the rice-growing communities of Thailand and Vietnam was developed by Oxenham (2000, 2006: 285), who has argued that in northern Vietnam most rice was exported to imperial China, rather than being consumed locally. In Thailand, wetland rice agriculture was apparently combined with broad-spectrum gardening (O'Connor 1995; White 1995), resulting in a fairly diverse and fiber-rich diet. Consequently, the difference in caries rates between the rice-growing populations of Japan and Southeast Asia may be explained by differences in the relative contributions of noncereal foods to the human diet in the respective areas.

Table 18.5 summarizes differences between males and females in the respective frequencies of carious teeth for the collections considered in this study. As is common in skeletal collections worldwide (Lukacs and Largaespada 2006), frequencies of carious lesions for females were higher than those for males in the overwhelming majority of the series examined. In collections from the Central Plains of China, statistically significant differences between males and females were found only in the chronologically more recent series, including those from Middle/Late Yangshao (Guanjia and Xishan), Longshan (pooled), Erlitou, and the Eastern Zhou collection from Xiyasi. Overall, a more marked decline in oral health through the millennia was manifested on female dentitions than on those of males, which makes it difficult to compare caries rates among skeletal series for which the ratio of males to females is unknown.

Indicators of Acquired Anemia: Porotic Hyperostosis and Cribra Orbitalia

Porotic lesions associated with thickening of the bones of the cranial vault—porotic hyperostosis and cribra orbitalia—are commonly recognized as manifestations of red bone marrow hyperplasia in response to anemia, whether acquired or congenital (Hill and Armelagos 1990; Hershkovitz et al. 1997; Hill 2001: 30). Other conditions, including vitamin C deficiency, age-related osteoporosis, and even the normal growth of cranial bones may result in mild porotic lesions that can be confused with porotic hyperostosis (El-Najjar 1979; Ortner and Putschar 1985; Ortner et al. 1999; Schultz 2001; Walker et al. 2009). Nevertheless, a recent reevaluation of clinical studies suggests that elevated erythropoietic activity due to iron-deficiency anemia is a very likely cause of porotic hyperostosis lesions on the cranial bones (Oxenham and Cavill 2010).

The low iron content of all cereals and limited absorption of nonchelated plant iron in the intestines were likely responsible for an increase in anemia indicators for many prehistoric populations experiencing a transition to cereal agriculture. In a number of fishing communities, this condition may have resulted from contracting intestinal parasites from fish and from upstream neighbors, as intestinal parasites apparently can also produce severe iron-deficiency anemia (Walker 1985; Blom et al. 2005). Elevated frequencies of anemia indicators have also been documented in skeletal series from large, overcrowded settlements, with their implications of poor sanitation (Kent 1986; Facchini et al. 2004).

Table 18.6 summarizes the frequencies of porotic hyperostosis and cribra orbitalia in those skeletal series from East and Southeast Asia. From this table, it can be seen that small sample size, especially with respect to juveniles, is a major impediment to interpopulation comparisons. Frequencies of cribra orbitalia ranged from 0 percent to 56 percent, with the highest frequency found in a pooled Western Zhou collection from Shaanxi Province. The range of variation in rates of porotic hyperostosis was similarly high, with the maximal frequency of 50 percent found in the Meishan series (Longshan culture).

According to evidence from cranial series originating on China's Central Plains, there seems to have been a trend toward increasing frequencies of porotic hyperostosis and cribra orbitalia over time. The Peiligang series from Jiahu, with relatively high levels of both porotic hyperostosis and cribra orbitalia (CO = 25 percent, PH = 19 percent) already evident on its human remains from the Early Neolithic, stands apart from the general temporal trend. Frequencies of porotic hyperostosis and cribra orbitalia were very low for the Early Yangshao collections from Beiliu, Jiangzhai, and Shijia. Frequencies increased slightly for the Middle Yangshao collections, Guanjia, Xipo, and particularly Xishan. The Xishan collection evidences significantly higher frequencies of both PH and CO (15.5 percent and 14 percent, respectively) than in earlier Yangshao collections. Three cases of PH in this collection were particularly severe in degree of bone involvement and bone thickening. In chapter 12 of this volume we suggest that living toward the periphery of Yangshao dominion, within the Dawenkou/Yangshao interaction zone, may have placed additional stresses on Xishan residents. Statistically significantly higher frequencies of CO and PH were also found in the collections from more recent time periods.

The pattern of variation in the distribution of anemia indicators across the

Table 18.6. Frequencies of porotic hyperostosis and cribra orbitalia in skeletal collections from East and Southeast Asia

Collection	Cribra orbitalia						Porotic hyperostosis		
	Juveniles (0–15)			Adults (15+)			Adults (15+)		
	#	Aff.	%	#	Aff.	%	#	Aff.	%
Middle to Final Jomon[a]	24	12	50.0	209	18	8.6			
Yayoi[a]	33	17	51.5	111	11	9.9			
Frontier area[b]									
Nomadic pastoralists	74	17	23.0	190	22	11.6	198	4	2.0
Agropastoralists	30	11	36.7	306	20	6.5	332	3	0.9
Agricultural	4	0	0å	22	1	4.5	22	0	0
Taojiazhai				75	18	24.0	77	15	19.5
Central Plains[c]									
Jiahu				28	7	25.0	37	7	18.9
Beiliu				6	0	0	6	0	0
Jiangzhai	6	1	16.7	28	5	17.9	28	0	0
Shijia	5	1	20.0	38	1	2.6	39	9	2.3
Guanjia	6	6	100.0	31	4	12.9	37	4	11
Xipo	2	0	0	21	3	14	23	2	8
Xishan				43	6	14	45	7	15.5
Meishan	7	0	0	6	3	50	6	3	50
Mengzhuang				5	2	40	7	1	14
Nanzhai				8	2	25	12	4	33
Western Zhou				18	10	56	18	8	44
Xiyasi				51	13	25	61	9	15
Tang dynasty				12	4	33	12	3	25
Thailand									
Khok Phanom Di[d]	13	10	77	57	3	5			
Non Nok Tha:[e]									
Early	9	0	0	31	6	19			
Late	2	0	0	27	1	4			
Ban Chiang:[e]									
Early	9	5	56	23	2	9			
Late	6	1	17	10	4	40			

[a] Based on Temple 2007a.
[b] Based on Eng 2007.
[c] Based on Pechenkina et al. 2007; this study.
[d] Based on Tayles 1996.
[e] Based on Douglas and Pietrusewsky 2007.

Chinese Central Plains collections raises several questions, which will be answered only by results from future exploration of larger skeletal series that include the remains of both adults and subadults. It is not clear what factors were primarily responsible for a generally steady increase in rates of porotic hyperostosis through the Middle to Late Neolithic and into the early Bronze Age. If, as we have suggested for the pastoral and agropastoral populations of the frontier, intestinal parasites contracted from domestic animals were an important factor in determining the prevalence of anemia, then fairly high rates of anemia would be expected for the cranial series dating to Early Yangshao, as pig tending was already well established by that time. It is possible that relatively low population density during Early Yangshao still permitted sufficient access to unpolluted fresh water to ameliorate the adverse effects of close contact with domesticated animals.

Cranial series from the frontier area of China also seem to suggest that neither increasing reliance on cereal products nor increasing sedentism affected the likelihood of suffering iron deficiency anemia: frequencies of cribra orbitalia and porotic hyperostosis for the agricultural populations from Inner Mongolia were very low (CO = 5 percent, PH = 0 percent) (Eng 2007). However, the crania of nomadic pastoralists displayed a somewhat elevated frequency of cribra orbitalia (23 percent of juvenile crania and 12 percent of adult crania). Among agropastoralists, the frequency of this pathology was especially high for subadults (37 percent) and moderate for adults (7 percent) (Eng 2007). It is tempting to speculate that the elevated frequencies of anemia for nomadic pastoralists and agropastoralists inferred from the frequencies of cribra orbitalia were caused by contracting intestinal parasites carried by domesticated herbivores. This inference is supported by evidence of relatively high frequencies of cribra orbitalia (28.7 percent) for the Chandman cranial series from Bronze Age western Mongolia (Bazarsad 2007). The degree of mobility of the people whose skeletons constitute the Chandman series, as well as the array of domesticated animals they herded, likely were analogous to the lifestyles of the people included in Eng's nomadic pastoralist pooled sample.

A large proportion of the pooled agriculturalist sample reported on in Eng's (2007) dissertation was derived from Miaozigou, a Neolithic archaeological site. Therefore, the low rate of anemia indicators found for this sample is not surprising, given the relatively low density of human population during that time. At the same time, continuing reliance for food on both wild and domestic animals, as well as on aquatic resources, as suggested by the faunal assemblage from this site (Inner Mongolia Archaeology Research Institute 2003: 599–600), would have enabled sufficient consumption of dietary iron.

Contrary to an expectation of increased anemia levels with a greater reliance on agricultural products, accompanied by population growth, samples from some geographical areas considered here evidence an opposing trend in the distribution of anemia indicators; in other areas there was no change over time at all. For instance, in skeletal series from the Japanese archipelago, frequencies of cribra orbitalia were high for juvenile crania from both Jomon and Yayoi (50.0–51.5 percent), with no statistically significant difference between the two periods (Temple 2007a). Among the adult crania from Japan, frequencies of this skeletal marker were moderate (8.6–9.9 percent), again with no difference between Jomon and Yayoi (Temple 2007a; see also chapter 14), suggesting that the transition to wetland rice agriculture did not have a marked impact on the prevalence of anemia. Similar to the case of findings reported by Liu and colleagues (chapter 17) for a Taiwanese population, intestinal parasites contracted from marine foods by coastal people during both Japanese cultural phases appear to have largely determined high rates of anemia, regardless of the degree of reliance on agricultural products.

For Southeast Asia, interpretation of porotic hyperostosis and cribra orbitalia is complicated by the presence of congenital hemoglobinopathias, which in malaria risk areas provide resistance to plasmodium infection and consequently are selected for (Allison 1954). Congenital anemias are often expressed on crania by severe cribra orbitalia or porotic hyperostosis (Tayles 1996). Of 30 juveniles from Khok Phanom Di exhibiting signs of cribra orbitalia, Tayles attributes 10 cases to genetic anemia, based on both the severity of the lesions and the concomitant skeletal pathology.

Juvenile series from other Southeast Asian archaeological sites are too small to lend conclusive evidence about temporal trends in the prevalence of anemia. Analyses of the Non Nok Tha and Ban Chiang series seem to suggest opposing trajectories in the distribution of this pathology among adults, which Douglas and Pietrusewsky (2007) attributed to different degrees of mobility represented at the two sites. They suggest that the Non Nok Tha assemblage was formed by multiple small, relatively mobile groups, while the Ban Chiang series consisted of multiple generations of a single sedentary population. The frequency of cribra orbitalia was statistically significantly higher for crania dating to late Ban Chiang than for samples from the earlier strata at the same site. This increase in anemia over time at Ban Chiang coincided with a decrease in life expectancy, as estimated from age-at-death distribution across the series (Douglas and Pietrusewsky 2007).

When observations from different parts of both East and Southeast Asia are taken into account, it can be suggested that increasing local population densities, combined with poor sanitation and more intimate contact with domesticated animals serving as reservoirs of intestinal parasites, could explain why Late Neolithic and Early Dynastic series from the Central Plains of China evidence considerably higher rates of anemia than do collections from the earlier Yangshao culture. Contracting intestinal parasites, whether from domesticated herbivores by pastoral peoples in the frontier area of northern China and Mongolia or by the Japanese from fish (Temple 2007a), might have been more important than the other particulars of diet in determining overall frequencies of anemia in those populations. However, it remains unclear why we find so little evidence of parasite-related anemia in either the Miaodigou collection from Inner Mongolia or from a number of Early Yangshao sites on the Chinese Central Plains, despite continuous exposure of those populations to parasites presumably carried by *Sus scrofa* (Furenbratt 2008). The only plausible explanation seems to be a continuing availability of unpolluted water and adequate sanitary conditions in some early agricultural settlements still benefiting from relatively low local population densities.

Finally, the apparent correspondence between increasing sexual dimorphism and diminishing oral health, particularly among females, alongside an increase in PH/CO during the Bronze Age, seems to argue against Stini's (1985) hypothesis that relates increased sexual dimorphism to amelioration of stress removing constraints on male growth. Instead, it appears that an overall increase in physiological stress and increasing reliance on cereal agriculture affected female health more strongly than that of males, likely because concurrent changes in gender defined status limited female access to resources.

Conclusions

Considering the array of different subsistence strategies and their variants practiced in East Asia during the Holocene, it is not surprising that no singular trajectory of health changes can be detected based on the distribution of health markers in skeletal series from this part of the world. Changes in East Asian community health generally followed a distinctive pattern in each ecological setting, contingent on the varied contribution to human subsistence of particular cereals, noncereal cultivars, specific domesticated animals, and wild resources, as well as changes in gender roles and interaction with neighboring communities.

An increase in sexual dimorphism over time was found almost in all subregions, which likely marks the increasing divergence of gender roles. Similarly, in those areas where the frequency of carious teeth increased over time, a gap between male and female oral health also increased, as the teeth of females were affected by caries to a significantly greater degree.

Local reliance on different staple cereals, in conjunction with varied cooking and food processing techniques, apparently resulted in differing distributions of carious lesions on dental crowns. Cooked millet appears to be quite cariogenic. However, its adverse effects on dental health can be ameliorated, provided that other components of the diet are fairly abrasive. This is evidenced by the reasonably good oral health of the Early Yangshao communities that still relied to some degree on foraging and hunting. In comparison with millet, rice appears to be less cariogenic. Nevertheless, when consumed in combination with other starchy foods, rice can lead to an increase in caries, as evidenced in post-Jomon skeletal series from Japan. Wheat- and barley-rich diets appear to produce a considerable increase in dental root caries, probably because stone grinding of these cereals can introduce grit particles into the mouth that lead to irritation of the gingiva and consequent alveolar recession.

An expected decline in community health with the transition to agriculture in East Asia was clearly evident only in the case of the Central Plains of China; even there, health changes were somewhat diachronic. While an increase in the rate of carious lesions between Early and Middle Yangshao is clear for dental series dated to circa 4000–3000 BC, other changes in health lagged behind staple dependence on millet agriculture and domesticated pigs. A shift toward wheat and barley as the major crop plants and the introduction of domesticated soybeans during the Bronze Age apparently had positive effects on at least some aspects of community health, as suggested by taller adult statures estimated for the Eastern Zhou skeletal series.

Increasing achieved adult stature in the pastoral and agropastoral communities of the northern Chinese frontier suggests that nutrition status was improved by increasing reliance on domesticated herbivores. At the same time, a fairly high rate of anemia markers on Bronze and Iron Age crania from this same area suggests diminished standards of sanitation and a consequent increase in parasitic loads. A transition to rice agriculture in Southeast Asia also does not seem to have led to an overall decline in community health. Increasing achieved adult stature over time in Thailand actually points to improved nutritional status with the intensification of farming, while the frequency of anemia increased in some areas and diminished in others, probably in accord with the historical ecological particulars of the local settings.

For the Japanese archipelago, there were considerable differences in health status between coastal and inland populations, not surprising given their differing access to marine resources and differing degrees of dependence on cultivated and wild plants. Although deterioration in oral health from Jomon to Yayoi was considerable, progressively increasing reliance on farming does not seem to have had any discernible effect on the prevalence of anemia. Adult stature increased rapidly during Early Yayoi, most likely as a consequence of significant migration from continental East Asia.

Considering the trends in East Asian community health suggested in this paper, it is important to keep in mind that our reconstructions still rely on minuscule sample sizes and are therefore tentative. Moreover, precise identification of the underlying factors that shaped some aspects of these changing trajectories in East Asian community health remains elusive. Future analysis of larger skeletal samples and their archaeological contexts, with broader geographical coverage and increased time depth, will be required to validate these apparent patterns.

Literature Cited

Aikens CM, Higuchi T. 1982. *Prehistory of Japan*. New York: Academic Press.

Aires CP, Tabchoury CP, Del Bel Cury AA, Koo H, Cury JA. 2006. Effect of sucrose concentration on dental biofilm formed in situ and on enamel demineralization. *Caries Research* 40: 28–32.

Allan W. 1970. Ecology, techniques and settlement patterns. In: Ucko PH, Tringham R, Dimbleby GW, editors. *Man, settlement and urbanism*. London: Duckworth. Pp. 211–26.

Allison AC. 1954. Protection afforded by sickle-cell trait against subtertian malarial infection. *British Medical Journal* 4857: 290–94.

Barfield TJ. 1993. *The nomadic alternative*. Englewood Cliffs, NJ: Prentice Hall.

Bazarsad N. 2007. Iron-deficiency anemia in early Mongolian nomads. In: Cohen MN, Crane-Kramer GMM, editors. *Ancient health: Skeletal indicators of agricultural and economic intensification*. Gainesville: University Press of Florida. Pp. 250–54.

Blom DE, Buikstra JE, Tomczak PD, Keng L, Shoreman E, Stevens-Tuttle D. 2005. Anemia and childhood mortality: Latitudinal patterning along the coast of pre-Columbian Peru. *American Journal of Physical Anthropology* 127: 152–69.

Bocquet-Appel JP, Naji S. 2006. Testing the hypothesis of a world wide Neolithic demographic transition. *Current Anthropology* 47: 341–66.

Bogin B. 1999. *Patterns of human growth*. 2nd ed. Cambridge: Cambridge University Press.

Bowlby J. 1969. *Attachment and loss*. Vol. 1: *Attachment*. New York: Basic Books.

Brace CL, Nagai M. 1982. Japanese tooth size: past and present. *American Journal of Physical Anthropology* 59: 399–411.

Chen S. 1980. *Osteology for Medical Examiners* (法医骨学). Beijing: Public Publishing House.

Chisholm B, Koike H, Nakai N. 1992. Carbon isotopic determination of paleodiet in Japan: Marine versus terrestrial resources. In: Aikens CM, Nai Rhee S, editors. *Pacific Northeast Asia in prehistory: Hunter-fisher-gatherers, farmers, and sociopolitical elites*. Pullman: Washington State University Press. Pp. 69–74.

Cohen MN, Armelagos GJ, editors. 1984. *Paleopathology at the origins of agriculture*. Orlando, FL: Academic Press.

Cohen MN, Crane-Kramer GMM, editors. 2007. *Ancient health: Skeletal indicators of agricultural and economic intensification.* Gainesville: University Press of Florida.

Crawford GW. 1983. *Paleoethnobotany of the Kameda Peninsula Jomon.* Ann Arbor: Museum of Anthropology, University of Michigan.

Crawford GW. 2006. East Asian plant domestication. In: Stark ML, editor. *Archaeology of Asia.* Malden, MA: Blackwell. Pp. 77–95.

Crawford GW. 2008. The Jomon in early agriculture discourse: issues arising from Matsui, Kanehara, and Pearson. *World Archaeology* 40: 445–65.

Crawford GW, Hurley W, Yoshizaki M. 1976. Implications of plant remains from the Early Jomon Hamanasuno Site, Hokkaido. *Asian Perspectives* 19: 145–55.

Crawford GW, Lee G. 2003. Agricultural origins in the Korean Peninsula. *Antiquity* 77: 87–95.

Cury JA, Francisco SB, Del Bel Cury AA, Tabchoury CP. 2000. In situ study of sucrose exposure, mutans streptococci in dental plaque and dental caries. *Brazilian Dental Journal* 12: 101–4.

D'Andrea AC, Crawford GW, Yoshizaki M, Kudo T. 1995. Late Jomon cultigens in northeastern Japan. *Antiquity* 69: 146–52.

Di Cosmo N. 1994. Ancient Inner Asian nomads: Their economic basis and its significance in Chinese history. *The Journal of Asian Studies* 53: 1092–1126.

Domett KM. 2001. *Health in late prehistoric Thailand.* BAR International Series no. 946. Oxford, UK: Archaeopress.

Domett K, Tayles N. 2007. Population health from the Bronze to the Iron Age in the Mun River valley, northeastern Thailand. In: Cohen MN, Crane-Kramer GMM, editors. *Ancient health: Skeletal indicators of agricultural and economic intensification.* Gainesville: University Press of Florida. Pp. 286–99.

Douglas MT, Pietrusewsky M. 2007. Biological consequences of sedentism: Agricultural intensification in northeast Thailand. In: Cohen MN, Crane-Kramer GMM, editors. *Ancient health: skeletal indicators of agricultural and economic intensification.* Gainesville: University Press of Florida. Pp. 300–319.

El-Najjar M. 1979. Human treponematosis and tuberculosis: Evidence from the New World. *American Journal of Physical Anthropology* 51: 599–618.

Eng JT. 2007. Nomadic pastoralists and the Chinese empire: A bioarchaeological study of China's northern frontier. Ph.D. dissertation, University of California, Santa Barbara.

Erdal YS, Duyar I. 1999. A new correction procedure for calibrating dental caries frequency. *American Journal of Physical Anthropology* 108: 237–40.

Eshed V, Gopher A, Hershkovitz I. 2006. Tooth wear and dental pathology at the advent of agriculture: New evidence from the Levant. *American Journal of Physical Anthropology* 130: 145–59.

Facchini F, Rastelli E, Brasili P. 2004. Cribra orbitalia and cribra cranii in Roman skeletal remains from the Ravenna area and Rimini (I–IV century AD). *International Journal of Osteoarcheology* 14: 126–36.

FAO. 1972. *Food composition table for use in East Asia.* Rome: Food Policy and Nutrition Division, Food and Agriculture Organization of the United Nations.

Fitzgerald RJ, Keyes PH. 1963. Ecologic factors in dental caries: The fate of antibiotic-resistant cariogenic streptococci in hamsters. *American Journal of Pathology* 42: 759–72.

Fuji A. 1960. On the relation of limb bone length to stature. *Bulletin of School of Physical Education* (Juntendo University) 3: 49–61.

Fully G. 1956. Une nouvelle methode de determination de la taille. *Annales de Medecine Legale, Criminologie, Police Scientifique et Toxicologie* 35: 266–73.

Furenbratt M. 2008. The prevalence of parasites of wild boar (*Sus scrofa*) in faeces: A pilot study in Sweden. University of Halmstad. Unpublished essay.

Geddes DA. 1994. Diet patterns and caries. *Advances in Dental Research* 8: 221–24.

Goodman AH, Armelagos GJ. 1985. Factors influencing the distribution of enamel hypoplasias within the human permanent dentition. *American Journal of Physical Anthropology* 68: 479–93.

Habu J. 2004. *Ancient Jomon of Japan*. Cambridge: Cambridge University Press.

Hershkovitz I, Rothschild BM, Latimer B, Dutour O, Leonetti G, Greenwald CM, Rothschild C, Jellema LM. 1997. Recognition of sickle cell anemia in skeletal remains of children. *American Journal of Physical Anthropology* 104: 213–26.

Hill MC. 2001. Porotic hyperostosis as an indicator of anemia: An overview of correlation and cause. Ph.D. dissertation, University of Massachusetts, Amherst.

Hill MC, Armelagos GJ. 1990. An evaluation of the biocultural consequences of the Mississippian transformation. In: Dye DH, Cox CA, editors. *Towns and temples along the Mississippi*. Tuscaloosa: University of Alabama Press. Pp. 16–37.

Hillson S. 2001. Recording dental caries in archaeological human remains. *International Journal of Osteoarchaeology* 11: 249–89.

Holden C, Mace R. 1999. Sexual dimorphism in stature and women's work: A phylogenetic cross-cultural analysis. *American Journal of Physical Anthropology* 110: 27–45.

Imamura K. 1996a. Jomon and Yayoi: The transition to agriculture in Japanese prehistory. In: Harris DR, editor. *The origins of agriculture and pastoralism in Eurasia*. Washington, DC: Smithsonian Institution Press. Pp. 442–64.

Imamura K. 1996b. *Prehistoric Japan: New perspectives on insular East Asia*. Honolulu: University of Hawai'i Press.

Inner Mongolia Archaeology Research Institute. 2003. *Miaozigou and Dabagou: The report of excavation of ancient sites of primitive inhabitant tribes in the New Stone Age*. Vol. 2. Beijing: Encyclopedia of China Publishing House.

Islam B, Khan SN, Khan AU. 2007. Dental caries: From infection to prevention. *Medical Science Monitor* 13: 196–203.

Jackes M, Lubell D, Meiklejohn C. 1997. Healthy but mortal: Human biology and the first farmers of Western Europe. *Antiquity* 71: 639–58.

Johnston FE, Wainer H, Thissen D, MacVean R. 1976. Hereditary and environmental determinants of growth in height in a longitudinal sample of children and youth of Guatemalan and European ancestry. *American Journal of Physical Anthropology* 44: 469–76.

Kanazawa S, Novak D. 2005. Human sexual dimorphism in size may be triggered by environmental cues. *Journal of Biosocial Science* 37: 657–65.

Kent S. 1986. The influence of sedentism and aggregation on porotic hyperostosis and anaemia: A case study. *Man* 21: 605–36.

Larsen CS. 1987. Bioarchaeological interpretations of subsistence economy and behavior from human skeletal remains. In: Schiffer MB, editor. *Advances in archaeological method and theory*. New York: Academic Press. Pp. 339–445.

Larsen CS. 1997. *Bioarchaeology: Interpreting behavior from the human skeleton*. Cambridge: Cambridge University Press.

Larsen CS, Shavit R, Griffins MC. 1991. Dental caries evidence for dietary change: an archaeological context. In: Kelley MA, Larsen CS, editors. *Advances in dental anthropology*. New York: Wiley-Liss. Pp. 179–202.

Lee G, Crawford G, Chen X. 2007. Plants and people from the Early Neolithic to Shang periods in North China. *Proceedings of the National Academy of Sciences* 104: 1087–92.

Leutenegger W, Kelly JT. 1977. Relationship of sexual dimorphism in canine size and body size to social, behavioral, and ecological correlates in anthropoid primates. *Primates* 18: 117–36.

Li Fajun. 2004. An examination of the human skeletons at Neolithic site of Jiangjialiang, Yangyuan, Hebei Province, China (河北阳原姜家梁新石器时代人骨研究). Ph.D. thesis, Jilin University.

Lu T. 1999. *The transition from foraging to farming and the origin of agriculture in China.* BAR International Series 774. Oxford: British Archaeological Reports.

Lu T. 2002. A green foxtail (*Setaria viridis*) cultivation experiment in the middle Yellow River valley and some related issues. *Asian Perspectives* 41: 1–14.

Lukacs JR, Largaespada LL. 2006. Explaining sex differences in dental caries prevalence: Saliva, hormones, and "life-history" etiologies. *American Journal of Human Biology* 18: 540–55.

Luoyang Archaeological Team of Culture and Relics. 2002. *Luoyang Zaojiaoshu: Excavation report on Erlitou settlement site of Zaojiaoshu, Luoyang, between 1992 and 1993.* Beijing: Science Press.

Ma X. 2005. *Emergent social complexity in the Yangshao culture: Analyses of settlement patterns and faunal remains from Lingbao, Western Henan, China (c. 4900–3000 BC).* Oxford: Archaeopress.

Matsui A. 1996. Archaeological investigation of anadromous salmon fishing in Japan. *World Archaeology* 27: 444–60.

Matsui A, Kanehara M. 2006. The question of prehistoric plant husbandry during the Jomon period in Japan. *World Archaeology* 38: 259–73.

Molnar S. 1992. *Human variation: Races, types, and ethnic groups.* Englewood Cliffs, NJ: Prentice Hall.

Molnar S, Molnar I. 1985. Observations of dental diseases among prehistoric populations of Hungary. *American Journal of Physical Anthropology* 67: 51–63.

Nakahashi T. 1995. Temporal craniometric changes from the Jomon to the Modern period in western Japan. *American Journal of Physical Anthropology* 90: 409–25.

Nakahashi T, Minchang L, Yamaguchi B. 2002. Anthropological study on the cranial measurements of the human remains from Jiangnan region, China. In: Nakahashi T, Minchang L, editors. *Ancient people in the Jiangnan region, China: Anthropological study on the origin of the Yayoi people in northern Kyushu.* Kyushu: Kyushu University Press. Pp. 17–33.

O'Connor RA. 1995. Agricultural change and ethnic succession in Southeast Asian states: A case for regional anthropology. *Journal of Asian Studies* 54: 968–96.

Oda S, Keally CT. 1986. A critical look at the Palaeolithic and "Lower Palaeolithic" research in Miyagi Prefecture, Japan. *Journal of the Anthropological Society of Nippon* 94: 325–61.

Ono A, Sato H, Tsutsumi T, Kudo Y. 2002. Radiocarbon dates and archaeology of the Late Pleistocene in the Japanese islands. *Radiocarbon* 44: 477–94.

Ortner DJ, Kimmerle EH, Diez M. 1999. Probable evidence of scurvy in subadults from archeological sites in Peru. *American Journal of Physical Anthropology* 108: 321–31.

Ortner DJ, Putschar WGJ. 1985. *Identification of pathological conditions in human skeletal remains.* Washington, DC: Smithsonian Institution Press.

Oxenham MF. 2000. Health and behaviour during the Mid-Holocene and Metal period of Northern Viet Nam. Ph.D. dissertation, Northern Territory University.

Oxenham MF. 2006. Biological responses to change in prehistoric Vietnam. *Asian Perspectives* 45: 212–39.

Oxenham MF, Cavill I. 2010. Porotic hyperostosis and cribra orbitalia: The erythropoietic response to iron-deficiency anaemia. *Anthropological Science* 118: 199–200.

Pearson K. 1899. Mathematical contributions to the theory of evolution, V: On the reconstruction of the stature of prehistorical races. *Philosophical Transactions of the Royal Society of London*, Series A, 192: 169–244.

Pechenkina EA, Ambrose SH, Ma X, Benfer RA Jr. 2005. Reconstructing northern Chinese Neolithic subsistence practices by isotopic analysis. *Journal of Archaeological Science* 32: 1176–89.

Pechenkina EA, Benfer RA Jr. 2002. The role of occlusal stress and gingival infection in the formation of exostoses on mandible and maxilla from Neolithic China. *Homo* 53: 112–30.

Pechenkina EA, Benfer RA Jr., Ma X. 2007. Diet and health in the Neolithic of the Wei and middle Yellow River basins, northern China. In: Cohen MN, Crane-Kramer GMM, editors. *Ancient health: Skeletal indicators of agricultural and economic intensification*. Gainesville: University Press of Florida. Pp. 255–72.

Pechenkina EA, Benfer RA Jr., Wang Z. 2002. Diet and health changes at the end of the Chinese Neolithic: The Yangshao/Longshan transition in Shaanxi province. *American Journal of Physical Anthropology* 117: 15–36.

Pietrusewsky M. 1999. Multivariate craniometric investigations of Japanese, Asians, and Pacific Islanders. In: Omoto K, editor. *Interdisciplinary perspectives on the origins of the Japanese*. Proceedings of the 11th International Symposium of the International Research Center for Japanese Studies, Kyoto 1996. Pp. 65–104.

Pinhasi R, Stock JT, editors. 2011. *Human bioarchaeology of the transition to agriculture*. Chichester, UK: Wiley-Blackwell. Pp. 235–64.

Rhen T, Cidlowski JA. 2005. Antiinflammatory action of glucocorticoids—New mechanisms for old drugs. *New England Journal of Medicine* 353: 1711–23.

Rose JC, Marks MK, Tieszen LL. 1991. Bioarchaeology and subsistence in the central and lower portions of the Mississippi Valley. In: Powell ML, Bridges PS, Mires AMW, editors. *What mean these bones? Studies in southeastern bioarchaeology*. Tuscaloosa: University of Alabama Press. Pp. 7–21.

Rudney JD, Katz RV, Brand JW. 1983. Interobserver reliability of methods for paleopathological diagnosis of dental caries. *American Journal of Physical Anthropology* 62: 243–48.

Sangvichien SJ, Srisurin V, Walthanayingsakol V. 1985. Estimation of stature of Thai and Chinese from the length of femur, tibia, and fibula. *Siriraj Hospital Gazette* 37: 85.

Sangvichien SJ, Srisurin V, Wattanayinsakul V, Theerarattakul P, Rakvanichpong S. n.d. Equations for estimation of the Thai's stature from the length of long bones. Preliminary report. Department of Anatomy, Faculty of Medicine, Siriraj Hospital, Mahidol University. Pp. 11–13.

Sato Y. 1999. Origin and dissemination of cultivated rice in Asia. In: Omoto K, editor. *Interdisciplinary perspectives on the origins of the Japanese*. Proceedings of the 11th International Symposium of the International Research Center for Japanese Studies, Kyoto 1996. Pp. 143–53.

Schollmeyer KG, Turner CG II. 2004. Dental caries, prehistoric diet, and the Pithouse to Pueblo transition in southwestern Colorado. *American Antiquity* 69: 569–82.

Schultz M. 2001. Paleohistopathology of bone: A new approach to the study of ancient diseases. *American Journal of Physical Anthropology* 33: 106–47.

Shao X. 1985. *Handbook of body measurement* (人体测量手册). Shanghai: Shanghai Dictionary Publishing House.

Shelton DR, Lee WJ. 2000. Cereal carbohydrates. In: Kulp K, Ponte JG, editors. *Handbook of cereal science and technology*. 2nd ed. New York: Marcel Dekker. Pp. 385–416.

Shen S, Samaranayake LP, Yip HK. 2004. In vitro growth, acidogenicity and cariogenicity of predominant human root caries flora. *Journal of Dentistry* 32: 667–78.

Smith BD. 2007. Niche construction and the behavioral context of plant and animal domestication. *Evolutionary Anthropology* 16: 188–99.

Smith BL. 2005. Diet, health, and lifestyle in Neolithic North China. Ph.D. dissertation, Harvard University.

Stevenson PH. 1929. On racial differences in stature long bone regression formula, with special reference to stature reconstruction formulae for the Chinese. *Biometrika* 21: 303–18.

Stini WA. 1971. Evolutionary implications of changing nutritional patterns in human populations. *American Anthropologist* 73: 1019–30.

Stini WA. 1985. Growth rates and sexual dimorphism in evolutionary perspective. In: Gilbert RI, Mielke JH, editors. *The analysis of prehistoric diets.* Orlando, FL: Academic Press. Pp. 191–222.

Stinson S. 1985. Sex differences in environmental sensitivity during growth and development. *Yearbook of Physical Anthropology* 28: 123–47.

Stinson S. 2000. Growth variation: Biological and cultural factors. In: Stinson S, Bogin B, Huss-Ashmore R, O'Rourke D, editors. *Human biology: An evolutionary and biocultural perspective.* New York: Wiley-Liss. Pp. 425–65.

Tayles N. 1996. Anemia, genetic diseases, and malaria in prehistoric mainland Southeast Asia. *American Journal of Physical Anthropology* 101: 11–27.

Tayles N, Domett KM, Nelson K. 2000. Agriculture and dental caries? The case of rice in prehistoric Southeast Asia. *World Archaeology* 32: 68–83.

Temple DH. 2007a. Human biological variation during the agricultural transition in prehistoric Japan. Ph.D. dissertation, Ohio State University.

Temple DH. 2007b. Dietary variation and stress among prehistoric Jomon foragers from Japan. *American Journal of Physical Anthropology* 133: 1035–46.

Temple DH. 2008. What can stature variation reveal about environmental differences between prehistoric Jomon foragers? Understanding the impact of systemic stress on developmental stability. *American Journal of Human Biology* 20: 431–39.

Temple DH, Larsen CS. 2007. Dental caries prevalence as evidence for agriculture and subsistence variation during the Yayoi period in prehistoric Japan: Biocultural interpretations of an economy in transition. *American Journal of Physical Anthropology* 134: 501–12.

Trivers RL. 1972. Parental investment and sexual selection. In: Campbell B, editor. *Sexual selection and the descent of man: 1871–1971.* Chicago: Aldine. Pp. 136–79.

Trotter M, Gleser GC. 1958. A re-evaluation of estimation of stature based on measurements of stature taken during life and of long bones after death. *American Journal of Physical Anthropology* 16: 79–123.

Tsude H. 2001. Yayoi farmers reconsidered: New perspectives on agricultural development in East Asia. *Bulletin of the Indo-Pacific Prehistory Association* 5: 53–59.

Turner CG II. 1979. Dental anthropological indications of agriculture among the Jomon people of central Japan. *American Journal of Physical Anthropology* 51: 619–36.

Turner CG II. 1990. Major features of Sundadonty and Sinodonty, including suggestions about East Asian microevolution, population history, and Late Pleistocene relationships with Australian Aboriginals. *American Journal of Physical Anthropology* 82: 295–317.

Walker PL. 1985. Anemia among prehistoric Indians of the American Southwest. In: Merbs CF, Miller RJ, editors. *Health and disease in the prehistoric Southwest.* Arizona State University Anthropological Research Papers 34. Tempe. Pp. 139–64.

Walker PL, Bathurst RR, Richman R, Gjerdrum T, Andrushko VA. 2009. The causes of porotic hyperostosis and cribra orbitalia: A reappraisal of the iron-deficiency-anemia hypothesis. *American Journal of Physical Anthropology* 139: 109–25.

Wesolowski V. 2006. Caries prevalence in skeletal series—is it possible to compare? *Memórias Do Instituto Oswaldo Cruz, Rio de Janeiro* 101: 139–45.

White JC. 1995. Modeling the development of early rice agriculture: Ethnoecological perspectives from northeast Thailand. *Asian Perspectives* 34: 37–68.

Xie J. 1972. The bases of Xiongnu subsistence. *Zhongyang Yanjiuyuan Minzuxue Yanjiusuo Jikan* 32: 163–90.

Yan W. 1992. Origins of agriculture and animal husbandry in China. In: Aikens CM, Rhee SN, editors. *Pacific Northeast Asia in prehistory: Hunter-fisher-gatherers, farmers, and sociopolitical elites.* Pullman: Washington State University Press. Pp. 113–23.

Yan W. 2005. The beginning of farming. In: Allan S, editor. *The formation of Chinese civilization: An archaeological perspective.* New Haven, CT: Yale University and New World Press. Pp. 27–42.

Yuan J, Flad RK. 2002. Pig domestication in ancient China. *Antiquity* 76: 724–32.

Zhang J. 2008. The research on the human Skeletons of Han and Jin dynasties from Taojiazhai graveyard in Xining city of Qinghai Province. Ph.D. dissertation, Jilin University.

Zhao Z. 2002. What was the staple crop in Shang agriculture. *Research Center for Ancient Civilization, Chinese Academy of Social Sciences* (中国古代文明研究中心) 3: 52.

Zhao Z, He N. 2006. Results and analysis of 2002 soil sample flotation from Taosi. *Kaogu* (考古) 5: 77–90.

Zohary D, Hopf M. 2001. *Domestication of plants in the Old World: The origin and spread of cultivated plants in West Asia, Europe, and the Nile Valley.* Oxford: Oxford University Press.

19

East Asian Bioarchaeology

Major Trends in a Temporally, Genetically,
and Eco-Culturally Diverse Region

MARC OXENHAM AND KATE PECHENKINA

One of the most significant aspects of this volume is the breadth of coverage of what is a vast and extremely complex region of the globe: mainland and insular East Asia. Moreover, this is the first attempt at collating such a diverse set of bioarchaeological studies of the region by scholars from very different schools of thought; the areas of interest range from Xinjiang and Mongolia on the one hand to central China and Manchuria, as well as the Japanese archipelago and Taiwan, on the other. A synthesis implies the exploration of large-scale trends that might otherwise be lost in the detail of individual contributions. This is a big task in any endeavor, and while we are unsure whether we will meet everyone's expectations, we believe this final chapter will draw together the various and disparate bioarchaeological threads, often scattered across a broad geographic and culturally diverse landscape, into a more or less coherent form.

Movement of Human Populations

One of the major themes of this volume is the exploration of population history in the wide area defined as our study region. Clearly the most detailed analyses concern three major subregions: the northern peripheral zones of China (Xinjiang through Mongolia, southern Siberia, and Manchuria, as well as eastern Siberia), discussed in chapters 3, 4, and 5 by Lee, Tumen, and Erdene, respectively; the Japanese archipelago, explored by Pietrusewsky in chapter 7; and finally the relationship between Northeast and Southeast Asia, as detailed by Pietrusewsky and by Matsumura and Oxenham in chapter 8.

Lee, in discussing the population history of mainland North and Northeast Asia using epigenetic traits, suggests that each broad temporal period from the Bronze Age through the Medieval period was characterized by different patterns of inter- and intraregional population dynamics. She argues for a long history of essentially Asian and European genetic interaction, beginning at least as early as the Bronze Age. Moreover, relatively elevated levels of population movement and interaction appear to have characterized the Bronze Age. In examining Lee's data we suggest that more circumscribed spheres of human interaction are potentially illuminated. For instance, the Bronze Age dendrogram (chapter 3, fig. 3.2) shows what at face value would seem like a tight clustering of three apparently geographically unlikely groups: Shang-Zhou (from the Central Plains), closely grouped with Xindian (Western Regions), and with Xiajiadian (Manchuria) as a somewhat more distant companion. Nonetheless, the Shang (Henan Province), Zhou (Shanxi Province) and Xindian (Qinghai and Gansu Provinces) are geographically proximate, with a shared genetic heritage in the Bronze Age not an unexpected finding. Furthermore, Xiajiadian (southeastern Inner Mongolia and northern Hebei) is not particularly geographically distant from the Shang-Zhou and Xindian samples, making a relatively close genetic relationship with these samples a reasonable finding. The second major clustering occurs between the Northern Zone (Slab Grave) and western Mongolia (Chandman). The Slab Grave culture samples are quite dispersed throughout the Northern Zone (essentially Mongolia), while the Chandman sample in fact derives from western Mongolia. Again, with some further resolution regarding the exact nature of the Slab Grave culture samples, a close resemblance to the Chandman sample does not necessarily indicate widespread population mobility and genetic exchange.

Regarding the Manchurian and western zone clusterings, as well as the isolated Central Plains group found in the Iron Age, we agree with Lee that this may be evidence for reduced population movement in the face of the emergence of large sociopolitical entities at that time. However, it may be useful to explore alternative reasons for the apparent fragmentation argued for the Medieval period. There is a close association between the only Central Plains sample (Zhenzishan, arguably Inner Mongolian or Manchurian) and the Manchurian sample from Qidan. However, the Manchurian Wanggu and northern zone Mongol samples are quite distant from each other and the Zhenzishan-Qidan cluster. Little can be said regarding the single, and isolated, northern zone sample. The main evidence for Lee's fragmentation lies in the large separation between the Manchurian samples from Qidan and Wanggu. Whatever the reason for this, a much larger data set is required before Medieval Manchurian population dynamics can be elucidated.

An interesting pattern seen in Tumen's craniometric analysis of North and Northeast Asian samples devolves from distinct geographic clusterings, particularly in the Neolithic and Xiongnu periods. In the Neolithic, there is a clear east–west divide with western Mongolian and southern Siberian samples (just to the northwest of Mongolia) on the one hand and eastern Mongolian and southern Siberian (just to the north and east of Mongolia) on the other. Furthermore, a distinct northern central Chinese clustering is seen, with offshoots of this population in Korea.

While an east–west division is maintained in the Bronze/Iron Ages in Mongolia, the situation is much more complex in the sample-rich southern Siberian region to the north of Mongolia. Southern Siberia at this time can be characterized as displaying a high degree of cranio-morphological diversity. By the Xiongnu period the picture has changed considerably, with a homogenization of the Mongolian population from west to east and a similar homogenization of the southern Siberian populations.

Erdene, like Lee, employed cranial nonmetric traits to explore aspects of the population history of Mongolia, in particular, from Neolithic to modern times. When the Mongolian samples are dealt with separately, with the exception of the inclusion of the Korean comparative data set, there is a clear dichotomization into Bronze/Iron Age and Neolithic on the one hand and Xiongnu, Mongolian period, and modern Mongolian on the other hand. This early versus late Mongolian separation is maintained even when a much larger comparative sample is included, although the Neolithic Mongolian sample appears to cluster with populations to the north of Mongolia, from Xinjiang in the west to what are essentially Manchurians in the east.

Nonetheless, it needs to be noted that Erdene's Neolithic Mongolian sample is extremely small and not likely to be representative of this period and region. What is particularly intriguing is that Erdene's analysis suggests the presence of four cohesive populations, linked more by geographic propinquity than anything else: (1) a Mongolian cluster limited to the modern geographic confines of Mongolia; (2) a south of Siberia/Xinjiang grouping (just to the south of Mongolia) with an outlier in northern Siberia (Yakut); (3) a population limited in geographic scope to the Japanese archipelago; and (4) a geographically dispersed grouping extending from southern to northern and even eastern Siberia. At least regarding the population history of Mongolia, Erdene's analysis could be seen as support for a great deal of cohesiveness in Mongolian genetic history over a vast period of time, something not supported by the analyses of either Lee or Tumen. An intriguing feature of Erdene's analysis is the ostensibly close similarity between her Mongolian and Korean samples. Yet the apparent link between these two groups is not unexpected when considering Riotto's (2009) extensive review of historical sources, which suggest extensive cultural, and perhaps genetic, exchange between the Xiongnu and the ancient Korean kingdom of Goguryeo. This is clearly an area that requires more research.

In distinction to the work by Lee, Tumen, and Erdene, Pietrusewsky (chapter 7) focuses his attention on the population history of Japan, as well as addressing the topical and current debate over the origins of modern Southeast Asian people. Matsumura and Oxenham (chapter 8) also concentrate their attention on this latter issue in exploring the competing models of regional continuity (supported by Pietrusewsky) and population replacement in Southeast Asia (which they support).

Pietrusewsky provides convincing support for the consensus view of a close biological relationship between Jomon and modern Ainu peoples, although he finds little evidence for a close relationship between Jomon and Ainu on the one hand and Ryuku Islanders on the other. Nonetheless, his results clearly support a model that sees the ultimate origins of all Japanese in North/Northeast Asia, rather than Southeast Asia.

Suzuki's (chapter 6) review of the evidence for tuberculosis (TB) is also of relevance in this discussion. While Suzuki argues that there is evidence for TB in East Asia beginning approximately 4000 years BP, the first clear evidence for its presence in the Japanese archipelago dates from as recently as less than 2500 years ago, during the Yayoi period migrations originating in mainland East Asia. Nonetheless, the lack of evidence for TB in Jomon period populations may not necessarily be surprising, with clear evidence for TB in the Americas dating to around 2000 BP (Allison et al. 1981) or perhaps as early as 3700–3300 BC (Rathbun et al. 1980), and with the disease having likely being introduced to the Americas by the first colonists well over 10,000 years ago. TB also has a low frequency of skeletal involvement (1 percent), at least in modern clinical settings (Aufderheide and Rodriguez-Martin 1998: 133) and, given its association with crowding (Johnston 1993), can survive in small communities with appropriate levels of close contact; large population size is not a requirement.

Wilbur and colleagues (2008) have proposed an explanatory model that links the availability of dietary protein and iron to immune function in response to *Mycobacterial* infection. They make a set of predictions regarding the likelihood of osseous tuberculosis in terms of a population's dietary status and furthermore make predictions regarding the likelihood of osseous tuberculosis based on observed frequencies of carious lesions and indicators of iron deficiency anemia in adults (i.e., unremodeled cribra orbitalia and cribra cranii; see Oxenham and Cavill 2010 for a recent discussion of the role of iron deficiency in the formation of these lesions). Following their model, dissemination of *Mycobacteria* into the skeletal tissue and survival long enough to elicit lesion formation is expected either in populations with adequate intake of both iron and protein (Wilbur's category 1) or, in contrast, deficient in both (Wilbur's category 4). Early cases of tuberculosis in East Asia (Suzuki and Inoue 2007; Pechenkina et al. 2007; Suzuki, this volume) seem to fall within Wilbur's category 4, representing populations that shifted their dietary emphasis to carbohydrate-rich and iron-poor dietary sources.

It is still unclear whether evidence for the emergence of TB during the Yayoi indicates that the pathogen was introduced to Japan by Yayoi immigrants, or that the disease became archaeologically visible in response to the development of ideal conditions for its dissemination (i.e., major increases in densely populated communities during the Yayoi period).

Interestingly, Temple and Larsen (chapter 14) argue for a decline in the frequency of chronic systemic infectious disease from the Jomon to the Yayoi, albeit in tandem with an apparent increase in infectious disease diversity. In support of such a view, an increase in the diversity of infectious disease with the adoption/introduction of intensive agriculture has been noted for northern Vietnam (Oxenham et al. 2005).

Similarly, Zhang's (chapter 13) analysis of a large skeletal series from Early Imperial China also documents the presence of a variety of infectious diseases, including treponematosis, that do not seem to be evident in collections from earlier time periods. Quite likely the increased population movement leading to progressive homogenization of steppe populations seen by the Xiongnu period (chapters 3 and 5) led to an interpopulation pathogen exchange and thus diversification in human-specific pathogenic strains. While some of infectious diseases remain invisible through the skeletal record, early historical records from China give accounts of the introduction of new infections. An alchemist and writer of the Jin dynasty, Ge Hong (葛洪, AD 283–343), describes the spread of an acute infectious disease, likely smallpox, during the Jianwu period (AD 25–56) of the Eastern Han dynasty in his work *Zhou Hou Fang* (肘后方). According to Ge Hong, an extremely virulent strain of a sore-causing infection—referred to in writing as "captive's sore" (虏疮)—was introduced into the Central Plains of China by soldiers and captives after a battle in Nanyang (Henan Province) with a steppe population, the Yue people (Hanson 2006: 133).

Turning to the question of the population history of Southeast Asia, Pietrusewsky argues for an East/Northeast Asia–Southeast Asian population dichotomy, in which island and mainland Southeast Asian populations show a close genetic affinity with each other. Moreover, this dichotomization is seen as evidence for long-term population continuity within each region and is thus incompatible with a displacement or migration model that would imply large-scale gene flow into Southeast Asia from the north.

Matsumura and Oxenham (chapter 8) have approached the question of the population history of Southeast Asia from a somewhat different perspective. While they focus on dental morphology for the most part, in contrast with Pietrusewsky's craniometric approach, they incorporate late Pleistocene/early Holocene samples from Southeast Asia into their analysis. Perhaps their most important finding is the marked discontinuity or dichotomy between early pre-Neolithic samples in Southeast Asia and later Neolithic and Metal Age samples in the same area. While there are complex groupings of individual samples within these pre-Neolithic and Neolithic clusters, a clear separation of North/Northeast Asian and Southeast Asian Neolithic samples through the Metal Age and beyond does not occur. Apparent anomalies, such as the close affinities of Neolithic Ban Chiang with Northeast Asian samples, a relationship also noted by Pietrusewsky (chapter 7), can be explained, and are indeed argued to be expected, by the immigration hypothesis, in that the major population movements occurred with the spread of farming communities from the southern regions of China sometime between 4500 and 4000 years ago. Not only does this model predict relatively close affinities between early Southeast Asian Neolithic assemblages, such as Ban Chiang, and Northeast Asian migration source populations, but it also predicts the presence of local or indigenous populations that were being assimilated by newly migrating peoples. The latter situation is exactly what is seen in the exceptionally heterogeneous Man Bac population, situated on the front line, as it were, of demic expansion into the region (see a more detailed discussion of this in Oxenham and Matsumura 2011).

Population Health

While several chapters in the section on human mobility refer to changes in human health and traumatic injuries as evidentiary sources of interpopulation contacts, chapters in the section on population health often discuss human mobility as a factor affecting various aspects of paleohealth. Two major themes can be underscored based on this section of the volume. The first concerns morbidity, trauma, and the growth profiles of populations in the contact situation and of those resident in the frontier zone or on the periphery, as opposed to in the core areas of their respective cultures. The second theme concerns the impact of different modes of subsistence and subsistence shifts with the introduction of new crop plants, as well as the effects of later sociopolitical changes, on the human condition in East Asia.

With respect to the first theme, Eng and Zhang examine the frequency and patterning of traumatic injuries in frontier populations from Xinjiang Province (Nileke, Yanghai; far from the imperial Chinese sphere of normal interaction) and Manchuria (Jinggouzi; a zone contested by nomadic pastoralists and agriculturalist Chinese alike) as compared to what are referred to as a "pacified-zone" sample of agropastoralists (Lamadong), essentially a population more or less assimilated into the Chinese imperial sphere. The frequency of nonspecific trauma (that could be related to either misadventure or interpersonal violence) was relatively low in all samples assessed; in fact, it was not dissimilar to frequencies reported from Southeast Asia (Oxenham et al. 2001; Domett and Tayles 2006).

Turning to trauma with a probable interpersonal conflict etiology, craniofacial injuries, Eng and Zhang (chapter 9) found similarly elevated rates of such lesions in the Xinjiang and Manchurian samples but a rather low frequency in the pacified zone sample. However, the Manchurian sample was unique not only in that it showed the highest rate of cranial trauma but also that in all instances females were the recipients of injury. Whatever the reason for the pattern in the Manchurian Jinggouzi assemblage (Eng and Zhang provide some possibilities), the causes of cranial trauma at Jinggouzi would appear at face value to be quite distinct from those operating in the Xinjiang samples, which are consistent with the violence associated with skirmishing and warfare in general. We suggest that it is not implausible, in a situation in which males were absent (when engaged in pastorally related activities) from permanent and semipermanent camps for long periods of time, that Jinggouzi women were involved in territorial defense. This should not be seen as unusual, as well-documented evidence for female participation, and also training, in martial behaviors occurred, for example, in Iron Age England (Redfern 2009). Such a scenario would imply that the Jinggouzi community living within this pastoralist–Chinese agriculturalist interaction zone were the recipients of violence, rather than being responsible for initiating intergroup conflict. Given the logistical difficulties associated with Chinese-nomadic conflict in Xinjiang, it is probable that the interpersonal violence evident in these populations was intertribal in nature.

Remaining on the periphery, Zhang (chapter 13) also looked at the frequency and patterning of trauma in a large sample from Qinghai Province, which could be seen as a frontier or buffer zone between imperial China and Xinjiang, Tibet, and Mongolia. The long bone fracture rate was comparable to the rates seen in the temporally more recent (c. 500 years) series examined by Eng and Zhang (chapter 9): 2.1 percent of long bones evidenced trauma compared to 3.5 percent at Jinggouzi and 1.9 percent at Lamadong. Low levels of facial fractures (four individuals) were noted, although five separate instances of sharp-force injury were seen (nominally, a rate of 1.3 percent). The rate and patterning of traumatic injury in the Qinghai sample is clearly difficult to interpret. The type and frequency of trauma, at least, is consistent with interpersonal conflict. The evidence for sharp-force trauma is also clearly consistent with interpersonal violence, although the low rate suggests small-scale and infrequent violence.

Machicek and Beach (chapter 10) have also provided some insights into human behavior with their assessment of degenerative joint disease (DJD) and oral health in a Manchurian (Inner Mongolian) sample of probable agropastoralists (the Tuchengzi sample, dated to 475 BC–AD 220) and a northern Mongolian sample of probable pastoralists (Egiin Gol, dated to 300 BC–AD 100). While sample sizes are quite small, and age-at-death data was not available for all samples, some interesting testable hypotheses have been generated. Significant differences in the frequency of DJD in the Mongolian sample potentially points to a sexual division of labor, possibly related to horse-riding activities. The lack of such a significant distinction among male and female Inner Mongolians may speak to a lower level, or lack, of gender-based activities sensitive to DJD, something perhaps not unexpected in a more complex or behaviorally diversified agropastoralist community. While the oral health findings need to be examined without recourse to the age-at-death profile of the sample, it is somewhat interesting to note the lack of caries in this much later (13th–14th century AD) Mongolian sample. Clearly this is an interesting area for further research with larger samples and a more detailed comparative framework.

Pechenkina and colleagues (chapter 12) examine the core versus frontier situation during the Neolithic period from the point of view of oral health. In their study, the Xishan population of a Yangshao cultural entity resident on the Yangshao/Dawenkou frontier exhibits a wider range of specialized dental wear patterns than do the populations from the core of the Yangshao area of influence. A somewhat elevated frequency of porotic hyperostosis and its active (not-healed) state in the same series (15.5 percent as opposed to 8 percent and 11 percent in the other two Yangshao collections from approximately the same time period) seems to vouch either for a shortage of dietary iron or for greater parasitic loads in this border area (see chapter 18).

Moving from the generalized behaviors to somewhat specific, or at least specifiable, subsistence lifeways, Wei and colleagues (chapter 11) assess a range of oral health signatures in a small sample of early Qin agriculturalists.

The level of caries (10.7 percent tooth count) is well within the range of ex-pectations for an agricultural population with a probable millet subsistence base. The relatively elevated level of caries in this sample is intriguing in that it is consistent with global evidence for a decline in oral health with the adop-tion and/or intensification of agriculture (Turner 1979; Lukacs 1992), but not for the pattern seen in Southeast Asia (see Oxenham et al. 2006). The role of potentially more cariogenic millet, as opposed to rice, may be impli-cated here (this issue is dealt with in more detail below). Moreover, the fre-quency of caries by tooth class and age cohort is consistent with expectations, as is the higher rate of female caries (see Lukacs 2008 for a discussion of this with respect to elevated fertility).

Because the work of Wei and colleagues needs to be examined within a deeper temporal and broader geographic context, the contributions by Pech-enkina and colleagues are useful to have at hand. In chapter 18, they pres-ent one of the few multisample reviews of the bioarchaeological evidence for health trends in mainland and insular East Asia, considering three im-portant health indicators: stature, caries, and cribra orbitalia. While noting a clear trend in stature reduction over the course of Jomon, Pechenkina and colleagues underscore Temple's (2008) assertion that stature heterogeneity should be seen in the context of geographic (and by implication dietary) dif-ferences in sampled populations. A marked trend in stature decline is seen in central China, particularly between the Yangshao and Longshan periods, which seems to coincide with millet intensification. In contrast, adult stature increases from the Bronze Age to the Iron Age in the northern frontier re-gions of central China, as well as in Xinjiang and Inner Mongolia, where the chief subsistence economy was nomadic pastoralism.

With regard to early assemblages in Thailand, Pechenkina and colleagues note an increase in stature from the earlier phases of Ban Chiang and Non Nok Tha as compared to the later phases of these sites. Moreover, the early site of Khok Phanom Di has the lowest adult stature of any early assemblage in Thailand. Their suggestion that reduced stature in the early assemblages may be due to a microevolutionary adaptation to a tropical forest forager life-style sounds reasonable; the only problem is that all of these assemblages are Neolithic, in the sense that they were primarily food producers. Early Ban Chiang and Non Nok Ta, as well as Khok Phanom Di, in fact represent some of the first food-producing communities in Southeast Asia. Moreover (see Matsumura and Oxenham, chapter 8, for a more extensive discussion), such sites are more than likely the vanguard of the Neolithic transition front (see Bellwood and Oxenham 2008) for the region. For relatively recent agricul-tural colonists in a new and unmodified landscape, reduced stature would be a predicted side effect. Increasing stature in later, more established food-producing phases would also be expected and is exactly what seems to have happened. With regard to the situation in northern Vietnam, there is a clear reduction in stature from the pre-Neolithic Da But (Con Co Ngua cemetery assemblage) in comparison to later Metal Age agriculturalist samples (Oxenham 2000).

Pechenkina and colleagues also note a marked decline in oral health with the intensification of agriculture in central China. Rather than place the blame squarely on the intensification of millet agriculture, they make the more nuanced argument that changes in dietary complexity—not specific foodstuffs in and of themselves—are important here. For instance, they argue that reduced supplementary foraging in the late phases of Yangshao radically altered food composition and texture and led to elevated caries rates (the oral health of Yangshao period samples is detailed by Pechenkina and colleagues in chapter 12). Caries rates also increased in Japan, even over the Jomon period, and peaked in the wet-rice agricultural Yayoi period. In terms of the general global thesis of reduced oral health with the adoption/intensification of agriculture this finding seems reasonable; however, it is inconsistent with the evidence from Southeast Asia, where rice was also the main subsistence crop (this is discussed below).

Moving our attention from the mainland to insular East Asia, we have several contributions specifically focused on various parts of the Japanese archipelago (Temple and Larsen in chapter 14; Okazaki in chapter 15; and Oxenham and colleagues in chapter 16) and one that looks at various aspects of paleohealth in Taiwan (Liu and colleagues in chapter 17). Temple and Larsen document a series of health indicators for the Jomon through Yayoi periods. They note a significant increase in caries during the Yayoi, coincidental with the introduction of wet-rice cultivation. This is an intriguing finding given the low caries rates associated with rice agriculture reported in Vietnam and Thailand (see Oxenham et al. 2006). Temple and Larsen argue that the high starch content of rice makes it cariogenic by definition and suggest that the low caries rates seen in Southeast Asia are potentially associated with "less refined" rice. Presumably this refers to various forms of processing (milling and polishing) that would remove the bran and germ layers from the rice grain, thus excluding the natural abrading and tooth-cleansing properties of the fibrous bran (see Tayles et al. 2000 for a discussion of this). Leaving aside the issue of rice processing, because information on this is not available for Neolithic Southeast Asia, the species of rice used in Yayoi Japan may be relevant. The main starch component of Japonica is amylopectin, which causes a very sticky type of rice (potentially more difficult to clear from the oral cavity) when cooked. While the variety of domesticated rice grown in ancient Southeast Asia has not been identified to date, long grain rice has been found in Phung Nguyen contexts (associated with the earliest agriculture in the region) in northern Vietnam. Long grain rice contains high levels of amylose, creating a soft, nonsticky rice when cooked.

It may also be relevant to reflect on the way in which rice is prepared for consumption, which is possibly more critical in terms of oral disease than the starch content of the grain itself is. Rice, unlike all other potentially cariogenic grains, is cooked and consumed whole and not (except in certain circumstances) milled into flour and prepared as a sticky form of "bread" or "cake," thus markedly reducing its cariogenicity. Temple and Larsen suggest that yams (*Dioscorea japonica*: see also Temple and Larsen 2007: 507) potentially contributed to elevated caries rates in Japan, which in our view is a much more likely scenario, particularly given the demonstrated low caries rates associated with rice agriculturalists in Southeast Asia (see Oxenham et al. 2006), as noted previously. Incidentally, tubers have been suggested as likely contributors to high caries rates at Khok Phanom Di in ancient Thailand (Tayles 1999) and the somewhat contemporaneous, if not earlier, food-producing site Man Bac in northern Vietnam (Oxenham and Matsumura 2011).

Apart from their intriguing oral health findings, Temple and Larsen note the rather unexpected outcome that the evidence for nonspecific systemic infectious disease decreases with the adoption and intensification of agriculture: elevated rates in the Jomon decline in the Yayoi. This is despite the first evidence for specific infectious diseases such as tuberculosis in the Yayoi, as well as the main ingredients for increasing levels of infectious disease: sedentism, population growth, and increased population densities. They suggest that the critical mass in terms of population density was not seen until much later, in the Kofun and Medieval periods, which saw a marked increase in the frequency of infectious disease.

While also looking at markers of health in Japan, Oxenham and colleagues placed their focus on Hokkaido, where they argued that meaningful comparative samples were to be found in subarctic and arctic North America, rather than Japanese islands south of Hokkaido. The highly specialized sea mammal–hunting subsistence economies of the Hokkaido Jomon and Okhotsk cultures, as well as the extremes of Hokkaidan ecology, are argued to limit the value of comparisons with other, more temperately adapted, Jomon assemblages. The evidence for both severe and debilitating infectious disease in cold-adapted Hokkaidans, unusual at face value, is seen to be consistent with the high disease loads experienced by other cold-climate populations in North America. Further, it is suggested that Hokkaidan populations may have been more susceptible to infectious disease in light of elevated levels of other physiological stress indicators: cribra orbitalia and linear enamel hypoplasia. Finally, it was found that despite the extreme nature of the environment, as well as the very demanding lifestyle of these large marine mammal hunters, they endured quite debilitating conditions: serious trauma and diffuse idiopathic skeletal hyperostosis (DISH), for instance.

The final chapter to deal with Japanese data, by Okazaki, focuses on a single measure of population health, subadult growth, assessing samples representing the Jomon, through Yayoi and Modern periods in Japan. Okazaki argues that Jomon populations were already relatively sedentary before the Yayoi migrations and that the Yayoi, while bringing a ready-made agricultural subsistence economy, supplemented this with a range of foraging activities during the early phase of their colonization of the Japanese archipelago.

In agreement with Okazaki's findings, Crawford (2008) emphasizes the significant role for food/resource production for Jomon populations and has argued that their interaction with the environment might have been quite similar to that of later farming populations. Okazaki's interpretation is somewhat consistent with Bellwood and Oxenham's (2008: 18) friction zone in discussing agricultural trajectories, which is "characterized by genetic admixture and cultural reticulation between hunters and farmers." It is also worth noting that the reduction in Jomon adult stature, both regionally and temporally, noted by Temple (2008; see also chapter 18, this volume), would be consistent with Okazaki's model of an increasing trend to sedentism over time during the Jomon. Such elevated levels of sedentism in otherwise foraging communities may have better facilitated varying levels of articulation with incoming sedentary agriculturalists that also appear to have supplemented their dirt farming with foraging to some degree or another (after Okazaki, this volume).

Finally, Liu and colleagues look at issues of health and behavior on the smallest island dealt with in this volume, during one of the more recent time periods addressed: the Iron Age coastal site of Shih-san-hang in Taiwan (2000 to 1000 years BP). An intriguing finding was the very low rates of dental disease (caries, antemortem tooth loss, and alveolar defects), comparable to those of Northeast Asian hunter-gatherers (Oxenham and Matsumura 2007) and also many agricultural Southeast Asian assemblages (Oxenham et al. 2006). Liu and colleagues suggest a mixed diet, with the possibility of a rice component.

It is interesting to interpret observations on gross pathology at Shih-san-hang in the context of archaeological finds suggesting intensive metallurgy at the site. Very low frequencies of oral pathologies including caries, antemor-

tem tooth loss, and abscessing suggest a diet with limited amounts of carbohydrates, yet skeletal markers of physiological stress indicate high rates of
iron-deficiency anemia and frequent incidents of growth arrest during early
childhood at Shih-san-hang. A higher frequency of linear enamel hypoplasias
(LEH) was seen in younger as compared to older age classes, potentially suggesting that LEH (whatever the underlying etiology) mediated increased risk
of death and/or selective mortality. While the authors attribute an elevated
rate of stress indicators to heavy parasitic loads contracted through exploitation of marine resources, general environmental pollution proceeding from
ore smelting was another likely cause of physiological stress in this population. Furthermore, the shoulder deformity and an asymmetric muscle deformity described for the skeleton of a middle-aged female could in fact represent the consequences of a physically taxing metallurgy-related occupation.

Conclusions

At the beginning of this chapter we promised to distill out, as it were, any
meta-trends apparent in the wealth of detail provided by the contributing
authors to this volume. It is clear from the chapters addressing the population
history of the region that major lacunae exist, in the sense that the core area of
China is not dealt with in any detail, and then mainly with respect to its ever-
fluctuating northern peripheral zones. That is a piece of the jigsaw puzzle that
will no doubt be filled in the coming years. Apart from this, we can say that
considerable light has been shed on various aspects of population dynamics
north of China, to some extent in the Japanese archipelago, and even in the
interaction zone between southern China and Southeast Asia.

The northern zone (including the northern borders of modern-day China,
Xinjiang, Inner Mongolia, Mongolia, Manchuria, and southern Siberia) can
be characterized as having experienced a great deal of flux over prehistory.
In very general terms, the Neolithic to the Bronze Age saw the highest levels of population heterogeneity, which suggests more isolated communities
with somewhat limited levels of population mobility. By the Xiongnu period,
a much greater degree of population homogeneity is seen throughout the
northern zone, which was likely related to a significant increase in population mobility and intercommunity contacts, as well as, of course, genetic exchange. This could well have been facilitated through intensification in the
use of the domesticated horse, although dating horse domestication and the
history of its adoption by northern zone populations is problematic (Olsen
2006).

While there is some degree of consensus regarding human mobility in the northern zone, quite the reverse is apparent when addressing the issue of Southeast Asian origins, a question intimately linked to the population history of Northeast/East Asia. Pietrusewsky makes a strong argument for limited, if any, Northeast Asian genetic contributions to the formation of modern Southeast Asian peoples. In contrast, Matsumura and Oxenham equally vigorously refute this model and argue for major Northeast Asian genetic contributions in the emergence of Southeast Asian populations, beginning in the Neolithic or a little less than 4000 years ago. While there are clearly differences in methodological approach, the samples considered, temporal focus, and the specifics of the questions addressed by these chapters, those factors cannot alone account for the very different conclusions reached. This is clearly an area of research in population history and mobility that requires considerably more attention.

In regard to population health, the two chief foci include biological responses to change in terms of (1) contact/friction zone communities; and (2) communities undergoing significant subsistence reorientation. The two main studies of trauma that deal with samples in contact/friction zones do, perhaps unsurprisingly, find slightly elevated levels of trauma with a likely interpersonal conflict etiology; however, rates are low enough to be interpreted as the results of minor skirmishing rather than large-scale warfare. Life on these ancient frontiers may not have been as dangerous as one would suppose. Nonetheless, such populations did evince elevated levels of physiological stress, as Pechenkina and colleagues demonstrate with their comparison of frontier versus core area Yangshao samples.

In terms of the pattern of paleohealth in the core regions of China, and indeed Japan, a clear pattern of declining health (oral health and stature declines, for instance) with the adoption and/or intensification of agriculture is visible. Taiwan, as examined through the lens of a single Iron Age site, was also broadly consistent with paleohealth expectations, although oral health was relatively good for such a temporally late site. The authors attribute this to a mixed diet, one not reliant on any particular staple grain. Regarding central China, this involved the adoption of millet, while in Japan rice was the chief grain adopted. The situations in both China and Japan suggest that the adoption of one particular staple grain or another is not a sufficient explanation of marked declines in oral health.

In China, differential levels and patterns of supplementary foraging, in concert with the development of millets as a staple, may have had a pivotal impact on oral health. In Japan, a similar situation may have been in play, although this has not been explored to date. However, another significant factor in the Jomon-Yayoi transition in Japan may be the type of rice used, for

Yayoi populations imported a sticky, and potentially more cariogenic, form of rice into the archipelago. Much more research into the cariogenicity of rice, particularly for diets containing rice in various forms (japonica vs. indica) and with a range of processing technologies (white vs. brown rice; boiled vs. processed rice flour cakes, for example), is required.

Finally, a number of chapters deal with the frequency and patterning of infectious disease, with the most intriguing findings coming from the Japanese archipelago. Temple and Larsen argue that the prevalence of infectious disease actually declined with the adoption of intensive wet-rice agriculture in Japan during the Jomon-Yayoi transition but did so in the face of an increase in the diversity of specific infectious diseases. One of these specific infectious diseases is tuberculosis, which has virtually become a signature disease for the emergence of the Yayoi in Japan. TB may well have been a new, and somewhat unwelcome, migrant to the archipelago, as Suzuki suggests. Alternatively, its emergence may be more a function of greater susceptibility to a microorganism that had been around for millennia but was only able to gain a foothold with the move to a more carbohydrate-rich and iron-poor diet during the Yayoi transition. Whatever the underlying causes for the skeletally visible appearance of TB in the archipelago, this is clearly an important area of future research.

A further, somewhat unintuitive, finding is the presence at a somewhat elevated level of infectious disease in the extreme cold of Hokkaido. Clearly, cold barriers to microorganisms responsible for disease are not infallible and in fact may not really be barriers at all. Moreover, this is a good example of the caution that needs to be employed in making intersample comparisons: the Hokkaidan Jomon, at least, cannot meaningfully be compared to southern Jomon samples, despite the appellation of Jomon, because of a vastly different climate and subsistence prehistory.

From the vast temporal and geographic spread that characterizes mainland and insular East Asia, an equally diverse series of chapters have been presented addressing key questions regarding human movement, contact, and health. Furthermore, while each author is a specialist in the area and topic dealt with, a majority of the contributors are local researchers writing about their own prehistories within their own particular academic traditions, an important strength of this book. At the beginning of the chapter we noted that "a synthesis implies the exploration of large-scale trends that might otherwise be lost in the detail of individual contributions." Clearly, such large-scale patterns are evident within the detail of the chapters included in this volume. Moreover, while some of those patterns may seem intuitively obvious, others clearly were not. Minimally, we trust that this volume will serve as a springboard from which a great deal more bioarchaeological research into East Asian issues will be launched. There is much within these pages that many will agree with, and perhaps equally as much that some will disagree with. In the scientific tradition, it is likely those who disagree will more vigorously take the bioarchaeology of East Asia into its next phase of development. The reader will find no lack of hypotheses begging to be tested, and what better purpose can any book hope to achieve?

Literature Cited

Allison M, Gerszten E, Munizaga J, Santoro C, Mendoza D. 1981. Tuberculosis in pre-Columbian Andean populations. In: Buikstra J, editor. *Prehistoric tuberculosis in the Americas.* Evanston, IL: Northwestern University Archaeological Program. Pp. 49–51.

Aufderheide AC, Rodriguez-Martin C. 1998. *The Cambridge encyclopedia of human palaeopathology.* Cambridge: Cambridge University Press.

Bellwood P, Oxenham M. 2008. The expansions of farming societies and the role of the Neolithic demographic transition. In: Bocquet-Appel J-P, Bar-Yosef O, editors. *The Neolithic demographic transition and its consequences.* Dordrecht: Springer. Pp. 13–34.

Crawford GW. 2008. The Jomon in early agriculture discourse: Issues arising from Matsui, Kanehara, and Pearson. *World Archaeology* 40: 445–65.

Domett KM, Tayles N. 2006 Adult fracture patterns in prehistoric Thailand: A biocultural approach. *International Journal of Osteoarchaeology* 16: 185–99.

Hanson ME. 2006. The significance of Manchu medical sources in the Qing. In: Wadley S, Naeher C, Dede K, editors. *Proceedings of the First North American Conference on Manchu Studies (Portland, OR, May 9–10, 2003).* Tunguso Sibirica 15, Vol. 1: Studies in Manchu Literature and History. Weisbaden: Harrassowitz. Pp. 131–75.

Johnston WD. 1993. Tuberculosis. In: Kiple KF, editor. *The Cambridge world history of human disease.* New York: Cambridge University Press. Pp. 1059–68.

Li J. 1985. Science of medicine in ancient China (中国古代医学科学技术发明举隅). In: *Selected papers from 30 years of Chinese Academy of Traditional Medicine* (中国中医研究院三十年论文选). Publishing House of Chinese Ancient Medical Texts (中医古籍出版社).

Lukacs JR. 1992. Dental paleopathology and agricultural intensification in South Asia: New evidence from Bronze Age Harappa. *American Journal of Physical Anthropology* 87: 133–50.

Lukacs JR. 2008. Fertility and agriculture accentuate sex differences in dental caries rates. *Current Anthropology* 49: 901–14.

Olsen SL. 2006. Early horse domestication on the Eurasian steppe. In: Zeder MA, Bradley DG, Emschwiller E, Smith BD, editors. *Documenting domestication: New genetic and archaeological paradigms.* Berkeley: University of California Press. Pp. 245–69.

Oxenham MF. 2000. Health and behaviour during the Mid-Holocene and Metal period of Northern Viet Nam. Ph.D. dissertation, Northern Territory University.

Oxenham MF. 2006. Biological responses to change in prehistoric Vietnam. *Asian Perspectives* 45: 212–39.

Oxenham MF, Cavill I. 2010. Porotic hyperostosis and cribra orbitalia: The erythropoietic response to iron-deficiency anaemia. *Anthropological Science* 1818: 199–200.

Oxenham MF, Matsumura H. 2007. Oral and physiological palaeohealth in cold adapted peoples: Northeast Asia, Hokkaido. *American Journal of Physical Anthropology* 135: 64–74.

Oxenham MF, Matsumura H. 2011. Man Bac: regional cultural and temporal context. In: Oxenham MF, Matsumura H, Nguyen KD, editors. *Man Bac: The excavation of a Neolithic site in Northern Vietnam; The Biology.* Terra Australis 33. Canberra: ANU E Press, Australian National University.

Oxenham MF, Nguyen KT, Nguyen LC. 2005. Skeletal evidence for the emergence of infectious disease in Bronze and Iron Age northern Vietnam. *American Journal of Physical Anthropology* 126: 359–76.

Oxenham MF, Nguyen LC, Nguyen KT. 2006. The oral health consequences of the adoption and intensification of agriculture in Southeast Asia. In: Oxenham M, Tayles N, editors. *Bioarchaeology of Southeast Asia.* Cambridge: Cambridge University Press. Pp. 263–89.

Oxenham MF, Walters I, Nguyen LC, Nguyen KT. 2001. Case studies in ancient trauma: Mid-Holocene through Metal Periods in Northern Viet Nam. In: Henneberg M, Kilgariff J, editors. *The causes and effects of biological variation.* Adelaide: Australasian Society for Human Biology, University of Adelaide. Pp. 83–102.

Pechenkina EA, Benfer RA Jr., Ma X. 2007. Diet and health in the Neolithic of the Wei and middle Yellow River basins, northern China. In: Cohen MN, Crane-Kramer GMM, editors. *Ancient health: Skeletal indicators of agricultural and economic intensification.* Gainesville: University Press of Florida. Pp. 255–72.

Rathbun T, Sexton J, Michie J. 1980. Disease patterns in a formative period South Carolina coastal population. *Tennessee Anthropological Association Miscellaneous Paper* 5: 52–74.

Redfern RC. 2009. Does cranial trauma provide evidence for projectile weaponry in late Iron Age Dorsett? *Oxford Journal of Archaeology* 28: 399–424.

Rotto M. 2009. Ancient Koreans and Xiongnu: What was the nature of their relationship. *Journal of Northeast Asian History* 6: 5–35.

Suzuki T, Inoue T. 2007. Earliest evidence of spinal tuberculosis from the aneolithic Yayoi period in Japan. *International Journal of Osteoarchaeology* 17: 392–402.

Tayles N. 1999. *The excavation of Khok Phanom Di: A prehistoric site in Central Thailand.* Vol. 4: *The people.* London: Society of Antiquaries of London/Oxbow Books.

Tayles N., Domett K., Nelsen K. 2000. Agriculture and dental caries? The case of rice in prehistoric Southeast Asia. *World Archaeology* 32 (1): 68–83.

Temple DH. 2008. What can stature variation reveal about environmental differences between prehistoric Jomon foragers? Understanding the impact of systemic stress on developmental stability. *American Journal of Human Biology* 20: 431–39.

Temple DH, Larsen CS. 2007. Dental caries prevalence as evidence for agriculture and subsistence variation during the Yayoi period in prehistoric Japan: Biocultural interpretations of an economy in transition. *American Journal of Physical Anthropology* 134: 501–12.

Turner CG II. 1979. Dental anthropological indications of agriculture among the Jomon people of central Japan. X: Peopling of the Pacific. *American Journal of Physical Anthropology* 51: 619–36.

Wilbur AK, Farnbach AW, Knudson KJ, Buikstra JE. 2008. Diet, tuberculosis, and the paleopathological record. *Current Anthropology* 49: 963–77.

Contributors

Jeremy J. Beach, Department of Anthropology, University of Indianapolis, Indianapolis, USA

Allison Drake, School of Archaeology and Anthropology, Australian National University, Canberra, Australia

Jacqueline T. Eng, Department of Anthropology, Western Michigan University, Kalamazoo, Michigan, USA

Erdene Myagmar, Department of Anthropology and Archaeology, School of Social Sciences, National University of Mongolia, Ulaanbaatar-46, Mongolia

Fan Wenquan, Henan Provincial Institute of Cultural Relics and Archaeology, Zhengzhou, P.R. China

John Krigbaum, Department of Anthropology, University of Florida, Gainesville, Florida, USA

Clark Spencer Larsen, Department of Anthropology, Ohio State University, Columbus, Ohio, USA

Christine Lee, Chinese Academy of Sciences, Institute of Vertebrate Paleontology and Paleoanthropology, Beijing, P.R. China

Liu Chinhsin, Department of Anthropology, University of Florida, Gainesville, Florida, USA

Liu Yichang, Institute of History and Philology, Academia Sinica, Taipei, Taiwan

Liu Wu, Institute of Vertebrate Paleontology and Paleoanthropology, Chinese Academy of Sciences, Beijing, P.R. China

Ma Xiaolin, Henan Administration of Cultural Heritage, Zhengzhou, P.R. China

Michelle L. Machicek, Smithsonian Institution, Department of Anthropology, National Museum of Natural History, Washington, D.C., USA

Hirofumi Matsumura, Department of Anatomy, Sapporo Medical University, Sapporo, Japan

Kenji Okazaki, Division of Morphological Analysis, Faculty of Medicine, Tottori University, Tottori, Japan

Marc Oxenham, School of Archaeology and Anthropology, Australian National University, Canberra, Australia

Kate Pechenkina, School of Social Sciences at Queens College of the City University of New York

Michael Pietrusewsky, Department of Anthropology, University of Hawai'i, Honolulu, USA

Takao Suzuki, Department of Epidemiology, Tokyo Metropolitan Institute of Gerontology, Tokyo, Japan

Daniel H. Temple, Department of Anthropology, University of North Carolina at Wilmington, North Carolina, USA

Tsang Chenghwa, Institute of History and Philology, Academia Sinica, Taipei Taiwan

Tumen Dashtseveg, Department of Anthropology and Archaeology, School of Social Sciences, National University of Mongolia, Ulaanbaatar-46, Mongolia

Wang Changsui, Graduate University of Chinese Academy of Sciences, Beijing, P.R. China

Wang Tao, Graduate University of Chinese Academy of Sciences, Beijing, P.R. China

Wei Dong, Research Center for Chinese Frontier Archaeology, Jilin University, Changchun, Jilin Province, P.R. China

Wei Miao, Lao She Memorial, Beijing, P.R. China

Zhang Jinglei, History Department, Nanjing University, P.R. China

Zhang Quanchao, Research Center for Chinese Frontier Archaeology, Jilin University, Changchun, Jilin Province, P.R. China

Zhao Congcang, Department of Archaeology, Northwest University, Xi'an, Shaanxi, China

Index of Subjects

Page numbers in *italics* refer to illustrations.

ablation. *See* tooth ablation

Afanasevo culture, 86, *90*, 98

age at death, assessment of, 12–13, 223, 269, 348; for juveniles, 372–73, 386, 388

agricultural colonization model, 138, 145

agricultural transition, influence on human health of, 444–45; in Japan, 344–45, 356, 359–60, 368; in Korea, 56–57

agropastoralism, 218, 219, 221, 323, 446, 462, 463, 465, 470, 471, 474, 488–89

Ainu, 9, 112, 113, 153, 157, 158; and Jomon, 10, 32, 144, 170, 173

Aira-Tanzawa phases, 32

Aleuts, 400, 403, 410; pyogenic lesions in skeletal remains of, 408, 409, 411–13; trauma in, 409, 414

Altai-Sayan culture variant, 85

alveolar breadth, 153, 154, 156

alveolar crypts, 258

alveolar prognathism, 101, 180, 193, 195

Amami Islands. *See* Ryukyu Islands

American Museum of Natural History, 4–5

amoebiasis, 410

Ancylostomatidae. See hookworm

Andersson, Johan Gunnar, 5; Yangshao discovery, 7

Andrews, Roy Chapman, 5

Andronovo culture, 39, *90*, 98

anemia, congenital, 433

anemia, iron-deficiency, 350, 433–36, 438, 444, 468–69, 494; on the Central Plains, 471–75; and tuberculosis, 485–86

animal husbandry, 33, 39–40, 220, 222, 238, 272, 279, 284, 341, 425. *See also* pastoralism

ankylosing spondylitis, 15, 336

antemortem tooth loss, 268–69, 280, 460, 493, 494; on Iron Age Taiwan, 421, 423, 426–28; during the Mongolian period, 258–59; among the Qin people, 270, 273, 280–81, 283; in the Qinghai collection, 340–41; in the Yangshao collections, 293, 296, 301–6, 315, 316

An Tesheng. *See* Andersson, Johan Gunnar

arboriculture, xviii, 44, 45, 445

Arizona State University dental anthropology system, 74, 75

armor, during Eastern Zhou, 236

Ascaris sp., 357, 411

asterionic bone, 116

Atayal, 149, 153, 157, 158, 159–66 *passim*, 188, 420

Australo-Melanesians, 172, 180, 181, 185, 196

Baitag culture, 86

Balz, Erwin, 10

Banpo Culture, *89*, 290

barley, 36; on the Central Plains, 444, 445, 459, 460, 466–67, 474; dispersal into China of, 37, 41; during Jomon, 45; in Mongolia, 250; during Yayoi, 48

basion-nasion, 154, 156

Bering Strait, 139

biasterionic breadth, 154, 156

biasterionic suture, 116

biauricular breadth, 154, 156

bifrontal breadth, 153, 154, 156

bimaxillary breadth, 154, 156

biorbital breadth, 154, 156

bistephanic breadth, 154, 156

Bitsalmuni. *See* Chulmun culture

Black, Davidson, 5, 7

Blakely, Robert, 1

Bohlin, Birger, 5

Borneo, 148, 153, 157, 159–64, 188

botulism, 410

Index of Archaeological Sites
and Skeletal Collections

Bioarchaeological Interpretations of the Human Past: Local, Regional, and Global Perspectives

Clark Spencer Larsen, Editor
Marin A. Pilloud, Co-Editor

Ancient Health: Skeletal Indicators of Agricultural and Economic Intensification, edited by Mark Nathan Cohen and Gillian M. M. Crane-Kramer (2007; first paperback edition, 2012)

Bioarchaeology and Identity in the Americas, edited by Kelly J. Knudson and Christopher M. Stojanowski (2009; first paperback edition, 2010)

Island Shores, Distant Pasts: Archaeological and Biological Approaches to the Pre-Columbian Settlement of the Caribbean, edited by Scott M. Fitzpatrick and Ann H. Ross (2010; first paperback edition, 2017)

The Bioarchaeology of the Human Head: Decapitation, Decoration, and Deformation, edited by Michelle Bonogofsky (2011; first paperback edition, 2015)

Bioarchaeology and Climate Change: A View from South Asian Prehistory, by Gwen Robbins Schug (2011; first paperback edition, 2017)

Violence, Ritual, and the Wari Empire: A Social Bioarchaeology of Imperialism in the Ancient Andes, by Tiffiny A. Tung (2012; first paperback edition, 2013)

The Bioarchaeology of Individuals, edited by Ann L. W. Stodder and Ann M. Palkovich (2012; first paperback edition, 2014)

The Bioarchaeology of Violence, edited by Debra L. Martin, Ryan P. Harrod, and Ventura R. Pérez (2012; first paperback edition, 2013)

Bioarchaeology and Behavior: The People of the Ancient Near East, edited by Megan A. Perry (2012; first paperback edition, 2018)

Paleopathology at the Origins of Agriculture, edited by Mark Nathan Cohen and George J. Armelagos (2013)

Bioarchaeology of East Asia: Movement, Contact, Health, edited by Kate Pechenkina and Marc Oxenham (2013; first paperback edition, 2025)

Mission Cemeteries, Mission Peoples: Historical and Evolutionary Dimensions of Intracemetery Bioarchaeology in Spanish Florida, by Christopher M. Stojanowski (2013)

Tracing Childhood: Bioarchaeological Investigations of Early Lives in Antiquity, edited by Jennifer L. Thompson, Marta P. Alfonso-Durruty, and John J. Crandall (2014)

The Bioarchaeology of Classical Kamarina: Life and Death in Greek Sicily, by Carrie L. Sulosky Weaver (2015)

Victims of Ireland's Great Famine: The Bioarchaeology of Mass Burials at Kilkenny Union Workhouse, by Jonny Geber (2015; first paperback edition, 2018)

Colonized Bodies, Worlds Transformed: Toward a Global Bioarchaeology of Contact and Colonialism, edited by Melissa S. Murphy and Haagen D. Klaus (2017; first paperback edition, 2021)

www.ingramcontent.com/pod-product-compliance
Lightning Source LLC
Chambersburg PA
CBHW032336280326
41935CB00008B/357